Peterson's®

MASTER THE DSST® EXAMS, VOLUME I

THE ULTIMATE GUIDE TO MASTERING THE DSST® EXAMS

About Peterson's

To succeed on your lifelong educational journey, you will need accurate, dependable, and practical tools and resources. That is why Peterson's is everywhere education happens. Because whenever and however you need education content delivered, you can rely on Peterson's to provide the information, know-how, and guidance to help you reach your goals. Tools to match the right students with the right school. It's here. Personalized resources and expert guidance. It's here. Comprehensive and dependable education content—delivered whenever and however you need it. It's all here.

For more information about Peterson's range of educational products, contact Peterson's, 3 Columbia Circle, Suite 205, Albany, NY 12203, 800-338-3282 Ext. 54229; or find us online at www.petersons.com.

ISBN-13: 978-0-7689-4110-4

Printed in the United States of America
10 9 8 7 6 5 4 3 2 1   18 17 16

First Edition

www.petersonspublishing.com/publishingupdates

Check out our website at www.petersonspublishing.com/publishingupdates to see if there is any new information regarding the test and any revisions or corrections to the content of this book. We've made sure the information in this book is accurate and up-to-date; however, the test format or content may have changed since the time of publication.

Prometric™

Prometric, the DSST® program provider, has reviewed the contents of *Master the DSST® Exams, Volume I* and found this study guide to be an excellent reflection of the content of the respective DSST tests. However, passing the sample tests provided in any study material does not guarantee you will pass the actual tests.

Contents

Before You Begin

HOW THIS BOOK IS ORGANIZED

Peterson's *Master the DSST ® Exams, Volume I* provides diagnostic tests, subject-matter reviews, and post-tests for twelve DSST exams. The following table provides a summary of the information covered in each chapter.

Chapter 1: Ethics in America	Contemporary foundational issues such as Relativism, Subjectivism, Determinism and Free Will, and relationships between morality and religion; development of ethical traditions from Greeks to modern philosophers; ethical analysis of various issues such as war, capital punishment, sexuality, and poverty
Chapter 2: General Anthropology	Methodologies and disciplines of anthropology; history and theory; physical anthropology; archaeology; cultural systems and processes; social, economic, and political organization; religion; and modernization and application of anthropology
Chapter 3: Health and Human Development	Health, wellness, mind/body connection; human development and relationships; addiction; fitness and nutrition; risk factors, disease, disease prevention; safety, consumer awareness, and environmental concerns
Chapter 4: Computing and Information Technology	Computer organization and hardware; systems software; application software; data communications and networks; software development; and social impact and history

Chapter 5: Introduction to Business	Foundations of business, functions of business, including management, marketing, finance, accounting, management information systems and human resources, and contemporary issues, including social responsibility and global business
Chapter 6: Introduction to World Religions	Definition and origins of religion, indigenous religions, Hinduism, Buddhism, Confucianism, Daoism, Shinto-ism, Judaism, Christianity, Islam, and Syncretism
Chapter 7: Management Information Systems	Computer hardware/software, telecommunications and networks, business information systems, systems analysis and design, managing data resources, business decision making, MIS and the organization, and MIS issues
Chapter 8: Money and Banking	The roles and kinds of money, commercial banks and other financial intermediaries, money and macroeconomic activity, central banking and the Federal Reserve, monetary policy in the United States, and the international monetary system
Chapter 9: Personal Finance	Foundations of personal finance, credit and debt, major purchases, taxes, insurance, investments, retirement and estate planning
Chapter 10: Principles of Supervision	Roles and responsibilities of managers and supervisors, management functions, and organizational environment
Chapter 11: History of the Soviet Union	Russia under the old regime, the Revolutionary Period (1914–1921), prewar Stalinism, the Second World War, postwar Stalinism, the Khrushchev years, the Brezhnev era, and reform and collapse
Chapter 12: Substance Abuse	Substance abuse and dependence, classification of drugs, pharmacological and neurophysiological principles, alcohol, antianxiety and sedative-hypnotics, inhalants, tobacco and nicotine, psychomotor substances, opioids, cannabinoids, hallucinogens, other drugs of abuse, antipsychotic drugs, and antidepressants and mood stabilizers

Each chapter of the book is organized in the same manner:

- **Diagnostic Test**—Twenty questions, followed by an answer key and explanations
- **Assessment Grid**—a chart designed to help you identify areas you need to focus on based on your test results
- **Subject-Matter Review**—General overview of the exam subject, followed by a review of the relevant topics and terminology covered on the exam.
- **Post-Test**—Sixty questions, followed by an answer key and explanations

The purpose of the diagnostic test is to help you figure out what you know . . . or don't know. The twenty multiple-choice questions are similar to the ones found on the DSST exam, and they should provide you with a good idea of what to expect. Once you take the diagnostic test, check your answers to see how you did. Included with each correct answer is a brief explanation regarding why a specific answer is correct and, in many cases, why other options are incorrect. Use the assessment grid to identify the questions you miss so that you can spend more time reviewing that information later. As with any exam, knowing your weak spots greatly improves your chances of success.

Following the diagnostic test in each chapter is a subject matter review. The review summarizes the various topics covered on the DSST exam. Key terms are defined; important concepts are explained; and, when appropriate, examples are provided. As you read the review, some of the information may seem familiar while other information may seem foreign. Again, take note of the unfamiliar because that will most likely cause you problems on the actual exam. If you need more information about a topic than what the review provides, refer to one of the textbooks recommended for the test.

After studying the subject-matter review, you should be ready for the post-test. The post-test for each chapter contains sixty multiple-choice items, and it will serve as a dry run for the real DSST exam. Take the time to answer all of the questions because they are similar to those found on the DSST exam for that particular subject. As with the diagnostic test, post-test answers and explanations are at the end of each chapter.

SPECIAL STUDY FEATURES

Peterson's *Master the DSST® Exams, Volume I* is designed to be as user-friendly as it is complete. To this end, it includes two features to make your preparation more efficient.

Overview

Each chapter begins with a bulleted overview listing the topics covered in the chapter. This overview will allow you to quickly target the areas in which you are most interested and need to review.

Summing It Up

Each review chapter ends with a point-by-point summary that captures the most important information in the chapter. The summaries offer a convenient way to review key points.

EXPAND YOUR DSST® TEST PREP ARSENAL

Peterson's *Master the DSST® Exams, Volume I* is the first of a two-volume set designed to give you the most comprehensive test prep resource available for the DSST exams. Peterson's *Master the DSST® Exams, Volume II* features the same effective test preparation strategies provided in this publication for twelve additional DSST exams: Advanced English Composition (new exam for 2017), Civil War and Reconstruction, Criminal Justice, Cybersecurity, Environment and Humanity: The Race to Save the Planet, Introduction to Law Enforcement, Human Resource Management, Math for Liberal Arts (new exam for 2017), Organizational Behavior, Principles of Public Speaking, Principles of Statistics, and Technical Writing.

YOU'RE WELL ON YOUR WAY TO SUCCESS

You've made the decision to take a DSST exam and earn college credit for your life experiences. Peterson's *Master the DSST® Exams, Volume I* will help prepare you for the steps you'll need to achieve your goal—scoring high on the exam!

GIVE US YOUR FEEDBACK

Peterson's publishes a full line of resources to help guide you through the exam process. Peterson's publications can be found at college libraries and career centers and at your local bookstore or library.

Publishing Department

Peterson's, a Nelnet company

3 Columbia Circle, Suite 205

Albany, NY 12203

About DSST

OVERVIEW

- **What is DSST®?**
- **Why Take a DSST® Exam?**
- **DSST® Test centers**
- **How to Register for a DSST® Exam**
- **Preparing for a DSST® Exam**
- **Test Day**

WHAT IS DSST®?

The DSST program provides the opportunity for people to earn college credit for what they have learned outside of the traditional classroom. Accepted or administered at over 1,900 colleges and universities nationwide and approved by the American Council on Education (ACE), the DSST program enables people to use the knowledge they have acquired outside the classroom to accomplish their educational and professional goals.

WHY TAKE A DSST® EXAM?

Previously known as DANTES Subject Standardized Tests, DSST exams offer a way for you to save both time and money in your quest for a college education. Why enroll in a college course in a subject you already understand? For over 30 years, the DSST program has offered the perfect solution for people who are knowledgeable in a specific subject and who want to save both time and money. A passing score on a DSST exam provides physical evidence to universities of proficiency in a specific subject. Over 1,900 accredited and respected colleges and universities across the nation award undergraduate credit for passing scores on DSST exams. With the DSST program, individuals can shave months off the time it takes to earn a degree.

The DSST program offers numerous advantages for people in all stages of their educational development:

- Adult learners
- College students
- Military personnel

Adult learners desiring college degrees face unique circumstances—demanding work schedules, family responsibilities, and tight budgets. Yet adult learners also have years of valuable work experience that can be applied toward a degree through the DSST program. For example, adult learners with on-the-job experience in business and management might be able to skip the Business 101 courses if they earn passing marks on DSST exams such as Introduction to Business and Principles of Supervision.

Adult learners can put their prior learning into action and move forward with more advanced course work. Adults who have never enrolled in a college course may feel a little uncertain about their abilities. If this describes your situation, then sign up for a DSST exam and see how you do. A passing score may be the boost you need to realize your dream of earning a degree. With family and work commitments, adult learners often feel they lack the time to attend college. The DSST program enables adult learners the unique opportunity to work toward college degrees without the time constraints of semester-long course work. DSST exams take 2 hours or less to complete. In one weekend, you could earn credit for multiple college courses.

The DSST exams also benefit students who are already enrolled in a college or university. With college tuition costs on the rise, most students face financial challenges. The fee for each DSST exam starts at $80 plus administration fees charged by some testing facilities—significantly less than the $750 average cost of a 3-hour college class. Maximize tuition assistance by taking DSST exams for introductory or mandatory course work. Once you earn a passing score on a DSST exam, you are free to move on to higher-level course work in that subject matter, take desired electives, or focus on courses in a chosen major.

Not only do college students and adult learners profit from DSST exams, but military personnel reap the benefits as well. If you are a member of the armed services at home or abroad, you can initiate your post-military career by taking DSST exams in areas with which you have experience. Military personnel can gain credit anywhere in the world, thanks to the fact that almost all of the tests are available through the Internet at designated testing locations. DSST testing facilities are located at over 500 military installations, so service members on active duty can get a jump-start on a post-military career with the DSST program. As an additional incentive, DANTES (Defense Activity for Non-Traditional Education Support) provides funding for DSST test fees for eligible members of the military.

Over thirty subject-matter tests are available in the fields of Business, Humanities, Math, Physical Science, Social Sciences, and Technology.

Available DSST® Exams	
Business	**Social Sciences**
Business Ethics and Society Business Mathematics Human Resource Management Introduction to Business Introduction to Computing Management Information Systems Money and Banking Organizational Behavior Personal Finance Principles of Finance Principles of Supervision	A History of the Vietnam War Art of the Western World Criminal Justice Foundations of Education Fundamentals of Counseling General Anthropology History of the Soviet Union Human/Cultural Geography Introduction to Law Enforcement Lifespan Developmental Psychology Substance Abuse The Civil War and Reconstruction
Humanities	**Physical Science**
Ethics in America Introduction to World Religions Principles of Public Speaking	Astronomy Environment and Humanity: The Race to Save the Planet Health and Human Development Principles of Physical Science I
Math	**Technology**
Fundamentals of College Algebra Principles of Statistics	Fundamentals of Cybersecurity Technical Writing

As you can see from the table, the DSST program covers a wide variety of subjects. However, it is important to ask two questions before registering for a DSST exam.

1. Which universities or colleges award credit for passing DSST exams?

2. Which DSST exams are the most relevant to my desired degree and my experience?

Knowing which universities offer DSST credit is important. In all likelihood, a college in your area awards credit for DSST exams, but find out before taking an exam by contacting the university directly. Then review the list of DSST exams to determine which ones are most relevant to the degree you are seeking and to your base of knowledge. Schedule an appointment with your college adviser to determine which exams best fit your degree program and which college courses the DSST exams can replace. Advisers should also be able to tell you the minimum score required on the DSST exam to receive university credit.

DSST® TEST CENTERS

You can find DSST testing locations in community colleges and universities across the country. Contact your local college or university to find out if the school administers DSST exams, or check the DSST website (www.getcollegecredit.com) for a location near you. Keep in mind that some universities and colleges administer DSST exams only to enrolled students. DSST testing is available to men and women in the armed services at over 500 military installations around the world.

HOW TO REGISTER FOR A DSST® EXAM

Once you have located a nearby DSST testing facility, you need to contact the testing center to find out the exam administration schedule. Many centers are set up to administer tests via the Internet, while others use printed materials. Almost all DSST exams are available as online tests, but the method used depends on the testing center. The cost for each DSST exam starts at $80, and many testing locations charge a fee to cover their costs for administering the tests. Credit cards are the only accepted payment method for taking online DSST exams. Credit card, certified check, and money order are acceptable payment methods for paper-and-pencil tests.

Test-takers are allotted two score reports—one mailed to them and another mailed to a designated college or university, if requested. Online tests generate unofficial scores at the end of the test session, while individuals taking paper tests must wait four to six weeks for score reports.

PREPARING FOR A DSST® EXAM

Even though you are knowledgeable in a certain subject matter, you should still prepare for the test to ensure you achieve the highest score possible. The first step in studying for a DSST exam is to find out what will be on the specific test you have chosen. Information regarding test content is located on the DSST fact sheets, which can be downloaded at no cost from **www.getcollegecredit.com**. Each fact sheet outlines the topics covered on a subject-matter test, as well as the approximate percentage assigned to each topic. For example, questions on the Principles of Supervision exam are distributed in the following way: 20 percent on the roles and responsibilities of the supervisor, 30 percent on organizational environment, and 50 percent on management functions.

In addition to the breakdown of topics on a DSST exam, the fact sheet also lists recommended reference materials. If you do not own the recommended books, then check college bookstores. Avoid paying high prices for new textbooks by looking online for used textbooks. Don't panic if you are unable to locate a specific textbook listed on the fact sheet; the textbooks are merely recommendations. Instead, search for comparable books used in university courses on the specific subject. Current editions are ideal, and it is a good idea to use at least two references when studying for a DSST exam. Of course, the subject matter provided in this book will be a sufficient review for most test-takers. However, if you need additional information, then it is a good idea to have some of the reference materials at your disposal when preparing for a DSST exam.

Fact sheets include other useful information in addition to a list of reference materials and topics. Each fact sheet includes subject-specific sample questions like those you will encounter on the DSST exam. The sample questions provide an idea of the types of questions you can expect on the exam.

Test questions are multiple choice with one correct answer and three incorrect choices. The fact sheet also includes information about the number of credit hours that ACE has recommended be awarded by colleges for a passing DSST exam score. However, you should keep in mind that not all universities and colleges adhere to the ACE recommendation for DSST credit hours. Some institutions require DSST exam scores higher than the minimum score recommended by ACE. Once you have acquired appropriate reference materials and you have the outline provided on the fact sheet, you are ready to start studying, which is where this book can help.

TEST DAY

After reviewing the material and taking practice tests, you are finally ready to take your DSST exam. Follow these tips for a successful test day experience.

1. **Arrive on time.** Not only is it courteous to arrive on time to the DSST testing facility, but it also allows plenty of time for you to take care of check-in procedures and settle into your surroundings.

2. **Bring identification.** DSST test facilities require that candidates bring a valid government-issued identification card with a current photo and signature. Acceptable forms of identification include a current driver's license, passport, military identification card, or state-issued identification card. Individuals who fail to bring proper identification to the DSST testing facility will not be allowed to take an exam.

3. **Bring the right supplies.** If your exam requires the use of a calculator, you may bring a calculator that meets the specifications. For paper-based exams, you may also bring No. 2 pencils with an eraser and black ballpoint pens. Regardless of the exam methodology, you are NOT allowed to bring reference or study materials, scratch paper, or electronics such as cell phones, personal handheld devices, cameras, alarm wrist watches, or tape recorders to the testing center.

4. **Take the test.** During the exam, take the time to read each question-and-answer option carefully. Eliminate the choices you know are incorrect to narrow the number of potential answers. If a question completely stumps you, take an educated guess and move on—remember that DSSTs are timed; you will have 2 hours to take the exam.

With the proper preparation, DSST exams will save you both time and money. So join the thousands of people who have already reaped the benefits of DSST exams and move closer than ever to your college degree.

Ethics in America

OVERVIEW

Chapter 1

The DSST® Ethics in America exam consists of 100 multiple-choice questions that cover contemporary foundational ethics issues such as relativism, subjectivism, determinism and free will; relationships between morality and religious traditions; the development of ethical traditions from Greeks to modern philosophers; and ethical analysis of various issues such as war, capital punishment, human rights, racism and affirmative action, biomedical ethics, and economic inequity. Critical thinking and logical analysis will be as important as your knowledge of ethical concepts and theories.

DIAGNOSTIC TEST ANSWER SHEET

1. Ⓐ Ⓑ Ⓒ Ⓓ   5. Ⓐ Ⓑ Ⓒ Ⓓ   9. Ⓐ Ⓑ Ⓒ Ⓓ   13. Ⓐ Ⓑ Ⓒ Ⓓ   17. Ⓐ Ⓑ Ⓒ Ⓓ

2. Ⓐ Ⓑ Ⓒ Ⓓ   6. Ⓐ Ⓑ Ⓒ Ⓓ   10. Ⓐ Ⓑ Ⓒ Ⓓ   14. Ⓐ Ⓑ Ⓒ Ⓓ   18. Ⓐ Ⓑ Ⓒ Ⓓ

3. Ⓐ Ⓑ Ⓒ Ⓓ   7. Ⓐ Ⓑ Ⓒ Ⓓ   11. Ⓐ Ⓑ Ⓒ Ⓓ   15. Ⓐ Ⓑ Ⓒ Ⓓ   19. Ⓐ Ⓑ Ⓒ Ⓓ

4. Ⓐ Ⓑ Ⓒ Ⓓ   8. Ⓐ Ⓑ Ⓒ Ⓓ   12. Ⓐ Ⓑ Ⓒ Ⓓ   16. Ⓐ Ⓑ Ⓒ Ⓓ   20. Ⓐ Ⓑ Ⓒ Ⓓ

POST-TEST ANSWER SHEET

1. Ⓐ Ⓑ Ⓒ Ⓓ   13. Ⓐ Ⓑ Ⓒ Ⓓ   25. Ⓐ Ⓑ Ⓒ Ⓓ   37. Ⓐ Ⓑ Ⓒ Ⓓ   49. Ⓐ Ⓑ Ⓒ Ⓓ

2. Ⓐ Ⓑ Ⓒ Ⓓ   14. Ⓐ Ⓑ Ⓒ Ⓓ   26. Ⓐ Ⓑ Ⓒ Ⓓ   38. Ⓐ Ⓑ Ⓒ Ⓓ   50. Ⓐ Ⓑ Ⓒ Ⓓ

3. Ⓐ Ⓑ Ⓒ Ⓓ   15. Ⓐ Ⓑ Ⓒ Ⓓ   27. Ⓐ Ⓑ Ⓒ Ⓓ   39. Ⓐ Ⓑ Ⓒ Ⓓ   51. Ⓐ Ⓑ Ⓒ Ⓓ

4. Ⓐ Ⓑ Ⓒ Ⓓ   16. Ⓐ Ⓑ Ⓒ Ⓓ   28. Ⓐ Ⓑ Ⓒ Ⓓ   40. Ⓐ Ⓑ Ⓒ Ⓓ   52. Ⓐ Ⓑ Ⓒ Ⓓ

5. Ⓐ Ⓑ Ⓒ Ⓓ   17. Ⓐ Ⓑ Ⓒ Ⓓ   29. Ⓐ Ⓑ Ⓒ Ⓓ   41. Ⓐ Ⓑ Ⓒ Ⓓ   53. Ⓐ Ⓑ Ⓒ Ⓓ

6. Ⓐ Ⓑ Ⓒ Ⓓ   18. Ⓐ Ⓑ Ⓒ Ⓓ   30. Ⓐ Ⓑ Ⓒ Ⓓ   42. Ⓐ Ⓑ Ⓒ Ⓓ   54. Ⓐ Ⓑ Ⓒ Ⓓ

7. Ⓐ Ⓑ Ⓒ Ⓓ   19. Ⓐ Ⓑ Ⓒ Ⓓ   31. Ⓐ Ⓑ Ⓒ Ⓓ   43. Ⓐ Ⓑ Ⓒ Ⓓ   55. Ⓐ Ⓑ Ⓒ Ⓓ

8. Ⓐ Ⓑ Ⓒ Ⓓ   20. Ⓐ Ⓑ Ⓒ Ⓓ   32. Ⓐ Ⓑ Ⓒ Ⓓ   44. Ⓐ Ⓑ Ⓒ Ⓓ   56. Ⓐ Ⓑ Ⓒ Ⓓ

9. Ⓐ Ⓑ Ⓒ Ⓓ   21. Ⓐ Ⓑ Ⓒ Ⓓ   33. Ⓐ Ⓑ Ⓒ Ⓓ   45. Ⓐ Ⓑ Ⓒ Ⓓ   57. Ⓐ Ⓑ Ⓒ Ⓓ

10. Ⓐ Ⓑ Ⓒ Ⓓ   22. Ⓐ Ⓑ Ⓒ Ⓓ   34. Ⓐ Ⓑ Ⓒ Ⓓ   46. Ⓐ Ⓑ Ⓒ Ⓓ   58. Ⓐ Ⓑ Ⓒ Ⓓ

11. Ⓐ Ⓑ Ⓒ Ⓓ   23. Ⓐ Ⓑ Ⓒ Ⓓ   35. Ⓐ Ⓑ Ⓒ Ⓓ   47. Ⓐ Ⓑ Ⓒ Ⓓ   59. Ⓐ Ⓑ Ⓒ Ⓓ

12. Ⓐ Ⓑ Ⓒ Ⓓ   24. Ⓐ Ⓑ Ⓒ Ⓓ   36. Ⓐ Ⓑ Ⓒ Ⓓ   48. Ⓐ Ⓑ Ⓒ Ⓓ   60. Ⓐ Ⓑ Ⓒ Ⓓ

ETHICS IN AMERICA DIAGNOSTIC TEST

Directions: Carefully read each of the following 20 questions. Choose the best answer to each question and fill in the corresponding circle on the answer sheet. The Answer Key and Explanations can be found following this Diagnostic Test.

1. Which of the following thinkers developed the philosophy of utilitarianism?
   A. Bentham
   B. Nozick
   C. Smith
   D. Mill

2. For a Stoic, the ethical evaluation of a decision to commit suicide depends on whether it
   A. adheres to basic liberties.
   B. seems to be a reasonable act.
   C. appears to be God's will.
   D. increases overall happiness.

3. The Universal Declaration of Human Rights (UDHR)
   A. was issued after the Rwandan genocide in 1994.
   B. has proven ineffective because it is not legally binding anywhere in the world
   C. was drafted by the International Criminal Court.
   D. has influenced nations to adopt laws to preserve basic human rights for their citizens.

4. Intentionally withholding treatment in order to allow a patient to die is
   A. active euthanasia.
   B. suicide.
   C. passive euthanasia.
   D. murder.

5. Compatibilists believe that an individual's actions and decisions
   A. are completely governed by uncontrollable natural forces.
   B. cannot influence future events.
   C. are only mental processes.
   D. can involve the exercise of free will.

6. The Hippocratic Oath is a foundational text in what field?
   A. Political science
   B. Biomedical ethics
   C. Feminism
   D. Academia

7. A supporter of affirmative action would argue that
   A. cultural diversity is not important.
   B. ethnicity and income should be factors in college admissions.
   C. the history of racial segregation is no longer relevant.
   D. college applicants should be evaluated solely by standardized test scores.

8. From what text do both Jews and Christians derive moral principles?
   A. Old Testament
   B. New Testament
   C. The Talmud
   D. The Catechism

9. Which of the following philosophies bases morality on the consequences of a behavior?
   A. Determinism
   B. Objectivism
   C. Utilitarianism
   D. Idealism

10. For a subjectivist, the statement "murder is wrong" is
    A. an objective truth.
    B. an expression of personal perception.
    C. supported by scientific evidence.
    D. an objective falsehood.

11. Relativism is the philosophical theory that
    A. some moral systems are inherently more valid than others.
    B. different people have different standards of behavior.
    C. rights are decided by popular consensus.
    D. morality involves absolute truths.

12. Which of these is **NOT** a goal of rehabilitative punishment?
    A. Improve quality of life for inmates
    B. Reduce overall crime rate
    C. Prevent criminals from reentering society
    D. Provide inmates with useful skills and education

13. Which of the following is **NOT** a monotheistic religion?
    A. Islam
    B. Judaism
    C. Hinduism
    D. Christianity

14. According to Just War theory, all of the following are important criteria for war **EXCEPT**:
    A. Right intentions
    B. Majority in favor
    C. Possibility of success
    D. Matches provocation

15. Which of the following statements best describes *anthropocentrism*?
    A. Humans are the most important living organisms.
    B. Men are superior to women.
    C. All creatures are equally important.
    D. Humans should not control the lives of animals.

16. For a utilitarian, the ethical evaluation of the decision to have an abortion will **NOT** depend on whether the abortion will
    A. cause emotional pain for the woman's family.
    B. eliminate pain for the woman having the abortion.
    C. cause suffering for the woman having the abortion.
    D. instigate change for the woman and her family.

17. The approach that women take when making moral decisions is known as
    A. ethics of feminists.
    B. ethics of justice.
    C. ethics of care.
    D. ethics of empathy.

18. Which Hindu term refers to a person's actions determining what happens to them in the future?
    A. Nirvana
    B. Karma
    C. Dharma
    D. Ahisma

19. Supporters of distributive justice are primarily concerned with what societal issue?
    A. Institutional racism
    B. Economic inequality
    C. Misogyny
    D. Homophobia

20. Aquinas was able to draw a connection between
    A. mathematics and knowledge.
    B. happiness and morality.
    C. theology and science.
    D. faith and virtue.

ANSWER KEY AND EXPLANATIONS

1. A	**5.** D	**9.** C	**13.** C	**17.** C
2. B	**6.** B	**10.** B	**14.** B	**18.** B
3. D	**7.** B	**11.** B	**15.** A	**19.** B
4. C	**8.** A	**12.** C	**16.** D	**20.** C

1. **The correct answer is A.** Jeremy Bentham first developed the concept of British utilitarianism. Mill (choice D) was a utilitarian inspired by Bentham, but he did not first develop the philosophy. Nozick (choice B) and Smith (choice C) were not utilitarian philosophers.

2. **The correct answer is B.** For a Stoic, the ethical evaluation of a decision to commit suicide depends on whether it seems to be a reasonable act. In cases where a person has a debilitating disease for which there is no treatment, suicide would most likely be considered moral to a Stoic. A utilitarian bases decisions on whether overall happiness increases (choice D). Choices A and C are incorrect.

3. **The correct answer is D.** The Universal Declaration of Human Rights (UDHR) was issued by the United Nations in 1948; thus choices A and C are incorrect. Although it is not legally binding anywhere in the world, some or all of its thirty articles have been adapted by sovereign nations for use in their own laws. It has been used in various international treaties and other human rights-related documents around the world, including the International Bill of Rights, so it is far from being ineffective (choice B).

4. **The correct answer is C.** Passive euthanasia refers to the act of intentionally withholding treatment in order to allow a patient to die. Active euthanasia (choice A) refers to intentionally killing a patient by lethal injection, smothering, or some other method. Suicide (choice B) and murder (choice D) are incorrect.

5. **The correct answer is D.** Compatibilists believe that the theories of determinism and free will are compatible and that an individual's actions and decisions, while influenced by prior causes, also involve the exercise of free will. Hard determinists, on the other hand, believe that actions and decisions are completely governed by uncontrollable natural forces (choice A). Compatibilists believe that an individual can influence future events and that decisions are more than only mental processes, making choices B and C incorrect.

6. **The correct answer is B.** The Hippocratic Oath is a foundational text in biomedical ethics. Composed by the Greek physician Hippocrates in the fifth century BCE, the oath establishes ethical standards that most modern doctors follow, such as maintaining patient confidentiality and not causing intentional injury. Choices A, C, and D are incorrect.

7. **The correct answer is B.** Supporters of affirmative action believe that diversity is important in schools and workplaces and that traditional markers of success, such as high standardized test scores, cannot always be achieved by students and applicants disadvantaged by racism and economic inequality. They therefore enact admissions and hiring policies that give special consideration to factors such as race, ethnicity, and income, alongside other academic and/or career achievements. Therefore, choices A, C, and D are incorrect.

8. **The correct answer is A.** Jews and Christians both derive moral values from the Old Testament, which includes the Five Books of Moses (Genesis, Exodus, Leviticus, Numbers, and Deuteronomy). The New Testament (choice B) is a source of ethical teachings for Christians only, while the Talmud (choice C) is a series of Jewish legal

books. The Catechism (choice D) is a core
text of the Catholic Church and is not read
by Jews.

9. **The correct answer is C.** Utilitarianism,
which is also known as consequentialism,
is the philosophy that actions are morally
acceptable if good consequences outweigh
bad consequences. On the other hand, an
action is considered immoral if bad consequences outweigh good consequences.
Determinism asserts that events occur
because of natural laws, so choice A is
incorrect. Choices B and D are not based
on consequences.

10. **The correct answer is B.** Subjectivism is the
philosophical theory that there is no absolute
truth, but rather, all statements are reducible
to personal preferences and perceptions.
Empiricism is the philosophical theory that
absolute truths can be determined through
scientific experimentation and evidence
(choice C). Choices A and D are incorrect.

11. **The correct answer is B.** Moral relativism
is the philosophical theory that different
people have different standards of behavior.
A relativist might argue, for example, that
cannibalism is no less moral than eating a
vegetarian diet. The theory that rights are
determined by popular consensus (choice C)
is typically associated with Immanuel Kant's
notion of the "common good." Choices A
and D are incorrect.

12. **The correct answer is C.** Rehabilitation
provides convicted criminals an education
and other opportunities for personal growth
while they are imprisoned. The objective of
a rehabilitative prison system is to make
life inside prison more productive and
harmonious and to prepare prisoners for
their eventual release. Because educated and
skilled individuals are considered less likely
to commit further crimes, rehabilitated
prisoners are allowed to reenter society.
Therefore, choices A, B, and D are incorrect.

13. **The correct answer is C.** There are many
Hindu gods according to followers of Hinduism. Islam, Judaism, and Christianity
are monotheisms, meaning that followers
believe in the existence of one God and no

other higher beings. Thus, choices A, B, and
D are incorrect.

14. **The correct answer is B.** According to Just
War theory, a war is justified if it is fought
with the right intentions (choice A), if there
is a reasonable chance for success (choice C),
and if the actions match the provocation
(choice D). The opinion of the majority
(choice B) is not a criterium.

15. **The correct answer is A.** Anthropocentrism
is the philosophical theory that humans are
inherently superior to other living organisms,
and thus, humans have the right to exert
control over natural processes. Choice B
describes *androcentrism*—a male-focused
philosophical perspective—rather than
anthropocentrism. Choices C and D are
incorrect.

16. **The correct answer is D.** A utilitarian views
ethical decisions in terms of good and bad
consequences. If the overall consequences
are bad, then a decision is immoral. Choices
A, B, and C affect the overall happiness
or unhappiness of the people involved, so
these are factors in the decision. Choice D
is irrelevant, which means it is the correct
answer.

17. **The correct answer is C.** The concept of
ethics of care was developed by psychologist
Carol Gilligan, who asserts that women
consider responsibilities and relationships
when making decisions. The moral decisions
made by women often appeal to such emotions as sympathy, love, and concern. The
ethics of justice (choice B) is what Gilligan
believes is the male approach to decision
making, based on application of rules and
minimizing emotions. Choices A and D are
incorrect.

18. **The correct answer is B.** Karma is the
Hindu and Buddhist principle that a person's
actions determine what happens to them
in the future and in future reincarnations.
Nirvana refers to a state of bliss, so choice
A is incorrect. Dharma (choice C) refers to
the duties that must be fulfilled based on a
person's caste. Ahisma (choice D) is the way
a person acts or feels about others.

19. **The correct answer is B.** Proponents of distributive justice are concerned with economic inequality. They argue that wide disparities in income are detrimental to the common good and that with redistribution of money, goods, and services—such as welfare, educational scholarships, and health care—society can be more just and harmonious. Choices A, C, and D are incorrect.

20. **The correct answer is C.** St. Thomas Aquinas was a thirteenth-century Catholic priest who drew a connection between theology and science. Aquinas believed that learning about nature was a way to learn about God. Choices A, B, and D are incorrect.

answers diagnostic test

DIAGNOSTIC TEST ASSESSMENT GRID

Now that you've completed the diagnostic test and read through the answer explanations, you can use your results to target your studying. Find the question numbers from the diagnostic test that you answered incorrectly and highlight or circle them below. Then focus extra attention on the sections within the chapter dealing with those topics.

Ethics in America		
Content Area	**Topic**	**Question #**
Ethical Traditions	• Greek views • Religious traditions • Law and justice • Consequentialist ethics • Feminist/Womanist ethics	1, 2, 9, 13, 17 18, 20
Contemporary Foundational Issues	• Relativism • Subjectivism • Determinism and free will • Relationship between morality and religion	5, 8, 10,11
Ethical Analysis of Issues and Practical Applications	• Morality, relationships, and sexuality • Life and death issues • Economic issues • Civil Rights • Punishment • War and peace • Life-centered and human-centered ethics • Human rights • Biomedical ethics	3, 4, 6, 7, 12, 14, 15, 16, 19

GET THE FACTS

To see the DSST® Ethics in America Fact Sheet, go to **http://getcollegecredit.com/exam_fact_sheets** and click on the **Humanities** tab. Scroll down and click the **Ethics in America** link. Here you will find suggestions for further study material and the ACE college credit recommendations for passing the test.

ETHICAL TRADITIONS

Ethics refers to the academic discipline of analyzing morality. Reasoning, rules, and logic form the basis of ethical philosophy. The foundation of American ethics began thousands of years ago in Ancient Greece when philosophers such as Socrates, Plato, and Aristotle first began discussing virtue, justice, and politics.

GREEK VIEWS

Since at least 1200 BCE, myths and stories provided explanations for virtually everything in Greek life from floods to war battles. Greek gods and goddesses resembled human beings, and mythology focused on the activities of Earth's residents. The Greek worldview considered people the center of everything, and the world was a playground for traveling, building societies, and engaging in warfare. Change occurred in the sixth century BCE when pre-Socratic philosophers raised questions about the natural world. How was the world made? How does the world work? The theories of cosmology and cosmogony developed at this time. **Cosmology** is the study of the physical world, such as what it is made of and how it works. **Cosmogony** is the study of the origin of the universe, such as how it came into existence.

One of the most notable pre-Socratic philosophers was Pythagoras, who was also a mathematician and a cosmologist. Since Pythagoras wrote nothing, his exact philosophy is uncertain. However, evidence suggests that beliefs in the magic of numbers and reincarnation were aspects of his philosophy. The philosopher had a significant number of followers, perhaps because people believed he had miraculous powers.

The Sophists

The first philosophers in Greece studied nature, but philosophical focus shifted to man toward the second half of the fifth century BCE. The democratic system in Athens was evolving, and it was the duty of every free adult male to participate in government. Because of the interest in society and politics among Athens citizens, a group of teachers known as the Sophists emerged. The Sophists traveled throughout Greece giving lectures about various popular topics, such as rhetoric, history, mathematics, and politics. Sophists received large sums of money in exchange for their presentations, unlike the wise men of Greece who freely shared their thoughts with the public.

The public viewed the first Sophists as teachers of virtue and excellence rather than as philosophers. Protagoras, one of the earliest and most respected Sophists, is best known for stating, "Man is the measure of all things." The statement suggests that people rather than nature determine behavior. Many experts consider the Sophists the first relativists. Ethical relativism proposes that every point of view is equally valid and that different people have different standards of behavior. Relativists often rely more heavily on persuasion than on truth. In addition, Protagoras questioned the existence of gods and thought that individuals should act according to their best interests without searching for wisdom from a higher power.

While many early Sophists were admired, others drew criticism for being untrustworthy. Some Sophists made boastful assertions that they could prove any position without knowledge of the subject

TIP

Most of the criticism aimed against the Sophists regarded their reliance on persuasion and manipulation, rather than the truth.

matter. The term *sophistry,* which means to use purposely deceptive and invalid arguments, derives its meaning from actions of the Sophists. Despite the fact that the Sophists emphasized persuasive skills rather than the honest analysis of issues, they set the stage for intellectual discussion in Athens.

Thucydides

In 431 BCE, war broke out between Athens and Sparta. Thucydides, a Greek historian, wrote *The History of the Peloponnesian War* as a report of the battle that lasted until 404 BCE. *The History of the Peloponnesian War* provides a graphic and exact account of military actions. Thucydides objectively presented the factual events of the war without any attribution to mythological beings. Yet he added drama to the document with the inclusion of fictional speeches that are factual in content. Considered one of the first and greatest historians, Thucydides raised questions in his publication about the ethics of war, especially with regard to justice and power.

Socrates

Socrates, one of the most influential thinkers of all times, lived in Athens during the fifth century BCE. Socrates was an outspoken critic of the Sophists, Athenian politics, and religious institutions. Socrates considered the teachings of the Sophists empty and manipulative, and he debated with them frequently. Socrates sought to uncover truth and spent much of his time discussing virtue, justice, and morality with the citizens of Athens. During the time of Socrates, most people equated virtue with beauty, and the philosopher hoped to change that notion. Socrates hoped to elevate the moral and intellectual nature of the city, and he sacrificed everything he had in this attempt.

Most information about Socrates' teachings stems from the writings of his most famous student, Plato, because Socrates never wrote any books. Socrates is renowned more for the way in which he taught than a specific philosophy. Socrates employed a questioning technique, later termed the Socratic Method or dialectic, to discuss philosophical issues with people. The method involves asking a series of questions and drawing out answers from students to develop understanding and insight about a particular issue. Socrates' series of questions eventually weakened the other person's argument by pointing out contradictions. Most of the time, Socrates claimed that he lacked any knowledge of the subject to illustrate that answers existed in the mind of the student.

Plato

Socrates' most famous student, Plato, was a philosopher and mathematician. After the death of Socrates, Plato continued with his teacher's work and established **the Academy** in 387 BCE. The Academy, which is considered the first university, served as the most significant institution of higher learning in the Western world. There, teachers and students discussed and researched mathematics, astronomy, politics, and natural history. Plato's earliest writings, the Socratic dialogues, convey the ideas of his deceased teacher. A dialogue is a method of presenting ideas in the format of a fictional discussion with other people, which for Plato was usually Socrates.

Plato's most famous and influential work is *The Republic.* The text uses dialogues to examine whether it is always better to be just than unjust. Unhappy with the democracy and tyranny of Greek government, Plato believed that selfish individuals wielded too much power. Plato's discussion of an ideal republic, known as utopian thinking, led to his conclusion that the ideal state is divided into three classes of citizens. The guardians of society are philosopher-kings. Philosopher-kings are capable of understanding truth and justice and are guided by wisdom rather than self-interest. Soldiers serve as the next level of Plato's ideal society because they are unselfish, moral, and courageous. The final societal level consists of workers or producers who are motivated by a certain level of greed, which Plato refers to as appetite. In Plato's ideal state, political justice replaces democracy and tyranny.

In *The Republic*, Plato employed an extended metaphor known as the Allegory of the Cave to compare untutored people to prisoners in a cave. The prisoners misinterpret shadows on a wall as reality. The parable and the rest of *The Republic* illustrate Plato's primary philosophical convictions:

- The world experienced through the senses is not the real world, which can only be understood intellectually.
- Some people are less virtuous than others, which is why government is necessary.
- Enlightened people have a responsibility to society.

As with other Greeks of the fourth and fifth century BCE, Plato believed in pursuing personal excellence to achieve peace in a troubled world. Plato explains in *The Republic* that the world may not acknowledge or reward virtue, but ultimate happiness can only be achieved through virtue.

Aristotle

One of the most renowned students of Plato's Academy in Athens was the philosopher Aristotle. In addition to being a philosopher, Aristotle was an authority on nearly every subject, including ethics, physics, biology, and psychology. However, Aristotle's approach to philosophy differed significantly from his teacher's methods. Whereas Plato viewed the world in abstracts, Aristotle concentrated on observations and experiences, or empirical knowledge. Learning about so many subjects corresponds with two key beliefs of Aristotle:

1. Everything has a purpose.
2. Change is both necessary and natural.

According to Aristotle, living virtuously is the purpose of human beings in the world. In his book *Nicomachean Ethics*, Aristotle states that physical pleasures derived from money, work, and sex fail to bring ultimate happiness. Aristotle equates virtue to happiness, and he distinguishes between two types of virtues—moral excellence and intellectual excellence. Moral virtues, which indicate excellence of character, include self-control, bravery, self-respect, gentleness, truthfulness, and generosity. Intellectual virtues include scientific knowledge, intuitive reason, practical wisdom, and skill. From Aristotle's perspective, maintaining balance and not going to the extreme in either direction is the key to happiness. This concept is known as the **golden mean**.

Stoics and Hedonists

From the fourth through the first centuries BCE, the philosophy of Plato and Aristotle spread to other countries along the Mediterranean Sea. During this period, multiple groups of thought emerged, including the Stoics and the Hedonists.

Founded around 300 BCE by a philosopher named Zeno, **Stoicism** later influenced Christian thinkers and experienced a revival during the Renaissance. Stoicism is a philosophy based on the idea that absolute law rules the universe and that humans cannot change fate. According to Stoic ethics, virtue requires living and acting according to reason and self-control. Wise and happy people are content with whatever occurs in life because they realize everything is inevitable. Unhappiness occurs when a person feels disappointment or regret about a certain course of events. Epictetus, one of the most prominent Stoics of the second century AD, encouraged his students to "live according to nature." Epictetus, a Roman slave often tortured by his master, exemplified the Stoic philosophy by refusing to moan during beatings because he accepted his fate in life.

Also around 300 BCE, the philosophy of **hedonism**, or **Epicureanism,** emerged under the guidance of Epicurus. The philosopher asserted that happiness was the purpose of life. According to hedonism, achieving happiness involves avoiding pain and increasing pleasure. Epicurus asserted that the universe was created by an accidental collision of atoms rather than by Greek gods. While Epicurus did not deny the existence of gods and goddesses, he suggested that they are indifferent to the activities of humans. Upon death, people's souls and bodies would dissolve back into atoms. As a result, hedonists felt free to enjoy life to the greatest extent without worrying about retribution from the gods.

RELIGIOUS TRADITIONS

The Bible has been the most popular tool for teaching morality in the Western world and serves as the center point for Judeo-Christian ethics. The Bible was first translated into Greek around 250 BCE, and it offered a completely different approach to ethics than the Greek philosophers did. For the Israelites, morality resided in one righteous God, and God's teachings were the basis of their laws.

Jews and Christians share the moral principles found in the Hebrew Bible, or Old Testament. The Ten Commandments are a list of rules indicating that it is immoral to murder, commit adultery, steal, and covet. Stories throughout the Old Testament indicate the importance of obeying God, taking responsibility, and exhibiting willpower. Whereas Judaism is based only on the Old Testament, Christianity also includes the teachings of Jesus Christ, found in the New Testament. The New Testament provides numerous ethical principles, most of which are focused on the concept of love. Christians are instructed to love God above all else and to love their neighbors, as indicated by the story of the Good Samaritan.

Although the Bible has been the most significant source of morality in America since the first colonists arrived, other religious traditions have had an effect on Western society as well. The following table provides a general overview of the major world religions.

Major World Religions	
Christianity	Bible instructs that personal salvation occurs through faith and that God is merciful and all knowing.
Judaism	As the oldest monotheistic religion, Judaism places importance on history, laws, and religious community and is responsible for influencing both Islam and Christianity.

Major World Religions	
Islam	Koran believed to have been written by the prophet Mohammed under the direction of God. Muslims are instructed to be generous and obedient and to avoid being greedy or prideful.
Hinduism	Moral guidance based on a principle called ahimsa, which is the principle of nonviolence. Ahisma involves both behavior and feelings towards others, so hatred for another violates ahisma. Emphasis is on being detached from pain and desire and choosing actions that cause the least amount of harm.
Buddhism	Moral code does not have a divine origin. Dalai Lama asserts that morality helps people achieve happiness many times through reincarnation. Happiness to self and others derives from being loving, compassionate, patient, forgiving, and responsible.

The concepts of *karma* and *dharma* are connected with both Hinduism and Buddhism. Karma is the principle that a person's actions determine what happens to them in the future and in future reincarnations. Dharma refers to the righteous duties of a person toward people and gods. In contrast, the three monotheistic religions—Judaism, Christianity, and Islam—consider events in life as being the will of God. *Monotheism* means belief in only one god rather than multiple gods.

Many countries around the world have a national religion. In some, religious concepts of morality and justice heavily influence the law of the land. In the United States, numerous laws reflect the Judeo-Christian morality of some of the nation's founders, as well as the moral perspectives of a majority of the current population. Laws prohibiting murder, theft, and slavery, for example, can be traced back to Biblical precepts. Yet there is also a commonly accepted "separation of church and state." Though that phrase does not technically appear in the Constitution, the First Amendment does state: "Congress shall make no law respecting an establishment of religion, or prohibiting the free exercise thereof." Most legal scholars interpret this statute as saying that while everyone is free to practice (or not practice) religion, religious morals and rules do not override secular law. Conversely, the First Amendment also protects religious institutions from government intrusion.

LAW AND JUSTICE

Natural law theories are based on the idea that the moral standards guiding human behavior originate in human nature and the universe. Deviating from the norm is immoral, sinful, evil, and harmful. However, the disorder caused by deviation forces a reasoning individual to restore events back to normal. Such logic is based on the idea that the universe is morally neutral and that moral laws are part of nature. The attraction of natural law is its ability to provide meaning for life and behavior. Elements of natural law are evident in the beliefs of the Ancient Greeks and the Stoics.

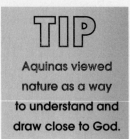

TIP

Aquinas viewed nature as a way to understand and draw close to God.

Aquinas's Natural Law Theory

Many medieval philosophers adopted natural law theories in an attempt to explain the relationship between God and humanity. Thirteenth-century Catholic priest St. Thomas Aquinas believed that faith and reason could exist together, and that theology and science were not contradictory. Well versed in the philosophy of Aristotle, Aquinas wrote that learning about nature is a way to learn about God. Aquinas's **theory of natural law** asserts that the laws discovered in nature stem from the eternal God. Human beings are naturally rational, so it is moral for humans to behave rationally.

Political Theories

In addition to questions about nature, numerous philosophers have raised questions about political authorities and the best way to manage societies. **Social contract theory** refers to the idea that the right to rule and the obligation to obey are based upon an agreement between an individual and society. The moral code put forth in a social contract creates a harmonious society in which all parties work together for mutual advantage. Thomas Hobbes, John Locke, and Jean-Jacques Rousseau wrote about social contract theory during the seventeenth and eighteenth centuries. As the most well-known social contract theorists, they attempted to explain how people join society for the purpose of security and societal order.

Thomas Hobbes

Thomas Hobbes, an English political philosopher, developed a theory suggesting that humans live fearfully in a natural world full of insecurity and violence. *Leviathan*, which Hobbes wrote during the English Civil War, describes the relationship between civil law and natural law. According to Hobbes, fear and insecurity force people into surrendering their natural rights to a sovereign ruler and forming a social contract. Failure to submit to a ruler, even a bad one, will result in conflict and savagery. Hobbes viewed virtues such as gratitude and modesty as traits that help people live harmoniously with the rest of society. He believed that it is in the self-interest of individuals to have such characteristics.

John Locke

Seventeenth-century British philosopher John Locke provided his thoughts about government in numerous writings, and he is often associated with the concept of empiricism. **Empiricism** refers to the notion that reliable knowledge is acquired by testing ideas against sensory evidence. Locke proposed that humans are not born with any ideas because the mind is a blank slate at birth. Understanding develops as people see, hear, and touch things.

Locke spent much of his efforts questioning the structure of British government. For centuries, people held that kings were direct descendants of Adam and thus had the divine right to rule. However, the bloodshed resulting from recent wars caused Locke to raise concerns about the monarchy. In *Two Treatises of Government,* Locke explains the function of political authority and proposes that individuals have certain natural rights:

- The right to live without being harmed by others
- The right to make their own choices
- The right to own property

According to Locke, the purpose of political authority is to protect individual rights to life, liberty, and property. Underlying Locke's theory is the idea that people have the right to resist unjust political authority. When a political power fails to uphold its half of a social contract, citizens should resist and revolt to protect their rights.

Locke's revolutionary ideas about government influenced many others, including Thomas Jefferson and the Founding Fathers in writing the U.S. Declaration of Independence:

> *We hold these truths to be self-evident, that all men are created equal, that they are endowed by their Creator with certain unalienable rights, that among these are life, liberty, and the pursuit of happiness.*

Jean-Jacques Rousseau

Locke also influenced Jean-Jacques Rousseau, the eighteenth-century French philosopher. Rousseau believed that human beings are innately good but that society, with its desires and greed, corrupts them. Rousseau developed the concept of **general will** in *Discourse on Political Economy* and *The Social Contract*. Under general will, citizens act as legislators to determine, as a collective body, the laws and legislation of society. According to the concept of general will, power rests with the citizens, and society becomes highly democratic. The French government banned Rousseau's controversial writings, and the philosopher fled to Switzerland.

John Rawls and Robert Nozick

Two American philosophers of the twentieth century are known for their ideas regarding political philosophy. John Rawls, author of *A Theory of Justice*, revived the social contract theory. Most of Rawls's writings raised questions about **distributive justice**, which refers to the way in which benefits and burdens are allocated within a society. Rawls attempted to refute the philosophy of utilitarianism based on the concept of "justice as fairness":

- **First principle:** Each person is to have an equal right to the most extensive total system of equal basic liberties compatible with a similar system of liberty for all.
- **Second principle:** Social and economic inequalities are to be arranged so that they are both: A. to the greatest benefit of the least advantaged, and B. attached to offices and positions open to all under conditions of fair equality of opportunity.

According to Rawls, the first principle has priority over the second principle, which is known as the difference principle. So, basic liberties, like freedom of speech, should not be hindered to improve life for the least advantaged individuals in a society. Rawls summed up his philosophy when he stated, "Injustice is simply inequalities that are not to the benefit of all."

One of Rawls's colleagues at Harvard, Robert Nozick, also addressed the concept of distributive justice. However, Nozick compared income tax to forced labor and stated that the redistribution of wealth is only justifiable when it is resolving a past injustice.

Immanuel Kant

Eighteenth-century German philosopher Immanuel Kant is one of the greatest influences on Western philosophy. Much of Kant's work attempts to answer three primary questions:

1. What can I know?
2. What should I do?
3. What can I hope for?

The concept of **transcendental idealism** plays a significant role in Kant's philosophy, as well as the philosophy of other German idealists. *Transcendence* means to be beyond the experience. Transcendental idealism is the concept that appearances should be viewed as only representations and not as things themselves. In other words, both the mind and understanding create reality. Kant used four categories of understanding—space, time, causality, and substance—to explain how the mind structures reality and enables people to make sense of experiences. Kant referred to these four concepts as *a priori* concepts to explain that the concepts occurred before a person's existence.

In addition, Kant developed two categories of moral thought: practical reason and pure reason. Practical reason is reasoning about how people should act, and pure reason is reasoning about what actually exists. Categorical imperatives are universal moral laws that act as the basis of practical reason and that help people behave morally. According to Kant, a behavior conforms to a categorical imperative if it is moral for all human beings.

CONSEQUENTIALIST ETHICS

Moral Egoism

Best known as the author of *The Wealth of Nations*, Adam Smith was more than a founder of **capitalism.** He was also an eighteenth-century moral philosopher. Smith proposed that the common good of society advances when individuals focus on benefiting themselves, a concept related to moral egoism. The theory of moral egoism asserts that it is always moral to act in a manner that benefits self-interest. According to Smith, individuals are able to achieve happiness in life when they focus on their own happiness rather than the happiness of others.

Ayn Rand, a twentieth-century Russian philosopher, also falls into the category of **moral egoist.** Rand asserted that pursuing self-interests and personal happiness are "the highest moral purpose" of life. According to Rand's philosophy of objectivism, doing anything for another person will sacrifice happiness unless there is a material or psychological reward involved. Rand's writings indicate her objection to the weak exploiting the strong and her admiration for individual accomplishment.

Utilitarianism

Utilitarianism, or **consequentialism**, refers to the theory that actions are morally acceptable if good consequences outweigh bad consequences. Similarly, if bad consequences outweigh good consequences, an action is morally wrong. Therefore, morality is completely about the results of any behavior. A utilitarian does not seek answers to ethical dilemmas from the universe, but from within. Behavior that brings pleasure is moral, while behavior that brings pain is immoral.

Jeremy Bentham (1748–1832) modified the philosophy of Epicurus, the first utilitarian, by arguing that service to society generates more pleasure than service to self. As the founder of British utilitarianism, Bentham asserted that behavior is wrong if it reduces overall happiness. For Bentham, behavior that produces long-term happiness to the community is preferred to short-term personal happiness. Bentham defines happiness as experiencing pleasure and avoiding pain. Bentham's ideas motivated the Philosophical Radicals, a group of social reformers in the early part of the nineteenth century. The Radicals advocated universal male suffrage and politics geared toward human happiness instead of natural rights.

Bentham's work inspired nineteenth-century British philosopher John Stuart Mill, whose father was a member of the Radicals. Mill conveyed his utilitarian ideas in numerous pieces, but his essay *On Liberty* is the best-known. In the essay, Mill asserts that the only time a government has the moral authority to limit a person's liberty is when harm may occur otherwise. In all other situations, people should be allowed the freedom to behave as desired. Continuing with utilitarian concepts, Mill wrote *The Subjugation of Women* as an argument in favor of women's equality. Mill asserts that the marital relationship improves when both partners have equal roles.

FEMINIST/WOMANIST ETHICS

Feminism refers to the philosophical and political discourse geared toward exposing, analyzing, and addressing sexual inequality. Feminist philosophy emerged in the 1960s for a number of reasons. First, it was believed that the bulk of philosophical research omitted women from major studies. Second, it was believed that there was a masculine bias in philosophical research, so an accurate assessment of women's morals was either neglected or distorted.

Carol Gilligan is a psychologist best known for her research and writings about the moral development of women. Unlike feminists who assert that there are no differences between men and women, Gilligan indicates that women and men have different approaches to making moral decisions. Men, she believes, have an ethics of justice and focus on applying rules and minimizing emotions when making decisions. For example, Kant's categorical imperatives and utilitarianism are both masculine approaches to making decisions. In contrast, she contends that women have an ethics of care and consider responsibilities and relationships when making decisions. The moral decisions made by women often appeal to such emotions as sympathy, love, and concern. Gilligan argues that both types of ethics are valuable to society.

Philosopher Nel Noddings also studies the concept of ethics of care. Noddings has focused her research on the origins of care within the home, such as parent-child relationships. Noddings asserts that studying how people care for those around them leads to understanding how to care for people within society.

CONTEMPORARY FOUNDATIONAL ISSUES

DETERMINISM AND FREE WILL

Do we as human beings have the ability to make spontaneous choices and exercise free will? Or is every action and decision predetermined by unchangeable natural processes? Can we know that we are free, and does it matter—morally or legally—whether we are or aren't? These are the questions at the heart of the theory of **determinism.**

Determinists assert that everything results from a cause, whether known or hidden, and that prior events directly influence future events. Determinism is not as rigid as the theory of fatalism, which argues that the origins of the universe set in motion an absolutely inescapable course of history and that all events proceed according to one certain destiny. Nevertheless, determinists do assert that certain causes necessarily produce certain effects. These causes can range from the physical laws of the universe, such as the movement of electrons within an atom, to social and environmental factors, such as education and childhood experiences. The eighteenth-century philosopher Baron d'Holbach theorized that, because the chemical matter in the human brain is subject to the laws of physics and biology, all human thought and perception is determined by those laws as well. Thus all actions, from taking a single step to committing a violent crime, should be seen as a consequence of chemical reactions rather than the outcome of independent moral choice.

More recently, the psychologist B.F. Skinner proposed that free will was an illusion and that external stimuli such as positive reinforcement, negative reinforcement, and punishment determine our patterns of behavior. He demonstrated, through laboratory experiments on rats, that introducing or withholding certain stimuli to a situation greatly increased the probability of certain behaviors and actions. He called this practice "operant conditioning." As with d'Holbach's theory, Skinner's experiments raised significant questions about whether an individual can be held morally or legally responsible for his or her actions, if inputs such as punishment or reward make certain future actions inevitable.

Compatibilists, by contrast, argue that while the laws of nature do influence our behavior, we can also make choices that subvert established patterns and prevent supposed inevitabilities. Put simply, compatibilists believe free will is not an illusion. Some ethicists take this position on theological grounds, such as the early Christian philosopher Augustine, who argued that God granted humans the freedom to act or not act based on our impulses. Others take a more secular approach, pointing at scientific evidence that shows that despite the laws of physics, random and unpredictable events can and do occur. The question of moral responsibility is thus arguably less complicated for compatibilists; if free will does exist, then individuals who commit moral and legal offenses do so knowingly and by their own volition. Members of society may then exercise their own volition to punish (or not punish) the offender accordingly.

Relativism and Subjectivism

Humans abide by (and likewise reject) countless moral and ethical systems, many of which we have explored: stoicism, hedonism, utilitarianism, moral egoism, idealism, feminism, etc. Many of these systems, such as hedonism and moral egoism, are compatible and have overlapping principles and values. Others, particularly religious belief systems, have less in common, and their differences have historically created tension and conflict.

Which one of these ethical systems is inherently better than all the others? Which one should you personally follow? Which will produce the most happiness—that is, if being happy is the purpose of life after all? Two philosophical theories, relativism and subjectivism, do not provide precise instruction for living a meaningful life or compel followers to adhere to certain norms. Rather, they are "meta-ethical" theories. They analyze the relationships *between* ethical systems; explore the value and effect of ethical statements and judgments; and consider whether any absolute ethical truth is ever possible.

Relativism is the theory that there is no such thing as an unconditional or universal ethical truth. Rather, all ethical practices are circumstantial—they reflect social, cultural, or personal situations. Different practices and ethics may be right for different people at different places and times. When traveling to another country, for example, it is typical to set aside the customs practiced at home and adopt the hosts' customs, reflecting a belief that there is inherent value to ways of life other than one's own. Relativists also make the point that social mores and scientific ideas have changed greatly over several millennia, and that we should thus be wary of anyone expressing supposedly absolute claims or infallible truths. Enforcing rigid moral rules and shutting out alternatives can prevent cultural growth and progress.

Subjectivism is the related theory that that there is no such thing as an unconditional or universal ethical truth, specifically because all statements reflect *only* the personal perception of the person saying them. Thus if you said "Rainy days are the worst," you wouldn't be objectively "right," and someone else who loved playing in the rain wouldn't be objectively "wrong"—the two of you would simply have different, yet equally valid perceptions. At first glance, subjectivism would appear to make it impossible for members of society to act and think collectively, since we all exist in our own moral bubbles. In practice, however, many people can and do act on the same common-sense beliefs and instincts, and where there is disagreement, subjectivism suggests compromise and tolerance of others' attitudes. In the subjectivist perspective, ethical statements can gain in value and become actionable when people listening to the statement agree: If millions agree that "murder is a crime," for example, they can build a society and pass laws that reflect that preference, even while recognizing that it's not an absolute truth or fact.

RELATIONSHIP BETWEEN MORALITY AND RELIGION

To discuss the relationship between morality and religion, one must first determine if there is an interconnection between religious views and morals. Many religions provide a framework for values designed to guide members regarding personal behavior and in determining between right and wrong through sources such as holy books, oral and written traditions, and religious leaders. Within the wide range of ethical traditions, religious traditions often share tenets with secular ethical theories such as consequentialism and utilitarianism.

Although the two concepts can be considered as closely related, many ethicists believe religion and morality are not synonymous and that, both in principle and theory, morality and a religious value system are two distinct guides for behavior. Religious values vary greatly, which can affect one's interpretation of what is considered moral. Modern monotheistic religions, such as Christianity, Islam, and Judaism, define right and wrong by the laws and rules set forth by their respective gods and as interpreted by religious leaders within the respective faith. Polytheistic religious traditions, however, tend to be less definitive. For example, in the Buddhist faith, an individual's intention and the circumstances involved in a given situation both play roles in determining whether an action is right or wrong.

For many religious people, morality and religion are the same or inseparable; for them, either morality is a result of practicing their religion or their religion is their morality. For others, especially those who do not adhere to any religion, morality and religion are distinct and separate; religion may be immoral or completely unrelated to morality, and morality may or should have no connection to religion. Debate continues as to whether a moral life can be lived without an absolute lawgiver (a deity) as a guide, and if moral behavior is dependent upon religious beliefs. This controversy is further fueled when questions of ethics arise regarding religions with beliefs that conflict with current social standards.

ETHICAL ANALYSIS OF REAL WORLD ISSUES

The previous section of this review focused on the ethical concepts developed by different philosophers in world history. This section provides a brief overview of some of the ethical issues facing American citizens today.

MORALITY, RELATIONSHIPS, AND SEXUALITY

Morality regarding sexuality often centers on the idea of sex without marriage, and most of the attention garnered by this topic relates to teens having premarital sex. Many people consider sex outside of marriage morally wrong because God forbids it. However, there are also non-theological perspectives regarding morality and sexuality. According to utilitarianism, if the overall happiness of an unmarried couple increases by having sex, then it is morally acceptable. Yet, possible problems include guilt, sexually transmitted diseases, and unintentional pregnancy, which would all tip the happiness scale in the opposite direction. Both Aristotle and the Dalai Lama focus on long-term rather than temporary happiness, which might not be achieved through a sexual relationship outside of marriage.

Another related issue involves the morality of homosexuality, which raises strong opinions on both sides. While some people believe homosexuality disobeys the will of God or condemn homosexuality because they consider it unnatural, many others argue that sexual orientation—like skin color or left- or right-handedness—is biologically determined and thus should not be subject to discrimination. The argument of natural versus unnatural raises questions about the definition of *natural*. If the meaning of *natural* is *normal*, then some might argue that abnormality does not equal immorality. For example, it is abnormal to jump four feet off the ground, but it is not immoral. Others argue that procreation is the purpose of sexual organs, and homosexual acts are an unnatural use of the body. Based on such a theory, is it immoral to use a foot for propping open a door? Some of the philosophers discussed in the previous section may not have written their views about sexuality, but an understanding of the different theories should provide the basis of an educated guess.

Issues regarding sexuality are often debated within the American legal system. In two Supreme Court cases in the twenty-first century, for example, the court determined that some state laws unfairly discriminated against gay men and women and limited their civil rights. In *Lawrence v. Texas* (2003), the court ruled that laws prohibiting same-sex sexual activity violated the constitutional right to privacy, and in *Obergefell v. Hodges* (2015), the court ruled that laws prohibiting same-sex marriage violated the constitutional right to equal protection under the law.

Opponents frequently contend that while legal protections of homosexuality might benefit some groups and individuals, they might also violate others' rights. For example, the right to religious freedom, protected by the First Amendment, could be threatened if the religiously-based refusal to serve gay customers is a crime punishable by law. The religious perspective on this matter is not monolithic, however. There is an ongoing debate within religious communities about tolerance of LGBT (lesbian, gay, bisexual, and transgender) people: some leaders and adherents argue that texts such as the Bible and Koran compel people to "love their neighbor," while others argue that those texts explicitly prohibit non-heterosexual activity and that laws should reflect that.

LIFE AND DEATH ISSUES

Abortion

Abortion has long been a controversial issue in America, especially since the 1973 U.S. Supreme Court handed down its decision in *Roe v. Wade*. In that case, the justices determined that states could not prevent a woman from having an abortion during the first trimester of pregnancy, but could enact regulations related to maternal health in the second trimester and prohibit abortion in the third trimester with exceptions for extraordinary circumstances where it would preserve the life or health of the mother. The justices in the majority based their decision on the right to privacy guaranteed by the U.S. Constitution. The decision in *Roe* has never been reversed entirely, but numerous states have since enacted regulations on abortions in the second and third trimesters of pregnancy.

In the decades since *Roe* was decided, the ethics and politics of abortion have remained heavily debated in the United States. Right-to-life advocates assert that abortion is immoral because the fetus is a living human being from the moment of conception. In contrast, the most liberal view of abortion holds that a woman always has the right to decide what happens to her body at any point during a pregnancy. While these two opinions may represent extremes of the spectrum, many people grapple with whether and when abortion is moral. The following questions are often raised in the abortion debate:

- At what stage of fetal development is abortion acceptable?
- What is the point of viability (when a fetus can live outside of the womb)?
- What are the reasons for seeking an abortion? Rape? Teen pregnancy? Career?

Recent advancements with infertility treatment also raise ethical questions about human life. For many women who are trying to conceive, such treatments are the best or only option to do so. During the process, a medical professional extracts several eggs from a prospective mother's ovaries and artificially inseminates the eggs with sperm from her husband, partner, friend, or an anonymous donor. Later, tests show which eggs have become viable embryos. In a case in which several embryos are viable, should the mother be responsible for carrying them all to term? Some ethicists argue that destroying a viable embryo is morally justifiable, as it is not yet recognizably human, but rather a cluster of cells incapable of thought or feeling. Others argue that all embryos contain potential human life that must be protected, and thus all viable embryos should be implanted or donated intact.

In addition, parents in some cultures desire male babies instead of female babies, so they abort girls. The public funding of abortions raises another concern. Opponents assert that the government should not fund an immoral activity, while advocates claim that a legal abortion should be available to everyone and not just the wealthy.

Suicide

Debate has raged for thousands of years about the morality or immorality of suicide. According to Plato, suicide is wrong unless the gods encourage it. In later writings, Plato indicates disapproval for suicide that occurs from "unmanly cowardice," but he seems to suggest that suicide is acceptable if a person faces hardship, disgrace, or extreme stress. Aristotle apparently agrees that suicide to "fly from evil" is acceptable, but suicide used to "escape from poverty or love" is not. Stoics believe suicide is acceptable when it seems like a reasonable and justifiable act, such as not having to live with a debilitating disease or avoiding being tortured into revealing information to a state enemy. Moreover, many Jews and Christians believe that God prohibits suicide based on the Commandment stating, "You shall not murder."

As indicated by both Plato and Aristotle, the reason for committing suicide often determines whether people view the act as moral or immoral. For example, if a person's quality of life has significantly diminished due to a terminal illness or a crippling disease, then suicide may be a reasonable alternative to living. In other cases, suicide is considered honorable, such as when Buddhist monks burned themselves to death in protest of the Vietnam War. A utilitarian would find suicide moral only if it increased the total happiness of everyone involved. However, Kant thought that suicide was always an immoral act.

Euthanasia

Euthanasia refers to killing or allowing the death of a sick or injured person for the sake of mercy. The act may involve killing someone, perhaps by giving a high dosage of drugs, or letting someone die without attempting to save them. While euthanasia is typically associated with the elderly, the issue relates to all stages of life:

- What should parents do when their infants are born with severe physical defects like an incomplete brain? Should they allow the child to die naturally or allow physicians to inject a lethal drug that will cause a peaceful death?

- What about a young adult with severe brain damage who is living in a persistent vegetative state? Do family members wait for an unlikely recovery or remove life support?

- What about a middle-aged man diagnosed with an untreatable and fatal form of cancer that is severely weakening his body? What if he wants to end the suffering and his family approves his decision?

Before deciding when or if euthanasia is morally acceptable, it is important to understand various relevant terms.

Euthanasia Terminology	
Passive euthanasia	Intentionally withholding treatment to allow a patient to die
Active euthanasia	Intentionally killing a patient by lethal injection, smothering, or some other method
Extraordinary treatment	Surgery, medication, dialysis, oxygen, CPR, or any other treatment needed to help an unhealthy patient
Ordinary care	Food, water, and any other care people need regardless of their health
Voluntary euthanasia	A competent and completely informed patient freely requests or consents to euthanasia
Nonvoluntary euthanasia	An incompetent patient or one who has not given consent undergoes euthanasia
Involuntary euthanasia	Intentionally killing a patient against his or her will—considered murder

As indicated by the table, informed consent is required for voluntary euthanasia. Philosophers use the term *autonomy* when referring to the idea of informed consent. Actions are autonomous when they are intentional, understood, and chosen freely. Both Aristotle and Kant, for example, place great value in autonomy when making decisions.

Voluntary euthanasia is mostly illegal in the United States. However, some ethicists and activists campaign for the "right to die," arguing that it is morally unjustifiable for individuals to experience continuous and unnecessary suffering, particularly when it is due to terminal illness. Instead, "right-to-die" activists believe patients should not only have the right to refuse extraordinary treatment and reject efforts to extend their lives through artificial means, they should also be allowed to hire a medical professional to administer active euthanasia. This alternative is frequently referred to as "death with dignity," which implies that the patient is acting autonomously and that death prevents further degradation in quality of life. A common method of voluntary euthanasia is physician-assisted suicide, which currently can result in imprisonment and fines for the doctor in much of the country. This raises the question of whom the law is intended to protect if the victim of the crime is someone who has consented to it.

ECONOMIC ISSUES AND CIVIL RIGHTS

Economic Inequality

The distribution of wealth and resources both within the United States and around the world raises ethical issues about economic inequality. John Rawls asserted that economic inequality is justified only when it benefits everyone, such as to encourage people to be more productive. Rousseau believed that an excessive degree of inequality destroys freedom if wealthy citizens act as tyrants in a society.

Opponents of economic equality claim that diversity within a society is highly valuable and that people should have the freedom to keep what they have earned. They argue that economic redistribution, which refers to taking from those who have many resources and giving to those who have few resources, violates the rights of the individuals who acquired the resources in the first place.

Affirmative Action

Affirmative action refers to policies and programs that consider race, gender, or ethnicity for a range of purposes. A moderate type of affirmative action program might attempt to increase the diversity of applicants for a school or a job. For example, a university might include pictures in its admissions brochures that show people of different races and ethnic backgrounds to convey the idea that the campus is diverse. Preferential treatment is a controversial method of implementing affirmative action that involves promoting certain college or job applicants based primarily on their race, gender, or ethnicity. Preferential treatment often assigns less importance to factors such as standardized tests, as some studies show that they do not assess intelligence or probability of academic success in a consistent manner across social groups.

Affirmative action advocates claim that the preferential treatment for African Americans is justified because historical forms of oppression and discrimination, such as slavery and "separate but equal" segregation laws, produced societal disadvantages and inequalities that still exist today. Affirmative action is thus proposed as a way to "level the playing field" and provide minorities with opportunities now that were not available to them in the past. It is also proposed as a remedy for institutional racism, a term some use to describe prejudice in systems such as education, criminal justice, housing, and the economy. Advocates of affirmative action often assert that those institutions both actively and passively discriminate against minorities and thus present obstacles to success. To illustrate that point, they refer to statistics that show that African Americans are disproportionately likely to be imprisoned for minor offenses, face challenges in securing loans for homes and businesses, and are less likely to graduate from high school or attend college.

Critics of affirmative action argue that the economic and social circumstances of minorities are better now than they have ever been in the past, and that America's legal, political, and social structures are designed to be fair for everyone. For example, critics point to laws such as the Fair Housing Act and the Civil Rights Act, which prohibit discrimination based on race, color, religion, nationality, and familial status.

CRIME AND PUNISHMENT

The majority of Americans view crime reduction as an important objective, but the best method of reducing crime remains debatable. Some people argue that the threat of punishment deters criminal activity, while others assert that focusing on societal problems like alcoholism, poverty, and drug abuse deters crime. However, giving attention to the causes of crime will most likely not eliminate all criminal activity. Moreover, most people believe that criminals should be punished. In general, punishment should match the crime, but such a concept raises many questions: How long should prison sentences be? What should the conditions in prison be like? How should youthful offenders be punished? What about criminals with mental disabilities?

Three general types of punishment are available within the American criminal justice system:

1. *Disablement*: placing a convicted criminal in prison or executing a criminal
2. *Deterrence:* when punishment is considered as a consequence, it can prevent (or deter) an individual from committing a crime.
3. *Rehabilitation*: prisoners spend time earning an education or learning a trade that can be used once released from prison to avoid the lure of criminal activity

Capital punishment is a controversial topic in the United States. Supporters of the death penalty assert that the threat of capital punishment is more effective than the threat of imprisonment for potential murderers. Advocates claim that capital punishment is morally acceptable because it protects society from the worst criminals. Additional arguments in favor of capital punishment include the idea that murderers deserve to die and that the death penalty provides closure for victims' families.

In contrast, opponents of capital punishment claim that life imprisonment satisfactorily removes a murderer from society. They also assert that imprisonment is just as effective in deterring crime as the death penalty. According to research studies, the likelihood of apprehension, conviction, and punishment is a more significant deterrent than the severity of the punishment when people decide whether to commit crimes. Mistakes made in the criminal justice system and questions regarding discrimination are issues continually raised in the death penalty debate as well. In 1972, the Supreme Court instituted a moratorium on capital punishment nationwide, after deciding that it constituted cruel and unusual punishment and was frequently imposed unfairly. The moratorium was later lifted, and now individual states can decide whether the death penalty is legal or not.

Quality of life for inmates is also a heavily debated topic in America. Many ethicists and lawmakers argue that prisons should be reformed to be more humane and less crowded with minor offenders. There are historical precedents for this modern discourse of prison reform. In the eighteenth and nineteenth centuries, the philosopher Jeremy Bentham analyzed contemporary methods of punishment and theorized that it would be more worthwhile to educate inmates and provide them with moral instruction than it would be to isolate and torture them, as was common at the time. An educated and repentant criminal, he argued, could eventually become a contributing member of society. He devised a model prison called the Panopticon that promoted civility, order, and virtue through a practice of constant surveillance.

Today, prison reform advocates take a similar position, arguing that while heinous crimes cannot go unpunished, many criminals, even violent ones, are capable of rehabilitation and reentry into society. Many advocates campaign to end solitary confinement, which is seen as a form of cruel and unusual punishment, as well as to curb abuse of inmates by prison officers. Reducing inmate populations is also a major goal of prison reform. One proposed means of achieving that is eliminating mandatory minimum sentences—for example, imposing a mandatory five-year sentence for drug trafficking. Supporters of mandatory minimum sentences, on the other hand, say that such laws are an appropriate way to ensure equal application of the law, as in the past, prison sentences may have been administered in a discriminatory fashion.

WAR AND PEACE

Wars have been fought for thousands of years and continue in modern society. War occurs for a variety of reasons—defending from attack, protecting natural resources, acquiring territory, and settling disputes. The way in which militaries fight wars varies as well and may include bombings, assassinations, and biological weapons. There are two primary questions related to the morality of war that must be asked by government leaders, soldiers, and regular citizens:

1. When is it morally acceptable to ensue in war?
2. What are the moral limits, if any, during a war?

Peace refers to the absence of fighting, but non-warring conditions can vary. Peace occurred at the end of the U.S. Civil War when over 600,000 soldiers lay dead. Peace existed between the United States and the Soviet Union during the Cold War, although weapons on both sides were ready to go at any moment. Peace occurs at times between Israel and the Palestinians, but it is always tenuous.

While many people take the view that peace requires preparation for war, pacifists believe war is never morally acceptable or justified. Pacifists think that war is an immoral way to achieve any goal and that war is ineffective because violence leads to more violence. Some pacifists cite the Hebrew Bible and the New Testament in protest of war. Other pacifists argue against war on pragmatic rather than moral or religious grounds and contend that there are more practical and effective ways, such as diplomacy, to resolve conflicts between nations and peoples.

Just War theory considers both the ethical and historical aspects of war. A war is justified under this theory if it meets certain criteria:

1. It is declared by a competent authority.
2. It is fought for a just cause.
3. It is fought with the right intentions.
4. It is appropriate for the provocation.
5. It is used as a last resort.
6. There is a reasonable chance for success.

The Just War tradition stems from the Roman Catholic Church, and St. Thomas Aquinas is linked to the first three justifications.

LIFE- AND HUMAN-CENTERED ETHICS

Environmental Ethics

Environmental ethics is a relatively new field of philosophy that focuses on human responsibility to nature. Protecting the natural environment is viewed as both practical and ethical for the future of humanity.

Much has been said in recent years about environmental threats such as global warming, air pollution, and energy consumption. The following list indicates the major environmental issues facing America and the rest of the world:

- Air pollution
- Deforestation
- Energy consumption
- Global warming
- Ozone depletion
- Population growth
- Water pollution
- Wilderness preservation

While everyone generally agrees on the causes of some environmental concerns, such as water pollution, other issues are highly debatable. For example, some scientists blame the burning of fossil fuels for global warming, while other experts attribute climate change to natural planetary and solar fluctuations. Energy consumption is another topic that triggers debate. Should the United States focus on developing alternative energy sources, or should it drill for oil where it is known to exist? Not only do environmental concerns raise ethical questions, but they raise issues about government policies as well.

Within ethical debates about the environment, some take the position that humans are equal to all other parts of nature, and others express a human-centered perspective, often referred to as *anthropocentrism*. The twentieth-century philosopher and naturalist Arne Naess developed an ethical theory known as "deep ecology." Naess argued that human beings are interconnected with all other forms of life on Earth and need to undergo a change of moral, philosophical, and political perspective in order to prevent impending ecological disaster. Naess was critical of capitalism and modern technological advances that endangered ecosystems and animal habitats.

Naess devised this eight-point platform for the **deep ecology movement:**

1. All life has value in itself, independent of its usefulness to humans.
2. Richness and diversity contribute to life's well-being and have value in themselves.
3. Humans have no right to reduce this richness and diversity except to satisfy vital needs in a responsible way.
4. The impact of humans in the world is excessive and rapidly getting worse.
5. Human lifestyles and population are key elements of this impact.
6. The diversity of life, including cultures, can flourish only with reduced human impact.

7. Basic ideological, political, economic, and technological structures must therefore change.

8. Those who accept the foregoing points have an obligation to participate in implementing the necessary changes and to do so peacefully and democratically.

Anthropocentrism is not necessarily opposed to the values of deep ecology. Ethicists who take this position often agree with environmentalists like Naess that the beauty, stability, and integrity of our natural resources should be maintained. However, rather than considering all living organisms as inherently equal in value, anthropocentric theorists contend that humans do have significant advantages over other forms of life; for example, higher intellectual ability and a refined sense of morality. In some cases, thus, anthropocentrism allows for the prioritization of human needs over other forms of life.

HUMAN RIGHTS

Since Ancient Greek civilization, philosophers have debated what inherent rights and privileges individuals are born with or are endowed with by God or nature. For much of recorded history, many of these rights have belonged only to certain categories of people, such as men or individuals with wealth, a certain skin color, or noble lineage. More recently, however, the concept of universal human rights has become more widely acknowledged, celebrated, and legally enforced. Around the world, women, minorities, and other groups that have historically been marginalized now have the right to vote, the right to own property, the right to freely express opinions, and the right to marry. However, there remain considerable inequalities, and in many nations, individuals still live in slavery or under repressive governments.

The **Universal Declaration of Human Rights** (UDHR) was one of the first efforts to define and protect human rights in the past century. The United Nations issued the UDHR in 1948, claiming that the two world wars demonstrated an urgent need to protect individual freedoms and end widespread oppression. The UDHR outlines more than thirty fundamental rights that belong to everyone, irrespective of race, color, sex, language, religion, political opinion, national origin, or other status. These include the following:

- "No one shall be subjected to arbitrary arrest, detention, or exile."
- "Everyone has the right to a nationality."
- "Everyone has the right to a standard of living adequate for the health and well-being of himself and of his family."
- "Everyone, without any discrimination, has the right to equal pay for equal work."
- "Everyone has the right to education."

The UDHR has inspired many sovereign nations to adopt laws that preserve these rights for its citizens. While the UDHR is not legally binding anywhere in the world, there are some judicial systems, such as the International Criminal Court, which prosecute and punish individuals for genocide and other violations of human rights.

There is an active debate about whether women, LGBT (lesbian, gay, bisexual, and transgender) individuals, minorities, children, and other social groups deserve special considerations under the law, or whether general recognition of human rights sufficiently protects all members of society.

BIOMEDICAL ETHICS

Due to advances in medical technology, such as vaccinations, organ transplants, and cancer treatment, humans are living longer than ever before. Despite these advances, however, we are still ultimately mortal and vulnerable to disease, pain, and suffering. As it has been throughout history, we entrust experts and professionals to help us live healthy and fulfilling lives, which raises many ethical questions.

Physicians, nurses, emergency medical technicians, insurance companies, and other health care providers make decisions every day about how to properly preserve patients' health and when to potentially allow a patient to die or experience extreme pain. How long is it necessary to prolong life for a mortally wounded, terminally ill, or comatose patient? Who receives medical treatment when resources are scarce, such as during a disease outbreak or war? Who is entitled to know confidential details about another person's medical history? Can a physician fulfill a patient's wishes to end his or her life through euthanasia?

These questions, and many others, are addressed in biomedical ethics, a field that can be traced back to Hippocrates. The fifth-century BCE Greek physician composed the **"Hippocratic Oath,"** to which many medical professionals still adhere today. The oath compels physicians to take every possible measure to ensure patients' health, to avoid harming patients, to respect patients' privacy, and to treat patients with dignity and respect. Yet this historic document also has many detractors who believe that profound and sweeping changes in technology, politics, and culture, as well as increasing specialization in medical fields, has made the oath outdated. Some of the questions raised by detractors include: Should physicians with specialties as different as dermatology and brain surgery have to swear to the same oath? In an era in which abortion is widely legal, how do we interpret the provision to "do no harm"? Should violating the oath carry any penalties?

More recently, the ethicists Tom Beauchamp and James Childress outlined four broad principles of biomedical ethics, which are frequently applied by medical professionals facing difficult decisions in the course of everyday treatment.

1. *Autonomy:* Every individual has the right to make his or her own choices. For example, a patient can sign a "do not resuscitate" form, which indicates a personal decision to refuse extraordinary care in the event of a medical emergency.

2. *Beneficence*: Medical professionals should act with the best interests of the patient in mind. Applying this principle, a physician might prescribe antibiotics to a patient suffering from a bacterial infection.

3. *Justice*: Medical services and resources should be distributed in a way that is fair. Applying this principle, during a disease outbreak, a team of doctors might perform "triage"—that is, decide which individuals or groups have the most urgent needs—and provide vaccinations to patients with the weakest immune systems.

4. *Non-maleficence:* Medical professionals should not intentionally cause harm to a patient. Applying this principle, a dental surgeon might administer anesthesia to a patient undergoing a root canal, so as to not cause excessive and unnecessary pain during the surgery.

In the United States, these ethical principles are often enforced through laws and regulations, for example, the 1996 Health Insurance Portability and Accountability Act (HIPAA). The act establishes guidelines for maintaining the privacy and security of information about patients' health. For example, the law disallows most employers from soliciting information about employees' and job applicants' medical history, in order to prevent discrimination.

Other topics of concern to biomedical ethicists include cloning, stem cell research, and human genetic engineering. Modern technology allows for many sophisticated and potentially dangerous decisions to be made about human life. For example, scientists now know the sequence and purpose of the entire human genome, which includes more than 20,000 individual genes that determine traits ranging from eye color to likelihood of contracting certain diseases. The availability of such information, combined with the practice of genetic screening, could eventually lead to discrimination against individuals applying for jobs or college, who have allegedly "inferior" innate characteristics. It is also conceivable that someday, attempts could be made to genetically engineer more "perfect" humans without handicaps or physical abnormalities or with only one skin color or body size—a widely condemned practice known as eugenics.

Should the possibility that research may eventually be used for dangerous or inhumane ends prevent modern scientists from making great advances? Must scientists weigh ethical dilemmas of the future against the possibility of curing cancer or AIDS today? The complexity and evolving challenges posed by biomedical ethics are no doubt why medical organizations are among the top employers of professional ethicists in the world today.

SUMMING IT UP

- **Ethics** refers to the academic discipline of analyzing morality. Reasoning, rules, and logic form the basis of ethical philosophy.

- **Cosmology** is the study of the physical world—what it is made of and how it works. **Cosmogony** is the study of the origin of the universe—how it came into existence.

- **Pythagoras**, one of the most notable pre-Socratic philosophers, was also a mathematician and a cosmologist. No writings of his exist, but evidence shows his philosophy was based on beliefs in the magic of numbers and reincarnation.

- The **Sophists** were traveling teachers who lectured about various topics for fees. Protagoras, a well-respected Sophist, is best known for stating, "Man is the measure of all things," suggesting that people rather than nature determine behavior.

- **Thucydides**, a Greek historian, wrote *The History of the Peloponnesian War* as a report of the battle between Athens and Sparta (431–404 BCE). He objectively presented factual events and questioned the ethics of war.

- **Socrates** lived in Athens during the fifth century BCE. An outspoken critic of the Sophists, and Athenian politics and religious institutions, he believed that virtue equaled knowledge and that a person who is knowledgeable about morality will behave with morality.

- Socrates' most famous student, **Plato**, was a philosopher and mathematician. After Socrates' death, Plato established the Academy in 387 BCE. His most influential work, *The Republic*, examines whether it is always better to be just than unjust.

- **Aristotle**, a renowned student of Plato's Academy, was a philosopher and an authority on nearly every subject. Aristotle believed everything had a purpose and change is both necessary and natural.

- **Stoicism** is a philosophy based on the idea that absolute law rules the universe and that humans cannot change fate. Epictetus was one of the most prominent Stoics of the second century AD.

- Around 300 BCE, hedonism or **Epicureanism** emerged under the guidance of Epicurus, who asserted that happiness was the purpose of life and that the universe was created by an accidental collision of atoms rather than by Greek gods.

- The **Bible** has been the most popular tool for teaching morality in the Western world and serves as the center point for Judeo-Christian ethics. While these ethics have had a major influence on law and customs in the United States, the Constitution implies that there should ultimately be a separation of church and state.

- **The major world religions include Christianity, Judaism, Islam, Hinduism, and Buddhism.** Judaism, Christianity, and Islam are **monotheistic religions**—they believe in only one god rather than in multiple gods. Hinduism and Buddhism share the concepts of karma and dharma.

- **Natural law theories** are based on the idea that the moral standards guiding human behavior originate in human nature and the universe and that deviating from the norm is immoral, sinful, evil, and harmful. Many medieval philosophers adopted natural law theories to explain the relationship between God and man, including St. Thomas Aquinas, who believed that faith and reason could exist together.

- **Social contract theory** refers to the idea that the right to rule and the obligation to obey are based upon an agreement, a moral code, between an individual and society. Thomas Hobbes, John Locke, and Jean-Jacques Rousseau wrote about social contract theory during the seventeenth and eighteenth centuries.

- **John Rawls** and **Robert Nozick**, twentieth-century American philosophers, were known for their ideas regarding political philosophy.

- **Transcendental idealism**, a concept most often associated with eighteenth-century German philosophers, such as **Immanuel Kant**, contends that appearances should be viewed only as representations and not as things themselves—that both the mind and understanding create reality.

- **Adam Smith**, an early theorist of capitalism, proposed that the common good of society advances when individuals focus on benefiting themselves, a concept related to the theory of **moral egoism**.

- **Ayn Rand**, twentieth-century Russian philosopher and moral egoist, asserted that pursuing self-interests and personal happiness are "the highest moral purpose" of life.

- **Utilitarianism** (consequentialism) is the theory that actions are morally acceptable if good consequences outweigh bad consequences. Utilitarian philosophers include **Jeremy Bentham** and **John Stuart Mill**.

- **Feminism** is the philosophical and political discourse aimed at exposing, analyzing, and addressing gender inequality. Feminist philosophy emerged in the 1960s.

- Psychologist **Carol Gilligan** asserts that women and men have different approaches to making moral decisions—men focus on applying rules and minimizing emotions, and women appeal to emotions such as sympathy, love, and concern.

- Philosopher **Nel Noddings** studies the concept of **ethics of care**, focusing on the origins of care within the home, such as parent-child relationships.

- **Determinism** is the philosophical theory that past events, combined with the laws of nature, make certain outcomes inevitable. **Compatibilism** is the theory that behaviors and decisions are heavily influenced by natural forces, but that individuals can exercise free will as well.

- **Relativism** is the philosophical theory that there is no absolute moral truth and, instead, ethics and values are circumstantial or context-specific; what is moral here and now may not be moral somewhere else or in the future. **Subjectivism** is the theory that all ethical statements are an expression of personal perception rather than an indicator of absolute, verifiable truth.

- Current **ethical issues** include morality and sexuality, abortion, suicide, euthanasia, economic inequality, affirmative action, crime and punishment, war and peace, environmentalism, and biomedical ethics.

ETHICS IN AMERICA POST-TEST

Directions: Carefully read each of the following 60 questions. Choose the best answer to each question and fill in the corresponding circle on the answer sheet. The Answer Key and Explanations can be found following this post-test.

1. The U.S. Supreme Court suspended the death penalty in 1972, because it
   A. violated the principles of federalism.
   B. constituted cruel and unusual punishment.
   C. violated the right to a fair trial.
   D. constituted murder.

2. Which of these is a limitation of the Universal Declaration of Human Rights?
   A. It is not legally binding in any country.
   B. It was never adopted by the United Nations.
   C. It has had no influence on laws around the world.
   D. It does not renounce slavery.

3. For a follower of Kant, the ethical evaluation of a decision to commit adultery depends on whether
   A. the adulterer is a Christian.
   B. adultery is a reasonable action.
   C. the adulterer will be happy.
   D. adultery is moral for everyone.

4. According to which of the following is it immoral to engage in war?
   A. Smith, because war serves no self-interests
   B. Gandhi, because war is never justified
   C. Rawls, because war destroys freedom
   D. Mill, because war is irrational

5. Which of these businesses would a follower of Arne Naess most likely support?
   A. One that maximized profits
   B. One that used technology to make work more efficient
   C. One that undertook "green" or sustainability initiatives
   D. One that resisted paying income taxes

6. The idea that all events occur because of previous actions and the laws of nature is
   A. rationalism.
   B. existentialism.
   C. determinism.
   D. scholasticism.

7. Which of the following is equivalent to murder in most cases?
   A. Passive euthanasia
   B. Involuntary euthanasia
   C. Active euthanasia
   D. Nonvoluntary euthanasia

8. According to Rawls, in which of the following situations is economic inequality ethical and justified?
   A. When citizens are required to share resources
   B. When the wealthy rule government offices
   C. When citizens need to be more productive
   D. When society has become too diverse

9. Plato uses the Allegory of the Cave to illustrate which of the following concepts?
   A. The world can only be understood intellectually.
   B. Happiness can be attained through physical experiences.
   C. The world can only be understood through the senses.
   D. Courage and morality are necessary in difficult situations.

10. The ethics of Judaism are based on the teachings of
   A. the Old Testament.
   B. Jesus Christ.
   C. Mohammed.
   D. the New Testament.

11. Which of these circumstances best describes a direct conflict between beneficence and non-maleficence?
   A. A hospital bans smoking in the lobby.
   B. A patient confides to his physician that he is gay.
   C. A promising experimental cancer treatment causes severe side effects.
   D. A patient asks her family to make medical decisions on her behalf.

12. According to which of the following philosophies is premarital sex most likely immoral?
   A. Moral egoism, because increasing knowledge is the most important goal
   B. Hedonism, because the gods will disapprove
   C. Transcendental idealism, because logical thinking equals happiness
   D. Stoicism, because self-control is virtuous

13. Determinism poses a challenge to the idea of moral responsibility in suggesting that
   A. God forgives immoral actions after repentance.
   B. individuals' actions are caused by natural forces.
   C. no one can objectively judge others' morality.
   D. all actions that benefit oneself are moral.

14. The statement "To each according to need" is an example of the principles of
   A. retributive justice.
   B. economic rationalism.
   C. distributive justice.
   D. social virtue.

15. According to which of the following philosophers is economic equality moral?
   A. Smith, because the purpose of society is to share wealth
   B. Rand, because helping others is the greatest moral purpose
   C. Bentham, because individual happiness is the purpose of life
   D. Rousseau, because excessive inequality undermines freedom

16. What was the Supreme Court's ruling in the 1973 case *Roe v. Wade*?
   A. Most abortion procedures are legal, because privacy is a right.
   B. All abortion procedures are legal, including during the third trimester.
   C. All abortion procedures are illegal, because they are a form of euthanasia.
   D. Abortion is legal only through the first four weeks of pregnancy.

17. What do "right-to-die" activists want to legalize?
   A. Capital punishment
   B. Abortion
   C. Voluntary euthanasia
   D. Involuntary euthanasia

18. A lawmaker who agreed with Mill's thesis in *The Subjugation of Women* would likely vote for a bill that

    A. establishes college scholarships for women.

    B. overturns women's suffrage.

    C. legalizes polygamy for certain religious groups.

    D. allows a man to take his ex-wife's property in a divorce.

19. According to Smith, which of the following is the best way to find happiness in life?

    A. Share resources with others.

    B. Accept life the way it is.

    C. Refrain from showing emotion.

    D. Focus on personal interests.

20. According to Locke, what should citizens do when ruled by an unjust political authority?

    A. Resist and revolt.

    B. Search for answers.

    C. Submit to authority.

    D. Accept the fate of nature.

21. An advocate for affirmative action would agree that

    A. standardized testing is the best indicator of intellectual ability.

    B. universities should enforce moral virtues.

    C. minority students are intellectually superior.

    D. "separate but equal" laws have left a lasting impact on society.

22. "Deep ecology" is a form of environmental ethics that

    A. is anthropocentric.

    B. values animal and plant life over human life.

    C. is compatible with the current state of industrial capitalism.

    D. critiques modern patterns of consumption and development.

23. Sophism most likely arose in Ancient Greece because of the

    A. condemnation of Socrates.

    B. war between Athens and Sparta.

    C. opening of the Athens Academy.

    D. growing democratic system.

24. For an Epicurean, the ethical evaluation of a decision to perform euthanasia will depend on whether the action will

    A. adhere to the natural laws of the world.

    B. avoid pain and increase happiness.

    C. maximize utility for everyone.

    D. lead to retribution from the gods.

25. A hospital managing vaccines during a disease outbreak will be most concerned about which principle of biomedical ethics?

    A. Autonomy

    B. Orthodoxy

    C. Referral

    D. Justice

26. The idea that the universe is morally neutral is a concept related to

    A. feminist ethics.

    B. Indian philosophy.

    C. natural law theories.

    D. social contract theories.

27. A "do not resuscitate" form, signed by a competent patient, constitutes a rejection of

    A. active euthanasia.

    B. autonomy.

    C. extraordinary treatment.

    D. ordinary care.

28. Which of the following writings develops the concept of the general will in society?

    A. *Discourse on Political Economy* by Rousseau

    B. *A Theory of Justice* by Rawls

    C. *The Wealth of Nations* by Smith

    D. *On Liberty* by Mill

29. Advocates of prison reform are most critical of what kind of punishment?
    A. Disablement
    B. Deterrence
    C. Rehabilitation
    D. Probation

30. Which of these positions would a pragmatic pacifist most strongly support?
    A. All violence is inherently immoral.
    B. Diplomacy is more effective than warfare.
    C. Wars that depose brutal dictators can be justified.
    D. Wars that result in the spread of democracy can be justified.

31. Which statement would most likely convince a follower of John Rawls to support an affirmative action policy?
    A. It recognizes everyone's right to equal opportunity.
    B. It reconciles past societal injustices.
    C. It was approved by the democratically elected student government.
    D. It will benefit you personally.

32. Which of the following would most likely disagree with the concept of redistributing wealth?
    A. Hobbes, because it is an irrational concept
    B. Rand, because of the personal sacrifices required
    C. Rawls, because of the burden placed on some citizens
    D. Kant, because of an individual's right to property

33. For a Kantian, the ethical evaluation of capital punishment mostly depends on
    A. natural and civil laws.
    B. assessing consequences.
    C. long-term societal benefits.
    D. developing a universal law.

34. Which of the following statements best explains ethical relativism?
    A. Knowledge is derived from observations.
    B. Every point of view is equally valid.
    C. Reality consists of one substance.
    D. Nothing in life actually matters.

35. In which way are determinism and deep ecology philosophically compatible?
    A. Both agree that humans determine their own destinies.
    B. Both agree that humans have dominion over nature.
    C. Both agree that human life is interconnected with nature.
    D. Both agree that humans cannot change their behavior.

36. All of the following are assertions made by Locke in *Two Treatises of Government* EXCEPT:
    A. People have the right to own property.
    B. People have the right to form militias.
    C. People have the right to make their own choices.
    D. People have the right to live without being harmed by others.

37. According to Rousseau, which of the following best explains why people commit crimes?
    A. Society has corrupted them.
    B. People are innately selfish.
    C. People lack moral knowledge.
    D. Natural laws encourage immorality.

38. Which of the following concepts are most closely associated with Hinduism and Buddhism?
    A. Love and salvation
    B. Laws and responsibilities
    C. Obedience and remorse
    D. Actions and duties

39. In the United States, what do HIPAA standards enforce?

A. Affirmative action policies for hospitals

B. Patient privacy

C. Universal healthcare

D. Nondiscrimination for preexisting conditions

40. According to Socrates, a man who robs a store at gunpoint is most likely

A. acting out of personal freedom.

B. immoral because he wants to be.

C. behaving in the way nature intended.

D. immoral because he lacks knowledge.

41. Which of the following best describes how Aquinas viewed nature?

A. As a way to understand humanity

B. As the ultimate source of life

C. As an accidental collection of atoms

D. As a way to draw close to God

42. Which of these phrases appears in the United States Constitution?

A. "Separation of church and state"

B. "No law respecting an establishment of religion"

C. "Right to practice religion freely"

D. "A national religion shall not be established."

43. According to which of the following philosophers is it immoral to tax people's income?

A. Rawls, because income taxes burden the wealthy

B. Smith, because income taxes discourage productivity

C. Nozick, because income tax is equivalent to forced labor

D. Noddings, because income tax does not create equity

44. According to Gilligan, when a woman faces a moral decision, she is most likely to

A. consider relationships.

B. minimize emotions.

C. apply standard rules.

D. assess ethical principles.

45. Subjectivism is the philosophical theory that

A. mental processes are not real.

B. human decisions are shaped by natural forces.

C. all citizens should be subject to the same legal standards.

D. all ethical statements are expressions of personal perception.

46. Which of the following is an example of triage?

A. Allowing women and children to board a lifeboat first

B. Performing elective cosmetic surgery

C. Medicating a patient against his consent

D. Prescribing chemotherapy to a late-stage cancer patient

47. What did the U.S. Supreme Court legalize nationwide in the 2003 case, *Lawrence v. Texas*?

A. Contraception access

B. Same-sex sexual activity

C. Same-sex marriage

D. Pornography

48. Which of the following statements is a core belief of Aristotle?

A. Change is a man-made process.

B. Virtue is a transcendent quality.

C. Everything in life has a purpose.

D. Wisdom brings contentment.

post-test

49. Which of the following thinkers believed that humans cannot change fate because absolute law rules the universe?

   A. Aquinas

   B. Epictetus

   C. Gandhi

   D. Epicurus

50. A concept in which citizens act as legislators to determine collectively the laws of a society is known as

   A. distributive justice.

   B. social constructivism.

   C. social contract theory.

   D. general will.

51. Which of the following questions would most likely be asked by a utilitarian when making an ethical decision about an affirmative action policy?

   A. Will an affirmative action policy benefit more people than it will harm?

   B. How does an affirmative action policy correspond with natural laws?

   C. Will an affirmative action policy allocate resources fairly and equally?

   D. What do the majority of people think about an affirmative action policy?

52. Which of the following is a similarity between Kant's categorical imperatives and utilitarianism?

   A. Both are methods for addressing societal immorality.

   B. Both are ways to conceptualize people and decisions.

   C. Both are preventive techniques for avoiding immorality.

   D. Both are masculine approaches to ethical decision making.

53. Which of the following was the main criticism against the Sophists?

   A. Their disbelief in the existence of the gods

   B. Their support of the ideas presented by Socrates

   C. Their domination in the Athenian government

   D. Their reliance on persuasion instead of truth

54. Which of the following best describes Plato's ideal state in *The Republic*?

   A. A society ruled by a political tyrant

   B. A society based upon political justice

   C. A society ruled by the general will

   D. A society based upon a social contract

55. Which of the following is a type of moral excellence according to Aristotle?

   A. Gentleness

   B. Wisdom

   C. Reason

   D. Skill

56. Which of these statements best describes institutional racism?

   A. Many people do not socialize outside of their own racial or ethnic groups.

   B. A business owner overcharges minority customers.

   C. Members of minority groups are frequently harassed by fellow citizens.

   D. Racial biases are pervasive in education, criminal justice, and politics.

57. For a Hindu, the ethical evaluation of a decision to drill for oil in the Alaska wilderness depends on whether drilling

A. serves the self-interests of the citizens of Alaska.

B. causes minimal harm to citizens and the environment.

C. follows the desires of the majority of people in America.

D. reduces American dependency on foreign oil.

58. Which of the following is better known for his manner of teaching than his philosophy?

A. Plato

B. Aristotle

C. Socrates

D. Pythagoras

59. Which of the following thinkers provides the most pessimistic view of society?

A. Hobbes, because he views society as a violent and insecure place

B. Mill, because he views citizens as weak against the government

C. Rousseau, because he views the monarchy as untrustworthy

D. Locke, because he views citizens as immoral and irrational

60. Which of the following concepts is suggested in the works of Plato?

A. Creating and appreciating beauty leads to contentment.

B. Enlightened people receive their abilities from nature.

C. Courage and morality lead societies out of darkness.

D. Pursuing excellence helps attain peace in the world.

post-test

ANSWER KEY AND EXPLANATIONS

1. B	**13.** B	**25.** D	**37.** A	**49.** B
2. A	**14.** C	**26.** C	**38.** D	**50.** D
3. D	**15.** D	**27.** C	**39.** B	**51.** A
4. B	**16.** A	**28.** A	**40.** D	**52.** D
5. C	**17.** C	**29.** A	**41.** D	**53.** D
6. C	**18.** A	**30.** B	**42.** B	**54.** B
7. B	**19.** D	**31.** A	**43.** C	**55.** A
8. C	**20.** A	**32.** B	**44.** A	**56.** D
9. A	**21.** D	**33.** D	**45.** D	**57.** B
10. A	**22.** D	**34.** B	**46.** A	**58.** C
11. C	**23.** D	**35.** C	**47.** B	**59.** A
12. D	**24.** B	**36.** B	**48.** C	**60.** D

1. **The correct answer is B.** In the 1972 Supreme Court case *Furman v. Georgia*, the majority decided that the death penalty constituted cruel and unusual punishment, though the justices disagreed on why that was the case. Some argued that the penalty was imposed in an inconsistent manner, and others proposed that the capital punishment was in itself cruel, though not legally murder. Justices in the majority did not cite the Sixth Amendment, which guarantees the right to a fair trial, nor the Tenth Amendment, which reinforces the principle of federalism. Therefore, choices A, C, and D are incorrect.

2. **The correct answer is A.** The Universal Declaration of Human Rights (UDHR) is not legally binding anywhere in the world. Nevertheless, it was formally adopted by the United Nations in 1948, so choice B is incorrect. Many sovereign nations have adopted their own laws that are inspired by the UDHR's principles, so choice C is incorrect. Article 4 of the UDHR states that "No one shall be held in slavery or servitude," so choice D is incorrect.

3. **The correct answer is D.** The basis of morality for followers of Kant is whether the behavior is moral or immoral for all human beings according to universal moral laws. God, reason, and happiness are not important factors in ethical decisions based on Kant's philosophy, so choices A, B, and C are incorrect.

4. **The correct answer is B.** Gandhi was a pacifist, and pacifists believe that war is never moral or justified. According to pacifists, war is an immoral method to attain a goal in all situations. In many cases, war brings freedom and is a rational choice, so choices C and D are incorrect. Wars can be self-serving if they are a way to acquire land or other resources, so choice A is incorrect.

5. **The correct answer is C.** Arne Naess was one of the primary thinkers of the twentieth-century "deep ecology" movement, and he laid out ethical principles that centered on protecting natural resources and ecosystems. In particular, Naess sought to protect the soil and wrote that human thinking needed to undergo a paradigm shift—away from rampant technological development and profitmaking and toward respect for Earth. Choices A and B are thus incorrect. Tax resistance (choice D) is more closely aligned with the thinking of John Rawls.

6. **The correct answer is C.** The concept that all events occur because of previous actions and the laws of nature is determinism. Rationalism (choice A) is the idea that knowledge can be gained without having experiences. Existentialism (choice B) is the idea that people have to determine what life means.

answers post-test

The philosophy of scholasticism (choice D) combines logic with a belief in God.

7. **The correct answer is B.** Involuntary euthanasia involves killing a patient against his or her will, which is considered murder in most cases. Passive euthanasia involves withholding treatment to allow a patient to die, while active euthanasia involves actively killing a patient, perhaps by lethal injection. Nonvoluntary euthanasia occurs when an incompetent patient undergoes euthanasia. Choices A, C, and D do not involve going against the will of the patient.

8. **The correct answer is C.** Rawls asserted that economic inequality is justified only when it benefits everyone, such as to encourage people to be more productive. Sharing resources would bring about equality, so choice A is incorrect. Rawls might argue that choice B is a reason for equality. The lack of diversity is an argument used against inequality, so choice D is incorrect.

9. **The correct answer is A.** The Allegory of the Cave illustrates the idea that the world experienced through the senses is not the real world. The world can truly be understood only on an intellectual level. Plato believed that happiness could be attained only through virtue, so choice B is incorrect.

10. **The correct answer is A.** The Old Testament, which is also known as the Hebrew Bible, is the ethical source for Judaism. Christians find ethical principles in both the Old Testament and the New Testament, which contains the teachings of Jesus Christ. Muslims turn to the words of the prophet Mohammed, so choice C is incorrect.

11. **The correct answer is C.** Beneficence is the biomedical ethics principle that physicians should take actions that are in the best interest of their patients' health and comfort. Non-maleficence is the biomedical ethics principle that physicians should not cause their patients any harm. A promising experimental cancer treatment would likely benefit a patient's health, but the severe side effects would likely cause some harm, thus bringing the two principles into conflict. Smoking bans both benefit and cause no harm to patients, so choice A is incorrect. Choices B and D primarily concern the principles of confidentiality and autonomy, so they are incorrect.

12. **The correct answer is D.** Stoicism finds self-control and reasoning the greatest virtues, and premarital sex most likely shows a lack of self-control. Stoics also advocated experiencing a passionless life. Moral egoism (choice A) focuses on self-interests, which may or may not be gained through premarital sex. Hedonists approved of anything pleasurable, so choice B is incorrect. Choice C is incorrect.

13. **The correct answer is B.** Moral responsibility presumes that individuals can exercise free will and choose between right and wrong. It would thus be difficult to hold an individual responsible for a crime or other offense if, as determinism suggests, all of our actions and decisions are predetermined by natural forces that we cannot control. Subjectivism suggests that no one can objectively judge others' morality, so choice C is incorrect. Moral egoism suggests that actions that benefit oneself are moral, so choice D is incorrect. Choice A is incorrect.

14. **The correct answer is C.** The statement "To each according to need" is an example of the principles of distributive justice. Distributive justice refers to the appropriate way of allocating benefits and obligations in a society. Retributive justice refers to what type of punishment is appropriate for a crime. Choices B and D are incorrect.

15. **The correct answer is D.** Rousseau believed that an excessive degree of inequality destroys freedom if wealthy citizens act as tyrants in a society. Smith and Rand advocated moral egoism and the protection of personal rather than societal interests, making choices A and B incorrect. Bentham believed people should improve happiness within society rather than increase personal happiness, so choice C is incorrect.

16. **The correct answer is A.** In a 7-2 decision, the U.S. Supreme Court ruled in *Roe v. Wade* that abortions during the first trimester of pregnancy were legal, because of the right

to privacy guaranteed by the Fourteenth Amendment, and that second trimester abortions could be regulated somewhat, so choices C and D are incorrect. The Supreme Court left the legality of third trimester abortions to be decided by individual states, so choice B is incorrect.

17. **The correct answer is C.** "Right-to-die" activists campaign to legalize voluntary euthanasia, in which a mentally competent individual consents to being assisted in ending his or her life by a doctor or third party through an active or passive method of euthanasia. They also campaign to make euthanasia and suicide more societally acceptable practices, especially for terminally ill patients. "Right-to-die" activists do not support involuntary euthanasia, which is terminating the life of an individual without that individual's consent, so choice D is incorrect. Abortion (choice B) is typically advocated by "pro-choice" activists. Choice A is incorrect.

18. **The correct answer is A.** In *The Subjugation of Women*, the nineteenth-century British philosopher John Stuart Mill used a utilitarian approach to argue in favor of women's equality and their right to receive a good education. He supported a woman's right to vote, so choice B is incorrect. He also criticized the institution of marriage, and stated that marriage—if a woman freely consented to it—should be the union of two equal, independent partners, so choices C and D are incorrect.

19. **The correct answer is D.** Focusing on personal interests is the way to find happiness in life according to Smith. As a moral egoist, Smith asserted that the happiness of oneself is more important than the happiness of others. Choices B and C describe Stoics.

20. **The correct answer is A.** Locke asserted that people have the right to reject and resist any unjust political authority. Hobbes stated that failure to submit to an unjust ruler results in conflict. Stoics live their lives accepting what happens as fate.

21. **The correct answer is D.** One popular argument in favor of affirmative action is that injustices such as "separate but equal" (or "Jim Crow") laws have lasting impacts on society and continue to create disadvantages for African Americans and other minorities. Advocates for affirmative action usually argue that standardized testing is unfairly biased in favor of wealthier students who have access to tutors, so choice A is incorrect. Advocates do not argue that any type of student is intellectually superior, but rather that some have been unfairly marginalized because of who they are, so choice C is incorrect. Choice B is incorrect.

22. **The correct answer is D.** Deep ecology is the ethical theory that humankind is simply one element of a vast, interconnected ecosystem on Earth, and that all living organisms are equal in value and importance. It is thus highly critical of modern patterns of consumption and development, as well as modern industrial capitalism, which tend to destroy natural resources and endanger animals. Choices A, B, and C are incorrect.

23. **The correct answer is D.** The burgeoning democratic system in Ancient Greece most likely led to Sophism. The Sophists traveled around discussing politics and justice with the citizens of Athens, many of whom were required to participate in government. Socrates's condemnation by the Greek government (choice A), and Plato's opening of the Athens Academy (choice C) occurred after Sophism developed. The Peloponnesian War (choice B) was less influential than democracy on Sophism.

24. **The correct answer is B.** For an Epicurean, the ethical evaluation of a decision to perform euthanasia will depend on whether the action will avoid pain and increase happiness. Epicureans do not worry about retribution from the gods or nature, so choices A and D are incorrect. A utilitarian would be concerned about maximizing utility for everyone, so choice C is incorrect.

25. **The correct answer is D.** Justice is the principle of biomedical ethics that pertains to the fair and equitable distribution of scarce resources, such as vaccines. The principle of autonomy pertains to a patient's right

to make decisions for himself or herself, so choice A is incorrect. Orthodoxy (choice B) and referral (choice C) are not principles of biomedical ethics, so they are incorrect.

26. **The correct answer is C.** The idea that the universe is morally neutral is a concept related to natural law theories. Natural law theories also assume that moral laws are part of nature. Social contract theories (choice D), feminist ethics (choice A), and Indian philosophies (choice B) are not based on assumptions regarding a morally neutral universe.

27. **The correct answer is C.** A competent patient who signs a "do not resuscitate" (DNR) form thereby requests that medical professionals *do not* attempt to administer extraordinary treatment such as CPR or defibrillation if his or her heart or breathing stops. A DNR form explicitly indicates consent and is an expression rather than a rejection of autonomy, so choice B is incorrect. Choices A and D are incorrect.

28. **The correct answer is A.** Rousseau develops the idea of the general will in society in *Discourse on Political Economy*. Under general will, citizens act as legislators to determine as a collective body the laws and legislation of society. Choices B, C, and D are incorrect.

29. **The correct answer is A.** Objectives of prison reform include reducing prison populations, making life in prison safer and more rehabilitative for inmates, and creating favorable conditions for inmates re-entering society on probation or parole. Prison reform advocates criticize minimum sentencing requirements as a factor that increases prison populations unnecessarily. Prison reformers tend to support deterrence (choice B), rehabilitation (choice C), and probation (choice D) as methods of addressing crime.

30. **The correct answer is B.** Pragmatic pacifists argue that violence and warfare are unnecessary and wrong, given that there are many other means, including diplomacy, to resolve disputes between nations and peoples. The idea that all violence is inherently immoral pertains to moral pacifism, so choice A is incorrect. Choices C and

D pertain to Just War theory and are not pacifist principles.

31. **The correct answer is A.** John Rawls's first principle of justice is that "Each person is to have an equal right to the most extensive total system of equal basic liberties," so a follower of his would most likely be convinced by an appeal to equal rights. The reconciliation of past injustices is more so a concern of Robert Nozick, so choice B is incorrect. Democratic consensus is more so a concern of Immanuel Kant, so choice C is incorrect. Personal benefit is more so a concern of a moral egoist like Ayn Rand, so choice D is incorrect.

32. **The correct answer is B.** Rand would most likely disagree with the concept of redistributing wealth because she believed that doing anything for another person sacrificed personal happiness. In addition, she objected to what she viewed as the weak exploiting the strong. Rawls (choice C) was an advocate of distributive justice, so he would support wealth redistribution. Choices A and D are incorrect.

33. **The correct answer is D.** A follower of Kant makes an ethical evaluation of capital punishment based on the development of a universal law. In other words, capital punishment is moral if it is moral for all human beings. A Kantian would focus less on natural and civil laws (choice A), consequences (choice B), and long-term societal benefits (choice C).

34. **The correct answer is B.** According to ethical relativism, every point of view is equally valid, and different people have different behavior standards. Choice A refers to empiricism, and choice C refers to monism, a theory held by pre-Socratic philosophers. Choice D describes stoicism.

35. **The correct answer is C.** Hard determinism is the theory that our actions and decisions are completely controlled and predetermined by natural forces, and deep ecology is the theory that all living organisms on earth are connected and interdependent; therefore, they would agree that human life is interconnected with nature. Determinists do

not believe in free will, so choices A and D are incorrect, and supporters of deep ecology believe that all organisms have equal claim to Earth, so choice B is incorrect.

36. **The correct answer is B.** In *Two Treatises of Government*, Locke asserts that people have three primary rights—life, liberty, and property. A modified version of these rights was included in the U.S. Declaration of Independence. The right to form militias is the Second Amendment to the U.S. Constitution, but it was not one of Locke's propositions.

37. **The correct answer is A.** Rousseau asserted that people are born innately good but that the greed and corruption in society corrupts them, which rules out choice B. The Greek philosophers believed that knowledge led to virtue, so choice C is incorrect. Rousseau did not blame natural laws for immorality, so choice D is incorrect.

38. **The correct answer is D.** Hinduism and Buddhism are most closely linked to actions and duties, or karma and dharma. *Karma* is the idea that a person's actions determine the future. *Dharma* refers to the righteous duties a person has toward people and gods. Choices A, B, and C are less associated with Buddhism and Hinduism.

39. **The correct answer is B.** HIPAA is the acronym for the Health Insurance Portability and Accountability Act, a law that regulates which entities can and cannot disclose private information about patients' medical histories. The Affordable Care Act, enacted later, guarantees that patients cannot be discriminated against by healthcare companies because of preexisting conditions, so choice D is incorrect. Choices A and C are incorrect.

40. **The correct answer is D.** According to Socrates, a man who robs a store at gunpoint is most likely immoral because he lacks knowledge. Socrates believed that virtue equaled knowledge, and wickedness resulted from ignorance. Choice B is incorrect because Socrates thought that people did not knowingly act immorally. Nature and personal freedom were less significant factors in morality than knowledge.

41. **The correct answer is D.** Aquinas viewed nature as a way to understand and draw close to God. Aquinas states that the laws discovered in nature stem from God. Aquinas attempted to understand the relationship between God and humanity, but he viewed nature as a way to understand God, not humans. Epicurus believed the universe was created by an accidental collision of atoms, so choice C is incorrect.

42. **The correct answer is B.** The First Amendment to the U.S. Constitution begins, "Congress shall make no law respecting an establishment of religion." Thomas Jefferson, as well as many legal scholars and Supreme Court justices, have interpreted this as establishing a "separation of church and state," but that phrase is not explicitly stated in the Constitution, so choice A is incorrect. Choices C and D express ideas that are in the First Amendment, but they are also not part of the actual text and are thus incorrect.

43. **The correct answer is C.** Nozick compared income taxes to forced labor. Rawls advocated distributive justice, so he would probably think taxes are moral. Smith wrote about capitalism in *The Wealth of Nations*, but he does not indicate that taxes discourage productivity. Noddings has focused her work on the ethics of care.

44. **The correct answer is A.** Gilligan found that women are more likely than men to consider responsibilities and relationships when making decisions. Men are more likely to minimize emotions and apply standard rules and principles when reaching a moral decision. Therefore, choices B, C, and D are incorrect.

45. **The correct answer is D.** Subjectivism is the philosophical theory that all statements about ethics are expressions of personal perception. Thus for a subjectivist, the expression "murder is wrong" is not a universal truth, but rather just the belief or common sense of the person expressing it. Choices A, B, and C are incorrect.

46. **The correct answer is A.** Triage, related to the biomedical ethics principle of justice, relates to the equitable distribution of resources, which often amounts to the decision of who lives and who dies. Allowing women and children to board a lifeboat first is just such a decision, as it allocates a scarce resource—space—to certain individuals but not others. Medicating a patient against his consent has more to do with autonomy than justice, so choice C is incorrect. Prescribing chemotherapy to a late-stage cancer patient is more relevant to the principles of beneficence and non-maleficence than justice, so choice D is incorrect. Choice B is also incorrect.

47. **The correct answer is B.** The majority decision in *Lawrence v. Texas* struck down sodomy laws, which had previously made same-sex sexual activity illegal in some states. Contraception access (choice A), same-sex marriage (choice C), and some types of pornography (choice D) were all legalized nationwide in other Supreme Court cases.

48. **The correct answer is C.** The idea that everything in life has a purpose was one of Aristotle's core beliefs. The other one is that change is both necessary and natural, so choice A is incorrect. Aristotle was extremely wise and learned, yet he continued to gain more knowledge, which means choice D is incorrect. Aristotle believed that virtue could be achieved through balance in life, so choice B is incorrect.

49. **The correct answer is B.** Stoics, such as Epictetus, believe that human beings cannot change fate because absolute law rules the universe. Epicurus was a hedonist who believed the universe was created by atoms colliding accidentally, so choice D is incorrect. Aquinas (choice A) was a Catholic priest who believed in God rather than fate. Hindus, such as Mohandas Gandhi (choice C) believe in many gods and karma rather than absolute law.

50. **The correct answer is D.** According to Rousseau's concept of general will, citizens act as legislators to determine as a collective body the laws and legislation of society. Rousseau is a social contract theorist, but

the definition given is of general will rather than social contract theory.

51. **The correct answer is A.** A utilitarian views issues in terms of consequences and results. A utilitarian will most likely ask if an affirmative action policy will benefit more people than it will harm because the question addresses the benefits of the policy. Utilitarians are not concerned with natural laws, so choice B is incorrect. Choice C relates to a policy of distributive justice rather than utilitarianism. The opinion of the majority is insignificant to utilitarians, so choice D is incorrect.

52. **The correct answer is D.** Both Kant's categorical imperatives and utilitarianism are masculine approaches to ethical decision making. Carol Gilligan researched how men and women make moral decisions, and men typically focus on rules, as with Kant's method and utilitarianism. Choices A, B, and C are not similarities between the two philosophies.

53. **The correct answer is D.** Most of the criticism against the Sophists regarded their reliance on persuasion and manipulation instead of truth. The Sophists questioned the existence of the gods, but that was not a primary criticism against them. Socrates was the most vocal critic of the Sophists, so choice B is incorrect. The Sophists did not dominate the government (choice C), although they were influential.

54. **The correct answer is B.** In *The Republic*, society is based on political justice. Democracy, which is similar to Rousseau's general will, and tyranny are replaced, so choices A and C are incorrect. The idea of a social contract was not developed until the seventeenth century, so choice D is incorrect.

55. **The correct answer is A.** Gentleness is one of the moral virtues proposed by Aristotle in his book *Nicomachean Ethics*. Self-respect, bravery, truthfulness, and generosity are other moral virtues. Wisdom (choice B), reason (choice C), and skill (choice D) are examples of intellectual virtues.

56. **The correct answer is D.** The term *institutional racism* refers to how racial biases are

prevalent in formal societal systems such as education, criminal justice, and politics. Self-selecting social groups (choice A), dishonest business practices (choice B), and harassment (choice C) can all involve racially biased sentiments or motivations, but they are different from institutional racism because they occur at the level of interpersonal relations rather than at the level of formal social and political institutions.

57. **The correct answer is B.** A Hindu would base a decision to drill for oil in the Alaska wilderness on the amount of harm it would cause. Hinduism advocates choosing actions that cause the least amount of harm, which in this case involves people and the environment. The opinion of the majority (choice C) and self-interests (choices A and D) would not be relevant factors in the decision-making process.

58. **The correct answer is C.** Socrates is better known for his method of teaching than for a specific philosophy. Socrates employed what is now known as the Socratic Method, which involves asking a student a series of questions in order to draw out the truth. Plato (choice A) and Aristotle (choice B) are both highly regarded for their philosophies. Pythagoras (choice D) was better known as a mathematician.

59. **The correct answer is A.** Hobbes holds the most pessimistic view of society, which he considers savage and full of conflict. He developed the social contract theory because he felt it was better for people to surrender some of their rights for the protection offered by a society. Rousseau (choice C) and Locke (choice D) were also social contract theorists, but they did not view the world as such a violent place like their peer. Mill (choice B) was a utilitarian who believed that the government had very limited moral authority over people.

60. **The correct answer is D.** Plato believed in pursuing personal excellence to achieve peace in a troubled world. During Plato's time, many people believed beauty equaled virtue, but Plato believed enlightenment gained from knowledge, not nature, was the key to virtue. Although the soldiers in Plato's *The Republic* are courageous and moral, the wise philosopher is the ruler, which means choice C is incorrect.

General Anthropology

OVERVIEW

Chapter 2

The DSST® General Anthropology exam consists of 100 multiple-choice questions that cover the four fields of anthropology: physical anthropology, archaeology, cultural anthropology, and linguistic anthropology. The exam focuses upon the following topics: methodologies and disciplines; cultural systems and processes; history and theory; social organization; economic and political organization; religion; and the modernization and application of anthropology. Careful reading, critical thinking, and logical analysis will be as important as your anthropological knowledge.

DIAGNOSTIC TEST ANSWER SHEET

1. Ⓐ Ⓑ Ⓒ Ⓓ   5. Ⓐ Ⓑ Ⓒ Ⓓ   9. Ⓐ Ⓑ Ⓒ Ⓓ   13. Ⓐ Ⓑ Ⓒ Ⓓ   17. Ⓐ Ⓑ Ⓒ Ⓓ

2. Ⓐ Ⓑ Ⓒ Ⓓ   6. Ⓐ Ⓑ Ⓒ Ⓓ   10. Ⓐ Ⓑ Ⓒ Ⓓ   14. Ⓐ Ⓑ Ⓒ Ⓓ   18. Ⓐ Ⓑ Ⓒ Ⓓ

3. Ⓐ Ⓑ Ⓒ Ⓓ   7. Ⓐ Ⓑ Ⓒ Ⓓ   11. Ⓐ Ⓑ Ⓒ Ⓓ   15. Ⓐ Ⓑ Ⓒ Ⓓ   19. Ⓐ Ⓑ Ⓒ Ⓓ

4. Ⓐ Ⓑ Ⓒ Ⓓ   8. Ⓐ Ⓑ Ⓒ Ⓓ   12. Ⓐ Ⓑ Ⓒ Ⓓ   16. Ⓐ Ⓑ Ⓒ Ⓓ   20. Ⓐ Ⓑ Ⓒ Ⓓ

POST-TEST ANSWER SHEET

1. Ⓐ Ⓑ Ⓒ Ⓓ   13. Ⓐ Ⓑ Ⓒ Ⓓ   25. Ⓐ Ⓑ Ⓒ Ⓓ   37. Ⓐ Ⓑ Ⓒ Ⓓ   49. Ⓐ Ⓑ Ⓒ Ⓓ

2. Ⓐ Ⓑ Ⓒ Ⓓ   14. Ⓐ Ⓑ Ⓒ Ⓓ   26. Ⓐ Ⓑ Ⓒ Ⓓ   38. Ⓐ Ⓑ Ⓒ Ⓓ   50. Ⓐ Ⓑ Ⓒ Ⓓ

3. Ⓐ Ⓑ Ⓒ Ⓓ   15. Ⓐ Ⓑ Ⓒ Ⓓ   27. Ⓐ Ⓑ Ⓒ Ⓓ   39. Ⓐ Ⓑ Ⓒ Ⓓ   51. Ⓐ Ⓑ Ⓒ Ⓓ

4. Ⓐ Ⓑ Ⓒ Ⓓ   16. Ⓐ Ⓑ Ⓒ Ⓓ   28. Ⓐ Ⓑ Ⓒ Ⓓ   40. Ⓐ Ⓑ Ⓒ Ⓓ   52. Ⓐ Ⓑ Ⓒ Ⓓ

5. Ⓐ Ⓑ Ⓒ Ⓓ   17. Ⓐ Ⓑ Ⓒ Ⓓ   29. Ⓐ Ⓑ Ⓒ Ⓓ   41. Ⓐ Ⓑ Ⓒ Ⓓ   53. Ⓐ Ⓑ Ⓒ Ⓓ

6. Ⓐ Ⓑ Ⓒ Ⓓ   18. Ⓐ Ⓑ Ⓒ Ⓓ   30. Ⓐ Ⓑ Ⓒ Ⓓ   42. Ⓐ Ⓑ Ⓒ Ⓓ   54. Ⓐ Ⓑ Ⓒ Ⓓ

7. Ⓐ Ⓑ Ⓒ Ⓓ   19. Ⓐ Ⓑ Ⓒ Ⓓ   31. Ⓐ Ⓑ Ⓒ Ⓓ   43. Ⓐ Ⓑ Ⓒ Ⓓ   55. Ⓐ Ⓑ Ⓒ Ⓓ

8. Ⓐ Ⓑ Ⓒ Ⓓ   20. Ⓐ Ⓑ Ⓒ Ⓓ   32. Ⓐ Ⓑ Ⓒ Ⓓ   44. Ⓐ Ⓑ Ⓒ Ⓓ   56. Ⓐ Ⓑ Ⓒ Ⓓ

9. Ⓐ Ⓑ Ⓒ Ⓓ   21. Ⓐ Ⓑ Ⓒ Ⓓ   33. Ⓐ Ⓑ Ⓒ Ⓓ   45. Ⓐ Ⓑ Ⓒ Ⓓ   57. Ⓐ Ⓑ Ⓒ Ⓓ

10. Ⓐ Ⓑ Ⓒ Ⓓ   22. Ⓐ Ⓑ Ⓒ Ⓓ   34. Ⓐ Ⓑ Ⓒ Ⓓ   46. Ⓐ Ⓑ Ⓒ Ⓓ   58. Ⓐ Ⓑ Ⓒ Ⓓ

11. Ⓐ Ⓑ Ⓒ Ⓓ   23. Ⓐ Ⓑ Ⓒ Ⓓ   35. Ⓐ Ⓑ Ⓒ Ⓓ   47. Ⓐ Ⓑ Ⓒ Ⓓ   59. Ⓐ Ⓑ Ⓒ Ⓓ

12. Ⓐ Ⓑ Ⓒ Ⓓ   24. Ⓐ Ⓑ Ⓒ Ⓓ   36. Ⓐ Ⓑ Ⓒ Ⓓ   48. Ⓐ Ⓑ Ⓒ Ⓓ   60. Ⓐ Ⓑ Ⓒ Ⓓ

GENERAL ANTHROPOLOGY DIAGNOSTIC TEST

Directions: Carefully read each of the following 20 questions. Choose the best answer to each question and fill in the corresponding circle on the answer sheet. The Answer Key and Explanations can be found following this Diagnostic Test.

1. Anthropology traditionally includes which four subdisciplines?
   A. Physical anthropology, archaeology, ethnobotany, and cultural anthropology
   B. Cultural anthropology, physical anthropology, anthropological linguistics, paleontology
   C. Anthropological linguistics, physical anthropology, archaeology, and economics
   D. Cultural anthropology, linguistic anthropology, archaeology, and physical anthropology

2. Absolute dating of a fossil is important to paleoanthropologists because
   A. fossils disintegrate quickly.
   B. the age of human bones can only be tested with absolute dating methods.
   C. it helps them more accurately reconstruct the timeline of human evolution.
   D. relative dating methods are accurate for anything younger than 100 years old.

3. What is the difference between innovation and invention?
   A. Innovation refers to an improvement or change to something that already exists. Invention refers to the development or discovery of something completely new.
   B. Invention refers to an improvement or change to something that already exists. Innovation refers to the development or discovery of something completely new.
   C. Invention and innovation both refer to the improvements made to existing products or services.
   D. Innovation and invention both refer to the development of a new product or service.

4. Tribal political organizations are usually found in which type of society?
   A. Pastoralists
   B. Agriculturalist
   C. Band
   D. Foraging

5. What is applied anthropology?
   A. Using an anthropological perspective to solve modern problems
   B. An anthropological technique that started in the 1980s
   C. Anthropologists working with paleontologists digging for dinosaurs
   D. An anthropological study of employment

6. Anthropologists say that agriculture is a necessary precursor to the development of urban society because
  A. human societies evolve through the same stages.
  B. intensive food production is required to feed large populations
  C. humans finally had time to develop tools.
  D. writing allowed people to share farming techniques with one another.

7. What is the primary difference between historic archaeologists and prehistoric archaeologists?
  A. Prehistoric archaeologists are interested in terrestrial research sites, while historic archaeologists are interested in underwater research sites.
  B. Prehistoric archaeologists are interested in human culture prior to the advent of written records, while historic archaeologists are interested in human cultures who used some form of writing.
  C. Prehistoric archaeologists are interested in artifacts, while historic archaeologists are interested in written documents.
  D. Prehistoric archaeologists are interested in dinosaurs, while historic archaeologists are interested in modern humans.

8. Bronislaw Malinowski proposed his theory of Functionalism after years of conducting fieldwork where?
  A. The Philippines
  B. The Trobriand Islands
  C. The Marshall Islands
  D. The island of Malta

9. From an anthropological perspective, what is an age group?
  A. People of the same age who share common interests
  B. A kinship term
  C. A survey category
  D. People of the same age who experience culturally relevant experiences at the same time

10. Which anthropologists could use their skills to develop programs to help multilingual students succeed in school?
  A. Physical anthropologists
  B. Structural linguists
  C. Historic archaeologists
  D. Sociolinguists

11. What are random changes in DNA that may lead to beneficial, harmful, or neutral traits for an organism?
  A. Genetic drift
  B. Gene flow
  C. Mutation
  D. Phenotype

12. Which anthropologist would be most likely to research the translation of writing on a stone table?
  A. Primatologist
  B. Historic archaeologist
  C. Forensic anthropologist
  D. Physical anthropologist

13. What is the name of the theory that states cultural institutions function to fulfill basic human biological needs and support the workings of society?
  A. Functionalism
  B. Anthropology and Gender
  C. Postmodernism
  D. Globalization

14. "People shouldn't eat fried grasshoppers for protein because that's gross and unnatural. Meat is the only protein people should eat." This statement is an example of what perspective?

    A. Ethnocentric perspective

    B. Holistic perspective

    C. Four-field perspective

    D. Culturally relative perspective

15. What is a gene pool?

    A. A laboratory sample of an individual's DNA

    B. All of the possible genetic variations within the human species

    C. The product of a sperm fertilizing an egg

    D. The visible traits of a population

16. Rituals that mark an individual's movement from one social status or stage of life to another are

    A. rites of witchcraft

    B. rites of intensification

    C. rites of passage

    D. rites of purification

17. Enculturation of the individual happens

    A. at birth.

    B. during childhood.

    C. as a teenager becomes an adult.

    D. throughout a person's entire life.

18. Which statement best describes the incest taboo from an anthropological perspective?

    A. The prohibitions of an incest taboo differ between cultures.

    B. The incest taboo is one of the four forces of evolution.

    C. Societies prefer monogamous marriages to avoid incest.

    D. The prohibitions of an incest taboo are the same between cultures.

19. Pastoralism is a subsistence strategy that relies on which of the following for survival?

    A. Long-term breeding of livestock

    B. Large territories for agriculture

    C. Caring for and keeping herds of domesticated animals

    D. Communal gardens

20. A shaman is a

    A. priestess.

    B. healer.

    C. totem.

    D. pilgrim.

diagnostic test

ANSWER KEY AND EXPLANATIONS

1. D	**5.** A	**9.** D	**13.** A	**17.** D
2. C	**6.** B	**10.** D	**14.** A	**18.** A
3. A	**7.** B	**11.** C	**15.** B	**19.** C
4. A	**8.** B	**12.** B	**16.** C	**20.** B

1. **The correct answer is D.** Anthropology studies the entirety of the human experience: the biological history and diversity of humanity (physical anthropology); the study of prehistoric and historic human cultures based on their material remains (archaeology); the study of human language (linguistic anthropology); and human cultural diversity (cultural anthropology). Choice A is incorrect because ethnobotany is the study of the relationship between plant life and humans. Choice B is incorrect because paleontology is the study of life on earth prior to the emergence of anatomically modern human beings. Choice C is incorrect because economics studies human decision-making regarding goods and services.

2. **The correct answer is C**. Since paleoanthropologists have identified many possible relatives of *Homo sapiens*, an accurate age of the fossils could help them determine when these other groups were alive on earth. It would then be easier to reconstruct the evolutionary changes that occurred over time. Choice A is incorrect because fossils are usually preserved as rock. Choice B is incorrect because the age of human bones can be determined through stratigraphy, an example of a relative dating method. Choice D is incorrect because relative dating methods can date fossils to millions of years ago.

3. **The correct answer is A.** The difference between invention and innovation is important. *Invention* refers to the development or discovery of something completely new. This may refer to a new idea, product, service, tool, etc. *Innovation* refers to an improvement or change to something that already exists—that is, something that has already been invented. Choice B is incorrect

because the definition is mismatched to the words. Choices C and D are incorrect because the words are not synonyms.

4. **The correct answer is A.** A tribe, which is usually found in pastoralist or horticulturalist cultures, is made up of groups related by kinship or family ties. Choice B is incorrect because agriculturalists usually organize themselves through a state system. Choices C and D are incorrect because foragers are usually organized into bands.

5. **The correct answer is A.** Applied anthropology uses the perspective and tools of physical, archaeological, linguistic, and cultural anthropology to solve a variety of problems. Choice B is incorrect because applied anthropology dates to the early 1940s. Choice C is incorrect because anthropologists do not excavate sites for dinosaurs. Choice D is incorrect because applied anthropology does not refer to an ethnographic study.

6. **The correct answer is B.** Agriculture allowed people to settle in one place and, over time, begin growing enough food to sustain larger and larger populations. Choice A is incorrect because human societies do not evolve through the same stages. Each society changes at its own pace and in its own way. Choice C is incorrect because humans have been developing tools for thousands of years prior to the emergence of large urban societies. Choice D is incorrect because people did not need writing to exchange information with one another. Agriculture likely emerged in the prehistoric, not historic, era.

7. **The correct answer is B.** Many archaeologists focus upon prehistoric archaeology (human culture prior to written historical

records). Others specialize in historic archaeology, analyzing both the cultural artifacts and written evidence to understand a group of people. Choice A is incorrect because prehistoric and historic archaeologists can conduct research at underwater and terrestrial sites. Choice C is incorrect because historic archaeologists are also interested in artifacts. Choice D is incorrect because paleontologists, not archaeologists, study dinosaurs.

8. **The correct answer is B.** Bronislaw Malinowksi is most famous for his work among the Trobriand Islands communities. Choices A, C, and D are incorrect.

9. **The correct answer is D.** An age group is a group of people of the same age who experience culturally relevant experiences, such as rites of passage, at the same time. Choice A is incorrect because associations based on age do not necessarily mean they have culturally relevant experiences together. Choice B is incorrect because kinship terms are defined as specific ways relatives are labeled or referred to. Choice C is incorrect because an age group means something more than a survey category in anthropology.

10. **The correct answer is D.** Sociolinguists study verbal and nonverbal communication in a variety of social contexts. They use their training to research a particular issue related to human language and develop an appropriate program. Choice A is incorrect because physical anthropologists focus on the biological history and diversity of humanity. Choice B is incorrect because structural linguists examine the construction (the grammar and syntax, for example) of languages. Choice C is incorrect because historic archaeologists analyze both the cultural artifacts and written evidence to understand a group of people.

11. **The correct answer is C.** Mutation refers to random changes in DNA that may lead to beneficial, harmful, or neutral traits for an organism. Choice A is incorrect because genetic drift occurs when random events, such as an earthquake, cause an individual to die without reproducing. Choice B is incorrect because gene flow refers to an individual or individuals from one gene pool introducing genetic material to another gene pool through producing offspring. Choice D is incorrect because phenotype refers to an individual's physical trait or expression of the genotype.

12. **The correct answer is B.** Historic archaeologists analyze both the cultural artifacts and written evidence to understand a group of people. Choices A, C, D are incorrect because those anthropologists are all physical anthropologists. Physical anthropologists focus on the biological history and diversity of humanity. Primatologists conduct biological research and observation of nonhuman primates to shed light on human evolution. Forensic anthropologists use applied biological anthropology to conduct an analysis of skeletal remains.

13. **The correct answer is A.** Bronislaw Malinowksi and others proposed the idea that cultural institutions function to fulfill basic human biological needs and support the workings of society. Choice B is incorrect because the Anthropology and Gender theory focuses on women's roles and how gender is important to understanding culture. Choice C is incorrect because Postmodernism argues that cultural descriptions are subjective, often reflect the anthropologist's bias, and can therefore never be accurately or fully described. Choice D is incorrect because the Globalization theory argues that culture must be understood within the context of the global network connecting capital, resources, goods, and services.

14. **The correct answer is A.** An ethnocentric perspective refers to the belief that one's own norms and values are the only correct standard for living and should be used to judge others. Choice B is incorrect because the holistic perspective refers to the way anthropologists understand cultural components by how they interact with one another. Choice C is incorrect because the four-field perspective refers to the four subfields of anthropology (physical, linguistic, archaeology, and cultural) and how they are used to study humanity. Choice D is incorrect because a culturally relative

perspective argues that each culture must be understood by its own norms and values and not be immediately judged by the standards of other cultures.

15. **The correct answer is B.** Scientists refer to all of the possible genetic variations within the human species as the gene pool. Choice A is incorrect because a gene pool refers to the entire species. Choice C is incorrect because the product of a sperm fertilizing an egg is a zygote (becomes an embryo after implantation). Choice D is incorrect because the gene pool refers to the genetic differences among humans.

16. **The correct answer is C.** Rites of passage are rituals that mark an individual's movement from one social status or stage of life to another. These include ceremonies for birth, marriage, aging, and death. Choice A is incorrect because witchcraft refers to magical rituals used to cause harm. Choice B is incorrect because rites of intensification (such as going to weekly prayer service) bind a group together and reinforce the norms and values of that group. Choice D is incorrect because rites of purification ritually cleanse a person or group when a taboo has been violated.

17. **The correct answer is D.** From the moment a person is born until the moment he or she passes away, the person is learning to be part of a cultural group, a process called enculturation. Since enculturation is a lifelong process, choices A, B, and C are incorrect.

18. **The correct answer is A.** Every society has rules prohibiting sexual relationships between family members. These incest taboos, however, do not all define family in the same way. Some cultures prohibit relationships between blood relatives. Other cultures encourage marriage between certain cousins but not others. Choice B is incorrect because the four forces of evolution are mutation, genetic drift, gene flow, and natural selection. Choice C is incorrect because the preference for monogamous marriage is not related to the incest taboo. Choice D is incorrect because prohibitions of an incest taboo differ between cultures.

19. **The correct answer is C.** Pastoralists care for and keep herds of domesticated animals such as goats, cattle, or camels. Choice A is incorrect because the long-term breeding of livestock is part of the subsistence strategy of agriculturalists. Choice B is incorrect because pastoralists need large areas for their animals to graze and eat grass. Choice D is incorrect because communal gardens are generally found in horticultural societies.

20. **The correct answer is B.** Shamans are often healers, people who treat and cure medical and spiritual illnesses. Choice A is incorrect because priestesses (and priests) hold a full-time position in the group and are expected to conduct rituals, interact with the supernatural, and lead the community. Choice C is incorrect because some religious groups believe ancestral spirits bind them together as one people and, as a result, have a special relationship with an animal, plant, or other object that represents that spirit (totemism). Choice D is incorrect because, in the religious sense, a pilgrim is someone who travels to a sacred site to prove one's dedication to the faith.

DIAGNOSTIC TEST ASSESSMENT GRID

Now that you've completed the diagnostic test and read through the answer explanations, you can use your results to target your studying. Find the question numbers from the diagnostic test that you answered incorrectly and highlight or circle them below. Then focus extra attention on the sections within the chapter dealing with those topics.

General Anthropology		
Content Area	**Topics Covered**	**Questions**
Anthropology: Methodologies and Disciplines	• Physical anthropology • Cultural anthropology • Linguistics • Archaeology • Applied anthropology	1, 7
History and Theory	• Ethnographies and perspectives • Sex and gender • Race and ethnicity • Cultural ecology and evolution	8, 13

Physical Anthropology	• Genetic principles
	 • Evolutionary principles
	 • Primatology:
	 • Paleontology:
	   1. Relative and absolute dating
	   2. Fossil hominids
		2, 11, 15

Archaeology	• Methodology • Paleolithic and Mesolithic • Neolithic • Development of civilization and urban societies	6, 12
Cultural Systems and Processes	• Components of culture • Symbolic systems • Language and communication • Cultural diffusion and power • Cultural universals, sub-cultures and counter cultures • World system and colonialism • Arts	3, 14, 17

General Anthropology		
Content Area	**Topics Covered**	**Questions**
Social Organization	• Marriage and family patterns: mate choice, residence, monogamy, polygamy, family of orientation–conjugal, natal family, incest, exogamy, divorce • Kinship and descent groups: kindred, lineage, clan, phratry, moiety, bilateral vs. unilateral descent, matrilineal, patrilineal, kinship terminology • Groups and associations (e.g., age, sex) • Social stratification: caste, class, slavery, status (achieved and ascribed), role, rank	9, 18
Economic and Political Organizations	• Bands, tribes, chiefdoms, and states • Subsistence and settlement patterns • Trade, reciprocity, redistribution, and market exchange • Modern political systems • Globalization and the Environment	4, 19
Religion	• Belief Systems • Formal institutions • Informal organizations • Religious practices and practitioners • Rituals	16, 20

Modernization and Application of Anthropology	• Applied anthropology
	• Cultural preservation
	• Directed and spontaneous cultural change
	• Future directions:
	  1. Environment
	  2. Cultural resource management
	  3. Indigenous survival and global culture
		5, 10

GET THE FACTS

To see the DSST® General Anthropology Fact Sheet, go to **http://getcollegecredit.com/exam_fact_sheets** and click on the **Social Sciences** tab. Scroll down and click the **General Anthropology** link. Here you will find suggestions for further study material and the ACE college credit recommendations for passing the test.

ANTHROPOLOGY: METHODOLOGIES AND DISCIPLINES

From the Greek *anthropos* ("human") and *logia* ("study"), anthropology is the study of humankind from our earliest hominid ancestors to current cultures and societies. The discipline covers the whole of human existence, as seen through its four major subdisciplines: physical, cultural, linguistic, and archaeology.

PHYSICAL ANTHROPOLOGY

Physical anthropology focuses on the biological history and diversity of humanity. Physical anthropologists (also known as biological anthropologists) study human evolution: adaptation to the environment over the millennia. Researchers in this subdiscipline might further specialize in one of several branches. We'll review the following three in this chapter:

1. *Human variation*: study of biological differences (physiology, genetics, etc.) within the human species

2. *Primatology*: biological research and observation of nonhuman primates to shed light on human evolution

3. *Paleoanthropology*: reconstruction of humanity's evolutionary past using the fossil record

Later on, we will explore important terms and concepts (such as fossil hominids, genetics, and living primates) associated with physical anthropology and these specializations.

CULTURAL ANTHROPOLOGY

Cultural anthropology focuses on researching and comparing patterns of human cultural diversity. An **ethnographer** spends an extended period of time with a group of people observing, interviewing, and participating in the activities of their everyday lives. Based on the data collected, the ethnographer will often produce a written account (called an **ethnography**) of that time period with detailed descriptions of the shared behavioral patterns, values, and norms of that group. The practice of comparing and contrasting the cultural patterns of one group with other ethnographic examples is referred to as **ethnology**. Later in this chapter we will discuss some of the different structures found in cultural groups such as religion, kinship, and economic and political organizations.

LINGUISTIC ANTHROPOLOGY

Linguistic anthropology is the study of human language. Three specific branches within this sub-discipline examine the complex variations in human communication:

1. *Historical linguistics* is concerned with the connection between languages and how these languages change over time.

2. *Descriptive* or *structural linguistics* examines the construction (the grammar and syntax, for example) of languages.

3. *Sociolinguistics* studies verbal and nonverbal communication in a variety of social contexts. We will review linguistic anthropology in relationship to the concept of culture and highlight important terms and definitions (see Cultural Systems and Processes).

ARCHAEOLOGY

Archaeology is the study of prehistoric and historic human cultures based on their material remains. Through the excavation of sites with evidence of human activity, archaeologists carefully recover, catalog, and study items created and/or shaped by people (artifacts). These sites, which may be terrestrial (on land) or aquatic (underwater), can yield information that predates written history. Therefore, many archaeologists focus on prehistoric archaeology (human culture prior to written historical records). Others specialize in historic archaeology, analyzing both the cultural artifacts and written evidence to understand a group of people.

We will review these topics in greater detail, including the differences between the Paleolithic, Mesolithic, and Neolithic eras and the rise of civilization and urban societies.

APPLIED ANTHROPOLOGY

While anthropology is typically divided into the four subfields, anthropologists are debating the inclusion of a fifth subdiscipline: **applied anthropology**. As the name suggests, this subdiscipline uses the perspective and tools of physical, archaeological, linguistic, and cultural anthropology to solve a variety of problems. At the end of this chapter, we will go over examples of applied anthropology and highlight situations where an anthropological perspective might be the most useful.

Regardless of the number of subdisciplines and specializations, one of the unifying principles of anthropology is the **holistic perspective**. The holistic perspective explains, in part, the four-field approach in anthropology. Anthropologists strive to understand the totality of human existence and believe that in order to do so, we must examine how all of the different components (cultural, biological, material, etc.) interact with one another. We will revisit this idea throughout the chapter.

HISTORY AND THEORY

ETHNOGRAPHIES AND PERSPECTIVES

The early history of anthropology was characterized by what some call "armchair anthropology." Instead of participant observation, scholars of the late nineteenth century would read accounts about other cultures (from explorers, missionaries, reporters, historians, etc.) and draw conclusions based on that information. Lewis Henry Morgan and Edward Burnett Tylor were among the most famous of these anthropologists who worked out of an office or study and made sweeping generalizations about a world they never experienced. Morgan and Tylor were the chief authors, for example, of the theory of **cultural evolution**. Based on their readings, they argued that every cultural group in the world should evolve through three stages: savagery, barbarism, and civilization. Morgan's and Tylor's ethnocentric perspective was that their own Western society was the most evolved and therefore the highest standard everyone should aspire to.

Franz Boas was a United States-based anthropologist and fierce critic of cultural evolution. He lived and conducted research among the North American Inuit on Baffin Island. Boas's subsequent research among other indigenous groups convinced him that cultures should be understood by their own internal norms and values. Cultural evolutionism, he argued, was constructed of racist categories based on misinformation and little to no understanding of the realities of the world's cultural diversity. Boas's research philosophy and the work of his students (who would later become his peers) influenced the discipline's rejection of ethnocentrism and cultural evolution. They focused on cultural relativism and **cultural determinism** (how culture shapes an individual's personality).

Boas was an example of an **ethnographer**: a cultural anthropologist who spends an extended period of time with a group of people observing, interviewing, and participating in the activities of their everyday lives. This activity is referred to as **participant observation**. Anthropologists focus on understanding the **emic** perspective: the point of view of the person who is part of that cultural group.

Based on the data collected, the anthropologist will often produce a written account (called an **ethnography**) of that time period with detailed descriptions of that culture. The analysis of those cultural patterns is usually written from the **etic** perspective: the point of view of someone who is outside of that cultural group. The practice of comparing and contrasting the cultural patterns of one group with other ethnographic examples is referred to as **ethnology**.

Polish-born anthropologist Bronislaw Malinowski pioneered the core anthropological method of participant observation. He spent several years (1915–1918) among the people of the Trobriand Islands and concluded that cultural groups must be understood by their own internal logics—not by the logics of others.

Since the time of Boas and Malinowski, anthropologists have continued researching cultural groups, introducing different methods and debating about the relationship between people and culture.

Cultural ecology, for example, focuses specifically on how the physical environment is the main reason for culture change. Over time, these debates and discussions have been categorized by how they help anthropologists explain and interpret culture.

The following chart briefly summarizes some of these anthropological theories.

Theory	Explanations and Interpretations of Culture	Key Contributors
Cultural Evolution	Cultural development evolves through universal stages.	Lewis Henry Morgan Edward Tylor
Historical Particularism	Cultures must be understood through the history that produced them.	Franz Boas Alfred Kroeber Benjamin Whorf
Functionalism	Cultural institutions function to fulfill basic human biological needs and support the workings of society.	Bronislaw Malinowski A.R. Radcliffe-Brown
Culture and Personality	Culture shapes and is shaped by the personalities of each individual.	Ruth Benedict Margaret Mead
Cultural Ecology and Neo-evolutionary Thought	Culture adapts to the physical environment.	Julian Steward Leslie White
Ecological Materialism	Environment and people influence culture and vice versa.	Morton Fried Marvin Harris
Structuralism	A universal human culture is the product of the human brain.	Claude Lévi-Strauss
Ethnoscience and Cognitive Anthropology	Culture reveals how people categorize the world, which, in turn, reveals how the human mind functions.	Harold Conklin Stephen Tyler
Sociobiology	Culture is a product of human genetics.	E.O.Wilson

Theory	Explanations and Interpretations of Culture	Key Contributors
Anthropology and Gender	Women's roles and how gender is construed is important to understanding culture.	Sherry Ortner Sally Slocum
Symbolic and Interpretive Anthropology	Understanding a culture means studying the significance of the symbols it uses.	Mary Douglas Clifford Geertz Victor Turner
Postmodernism	Cultural descriptions are subjective, often reflect the anthropologist's bias, and can therefore never be accurately or fully described.	Renato Rosaldo Vincent Crapanzano
Globalization	Culture must be understood within the context of the global network connecting capital, resources, goods, and services.	Arjun Appadurai James Ferguson Akhil Gupta

SEX AND GENDER

In anthropology, the terms **sex** and **gender** are defined differently. **Gender** commonly refers to the cultural norms, values, expectations, and categories of what is "masculine" and "feminine." In the past century of anthropological study, the meaning of the word *gender* has shifted and now encompasses perspectives that no longer conform to long-held beliefs and assumptions about the roles of men and women in society. For example, the Hijras of India are neither gender male or female and are referred to as "third gender." Other cultures have fourth or fifth genders. Gender male or female does not always correspond to sex male or sex female. People may be identified as belonging to a specific gender (at birth, for example) and people may self-identify as belonging to a particular gender (the Hijras of India, for example).

RACE AND ETHNICITY

Race refers to certain physical traits grouped together under specific labels and categories. As discussed above, human variations in skin tone, eye and hair color, height, etc., are due to evolution and other environmental factors. Genetic testing identifies each of us as belonging to a single human species. However, over time and often in relation to systems of stratification, the idea that humans were separate "races" became accepted as natural and correct. Human beings owning other human beings who are stripped of their rights and freedoms (**slavery**) occurred in many cultures over the centuries. However, slavery from the fifteenth through nineteenth centuries was justified, in part, by the idea that indigenous African peoples were of a different, lower "race" than Europeans. Although "race" does not exist biologically, it is still used to justify social stratification.

Ethnicity refers to being part of a select social group with a common cultural tradition and/or national origin. While race is based primarily on physical traits, ethnicity is often categorized in terms of one's common ancestry, a shared history, language, and regional culture.

To illustrate the difference between race and ethnicity, consider two people—one from the United States and one from Sweden. Based on their physical characteristics—light skin and eyes, thin lips, narrow noses, and straight hair—both would be considered members of the Caucasian race. However, their ethnicities could be quite different—they most likely would speak different languages, have different traditions, and perhaps different beliefs as a result of the environments in which they were raised.

PHYSICAL ANTHROPOLOGY

Physical (or **biological**) **anthropologists** focus on the biological history and diversity of humanity. Some choose specialization in different areas and focus on particular questions. Physical anthropologists interested in **human variation** ask, "What is the range of biological diversity within the human species, and how does it happen?" **Primatologists** research answers to the question, "What can biological study and observation of nonhuman primates tell us about human evolution?" A **paleoanthropologist** asks, "What does the fossil record tell us about the ancestors and relatives of *Homo sapiens?*"

Answers to these questions are rooted in Charles Darwin's Theory of Evolution. In the 1830s, Darwin was part of a scientific expedition that exposed him to animal and plant life in various coastal areas around the world. Based on his observations and extensive background knowledge of science and history, Darwin eventually proposed his now-famous theory of evolution by natural selection. Simply, Darwin argued that every species of plant and animal life exhibits a range of variation. These variations may help an organism survive or die in its environment. If a variation (also referred to as a **trait**) is considered advantageous, the organism possessing it will survive to reproduce and pass those traits to offspring. If the variation is considered disadvantageous, the organism dies and will not reproduce. Generation after generation, only those organisms with traits that help them survive the environment will live to reproduce and, eventually, new species will emerge.

However, Darwin did not have the answers to questions of how exactly these traits were passed on to offspring and why the variations occurred. Unbeknownst to Darwin, in 1866, a monk named Gregor Mendel published some of the information crucial to answering these questions. Mendel was a scientist who used the monastery garden to grow and study approximately 30,000 pea plants over ten years. He identified specific traits of the plants (flower color, height, etc.) and recorded how these traits were (or were not) passed along from one generation to the next. Based on these data, Mendel eventually identified specific patterns that are now referred to as **Mendel's Principles of Inheritance**, which we will discuss in more detail shortly.

GENETIC PRINCIPLES

Over the years, scientists have built on Darwin's and Mendel's work to give us a clearer understanding of what happens at the cellular and genetic level. You may remember from your life science classes that all animal and plant life is composed of cells. Under the power of a microscope, you can see chromosomes located in the cell nucleus.

These chromosomes are comprised of DNA (deoxyribonucleic acid) strands. **Genes**, which are also referred to as the units of heredity, are specific sections of DNA. In the human body, genes are the genetic blueprints for making proteins. These proteins drive the development and maintenance of the human body and are what cause people to have different traits such as eye or hair color and blood type.

Scientists have identified genes that may cause more than one version of a particular trait. For example, Mendel observed that pea plants grew to different heights. Scientists today could say that the gene for the height trait comes in a "tall gene" or "short gene" variety. To help clarify between these different terms, scientists today use the term **allele**. The height trait genes will cause a pea plant to be a different size because of presence of the "tall" trait allele or the "short" trait allele.

Mendel's Principles of Inheritance outline how these traits are inherited by offspring.

- **The principle of segregation** states that each organism usually has two alleles of each gene. When a sperm fertilizes an egg and the cell begins to reproduce, the offspring will receive one allele of each gene from each parent.

- **The principle of dominance** states one allele will dominate over the other. **Dominant alleles** will produce dominant traits. **Recessive alleles** will produce a trait only if a dominant allele is not present.

- **The principle of independent assortment** states that the genes for different traits are inherited independently of one another.

In humans, genes are responsible for the production of blood. Blood type is a trait that actually has three alleles: A, B, and O. Offspring will inherit one blood allele from each parent (**the principle of segregation**). Scientists have determined that the A allele is dominant to the O allele; the B allele is also dominant to the O allele (**the principle of dominance**). The A allele and B allele are actually co-dominant, which means that both traits of the allele will be expressed. Therefore, depending upon which allele is inherited from the parent, the offspring will have a blood type of A, B, AB, or O. Finally, the blood trait and hair trait (for example) are inherited independently of one another (**the principle of independent assortment**).

		Father's Blood Type				
		A	**B**	**AB**	**O**	
Mother's Blood Type	**A**	A or O	A, B, AB, or O	A, B, or AB	A or O	**Child's Blood Type**
	B	A, B, AB, or O	B or O	A, B, or AB	B or O	
	AB	A, B, or AB	A, B, or AB	A, B, or AB	A or B	
	O	A or O	B or O	A or B	O	

In addition to blood type, the diversity of physical traits among humans suggests a variety of possible allele combinations. A **genotype** refers to the genes and alleles each person possesses. The **phenotype** refers to the physical expression of the genotype. A person may have inherited alleles for dark (for example, black) and light (for example, blond) hair from their parents. However, because dark hair is a dominant allele trait and light hair is a recessive allele trait, a dark hair color will grow from the person's head. The dark hair allele expresses itself on the human body.

EVOLUTIONARY PRINCIPLES

Within the human species, all of these possible genetic variations are referred to as the **gene pool.** Returning to Darwin, how do scientists know if humans are evolving? The answer lies in how the frequency of alleles in the gene pool changes over time. The percentages of allele expression among the human population change over the years and centuries. Scientists have summarized the reasons why as **the four forces of evolution**:

1. *Mutation* refers to random changes in DNA that may lead to beneficial, harmful, or neutral traits for an organism.

2. *Genetic drift* occurs in smaller populations when random events such as an earthquake cause an individual to die without reproducing. That individual's genotype disappears from the gene pool, which decreases the number of available alleles to be passed on to the next generation.

3. *Gene flow* occurs when an individual or individuals from one gene pool introduces genetic material to another gene pool through producing offspring.

4. *Natural selection* is the process through which individuals who have traits that allow them to survive in their environment and reproduce pass along these traits to their offspring, thereby increasing the frequency of those alleles in the gene pool. The alleles of those who do not reproduce are lost, thereby reducing the frequency of those alleles in the gene pool.

Physical anthropologists ask, "What is the range of biological diversity within the human species and how does it happen?" The human gene pool is filled with a variety of alleles (genotypes) that may or may not express themselves physically (phenotypes). Adaptation to Earth's environment has produced humans with a broad range of body shapes, for example. Differences in other phenotypes, such as skin tone and eye and face shape, also have genetic explanations.

PRIMATOLOGY

Primatologists ask, "What can biological study and observation of nonhuman primates tell us about human evolution?" By learning how **living primates** such as gorillas and chimpanzees have adapted over time (evolution by natural selection), primatologists help us understand how humans may have changed over the millennia.

In the research field (forest, jungles, etc.), primatologists spend years observing various primate groups. The results of the anthropologists' studies have yielded a wide variety of insights as to how they live and survive in the wild.

- Orangutans (found in Sumatra and Borneo) are generally solitary creatures that tend to forage for food over broad areas. Female orangutans stay with their offspring until they have matured to self-sufficiency. These primates have been observed attempting to spear fish and catch termites with branches.

- Gorillas in sub-Saharan Africa eat plants, fruits, and insects. They live in groups: usually one older, dominant male with younger males, females, and offspring. Gorillas have been observed building nests of branches and leaves.

- Chimpanzees are found in East, Central, and West Africa and live in large groups of approximately sixty individuals. While they mostly eat fruit, like other primates they also eat insects and plants. Chimpanzees have also been seen eating meat. Primatologists have observed chimpanzees using sticks to pull termites out of a nest and rocks to break open nuts.

In a laboratory setting, primatologists study every aspect of these nonhuman primates. The same advances that allow research at the human genetic level have been used to discover that chimpanzees (for example) share 98 percent of the same DNA with humans. DNA also reveals how primates are related to one another. Primatologists study feces, hair, and teeth for clues about diet. The different skeletal structures of the primates are studied to determine why they move the way they do.

Primatologists contribute to the broader understanding of humans by studying our closest primate relatives. How have primates evolved in response to environmental pressures? How do they survive in the wild? How do they learn? How do they communicate with one another? Anthropologists compare the answers to these, and other questions, with similar research conducted with humans. Comparisons help us understand how much behavior is driven by nature (biology) and how much is driven by nurture (teaching, learning).

PALEONTOLOGY/PALEOANTHROPOLOGY

A **paleoanthropologist** asks, "What does the fossil record tell us about the ancestors and relatives of *Homo sapiens*?" **Fossil** refers to the preserved remains of an organism (plant, animal, human) found in the Earth's crust (or glaciers, marshes, etc.). When a paleoanthropologist discovers a fossil, he or she attempts to find out how old it is through relative and absolute dating.

- **Relative dating** methods can tell us only if a fossil is older or younger than another fossil. Stratigraphy is one example of a relative dating method. Generally, deeper layers of dirt and rock are older than the surface layer of dirt. Through a variety of other techniques, scientists have determined how old these layers are going back millions of years. Paleontologists can determine the age of a fossil based on how far below the ground's surface it is found; simply, the fossil's age is relative to the age of the earth around it.

- **Absolute dating** (also known as **calendar dating**) tells the age of something in actual years. For example, if human remains are found next to a coin with the year 1500 inscribed on it, scientists can tell that the remains date back to sometime during or after the year 1500. Another form of absolute dating is called carbon-14 (C-14) dating. Living organisms have the same amount of carbon-14 in their cellular structure. Once an organism dies, C-14 begins decreasing at a constant rate. Scientists test fossils for the amount of C-14 present, and, with that number, they can tell how long ago an organism lived.

The improvement of dating techniques has helped paleoanthropologists identify the biological origins of modern humans (*Homo sapiens*). Based on what we know about evolution, anthropologists generally accept that many species came before *Homo sapiens*. Over millions of years, their bodies adapted and changed in response to the environment. Those who had traits best suited for survival passed along those characteristics to offspring. Paleoanthropologists have grouped together fossils they believe represent specific groups of humanity's ancestors.

The following chart presents some of those groups.

Name	Approximate Dates Alive	Fossil Discovered at Sites in These Countries (partial list)	Distinguishing Physical Traits and Behaviors (partial list)	Cultural Characteristics (partial list)
Australopithecus afarensis	4–2.9 million years ago	• Ethiopia • Tanzania	• Ape-like features • Walked upright on two legs (also known as bipedal)	*Australopithecus afarensis* likely used tools like modern chimpanzees.
Homo habilis	2.8–1.5 million years ago	• Kenya • Tanzania	• Smaller teeth than *Australopithecus* • Larger brain than *Australopithecus*	• Oldowan stone tools are rocks shaped by striking flakes off. Both the core rock and flakes were used for cutting or slicing plants and animals.

Name	Approximate Dates Alive	Fossil Discovered at Sites in These Countries (partial list)	Distinguishing Physical Traits and Behaviors (partial list)	Cultural Characteristics (partial list)
Homo erectus	1.8 million to 300,000 years ago	• China • Indonesia • Kenya	• Large molars • More robust than average modern humans	• Acheulan stone tools are oval-shaped hand axes produced like Oldowan tools. • Some evidence suggests that the controlled use of fire dates from this time period.
Homo neander-thalensis	250,000 to 30,000 years ago	• Belgium • France • Iraq	• Shorter and stockier than modern humans • Powerful muscles • Thicker and heavier skeletal structure than modern humans	• Mousterian stone tools refer to the variety of objects, such as hand axes and wooden spears, found at various sites. • Anthropologists have discovered caves with fossils, which suggest *Homo neanderthalensis* deliberately buried their dead.

Name	Approximate Dates Alive	Fossil Discovered at Sites in These Countries (partial list)	Distinguishing Physical Traits and Behaviors (partial list)	Cultural Characteristics (partial list)
Homo sapiens	100,000 years ago to present	• Israel • South Africa	• Large brains • Smaller teeth	• Cave art discovered in France dates to over 30,000 years ago; tools date to over 40,000 years ago.

Advances in genetic testing and the discovery of other fossils have helped fill in some of the gaps in our understanding of human evolution. Anthropologists believe, for example, that humans evolved on the African continent and eventually migrated around the world. DNA testing suggests that *Homo sapiens* and *Homo neanderthalensis* likely interbred. New discoveries suggest other species existed that may or may not have been ancestors to humans.

Biological anthropology is the subfield that focuses on the biological history and diversity of humanity. In comparing human variation past and present, studying genetic relatives of *Homo sapiens*, and understanding the biological processes at work, anthropologists understand humanity down to its DNA. This is, however, only one piece of the human puzzle that must be understood in context with archaeology, linguistics, and cultural anthropology (**holism**).

ARCHAEOLOGY

METHODOLOGY

Archaeology is the study of prehistoric and historic human cultures based on their material remains. Archaeologists share similar methods with paleoanthropologists: both carefully excavate sites and use absolute and relative dating to help determine the age of fossils or artifacts (items created and/or shaped by people). These anthropologists carefully recover, catalog, and study their findings to give us a more compete history of humanity.

Archaeologists study sites with evidence of human activity; these sites may be terrestrial (on land) or underwater. Maritime archaeologists search for shipwrecks in oceans or lakes, for example, or search for evidence of coastal human settlements that have been submerged over time. Artifacts can yield information that predates written history. Therefore, many archaeologists focus upon **prehistoric archaeology** (human culture prior to written historical records). Others specialize in **historic archaeology,** analyzing both the cultural artifacts and written evidence to understand a group of people.

PALEOLITHIC, MESOLITHIC, AND NEOLITHIC ERAS

Archaeologists categorize the human past based on the type of tools used by our ancestors. These dates are approximate and subject to change based on new discoveries by anthropologists. Overlap between the dates is possible because changes in tool use happened gradually over time in different places.

Paleolithic (Old Stone Age)

- **Lower Paleolithic**: 2.8 million to 1.5 million years ago: *Homo habilis* used Oldowan stone tools, which refer to rocks that were shaped by striking flakes off with other rocks. Both the core rock and flakes were used for cutting or slicing plants and animals.

- **Middle Paleolithic**: 250,000 to 30,000 years ago: *Homo neanderthalensis* used Mousterian stone tools, which refer to the variety of objects, such as hand axes and wooden spears, found at various sites.

- **Upper Paleolithic**: 40,000 to 10,000 years ago: Cave art likely produced by *Homo sapien*s discovered in France dates to over 30,000 years ago. Tools found at other sites date to over 40,000 years ago.

Mesolithic (Middle Stone Age) refers to the transition era between the Paleolithic and the Neolithic. Humans inhabit every continent on Earth.

Neolithic (New Stone Age)

- **Early Neolithic**: 12,000 to 10,000 years ago: *Homo sapiens* manufactured, among other things, arrowheads and blades. Humans began engaging in food production, also known as **agriculture**.

- **Late Neolithic**: 10,000 to 5,000 years ago: *Homo sapiens* manufactured, among other things, pottery. The emergence of writing and record keeping mark the end of the prehistoric era.

During the Paleolithic era, humans survived by **foraging**: collecting plants, fishing, and hunting animals in order to survive. Humans probably lived in small groups, moving from place to place as the seasons changed, vegetation died and grew, and animals moved. The Neolithic era marks a profound shift in how humans survived. Archaeological evidence suggests that **agriculture**, the deliberate production of food by growing crops and tending animals, slowly emerged in many (but not all) cultures around the world. Depending on the environmental factors (temperature, soil, etc.), availability of plants, variety of animals to domesticate, and availability of materials to make tools with means this **Neolithic Revolution** did not happen abruptly. Each cultural group learned agricultural techniques at its own pace, although most of these changes occurred 12,000 to 10,000 years ago.

DEVELOPMENT OF CIVILIZATION AND URBAN SOCIETIES

The transition from foraging to agriculture meant that people could stay in one place rather than move on a regular basis. Humans began guiding the growth of plants and the reproduction of animals (also referred to as **domestication**). People had a relatively consistent source of food. Increased food production and population growth transformed small villages into larger towns. As technology improved, agriculture became even more productive. Farmland could now support larger city centers.

Governments emerged to manage the needs of the large populace. Social hierarchies meant people began experiencing unequal access to important resources (**social stratification**).

Archaeology is the subfield of anthropology that focuses on the study of material remains. From tools found with our earliest ancestors to vases in the hull of a ship on the ocean floor, artifacts tell stories of the human experience. However, the interpretation of these artifacts happens within a larger context. While **processual** archaeologists believe they can come to an objective conclusion about the significance of an artifact, **post-processual** archaeologists argue that all interpretation is subject to bias. Is an artifact significant? What is the meaning of this artifact to the people who produced it? Is this artifact representative of one cultural group or another?

To avoid interpretations that only reflect the archaeologist's viewpoint, post-processual archaeologists say the answers to these and other questions should be supported (when possible) with other evidence. This is another interpretation of the anthropological focus on the holistic perspective. In archaeology, the artifacts should be understood in relationship to other available information. In prehistoric archaeology, this might mean biological and chemical analysis of the soil around the artifact. In historic anthropology, written records can be consulted to help reconstruct the significance of artifacts.

Broadly, archaeologists' research also adds another piece to the human puzzle: physical anthropologists help us understand our human biology. Archaeology helps us understand how we physically interact with the world around us.

Linguistic and cultural anthropology add to the physical pieces we've already covered to help us understand the rest of the human experience.

CULTURAL SYSTEMS AND PROCESSES

COMPONENTS OF CULTURE

Another perspective that helps unify the four fields of anthropological research is the concept of **culture**. Physical anthropologists explore human biology and its relationship to culture. Archaeologists study artifacts and the culture. Linguistic anthropologists research our human capacity for language and how it is directly related to culture. Cultural anthropology focuses on researching and comparing patterns and components of human cultural diversity. What is culture?

Culture Is Learned

Unlike the physical traits we discussed in the section on genetic principles, culture is *not* passed along to the next generation through our DNA. From the moment we are born until the moment we pass away, we are learning to be part of a cultural group, a process called **enculturation**. Like nonhuman primates, we learn through observation of the world around us. However, we also learn the culturally appropriate behavioral patterns, values, and norms from other people (caregivers, peers, professors, etc.). Communication through language, gestures, pictures, and written records helps us learn the information and skills we need to survive in our environment.

TIP

The soil around some remains of *Homo neanderthalensis* and Mousterian tool sets have revealed ancient traces of pollen, which helps anthropologists reconstruct which plants were possibly important to Neanderthals.

Culture Is Shared

Cultural groups define their **norms** (the way things should be done) and **values** (standards for what is good, correct, ethical, and moral). Being a part of that cultural group generally means a shared acceptance of those norms and values. However, anthropologists have observed a difference between **real** and **ideal culture**. A group may state certain norms and values (**ideal culture**) but those norms and values are not necessarily acted out in reality (**real culture**). For example, a cultural group may say that an ideal marriage is monogamous and based in romantic love. However, the reality may be that people marry for any number of reasons, including financial gain or family pressure.

Culture Is a System of Symbols

As we discussed earlier, symbols represent something else. In human language, words (spoken and written) are symbols because they represent ideas, actions, objects, people, animals, plants, etc. Objects—such as flags for example—can also be symbols if they are significant to a cultural group. All of these symbols help people organize and understand the world around them. We have words and names for the things around us. We can communicate about what we see, hear, touch, and imagine. We can transmit information about our norms and values through the objects we create or shape (our material culture or, from an archaeological perspective, artifacts).

Culture Is an Integrated System

Anthropologists recognize many different aspects of culture, including economic systems, political organization, religion, kinship, and others we will review later. These systems interact with one another; in order to understand a culture, they must be understood in relationship to one another. Anthropologists study how well (or poorly) these pieces are integrated and function together.

Culture Is Adaptive

As you may recall from our earlier discussion about biological anthropology, humans evolve biologically in response to changing environments. Human culture also changes and adapts to give people a better chance to survive and reproduce in their environment. For example, in the space of a few years, a cultural group who is used to hunting game and gathering food in a forest might find its territory destroyed due to natural disaster like a drought. In order to survive, the group will develop new cultural practices to find and process food from other sources.

Culture Is Constantly Changing

Cultural change happens quickly or slowly, and cultures change at different speeds from one another. There is no blueprint or chart for when and how a cultural group might experience any change. Why do cultures change? Environmental pressures, disease, natural disasters are some reasons; conflict within the group or from outside of the group is another reason. Cultures may also change due to **invention** (the development or discovery of something completely new) or **innovation** (the improvement or change to something that already exists). **Diffusion** is also responsible for culture change: ideas, devices, and/or innovations that spread from one culture to another.

Debates About Culture

Cultural universals refer to something that is present in all cultures. Anthropologists debate about what counts as a universal and if they do, in fact, exist in all cultures. Biologically, for example, all humans need to eat, drink, and sleep. However, different norms exist about what is considered "food" and where someone should sleep. Cultural anthropologists have observed patterns of human behavior that seem to exist in multiple, but certainly not all, cultures.

Similarly, some anthropologists continue debating the components of culture. Can culture be compartmentalized? Early anthropologist Edward Tylor first proposed a definition of culture: "Culture… taken in its broad, ethnographic sense, is that complex whole which includes knowledge, belief, art, morals, law, custom, and any other capabilities and habits acquired by man as a member of society." Since then, some anthropologists suggest the basic components of culture are its symbols, language, norms and values. Other argue that beliefs or technology (and other categories) belong on the list.

Culture shapes who we are, what we think, and what we do. Anthropologists argue over **agency**: people's ability to make choices and exercise their free will. Are we ever truly free to behave outside cultural norms, and values? What happens when an individual identifies as part of a culture but rejects some of those norms and values? Is it possible to measure how much of an individual's decision making is rooted in enculturation or his or her own free will?

Studying Culture

A cultural anthropologist may decide to focus on a specific **culture**: a group that shares behavioral patterns, values, and norms. Anthropologists ask questions about **society**, a group of people who usually (but not always) share the same culture, live in a specific territory, and share common goals.

Most cultural anthropologists, like post-processual archaeologists, are particularly aware of their own biases. Anthropologists argue against **ethnocentrism**, the belief that one's own norms and values are the only correct standard for living and should be used to judge others. Anthropologists begin with a method referred to as **cultural relativism**, which argues that each culture must be understood by its own norms and values and not be immediately judged by the standards of other cultures.

Art, for example, is often subject to fierce debates. **Art** is broadly defined as expression of the human imagination and includes, but is not limited to, music, song, dance, drawing, carving, paintings, poems, and stories. What fits into the categories of art and how it is valued depends on each cultural group.

SYMBOLS, LANGUAGE, AND COMMUNICATION

Linguistic anthropology is the study of human language: a system of communication that includes symbols, sounds, and gestures. A **symbol** is something that represents something else. In human language, spoken and written words are symbols because they represent ideas, actions, objects, people, animals, plants, etc. In the English language, for example, individual letters combine to form the word *rose*, which represents a specific type of flower. Humans also combine sounds to produce words, which we can use to communicate with others. Finally, body movements (hand gestures, facial expression, etc.) also communicate specific moods, ideas, and emotions.

Language allows humans to communicate complex ideas, accumulate information (through writing or oral history, for example), and discuss events that occurred in the past, are happening in the present, or could happen in the future. Scientists suggest that animals are able to communicate with one another and, to a certain extent, with humans. However, the evidence suggests that humans' capacity for language and what it helps us accomplish is unmatched by any other species.

Three specific branches within this subdiscipline examine the complex variations in human communication:

1. *Descriptive* or *structural linguistics* examines the construction of languages. **Phonology** studies the sounds of language and **morphology** examines how words are created from those sounds. Structural linguists also study the **grammar** (the rules of how a language is written and/or spoken) as well as **syntax** (the rules for constructing sentences). A structural linguist might go to a cultural group with no tradition of written history and try to record (through writing as well as video and audio) their language.

2. *Historical linguistics* is concerned with the connection between languages and how these languages change over time. A historical linguist might be interested in how Spanish, Italian, and French, for example, developed from Latin over hundreds of years.

3. *Sociolinguistics* studies verbal and nonverbal communication in a variety of social contexts. These anthropologists are interested in the relationship between culture (discussed extensively below) and language. Specifically, sociolinguists research how age, class, race, ethnicity, gender, and other aspects of a person's background and identity influence communication. For example, how do students communicate with peers compared with speaking to teachers?

SOCIAL ORGANIZATION

A society may be understood by its subsistence strategy, economic system, political organization, and social organization. Anthropologists distinguish between societies where individuals and groups may have different access to goods and services, wealth, status, and power. Anthropologists also study how societies organize themselves at the level of family and kin.

MARRIAGE AND FAMILY PATTERNS

Marriage is a cultural institution that defines the parameters of a union between two or more people, establishes rules for the responsibility of children, and clarifies the relationship between the kin of the married people. The rules regarding **divorce** (the end of a marriage) are also culturally determined.

Every society has rules prohibiting sexual relationships between family members. These **incest taboos**, however, do not all define family in the same way. Some cultures prohibit relationships between blood relatives. Other cultures encourage marriage between certain cousins, but not others.

Other culturally based rules require people marry within their own group (**endogamy**) or outside their own group (**exogamy**). These groups may include class, caste, religious, ethnic, racial, etc. Even the number of spouses one has can differ from group to group. **Monogamy** (only one spouse at a time) is the norm for many cultures but **polygamy** (multiple spouse marriage) also exists. **Polygyny** (the marriage of one man to several women) is sanctioned by some religious groups. **Polyandry** (the marriage of one woman to several men) has been observed in places like Tibet where brothers may marry one woman to keep land intact and within the family (rather than splitting the inheritance between several monogamous married couples).

Finding a spouse or spouses may be left up to the individual. However, anthropologists have also studied **arranged marriage**, where the families of potential spouses determine if their children would be a socially appropriate match.

After marriage, cultural rules determine where the spouses will live:

- **Neolocal**: spouses live separately from their parents in their own households
- **Bilocal** or **ambilocal**: spouses choose which family to live with or near
- **Matrilocal**: spouses live with or near the wife's family
- **Patrilocal**: spouses live with or near the husband's family
- **Avunculocal**: spouses live with or near the husband's mother's brother

Culture defines both marriage and **family.** A **nuclear family** (also known as a **conjugal family**) refers to the married partners and the children they are responsible for. **Extended family** refers to multiple generations of family members: grandparents, married offspring, and grandchildren. From the perspective of the individual, the **natal family** is the group they are born into. How that group is defined depends on the rules of kinship and **descent**.

KINSHIP AND DESCENT GROUPS

Descent is how a culture defines how individuals are related to their parents. In **bilateral descent**, descent is traced through both the paternal (father's) and maternal (mother's) line. An individual's **kindred** refers to their maternal and paternal blood relatives.

In **unilateral** (also known as unilineal) **descent**, descent is traced through either the **patrilineal** (male) or **matrilineal** (female) line. A **lineage** is a unilineal kinship group descended from a common ancestor. **Matrilineages** trace descent through the female line; **patrilineages** trace descent through the male line. A **clan** is often composed of many lineages who believe they are descended from a common ancestor many generations before. A **phratry** is at least two clans who believe they are related to one another. When a society is divided into two major descent groups, each half is referred to as a **moiety**. Each moiety usually consists of several clans.

Kinship refers to a network of relatives related by blood or marriage. **Kinship systems** are the ways in which a cultural group classify how people are related to one another. **Kinship terminology** refers to specific ways relatives are labeled. Three popular systems are named for the ethnographic example anthropologists use to describe each system.

The Eskimo system focuses on the nuclear family. Relatives share common labels, such as *aunt*, *uncle*, and *cousin*.

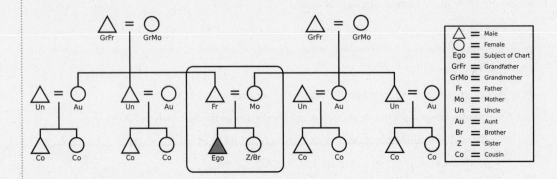

In the Hawaiian system, all of the relatives of the same generation and sex share the same label. An individual's mother, mother's sister, and father's sister share a single term (for example, *mother*). An individual's father, father's brother, and mother's brother share a single term (for example, *father*). An individual's cousins in the same generation are all brothers or sisters.

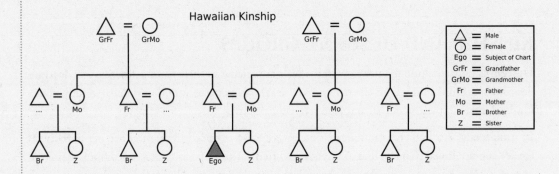

In the Iroquois system, an individual's father and father's brother share a single term (for example, *father*) and a mother and mother's sister share a single term (for example, *mother*). The children of the mother's sister or father's brother are **parallel cousins** to the individual and referred to as *brother* or *sister*.

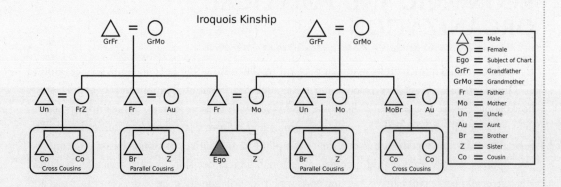

Iroquois Kinship

A father's sister may be referred to as an "aunt" and mother's brother may be referred to as an "uncle." The children of the mother's brother or the father's sister are **cross-cousins** to the individual.

SOCIAL AND ECONOMIC STRATIFICATION

In **egalitarian** societies, people generally have about the same access to goods and services, wealth, status, and power. Foraging societies tend to be egalitarian. In **rank** societies, chiefs or other people may have a higher status than others in the group, but everyone still has the same access to goods and services, wealth, status, and power. In **stratified** societies, social and economic hierarchies are normal and the different levels have unequal access to goods and services, wealth, status, and power. These hierarchies are referred to as **social stratification**.

State societies with large populations and economic specialization tend to be stratified societies. **Open class** refers to stratified systems where there is a possibility of moving between the different levels of a social hierarchy. In the open class system, where a person is located in the hierarchy is based on **achieved status**: what a person is able accomplish through their own actions. In the United States, the class system is theoretically open. The "American Dream" says that if people work hard enough, they can earn more money and access to material resources and become part of the upper class (the highest level of the social and economic hierarchy).

Closed class refers to stratified systems where there is no possibility of moving between the different levels of a social hierarchy. In the closed class system, a person's location in the hierarchy is based on **ascribed status**: the position a person was born into. In a **caste** system, one example of a closed class stratified system, a person's position is fixed for life and cannot be changed. Traditionally, the Hindu caste system of India strictly associates people born into it with specific occupations, dress, rituals, and customs.

ECONOMIC AND POLITICAL ORGANIZATION

Economics studies human decision-making regarding the finite amount of goods and services around us. Time, land, meat, vegetables, wood, water, minerals, etc., are in limited supply, and economists study how people choose to use, create, distribute, and work with these resources. Some anthropological debates about the relationship between economics and culture draw from economic theory. The **formalist-substantivist debate** is one such example. The **formalist** position is based on economic assumptions, which state that all people are rational, logical decision makers. Since all resources are scarce, all people will behave in a universal way: they will consider the costs, benefits, time, and energy required for an action, and they behave in a way that is the most beneficial to themselves. The **substantivists** argue that decision making is based on the norms and values of each culture. What is rational and beneficial for one person may be different for someone of another culture. Anthropologists have identified some patterns related to human economic behavior (decision making), which are also tied into subsistence strategies, political organization, and social organization.

SUBSISTENCE AND SETTLEMENT PATTERNS

To begin untangling some of the complexities, anthropologists start with identifying **subsistence strategies**: the ways people survive in their physical environment (foraging, pastoralism, horticulture, and agriculture). These strategies tend to support a certain **population size** based on if and where they **settle** (live) as a group. Research also suggests that other patterns relating to property ownership and land management are related to certain subsistence strategies.

Foraging

Foraging is collecting plants, fishing, and hunting animals in order to survive. The majority of food comes from foraging for plants, nuts, fruits, and vegetables. Foragers are able to identify a large number of plants and animals. Foragers move from place to place as the seasons change, vegetation dies and grows, and animals move. Since foragers must carry all of their belonging as they move, they tend to have few material possessions. Foragers use simple tools such as spears, digging sticks, and bows and arrows.

Pastoralism

Pastoralism is caring for and keeping herds of domesticated animals, such as goats, cattle, or camels. Some pastoralists move their animals throughout the seasons to areas where there are enough pastures for the herd. They leave behind people at the permanent village. In other types of pastoralist cultures, everyone moves with the herds. There are no permanent settlements. Pastoralists take care to eat or sell only the animals they can spare—they must maintain enough breeding stock throughout the year. Their diets often include the blood and milk of the animal because the animal does not have to be killed to use these resources. Pastoralists will also trade with neighbors for other food and materials they may need.

Horticulture

Horticulture is growing and cultivating crops with simple hand tools, such as digging sticks or hoes. Horticulturalists who live in tropical forests practice swidden farming (also known as slash-and-burn cultivation). In swidden farming, trees and plants in a specific area are cut down and then burned. Crops are planted in the ashes, which act as fertilizer. Horticulture can support villages of 100 to 1,000 people. These villages will also supplement their diet by hunting, fishing, or raising a few animals. There is a sense that the village gardens are **communal property** because the crops are dedicated to feeding and maintaining the group as a whole.

Agriculture

Agriculture is the deliberate production of food by growing crops and tending animals. Hand plows or plows pulled by animals, irrigation, and long-term breeding of livestock are all characteristic of this subsistence strategy. The methods lead to a surplus of food and animal resources, which then can be traded or sold. The idea of **private property** and ownership becomes more prevalent as people farm and claim lands as their own, which are then transferred to the next generation in the family. A steady supply of food transforms small villages into larger towns. As technology improves, agriculture becomes even more productive. Farmland could now support larger city centers and then states. Since food is available for purchase, people can specialize in other occupations. Governments emerge to manage the needs of the large populace. Social hierarchies allow people to experience unequal access to important resources (social stratification).

Industrialism

Few people, compared to the rest of the population, are involved with food production. Instead of selling food or goods they have produced themselves, people are selling their labor and working for others. Laborers earn wages in order to purchase goods, services, and food.

ECONOMIC SYSTEMS

Economic systems are the cultural norms and values that regulate the production, allocation, and consumption of goods and services. For **production**, each society has a **division of labor**: the person or group responsible for completing particular tasks. Generally in a foraging society, women tend to gather and men tend to hunt. In large-scale agricultural societies, the owners of the land and tools are separate from those who actually cultivate, grow, and harvest the crops.

Societies also **allocate** (distribute) and **consume** (use) goods and services in specific ways. People engage in **reciprocity** when they exchange goods and services that are of roughly equal value. For example, foragers will, over time, give one another food resources to maintain and preserve social ties. **Redistribution** occurs when goods are collected by a central person or office and then reallocated into the society. In industrialized societies, for example, a government collects taxes and returns them to the populace in the form of national health care, education, etc. In a **market exchange**, the buying and selling of goods and services are dependent upon how many of those goods and services exist and how many people need or want those things.

POLITICAL ORGANIZATIONS

Subsistence strategies and economic systems are also related to **political organization**: the ways in which societies maintain social order. Whether maintaining **customs** (traditional behaviors) or punishing the violation of formal codes of conduct (**laws**), political organizations regulate behavior for social cohesion. **Political associations** are often categorized as bands, tribes, chiefdoms, or states.

- **Bands** are small groups of people with no formal leadership. Foraging groups tend to live in bands and function through group consensus.

- A **tribe**, which is usually found in pastoralist or horticulturalist culture, is made up of groups related by kinship or family ties. These groups may believe they are descended from a common ancestor. Tribes may have leaders but these are informal positions based on prestige or popularity among people. Some anthropologists argue that tribes are more likely to engage in **war** (deliberate acts of violence between groups of people) although the reason why is unclear.

- **Chiefdoms** are ruled by a chief who collects and redistributes goods among the people. Chiefdoms are hierarchical and the leader controls the economic activities of the group (which are usually highly productive horticulturalists or pastoralists).

- In state societies, **governments** are the social structures that manage the society's territory, redistribute goods, manage services, maintain infrastructure, and keep law and order.

These modern political systems of government can take several forms and variations, including **democracies** (where all members of a state system make decisions about state affairs), **oligarchies** (where power and decision making lie in the hands of a powerful few), or **autocracies** (where a single person holds all power).

While foraging, pastoralism, horticulture, agriculture, industrialism and the various types of political organizations still exist in the present day, anthropologists study how these systems are changing and adapting. **Globalization** (the increasing interconnectedness of people around the world), for example, is closely examined in relationship to the environment. As more countries turn to industrialism and increased trade with one another, what is the environmental impact? How have cultures around the world dealt with these changes?

Anthropologists are also studying how economic and political organizations have changed over time as a result of **colonialism**: foreign powers establishing colonies and outposts in other countries, usually for the exploitation of people and resources. Specifically, the expansion of European powers throughout the world from approximately the fifteenth to the middle of the twentieth century is described as one of the catalysts for emergence of the **world system theory** (developed by Immanuel Wallerstein). Core countries, many of whose wealth and power were developed during the colonial era, continue dominating the world economic system by exploiting peripheral societies (usually poorer countries). For example, anthropologists study global powers like the European Union and its reliance on the labor of countries like the Philippines and Vietnam to produce inexpensive goods.

Groups and Associations

Cultural norms and values influence how people willingly associate or are unwillingly grouped together in other ways besides kinship. People may choose to come together for a specific purpose or because they share common interests (**associations**). Occupation associations (such as doctors' groups) or recreation groups (such as sports clubs) are examples of people voluntarily grouping themselves. Another example, grouping by **age**, means that in a society people of the same age experience culturally relevant experiences at the same time.

RELIGION

BELIEF SYSTEMS

Each culture shares a **worldview**: a broad set of ideas and beliefs about the nature of their reality. Part of that worldview is **religion**, an organized set of beliefs and practices related to the supernatural. **Spirituality** (sometimes defined separately from religion) refers to an individual's beliefs about the supernatural; participation in an organized religious group is not a necessary part of that belief. When religion begins to disappear from a group's worldview, this is described as **secularization**. People who self-identify as spiritual, for example, may group together through **informal organizations** to discuss their ideas. There may be no specific structure or set of rules to adhere to.

Anthropologists once believed that all religions passed through stages, starting with **animism** (the belief that everything is made of spirits or supernatural energies), then **polytheism** (the belief in many divine beings), and finally **monotheism** (the belief in a single divine being). Anthropologists no longer support the idea of stages and recognize that religion encompasses a wide range of beliefs, ideas, and practices. Anthropologists now try to identify patterns that emerge through the study of religions.

All religions have some sort of **sacred narrative** (or **myth**): sacred stories that explain the relationship between the supernatural and reality. For believers, these narratives are important for how the group functions and what they believe. Religious groups likely use symbols, such as religious pendants or masks used in rituals. Supernatural beings in religious practice include spirits, divine beings (for example gods and goddesses), or **ancestor spirits** (spirits who are relatives or kin to the group). Some religious groups believe ancestral spirits bind them together as one people and, as a result, have a special relationship with an animal, plant, or other objects that represents that spirit (**totemism**).

RELIGIOUS PRACTICES AND RITUALS

Religious practitioners are specialists in the religious group who carry out any number of duties. **Priestesses** and **priests** hold a full-time position in the group and are expected to conduct rituals, interact with the supernatural, and lead the community. **Shamans** are often **healers**, people who treat and cure medical and spiritual illnesses. Shamans can enter altered states of consciousness through rituals or by other means and communicate with the world of the supernatural.

Rituals, ceremonial acts designed for use during specific occasions, are also an important part of religious life. **Rites of passage** are rituals that mark an individual's movement from one social status or stage of life to another. These include ceremonies for birth, marriage, aging, and death. **Rites of purification** ritually cleanse a person or group when a taboo has been violated. **Rites of intensification** bind a group together and reinforce the norms and values of that group.

Some rituals involve **magic**: rituals involving actions (verbal, physical, and/or written) invoking supernatural power to try and effect some sort of change. **Imitative** or **sympathetic magic** is the belief that something that happens in a ritual will cause the same thing to happen outside the ritual. To harm a person, for example, someone might ritually harm a doll that is supposed to represent that person. **Contagious magic** is the idea that something keeps a connection with an object or person it was once in contact with. **Witchcraft** refers to magical rituals used to cause harm.

Other rituals include **prayer**: appeals to the supernatural. **Sacrifice** is an offering to supernatural beings to demonstrate faith and loyalty. Somewhat related to the idea of sacrifice is **pilgrimage**, traveling to a sacred site to prove one's dedication to the faith. **Divination** is a ritual that tries to discover hidden information or find lost people or objects.

Religious groups are also subject to cultural change. In response to great social changes and high levels of stress or unhappiness, **revitalization movements** may emerge. These movements promise widespread reforms, based on religious beliefs, which will improve life and end suffering. Some movements are **messianic**, believing that an individual will change the world into paradise. Other movements are **millenarian**, believing that a catastrophe will occur that will destroy most of the world but will eventually lead to heaven on earth. In response to culture change that brings two or more religious faiths together, **syncretism** sometimes occurs: the merging of two or more religions into a new faith.

MODERNIZATION AND APPLICATION

APPLIED ANTHROPOLOGY

While anthropology is typically divided into the four subfields we have just reviewed (physical anthropology, linguistics, cultural anthropology, and archaeology), anthropologists are debating the inclusion of a fifth subdiscipline: **applied anthropology**. What is applied anthropology? This subdiscipline uses the perspective and tools of physical, archaeological, linguistic, and cultural anthropology to solve a variety of problems. In 1941, the Society for Applied Anthropology was founded. During World War II, anthropologists such as Margaret Mead, Ruth Benedict, and George Murdock used their training to support the United States war effort. Today, anthropologists can be found conducting research in many different contexts.

For example, physical anthropologists often use their skills to conduct **forensic anthropology**, the analysis of skeletal remains. These remains may be part of an FBI or police investigation, and careful examination can provide the clues necessary to help solve a case. Nongovernment organizations wanting to identify the human remains found at a mass grave after wartime might employ a physical anthropologist to help with that work as well.

Some archaeologists choose to work in the field of **cultural resource management (CRM)**. Many countries and businesses around the world hire archaeologists to examine cultural remains in a variety of contexts. For example, say a construction company in San Francisco, California, has torn down a building and is preparing the ground for new development. If, during the course of the digging, construction workers come across any artifacts and/or human remains, they are legally required to call an archaeologist to the site. The archaeologists and their team will examine what has been found and will decide how to proceed. The artifacts may be excavated and studied or reburied, for example.

Linguistic anthropologists may work with a group of people whose language is in danger of dying out. Linguists can help with writing a dictionary, recording the grammar and syntax of the language and help the community preserve their heritage (also referred to as **cultural preservation**). In another example, linguistic anthropologists might develop programs to help multilingual students succeed in school.

Cultural anthropologists use their skills in many situations, from the medical field to large corporations to nongovernment organizations. Computer companies, for example, hire cultural anthropologists to design and carry out specific research projects. A laptop designer may want to know what sort of features to include in the equipment. An anthropologist who is used to living and working with the community might decide to spend time on a boat with deep sea fishermen. He or she could observe and speak with the captain and crew to figure out how they use their computers and what would be the most useful upgrades. In another example, an anthropologist might work as liaison between a shaman and Western-trained medical doctors to provide medical care to a community.

CULTURAL CHANGE AND THE FUTURE

Anthropologists from across the subdisciplines are also working with nongovernment organizations, government offices, human rights groups, and others to help insure that indigenous people have the power to represent their own interests. Historically, governments have been the cause of **directed cultural change**, which often forced people (indigenous Americans First-Nations or the Ju/'hoansi of southern African, for example) to give up their lands and cultures to satisfy territorial expansion. When possible, anthropologists have tried to aid indigenous groups if they request it and in ways that preserve the choices and dignity of those groups. All over the world, as culture change continues and globalization tightens connections between people and places, indigenous groups fight for **cultural survival**: the right to preserve, remember, and celebrate one's culture.

Anthropologists are also asked to consider future directions for research: specifically, what problems or challenges are in store for humans? Anthropologists continue studying the relationship between the environment and people, for example, to determine how cross-cultural responses to climate change may offer solutions to human survival. Other serious questions pose significant challenges. In light of globalization, for example, anthropologists consider if people from around the world are embracing a global culture of shared beliefs, behaviors, norms, and values. If so, what is that culture? What impact would such a culture have upon indigenous survival as historically subjugated groups fight to maintain their cultural heritage? What role can and should anthropology play in addressing current and future challenges?

SUMMING IT UP

- **Anthropology** studies the human existence via four major subdisciplines: **physical anthropology**, **archaeology**, **cultural anthropology**, and **linguistic anthropology**. Anthropologists also debate the inclusion of a fifth subdiscipline: **applied anthropology**. The holistic perspective of anthropology strives to understand the totality of human existence and how different components (cultural, biological, material, etc.) interact with one another.

- Charles Darwin's evolutionary theory of **natural selection** states every species of life exhibits a range of variation that helps it survive and reproduce or die in its environment. Gregor Mendel then explained how these traits are passed to offspring by identifying specific traits of plants and how these traits were (or were not) passed along from one generation to the next.

- Genes are the blueprints for making proteins, which maintain the human body and cause people to have different traits such as eye or hair color and blood type. Genes may cause more than one version of a particular trait (such as blue eyes or brown eyes, or tall vs. short), referred to as **alleles** of a gene. **Mendel's Principles of Inheritance** are the principle of segregation (each organism usually has two alleles of each gene, and offspring will receive one allele of each gene from each parent); the principle of dominance (one allele will dominate over the other); and the principle of independent assortment (genes for different traits are inherited independently of one another).

- Genetic variations in a species are the **gene pool**. Evolution refers to how the frequency of alleles in the gene pool changes over time. Changes are summarized by **the four forces of evolution**: mutation (random changes in DNA); **genetic drift** (when random events cause an individual to die without reproducing, eradicating a genotype from the gene pool); **gene flow** (when an individual or individuals from one gene pool introduces genetic material to another gene pool through producing offspring); and natural selection (the survival of individuals with traits that are best adapted to their environment).

- **Primatologists** study how living primates such as gorillas and chimpanzees have adapted over time to help us understand how humans may have changed over the millennia. Primatologists study feces, hair, and teeth for clues about diet. They try to determine how primates have evolved in response to environmental pressures and compare results with research conducted with humans to understand how much behavior is driven by nature and how much is driven by nurture.

- A **paleoanthropologist** studies fossil records to learn about the ancestors and relatives of *Homo sapiens*. Paleoanthropologists can attempt to find a fossil's age through relative dating (determining whether a fossil is older or younger than another fossil, sometimes by its placement within the ground) and absolute dating (its age in absolute years, sometimes found by carbon-14 dating).

- **Archaeologists** study prehistoric and historic human cultures based on their material remains. Archaeologists' research helps us understand human biology by determining how we physically interact with the world around us. They categorize the human past based on the type of tools used by our ancestors.

- During the **Paleolithic era**, humans survived by foraging and lived in small groups that moved from place to place due to environmental changes. In the **Neolithic era**, agriculture emerged in many cultures around the world, with most changes occurring 12,000 to 10,000 years ago. Transition from foraging to agriculture meant that people could stay in one place. This led villages to turn into towns, with farmlands supporting bigger city centers. Then, governments emerged to manage the needs of the large populace.

- **Linguistic anthropology** is the study of human language: a system that allows humans to communicate information and discuss events that occurred in the past, are happening in the present, or could happen in the future. **Descriptive** or **structural linguistics** examines the construction of languages; **historical linguistics** studies the connection between languages and how they change over time; **sociolinguistics** studies verbal and nonverbal communication in a variety of social contexts: the relationship between culture and language.

- **Cultural anthropology** focuses on researching and comparing patterns of human cultural diversity. The process of learning to be part of a cultural group through observation of the world and people around us is called **enculturation**. Anthropologists recognize many different aspects of culture, including economic systems, political organizations, and religions. Anthropologists study how well (or poorly) these systems integrate and function together. Human culture evolves to give people a better chance to survive and reproduce in their environment. Cultures change at different speeds from one another due to environmental pressures, disease, natural disasters, conflict within the group or from outside of the group, among other reasons. Cultures may also change due to invention, innovation, and diffusion.

- A cultural anthropologist, also known as an **ethnographer**, may decide to focus on a specific culture: a group that shares behavioral patterns, values, and norms. Anthropologists ask questions about society—a group of people who usually share the same culture, live in a specific territory, and share common goals. Anthropologists focus on the **emic** perspective: the point of view of the person who is part of that cultural group, and then often write an **ethnography** with detailed descriptions of that culture from the **etic** perspective: the point of view of someone who is outside of that cultural group.

- Anthropologists argue against **ethnocentrism**, the belief that one's own norms and values are the only correct standard for living and should be used to judge others. **Cultural relativism** argues that each culture must be understood by its own norms and values and not be immediately judged by the standards of other cultures.

- Lewis Henry Morgan and Edward Burnett Tylor were the chief authors of the theory of **cultural evolution**. They argued that every cultural group in the world should evolve through three stages: savagery, barbarism, and civilization; their ethnocentric perspective stated Western society was the most evolved and therefore the highest standard everyone should aspire to. Franz Boas conducted research among the North American Inuit on Baffin Island. He determined cultures should be understood by their own internal norms and values, and his research influenced the discipline's rejection of ethnocentrism and cultural evolution. It focused on cultural relativism and cultural determinism (how culture shapes an individual's personality). Bronislaw Malinowski pioneered the core anthropological method of participant observation and determined through research that cultural groups must be understood by their own internal logics.

- In the **formalist-substantivist debate**, the formalist position assumes people make rational decisions and will consider the costs, benefits, time, and energy to behave in a way beneficial to themselves. **Substantivists** argue that decision making is based on the norms and values of each culture. **Subsistence strategies** are the ways people survive in their physical environment and include foraging, pastoralism, horticulture, and agriculture.

- Economic systems are the cultural norms and values that regulate the production, allocation, and consumption of goods and services. Each society has a **division of labor**: the person or group responsible for completing particular tasks. People engage in **reciprocity** when they exchange goods and services that are of roughly equal value. **Redistribution** occurs when goods are collected by a central person or office and then reallocated into the society. In a **market exchange**, the buying and selling of goods and services are dependent upon the number of goods and services and the demand for them.

- **Political organizations** maintain social order in a society; they regulate behavior for social cohesion. **Political associations** are often categorized as bands (groups with no formal leadership), tribes (groups related by kinship or family ties), chiefdoms (ruled by a chief who collects and redistributes goods among the people), or states (run by governments that manage services and keep law and order).

- In **egalitarian** societies, all people have about the same access to goods and services, wealth, status, and power. In **rank** societies, some have a higher status than others, but everyone still has the same access to goods and services, wealth, status, and power. In **stratified** societies, different levels have unequal access to goods and services, wealth, status, and power. In an **open class system**, there is a possibility of moving between the different levels of a social hierarchy. In a **closed class system**, there is no possibility of moving between the different levels of a social hierarchy.

- **Marriage** is a cultural institution that defines the parameters of a union between 2 or more people, establishes rules for the responsibility of children, and clarifies the relationship between the kin of the married people. Culturally based rules require people marry within their own group (**endogamy**) or outside their own group (**exogamy**). Culture defines both marriage and family.

- **Descent** is how a culture defines how individuals are related to their parents. In **bilateral descent**, descent is traced through both the paternal (father's) and maternal (mother's) lines. In **unilateral descent**, descent is traced through either the **patrilineal** (male) or **matrilineal** (female) line. **Kinship** refers to a network of relatives related by blood or marriage, and **kinship systems** are the ways in which a cultural group classify how people are related to one another.

- **Sex** refers to the genetic combination of X and Y chromosomes. **Gender** commonly refers to the cultural norms, values, expectations, and categories of what is "masculine" and "feminine." Gender male or female does not always correspond to sex male or sex female.

- **Race** refers to certain physical traits grouped together under specific labels and categories. Though genetic testing identifies a single human species, over time the idea that humans were separate "races" became accepted as natural and correct. Although "race" does not exist biologically, it is still used to justify social stratification.

- **Religion** is an organized set of beliefs and practices related to the supernatural. **Spirituality** refers to an individual's beliefs about the supernatural. Anthropologists believe religion encompasses a wide range of beliefs, ideas, and practices and try to identify patterns that emerge through the study of religions. Religious groups are subject to cultural change.

- **Applied anthropology** uses the perspective and tools of physical, archaeological, linguistic, and cultural anthropology to solve problems. For example, **physical anthropologists** often use their skills to conduct forensic anthropology for FBI or police investigations. Some **archaeologists** work in **cultural resource management** (**CRM**), in which countries and businesses around the world hire archaeologists to examine cultural remains in a variety of contexts. **Linguistic anthropologists** might develop programs to help multilingual students succeed in school. All over the world, as indigenous groups fight for the right to preserve their culture, **cultural anthropologists** can be called upon to aid their cause.

GENERAL ANTHROPOLOGY POST-TEST

Directions: Carefully read each of the following 60 questions. Choose the best answer to each question and fill in the corresponding circle on the answer sheet. The Answer Key and Explanations can be found following this post-test.

1. Which subfield of physical anthropology reconstructs humanity's evolutionary past using the fossil record?
   A. Paleoanthropology
   B. Primatology
   C. Human variation
   D. Forensic anthropology

2. Whose theory of evolution by natural selection revolutionized the field of biology?
   A. Gregor Mendel
   B. Charles Darwin
   C. Franz Boas
   D. Bronislaw Malinowski

3. Prehistoric archaeology studies artifacts from which time period?
   A. Dating from 10 to 50 years old
   B. Dating from 100 to 500 years old
   C. Dating from 1,000 to 5,000 years old
   D. Dating from 10,000 to 50,000 years old

4. The theory of Structuralism is associated with which anthropologist?
   A. E.O. Wilson
   B. Bronislaw Malinowksi
   C. Ruth Benedict
   D. Claude Lévi-Strauss

5. A _____ is something that represents something else.
   A. syntax
   B. symbol
   C. grammar
   D. phonology

6. The Neolithic Revolution refers to
   A. the extinction of *Homo neanderthalensis*.
   B. the production of pottery.
   C. the emergence of agriculture.
   D. the earliest expression of human imagination through cave art.

7. Which primates are generally solitary creatures who tend to forage for food over broad areas?
   A. Gorillas
   B. Bonobos
   C. Chimpanzees
   D. Orangutans

8. Ethnography is best described as
   A. the science of observing people in a laboratory setting.
   B. a list of the number of people who live in a particular city.
   C. a written account of an anthropologist's fieldwork and research.
   D. a collection of newspaper articles about a cultural group.

9. Franz Boas's Historical Particularism was developed as a critique of which theory?
   A. Cultural Evolution
   B. The Four Forces of Evolution
   C. Neo-evolutionary Thought
   D. Cultural Relativism

10. Cultural determinism argues that
    A. one's own cultural norms are the only correct standard for living and should be used to judge others.
    B. culture moves through the three stages of savagery, barbarism, and civilization.
    C. culture shapes an individual's personality.
    D. culture is transmitted through genes.

11. A group may claim it holds certain cultural norms and values. However, those norms and values are not necessarily acted out in reality. This is best described as a tension between
    A. symbolic and nonsymbolic culture.
    B. adaptive and nonadaptive culture.
    C. shared and learned culture.
    D. real and ideal culture.

12. The emic perspective refers to
    A. the point of view of someone outside of a cultural group.
    B. the point of view of someone who is part of a cultural group.
    C. a religious world view.
    D. a secular world view.

13. Why do members of foraging groups own very few material possessions?
    A. Foragers are mostly interested in collecting vegetables, not material possessions.
    B. Foragers must carry all of their belongings as they move; lighter is better.
    C. Foragers share all possessions among the group.
    D. Foragers do not use tools.

14. Descent traced through either the patrilineal or matrilineal line is referred to as
    A. unilateral descent.
    B. bilateral descent.
    C. phratry.
    D. moiety.

15. What is an open class system?
    A. A society of relative equals
    B. A society of chiefs and commoners
    C. Stratified systems where there is a possibility of moving between the different levels of a social hierarchy
    D. Stratified systems where there is no possibility of moving between the different levels of a social hierarchy

16. Which anthropologist will be contacted if a shipwreck is discovered while an area is being prepared to construct a new building?
    A. Physical anthropologist
    B. Archaeologist
    C. Linguist
    D. Cultural anthropologist

17. What is a genotype?
    A. Genes and alleles each person possesses
    B. When one allele dominates over the other
    C. The four forces of evolution
    D. A numeric classification system for fossils

18. *Australopithecus afarensis'* most distinguishing feature is that it
    A. had human-like facial features.
    B. was bipedal.
    C. invented the wheel.
    D. existed at the same time as the dinosaurs.

19. Which subsistence strategy did humans rely on during the Paleolithic era?
    A. Agriculture
    B. Pastoralism
    C. Horticulture
    D. Foraging

20. What was the main reason Cultural Evolution was discredited as a theory?
    A. Morgan and Tylor were too biased as participant observers during fieldwork.
    B. The "industrial" stage was missing from "savagery," "barbarism," and "civilization."
    C. Morgan and Tylor gathered demographic data from Europe rather than the Americas.
    D. Cross-cultural comparisons support the idea that cultures change and innovate at their own pace.

21. An anthropologist who is interested in researching cultural universals might use which method?
    A. Ethnology
    B. Observation
    C. Interviewing
    D. Absolute dating

22. In the substantivist-formalist debates, the formalist argument is based on what assumption?
    A. People are rational, logical decision makers.
    B. People place the group's needs above their own.
    C. People are irrational, illogical decision makers.
    D. People place the needs of the family above their own.

23. Who are the Hijra?
    A. A pastoralist group in Nigeria
    B. A third gender in India
    C. A fourth gender in the Philippines
    D. A horticultural group in Vietnam

24. Within the subdiscipline of physical anthropology, primatology refers to
    A. research of primal foraging societies.
    B. cataloging the first fossils of *Homo sapiens* ancestors.
    C. the study of primordial cell development.
    D. the biological research and observation of nonhuman primates.

25. Why are prehistoric archaeologists interested in sites where *Homo habilis* has been discovered?
    A. Some *Homo habilis* sites contain Mousterian stone tools that are some of the earliest examples of human culture.
    B. Oldowan stone tools, some of the earliest evidence of tool making, have been discovered with *Homo habilis*.
    C. *Homo habilis* traded pottery with *Homo sapiens*.
    D. Evidence of intensive food production has been found with *Homo habilis*.

26. Anthropologist Marvin Harris studied the sacred cattle of India and proposed which theory?
    A. Cognitive Anthropology
    B. Ecological Materialism
    C. Functionalism
    D. Sociobiology

27. Diffusion drives culture change because
    A. it speeds up cultural evolution.
    B. culture contact leads people to become less innovative.
    C. ideas are forgotten, and people need to invent new technologies.
    D. new ideas, devices, and/or innovations often spread from one culture to another.

28. What are some ways societies maintain social control?
    A. Invention and innovation
    B. Foraging and agriculture
    C. Laws and customs
    D. Participant observation and interviewing

29. Kinship is best defined as
    A. a lineage.
    B. maternal and paternal blood relatives.
    C. a network of relatives related by blood or marriage.
    D. specific ways relatives are labeled or referred to.

30. What are sacred narratives?
    A. Myths that are inherently false
    B. Rituals invoking supernatural power to effect change
    C. Stories that explain the relationship between the supernatural and reality
    D. Rituals that try to discover hidden information or find lost people or objects

31. Which anthropologist will use his or her skills to conduct cultural resource management?
    A. Historical linguist
    B. Paleoanthropologist
    C. Archaeologist
    D. Ethnographer

32. A religious group's weekly prayer meetings are best described as a rite of
    A. passage.
    B. purification.
    C. intensification.
    D. syncretism.

33. Ascribed status is usually central to which type of society?
    A. Monogamous
    B. Polygamous
    C. Open class system
    D. Closed class system

34. What is a division of labor?
    A. The number of hours in a work day
    B. Different salaries for different types of jobs
    C. The person or group responsible for completing particular tasks
    D. Tasks that should be completed in a certain order

35. A _____ revitalization movement believes that an individual will change the world into paradise.
    A. messianic
    B. millenarian
    C. totemic
    D. secularization

36. The practice of comparing and contrasting the cultural patterns of one group with other ethnographic examples is referred to as
    A. ethnographer.
    B. ethnography.
    C. ethnology.
    D. ethnomusicology.

37. Magic, divination, and sacrifice are examples of
  A. myth.
  B. rituals.
  C. exogamy.
  D. reciprocity.

38. What is cultural survival?
  A. Another term for cultural universal
  B. Artifacts from early human cultures
  C. The right to preserve, remember, and celebrate one's culture
  D. Historic records

39. Which anthropologist would be the most interested in how languages have changed over time?
  A. Structural linguist
  B. Cultural anthropologist
  C. Historical linguist
  D. Historic archaeologist

40. Which human ancestor is associated with Acheulean stone tools?
  A. *Australopithecus afarensis*
  B. *Homo habilis*
  C. *Homo erectus*
  D. *Homo neanderthalensis*

41. The belief that everything is made of spirits or supernatural energies is referred to as
  A. sacrifice.
  B. witchcraft.
  C. syncretism.
  D. animism.

42. Which anthropologist would be most interested in researching how different genders speak with one another at the workplace?
  A. Historical linguist
  B. Descriptive linguist
  C. Sociolinguist
  D. Structural linguist

43. Primatologists observe and study nonhuman primates because
  A. chimpanzee DNA is the same as 50 percent of human DNA.
  B. unlike humans, orangutans do not know how to use tools.
  C. gorillas can help us understand how humans may have evolved over the millennia.
  D. meerkats display human-like behavior.

44. Franz Boas and Bronislaw Malinowski advocated for which method to be at the center of anthropological fieldwork?
  A. Absolute dating
  B. Relative dating
  C. Participant observation
  D. Armchair anthropology

45. Which phrase accurately describes "culture"?
  A. A group who shares values and norms
  B. A group who lives in a specific territory
  C. An individual's personality
  D. An individual's belief system

46. _____ occurs when goods are collected by a central person or office and then reallocated into society.
  A. Production
  B. Market exchange
  C. Reciprocity
  D. Redistribution

47. The emergence of social stratification is directly related to
  A. agriculture.
  B. tool use.
  C. cave art.
  D. migration.

48. Which is an example of relative dating?
    A. Stratigraphy
    B. Radiocarbon dating
    C. Dendrochronology
    D. Potassium-argon dating

49. Art is broadly defined as expression of the human imagination. The earliest form of human art, cave drawings, date back to which era?
    A. Lower Paleolithic
    B. Middle Paleolithic
    C. Upper Paleolithic
    D. Neolithic

50. Which anthropologist will use his or her skills to conduct forensic anthropology?
    A. Primatologist
    B. Cultural anthropologist
    C. Linguist
    D. Physical anthropologist

51. From an anthropological perspective what is a pilgrimage?
    A. A religious movement that promises widespread reform
    B. Traveling for tourism
    C. Migrating to a new country
    D. Traveling to a sacred site to prove one's dedication to the faith

52. Which anthropologist could conduct participant observation among computer gamers to research their preferences in personal computing hardware?
    A. Maritime archaeologist
    B. Primatologist
    C. Forensic anthropologist
    D. Cultural anthropologist

53. The physical expression of the genotype refers to
    A. DNA.
    B. genes.
    C. allele.
    D. phenotype.

54. What is directed culture change?
    A. When elites devise and enforce plans that force the less powerful to accept changes
    B. One of the forces of cultural evolution
    C. The practice of witchcraft to harm others
    D. Evidence of totemism among a religious group

55. Political associations are important because they
    A. organize voting.
    B. help maintain social order.
    C. led the Neolithic Revolution.
    D. moderated the formalist and substantivist debate.

56. In anthropological studies, domestication is best described as
    A. humans making stone tools.
    B. fieldwork conducted in the United States.
    C. women staying close to home to raise children.
    D. humans guiding the growth of plants and the reproduction of animals.

57. Individuals are said to be better adapted to the environment they live in if they are able to
    A. live past the age of 5.
    B. live to the age of 100.
    C. prepare for natural disasters.
    D. survive and reproduce.

58. The idea of cultural relativism developed out of which theoretical framework?

   A. Sociobiology

   B. Structuralism

   C. Historical particularism

   D. Anthropology and gender

59. After marriage, spouses live separately from their parents in their own household. What is the anthropological term for this type of residence?

   A. Neolocal

   B. Bilocal

   C. Avunculocal

   D. Ambilocal

60. What is an example of directed culture change?

   A. Random changes in DNA that may lead to beneficial, harmful, or neutral traits for an organism

   B. Events such as an earthquake that cause an individual to die without reproducing

   C. Understanding how different cultural components work with one another

   D. Indigenous people being forced to give up land to colonizers.

post-test

ANSWER KEY AND EXPLANATIONS

1. A	13. B	25. B	37. B	49. C
2. B	14. A	26. B	38. C	50. D
3. D	15. C	27. D	39. C	51. D
4. D	16. B	28. C	40. C	52. D
5. B	17. A	29. C	41. D	53. D
6. C	18. B	30. C	42. C	54. A
7. D	19. D	31. C	43. C	55. B
8. C	20. D	32. C	44. C	56. D
9. A	21. A	33. D	45. A	57. D
10. C	22. A	34. C	46. D	58. C
11. D	23. B	35. A	47. A	59. A
12. B	24. D	36. C	48. A	60. D

1. **The correct answer is A.** Paleoanthropology reconstructs humanity's evolutionary past through the fossil record. Choice B is incorrect because primatology is the biological research and observation of nonhuman primates to shed light on human evolution. Choice C is incorrect because human variation is the study of biological differences (physiology, genetics, etc.) within the human species. Choice D is incorrect because forensic anthropology is the analysis of skeletal remains as part of a formal investigation (for the police, the FBI, etc.).

2. **The correct answer is B.** Charles Darwin proposed the theory of evolution by natural selection in the mid-1800s. Gregor Mendel, choice A, is incorrect because his work was the basis of Mendel's Principles of Inheritance. Choices C and D are incorrect because Boas and Malinowski were scientists who revolutionized the field of anthropology.

3. **The correct answer is D.** Prehistoric archaeology focuses on human culture prior to written historical records. The late Neolithic period, which dates to 10,000 to 50,000 years ago, marks the end of the prehistoric era. Choices A, B, and C are incorrect because the artifacts that old would

date from the historic era (when writing and record keeping emerged).

4. **The correct answer is D.** Claude Lévi-Strauss is the anthropologist who established the theory of Structuralism. Choice A is incorrect because E.O. Wilson is associated with the Sociobiology theoretical school. Choice B is incorrect because Bronislaw Malinowksi is associated with the theory of Functionalism. Choice C is incorrect because Ruth Benedict is associated with the Culture and Personality theory.

5. **The correct answer is B.** A symbol is something that represents something else. Choice A is incorrect because syntax refers to rules for constructing sentences. Choice C is incorrect because grammar refers to the rules of how a language is written and/or spoken. Choice D is incorrect because phonology is the study of language sounds.

6. **The correct answer is C.** During the Neolithic era agriculture emerged: the deliberate production of food by growing crops and tending animals. Choice A is incorrect because the extinction of *Homo neanderthalensis* likely occurred prior to the emergence of agriculture. While the production of pottery,, (choice B) occurred during the Neolithic era, it is not considered the defining feature of the Neolithic Revolution. Choice D is

incorrect because the earliest expression of human imagination through cave art dates to the upper Paleolithic era.

7. **The correct answer is D.** Orangutans (found in Sumatra and Borneo) are generally solitary creatures who tend to forage for food over broad areas. Choices A, B, and C are incorrect because those primates tend to live in groups with others of their kind.

8. **The correct answer is C.** Anthropologists will often produce a written account of their time conducting fieldwork, complete with detailed descriptions of the culture they encountered and any patterns they may have observed. Choice A is incorrect because anthropologists prefer to participate in the everyday lives of people rather than in the controlled environment of a laboratory. Choice B is incorrect because an ethnography is a detailed description of a cultural group with more detail than a demographic list. Choice D is incorrect because an ethnography is usually an original work by one or more anthropologists written with a specific theoretical perspective.

9. **The correct answer is A.** Franz Boas's argument that cultures must be understood through the history that produced them is a direct critique of the idea that all cultures evolve through distinct states. Choice B is incorrect because the four forces of evolution is a concept from biology. Choice C is incorrect because Boas developed Historical Particularism decades before the emergence of neo-evolutionary thought. Choice D is incorrect because Boas was a supporter of cultural relativism, which argues that each culture must be understood by its own norms and values and not be immediately judged by the standards of other cultures.

10. **The correct answer is C.** Cultural determinism studies the role of culture in shaping a person's personality. Choice A is incorrect because the belief that one's own cultural norms are the only correct standard for living and should be used to judge others is referred to as ethnocentrism. Choice B is incorrect because cultural evolution argues that culture moves through the three stages of savagery, barbarism, and civilization.

Choice D is incorrect because culture is not transmitted through genes. People learn and share culture through communication.

11. **The correct answer is D.** Anthropologists often observe cultures where the ideal set of behaviors and beliefs (ideal culture) is different from how people behave (real culture). Choice A is incorrect because culture itself is referred to as a system of symbols; these symbols are not necessarily related to norms and ideal behavior. Choice B is incorrect because adaptive and nonadaptive culture refers to behavior that helps people survive changes in the environment. Choice C is incorrect because "shared and learned" refer to characteristics of culture, not tensions with cultures.

12. **The correct answer is B.** Anthropologists focus on understanding the emic perspective: the point of view of the person who is part of that cultural group. Choice A is incorrect as that refers to the etic perspective: the point of view of someone who is outside of a cultural group. Choices C and D are incorrect as the emic perspective simply refers to the social position of the person (inside of a group), not their religious or secular perspective.

13. **The correct answer is B.** Foragers move from place to place as the seasons change, vegetation dies and grows, and animals move. Since foragers must carry all of their belonging as they move, they tend to have few material possessions. Choice A is incorrect because while foragers are focused on gathering fruits, vegetables, and plants, that does not completely negate their interest in owning material possessions. Choice C is incorrect because foragers do own personal material items. Choice D is incorrect because foragers use simple tools such as spears, digging sticks, and bows and arrows.

14. **The correct answer is A.** Choice A is correct because in unilateral (also known as unilineal) descent, descent is traced through either the patrilineal or matrilineal lines. Choice B is incorrect because bilateral descent is traced through both the paternal and maternal lines. Choice C is incorrect because a phratry is at least two clans who believe they are related to one another.

Choice D is incorrect because a moiety refers to a society divided into two major descent groups; each half is referred to as a moiety. Each moiety usually consists of several clans.

15. **The correct answer is C.** Open class refers to stratified systems where there is a possibility of moving between the different levels of a social hierarchy. Choice A is incorrect because a society of relative equals is referred to as an egalitarian society. Choice B is incorrect because a society of chiefs and commoners is referred to as a rank society. Choice D is incorrect because stratified systems where there is no possibility of moving between the different levels of a social hierarchy is a closed class system.

16. **The correct answer is B.** Archaeologists are the experts at carefully recovering, cataloging, and studying items created and/ or shaped by people, in this case a ship. Choice A is incorrect because physical anthropologists focus on the biological history and diversity of humanity. Choice C is incorrect because linguists study human language. Choice D is incorrect because cultural anthropologists focus on human cultural diversity.

17. **The correct answer is A.** A genotype refers to the genes and alleles each person possesses. Choice B is incorrect because one allele dominating the other refers to Mendel's principle of dominance. Choice C is incorrect because the four forces of evolution are mutation, genetic drift, gene flow, and natural selection. Choice D is incorrect because there is no official numeric classification system for fossils.

18. **The correct answer is B.** Paleoanthropologists have discovered fossil evidence that supports the idea that *Australopithecus afarensis* was likely the first human ancestor to walk on two legs. Choice A is incorrect because *Australopithecus afarensis* likely had apelike features. Choice C is incorrect because there is no evidence that *Australopithecus afarensis* invented the wheel or any other complicated tool. Choice D is incorrect because *Australopithecus afarensis* did not exist during the time of the dinosaurs.

19. **The correct answer is D.** During the Paleolithic era, humans survived by foraging: collecting plants, fishing, and hunting animals in order to survive. Choice A is incorrect because agriculture emerged during the Neolithic era. Choice B is incorrect because the animal domestication that is necessary for pastoralism emerged during the Neolithic era. Choice C is incorrect because the agricultural techniques of horticulturalists emerged during the Neolithic era.

20. **The correct answer is D.** Cultures change and innovate at their own pace. Decades of ethnographic research and cross-culture comparisons refute the idea that cultures evolve through the same stages over time. Choice A is incorrect because Morgan and Tylor did not conduct ethnographic fieldwork. They were considered armchair anthropologists because they never went into the field. Choice B is incorrect because industrialism was considered part of the civilization stage. Choice C is incorrect because Morgan and Tylor collected second- and third-hand information from around the world.

21. **The correct answer is A.** Cultural universals refer to something that is present in all cultures. Anthropologists debate about what counts as a universal and if they do, in fact, exist in all cultures. Ethnology refers to the practice of comparing and contrasting the cultural patterns of one group with other ethnographic examples. This could potentially reveal something present in every world culture. Choice B is incorrect because although observation is an anthropological method, it does not, by itself, provide the necessary cross-cultural comparison. Choice C is incorrect because interviewing as the only anthropological technique would not provide the necessary cross-cultural data to study cultural universals. Choice D refers to a method in paleoanthropology or archaeology for determining the age of a fossil or artifact.

22. **The correct answer is A.** The formalist position is based on economic assumptions that state all people are rational, logical

decision makers. Since all resources are scarce, all people will behave in a universal way: they will consider the costs, benefits, time, and energy required for an action, and they behave in a way that is the most beneficial to themselves. Choices B and D are incorrect because the group or family needs will not be placed above those of the individual. Choice C is incorrect because the formalist position assumes people behave logically and rationally.

23. **The correct answer is B.** The number of genders present in a cultural group varies. The Hijras of India are neither gender male or female and are referred to as "third gender." Therefore, choices A, C, and D are incorrect.

24. **The correct answer is D.** Primatology is the biological research and observation of nonhuman primates to shed light on human evolution. Choice A is incorrect because archaeologists and cultural anthropologists usually research foraging societies. Choice B is incorrect because paleoanthropologists typically catalog *Homo sapiens* fossils. Choice C is incorrect because primordial cell development would interest physical anthropologists specializing in human variation.

25. **The correct answer is B.** Some *Homo habilis* sites contain Oldowan stone tools, some of the earliest evidence of tool making. Choice A is incorrect because *Homo neanderthalensis* used Mousterian stone tools (the variety of objects such as hand axes and wooden spears found at various sites). Choice C is incorrect because there is no evidence that *Homo habilis* existed at the same time as *Homo sapiens*. Choice D is incorrect because intensive food production occurred during the Neolithic era. *Homo habilis* lived during the Lower Paleolithic era.

26. **The correct answer is B.** Marvin Harris's famous article "The Cultural Ecology of India's Sacred Cattle" argues for a theory of Ecological Materialism. Choice A is incorrect because Cognitive Anthropology focuses on categories and the human mind. Choice C is incorrect because Functionalism argues that cultural institutions function to fulfill basic human biological needs and support the workings of society. Choice D is incorrect because Sociobiology studies the relationship between culture and genetics.

27. **The correct answer is D.** Diffusion refers to new ideas, devices, and/or innovations spread from one culture to another through migration, colonization, etc. Choice A is incorrect because cultural evolution does not exist; each culture changes at its own rate. There is no blueprint or chart for when and how a cultural group might experience any change. Choice B is incorrect because culture contact can lead to more innovation as shared ideas or items are changed to suit the needs of a different cultural group. Choice C is incorrect because diffusion is about ideas that are not forgotten but are, in fact, exchanged and passed along to others.

28. **The correct answer is C.** Whether maintaining customs (traditional behaviors) or punishing the violation of formal codes of conduct (laws), political organizations regulate behavior for social cohesion. Choice A is incorrect because invention and innovation are related to cultural change. Choice B is incorrect because foraging and agriculture are forms of subsistence strategy. Choice D is incorrect because participant observation and interviewing are anthropological research methods.

29. **The correct answer is C.** Kinship refers to a network of relatives related by blood or marriage. Choice A is incorrect because a lineage is a specific term referring to a unilineal kinship group descended from a common ancestor. Choice B is incorrect because maternal and paternal blood relatives are referred to as kindred. Choice D is incorrect because kinship terminology is defined as specific ways relatives are labeled or referred to.

30. **The correct answer is C.** Sacred narratives (also known as myths) are sacred stories that explain the relationship between the supernatural and reality. Choice A is incorrect because anthropologists do not categorize sacred narratives as true nor false. Choice B is incorrect because rituals invoking supernatural power to effect change refers to

magic. Choice D is incorrect because a ritual that tries to discover hidden information or find lost people or objects is referred to as divination.

31. **The correct answer is C.** Archaeologists conduct cultural resource management: conserving material culture in accordance with laws for historic preservation. Choice A is incorrect because historical linguists are concerned with the connection between languages and how those languages change over time. Choice B is incorrect because paleoanthropologists reconstruct humanity's evolutionary past using the fossil record. Choice D is incorrect because ethnographers are usually cultural anthropologists who are researching and comparing patterns of human cultural diversity.

32. **The correct answer is C.** Rites of intensification bind a group together and reinforce the norms and values of that group. Choice A is incorrect because rites of passage are rituals that mark an individual's movement from one social status or stage of life to another. These include ceremonies for birth, marriage, aging, and death. Choice B is incorrect because rites of purification ritually cleanse a person or group when a taboo has been violated. Choice D is incorrect because syncretism occurs when two or more religions merge into a new faith.

33. **The correct answer is D.** Closed class refers to stratified systems where there is no possibility of moving between the different levels of a social hierarchy. In the closed class system, a person's location in the hierarchy is based on ascribed status: the position a person was born into. Choices A and B are incorrect because monogamy refers to having one spouse at a time, while polygamy refers to having multiple spouses at a time. Choice C is incorrect because open class refers to stratified systems where there is a possibility of moving between the different levels of a social hierarchy. In the open class system, where a person is located in the hierarchy is based on achieved status: what a person is able to accomplish through their own actions.

34. **The correct answer is C.** Division of labor refers to cultural groups deciding which person or group will be responsible for completing particular tasks. Choice A is incorrect because the time spent working is not necessarily related to division of labor. Choice B is incorrect because not all work is salaried. Choice D is incorrect because division of labor refers to categories of workers, not a set of tasks.

35. **The correct answer is A.** In response to great social changes and high levels of stress or unhappiness, revitalization movements may emerge. These movements promise widespread reforms, based on religious beliefs, which will improve life and end suffering. Some movements are messianic, believing that an individual will change the world into paradise. Choice B is incorrect because a millenarian movement believes that a catastrophe will destroy most of the world but will eventually lead to heaven on earth. Choice C is incorrect because a totemic religious movement believes ancestral spirits bind them together as one people and, as a result, they have a special relationship with an animal, plant, or other object that represents that spirit. Choice D is incorrect because secularization is when a society moves away from a religious worldview.

36. **The correct answer is C.** Anthropologists will often conduct cross-cultural comparisons of observed patterns to determine if there are any significant parallels between cultural groups. This is called ethnology. Choice A is incorrect because ethnographer refers to the anthropologist conducting the study. Choice B is incorrect because an ethnography is the detailed written description of a cultural group. Choice D is incorrect because ethnomusicology is the study of the relationship between music and culture.

37. **The correct answer is B.** Magic, divination, and sacrifice are examples of rituals, ceremonial acts designed for use during specific occasions. Choice A is incorrect because myths are sacred stories that explain the relationship between the supernatural and reality. Choice C is incorrect because

exogamy is when an individual must marry outside his or her own group. Choice D is incorrect because reciprocity is when people exchange goods and services that are of roughly equal value.

38. **The correct answer is C.** All over the world, as culture change continues and globalization tightens connections between people and places, indigenous groups fight for cultural survival: the right to preserve, remember, and celebrate one's culture. Choice A is incorrect because a cultural universal is something that is found in every culture. Choice B is incorrect because artifacts from early human cultures are also referred to as material culture or cultural remains. Choice D is incorrect because cultures can be preserved in ways other than historical records, for example, art, literature, and multimedia.

39. **The correct answer is C.** Historical linguists are concerned with the connection between languages and how these languages change over time. Choice A is incorrect because structural linguists are focused on how a language is constructed (grammar, syntax, etc.). Choice B is incorrect because cultural anthropologists focus on cultural patterns of human behavior. Choice D is incorrect because historic archaeologists analyze both cultural artifacts and written evidence to understand a group of people.

40. **The correct answer is C.** Paleoanthropologists have discovered fossil evidence that *Homo erectus* was likely producing Acheulean stone tools, oval-shaped hand tools. Choice A is incorrect because *Australopithecus afarensis* likely used tools like a modern chimpanzee. Choice B is incorrect because *Homo habilis* is associated with Oldowan stone tools: rocks were shaped by striking flakes off. *Homo neanderthalensis* (choice D) is incorrect because they are associated with Mousterian stone tools: the variety of objects such as hand axes and wooden spears found at various sites.

41. **The correct answer is D.** Animism is the belief that everything is made of spirits or supernatural energies. Choice A is incorrect because sacrifice is an offering to supernatural beings to demonstrate faith and loyalty. Choice B is incorrect because witchcraft refers to magical rituals used to cause harm. Choice C is incorrect because syncretism is the merging of two or more religions into a new faith.

42. **The correct answer is C.** Sociolinguists study language use by different groups in various social contexts. Choices B and D are incorrect because descriptive and structural linguists refer to people who study the construction of languages. Choice A is incorrect because historical linguists are concerned with the connection between languages and how these languages change over time.

43. **The correct answer is C.** Gorilla social behavior, skeleton structure, and eating habits all give primatologists clues as to how humans may have evolved over time. Choice A is incorrect because chimpanzee DNA is 98 percent the same as human DNA. Choice B is incorrect because orangutans have been observed catching termites with branches and attempting to spear fish out of rivers. Choice D is incorrect because meerkats are not primates.

44. **The correct answer is C.** Boas and Malinowski practiced and taught their students participant observation: spending an extended period of time with a group of people observing, interviewing, and participating in the activities of their everyday lives. Choices A and B are incorrect because absolute and relative dating methods are used to determine the age of fossils or artifacts. Choice D is incorrect because armchair anthropology refers to reading accounts about other cultures (from explorers, missionaries, reporters, historians, etc.) and drawing conclusions based on that information—the opposite of participant observation.

45. **The correct answer is A.** Culture is best described as a set of behavioral patterns, norms, and values shared by a group. Choice B is incorrect because a cultural group may live in many territories. A single territory may have many cultural groups. Choices C and D are incorrect because, from an anthropological perspective, culture is shared

between people and is not limited to an individual's personality or belief system.

46. **The correct answer is D.** Redistribution occurs when goods are collected by a central person or office and then reallocated into the society. In industrialized state societies, for example, a government collects taxes and returns them to the populace in the form of national healthcare, education, etc. Choice A is incorrect because production refers to how resources are transformed into specific goods and services. Choice B is incorrect because a market exchange refers to the buying and selling of goods depending on supply and demand. Choice C is incorrect because people engage in reciprocity when they exchange goods and services that are of roughly equal value.

47. **The correct answer is A.** Agriculture allowed people to settle in one place and, over time, begin growing enough food to sustain larger and larger populations. Anthropological evidence suggests no large scale society has ever organized itself without social stratification (unequal access to resources). Choice B is incorrect because tool use emerged prior to large populations of human settlement. Choice C is incorrect because cave art dates back to the Upper Paleolithic era, likely prior to agriculture. Choice D is incorrect because people were moving from one place to another prior to the late Neolithic era.

48. **The correct answer is A.** Relative dating methods can only tell us if a fossil is older or younger than another fossil. Stratigraphy is one example of a relative dating method. Generally, deeper layers of dirt and rock are older than the surface layer of dirt. Choices B, C, and D are all examples of absolute dating and give us the age of something in actual years.

49. **The correct answer is C.** Evidence suggests that cave art was likely produced by *Homo sapiens* over 30,000 years ago, what archaeologists refer to as the Upper Paleolithic era. Choices A and B are incorrect because the Lower and Middle Paleolithic eras occurred before the Upper Paleolithic era.

Choice D is incorrect because the Neolithic era occurred after the Upper Paleolithic era.

50. **The correct answer is D.** Physical anthropologists often use their skills to conduct forensic anthropology, the analysis of skeletal remains. These remains may be part of an FBI or police investigation, and careful examination can provide the clues necessary to help solve a case. Choice A is incorrect because primatologists study nonhuman primates to shed light on human evolution. Choice B is incorrect because cultural anthropologists focus on researching and comparing patterns of human cultural diversity. Choice C is incorrect because linguists study human language.

51. **The correct answer is D.** A pilgrimage refers to traveling to a sacred site to prove one's dedication to the faith. Choice A is incorrect because a religious movement that promises widespread reform is a revitalization movement. Choice B is incorrect because traveling for tourism is simply tourism. Choice C is incorrect because migrating to a new country is known as immigrating.

52. **The correct answer is D.** Cultural anthropologists focus on researching and comparing patterns of human cultural diversity through participant observation. Choice A is incorrect because maritime archaeologists search for artifacts in bodies of water. Choice B is incorrect because primatologists study nonhuman primates to shed light on human evolution. Choice C is incorrect because forensic anthropologists analyze skeletal remains.

53. **The correct answer is D.** The phenotype refers to the physical expression of the genotype. A person may have inherited alleles for dark (for example, black) and light (for example, blond) hair from their parents. Choices A, B, and C are incorrect because an allele is a group of genes located on sections of DNA that can only be seen at the microscopic level.

54. **The correct answer is A.** Elites (governments, for example) historically have been the cause of directed culture change: when those with power (often the people at the top of a socially stratified society) develop

and enforce plans that force the less powerful to accept changes. Choice B is incorrect because there are no forces of cultural evolution. Choice C is incorrect because directed cultural change is not related to witchcraft. Choice D is incorrect because totemism is evidence of people having a special relationship with an animal, plant, or other object that represents ancestral spirits.

55. **The correct answer is B.** Political associations refer to the categories of bands, tribes, chiefdoms, or states; these are the ways cultural groups organize themselves to maintain social order. Choice A is incorrect because voter organization is one of the many ways of maintaining social order. Choice C is incorrect because the Neolithic Revolution occurred over a long period of time and was not a product of political associations. Choice D is incorrect because the formalist and substantivist debate was a theoretical debate, not an actual one.

56. **The correct answer is D.** During the Neolithic era, humans began guiding the growth of plants and the reproduction of animals. Choices A, B, and C are incorrect because none of these answers is directly connected to agriculture or the care of livestock.

57. **The correct answer is D.** Individuals who have traits that allow them to survive and reproduce are said to be better adapted to the environment they live in. Choices A and B are incorrect because successful adaptation means passing on the traits that helped the individual survive—reproduction. Choice C is incorrect because preparation for natural disasters is less directly related to reproduction.

58. **The correct answer is C.** Cultural relativism argues that each culture must be understood by its own norms and values and not be immediately judged by the standards of other cultures. This perspective has its roots in the work of Franz Boas and many of his students. Their work is collectively referred to as historical particularism. Choices A, B, and D are incorrect as those are all theoretical frameworks that emerged after historical particularism.

59. **The correct answer is A.** Neolocal refers to spouses living separately from their parents in their own households. Choices B and D are incorrect because bilocal and ambilocal refer to spouses choosing which family to live with or near. Choice C is incorrect because avunculocal refers to spouses living with or near the husband's mother's brother.

60. **The correct answer is D.** Elites (governments, for example) historically have been the cause of directed culture change: when those with power (often the people at the top of a socially stratified society) develop and enforce plans that force the less powerful to accept changes. Choice A is incorrect because random changes in DNA that may lead to beneficial, harmful, or neutral traits for an organism are referred to as mutation. Choice B is incorrect because an event such as an earthquake that causes an individual to die without reproducing is referred to as genetic drift. Choice C is incorrect because understanding how different cultural components work with one another is referred to as holism or the holistic perspective.

Health and Human Development

OVERVIEW

The DSST® Health and Human Development exam consists of 100 multiple-choice questions that cover human development and relationships; fitness and nutrition, disease and prevention; consumer awareness; psychological disorders and addiction intentional injuries; and violence. Careful reading, critical thinking, and logical analysis will be as important as your knowledge of health-related topics.

DIAGNOSTIC TEST ANSWER SHEET

1. Ⓐ Ⓑ Ⓒ Ⓓ   5. Ⓐ Ⓑ Ⓒ Ⓓ   9. Ⓐ Ⓑ Ⓒ Ⓓ   13. Ⓐ Ⓑ Ⓒ Ⓓ   17. Ⓐ Ⓑ Ⓒ Ⓓ

2. Ⓐ Ⓑ Ⓒ Ⓓ   6. Ⓐ Ⓑ Ⓒ Ⓓ   10. Ⓐ Ⓑ Ⓒ Ⓓ   14. Ⓐ Ⓑ Ⓒ Ⓓ   18. Ⓐ Ⓑ Ⓒ Ⓓ

3. Ⓐ Ⓑ Ⓒ Ⓓ   7. Ⓐ Ⓑ Ⓒ Ⓓ   11. Ⓐ Ⓑ Ⓒ Ⓓ   15. Ⓐ Ⓑ Ⓒ Ⓓ   19. Ⓐ Ⓑ Ⓒ Ⓓ

4. Ⓐ Ⓑ Ⓒ Ⓓ   8. Ⓐ Ⓑ Ⓒ Ⓓ   12. Ⓐ Ⓑ Ⓒ Ⓓ   16. Ⓐ Ⓑ Ⓒ Ⓓ   20. Ⓐ Ⓑ Ⓒ Ⓓ

POST-TEST ANSWER SHEET

1. Ⓐ Ⓑ Ⓒ Ⓓ   13. Ⓐ Ⓑ Ⓒ Ⓓ   25. Ⓐ Ⓑ Ⓒ Ⓓ   37. Ⓐ Ⓑ Ⓒ Ⓓ   49. Ⓐ Ⓑ Ⓒ Ⓓ

2. Ⓐ Ⓑ Ⓒ Ⓓ   14. Ⓐ Ⓑ Ⓒ Ⓓ   26. Ⓐ Ⓑ Ⓒ Ⓓ   38. Ⓐ Ⓑ Ⓒ Ⓓ   50. Ⓐ Ⓑ Ⓒ Ⓓ

3. Ⓐ Ⓑ Ⓒ Ⓓ   15. Ⓐ Ⓑ Ⓒ Ⓓ   27. Ⓐ Ⓑ Ⓒ Ⓓ   39. Ⓐ Ⓑ Ⓒ Ⓓ   51. Ⓐ Ⓑ Ⓒ Ⓓ

4. Ⓐ Ⓑ Ⓒ Ⓓ   16. Ⓐ Ⓑ Ⓒ Ⓓ   28. Ⓐ Ⓑ Ⓒ Ⓓ   40. Ⓐ Ⓑ Ⓒ Ⓓ   52. Ⓐ Ⓑ Ⓒ Ⓓ

5. Ⓐ Ⓑ Ⓒ Ⓓ   17. Ⓐ Ⓑ Ⓒ Ⓓ   29. Ⓐ Ⓑ Ⓒ Ⓓ   41. Ⓐ Ⓑ Ⓒ Ⓓ   53. Ⓐ Ⓑ Ⓒ Ⓓ

6. Ⓐ Ⓑ Ⓒ Ⓓ   18. Ⓐ Ⓑ Ⓒ Ⓓ   30. Ⓐ Ⓑ Ⓒ Ⓓ   42. Ⓐ Ⓑ Ⓒ Ⓓ   54. Ⓐ Ⓑ Ⓒ Ⓓ

7. Ⓐ Ⓑ Ⓒ Ⓓ   19. Ⓐ Ⓑ Ⓒ Ⓓ   31. Ⓐ Ⓑ Ⓒ Ⓓ   43. Ⓐ Ⓑ Ⓒ Ⓓ   55. Ⓐ Ⓑ Ⓒ Ⓓ

8. Ⓐ Ⓑ Ⓒ Ⓓ   20. Ⓐ Ⓑ Ⓒ Ⓓ   32. Ⓐ Ⓑ Ⓒ Ⓓ   44. Ⓐ Ⓑ Ⓒ Ⓓ   56. Ⓐ Ⓑ Ⓒ Ⓓ

9. Ⓐ Ⓑ Ⓒ Ⓓ   21. Ⓐ Ⓑ Ⓒ Ⓓ   33. Ⓐ Ⓑ Ⓒ Ⓓ   45. Ⓐ Ⓑ Ⓒ Ⓓ   57. Ⓐ Ⓑ Ⓒ Ⓓ

10. Ⓐ Ⓑ Ⓒ Ⓓ   22. Ⓐ Ⓑ Ⓒ Ⓓ   34. Ⓐ Ⓑ Ⓒ Ⓓ   46. Ⓐ Ⓑ Ⓒ Ⓓ   58. Ⓐ Ⓑ Ⓒ Ⓓ

11. Ⓐ Ⓑ Ⓒ Ⓓ   23. Ⓐ Ⓑ Ⓒ Ⓓ   35. Ⓐ Ⓑ Ⓒ Ⓓ   47. Ⓐ Ⓑ Ⓒ Ⓓ   59. Ⓐ Ⓑ Ⓒ Ⓓ

12. Ⓐ Ⓑ Ⓒ Ⓓ   24. Ⓐ Ⓑ Ⓒ Ⓓ   36. Ⓐ Ⓑ Ⓒ Ⓓ   48. Ⓐ Ⓑ Ⓒ Ⓓ   60. Ⓐ Ⓑ Ⓒ Ⓓ

answer sheets

HEALTH AND HUMAN DEVELOPMENT
DIAGNOSTIC TEST

Directions: Carefully read each of the following 20 questions. Choose the best answer to each question and fill in the corresponding circle on the answer sheet. The Answer Key and Explanations can be found following this Diagnostic Test.

1. Which of the following is a hereditary condition that causes the body to produce sticky mucus that impairs the lungs and intestinal tract?
   A. Huntington's disease
   B. Achondroplasia
   C. Cystic fibrosis
   D. Hemophilia

2. The highest level in Maslow's Hierarchy of Needs is
   A. social.
   B. physiological needs.
   C. esteem.
   D. self-actualization.

3. An important concept of wellness that involves choosing to focus on only what you can control is
   A. holistic health.
   B. empowerment.
   C. spirituality.
   D. exercise.

4. Which stage of an infection is most contagious?
   A. Incubation
   B. Peak
   C. Recovery
   D. Prodromal

5. Which of the following drugs is classified as an opioid?
   A. Morphine
   B. Marijuana
   C. Phencyclidine
   D. Valium

6. Exercise in which the body supplies oxygen to all body parts is called
   A. anaerobic.
   B. isometric.
   C. aerobic.
   D. isokinetic.

7. Which of the following gases has been linked to air pollution and damage to the earth's atmosphere?
   A. Hydrogen
   B. Nitrogen
   C. Argon
   D. Methane

8. According to Kubler-Ross, which of the following is the first stage in grieving?
   A. Depression
   B. Anger
   C. Denial
   D. Acceptance

9. The hardening of arteries is called
   A. arteriosclerosis.
   B. arthritis.
   C. atherosclerosis.
   D. angina.

10. Which of the following is a characteristic of secondary depression?
    A. Onset of depression for no apparent reason
    B. Onset of depression clearly defined by a traumatic event
    C. Depression attributed to brain chemistry
    D. Depression related to insufficient exposure to sunlight

11. Hypertrophic obesity is defined as
    A. the development of more fat cells in babies.
    B. the body's preference to maintain current weight, making it difficult to lose weight.
    C. obesity due to genetic factors.
    D. the growth of fat cells to accommodate increased intake of food.

12. During the transition stage of birth, the
    A. cervix begins to efface
    B. "bloody show" discharges from vagina.
    C. cervix dilates from seven to ten centimeters.
    D. placenta is delivered.

13. Your BAC is influenced by body weight, percentage of body fat, and
    A. the type of drink you consume.
    B. your sex.
    C. the amount of food in your stomach.
    D. the time of day.

14. Which type of cancer develops in connective tissue?
    A. Leukemia
    B. Melanoma
    C. Sarcoma
    D. Carcinoma

15. Which statement best describes the difference between barbiturates and tranquilizers?
    A. Barbiturates are addictive, but tranquilizers are not.
    B. Barbiturates cause sleep, and tranquilizers are used to cope during waking hours.
    C. Barbiturates are safe, and tranquilizers are dangerous.
    D. Barbiturates are no longer used, and tranquilizers are widely prescribed.

16. Which of the following is NOT one of the three stages of the GAS theory of stress?
    A. Alarm reaction
    B. Resistance
    C. Distress
    D. Exhaustion

17. Which energy source is most dense and provides stored energy for the body?
    A. Carbohydrates
    B. Vitamins
    C. Fats
    D. Proteins

18. The use of traditional free weights provides which form of exercise?
    A. Isometric
    B. Isotonic
    C. Isokinetic
    D. Aerobic

19. Which of the following can be detected by amniocentesis?
    A. Diabetes
    B. Cleft palate
    C. Down Syndrome
    D. Hemochromatosis

20. Which of the following is NOT a common residential safety principle?
    A. Having a fire escape plan
    B. Changing locks when moving into a new home
    C. Keeping noise at a reasonable level
    D. Asking for identification from strangers such as repairmen

ANSWER KEY AND EXPLANATIONS

1. C	5. A	9. A	13. B	17. C
2. D	6. C	10. B	14. C	18. B
3. B	7. D	11. D	15. B	19. C
4. B	8. C	12. C	16. C	20. C

1. **The correct answer is C.** Cystic fibrosis is a hereditary and often fatal disease that is caused by a genetic mutation. The defective gene causes a deficiency in essential enzymes produced in the pancreas, so the body doesn't properly absorb nutrients. Thick mucus impairs the function of the lungs and intestinal tract. Choice A is incorrect because Huntington's disease involves a degeneration of cells in certain areas of the brain. Choice B is incorrect because achondroplasia is the term used for dwarfism. Choice D is incorrect because hemophilia is a genetic disorder in which individuals are missing the factor necessary for blood to clot.

2. **The correct answer is D.** Self-actualization is the highest order according to Abraham Maslow's Hierarchy of Needs. He referred to people who reached this state as *transcenders* and Theory Z people. Self-actualization comes from the need for people to do what they were "meant" to do. Choice A is incorrect because social is the third level of Maslow's Hierarchy. Choice B is incorrect because physiological needs are the first level in the Hierarchy of Needs. Choice C is incorrect because esteem for self and others is the fourth level of the hierarchy.

3. **The correct answer is B.** Empowerment is choosing to focus on controlling only that which you have power over. Choice A is incorrect because holistic health focuses on taking care of your physical, psychological, social, intellectual, and spiritual self. Choice C is incorrect because spirituality involves focusing on your ability to understand the world and how you can serve others. Choice D is incorrect because exercise is only one aspect of life that you can control to promote overall wellness.

4. **The correct answer is B.** The peak stage is the most contagious phase of the disease and when the symptoms are most intense. Choice A is incorrect because the incubation stage occurs at the very beginning when an individual is capable of infecting others, but not as much as peak. Choice C is incorrect because the individual is least contagious during recovery. Choice D is incorrect because the prodromal stage is the second most contagious stage.

5. **The correct answer is A.** Narcotics such as opium, morphine, heroin, codeine, and methadone are classified as opioids. These drugs relieve pain, cause drowsiness, and induce euphoria. Choice B is incorrect because marijuana is derived from the plant cannabis and is not an opioid. Choice C is incorrect because phencyclidine is a dangerous hallucinogen also known as PCP or angel dust and is not an opioid. Choice D is incorrect because valium is classified as a tranquilizer.

6. **The correct answer is C.** During aerobic exercise, the body can supply oxygen to all body parts. Choice A is incorrect because during anaerobic exercise, the body cannot be oxygenated fast enough to supply needed energy. Choice B is incorrect because isometric refers to static exercises that focus on resistance. Choice D is incorrect because isokinetic exercise focuses on range of motion through mechanical devices used to provide resistance.

7. **The correct answer is D.** Methane is a gas linked to air pollution and harm to the earth's atmosphere. Choices A, B, and C are gases that are naturally and abundantly found in the earth's atmosphere and do not harm the atmosphere in their natural states.

8. **The correct answer is C**. According to Kubler-Ross, there are five stages in the process of coping with grief and tragedy. The first stage is denial, or refusal to accept the facts or any information about the situation. Choice A is incorrect because depression is the fourth step in grieving. Choice B is incorrect because anger is the second step. Choice D is incorrect because acceptance is the fifth stage of grieving.

9. **The correct answer is A**. The hardening of the arteries is known as arteriosclerosis. Choice B is incorrect because arthritis affects joints, not the heart. Choice C is incorrect because the buildup of plaque on inner walls of the arteries is called atherosclerosis. Choice D is incorrect because angina is a condition in which the heart doesn't receive enough oxygen.

10. **The correct answer is B**. The onset of secondary depression can clearly be attributed to a traumatic event such as death or divorce. Choices A and C are incorrect because the onset of depression for no apparent reason that is often linked to brain chemistry is defined as primary depression. Choice D is incorrect because depression linked to the amount of sunlight an individual is exposed to is classified as Seasonal Affective Disorder (SAD).

11. **The correct answer is D**. Adults typically take in more calories than they expend, causing fat cells to grow to accommodate the increased intake. This growth of fat cells is known as hypertrophic obesity. Choice A is incorrect because the development of more fat cells typically seen in babies who are overfed is known as hypercellular obesity. Choice B is incorrect because the idea that the body prefers to maintain its current weight is known as set-point theory. Choice C is incorrect because obesity due to genetic factors usually relates to thyroid or endocrine issues or metabolism.

12. **The correct answer is C**. Transition occurs during the first stage of labor when the cervix dilates from seven to ten centimeters. This is the shortest and most strenuous part of labor. Choice A is incorrect because effacement, or thinning of the cervix begins early in the first stage of labor. Choice B is incorrect because the thick mucus discharge called the "bloody show" is apparent before transition. Choice D is incorrect because the placenta is delivered during the final stage of birth, not during transition.

13. **The correct answer is B**. Blood alcohol concentration is determined by body weight, percent body fat, and gender. Choice A is incorrect because the type of drink is not as important as the amount of the drink ingested. Choice C is incorrect because the amount of food in the stomach will not alter the level of alcohol in the bloodstream. Choice D is incorrect because the time of day does not influence the BAC at all.

14. **The correct answer is C**. A sarcoma is a cancer that develops in connective tissue. Choice A is incorrect because leukemia is cancer involving the blood cells. Choice B is incorrect because melanoma is skin cancer. Choice D is incorrect because a carcinoma can be in many types of body parts but not in connective tissue.

15. **The correct answer is B**. The major difference between barbiturates and tranquilizers is that barbiturates are designed to induce sleep, and tranquilizers are used to help cope during waking hours. Choice A is incorrect because both are addictive. Choice C is incorrect because, when used properly, both drugs are safe. Choice D is incorrect because both drugs are still prescribed.

16. **The correct answer is C**. There is no stage of distress in Selye's theory on stress known as General Adaptation Syndrome, or GAS, theory. Choice A is incorrect because the first stage of GAS is alarm reaction, which is a physical "fight-or-flight" response to stress caused by the surge of adrenaline. Choice B is incorrect because the stage of resistance is the second stage of GAS; it is the point at which the body reaches homeostasis with respect to adrenaline and energy levels. Choice D is incorrect because the stage of exhaustion is the third stage of the GAS theory. This is the point at which a stressed body becomes tired.

17. **The correct answer is C.** Fats are an excellent energy source and are denser than carbohydrates. Fats store energy for long-term use. Choice A is incorrect because carbohydrates are also used for energy but they provide a short-term energy source and are less dense than fats. Choice B is incorrect because vitamins are not a source of energy. Choice D is incorrect because proteins are not a readily accessible source of energy.

18. **The correct answer is B.** Progressive resistance, or isotonic, exercises employ the use of traditional free weights to provide resistance. Choice A is incorrect because isometric exercise focuses solely on resistance. Choice C is incorrect because isokinetic resistance involves exercising through a range of motion. Choice D is incorrect because aerobic exercise has to do with the amount of blood supplied to muscles throughout the body.

19. **The correct answer is C.** Down Syndrome, or trisomy 21, is a disorder in which there is an extra chromosome 21. This can be detected during pregnancy with amniocentesis. Choice A is incorrect because diabetes isn't detected by amniocentesis and usually doesn't develop in young babies. Choice B is incorrect because a cleft palate is a physical birth defect, not a genetic defect. Choice D is incorrect because hemochromatosis, or an abnormally high level of iron in the body, is not detected by amniocentesis.

20. **The correct answer is C.** Keeping noise at a reasonable level is a principle of motor vehicle safety, not a residential safety principle. Choices A, and B, and D are all common residential safety principles. Other principles that fall into this category are installing a peep hole, keeping cooking and heating equipment in good working order, and storing poisonous substances away from children and pets.

answers diagnostic test

DIAGNOSTIC TEST ASSESSMENT GRID

Now that you've completed the diagnostic test and read through the answer explanations, you can use your results to target your studying. Find the question numbers from the diagnostic test that you answered incorrectly and highlight or circle them below. Then focus extra attention on the sections within the chapter dealing with those topics.

Health and Human Development		
Content Area	**Topics Covered**	**Questions**
Health, Wellness, and Mind/Body Connection	• Dimensions of wellness, health, and lifestyles • Healthy People 2020 • Prevention • Mental health and mental illness	2, 3, 10
Human Development and Relationships	• Reproduction • Sexuality • Intimate relationships • Healthy aging • Death and bereavement	8, 12, 19
Addiction	• Addictive behavior • Alcohol • Tobacco • Other drugs • Other addictions	5, 13, 15
Fitness and Nutrition	• Components of physical fitness • Nutrition and its effect	6, 11, 17, 18
Risk Factors, Disease, and Disease Prevention	• Infectious diseases • The cardiovascular system • Types of cancer • Immune disorders • Diabetes, arthritis, and genetic-related disorders • Stress management and coping mechanisms • Common neurological disorders	1, 4, 9, 14, 16

Health and Human Development		
Content Area	**Topics Covered**	**Questions**
Safety, Consumer Awareness and Environmental Concerns	• Safety • Intentional injuries and violence • Consumer awareness • Environmental concerns	7, 20

GET THE FACTS

To see the DSST® Health and Human Development Fact Sheet, go to **http://getcollegecredit.com/exam_fact_sheets** and click on the **Physical Science** tab. Scroll down and click on the **Health and Human Development** link. Here you will find suggestions for further study material and the ACE college credit recommendations for passing the test.

HEALTH, WELLNESS, AND MIND/BODY CONNECTION

Wellness is determined by overall health and vitality. Some aspects of health are not in our control; for example, age, gender, and genetic makeup are not things that we can control. However, wellness is determined in a large part by factors that we can control—such as diet, exercise, and relationships with others. Understanding that you can't control hereditary makeup, age, or gender helps achieve a feeling of empowerment, and empowerment is an important concept in overall wellness.

DIMENSIONS OF WELLNESS, HEALTH, AND LIFESTYLES

There are six dimensions to overall wellness: physical, emotional, spiritual, intellectual, interpersonal, and environmental. Each dimension is dependent on the others.

- **Physical wellness** includes not only the absence of disease but also fitness level and the ability to care for oneself. Physical wellness is determined by coordination, strength, and the five senses (sight, hearing, taste, touch, and smell).

- **Emotional wellness** reflects the ability to understand and cope with feelings or emotions. This also includes identifying any obstacles or factors that may affect emotional stability.

- **Spiritual wellness** involves developing a set of guided beliefs, principles, or values that give meaning and purpose to life.

- **Intellectual wellness** involves constantly challenging the mind and keeping it active. Continued creativity, problem solving, and processing information is essential for wellness.

- **Interpersonal wellness** is defined by the ability to develop and maintain healthy, satisfying, and supportive relationships with others. This includes participating in society in a positive way.

- **Environmental wellness** involves support from one's environment. The overall livability of the environment affects wellness, so it is important to make the world a cleaner, safer place to live.

Lifestyle choices include exercise, diet, and the choice to use alcohol or tobacco. People can influence their own lives by the lifestyle choices they make, but these four lifestyle choices play a major role in the leading causes of death in the United States.

HEALTHY PEOPLE 2020

Healthy People 2020 is a nationwide program created by the United States Office of Disease Prevention and Health Promotion designed to promote health and wellness. This program began in the late 1970s and has been updated periodically to include new information and changes that follow society and societal needs. The 2020 initiative added categories that cover blood disorders and transmission of infectious diseases, along with global health and preparedness in response to recent global outbreaks of certain infectious diseases. Healthy People 2020 has also included sections on lesbian, gay, bisexual, and transgender health in response to our changing society.

Healthy People 2020 researches and responds to the leading health indicators in each time period, including biological, social, economic, and environmental factors that interact and affect how people maintain their health. It strives to improve population health, eliminate health problems, and increase health awareness for everyone. One of the main goals of Healthy People 2020 is the promotion of quality of life and healthy development for individuals of all ages by increasing healthy behaviors through education, awareness, and availability of health resources.

Healthy People 2020 focuses on prevention of disease, disability, injury, and preventable death, while also promoting healthier lifestyles. There are forty-two topic areas that are covered, including substance use and abuse, heart disease, stroke, obesity, and mental health. One area that is seeing more attention is access to early and affordable detection and treatment. This initiative has found problems in availability, cost, lack of insurance coverage, and limited language access, all of which have led to individuals' inability to access preventative services and delays or failure to seek needed care. These factors ultimately lead to higher costs in health care as lengthy treatments and hospital stays that could have been prevented with early detection and treatment result.[1]

PREVENTION

Healthy People 2020 seeks to increase awareness of prevention efforts designed to reduce the need for hospitalization and invasive treatment procedures. As people actively become more aware of healthy practices and incorporate them, disease can be prevented. These healthy practices include regular well visits to the doctor and dentist, proper nutrition in diets, and exercise. Individuals need

TIP

The national Healthy People Initiative aims to improve the quality of life for Americans. Its two broad goals are to increase the quality and years of healthy life for individuals and to eliminate health disparities among population groups in the United States.

---

1. HealthyPeople.gov (n.d.). Healthy People 2020. Retrieved from: https://www.healthypeople.gov/.

to meet the guidelines of the food pyramid and exercise regularly. It is important to discuss changes in diet and exercise with a doctor to ensure that there are no problems with the changes beforehand.

One form of prevention is through holistic health methods. **Holistic health** includes understanding the importance of all six dimensions of wellness. It includes good diet, proper exercise, adequate sleep, preventative care, moderation in alcohol consumption, and no drug or tobacco use. Behavioral changes are also important in creating a healthy lifestyle. **Holistic medicine** seeks to create an entire healthy being through body, mind, spirit, and emotion. A holistic practitioner is open to using different forms of healthcare prevention and treatment, including conventional and alternative methods. A visit to a holistic medicine practitioner for back pain might result in an examination of many different potential issues that could be causing the pain, including sleep position, stress, diet problems, and physical activity. An individual might leave the office with a prescription for medications to alleviate the pain but will also leave with suggestions of lifestyle modifications to help prevent the continuance of the back pain.

Holistic medicine operates under certain principles, including the presence of innate healing powers in all individuals. Because patients are people not diseases, treatment occurs through teamwork between the patient and the doctor. Treatment addresses all aspects of the patient and involves treating the condition not just the symptoms. Types of treatment could include patient education of lifestyle changes and healthy self-care practices, complementary and alternative therapies that could include reiki, homeopathy, aromatherapy, acupuncture, and massage therapy, to name a few. Holistic treatment does include medications and surgical procedures based on traditional practices. The treatment professional could be a doctor of medicine, doctor of osteopathy, chiropractor, or homeopathic doctor, in addition to other holistic health professionals. Since there is such a wide variety of professionals involved, it is very important to check the credentials and reputation of any holistic practitioner before entrusting health matters to them. 2

The **transtheoretical**, or stages of change, model is an effective approach to lifestyle management. The stages of change include the following:

- **Precontemplation**: An individual doesn't think he or she has a problem and doesn't intend to change.

- **Contemplation**: An individual recognizes he or she has a problem and intends to change in six months.

- **Preparation**: An individual plans to take action to change a behavior within a month or has begun to make a change already.

- **Action**: An individual outwardly modifies his or her behavior.

- **Maintenance**: An individual has maintained a healthier lifestyle for at least six months.

- **Termination**: An individual has exited the cycle of change and is not tempted to lapse back into old behaviors.

---

2. WebMD (n.d.). What is holistic medicine? Retrieved from: http://www.webmd.com/balance/guide/what-is-holistic-medicine

MENTAL HEALTH AND MENTAL ILLNESS

People who are mentally healthy are comfortable with who they are and feel confident that they can meet the demands of life. When mentally healthy people are faced with negative feelings of disappointment, anger, jealousy, or regret, they are able to deal with the feelings without succumbing to them. Abraham Maslow developed the **Hierarchy of Needs**, which suggests that most people are motivated to fulfill basic needs before moving on to more complex needs. The needs are arranged in a pyramid. As one progresses up the steps of the pyramid, the needs become more complex.

- The lowest level is made up of the most basic **physiological needs**, including food, shelter, sleep, clothing, and compensation.

- The next level is the need for **safety and security**.

- Next is the need for **love and belonging**, including social relationships, family, friends, and social interaction.

- Next is the need for **esteem**, including self-esteem, confidence, achievement, respect for others, and respect from others.

- The final level is **self-actualization**, which is the point at which individuals are finally doing what they are meant to do. This level includes morality, creativity, spontaneity, problem solving, lack of prejudice, and acceptance of facts. Maslow calls self-actualized individuals *transcenders*, or Theory Z people.

Responses to challenges in life influence the personality and identity of individuals. Psychologist Erik Erikson proposed eight stages that extend throughout an individual's lifetime. Each stage is characterized by a turning point or a crisis. One must master a stage successfully before being able to progress to the next stage.

1. The *first stage at birth year to 1* involves developing a trust that others will respond to your needs.

2. The *second stage from 1 to 3 years* involves learning self-control without losing the capacity for assertiveness.

3. From *3 to 6 years*, individuals develop a conscience based on parental prohibitions.

4. From *6 to 12 years*, individuals learn the value of accomplishment and perseverance without feeling inadequate.

5. In *adolescence*, individuals develop a stable sense of who they are based on needs, abilities, style, and values.

6. During *young adulthood*, individuals learn to live with and share intimately with others, often in a sexual relationship.

7. *Middle adulthood* includes doing things for others, such as parenting and becoming involved in civic activities.

8. *Older adulthood* includes affirming life's value and ideals.

Psychological Disorders

There are several types of psychological, or mental, disorders with varying degrees of severity: mood or affective disorders, schizophrenia, dissociative disorders, and somatoform.

Mood or affective disorders create emotional disturbances that are intense enough to affect the normal functioning of an individual. Electroconvulsive therapy is effective for severe depression, if no other treatments succeed. The three most common mood disorders are anxiety disorders, depression, and bipolar disorder.

- **Anxiety disorders** are mood disorders based on fear. They cause physical symptoms such as rapid heartbeat and tenseness. There are several types of anxiety disorders.
    - **Simple phobia** is a fear of something definite, such as heights or closed spaces.
    - **Social phobia** is the fear of humiliation or embarrassment within a social setting. Shyness is associated with social phobia.
    - **Panic disorder** is the sudden and unexpected surge in anxiety and can lead to agoraphobia, which in its extreme is the fear of leaving home.
    - **Generalized anxiety disorder (GAD)** occurs when worries push out other thoughts and a person cannot banish these worrying thoughts.
    - **Obsessive-compulsive disorder (OCD)** includes irrational thoughts and impulses and the compulsion to do things over and over again. People with OCD feel out of control and embarrassed.
    - **Post-traumatic stress disorder (PTSD)** is a reaction to severely traumatic events, such as physical violence, natural disasters, and accidents.

- **Depression** is the most common mood disorder and is an overwhelming feeling of worthlessness, despair, and sadness in such a way that reality is distorted.
    - **Primary depression** seems to start for no apparent reason and is usually attributed to brain chemistry. The most successful treatment for primary depression is antidepressant medication.
    - **Secondary depression**, also known as **reactive depression**, is brought about by a traumatic event. The most successful treatments for this type of depression include counseling and other therapies.
    - **Seasonal affective disorder (SAD)** is directly related to the amount of sunlight an individual is exposed to. This disorder worsens during winter months, and phototherapy is an effective treatment.

- **Bipolar disorders** are another type of mood disorder. People who swing between a manic state and a depressive state have a bipolar disorder. People who experience mania are often restless, have a great deal of energy, need very little sleep, and talk incessantly. Medications such as the salt lithium carbonate can help prevent mood swings. Moods can also be stabilized with anticonvulsant drugs, such as Tegretol and Lamictal, which are generally used to prevent seizures.

- **Schizophrenia** has a number of symptoms, including auditory hallucinations, delusions of grandeur, persecution, inappropriate emotions, disorganized thoughts, and deteriorating social and work function. Schizophrenia is likely caused by a combination of genetics and environmental factors during pregnancy. Being born to older fathers or prenatal exposure to certain infections or medications can make an individual more susceptible to schizophrenia.

- **Dissociative disorders** cause a sudden, but temporary, change in identity or consciousness of an individual. Psychogenic amnesia is the inability to recall a stressful event, and psychogenic fugue occurs when an individual moves to a new place and assumes a new identity after a stressful event.

- **Somatoform disorders** are physical ailments without a medical condition to support them. Hypochondria is the belief that the person is sick when there is no medical evidence, and a conversion disorder is the unexplained loss of function of a body part.

HUMAN DEVELOPMENT AND RELATIONSHIPS

Over the course of a lifetime, a person will meet many people, have a variety of relationships, and live to see some family and friends die. Healthy living is the process of growing into a productive adult; coping with midlife issues; and aging and facing mortality in a positive, healthy way.

REPRODUCTION

The sex organs necessary for reproduction are different for women and men, but arise from the same structures and carry out similar functions. The gonads of females are called the **ovaries**, and the gonads of males are called the **testes**. The testes and ovaries produce sex hormones (androgens, estrogens, and progestins) that trigger the development and function of the reproductive system. Within the gonads, germ cells develop into gametes (**sperm** in males and **eggs** (or **ova**) in females), which merge during the fertilization process.

The external genitals of the female are the vulva and the labia majora and the labia minora, which are two paired folds of skin. Inside these folds are the clitoris, the opening of the urethra, and the opening of the vagina. The external genitals of the male are the penis and the scrotum. The scrotum contains the testes, which keeps the sperm at a temperature five degrees below normal body temperature.

The biological sex of an individual is determined by the sperm that fertilizes an ovum at the time of conception. All ova carry an X-chromosome, and sperm carry either an X- or a Y-chromosome. In females, progesterone and estrogen cause breast development, rounding of hips, and the start of the menstrual cycle. Maturation of the male reproductive system is about two years behind females. Testicular growth is the first sign of maturity. Body hair grows, the voice deepens, and height increases.

Conception and Infertility

The process of conception involves the fertilization of an ovum inside a woman by the sperm of a man during sexual intercourse. Once an egg is fertilized by a sperm, it becomes a **zygote**. As soon as fertilization occurs, the zygote starts the process of cell division, and moves through the fallopian tubes into the uterus. The cluster of growing cells forms a **blastocyst** that is implanted into the endometrial lining of the uterus. The blastocyst develops into a **fetus**.

Infertility is the inability to conceive a child after a year or longer of trying to do so. Most cases of infertility are treated with conventional medical therapies, such as surgery to correct anatomical problems or fertility drugs to help women ovulate. If these treatments don't work, assisted reproductive technology (ART) may be used. ART methods include intrauterine insemination, *in vitro* fertilization (IVF), gamete intrafallopian transfer (GIFT), and zygote intrafallopian transfer (ZIFT).

Pregnancy

Pregnancy is divided into trimesters of about three months each. Some of the major physiological changes to the mother and baby are as follows:

- **Mother**: During the first trimester, the uterus enlarges to about three times its nonpregnant size. During the start of the second trimester, the abdomen begins to protrude. The circulatory system and the lungs become more efficient. In the third trimester, the increased needs of the fetus put a strain on the woman's lungs, heart, and kidneys. The average weight gain during pregnancy is about 27.5 pounds. Preliminary contractions called Braxton-Hicks contractions start in the third trimester. In the ninth month, the baby settles in the pelvic region, and this stage of pregnancy is known as lightening.

- **Baby**: During the first trimester, the blastocyst implants in the uterus about four days after fertilization, eventually becoming an embryo at about the end of the second week after fertilization. The inner cells of the blastocyst are divided into three layers: One layer becomes inner body parts such as the digestive and respiratory systems. The middle layer of cells becomes muscle and bones, blood, kidneys, and sex glands. The third layer of cells becomes skin, hair, and the nervous system. An outermost layer of cells becomes the placenta, the umbilical cord, and the amniotic sac.

  These components provide nutrients and oxygen to the fetus. During the second trimester, the fetus does a great deal of growing, and it needs large amounts of food, water, and oxygen, which are all supplied from the mother through the placenta. During the third trimester, the fetus gains most of its birth weight.

Only about 3 percent of babies born have a major birth defect. The health and sex of a baby can be determined with several testing methods. These methods include ultrasonography, amniocentesis, chorionic villus sampling, and quadruple screen marker tests. Ultrasonography and amniocentesis are the most frequent methods used to detect fetal abnormalities. An ultrasound is done so that measurements of the developing fetus can be taken. A discrepancy in a fetal measurement can indicate an abnormality. Further detail can be obtained through amniocentesis. During amniocentesis, a needle is injected into the mother's abdomen to remove some of the amniotic fluid. The amniotic fluid contains all of the genetic material of the fetus, and so genetic, neural, and chromosomal abnormalities, such as Down syndrome, Tay-Sachs syndrome, spina bifida, and cystic fibrosis, can be detected. However, the severity of the problem is not known through amniocentesis.

Birth Process

The birth process occurs in three stages, and the whole process takes anywhere from about 2 to 36 hours. Labor begins when contractions exert pressure on the cervix and cause it to thin (effacement) and open (dilation). The first stage of labor involves effacement and dilation of the cervix to 10 centimeters through contractions. The last part of the first stage is called transition and is characterized by stronger, more frequent contractions. The second stage of labor begins when the cervix is completely dilated to 10 centimeters and ends with the delivery of the baby. During the third stage of labor, the uterus continues to contract until the placenta is delivered.

Birth Control

Contraceptives are devices, substances, or techniques that are used to prevent pregnancy by preventing the fertilization of an egg or the implantation of a fertilized egg (ovum). Methods of contraception include the barrier method (condoms, cervical cones, diaphragms), intrauterine devices (create an unstable environment in the uterus; IUD), hormonal methods (birth control pills and skin patch), natural methods (rhythm and withdrawal), and surgical sterilization (tubal ligation or tubal sterilization in women and vasectomy in men).

SEXUALITY

The sexual response in humans follows a specific pattern of phases: excitement, plateau, orgasmic, and resolution. Two physiological responses explain the genital and bodily reactions caused by arousal and orgasm. These are vasocongestion (accumulation of blood in tissue) and muscular tension.

Any type of disturbance in sexual desire, performance ability, or satisfaction is referred to as sexual dysfunction. Some common sexual dysfunctions in men are erectile dysfunction, premature ejaculation, and retarded ejaculation. Female sexual dysfunction includes the lack of desire to have sex, failure to become aroused, and failure to achieve orgasm.

Sexual behavior is a result of many factors shaped by life experience and biological factors, and it is also influenced by gender identity. When a person's gender traits don't match his or her gender identity, that person is considered transgender. Transgender includes transsexuals (those whose gender does not match their gender identity); transvestites (those who enjoy wearing the clothing of the opposite gender); and intersexed, or androgynous, individuals (born without definitive sexual characteristics).

Most individuals engage in sexual intercourse as the ultimate sexual experience. Atypical sexual behaviors include fetishism, exhibitionism, voyeurism, sadism, masochism, and sadomasochism. Paraphilia is the term used to describe atypical sexual behaviors that cause harm to oneself or others. The use of force in a sexual relationship is a serious problem in human interaction. The most extreme forms of sexual coercion are rape, pedophilia, and sexual harassment.

INTIMATE RELATIONSHIPS

The first relationships formed outside the family are friendships. Friendships are based on companionship, respect, acceptance, help, loyalty, trust, mutuality, and reciprocity. Intimate partnerships are much like friendships, but these relationships include sexual desire, deeper levels of caring, and a greater demand for exclusiveness.

There are several stages of attraction between individuals.

- The initial stage of a relationship is defined as **marketing**, when individuals "market" their best selves while finding new friends and acquaintances.

- The next stage is **sharing of common values and beliefs**. If there is enough compatibility, then the relationship moves to the behavior stage.

- During the **behavior stage**, the relationship develops further into a friendship or a passionate love relationship.

- **Passionate love** is characterized by a temporary phase of intense feelings and attraction. This phase does not last very long and is often called infatuation or lust.

- Passionate love usually gives way to **companionate love**, which is a deep enduring attachment built on mutual support, empathy, and tolerance.

Friendship and marriage are based on many of the same characteristics of companionate love and the same level of deep commitment that strengthens over time. For most individuals, love, commitment, and sex are important parts of an intimate relationship.

Dating and Marriage

Most people in the United States find a romantic partner through dating someone who lives in the same region, is from a similar ethnic or cultural background, has a similar educational background, lives a similar lifestyle, and has the same ideas of physical attraction. Living together, or cohabitation, is one of the most rapid social changes in our society. Today, by age 30, about 50 percent of all men and women have cohabitated.

Sexual orientation in an intimate relationship refers to the gender that an individual is attracted to. There are three types of sexual orientation. Heterosexuals are attracted to individuals of the opposite sex, or gender; homosexuals are attracted to others of the same gender; and bisexuals are attracted to both genders.

The majority of Americans marry at some point in their life. Certain characteristics can predict whether a marriage will last; it is important that partners feel good about each other's personalities, have realistic expectations about the relationship, communicate well, agree on religious and ethical values, devise effective ways to resolve conflict, have an egalitarian role in the relationship, and have a good balance between individual and joint interests. Approximately 50 to 55 percent of U.S. marriages end in divorce, a fact that is likely due to extremely high expectations of emotional fulfillment.

Starting a family can be stressful, but couples who keep their commitment strong after the arrival of a baby have three characteristics in common: a strong relationship before having children, planning their family and wanting children very much, and communicating well about feelings and expectations. As individuals become parents, there are typically four general styles of parenting, which vary depending on the levels of demandingness and responsiveness of the parent. The four parenting styles are as follows:

1. Authoritarian (high demandingness, low responsiveness)
2. Authoritative (high demandingness, high responsiveness)
3. Permissive (low demandingness, high responsiveness)
4. Uninvolved (low demandingness, low responsiveness)

HEALTHY AGING

Through good habits, individuals can delay, lessen, prevent, and sometimes reverse some changes associated with aging.

Midlife

In midlife, there is a general feeling of starting anew and coming to terms with mortality, although there is a slow decline of body function in terms of loss of bone mass, compression of vertebrae, loss of lean body mass, vision loss, hearing loss, fertility loss, and decrease in sexual function.

Many people retire in middle age, and their children are grown and leave home. These changes can bring about increased leisure time and changes in economic status.

Later Life

During the final stages of life, a greater emphasis is put on maintaining physical function and independence. **Life expectancy** is the average length of time that an individual can expect to live. Life expectancy continues to increase, which means more individuals are reaching older adulthood. This has increased the need for later forms of healthcare and chronic health issue management, both physically and psychologically. **Health span** refers to the length of time that one is generally healthy and free from serious disease. **Rehabilitation** is the return to normal functioning after an injury or illness. **Remediation** is the restoring of function through alternative methods. Government aid to elderly individuals includes housing subsidies, Medicare, Medicaid, and food stamps.

DEATH AND BEREAVEMENT

Death and bereavement are a natural part of life and affect all individuals at one time or another. Death is the cessation of all body functions; the heart stops beating and breathing ceases. Life-support systems and respirators can sustain some body functions for a period of time, but if an individual does not regain independent breathing and heart functions, once life support is terminated, death occurs.

People prepare wills and other legal documents to express their wishes and dispense their estate (property and possessions) after death. Some people also leave instructions to donate their organs after their death, living wills that specify the medical treatment preferred in the event the individual cannot communicate his or her wishes, and orders not to resuscitate.

End-of-life care can be home care, hospital care, or hospice care, depending on the wishes of the individual. In some cases, when a patient is in a persistent vegetative state (unconscious and non-functioning) and cannot maintain normal body functions without artificial life support, life support is discontinued so as not to prolong life in a vegetative state. The practice of withholding medical treatment (such as feeding tubes and ventilators) that may prolong a life is called **passive euthanasia**. In **physician-assisted suicide**, the physician provides lethal drugs at the patient's request to end his or her life. **Active euthanasia** is the intentional act of ending the life of someone who suffers from an incurable and painful disease.

Based on Kubler-Ross' **Five Stages of Grief** (denial, anger, bargaining, depression, and acceptance), Charles A. Corr describes four main dimensions a person experiences while coping with a life-threatening illness: physical, psychological, social, and spiritual. Dr. Corr, a professor emeritus of philosophical studies at Southern Illinois University Edwardsville, has published extensively on the topic of death and dying and life and living.

Grief is a natural reaction to death or loss, and grief is present during the bereavement process. Psychologist William Worden identified four tasks of the mourning process:

1. Accepting reality
2. Working through pain
3. Adjusting to a changed environment without the presence of the deceased individual
4. Emotionally relocating the deceased and continuing with life

ADDICTION

The source or cause of an addiction can be the result of hereditary factors, personality, lifestyle, or environmental factors. Addictive behaviors are habits (usually bad habits) that are out of control and have negative effects on health and well-being.

ADDICTIVE BEHAVIORS

Drug addiction is defined as the compulsive desire for a drug, the need to increase drug dosage, harmful effects to the addicted individuals and those around them, and psychological and physical dependence. **Physical dependence** is the most dangerous effect of drug use. A physical dependence means that the body relies on the drug for normal function. Removal of a drug from an individual who is physically dependent can produce significant withdrawal symptoms, which often include irritability, depression, physical pain, and death. **Psychological dependence** includes an intense desire to continue using a particular drug or drugs.

Drug habituation shares the same characteristics as drug addiction without the same level of compulsion or increased need of higher doses. Drug habituation is accompanied by psychological dependence but not physical dependence. Drug users can develop a tolerance to drugs so that they need an increased dosage to get the same effects.3

---

3. Engs, Ruth C. "Addictive behaviors," *Alcohol and Other Drugs: Self Responsibility*. Bloomington, IN: Tichenor Publishing Co. 1987. Used by permission of the author. Available on: http://www.indiana.edu/~engs/rbook

ALCOHOL

Alcohol, or ethyl alcohol (ethanol), is a form of a psychoactive drug. The concentration of alcohol in a particular drink is reflected in its proof value, which is twice the percentage of alcohol in the beverage. A standard alcoholic drink, referred to by the term "one drink," is 0.6 ounces of alcohol. As an individual ingests alcohol, about 20 percent is rapidly absorbed from the stomach into the bloodstream. About 75 percent is absorbed through the upper part of the small intestine, and the remainder enters the bloodstream later and farther down in the intestinal tract. Once it enters the bloodstream, alcohol induces the feeling of intoxication. The rate of absorption can be affected by the type of drink or the presence of food in the intestine. Food slows down the absorption of alcohol into the bloodstream, but carbonation or artificial sweeteners in the drink increase the rate of absorption.

Alcohol is metabolized primarily in the liver. **Blood alcohol concentration (BAC)** is determined by the volume of alcohol consumed over a given time period and by individual factors, including a person's sex, body weight, and percentage of body fat. Drinking low concentrations of alcohol can lead to feelings of relaxation, joviality, and mild euphoria. Higher concentrations of alcohol lead to feelings of anger, sedation, and drowsiness and decreased internal body temperature. The effects of alcohol wear off slowly, and individuals often experience what is known as a hangover.

Drinking large quantities of alcohol over a short period of time can rapidly increase BAC levels to a lethal range. This leads to alcohol poisoning, which can result in death. Drinking alcohol in combination with taking illegal drugs is the leading cause of drug-related deaths. Alcohol crosses a restrictive layer of cells into the brain where it disrupts the function of neurotransmitters. This disruption creates many of the typical effects of drinking alcohol or drunkenness. With heavy alcohol consumption, these effects become permanent. Health problems related to chronic or excessive use of alcohol include diseases of the digestive and cardiovascular systems and cancers of the throat, mouth, esophagus, liver, and breast. During pregnancy, alcohol consumption presents health risks to both the mother and the developing fetus, and there is a strong chance of the baby developing fetal alcohol syndrome, an alcohol-related neurodevelopmental disorder. Alcohol abuse includes recurrent alcohol use that has negative consequences. Alcoholism involves more severe problems with alcohol use and a dependence on alcohol.

TOBACCO

Smoking tobacco is the most preventable cause of poor health, disease, and death in the United States, but millions of Americans still smoke. Regular tobacco use causes a physical dependence on nicotine, which is characterized by a loss of control (cannot stop smoking), a buildup of tolerance to nicotine, and withdrawal symptoms in the absence of nicotine.

Tobacco smoke is made up of hundreds of chemicals, including toxic and poisonous chemicals, such as acetone, toluene, and arsenic. When these particles are condensed, they form a brown sticky solid called cigarette tar. Cigarette smoke also contains carbon monoxide, a deadly gas that depletes the body's supply of oxygen.

Nicotine, the key psychoactive ingredient in tobacco, affects the nervous system and can act as a stimulant or a depressant. It stimulates the cerebral cortex of the brain, and it stimulates adrenal glands to release adrenaline. Nicotine inhibits the formation of urine, constricts blood vessels, accelerates heart rate, and elevates blood pressure. Other long-term effects of smoking are cardiovascular disease, especially coronary heart disease (CHD); lung cancer and other cancers; respiratory diseases; stroke; aortic aneurysm; chronic obstructive pulmonary disease (COPD); arteriosclerosis (hardening of the arteries); emphysema; chronic bronchitis; ulcers; impotence; reproductive health problems; dental (gum) disease; and diminished senses, such as taste and smell. CHD is the most widespread cause of death among cigarette smokers and is often the result of atherosclerosis (plaque buildup in the walls of arteries).

Other forms of tobacco use, such as chewing tobacco, cigars, pipes, clove cigarettes, e-cigarettes, and bidis, also cause nicotine addiction and health issues. Oral tobacco use can lead to leukoplakia, the development of white leathery patches on gums, tongue, and inside of cheeks. This can be benign or a sign of cancer.

Second-hand, or environmental, tobacco smoke (ETS) contains high levels of toxic chemicals and poisons that cause headaches, sinus problems, eye irritation, and nasal irritation. Long-term exposure to ETS is linked to lung cancer and heart disease. Children and infants of parents who smoke are at greater risk of health issues. Smoking during pregnancy leads to an increase in the rate of miscarriage, stillbirth, congenital abnormalities, low birth weight, and premature births.

OTHER DRUGS

Drug abuse is a harmful pattern of illegal or prescription drug use that persists in spite of negative consequences to health and psychological and social well-being. Dependence on drugs involves taking them compulsively despite any adverse effects that use might have.

Psychoactive drugs affect the mind and body function by altering brain chemistry. The properties of the drug and how it is used affect how the body or brain reacts to it. The effect of these drugs also is dependent upon user factors, such as psychological and physiological factors; and social factors, such as the social and physical environment surrounding the drug user. Psychoactive drugs include the following:

- **Opioids**, also called **narcotics**, or **narcotic analgesics**, are drugs used to relieve pain; they cause drowsiness and induce a state of euphoria. Opioids also reduce anxiety, produce feelings of lethargy and apathy, and affect the ability to concentrate. Some common opioids are opium, morphine, heroin, methadone, oxycodone, hydrocodone, methadone, and codeine. These drugs are typically injected or absorbed through snorting, sniffing, or smoking.

- **Central Nervous System** (**CNS**) **depressants** slow down the activity of the nervous system. They reduce anxiety and also cause mood changes, impair muscular coordination, slur speech, and induce sleep or drowsiness. Results of use can vary from mild sedation to death. CNS depressants include alcohol, barbiturates, and antianxiety drugs, also called tranquilizers or sedatives, such as valium and methaqualone. Barbiturates are used to help individuals calm down and sleep.

- **CNS stimulants** speed up the activities of the nervous system and cause an accelerated heart rate, a rise in blood pressure, dilation of the pupils and bronchial tubes, and an increase in gastric and adrenal secretions. Examples of some common CNS stimulants include cocaine, nicotine, and amphetamines, which include dextroamphetamine, methamphetamine, and crystal methamphetamine; ephedrine; and caffeine.

- **Marijuana** used in low doses causes euphoria and a relaxed attitude. Very high doses cause feelings of depersonalization and sensory distortion. The long-term effects of marijuana include chronic bronchitis and some cancers. Using marijuana during pregnancy can impair fetal growth.

- **Hallucinogens** alter perception, feelings, and thought and can also cause an altered sense of time, mood changes, and visual disturbances. Hallucinogens include LSD (lysergic acid diethylamide), mescaline, psilocybin, STP, DMT, MDMA, PCP, and ketamine.

- **Inhalants**, which are present in a number of common household products, can cause delirium, loss of consciousness, heart failure, suffocation, and death. Inhalants can be categorized as volatile solvents (paint thinner, glue, gasoline), aerosols (sprays containing propellants and solvents), nitrites (butyl nitrite and amyl nitrite), and anesthetics (nitrous oxide).

Treatment of drug addictions include medication, self-help groups, rehabilitation and drug treatment centers, peer counseling, and counseling for family members.

OTHER ADDICTIONS

Drugs do not provide the only form of addiction. Addiction is basically a compulsive need for some habit or substance that creates physiological symptoms of withdrawal. Some alternate forms of addiction could include food, such as ice cream, or behaviors, such as exercise, gambling, shopping, sex, online games, online social media, and even bingo. In some way, the behavior becomes life-altering, and choices in lifestyle revolve around the addiction.

Gambling, bingo, and shopping can become addictions when they become compulsive. The individual can feel a sense of excitement and euphoria when buying or gambling—bingo is considered a form of gambling. This high is sought continuously, often leading to a depletion of earnings and savings, and often a descent into heavy debt, stealing, and lying. The individual can lose his or her family, job, and home in the pursuit of these types of addictions.

Sex addiction is not necessarily about the gratification of the physical act as much as it is about the initial excitement experienced during a first-time encounter, such as a first kiss. There is an unmet need for love and attention that the individual continuously tries to fill. Behaviors often include frequent and multiple partner interactions, which can result in an inability to form lasting monogamous relationships, and unprotected sexual activity, which can lead to contracting sexually transmitted diseases.

Some individuals engage in exercise to an excessive extent in an effort to satisfy an obsession over body image. The body is never perfect enough in the individual's mind, driving him or her to continue to exercise and seek excellence in performance. The high is experienced as endorphins are released during the exercise, and the individual continues to need this exercise in order to feel good about himself or herself. This addiction can lead to physical problems as the individual pushes too hard and causes strained muscles.

Online addictions occur as individuals spend inordinate amounts of time online either gaming or engaging in social media interactions. The high is from the interaction with the computer and often occupies long periods of time that should be spent working or taking care of normal daily routines.

FITNESS AND NUTRITION

Part of having a healthy lifestyle is being physically fit and eating well. Regular exercise and proper diet are important wellness factors.

COMPONENTS OF PHYSICAL FITNESS

Exercise

Exercise lowers the risk of cardiovascular disease by lowering blood fat levels, reducing high blood pressure, and preventing arterial blockage. Exercise also reduces the risk of some cancers, osteoporosis, and diabetes; boosts the immune system; improves psychological health; and prevents injuries and lower back pain. There are two types of exercise: aerobic and anaerobic. During aerobic exercise, oxygen is supplied to all areas of the body. During anaerobic exercise, the body cannot be oxygenated fast enough to supply energy to muscles from oxygen alone. This type of exercise involves a high intensity of effort.

Endurance training is a form of aerobic activity. It improves the function of chemical systems in the body and enhances the body's ability to utilize food energy. It includes exercises with continuous rhythmic movements, such as walking, jogging, cycling, and aerobic dancing. An indicator of the level of aerobic activity performed is the calculation of one's target heart rate, which is between 60 to 80 percent of one's maximum heart rate, which can be calculated by multiplying the maximum heart rate (220 − age) by .65 to .85.

The **Dietary Guidelines for Americans** recommend that children and adolescents should engage in at least 60 minutes of physical activity every day. Adults should take part in at least 2 hours and 20 minutes of moderate intensity or 1 hour and 15 minutes of vigorous intensity aerobic physical activity per week. Aerobic activity should be performed in segments of at least 10 minutes per segment and should occur multiple times throughout the week. Older adults should try to engage in the same level of exercise as younger adults, but, if health concerns prevent this, they should take part in as much physical activity as their conditions allow.

Physical activity should be appropriate to the individual's current level of physical fitness and should increase gradually based on health and ability. If an individual has health concerns, it is important to check with a doctor first to determine which types of physical activity will work best. Someone who is not currently active should not start out with a rigorous aerobic workout. It is important to be safe and go slowly.

In addition to health benefits, regular physical activity can provide a means of socializing with others, improve physical appearance, aid in sleep quality, increase energy, and provide more opportunity for independent living for older adults. A 45-minute walk during lunch can increase healthy physical activity and provide an opportunity to socialize with coworkers and friends. Many people set up step goals. The Dietary Guidelines recommend walking 10,000 steps a day.

There are five components to physical fitness:

1. Cardiorespiratory endurance
2. Muscular strength
3. Muscular endurance
4. Flexibility
5. Body composition

Cardiorespiratory endurance is the ability to perform prolonged, large muscle, dynamic exercises at a moderate- to high-intensity level. It increases the strength of the heart and certain related physical functions: the heart pumps more blood volume per heartbeat, the resting heart rate and resting blood pressure decrease, blood supply to tissue improves, and the body is better able to cool itself.

Muscular strength and endurance involves exerting force against significant resistance (weight lifting). Strength training should be done about two nonconsecutive days a week and should involve 8 to 12 repetitions of 8 to 10 different exercises. Strength training improves physical fitness and increases muscle mass, which means the body will require more energy to sustain life. There are three ways to improve muscle strength and endurance:

1. *Isometric exercises* are static and focus only on resistance (for example: pushing against a wall). It is difficult to measure the effectiveness of an isometric exercise, so they are not used often.

2. *Progressive resistance exercises*, or isotonic exercises, are those that provide a fixed amount of resistance, such as the use of traditional free weights.

3. *Isokinetic exercises* are those that include a range of motion and resistance provided by a mechanical source. The development of muscular endurance includes the ability to keep a specific muscle group contracted for a long period of time or to continually contract the same muscle group for a long period of time.

Flexibility is defined as the ability to move joints through a full range of motion. Flexibility depends on the structure of a particular joint, the length and elasticity of its connective tissue, and nervous system activity surrounding the joint. Stretching can help to provide flexibility and prevent injury when exercising and should include exercises for all the major muscle groups and joints. Muscle and joint injury can be treated with the R-I-C-E method: Rest, Ice, Compression, and Elevation.

A healthy **body composition** includes a higher proportion of fat-free body mass than fat mass. The proportion of fat-free to fat mass varies by age and sex. A higher concentration of body fat, especially in the abdominal region, can lead to health issues, including high blood pressure, heart disease, stroke, joint problems, gall bladder disease, back pain, diabetes, and cancer. Body composition can be altered by proper exercise and a healthy diet.

Regular exercise lowers the risk of cardiovascular diseases, cancer, osteoporosis, and Type II diabetes.

Any exercise is better than no exercise, and benefits of exercise occur across all age groups and racial and ethnic groups. The more exercise an individual does, the more the individual realizes the benefits with stronger bones and muscles and increased lung capacity. Regular exercise with a steady progression can increase benefits, while minimizing risk of injury. Individuals should start slowly and increase and diversify their workouts as they go along.

Obesity

Many people exercise as part of a regimen to overcome obesity. Obesity can be caused by genetic factors or be due to the **set point theory**, which maintains that the body prefers to stay at its current weight, making it difficult for a person to drop below that weight. People who were overweight as babies may develop more fat cells, a condition known as **hypercellular obesity**, and this may make them more susceptible to being obese as adults. With the set point theory, there is more of an environmental influence as individual choices in food and exercise can influence how weight fluctuates. People who eat more calories than they expend have **hypertrophic obesity**, in which the fat cells expand to increase in volume and hold more fat tissue. People can remedy obesity through diet modification, physical intervention (appetite suppressants to control food intake), behavioral intervention (increased physical activity), or in extreme cases, bariatric surgery.

The prevalence of obesity has doubled among adults and tripled among children in the United States in recent decades. The easy availability of high-calorie, good-tasting, and inexpensive foods, along with larger portion sizes, have contributed to this trend in obesity. In addition to poor diet habits, technological advances and cutbacks in physical education programs in the schools have reduced physical activity in children. They do not develop good exercise habits when they are young, and this carries over to adulthood.

One way to measure body fat is through the **Body Mass Index (BMI)**. The BMI measures body fat based on height and weight and can indicate if an individual is underweight, normal, overweight, or obese. The healthy range of scores are from 20 to 25, with scores below 20 indicating that an individual is underweight, while scores over 25 indicate overweight and obese conditions. The BMI is calculated by dividing an individual's weight in pounds by their height in inches squared. This figure is then multiplied by 703. The BMI provides a guideline but is not completely accurate since it does not account for the variations in body type, height, and muscle mass.

NUTRITION AND ITS EFFECT

There are about forty-five essential nutrients that the body requires to maintain its maximum level of health and well-being. Food provides the essential nutrients and fuel that bodies require. The energy in foods is expressed in terms of kilocalories, commonly referred to as **calories**. **Macronutrients** include protein, fat, and carbohydrates, and each of these supplies energy to the body in differing amounts. Fat provides nine calories (kilocalories) per gram, protein provides four calories per gram, and carbohydrates provide four calories per gram.

Proteins are composed of chains of amino acids folded into a complex three-dimensional structure. Proteins form muscle and bone; are required for the production of blood, enzymes, hormones, and cell membranes; and are found in various forms in every cell of the body. Food obtained from animal sources (meat, eggs) provides complete proteins, but food from plant sources provides incomplete proteins.

Fats are the best source of energy for the body and are stored in the body for long-term energy use. Foods contain saturated or unsaturated fats or both. **Saturated fats** are solid at room temperature and generally found in animal products. **Unsaturated fats** generally come from a plant source and are liquid at room temperature. **Trans fatty acids** are unsaturated fats that have been altered so that their shape affects their behavior in the body.

Saturated and trans fats pose health risks, but some fats can be beneficial elements of a healthy diet. Omega-3 fatty acids are healthy polyunsaturated fats found in fish, nuts, and some plant-based foods like avocados. Omega-3 fatty acids reduce the tendency to form blood clots, inhibit inflammation, decrease abnormal heart rhythms, and help to reduce the risk of heart attacks, high blood pressure, and stroke in some people. **Carbohydrates** supply energy to cells and are the exclusive supply of energy for the brain and other parts of the nervous system and red blood cells. Carbohydrates are either simple or complex. Simple carbohydrates include sucrose, fructose, maltose, and lactose; these provide sweetness to foods. Complex carbohydrates are found in starches and dietary fiber; nondigestible carbohydrates in many plants. Fiber can help manage diabetes and high cholesterol levels and improve intestinal health. **Soluble fiber** turns into a gel in the intestine and binds to cholesterol to move it through the digestive tract. **Insoluble fiber** absorbs water and helps digestion.

There are thirteen vitamins needed for proper nutrition and for proper maintenance of chemical and cellular processes. Four vitamins are fat-soluble (Vitamins A, D, E, and K) and nine are water-soluble (C and the eight B-complex vitamins: thiamin, riboflavin, niacin, B-6, folate, B-12, biotin, and pantothenic acid). Deficiencies in these essential vitamins can cause serious illness or death. Water is required to digest and absorb food, transport substances to different areas of the body, lubricate joints and organs, and help maintain body temperature. Water is found in almost all food sources.

There are also seventeen essential minerals needed in a healthy diet. Minerals are inorganic substances, such as calcium, phosphorous, sulfur, sodium, potassium, and magnesium, that regulate body functions, help in growth and maintenance of body tissue such as teeth and muscles, and help in the release of energy from foods eaten.

Dietary Reference Intakes (**DRI**) are recommended intakes for essential nutrients that meet the needs for overall health and well-being. The Dietary Guidelines for Americans address the prevention of diet-related diseases (cancer, diabetes, cardiovascular disease). The Dietary Guidelines noted that while the rates of infectious diseases have decreased, the rates of diet-related issues have increased. Roughly half of all American adults have been diagnosed with diseases related to poor eating and exercise habits. The Guidelines include the following recommendations:

1. Follow healthy eating patterns throughout life. Healthy habits are lifelong and should include maintaining a healthy body weight through nutritious foods.

2. Focus on variety, nutrient density, and amount. Individuals should choose nutrient-dense foods from all food groups while limiting calories.

3. Limit calories from added sugars, sodium, and saturated fats. It is important to limit foods high in refined sugars and sodium, including beverages, and cut back on foods containing saturated fats.

4. Move to healthier foods and beverages, including water.

5. Support healthy eating patterns in all settings.

By law, almost all foods require labels that break down the composition of the food into fats, proteins, carbohydrates, fiber, and sodium. Serving sizes have been standardized, health claims of particular foods are regulated, and dietary supplements must also have food labels. Individuals should limit intake of added sugars and saturated fats to no more than 10 percent of total calories each per day. Sodium should be limited to fewer than 2,300 milligrams per day, and alcohol should be consumed in moderation (no more than one drink per day for women and two drinks or fewer per day for men). Some studies have indicated health benefits to drinking wine, yet it is not recommended that people who do not currently drink begin to drink as a result of these studies. A diet high in fruits, vegetables, and whole grains aids a healthy lifestyle. One rule of thumb is to create a plate of food that is comprised mainly of fruits, vegetables, and whole grains, with a little bit of meat or other protein.

RISK FACTORS, DISEASES, AND DISEASE PREVENTION

INFECTIOUS DISEASES

In order to contract an infectious disease, several components are required: an agent, an entry point, a reservoir, and an exit point. A disease-producing agent—a **pathogen**—can be bacterial, viral, or fungal. The entry point can be either direct (bodily fluids, droplets, or fecal matter) or indirect (inanimate objects or nonhuman organisms, for example, mosquitoes).

There are four basic stages of an infection:

1. *Incubation* is the silent stage where symptoms are not apparent, but an individual is capable of infecting others.

2. During the *prodromal stage*, the pathogen, or disease agent, multiplies rapidly. During this stage, the infected individual (host) will experience some symptoms and is more likely to infect others.

3. During the *peak*, or *acme stage*, the symptoms are most intense; this is the most contagious phase of the disease.

4. The final stage is the *recovery stage* when the body begins to heal from the effects of the disease.

When a foreign organism infects the body, a complex system of responses is activated, two of which are the inflammatory response and the immune response. The immune system is the body's defense system against disease, and defense is carried out by different types of white blood cells, which are produced in bone marrow: **neutrophils** (travel in bloodstream to site of infection), macrophages (devour pathogens and dead cells), **natural killer cells** (directly destroy virus- infected cells or cancerous cells), **dendrite cells** (eat pathogens and activate lymphocytes), and **lymphocytes** (travel through the bloodstream and the lymphatic system).

Within the lymphatic system, lymph nodes filter bacteria and other substances from the lymph. When the lymph nodes are fighting off an infection, they fill with cells and become swollen. The location of the swollen nodes can alert doctors to the area of an infection.

There are three types of immunity that can fight off an infection.

1. *Artificially Acquired Immunity* (*AAI*): Occurs when the body develops immunity from a vaccination or an infection

2. *Naturally Acquired Immunity* (*NAI*): Occurs when the body itself fights off an infection and develops a "memory" for the infection to prevent reinfection

3. *Passively Acquired Immunity* (*PAI*): Occurs when antibodies are used until the body develops a natural immunity against an infection

Bacterial infections can be treated with the administration of antibiotics that can kill bacteria. Vaccines can be administered to manipulate the immune system and cause the body to develop immunity to a certain infectious disease.

There are seven sexually transmitted diseases (STDs) that pose a major health threat:

1. *AIDS* (*Acquired Immune Deficiency Syndrome*): Most serious and life-threatening sexually transmitted disease. AIDS is caused by the virus known as HIV (human immunodeficiency virus), which compromises the immune system by attacking helper T cells (CD4 T cells). HIV is spread through bodily fluids, such as blood, semen, and vaginal secretions, and it can pass from mother to baby. There is a great variation in the incubation time of HIV: from about six months to up to ten years. There is no cure for AIDS or HIV, but there are medicines available that can reduce the rate of destruction of helper T cells.

2. *Chlamydia*: Causes painful urination in both men and women. Most women with chlamydia are asymptomatic, but it can lead to pelvic inflammatory disease (PID) if left untreated. It increases a woman's risk of infertility and ectopic pregnancies and can lead to male infertility. It is the most widely spread bacterial STD in the United States.

3. *Gonorrhea*: Causes urinary discomfort in men and has a yellowish, green discharge. Most women infected with gonorrhea are asymptomatic, but some experience painful urination, vaginal discharge, and severe menstrual cramps. This STD is treated with antibiotics.

4. *Human Papillomavirus* (*HPV*): Most common viral STD in the United States. About 6.2 million Americans are infected each year. Most people with HPV have no symptoms, and the virus can be cleared by the immune system without any treatment. However, if the infection persists, it can lead to genital warts (and common warts) and genital cancers, cervical cancers, penile cancers, and some forms of rectal and oropharyngeal cancers.

5. *Genital Herpes*: Infects about 1 in 5 adults in the United States, but most people don't know that they're infected. There are over fifty different herpes viruses, including chicken pox, shingles, and mononucleosis. There are two types of the herpes simplex virus: HSV-1 and HSV-2. HSV can be transmitted through sexual activity, including oral sex, and HSV infections usually last a lifetime. The virus can lie dormant for long periods of time and reactivate at any time. An infected individual is always contagious.

6. *Hepatitis B*: Causes inflammation of the liver and can cause serious and sometimes permanent damage. Hepatitis B is found in most body fluids and can be transmitted sexually, through intravenous drug use, and during pregnancy and delivery. Hepatitis B is similar to HIV, but it can spread through both sexual and nonsexual contact.

7. *Syphilis*: Caused by bacteria and can therefore be treated with antibiotics. After infection, an individual may be asymptomatic for four to ninety days.

Early diagnosis and treatment of STDs can help avoid complications and prevent their spread. Condom use is another effective way to help prevent the spread of some STDs.

THE CARDIOVASCULAR SYSTEM

The cardiovascular system consists of the heart and blood vessels. The heart pumps blood to the lungs through the pulmonary artery and to the body via the aorta. There are six major preventable risk factors for **cardiovascular disease** (**CVD**): smoking, high blood pressure, unhealthy cholesterol levels, inactive lifestyle, obesity or being overweight, and diabetes.

CVD can be prevented by making dietary changes, especially decreasing fat intake (saturated and trans fats) and increasing fiber intake; getting regular exercise; avoiding tobacco; managing blood pressure and cholesterol levels; and developing effective ways of dealing with anger and stress.

TYPES OF CANCER

Cancer can develop in all areas of the body. Treatment options depend on where the cancer is located, what type of cancer it is, and how far the cancer has progressed. Most cancers take the form of a tumor, which is a mass of tissues that serves no physiological purpose. Tumors may be **benign** (noncancerous) or **malignant** (cancerous). The spreading of cancer cells from one part of the body to another is called **metastasis**. The extent or spread of a cancer can be categorized into one of five progressive stages (stages 0 to IV). Malignant tumors are classified according to the type of cells the cancer is infecting.

- **Carcinomas** form from epithelial cells and account for 85 percent of all tumors. They can be in the skin, mouth, throat, intestinal tract, glands, nerves, breasts, genital structures, urinary tract, lungs, kidneys, and liver.
- **Sarcomas** are found in connective tissues, such as bones, cartilage, and membranes, that cover muscles and fat. Sarcomas account for about 2 percent of all cancers.
- **Melanomas** are skin cancers caused by prolonged sun exposure.
- **Lymphomas** are cancers of the lymph nodes or lymphatic system.
- **Leukemias** are cancers of blood-forming cells (bone marrow cells).
- **Neuroblastomas** generally affect children and start in the immature cells of the CNS.
- **Adenocarcinomas** are found in the endocrine glands.
- **Hepatomas** are found in liver cells.

Cancer is due to uncontrolled growth of cells because of genetics, exposure to mutagens, viral infection, and chemical substances in food and air. Dietary factors such as meat, certain types of fats, and alcohols can increase the risk of some cancers. Other risks include lack of exercise, obesity, certain types of infection, and exposure to chemicals and radiation. Diets that include a large variety of fruits and vegetables are linked to lower cancer rates. Also, self-monitoring and regular screening tests are essential to early cancer detection.

The following mnemonic devices are useful for self-monitoring and early cancer detection:

- The **ABCD test** for melanoma means checking a mole for asymmetry, border irregularity, color variation, and diameter greater than 6 millimeters.

- The acronym **CAUTION** promotes symptom awareness: C = change in bowel or bladder habits, A = a sore throat that does not heal, U = unusual bleeding or discharge, T = thickening or lump in breasts or elsewhere, I = indigestion or difficulty swallowing, O = obvious change in wart or mole, N = nagging cough or hoarseness.

Cancer treatment methods include surgery, chemotherapy, and radiation. Lifestyle choices can greatly reduce the risk of cancer: avoid smoking, control diet and weight, exercise, protect skin, and avoid environmental and occupational carcinogens.

IMMUNE DISORDERS

Immune disorders occur when the body comes under attack by its own cells (as is the case in cancers). The immune system often is able to detect cells that have recently transformed to cancer cells and is capable of destroying these cells. However, if the immune system starts to break down because of age, immune disorders like HIV, or chemotherapy, cells can grow out of control, often before the immune system can detect danger.

Another immune disorder occurs when the body confuses its own cells with foreign organisms. Some autoimmune disorders in which the immune system is too sensitive and attacks cells within the body include systemic lupus erythematosus and rheumatoid arthritis.

DIABETES, ARTHRITIS, AND GENETIC-RELATED DISORDERS

Diabetes is a disease in which the pancreas does not produce insulin normally. Insulin is a necessary biological chemical that is used to process sugar in the body. There are three types of diabetes: Type I diabetes, which usually occurs during childhood; Type II diabetes, most often an adult disease; and gestational diabetes, a temporary condition during pregnancy. An individual with Type I will spend a lifetime monitoring blood sugar levels and injecting insulin. Obesity is a risk factor for Type II diabetes and can often be controlled through diet and exercise.

Rheumatoid arthritis (RA) is an autoimmune response that occurs when the immune system attacks healthy joint tissue. Symptoms of RA include stiffness, joint pain, swelling, redness, throbbing, muscle atrophy, joint deformity, and limited mobility. **Osteoarthritis** is caused by the wear and tear on joints and is usually a problem in older people. There is no cure for arthritis, but pain management and therapy can help.

Genetic disorders are diseases inherited from biological parents. The following are some common genetic disorders:

- **Hemophilia**: Passed from gene-carrying mothers to sons; the individual is missing factors needed for blood clotting

- **Retinitis Pigmentosa**: Eye disease that causes light sensitivity and the degeneration of the retina leading to eventual blindness

- **Color Blindness**: Affects the ability to discern colors
- **Cystic fibrosis**: Fatal condition caused by a defective gene prompting the body to produce a sticky mucus in the lungs and elsewhere

STRESS MANAGEMENT AND COPING MECHANISMS

Stress can refer to two different things: the stressor and the stress response. The situation that triggers physical or emotional reactions is called the **stressor**, and the physical and emotional reactions are called the **stress response**. *Stress* is the general term used to describe the physical and emotional state that is part of the stress response.

Two body systems control the physical response to a stressor: the nervous system and the endocrine system. The autonomic nervous system consists of the parasympathetic division, which is in control when the body is relaxed, and the sympathetic division, which is activated during times of arousal. The sympathetic division triggers signals to tell the body to stop storing energy and to use it in response to crisis. This is carried out with the neurotransmitter norepinephrine. During times of stress, the sympathetic division of the nervous system triggers the endocrine system, where key hormones are released, including cortisol and epinephrine.

Hans Selye developed a theory of stress called the **General Adaptation Syndrome** (**GAS**), which has three stages.

1. The first stage is the *alarm reaction* when the body encounters the initial stressor and initiates the fight-or-flight response, which is triggered by a surge of cortisol into the bloodstream.

2. The next stage of GAS is the *stage of resistance*. The body cannot maintain the levels of energy and adrenaline, so, in this stage, the parasympathetic division of the nervous system takes over and restores a state of stability called homeostasis.

3. The third stage of GAS is *exhaustion*. The stressed body will be tired at this stage because the initial adrenaline surge and the return to homeostasis expend a large amount of energy. Stress triggered by a pleasant stressor is called eustress, and stress triggered by an unpleasant stressor is called *distress*.

Behavioral responses to stressors are controlled by the **somatic nervous system**. Personality types also play a role in how an individual deals with stress. Type A personalities have a high perceived stress level and usually have problems dealing with stress. Type B personalities are less frustrated by daily events and other people's behavior. Type C personalities have difficulty expressing emotion and suppress their anger. They have an exaggerated response to minor stressors.

Stress can be managed in a myriad of ways, including having a good support system, improving communication skills, developing a healthy lifestyle, improving time management, and learning to identify and moderate individual stressors. Spiritual wellness can also help individuals deal with stress and improve overall health. Keeping a diary, changing unhealthy thought patterns, and using relaxation techniques that trigger a relaxation response are other ways to cope with stress.

A **relaxation response** is a physiological state that results in a slowing of breathing, heart rate, and metabolism; a decrease in blood pressure and oxygen; an increase in blood flow to the brain and skin;

and a switch of brain waves to the relaxed alpha rhythm. Counterproductive strategies for coping with stress include alcohol and tobacco use, drug use, and unhealthy eating habits.

COMMON NEUROLOGICAL DISORDERS

Two common neurological disorders are **Rett syndrome** and **Huntington's disease**. Rett syndrome affects brain development and is similar to autism. It is most common in girls. Development of affected individuals slows after 18 months, and children begin losing motor function.

Huntington's disease is characterized by the degeneration of brain cells in certain parts of the brain, causing loss of intellect, muscle control, and emotional control. A child of a parent with Huntington's disease has a 50/50 chance of inheriting the gene and developing the disease.

SAFETY, CONSUMER AWARENESS, AND ENVIRONMENTAL CONCERNS

In contemporary society, anxiety and even fear of random violence have become daily concerns for many. Learning simple safety procedures for the home and workplace can provide some sense of security. Being good healthcare consumers and protecting the environment are other areas of interest to many.

SAFETY

Many injuries are caused by the interaction of humans with environmental factors. The chief areas of safety concern are personal, residential, recreational, motor vehicle, and gun use. To maintain personal safety, one must think carefully, be aware of one's surroundings, and avoid atypical patterns.

Some common residential safety principles are to have a fire escape plan, install a peep hole, change locks when moving into a new home, and ask strangers such as repairmen for identification. The home can contain many poisonous substances that should be kept safe and away from children and pets. Home fires can be prevented by being careful about where smoking is done and keeping cooking and heating equipment in good working order. Always be prepared for fire emergencies with a fire escape route and smoke detectors.

Many injuries during recreational activities are the result of misuse of equipment, lack of experience, use of alcohol, or failure to wear proper safety equipment, such as a bike helmet or seat belt. Practicing motor vehicle safety includes keeping a mechanical vehicle in good working order, avoiding drinking and driving, driving defensively, giving pedestrians the right of way, and keeping noise at a reasonable level.

The proper handling and storage of firearms can help prevent injuries. People should know the gun laws in their state, never point a gun at an unintended target, keep fingers off the trigger, educate children, and keep guns locked away.

INTENTIONAL INJURIES AND VIOLENCE

Violence is defined as the intent to inflict harm on another person through the use of physical force. Social factors, such as violence in the media, and interpersonal factors, such as age, gender, ethnic background, and socioeconomic background, often contribute to violence. Alcohol and drug use often play a role in violent behavior as well.

Battering and forms of child abuse occur at every socioeconomic level. The issue with this type of violence is the need for the abuser to control other people. Child sexual abuse most often results in serious trauma for the child because the abuser is usually a trusted adult. **Rape** is a form of sexual assault that occurs when a person is forced to have sexual intercourse against his or her will. When a person is raped by someone he or she knows socially, it is considered **acquaintance rape** or **date rape**, depending on the level of the relationship between the attacker and victim. In a 2010 CDC Intimate Partner and Sexual Violence Survey, it was reported that most rape victims know their assailants: 51 percent of female victims were sexually assaulted by a current or former intimate partner, and 41 percent were sexually assaulted by an acquaintance. Of men and boys, 52 percent report being sexually assaulted by an acquaintance. **Sexual harassment** is defined as unwelcome sexual advances or other conduct of a sexual nature that have a negative effect on an individual or create an intimidating or hostile environment.

CONSUMER AWARENESS

In general, a person should seek the help of a healthcare professional for symptoms that are severe, unusual, persistent, or recurrent. When new symptoms first occur, there are self-treatment options that may benefit some individuals and certain health issues. When using self-medication, it's important to follow some simple guidelines:

- Read the label and follow the directions carefully.
- Do not exceed the recommended daily dose.

When seeking professional medical treatment, patients have the option of choosing conventional medical care or **complementary and alternative medicine** (**CAM**). CAM practices are not part of conventional or mainstream healthcare or medical practice taught in U.S. medical schools. CAM practices include traditional Chinese medicine (TCM), acupuncture, energy therapies, mind-body interventions, and herbal remedies.

Conventional medicine, also called biomedicine or standard Western medicine, is based on the application of the scientific method. Professionals who practice conventional medicine include doctors of medicine, doctors of osteopathic medicine, podiatrists, optometrists, and dentists. Healthcare in the United States is financed by a combination of private and public insurance plans. Medicare, Medicare Advantage, Medigap, and Medicaid account for 45 percent of patient coverage in the United States.

ENVIRONMENTAL CONCERNS

Environmental health began with the effort to control communicable diseases. It has since expanded to include concern for air quality, global warming, and various forms of pollution, all of which play a role in some infectious and chronic diseases. Increased amounts of air pollutants are especially dangerous for children, elderly adults, and those with chronic health conditions. Some of the gases that are causing damage to our atmosphere and contributing to air pollution are carbon dioxide, carbon monoxide, chlorofluorocarbons (CFCs), methane, and nitrous oxide. Factors that contribute to poor air quality are heavy motor vehicle traffic, burning of fossil fuels, hot weather, and stagnant air.

The **greenhouse effect** occurs as thermal energy from the sun is trapped in the atmosphere by pollutants. This causes a rise in Earth's temperature that, in turn, causes droughts, ice melt, smog, and acid rain. In addition, the ozone layer that shields Earth's surface from the harmful UV rays of the sun is thinning and has developed holes in certain regions, including above Antarctica. Concerns for water quality worldwide focus on pathogenic organisms (bacterial, viral, or protozoan), chemical and hazardous waste, and water shortages, including shortages of clean drinking water. Land pollution is caused by landfills that release chemicals into the ground, pesticides, automobiles, accidental spills, radon gas, and nuclear reactors. Pollution also comes in the form of noise; loud and persistent noise can lead to hearing loss and stress.

SUMMING IT UP

- The six dimensions to overall wellness are physical, spiritual, emotional, intellectual, interpersonal, and environmental.
- The **transtheoretical model** is an effective approach to lifestyle management that includes pre-contemplation, contemplation, preparation, action, maintenance, and termination.
- Psychologist Abraham Maslow developed a pyramid expressing the **hierarchy of human needs**. According to Maslow, these needs move up the pyramid, starting with the most basic needs being **physiological**, then progressing to **safety and security**, **social relationships**, **self-esteem**, and finally, the highest level of need, **self-actualization**. Maslow called those who achieve self-actualization *transcenders*.
- Erik Erikson described eight stages of a human's lifespan:
    1. Birth to one year
    2. One to three years
    3. Three to six years
    4. Six to twelve years
    5. Adolescence
    6. Young adulthood
    7. Middle adulthood
    8. Older adulthood
- Types of **psychological disorders** include anxiety disorders, mood disorders, bipolar disorders, schizophrenia, dissociative disorders, and somatoform disorders.
- **Reproduction** refers to fertility, pregnancy, and various methods of birth control.
    o **Fertilization** starts the process of human development. **Infertility** can be overcome with several methods of treatment.

- **Pregnancy** is divided into three trimesters, each lasting about three months. The birth process takes place in three stages.

- The birth control methods that can be used to prevent unwanted pregnancies are **barrier method**, **intrauterine device**, **hormonal methods**, **natural methods**, and **surgical sterilization**.

- **Human sexual response** goes through the following phases: **excitement**, **plateau**, **orgasmic**, and **resolution**. Two physical responses to arousal are vasocongestion and muscular tension.

- Any type of disturbance in sexual desire, performance ability, or satisfaction is referred to as **sexual dysfunction**.
  - Common male sexual dysfunctions are erectile dysfunction, premature ejaculation, and retarded ejaculation.
  - Common female sexual dysfunction includes lack of desire to have sex, failure to become aroused, and failure to achieve orgasm.

- There are several stages of attraction between individuals: **marketing**, **sharing**, **behavior**, **passionate love**, and **enduring attachment**. Challenges that a relationship faces may include being open and honest, having unrealistic expectations, competitiveness, having unequal or premature commitment, balancing time spent together, jealousy, and supportiveness.

- The four general styles of parenting are **authoritarian**, **authoritative**, **permissive**, and **uninvolved**.

- **Healthy aging** is the process of growing into a productive adult, coping with midlife issues, and facing mortality in a positive, healthy way.

- Kubler-Ross proposed **Five Stages of Grief**:
  1. Denial
  2. Anger
  3. Bargaining
  4. Depression
  5. Acceptance

- **Addictive behaviors** involve habits that have become out of control. Factors leading to addictive behaviors include personality, lifestyle, heredity, social and physical environments, and the nature of the activity or substance.
  - **Drug addiction** is defined as the compulsive desire for a drug, the need to increase drug dosage, harmful effects to the addicted individual and those around him or her, and psychological and physical dependence.

- **Alcohol**, or ethyl alcohol (ethanol), is a form of a psychoactive drug. **Blood alcohol concentration** (BAC) is determined by the volume of alcohol consumed over a given time period and by individual factors, including body weight, percent body fat, and gender.
  - Health problems related to chronic or excessive use of alcohol include diseases of the digestive and cardiovascular systems and some cancers.

- **Nicotine** is the key psychoactive ingredient in tobacco. It affects the nervous system and can act as a stimulant or a depressant.

- Cardiovascular disease, especially **coronary heart disease** (**CHD**), is the most widespread cause of death among cigarette smokers. CHD is often the result of atherosclerosis.

- **Psychoactive drugs** affect the mind and body functions by altering brain chemistry. Psychoactive drugs include alcohol, opioids, central nervous system (CNS) stimulants and depressants, marijuana, hallucinogens, and inhalants.

- The five components of physical fitness are **cardiorespiratory endurance**, **muscular strength**, **muscular endurance**, **flexibility**, and **body composition**.

- There are thirteen vitamins, seventeen minerals, and about forty-five essential nutrients that the body requires to maintain its maximum level of health and well-being.
    - **Macronutrients** include protein, fat, and carbohydrates, and each of these supplies energy to the body in differing amounts.
    - Individuals should limit intake of added sugars and saturated fats to no more than 10 percent of total calories per day each.
    - Sodium should be limited to fewer than 2,300 milligrams per day, and alcohol should be consumed in moderation.

- In order to contract an infectious disease, **an agent**, **an entry point**, **a reservoir**, and **an exit point** are required.
    - The disease-producing agent is a **pathogen**. A pathogen can be **bacterial**, **viral**, or **fungal**.
    - The four basic stages of an infection are **incubation**, **prodromal**, **peak**, and **recovery**.

- The **immune system** is the body's defense system against disease, and defense is carried out by different types of white blood cells that are produced in bone marrow.

- Within the lymphatic system, **lymph nodes** filter bacteria and other substances from the lymph. When the lymph nodes are fighting off an infection, they fill with cells and become swollen. In the lymphatic system, there are two types of lymphocytes: (1) T cells and (2) B cells.

- There are **seven sexually transmitted diseases** (**STDs**) that pose a major health threat:
    1. AIDS
    2. Herpes
    3. Hepatitis
    4. Syphilis
    5. Chlamydia
    6. Gonorrhea
    7. Human papillomavirus (HPV)

- There are **six major preventable risk factors for cardiovascular disease** (**CVD**), including smoking, high blood pressure, unhealthy cholesterol levels, inactive lifestyle, overweight or obesity, and diabetes.

- **Cancer** is due to uncontrolled growth of cells because of genetics, exposure to a mutagen, viral infection, or chemical substances in food and air.

- **Autoimmune disorders** occur when the body comes under attack by its own cells.
  - **Rheumatoid arthritis** (**RA**) is an autoimmune response in which the immune system attacks healthy joint tissue.

- **Diabetes** is a disease in which the pancreas does not produce insulin normally. Insulin is a necessary biological chemical that is used to process sugar in the body. The three types of diabetes are Type I, Type II, and gestational diabetes.

- **Genetic disorders** are diseases that are inherited from biological parents.

- The **nervous system** and **endocrine system** control the body's physical response to stress. Behavioral responses to stressors are controlled by the **somatic nervous system**.

- Hans Seyle's theory on stress is the **General Adaptation Syndrome** (**GAS**), which has three stages:
  1. Alarm
  2. Resistance
  3. Exhaustion

- **Safety issues** include personal safety, residential safety, recreational safety, motor vehicle safety, and gun safety. **Violence** is defined as the intent to inflict harm on another person through the use of physical force.

- When seeking professional medical treatment, patients have the option of choosing **conventional medical care** or **complementary and alternative medicine** (**CAM**).

- **Environmental health** includes concern for air quality, global warming, and various forms of pollution, all of which play a role in some infectious and chronic diseases.

HEALTH AND HUMAN DEVELOPMENT POST-TEST

Directions: Carefully read each of the following 60 questions. Choose the best answer to each question and fill in the corresponding circle on the answer sheet. The Answer Key and Explanations can be found following this post-test.

1. Which type of psychological disorder is characterized as an affective disorder?
   A. Schizophrenia
   B. Stress
   C. Bipolar
   D. Somatoform

2. Which of the following is NOT a risk factor for heart disease that can be controlled?
   A. Weight
   B. Heredity
   C. Physical activity
   D. Hypertension

3. Which of the following are drugs derived from opium?
   A. Hallucinogens
   B. Tranquilizers
   C. Narcotic analgesics
   D. Barbiturates

4. What is the key psychoactive ingredient in tobacco?
   A. Acetone
   B. Toluene
   C. Arsenic
   D. Nicotine

5. Which of the following lists three of the five chief areas of safety concern?
   A. Recreational, residential, personal
   B. Recreational, fire, violence
   C. Experience, personal, residential
   D. Recreational, physical, violence

6. What is the term used for people who reach the highest level in Maslow's Hierarchy of Needs?
   A. Achievers
   B. Needy
   C. Transcenders
   D. Champions

7. The primary stage of Selye's General Adaptation Syndrome (GAS) is
   A. resistance.
   B. compulsion.
   C. exhaustion.
   D. alarm.

8. Which condition is a possible consequence of oral tobacco use?
   A. Scar tissue
   B. Swollen lymph nodes
   C. Leukoplakia
   D. HIV

9. Which type of stress is "good stress" according to Dr. Selye?
   A. Distress
   B. Eustress
   C. Astress
   D. Stressors

10. Which type of nutrient is the most calorie-dense?
    A. Carbohydrates
    B. Fats
    C. Proteins
    D. Fiber

11. Which of the following are fat-soluble vitamins?
    A. Calcium, magnesium, and iron
    B. A, B, C, and D
    C. A, D, E, and K
    D. B, C, and iron

12. Which of the following is an atypical sexual behavior that causes harm to one's self or others?
    A. Shared touching
    B. Transsexualism
    C. Paraphilia
    D. Masturbation

13. When referring to checking for melanoma, what does ABCD stand for?
    A. Abnormal, Blending, Color variation, Description
    B. Asymmetry, Border irregularity, Color variation, Diameter
    C. Asymmetry, Big, Color variation, Deformed
    D. Abnormal, Border irregularity, Color variation, Depth

14. What are the two forms of dietary fiber?
    A. Organic and inorganic
    B. Vegetable and mineral
    C. Soluble and insoluble
    D. Carbohydrate and fat

15. A vaccine can instill which type of immunity?
    A. Naturally acquired immunity
    B. Passively acquired immunity
    C. Artificially acquired immunity
    D. Actively acquired immunity

16. Which of the following hormones is responsible for breast development in females?
    A. Testosterone
    B. Progesterone
    C. Androgen
    D. Cortisol

17. What is the hormone cortisol secreted in response to?
    A. Puberty
    B. Release of ovum
    C. Exhaustion
    D. Stress

18. Which factor would be used to calculate your target heart rate for aerobic activity?
    A. Weight
    B. Body mass
    C. Age
    D. Muscle density

19. Which of the following refers to hardening of the arteries?
    A. Arteriosclerosis
    B. Atherosclerosis
    C. Angina pectoris
    D. Hypertension

20. What does HIV stand for?
    A. Human immune virus
    B. Human immunodeficiency virus
    C. Habitual immunodeficiency virus
    D. Habitual immune virus

21. Which of the following is best categorized as a way to ensure personal safety?
    A. Wear a bicycle helmet.
    B. Have a fire escape plan.
    C. Avoid atypical patterns.
    D. Drive defensively.

22. Which type of depression is best controlled by medication?
    A. Primary depression
    B. Secondary depression
    C. Seasonal affective disorder
    D. Loneliness

23. Which neurological disorder has traits similar to autism?
    A. Huntington's disease
    B. Rett syndrome
    C. Muscular dystrophy
    D. Neurofibromatosis

24. An agent or particle that causes disease is known as a(n)
   A. vaccine.
   B. antibody.
   C. antagonist.
   D. pathogen.

25. Which of the following is NOT considered an assisted reproductive technology (ART) treatment?
   A. *In vitro* fertilization.
   B. Intrauterine insemination
   C. Gonadatrophin injections
   D. Gamete intrafallopian transfer

26. Amniocentesis can detect which of the following abnormalities?
   A. Diabetes
   B. Cleft palate
   C. Cystic fibrosis
   D. Phocomelia

27. Which of the following types of cancer develops in connective tissue?
   A. Melanoma
   B. Sarcoma
   C. Leukemia
   D. Carcinoma

28. Which type of specialist would be considered part of CAM healthcare?
   A. Dentist
   B. Registered nurse
   C. Herbalist
   D. Midwife

29. The five stages of grieving according to Kubler-Ross are
   A. denial, anger, bargaining, depression, acceptance.
   B. denial, pleading, grief, rage, closure.
   C. sadness, anger, grief, closure, moving on.
   D. sadness, crying, anger, closure, moving on.

30. Unwelcome sexual advances that have a negative effect on an individual is the definition of
   A. sexism.
   B. sexual harassment.
   C. sexual misconduct.
   D. rape.

31. Which of the following would be classified as a CNS depressant?
   A. Hydrocodone
   B. Cocaine
   C. Valium
   D. Ephedrine

32. Which of the following psychological disorders is linked to anxiety?
   A. Phobias
   B. Depression
   C. Schizophrenia
   D. Bipolar

33. Which dimension of health focuses on understanding self-purpose?
   A. Physical
   B. Intellectual
   C. Emotional
   D. Spiritual

34. Which is the most dangerous type of drug dependence?
   A. Physical
   B. Psychological
   C. Emotional
   D. Tolerance

35. What is the most basic level of need according to Maslow?
   A. Love
   B. Physiological
   C. Esteem
   D. Self-actualization

36. Which of the following is a symptom of physical dependence on a drug?
    A. A drug user gets a headache shortly after using his/her drug of choice.
    B. A drug user gets a headache after not using his/her drug of choice for a prolonged period of time.
    C. A drug user gets a headache while self-administering his/her drug of choice.
    D. A drug user gets daily headaches whether using his/her drug of choice or not.

37. Which of the following is one of the goals of the National Healthy People Initiative?
    A. Eliminate economic disparities among Americans
    B. Eliminate health disparities among Americans
    C. Focus on holistic health for all Americans
    D. Focus on making alcohol and tobacco illegal

38. Which of the following is defined as an interpersonal factor that may contribute to violence and intentional injury?
    A. Social factors
    B. Gender
    C. Violence in the media
    D. Address

39. What does set point theory propose?
    A. Dieting is a successful way to lose weight and keep it off without problems.
    B. Environmental factors are the strongest indicators of weight fluctuation.
    C. The body has a weight it tends to remain at making weight change hard to accomplish.
    D. Eating nutritious foods will lower weight and readjust the body.

40. Which of the following describes an authoritative parenting style?
    A. High demandingness, low responsiveness
    B. High demandingness, high responsiveness
    C. Low demandingness, high responsiveness
    D. Low demandingness, low responsiveness

41. Where is the primary site of alcohol metabolism in the body?
    A. Intestines
    B. Stomach
    C. Liver
    D. Kidneys

42. What would identify tolerance in someone who uses alcohol or other forms of drugs?
    A. Headaches when the individual stops using the substance
    B. The need for greater amounts of a substance in order to maintain the same feeling
    C. Sudden onset of depression or anxiety
    D. The compulsive desire or need for the drug

43. Which of the following best describes anaerobic exercise?
    A. Respiration of oxygen in the lungs
    B. Insufficient oxygen supply to reach all muscles
    C. Cardiorespiratory endurance
    D. Continuous rhythmic movements

44. The belief that you are sick without any medical data to support this claim is a
    A. dissociative disorder.
    B. mood disorder.
    C. disorder.
    D. seasonal affective disorder.

45. How would a doctor initially check for the location of an infection in the lymph nodes?

    A. The doctor would need to look at an x-ray.

    B. The doctor would check for signs of heat.

    C. The doctor would have to run blood work.

    D. The doctor would look for swelling.

46. The initial stage of attraction between two individuals is

    A. behavior.

    B. sharing.

    C. marketing.

    D. mutual support.

47. Which type of fat provides health benefits?

    A. Saturated

    B. Trans fatty acid

    C. Hydrogenated oils

    D. Omega-3

48. The R-I-C-E method of treating muscle and joint injury includes

    A. rest, independence, compassion, and emotion.

    B. regular, intervals, conditioning, and endurance.

    C. rest, ice, conditioning, and endurance.

    D. rest, ice, compression, and elevation.

49. The cluster of cells that implants into the endometrial lining of the uterus is called a

    A. zygote.

    B. fetus.

    C. blastocyst.

    D. ovum.

50. Which type of white blood cell devours pathogens and dead cells as part of the body's immune system?

    A. Neutrophils

    B. Lymphocytes

    C. Dendrite cells

    D. Macrophages

51. Which STD is caused by an inflammation of the liver and can be transmitted through both sexual and nonsexual contact?

    A. Human immunodeficiency virus

    B. Human papillomavirus

    C. Genital herpes

    D. Hepatitis B

52. The most common viral STD in the United States is

    A. AIDS.

    B. HPV.

    C. HSV-1.

    D. HSV-2.

53. Which of the following best describes the greenhouse effect?

    A. Thermal energy is trapped in Earth's atmosphere by air pollutants.

    B. Sunlight is getting more powerful.

    C. Holes in the ozone layer allow more heat from the sun in the atmosphere.

    D. Many green plants are able to grow in certain regions of Earth.

54. Which of the following shields Earth's surface from the sun's harmful rays?

    A. Oxygen

    B. Methane

    C. Ozone

    D. Carbon

post-test

55. Which disease can occur when the pancreas does not produce insulin properly?
    A. Hemophilia
    B. Diabetes
    C. Huntington's disease
    D. Cystic fibrosis

56. What does the "U" stand for in the acronym CAUTION used to describe early detection of cancer?
    A. Unusual growths
    B. Unusual weight loss
    C. Unusual bleeding or discharge
    D. Unusual symptoms

57. Which of the following would increase the rate of absorption of alcohol into the bloodstream?
    A. Drinking with a full stomach
    B. Switching from beer to wine
    C. Carbonation in the alcoholic drink
    D. Heavier body weight

58. During which stage of labor is the cervix opened completely?
    A. First stage
    B. Second stage
    C. Third stage
    D. Postpartum stage

59. The most widespread cause of death among cigarette smokers is
    A. cancer.
    B. cardiovascular disease.
    C. bronchitis.
    D. chronic obstructive pulmonary disease (COPD).

60. Progressive resistance exercises are called
    A. isotonic.
    B. isokinetic.
    C. isometric.
    D. stretching.

ANSWER KEY AND EXPLANATIONS

1. C	13. B	25. C	37. B	49. C
2. B	14. C	26. C	38. B	50. D
3. C	15. C	27. B	39. C	51. D
4. D	16. B	28. C	40. B	52. B
5. A	17. D	29. A	41. C	53. A
6. C	18. C	30. B	42. B	54. C
7. D	19. A	31. C	43. B	55. B
8. C	20. B	32. A	44. C	56. C
9. B	21. C	33. D	45. D	57. C
10. B	22. A	34. A	46. C	58. A
11. C	23. B	35. B	47. D	59. B
12. C	24. D	36. B	48. D	60. A

1. **The correct answer is C**. Bipolar disorder is characterized as an affective or mood disorder. Choice A is incorrect because schizophrenic disorders are characterized by disorganized thought and distortions of reality. Choice B is incorrect because stress is a response to a change in environment, whether positive or negative, not a psychological disorder. Choice D is incorrect because somatoform disorders are physical ailments without a medical condition to support them.

2. **The correct answer is B**. An individual is not capable of controlling inherited factors, and some hereditary factors put individuals at a higher risk for heart disease. Choice A is incorrect because weight can be controlled by diet and exercise. Choice C is incorrect because an individual has control over his or her level of physical activity. Choice D is incorrect because hypertension can be controlled with exercise, diet, weight management, and medicine.

3. **The correct answer is C**. Drugs derived from opium are called narcotic analgesics. Choice A is incorrect because hallucinogens are either chemically synthesized or derived from mescaline (cactus). Choice B is incorrect because tranquilizers are sedatives produced synthetically. Choice D is incorrect because barbiturates are also produced by synthetic methods.

4. **The correct answer is D**. Nicotine is the key psychoactive ingredient in tobacco. Choices A, B, and C are incorrect because they are all poisonous chemicals in tobacco smoke but not the key psychoactive ingredient in tobacco.

5. **The correct answer is A**. Many injuries are caused by the interaction of humans with environmental factors, and the chief areas of safety concern are (1) personal, (2) residential, (3) recreational, (4) motor vehicle, and (5) gun use. Choice B is incorrect because fire and violence are not categories of individual safety. Choice C is incorrect because experience is not an area of safety concern, although lack of experience can be classified as a concern when operating motor vehicles. Choice D is incorrect because violence and physical concerns are not individual safety categories.

6. **The correct answer is C**. People who reach self-actualization, the highest level of Maslow's Hierarchy of Needs, are called transcenders.

7. **The correct answer is D**. The first stage of Dr. Hans Selye's GAS theory is alarm, also known as the fight-or-flight stage. Choice A is incorrect because resistance is the second stage in the GAS theory. Choice B

is incorrect because compulsion is not a stage of the GAS theory. Choice C is incorrect because exhaustion is the third stage of the GAS theory.

8. **The correct answer is C**. Leukoplakia is a condition characterized by white patches on the tongue that aren't easily removed and are usually the result of excess oral tobacco use. Choice A is incorrect because scar tissue isn't a result of too much tobacco use. Choice B is incorrect because swollen lymph nodes are a symptom of an infection. Choice D is incorrect because HIV is a virus that can lead to the development of AIDS.

9. **The correct answer is B**. The term *eustress* refers to good stress on the body, such as during exercise or stress induced by the desire to do well at something. Choice A is incorrect because distress is usually considered "bad stress." Choice C is incorrect because the term *astress* is not a psychological term. Choice D is incorrect because stressors are factors that can cause any type of stress.

10. **The correct answer is B**. Fats are the most calorie-dense nutrients; there are nine calories per one gram of fat. Choices A and C are incorrect because carbohydrates and proteins both have seven calories per gram. Choice D is incorrect because fiber is a type of carbohydrate and has seven calories per gram.

11. **The correct answer is C**. Fat-soluble vitamins include A, D, E, and K. Choice A is incorrect because calcium, magnesium, and iron are minerals, not vitamins. Choice B is incorrect because the B vitamins and vitamin C are water-soluble. Choice D is incorrect because iron is not a vitamin; it's a mineral.

12. **The correct answer is C**. Paraphilia is any sexual act that causes harm to one's self or others. Choice A is incorrect because shared touching is usually done with mutual consent between two individuals. Choice B is incorrect because transsexualism refers to cases where an individual's gender doesn't match gender identity. Choice D is incorrect because masturbation is a form of self-stimulation and is generally not harmful.

13. **The correct answer is B**. The ABCD test for melanoma refers to checking a mole for asymmetry, border irregularity, color variation, and a diameter larger than a quarter of an inch. Choices A, C, and D are incorrect because these aren't the criteria for checking for the properties of a melanoma.

14. **The correct answer is C**. The two forms of dietary fiber are soluble and insoluble. Both are derived from indigestible plant material. Choice A is incorrect because all fiber is organic material. Choice B is incorrect because fiber is not a mineral. Choice D is incorrect because all fiber derived from plants is a source of carbohydrates and fats are not fiber.

15. **The correct answer is C**. A vaccine is an injection of either an inactivated or a live virus that builds up immunity in the body. This is a form of artificially acquired immunity. Choice A is incorrect because naturally acquired immunity occurs when the body builds up immunity after being exposed to a disease. Choice B is incorrect because passively acquired immunity is the process of using antibodies to develop immunity. Choice D is incorrect because actively acquired immunity is not a type of immunity.

16. **The correct answer is B**. Progesterone and estrogen cause breast development in females. Choices A and C are incorrect because testosterone and androgen are responsible for genital development in males. Choice D is incorrect because Cortisol is a hormone released in response to stress.

17. **The correct answer is D**. Cortisol is a hormone that is released in conjunction with epinephrine in response to stress. Choice A is incorrect because cortisol is not a sex hormone that is elevated during puberty. Choice B is incorrect because estradiol and LSH are released during ovulation. Choice C is incorrect because cortisol is released as a response to stress, not exhaustion.

18. **The correct answer is C**. Choices A, B, and D are not used to calculate target heart rate. This leaves choice C as the correct answer. One's target heart rate for aerobic exercise is calculated by subtracting age from 220 and

then multiplying that number by a range of .65 to .85.

19. **The correct answer is A**. Choice B is incorrect because atherosclerosis refers to the buildup of plaque inside the walls of the heart. Choice C is incorrect because angina pectoris refers to chest pain caused by an insufficient amount of oxygen reaching the heart. Choice D is incorrect because hypertension refers to high blood pressure.

20. **The correct answer is B**. HIV is a virus that attacks the immune system and is called human immunodeficiency virus. All other choices are incorrect.

21. **The correct answer is C**. Avoiding atypical patterns, especially after dark, is one way to ensure personal safety. Choice A is incorrect because wearing a bicycle helmet is best categorized as recreational safety. Choice B is incorrect because planning a fire escape route is a part of residential safety. Choice D is incorrect because driving defensively is categorized as motor vehicle safety.

22. **The correct answer is A**. Antidepressants are most successful in the treatment of primary depression. Choice B is incorrect because secondary depression is linked to a traumatic event and best treated by therapy. Choice C is incorrect because seasonal affective disorder is related to the amount of sunlight a person receives and is treated with exposure to UV light. Choice D is incorrect because loneliness is not a form of depression.

23. **The correct answer is B**. Rett syndrome is a neurological disorder, most common in girls, with traits similar to autism. Choice A is incorrect because Huntington's disease is a genetic disorder in which there is a degeneration of brain cells. Choice C is incorrect because muscular dystrophy is a genetic disorder in which there is a degeneration of skeletal muscles. Choice D is incorrect because neurofibromatosis is a genetic disorder that causes tumors to grow in the nervous system.

24. **The correct answer is D**. Choice A is incorrect because a vaccine is used to prevent infection. Choice B is incorrect because antibodies are used to fight against infection.

Choice C is incorrect because an agent of infection is referred to as a pathogen, not an antagonist.

25. **The correct answer is C**. Gonadatrophin is a fertility drug used to help women ovulate, and administering injections of the drug is not considered an ART treatment. Choice A is incorrect because *in vitro* fertilization is the process of fertilizing several eggs with sperm outside the woman's body and then reinserting them. Choice B is incorrect because in intrauterine insemination is the placement of a man's sperm into a woman's uterus using a long, narrow tube. Choice D is incorrect because gamete intrafallopian transfer (GIFT) is removal of the egg from the ovary and mechanical insertion into the fallopian tube. Sperm is then added in hopes of fertilization. These three procedures fall under the category of ART treatments.

26. **The correct answer is C**. Cystic fibrosis, the fatal accumulation of too much mucus in the lungs, is the result of a genetic abnormality and can be detected through amniocentesis. Choice A is incorrect because diabetes isn't detected before birth. Choice B is incorrect because a cleft palate is a physical abnormality and isn't detected by amniocentesis. Choice D is incorrect because the short limbs associated with phocomelia are not detected by amniocentesis.

27. **The correct answer is B**. Sarcoma is cancer that begins in connective tissue. Sarcomas are very rare and only account for 2 percent of all cancers. Choice A is incorrect because melanoma originates in the skin. Choice C is incorrect because leukemia is a cancer that originates in the blood. Choice D is incorrect because carcinoma doesn't originate in connective tissue.

28. **The correct answer is C**. An herbalist would be considered a part of complementary and alternative medicine (CAM). Choices A, B, and D are incorrect because all of these professionals practice conventional medicine.

29. **The correct answer is A**. According to the process of grieving outlined by Kubler-Ross, the five stages of grief are denial, anger,

bargaining, depression, and acceptance. Choices B, C, and D are incorrect.

30. **The correct answer is B**. Sexual harassment is defined as unwelcome sexual advances or other conduct of a sexual nature that have a negative effect on an individual or create an intimidating or hostile environment. Choice A is incorrect because sexism is discrimination against an individual based on his or her sex. Choice C is incorrect because sexual misconduct is a more general term, whereas sexual harassment is more specific to the actions and language that are unwelcome. Choice D is incorrect because rape involves the act of sexual intercourse against an individual's will.

31. **The correct answer is C**. Valium is classified as a CNS depressant. It reduces anxiety and helps individuals calm down. Choice A is incorrect because hydrocodone is an opioid. Choices B and D are incorrect because cocaine and ephedrine are CNS stimulants.

32. **The correct answer is A**. Phobias are a psychological disorder linked to anxiety. Choice B is incorrect because depression is an affective disorder. Choice C is incorrect because schizophrenia is a disorder linked to hallucinations and distortion. Choice D is incorrect because bipolar is an affective disorder.

33. **The correct answer is D**. Spiritual health focuses on the ability to understand one's purpose in the world and the ability to serve others. Choice A is incorrect because physical health focuses on physical wellness. Choice B is incorrect because intellectual health focuses on creativity and problem solving. Choice C is incorrect because emotional health focuses on the ability to deal with stress and conflict and to have emotionally appropriate responses to external stimuli.

34. **The correct answer is A**. Physical dependence is the most dangerous type of drug dependence; bodily functions become dependent on a drug. Choice B is incorrect because psychological dependence is a mental state and easier to overcome than physical dependence. Choice C is incorrect because emotional dependence falls into the category of psychological dependence. Choice D is incorrect because tolerance isn't a type of drug dependence.

35. **The correct answer is B**. Physiological needs such as food and shelter are humans' most basic needs. Choice A is incorrect because according to Maslow, love falls under the third level of need. Choice C is incorrect because esteem is the fourth hierarchical level of need. Choice D is incorrect because self-actualization is the highest level of need.

36. **The correct answer is B**. Headaches (and other types of physical pain) are a symptom of physical drug dependence, and these can occur when a user stops using his/her drug of choice. Choices A, D, and C are incorrect because headaches typically do not develop in these scenarios.

37. **The correct answer is B**. The National Healthy People Initiative has two broad goals: to increase the quality and years of healthy life for, and to eliminate health disparities among, population groups in the United States. Choice A is incorrect because the Healthy People Initiative doesn't focus on economic measures. Choice C is incorrect because the Healthy People Initiative isn't limited to a holistic approach. Choice D is incorrect because the Healthy People Initiative isn't trying to eliminate tobacco and alcohol.

38. **The correct answer is B**. There are several interpersonal factors that contribute to violence: gender, age, ethnic background, and socioeconomic background. Choice A is incorrect because social factors are different contributing factors to violence. Choice C is incorrect because violence in the media is considered a social factor that contributes to violence and intentional injury. Choice D is incorrect because one's address is a social, not an interpersonal, factor.

39. **The correct answer is C**. Set point theory proposes that the body prefers to stay at its current weight, making it difficult for weight to adjust with diet. Choice A is incorrect because weight loss would be difficult to maintain. Choice B is incorrect because set point theory proposes genetic rather than

environmental influences, which also makes Choice D incorrect because nutritious foods would not influence the set weight.

40. **The correct answer is B**. An authoritative parenting style is one involving high demandingness and high responsiveness. Choice A is incorrect because high demandingness and low responsiveness is characteristic of an authoritarian style of parenting. Choice C is incorrect because low demandingness and high responsiveness is characteristic of a permissive parenting style. Choice D is incorrect because low demandingness and low responsiveness is characteristic of an uninvolved parenting style.

41. **The correct answer is C**. Choices A and B are incorrect because most alcohol is metabolized in the liver, not in the intestines or the stomach. Choice D is incorrect because only about 2 percent of alcohol is not metabolized in the liver and is excreted by the lungs, kidneys, and sweat glands.

42. **The correct answer is B**. Tolerance occurs as an individual needs an increasing amount of the substance in order to get the same feeling. Choice A is incorrect because headaches would be an indication of dependence and withdrawal. Choice C is incorrect because depression would be an indication of dependence and withdrawal. Choice D is incorrect because the need for the drug indicates addiction.

43. **The correct answer is B**. During anaerobic exercise, the body cannot be oxygenated fast enough to supply energy to muscles from oxygen alone. Choice A may seem like a good answer, but it doesn't relate to anaerobic exercise. Choices C and D are incorrect because they describe aerobic exercise.

44. **The correct answer is C**. With a somatoform disorder, an individual presents physical ailments without any medical condition to support these ailments. Choice A is incorrect because dissociative disorders can cause a sudden, but temporary, change in identity or consciousness. Choice B is incorrect because a mood disorder is itself a category of disorders. Choice D is incorrect

because seasonal affective disorder is a form of depression.

45. **The correct answer is D**. The doctor would be able to determine the location of the infection by looking for swelling in the lymph nodes. Choices A and C are incorrect because there would be no need for an x-ray or blood work to determine the location. Choice B is incorrect because heat would not necessarily be present.

46. **The correct answer is C**. There are several stages of attraction between two people, and the initial stage is defined as marketing, during which an individual will market his or her best self. Choice A is incorrect because the behavior stage of attraction is the third stage in which a relationship develops into friendship or passionate love. Choice B is incorrect because the sharing phase of attraction is the second stage. Choice D is incorrect because mutual support develops in the last stage of attraction.

47. **The correct answer is D**. Omega-3 fatty acids provide health benefits, including reducing the risk of heart attacks. Choice A is incorrect because saturated fats pose health risks. Choice B is incorrect because trans fats pose health risks. Choice C is incorrect because hydrogenated oils are trans fats.

48. **The correct answer is D**. Muscle and joint injuries can be treated with rest, ice, compression, and elevation. Choices A, B, and C are incorrect because they don't describe the components of the R-I-C-E method.

49. **The correct answer is C**. The cluster of cells that grows after an egg has been fertilized and implants in the endometrial lining is called a blastocyst. Choice A is incorrect because once the egg is fertilized by a sperm, it becomes a zygote. Choice B is incorrect because after the blastocyst implants in the endometrial lining, it develops into a fetus. Choice D is incorrect because an ovum is an unfertilized egg.

50. **The correct answer is D**. Macrophages devour pathogens and dead cells. Choice A is incorrect because neutrophils travel in the blood stream to the infection. Choice B is incorrect because lymphocytes travel

through the blood stream and the lymphatic system. Choice C is incorrect because dendrite cells eat pathogens and activate lymphocytes.

51. **The correct answer is D.** Hepatitis B causes inflammation of the liver and can be transmitted sexually, through intravenous drug use, and during pregnancy and delivery. Choice A is incorrect because human immunodeficiency virus compromises the immune system and is spread through bodily fluids. Choice B is incorrect because human papillomavirus is spread sexually and can cause genital warts and certain cancers. Choice C is incorrect because genital herpes is transmitted through sexual activity.

52. **The correct answer is B.** The human papillomavirus (HPV) is the most common STD, infecting approximately 6.2 million Americans each year. Choice A is incorrect because although AIDS is an STD, it isn't the most commonly spread STD. Choices C and D are incorrect because herpes simplex virus 1 and 2 are not more common than HPV.

53. **The correct answer is A.** The greenhouse effect occurs as thermal energy from the sun is trapped in the atmosphere by air pollutants, which causes Earth's temperature to rise. Choice B is incorrect because the sun's effects on Earth may be getting stronger, but the sun is not getting more powerful. Choice C is incorrect because holes in the ozone layer contribute to a rise in Earth's temperature, but it is air pollution that causes the greenhouse effect. Choice D is incorrect because it doesn't describe the greenhouse effect.

54. **The correct answer is C.** The ozone layer protects Earth's surface from the harmful UV rays of the sun. Choice A is incorrect because oxygen does not protect Earth's surface. Choices B and D are incorrect because in various forms methane and carbon are harmful to Earth's surface.

55. **The correct answer is B.** Diabetes is a disease in which the pancreas does not produce insulin normally. Hemophilia (choice A) is passed from gene-carrying mothers to sons. Huntington's disease (choice C) is characterized by degeneration of cells in certain parts of the brain. Cystic fibrosis (choice D) is a fatal condition caused by a defective gene prompting the body to produce a sticky mucus in the lungs.

56. **The correct answer is C.** The "U" in the CAUTION acronym stands for unusual bleeding or discharge, which is a possible sign of cancer. Choices A, B, and D are incorrect because they don't describe what the "U" stands for.

57. **The correct answer is C.** Carbonation in a drink can increase the rate of alcohol absorption into the bloodstream. Choice A is incorrect because drinking on a full stomach can decrease absorption. Choice B is incorrect because the type of drink does not matter for absorption, other than carbonation or artificial sweetener. Choice D is incorrect because the heavier body mass will not affect absorption rate.

58. **The correct answer is A.** During transition, the cervix dilates to ten centimeters and is fully open. Choice B is incorrect because during the second stage of labor, the cervix is already fully dilated and the mother pushes the baby out. Choice C is incorrect because the placenta is delivered in the third stage. Choice D is incorrect because during the postpartum phase, the body begins to return to its pre-pregnancy state.

59. **The correct answer is B.** The most widespread cause of death among cigarette smokers is cardiovascular disease and in particular coronary heart disease. Choice A is incorrect because, although cigarette smoking is a primary cause of lung cancer and can cause other cancers, cardiovascular disease is responsible for more deaths among cigarette smokers. Choice C is incorrect because bronchitis is a result of cigarette smoking, but it isn't a leading cause of death. Choice D is incorrect because COPD is a result of cigarette smoking but is not the leading cause of death among smokers.

60. **The correct answer is A.** Isotonic exercises are progressive resistance exercises that provide a fixed amount of resistance. Choice B is incorrect because isokinetic exercises are those that include a range of motion and resistance from a mechanical source. Choice C is incorrect because isometric exercises are static. Choice D is incorrect because stretching is done to increase flexibility and prevent injury.

answers post-test

Computing and Information Technology

OVERVIEW

Chapter 4

The DSST® Computing and Information Technology exam consists of 100 multiple-choice questions that cover the use and social impact of computers and related technology. The exam focuses upon the following topics: hardware; software licensing and development tools; development life cycles; data management; connectivity; privacy concerns; intellectual property; network etiquette; telecommunications law; and globalization. Careful reading, critical thinking, and logical analysis will be as important as your knowledge of computer systems.

Note: You will be allowed to use a nonprogrammable calculator during this test. Scratch paper for computations will be provided onsite. A calculator function is available to those taking the computer-based version of the test.

DIAGNOSTIC TEST ANSWER SHEET

1. Ⓐ Ⓑ Ⓒ Ⓓ   5. Ⓐ Ⓑ Ⓒ Ⓓ   9. Ⓐ Ⓑ Ⓒ Ⓓ   13. Ⓐ Ⓑ Ⓒ Ⓓ   17. Ⓐ Ⓑ Ⓒ Ⓓ

2. Ⓐ Ⓑ Ⓒ Ⓓ   6. Ⓐ Ⓑ Ⓒ Ⓓ   10. Ⓐ Ⓑ Ⓒ Ⓓ   14. Ⓐ Ⓑ Ⓒ Ⓓ   18. Ⓐ Ⓑ Ⓒ Ⓓ

3. Ⓐ Ⓑ Ⓒ Ⓓ   7. Ⓐ Ⓑ Ⓒ Ⓓ   11. Ⓐ Ⓑ Ⓒ Ⓓ   15. Ⓐ Ⓑ Ⓒ Ⓓ   19. Ⓐ Ⓑ Ⓒ Ⓓ

4. Ⓐ Ⓑ Ⓒ Ⓓ   8. Ⓐ Ⓑ Ⓒ Ⓓ   12. Ⓐ Ⓑ Ⓒ Ⓓ   16. Ⓐ Ⓑ Ⓒ Ⓓ   20. Ⓐ Ⓑ Ⓒ Ⓓ

POST-TEST ANSWER SHEET

1. Ⓐ Ⓑ Ⓒ Ⓓ   13. Ⓐ Ⓑ Ⓒ Ⓓ   25. Ⓐ Ⓑ Ⓒ Ⓓ   37. Ⓐ Ⓑ Ⓒ Ⓓ   49. Ⓐ Ⓑ Ⓒ Ⓓ

2. Ⓐ Ⓑ Ⓒ Ⓓ   14. Ⓐ Ⓑ Ⓒ Ⓓ   26. Ⓐ Ⓑ Ⓒ Ⓓ   38. Ⓐ Ⓑ Ⓒ Ⓓ   50. Ⓐ Ⓑ Ⓒ Ⓓ

3. Ⓐ Ⓑ Ⓒ Ⓓ   15. Ⓐ Ⓑ Ⓒ Ⓓ   27. Ⓐ Ⓑ Ⓒ Ⓓ   39. Ⓐ Ⓑ Ⓒ Ⓓ   51. Ⓐ Ⓑ Ⓒ Ⓓ

4. Ⓐ Ⓑ Ⓒ Ⓓ   16. Ⓐ Ⓑ Ⓒ Ⓓ   28. Ⓐ Ⓑ Ⓒ Ⓓ   40. Ⓐ Ⓑ Ⓒ Ⓓ   52. Ⓐ Ⓑ Ⓒ Ⓓ

5. Ⓐ Ⓑ Ⓒ Ⓓ   17. Ⓐ Ⓑ Ⓒ Ⓓ   29. Ⓐ Ⓑ Ⓒ Ⓓ   41. Ⓐ Ⓑ Ⓒ Ⓓ   53. Ⓐ Ⓑ Ⓒ Ⓓ

6. Ⓐ Ⓑ Ⓒ Ⓓ   18. Ⓐ Ⓑ Ⓒ Ⓓ   30. Ⓐ Ⓑ Ⓒ Ⓓ   42. Ⓐ Ⓑ Ⓒ Ⓓ   54. Ⓐ Ⓑ Ⓒ Ⓓ

7. Ⓐ Ⓑ Ⓒ Ⓓ   19. Ⓐ Ⓑ Ⓒ Ⓓ   31. Ⓐ Ⓑ Ⓒ Ⓓ   43. Ⓐ Ⓑ Ⓒ Ⓓ   55. Ⓐ Ⓑ Ⓒ Ⓓ

8. Ⓐ Ⓑ Ⓒ Ⓓ   20. Ⓐ Ⓑ Ⓒ Ⓓ   32. Ⓐ Ⓑ Ⓒ Ⓓ   44. Ⓐ Ⓑ Ⓒ Ⓓ   56. Ⓐ Ⓑ Ⓒ Ⓓ

9. Ⓐ Ⓑ Ⓒ Ⓓ   21. Ⓐ Ⓑ Ⓒ Ⓓ   33. Ⓐ Ⓑ Ⓒ Ⓓ   45. Ⓐ Ⓑ Ⓒ Ⓓ   57. Ⓐ Ⓑ Ⓒ Ⓓ

10. Ⓐ Ⓑ Ⓒ Ⓓ   22. Ⓐ Ⓑ Ⓒ Ⓓ   34. Ⓐ Ⓑ Ⓒ Ⓓ   46. Ⓐ Ⓑ Ⓒ Ⓓ   58. Ⓐ Ⓑ Ⓒ Ⓓ

11. Ⓐ Ⓑ Ⓒ Ⓓ   23. Ⓐ Ⓑ Ⓒ Ⓓ   35. Ⓐ Ⓑ Ⓒ Ⓓ   47. Ⓐ Ⓑ Ⓒ Ⓓ   59. Ⓐ Ⓑ Ⓒ Ⓓ

12. Ⓐ Ⓑ Ⓒ Ⓓ   24. Ⓐ Ⓑ Ⓒ Ⓓ   36. Ⓐ Ⓑ Ⓒ Ⓓ   48. Ⓐ Ⓑ Ⓒ Ⓓ   60. Ⓐ Ⓑ Ⓒ Ⓓ

COMPUTING AND INFORMATION TECHNOLOGY DIAGNOSTIC TEST

Directions: Carefully read each of the following 20 questions. Choose the best answer to each question and fill in the corresponding circle on the answer sheet. The Answer Key and Explanations can be found following this Diagnostic Test.

1. What term describes application software that is free to use on a trial basis?
   A. Commercial
   B. System
   C. Open source
   D. Shareware

2. Which of the following networks is typically limited to a single office building?
   A. WAN
   B. PAN
   C. MAN
   D. LAN

3. Which of the following involved the use of the first digital computer?
   A. World War I
   B. World War II
   C. Korean War
   D. Vietnam War

4. What is the term for a utility program that is used to block certain websites from children?
   A. Defragmenter
   B. Antivirus
   C. Filtering
   D. Backup

5. What is the term for sending fraudulent e-mails intended to fool users into revealing personal information?
   A. Phishing
   B. Encrypting
   C. Streaming
   D. Hacking

6. Which stage of the software life cycle usually involves testing the software?
   A. Investigation
   B. Analysis
   C. Development
   D. Design

7. What is the term for a tiny piece of silicon containing electronic circuits that serves as the CPU of personal computers?
   A. Server
   B. Hard disk
   C. Peripheral
   D. Microprocessor

8. What is the term for software that allows multiple users to collaborate on a project and share data?
   A. Groupware
   B. Freeware
   C. Shareware
   D. Demoware

9. Which of the following is a malicious program that repeatedly copies itself into a computer's memory?
   A. Worm
   B. Spam
   C. Firewall
   D. Key logger

10. ARPANET was developed in
    A. 1959.
    B. 1969.
    C. 1979.
    D. 1989.

11. Which of the following computers is built into devices such as digital cameras and MP3 players?
    A. Supercomputer
    B. Microcontroller
    C. Microcomputer
    D. Mainframe

12. Which of the following security tools requires a person's fingerprint before allowing computer access?
    A. Biometrics
    B. Encryption
    C. Firewall
    D. Password

13. Which of the following is a program that enables peripherals to communicate with a computer system?
    A. Utility software
    B. Operating system
    C. Device driver
    D. User interface

14. Which of the following licensing agreements is displayed on the screen during software installation?
    A. Shrink-wrap
    B. End-user
    C. Multiple-user
    D. Single-user

15. What is the term for a full-duplex device that connects computers to a network?
    A. Hub
    B. Node
    C. Switch
    D. Gateway

16. Which programming language is the oldest one used for business and finance-related systems?
    A. COBOL
    B. BASIC
    C. FORTRAN
    D. NOMAD

17. Which of the following is a textual portrayal of a writer's mood or intention often used in e-mails?
    A. Handshaking
    B. Netiquette
    C. Emoticon
    D. Blog

18. What is the term for the process of loading an operating system into the main memory of the computer?
    A. Booting
    B. Queuing
    C. Spooling
    D. Multitasking

19. What is the term for the temporary holding location for data and the operating system while the computer is on?
    A. ROM
    B. BMP
    C. RAM
    D. JPEG

20. Which application software program is considered a spreadsheet?
    A. Microsoft Excel
    B. Microsoft Word
    C. Oracle
    D. PeopleSoft

ANSWER KEY AND EXPLANATIONS

1. D	**5.** A	**9.** A	**13.** C	**17.** C
2. D	**6.** C	**10.** B	**14.** B	**18.** A
3. B	**7.** D	**11.** B	**15.** C	**19.** C
4. C	**8.** A	**12.** A	**16.** A	**20.** A

1. **The correct answer is D.** Shareware is software available at no cost on a trial basis. Users must pay to continue using shareware at the end of the trial. Commercial software costs money. System software manages the computer system and is not application software. Open source software may be free or sold, but it is not typically used on a trial basis.

2. **The correct answer is D.** Local area networks (LAN) serve limited geographical areas, such as single office buildings. Wide area networks (WAN) cover entire countries, so choice A is incorrect. Personal area networks (PAN) are very short range, so choice B is incorrect. Metropolitan area networks (MAN) typically cover 50-mile areas, so they would be able to serve more than one building.

3. **The correct answer is B.** The first digital computers were designed for World War II. The military used the computers to calculate missile trajectories and break enemy codes. Digital computers were not used during WWI, and they were already in full use by the time of the Korean and Vietnam Wars.

4. **The correct answer is C.** Filtering software is a utility used to prevent children from viewing inappropriate websites. Defragmenter utilities find and reorganize the scattered files on a hard drive to speed up operation. Antivirus utilities block viruses, spam, and pop-ups. Backup utilities make copies of a system's hard drive.

5. **The correct answer is A.** Phishing refers to sending fraudulent e-mails intended to fool users into revealing personal information. Encrypting is a method of protecting a computer or network. Streaming is a method for moving data so that it can be processed as a steady and continuous stream, as in streaming audio and video. Hackers often break into computers and networks for the challenge, but they are not necessarily associated with fraudulent e-mails. Crackers are the individuals who break into systems for malicious reasons.

6. **The correct answer is C.** The development stage of the software life cycle usually involves testing. Investigation relates to conducting a cost/benefit analysis of developing the software. Analysis calls for gathering and analyzing data. In the design stage, software engineers build a prototype.

7. **The correct answer is D.** A microprocessor chip is a small piece of silicon that contains millions of tiny electronic circuits. The microprocessor acts as the central processing unit (CPU) of personal computers. A server is a computer that processes requests from other computers, so choice A is incorrect. Choices B and C are incorrect.

8. **The correct answer is A.** Groupware allows multiple users to collaborate on a project and share data. Freeware is free software, so choice B is incorrect. Shareware (choice C) and demoware (choice D) are both available for a limited basis or with limited features.

9. **The correct answer is A.** Worms are malicious programs that repeatedly copy themselves into a system's memory, causing crashes. Spam and key loggers (choices B and D) are both security problems for computer users, but neither makes numerous copies. A firewall (choice C) is a security measure that attempts to protect systems from worms and viruses.

10. **The correct answer is B.** The U.S. Department of Defense developed ARPANET in 1969, and the small network was the starting point for today's Internet. ARPANET consisted of four linked computers at different university campuses and defense contractor offices. Choices A, C, and D are incorrect.

11. **The correct answer is B.** Microcontrollers, or embedded computers, are tiny microprocessors built into the devices that they control, such as digital cameras, cars, and MP3 players. A microcomputer is the same as a personal computer, so choice C is incorrect. Choices A and D are large and expensive.

12. **The correct answer is A.** Biometrics uses physical attributes like fingerprints, voices, faces, or eyes to confirm an individual's identity. Encryption involves scrambling data to prevent unauthorized access. Firewalls shield computers from intruders by filtering incoming and outgoing packets. Passwords are unique codes that restrict access.

13. **The correct answer is C.** A device driver is a software program that enables peripheral devices, such as printers and sound cards, to communicate with a computer system. Utility software enables users to monitor and configure the settings of hardware, application software, and the operating system. The operating system manages files, tasks, and security, while user interfaces enable users and computers to communicate.

14. **The correct answer is B.** The end-user license agreement (EULA) is displayed on the screen during installation of the software. Choice A appears on the package. Choices C and D are types of licensing agreements, but they are not specifically displayed on the screen during installation.

15. **The correct answer is C.** A switch is a full-duplex device that connects computers to a network. Full-duplex devices transmit data back and forth at the same time. Hubs are half-duplex devices that transmit data one direction at a time. Nodes are the devices that attach to networks, like PCs and printers. A gateway is an interface that allows different types of networks to communicate.

16. **The correct answer is A.** COBOL, one of the oldest programming languages, is used in business systems. BASIC serves as a teaching tool, so choice B is incorrect. FORTRAN (choice C) is an old language used for science and engineering applications. NOMAD (choice D) is a problem-oriented language not commonly used for business systems.

17. **The correct answer is C.** Emoticons, such as smiley faces, are textual portrayals of a writer's mood or intention used in e-mails. Emoticons are an example of netiquette, or Internet etiquette, so choice B is incorrect. Handshaking (choice A) is a process that enables two network devices to communicate. A blog (choice D) is a website on which a writer posts entries about personal opinions and experiences.

18. **The correct answer is A.** *Booting* refers to the sequence of events that loads an operating system into the main memory of the computer. Choices B and C are terms used for CPU task management. Multitasking (choice D) occurs when two or more programs run at nearly the same time on one computer.

19. **The correct answer is C.** Random-access memory (RAM) is the temporary holding location for data, software instructions, and the operating system while the computer is on. Read-only memory, or ROM (choice A), contains a computer's fixed startup instructions. Choices B and D are both format terms for bitmap files.

20. **The correct answer is A.** Microsoft Excel is an application software program that is considered a spreadsheet. Choice B is a graphical word processing program. Choices C and D are Relational Database Management Systems (RDBMS).

DIAGNOSTIC TEST ASSESSMENT GRID

Now that you've completed the diagnostic test and read through the answer explanations, you can use your results to target your studying. Find the question numbers from the diagnostic test that you answered incorrectly and highlight or circle them below. Then focus extra attention on the sections within the chapter dealing with those topics.

Computing and Information Technology		
Content Area	**Topics Covered**	**Questions**
Computer Organization and Hardware	• Processing components • Primary storage • Peripherals • Architectures • Data representation • Units of measurement	7, 11, 15, 19
Systems Software	• Operating systems • Utilities • User interfaces	13, 18
Application Software	• Word processing and desktop publishing • Spreadsheets • Presentation software • Personal communications • Multimedia • Databases • Graphics • Software licensing • Commercial application software	1, 8, 14, 20
Data Communications and Networks	• World Wide Web • Network access • Network architectures • Data communications • Safety and security • Mobile networks	2, 9, 12, 17

Computing and Information Technology		
Content Area	Topics Covered	Questions
Software Development	• Software life cycle • Programming methodology • Software development tools	6, 16
Social Impact and History	• History • Ethical/legal issues • Safety and security • Careers in computer science and information systems • Social issues	3, 4, 5, 10

GET THE FACTS

To see the DSST®Computing and Information Technology Fact Sheet, go to **http://getcollegecredit .com/exam_fact_sheets** and click on the **Technology** tab. Scroll down and click the **Computing and Information Technology** link. Here you will find suggestions for further study material and the ACE college credit recommendations for passing the test.

COMPUTER ORGANIZATION AND HARDWARE

COMPUTER TERMINOLOGY

Computers serve numerous purposes: accepting input, processing data, storing data, and producing output. Being familiar with basic terminology helps one understand how computers function, make purchasing decisions, and troubleshoot problems.

Basic Computer Terms	
File	Collection of data given a specific name; may be stored on a hard disk, CD, DVD, or flash drive
Hardware	Physical components or parts of a computer, such as the keyboard, screen, and the CPU
Input	Information placed into a computer through a device like a keyboard, thermostat, mouse, camera, or microphone
Microprocessor chip	Small piece of silicon that holds millions of tiny electronic circuits; serves as CPU for most computers; can be programmed to perform certain tasks
Motherboard	Main circuit board of a computer, also known as the system board; includes ports or connections to which the keyboard, mouse, and printer are attached; processor and memory chips are also attached to the motherboard; includes expansion slots for adding additional circuit boards, such as for video or sound
Network	Communication system
Output	Results generated by a computer, such as reports, graphs, and pictures that are provided by an output device like a screen or a printer
Peripheral device	Components or equipment that expand or enhance the input, output, and storage functions of a computer; includes printers, disk drives, scanners, joysticks, speakers, and digital cameras
Storage	Area where data is left permanently in files when not needed for processing; a hard disk drive inside a PC serves as the main storage device; also known as secondary storage

In 1993, Intel®
Corporation
released its first
Pentium® micropro-
cessor. The Pentium
product line
allowed the use of
graphics, music,
speech, 3-D
animation, video,
and music with
increasing speed
and became a part
of 90's pop culture.

PROCESSING COMPONENTS

Computers require processing and memory components in order to function. The processing components work together to gather the user's input and produce an output.

- **CPU:** Central processing unit that manipulates data. The CPU **fetches** the instruction from its memory and **executes** it after decoding the instruction.

- **ALU:** Arithmetic logic unit that contains the electronic circuitry that executes all arithmetic and logical operations or mathematical calculations. The ALU may need to perform a mathematical calculation in order to decode the instruction so that the CPU can **execute** the instruction.

- **RAM:** Random-access memory; temporary or working storage that holds data, software instructions, and the operating system for quick access; also known as primary storage or memory

- **Software:** Programs that instruct computers how to perform specific tasks

PRIMARY STORAGE

Random-access memory (**RAM**) is a temporary holding location for data, software instructions, and the operating system while the computer is running. When a person opens a word processing document, a copy of that file moves from the hard disk to RAM. As the person makes changes to the document, changes are made to the RAM copy rather than the version in the hard drive. As soon as the document is saved, the changed version moves from RAM back to the hard drive. Saving should occur frequently because RAM is volatile, which means RAM needs electrical power to hold data. Data in RAM is immediately and permanently lost when a computer's power is shut off.

Personal computers are installed with different amounts of RAM, which is measured in gigabytes. The amount of RAM needed for a personal computer depends on the software. A number of RAM chips are included in most personal computers:

- **DRAM:** Dynamic RAM; dynamic means that it needs to be refreshed constantly by the CPU or its contents are lost

- **SDRAM:** Synchronous dynamic RAM; synchronized by the system clock and faster than DRAM

- **SRAM:** Static RAM; faster than DRAM and holds on to its contents without needing to be refreshed by the CPU

- **DDR-SDRAM:** Double-data rate synchronous dynamic RAM; the newest and most popular RAM chip

Cache memory is random-access memory that the computer microprocessor can access quickly when needed. A cache stores program instructions that software programs frequently access. This storage allows the software programs to access these instructions faster, which allows the software to run quickly and efficiently and to use fewer resources. The cache has different memory levels:

- **Level 1 cache or L1** is a small cache that is embedded in the processor chip; although it is small, it is really fast.

- **Level 2 cache or L2** is larger than an L1 cache and it is usually located on a CPU or a separate chip. A high-speed alternative system bus connects the cache to the CPU to prevent it from slowing down when there is a lot of traffic (activity) on the main system bus.

- **Level 3 cache or L3** is typically double the random-access memory speed and is considered a specialized memory designed to improve the L1 and L2's performance. When an instruction is referenced in the L3 cache, it is usually elevated to a higher tier cache.

In addition to RAM, there are three other primary types of memory chips in computers. **Read-only memory (ROM)** chips contain a computer's fixed startup instructions loaded at the factory. The instructions in ROM cannot be erased, and ROM chips are not volatile like RAM chips. **CMOS (complementary metal-oxide semiconductor)** chips are battery powered, so they do not lose their contents when power is interrupted. CMOS chips hold flexible startup instructions kept up to date when the computer is not on, such as time and date. **Flash memory** chips store flexible programs in computers, cell phones, digital cameras, and MP3 players. Flash memory chips, which are nonvolatile, can be erased and reprogrammed.

Virtual memory is an imaginary memory area that some operating systems support. It exists as a main storage; however, data held in a secondary storage support most of virtual memory. It temporarily transfers pages of data from random-access memory to the disk storage, automatically allowing the transfer between the two as required.

PERIPHERALS

Peripheral devices are external auxiliary devices that connect to your computer. They can be used to input information in the computer, allow the computer to output some information, or can conduct both inputs and outputs. Below are some examples of peripheral devices and situations where they can be used with the computer.

- **Keyboard:** An input device that allows the user to type information into the computer or software program within the computer

- **Mouse:** An input device that allows the user to click icons or place the cursor in a location so that the user can perform a function on the keyboard to input information in the computer

- **Printer:** An output device that allows files to be printed from the computer as a hard copies

- **USB Flash Drive:** An input and output device that allows files to be stored and extracts files to the computer

- **Micro SD Card:** A small card that functions as an input and output device; it allows files to be stored and also extracts files to the computer

- **Monitor:** An output device that displays what the user is doing on the computer (e.g., typing, working with a software program, creating a document, clicking icons)

- **Speaker:** An output device that allows the user to hear audio from the computer

- **Secondary storage:** Additional storage that is separate from the main memory (secondary memory or auxiliary storage). Some examples of secondary storage are external hard drives, USB drives, Micro SD Cards.

- **Disk storage:** Storage that provides a means to record data by various electronic, magnetic, optical, or mechanical changes to a surface layer of one or more rotating disks. Some examples are hard disk drives, floppy disk drives, and optical disk drives. Internal storage space within the computer (hard drive storage) that allows the user to store files directly on the computer is one of the most common examples.

- **Biometrics:** Metrics that use human characteristics as a form of identification. Some examples are a fingerprint reader, facial recognition, and iris recognition.

- **Scanners:** Devices that scan and copy documents and convert them to an electronic format or digital data.

- **Communications hardware:** Devices that can transmit either analog or digital signals over cable, wireless technology, or telephone. The devices are installed on the computer within the internal memory. Some examples are Bluetooth devices, modems, network cards, Wi-Fi devices.

- **Cloud computing:** A means for storing and accessing files, data, and programs via the Internet.

ARCHITECTURES

Engineers build computers in a variety of sizes and shapes, and each type serves a particular function. While most people are familiar with personal computers because they use them at home or at work, it is important to have a general understanding of the other types of computers that serve useful purposes in the world.

- **Supercomputer:** High-capacity machine with thousands of microprocessors; fastest and most expensive type; able to process trillions of calculations every second; used for weather forecasting, physical simulations, and image processing

- **Mainframe computer:** Large, fast, and expensive computer typically used by large organizations, such as banks, airlines, universities, and government agencies; used to process, store, and manage large quantities of data; accessed from a computer terminal

- **Workstation:** Expensive and powerful personal computer (PC) designed for specific, complex tasks like medical imaging or computer-aided design (CAD); term also used to refer to a PC connected to a network

- **Microcomputer:** Computing device with a microprocessor intended to meet needs of individuals; also known as personal computer or PC; capable of handling e-mail, word processing, photo editing, and other applications; available as laptops, desktops, or handheld computers; may be connected to a computer network

- **Microcontroller:** Tiny, specialized microprocessor built into the device it controls; also known as an embedded computer; used in automobiles, MP3 players, digital cameras, and electronic appliances

- **Mobile Devices:** Small (mini-computers) devices that provide most of the same functions as a regular personal computer or laptop; some mobile devices can provide a means of telephonic communication; the most common are smart phones and tablets

DATA REPRESENTATION AND UNITS OF MEASUREMENT

The symbols a computer uses to represent facts and ideas, such as names, numbers, or colors, are data. Computers convert data into signals, marks, or binary digits that electronic circuitry is able to understand. The format in which data is stored, processed, and transmitted is known as data representation.

The electronic circuitry of computers requires the use of certain units of measurement. Computers use the binary number system, or **base-2 number system**. In the binary number system there are only two digits (**bits**): 0 and 1. Such a system enables computers to represent nearly any number with 0s and 1s. A group of eight binary digits is a **byte**, which is abbreviated with a capital B. A word is a unit of data that has a defined length. A 32-bit machine will have 32-bit-long words, and a 64-bit machine will have 64-bit-long words. Graphic and multimedia formats are also represented by bits.

A **kilobyte** (KB) equals 1,024 bytes and refers to small computer files. A **megabyte** (MB) is approximately 1 million bytes, a **gigabyte** (GB) is approximately 1 billion bytes, and a **terabyte** (TB) is approximately 1 trillion bytes, or 1000 GB. Megabytes are typically used to describe the size of medium to large computer files. Gigabytes are most often used when referring to a computer's storage capacity.

There is also a specific unit of measurement used when discussing processor speeds. This is usually measured in **gigahertz** (GHz). One GHz is 1000 megahertz (MHz), or one million hertz.

Some other units of measurement are as follows:

- **Microsecond:** One millionth of a second
- **Nanosecond:** One billionth of a second
- **Band:** Range of electromagnetic frequency
- **Bps:** bits per second or bits/sec

SYSTEMS SOFTWARE

Software provides electronic instructions to computers regarding the way to perform a specific task. Two types of software exist: **systems software** and **application software**.

Systems software serves as the link between the user, the application software, and the computer hardware. The four primary elements related to systems software are as follows:

1. Operating system
2. User interface
3. Device driver
4. Utility program

OPERATING SYSTEMS

The **operating system** controls activities occurring within the computer system and affects how a person is able to use a computer. Microsoft® Windows and Mac® OS are the operating systems most frequently installed into personal computers, while Linux is a popular system for servers. Numerous operating systems exist, including UNICOS, Unix, Mainframe, and BeOS. There are also operating systems for mobile devices. Two of the most commonly used mobile-device operating systems are Android and Apple®iOS. Each one is intended for use with specific computers. A computer's hardware is designed to accept only one kind of operating system.

The operating system of a computer interfaces with software, peripheral devices, and hardware, and it manages all of the hardware resources of the computer. A computer resource is any component that handles tasks, including the microprocessor, memory, storage, and peripheral devices like scanners and printers. The operating system works at specific tasks that typically go unnoticed but are critical to the performance of a computer:

- Booting
- CPU management
- File management
- Task management
- Security management

A computer's operating system first gets to work when the computer is turned on and the system is booted. *Booting* refers to the sequence of events that occur to load an operating system into the main memory of the computer. Operating systems are very large, so they are stored in the hard disk. The center module of the operating system is the kernel, and it manages memory, processes, tasks, and storage devices while the computer is on. The rest of the operating system stays in ROM until needed for specific tasks. The boot process involves six steps to obtain the operating system from the hard disk and load it into the computer's RAM:

1. Distribute power to the computer circuitry.
2. Start the bootstrap program stored in ROM that is used to load the operating system.
3. Activate diagnostic tests of various components.
4. Identify peripheral devices connected to the computer.
5. Load the operating system onto RAM from hard drive.
6. Check configurations and execute any specialized startup routine.

In addition to booting the computer, the operating system manages the central processing unit (CPU). The operating system monitors the main memory for the locations of programs and data. Only the essential data and programs stay in the main memory; the rest move to secondary storage until needed. Data and programs wait in queues, or lines, before processing occurs. Buffers are disk areas where programs or documents wait. For example, a print job is spooled, or placed, into a buffer where it waits in a queue for its turn with the printer.

Operating systems also manage files, tasks, and security. The operating system records the location of data files and program files, and it enables users to copy, rename, move, and delete files as needed. Organizing files into directories, subdirectories, and paths can also be accomplished through the operating system. Task management refers to the ability of the operating system to perform different tasks, such as storing, printing, and calculating. Most operating systems enable users to use more than one program at a time, such as typing information into a spreadsheet and listening to a music CD. This ability of an operating system to execute two or more programs by one user on one processor nearly at the same time is called **multitasking**. An operating system also enables users to control the security of their computers by requiring user names and passwords.

The operating system also manages resource allocation and job scheduling. Resource allocation occurs when a user opens a program. At that point it is considered a process. The operating system decides which resources will be used to run the selected program. Job scheduling allows the operating system to allocate system resources to different tasks. The system then attempts to complete jobs/tasks that are prioritized in a job queue. The operating system determines which job will be processed/completed based on the amount of time it takes to process/complete that particular job. Scheduling the jobs/tasks in this manner allows the operating system to ensure that the tasks are completed on time.

Virtual computing allows a user to download and use more than one operating system on the computer. It allows the one computer to act as if it is more than one or many computers (depending on the number of virtual machines installed). Users can perform similar functions on more than one computer using a virtual computer, and a user can access software programs from a single computer or an entire network.

UTILITIES

Utility programs help users monitor and configure the settings for computer hardware, application software, and the operating system. Diagnostic and maintenance tools, setup wizards, and security software are types of utility programs. Computers typically come with pre-installed utility programs, but utility programs may also be purchased separately. Most utility software programs focus on one specific task:

- **Antivirus software**, such as McAfee® Antivirus, is a popular method of dealing with viruses, pop-up ads, and spam.
- **Filtering software**, such as Net Nanny®, is a type of utility used by parents to prevent children from accessing inappropriate websites.
- **Backup utilities** make duplicate copies of a system's hard disk in case of hard drive failure.
- **Data recovery utilities** restore damaged or corrupted data caused by viruses or hardware failures.
- **Data compression utilities**, such as WinZip®, eliminate unneeded data and gaps in a computer's storage space so that less space is required.
- **Defragmenter utilities** find and reorganize the scattered files on a hard drive to speed up operation.

USER INTERFACES

A user interface is the hardware and software that enables users and computers to interact. A computer's user interface includes hardware, such as the monitor, mouse, and keyboard, and software mechanisms, such as icons, menus, and toolbars. In the past, computers used command-line interface to link users and computers. A command-line interface requires users to type commands in order to run programs. Today, computers have **graphical user interfaces (GUI)**. GUI allows users to choose icons or commands from menus with a mouse or a keyboard. Computers also allow users to select items and information by using touch and gestures on a touchscreen and by using a voice-user interface that recognizes speech.

APPLICATION SOFTWARE

Application software is any computer program that enables a user to perform a certain task, such as word processing or desktop publishing. Since people use computers for a multitude of purposes, there are many different kinds of application software available, including entertainment software, education software, and specialty software such as drawing, publishing, and computer-aided design. Productivity software refers to any application software that improves the work efficiency of users. Examples of productivity software include word processing, spreadsheets, desktop publishing, and database managers. At times, productivity software is bundled together into a single package, such as Microsoft® Office. In other cases, software companies sell productivity software as groupware, which is software that allows multiple users to work together on a project and share data and other resources.

WORD PROCESSING AND DESKTOP PUBLISHING

Word processing software enables users to create, edit, format, print, and store documents such as reports, letters, memos, and manuscripts. As the most commonly used software application, word processors easily replaced typewriters decades ago. Although numerous word processing programs are available, Microsoft® Word stands out as the one most commonly utilized.

The act of creating a word processing document involves entering text into the computer via the keyboard or through the diction function, if speech-recognition software is in use. The cursor, scrolling, and word wrap help users easily create documents with word processing software. The movable symbol on the display screen is the cursor. The cursor, which usually blinks, indicates the insertion point where text may be entered. Moving quickly up and down through text is known as scrolling. Word wrap is an automatic function that wraps text around to the next line when the user reaches the right margin.

Editing documents is simple with the numerous features offered by word processing software:

- **Insert/Delete:** Adding or inserting text can be done with the Insert key or by moving the cursor to a specific location. Deleting or removing text can be accomplished with the Delete or Backspace key.

- **Find/Replace:** Locate a word, phrase, or number with the Find or Search function. The Replace command enables users to replace a word, phrase, or number automatically with something else.

- **Cut/Copy and Paste:** Move text with Copy or Cut to the clipboard, a holding area in memory, and then use Paste to relocate the text somewhere else.

- **Spelling Checker:** This tests for incorrectly spelled words, which are indicated by a wavy line in Word.

- **Grammar Checker:** Grammar mistakes are highlighted but not automatically corrected.

- **Thesaurus:** On-screen thesaurus lists synonyms.

- **Readability Formula:** This analyzes the reading level of a document based on sentence length and vocabulary.

TIP

Most word processing applications have default settings automatically implemented unless the user overrides them.

Word processing applications are also useful in modifying the appearance of text, a function known as formatting. **Templates** and **wizards** are the two primary formatting tools in word processing software. Templates serve as preformatted style guides for structuring a document. Wizards are interactive utilities programs that lead users through steps to format a certain type of document, such as a memo or a resume. Additional formatting tools include font size and style, spacing, margins, headers, footers, page numbers, and tables.

The features available in most word processing programs are virtually endless. For example, the mail merge function automates the process of making customized documents by combining mailing list information with a form letter. The software is capable of numbering and positioning footnotes and generating indexes and tables of contents. Desktop publishing software is an advanced version of word processing that offers sophisticated graphic and design features. Software applications such as The Print Shop® and Adobe® InDesign™ enable users to create professional-grade newsletters and brochures.

SPREADSHEETS

Spreadsheet software, such as Microsoft® Excel, enables users to enter numerical data and formulas into rows and columns. The software then performs calculations based on the provided information to create tables. While spreadsheet software was originally popular among accountants and financial managers, it has since developed a following among other professions. The software is useful for creating budgets, balancing checkbooks, estimating costs, and maintaining a grade book. An especially helpful tool in spreadsheets is the what-if analysis. Users employ the recalculation function to see how changing one or more variables affects the outcome of the equation. For example, a user might wonder what a monthly car payment would be with different interest rates. By making changes to the interest rate and then recalculating, the user can see the effect on the monthly payment. With more than 16 million cells on every worksheet, electronic spreadsheets are extremely useful tools, and it is important to understand their specific terminology.

Spreadsheet Terms	
Cell	Location where a row and a column intersect
Cell address	Cell's position as designated by the column letter and row number
Formula	Instructions for calculations
Function	Built-in formula provided by software
Label	Text used to describe data
Range	Groups of cells next to each other
Values	Numbers or dates entered into a cell

In addition, spreadsheet software typically offers analytical graphics capabilities. Analytical graphics, or business graphics, are graphical forms, such as bar charts, line graphs, and pie charts that present data visually and enhance data comprehension.

PRESENTATION SOFTWARE

Presentation software, such as Microsoft® PowerPoint, allows users to create dynamic, engaging presentations without having to depend solely on note cards. The user can include the necessary visuals within the presentation and customize those visuals a number of different ways in order to grab the audience's attention. Images and photos can be incorporated, as can audio clips, video clips, and custom animations. Each page of a presentation is a slide, so live sessions are slide shows. However, the software offers the capability of printing the slides on paper, placing the presentation on the Web, or transferring the presentation as an electronic file. Some presentation software also allows users to embed documents and spreadsheets from other software programs into the presentation. For example, a person might be presenting information from the slides and need to show the audience some data and tables that were created in a spreadsheet such as Microsoft® Excel. The presenter can embed the spreadsheet within the presentation and retrieve it when reaching the particular slide where the information needs to be referenced.

Presentation software also allows users the ability to create presentations with embedded **hyperlinks.** The hyperlinks can be triggered by clicking the link on the slide, clicking an image that has the embedded link, or clicking text that contains the embedded link. Depending on what is included within the hyperlink, the presenter can link to a website, video, or some other media external to the presentation software.

PERSONAL COMMUNICATIONS

An amazing 60 billion e-mails cross through the Internet every day. People's ability to communicate with others so efficiently may be one of the primary reasons for the Internet explosion. Electronic mail can be transmitted through an e-mail program, such as Microsoft® Outlook Express, or a web-based e-mail program, such as Gmail.

While **e-mail** is probably the most popular form of communication, other electronic methods exist for interacting with people. **Instant messaging** (IM) allows for real-time communication through transmitted text messages. **Newsgroups** are electronic bulletin boards where users participate in written discussions about various subjects. **Social networking sites**, such as Facebook and Twitter, enable users to post pictures and messages about personal activities and interests for the viewing pleasure of others. **List servers** are software programs used to distribute messages to an online mailing list.

Conferencing software is another popular form of communication allowing users to communicate in real-time. Skype®, Adobe® Connect™, WebEx® and Go ToMeeting™ are conferencing software solutions allowing users to instant message each other, view attendees web cams, speak to attendees, listen to each other, share files, view videos and presentations, and write messages on a whiteboard. These conferencing software tools work well, not only for communicating with one person but also for communicating with multiple people.

As with other types of communication, e-mail writers should consider both the audience and the message when composing messages. **Netiquette,** or Internet etiquette, refers to various guidelines to ensure civil and effective communication when participating in online discussion groups or exchanging e-mails. For example, consult the FAQ (frequently asked questions) section of discussion groups to determine the behavior expectations. Avoid using obscene or inappropriate language, which is known as flaming. Instead, insert occasional emoticons, or smiley faces, to convey intention if the e-mail is not work-related. In addition, avoid sending large attachments that may slow down a recipient's computer system or at least request permission before doing so.

TIP

Using all capital letters in electronic communications is interpreted as shouting at the recipient.

MULTIMEDIA

Multimedia is the combination of multiple forms of media, including text, graphics, audio, video, animation, and interactive content. A computer capable of utilizing multimedia components will have a sound card, speakers, and multimedia software. CDs and DVDs are often considered to be multimedia formats because of their large data storage capacity since most multimedia content requires disk storage space. In general, there are two categories of video and audio software:

1. Software that can be used to record and edit video and audio

2. Media players that provide only playback options

Media players typically use icons to control their functions, including Play, Pause, Stop, Fast Forward, and various volume control options.

Most operating systems have a default multimedia player built in. For example, Windows® operating system includes Windows Media Player, and Mac OS® includes QuickTime® and iTunes®. There are many other media players available, however.

Many of today's media players are integrated with content provider services, for example, online stores for movies and TV shows, music, or streaming services. iTunes is one of the oldest and most popular of these types of media players, but others, such as Amazon and Pandora, have emerged as the demand for online media has increased.

DATABASES

A **database** is a collection of data stored on any type of computer. A wide range of information may be included in a database, such as inventory, addresses, and customer names. Databases organize interrelated files by common elements to simplify the process of retrieving data. Database software, such as Microsoft® Access and FileMaker Pro®, allows users to enter, locate, organize, and update information. Database software enhances data accuracy, reduces data repetition, and increases security.

Relational databases organize data into related tables with rows and columns. The columns are fields that contain one item of data. The rows are records that hold data for a single unit, which may be a person, place, thing, or event. A **record** is a complete set of fields. For example, a retail store's database contains a record of the contact information for each customer. Within each record are the separate fields—last name, first name, and address.

The ability to locate records efficiently is the chief benefit of database software. In order to find one record out of the thousands in a database, a user enters a query, which is a set of key words and commands describing the needed information. Database software provides at least one of the following methods for making queries:

- **Structured query language (SQL):** set of command words to instruct the computer to locate, sort, or modify data
- **Natural language query:** query constructed in human instead of machine language
- **Query by example:** examples of the data being sought

Four other types of databases exist in addition to relational databases—**hierarchical, network, object-oriented**, and **multidimensional**. The oldest database format is the hierarchical database in which fields and records are arranged in related groups similar to a family tree with lower-level (child) records subordinate to higher-level (parent) records. Network databases resemble hierarchical databases except each lower-level record can have more than one higher-level record. Object-oriented databases are used most often in manufacturing or scientific settings. Two types of object-oriented databases are **hypertext databases** with text links to other documents and **hypermedia databases** with links to graphics, audio, and video. Multidimensional databases are useful in analyzing large amounts of data that can be grouped in more than two dimensions. For example, data regarding country, year, and product could be placed into a three-dimensional data cube.

Data mining/analytics is a process where patterns or large data sets are discovered. Companies can turn raw data into user information by using data-mining software to find patterns in large batches of data. Some companies use data mining/analytics to increase sales and for identifying marketing targets.

GRAPHICS

Graphics software helps users create, manipulate, and print graphics such as drawings, photographs, and images that appear on a computer screen. Image editing software, or paint software, provides users with electronic pens, brushes, and paints to create images on a computer screen. The size, brightness, and quality of photographs can be adjusted with photo-editing software like Adobe® Photoshop™. Drawing software like Adobe® Illustrator™ offers lines, shapes, and colors that can be manipulated to create diagrams, logos, and other images. Computer-aided design (CAD) software is a type of 3-D graphics software used by architects and engineers to create product specifications and design blueprints.

SOFTWARE LICENSING AND COMMERCIAL APPLICATION SOFTWARE

Certain legal restrictions apply to both purchased and free computer software. A copyright gives the software's creator the exclusive right to copy, distribute, sell, and modify the software. A software license is a legal contract defining the way in which a program may be used. There are various types of software licenses:

- **Single-user license:** limits use of the software to one person at a time
- **Site license:** may be used on all computers at a specific location and is purchased for a flat fee
- **Multiple-user license:** price based on the number of users; specified number of users may use the software at any given time
- **Concurrent-use license:** priced per copy; specific number of copies may be used at the same time
- **Shrink-wrap license:** agreement printed on package that becomes effective when package is opened
- **End-user license (EULA):** displayed on screen during first installation

In general, there are two software categories: public domain and proprietary. **Public domain software** is available to the public without any restrictions. **Proprietary software,** which may be commercially sold or free, has restrictions on its use. Proprietary software is typically distributed as commercial software, demoware, shareware, freeware, open source software, enterprise software and software, as a service.

Types of Proprietary Software	
Commercial	Sold in stores and on websites
Shareware	Available for free on a trial basis; must pay to continue using it at end of trial period
Freeware	Available for free
Demoware	Commercial software available in a trial version that has limited features; often pre-installed on new computers
Open source	Includes source codes, so programmers can make modifications and improvements

Types of Proprietary Software	
Enterprise Software	Also known as enterprise application software or EAS; is used to satisfy an organization's needs, e.g., government, businesses, educational institutions, clubs and charities
Software as a Service (SaaS)	Software is licensed based on a subscription (typically monthly or yearly) and is considered to be an on-demand software choice

An additional type of software available illegally is pirated software. Individuals obtain pirated software from the Internet, friends, and foreign stores. Not only is using pirated software unethical, it may include a virus or may not function properly.

DATA COMMUNICATIONS AND NETWORKS

WORLD WIDE WEB

While many people believe the World Wide Web and the Internet are the same, the two are distinctly different, though related. The **Internet** is a worldwide communication infrastructure that connects computer networks. To access the Internet, one must have an Internet Service Provider (ISP). An ISP provides business and personal access to the Internet for a fee (usually monthly), and the provider typically provides the modem that is also needed to access the Internet.

In 1969, the U.S. Department of Defense developed **ARPANET**, the starting point for today's Internet. ARPANET consisted of four linked computers at different university campuses and defense contractor offices. By 1987, ARPANET linked the computers of 28,000 researchers and academics and provided text-based information. Since then, the World Wide Web has replaced ARPANET, and over 1 billion people use the Internet each day.

The **World Wide Web** is a collection of multimedia files linked and accessed through the Internet. Browsers, such as Microsoft Internet Explorer and Mozilla Firefox, enable people to access areas of the Web known as **websites**. Each website has a unique address or **URL** (**Uniform Resource Locator**) and is composed of one or more web pages or multimedia documents. Browsers find web pages through the URL, which consists of four elements. To illustrate, the web address for Big Bend National Park will be used to identify the different parts of URLs:

http://www.nps.gov/bibe/index.htm

URL Terminology		
Part	**Text**	**Definition**
Web protocol	http:// and https://	Hypertext Transfer Protocol (HTTP) refers to the communications rules enabling browsers to connect to web servers. HTTPS is the secure version of Hypertext Transfer Protocol.
Domain name	www.nps.gov	Location on the Internet; last three letters describe the domain type—gov (government), .com (commercial), .net (network), .org (nonprofit), .edu (educational), .mil (military), or .int (international organization)
Directory name	*bibe*	Name on the server for the directory from which the browser needs to retrieve a file
File name and extension	*index.htm*	File name is the specific page—*index.htm*; *.htm* is an extension of the file name that tells the browser that it is an HTML (Hypertext Markup Language) file; HTML is a standardized format that specifies the layout for web pages

Web Searches

With the extensive amount of information on the Web, it is helpful to search effectively and efficiently. Search engines, such as Google™ and Bing®, help users locate information on the Web. There are at least three search tools available to people who use search engines.

1. **Keyword index**—Search for information with one or more keywords, and the search engine displays a list of web pages containing the keywords.

2. **Subject directory**—Search for information by choosing lists of categories or topics, such as "Sports" or "Arts and Humanities." Yahoo!® and Galaxy® include subject directories.

3. **Metasearch engine**—Search more than one search engine at the same time. Webcrawler® and Dogpile® are metasearch engines.

Along with search engines, browsers, and HTML, there are also applets. An **applet** is a small application that can perform a specific function. It can be within a utility program. The Java applet, for example, is a program written in the Java programming language designed to be run on a web page that can run interactive animations or perform calculations.

NETWORK ACCESS AND ARCHITECTURE, AND DATA COMMUNICATIONS

Before people can locate information on the Internet or send e-mails to friends, they need network access. A **network** is a group of interconnected computers, phones, and other communications devices that are able to communicate with each other and share resources. Networks are differentiated by geographic range, size, and purpose as indicated by the following table.

Types of Networks		
Type	**Abbreviation**	**Function**
Local area network	LAN	Serves a very limited geographical area, such as one building
Metropolitan area network	MAN	Serves a 50-mile area; local Internet service providers and cable TV companies are often MANs
Neighborhood area network	NAN	Connects a limited geographical area, often several buildings
Personal area network	PAN	Uses short-range (30 feet) wireless technology for connecting personal digital devices
Wide area network	WAN	Covers a large geographical area, such as a country or the world, and typically consists of several smaller networks; the Internet is the world's largest WAN
Home area network	HAN	Connects the digital devices inside a home

Networks are structured as either client/server or peer-to-peer. In a **client/server network,** processing is divided between the clients, which are the workstations, and the server that manages shared devices such as printers and scanners. In client/server mode, the server acts as the most important resource. In a **peer-to-peer (P2P) network,** all workstations on the network communicate with each other without depending on a server. A P2P network is less costly than a client/server approach, but users sacrifice speed when more than twenty-five computers are connected.

The File Transfer Protocol (FTP) is a standard network protocol that uses separate control and data connections between the server and the client, and it is built on a client-server model architecture. FTP is used to transfer files on a computer network between the server and the client.

Telnet allows remote access to another person's computer. It is an underlying TCP/IP protocol for accessing remote computers. The remote user will log onto the remote computer as if he/she is a regular user in front of the remote computer, and the remote user is granted the same privileges as the regular user. This means that the remote user will be able to access any data or applications that are on the remote computer.

Within a network, data moves from one device to another through cables or through the air via wireless technologies. The following table consists of the various components found in most networks.

Network Components	
Component	**Function**
Host	Mainframe or midsize central computer that controls a client/server network
Node	Any device attached to a network, such as a PC, storage device, or scanner
Packet	Unit of data transmitted over a network; communications, such as e-mails, are divided into packets when sent and reassembled upon arrival
Protocol	Set of rules that govern the exchange of data between hardware and software components; each device in a network has a unique Internet protocol (IP) address so that data is routed properly
Hub	Common connection point for devices in a network where data arrives and is forwarded out; hubs are half-duplex devices that transmit data in both directions but only one direction at a time
Switch	Device that connects computers to a network; switches are full-duplex devices that transmit data back and forth at the same time
Bridge	Interface that connects the same types of networks like two LANs joined to create a larger network
Gateway	Interface allowing communication between different types of networks, such as between a LAN and a WAN
Router	Special computer that joins multiple networks together and directs communicating messages, such as e-mails and HTML files
Backbone	Main highway that connects an organization's computer networks
Network interface card	Circuitry that transmits and receives data on a LAN; often inserted into an expansion slot
Network operating system	Systems software that manages network activity, such as data flow and security

Since network connections need to move data quickly, **bandwidth,** which is the data transmission capacity of a communications channel, is an important factor. The broadband available from high-bandwidth communications systems like cable TV and DSL transmits high-speed data and high-quality audio and video. Systems with less capacity, such as dial-up Internet access, are narrowband or voice band.

Ethernet is a popular network architecture where nodes are connected by wire or cable. With small LANs, Ethernet prevents messages from colliding along the transmission line. When two workstations attempt to send data at the same time, Ethernet requires that the data be resent.

Networks use either wired or wireless connection systems. Wired networks with cables that connect devices offer high bandwidth, speed, security, and simplicity, but they lack the mobility of wireless networks. Wireless networks use a number of methods to connect devices:

- **Infrared transmission:** transports data with infrared-light waves that are just below the visible light spectrum

- **Microwave radio:** transmits voice and data with super-high-frequency radio that can be aimed in one direction; more carrying capacity than broadcast radio waves; Bluetooth, for example, involves short-range microwave transmissions

- **Broadcast radio:** sends data over long distances between states and countries; requires transmitters and receivers

- **Communications satellites:** microwave relay stations orbiting the earth; serve as basis for Global Positioning System (GPS)

Wireless fidelity—Wi-Fi—refers to an Ethernet-compatible wireless network that transmits data as radio waves. With Wi-Fi, people are able to use their Wi-Fi–equipped devices to work online wirelessly in areas with public access to Wi-Fi networks, such as airports.

SAFETY AND SECURITY

Along with the vast amount of information available on the Internet come annoyances, such as **spam.** In addition, **malware** poses serious problems to computer users. Malware, or malicious software, is any program designed to secretly infiltrate a computer and disrupt normal operations. **Spyware** is similar to malware because it also secretly enters a computer system, but the purpose is usually to gather a user's personal information for advertising purposes. The following table describes various intrusive elements of the Internet, some of which pose serious security risks.

Security Problems	
Type	**Definition/Danger Posed**
Browser hijacker	Spyware that secretly changes browser settings
Denial-of-service attack (DoS)	Repeated fraudulent requests of a computer system or network that result in a system overload

Security Problems	
Type	**Definition/Danger Posed**
Key logger	Spyware that records characters being typed and relays the information to other Internet users, making it possible for strangers to know passwords and other private information
Pharming	Redirecting users to fake websites
Phishing	Sending forged e-mail with the intention of fooling users into revealing private information
Pop-up generator	Type of spyware that tracks web surfing and online purchases so marketers can send unsolicited pop-up ads targeted to the user's interests; also known as adware
Search hijacker	Spyware that intercepts actual search requests and re-routes the user to other sites
Spam	Unsolicited e-mail, typically in the form of advertising or chain letters
Spoofing	Forging the name of an e-mail sender
Trojan horse	Program that appears to be useful but actually carries a virus or destructive instructions; typically offered for free in the form of a game or a screen saver; may invite backdoor programs that enable illegitimate users to gain control of a computer secretly
Virus	Deviant program that copies itself and infects computers; attaches to hard disks and destroys and corrupts data
Worm	Program that repeatedly copies itself into a computer's memory; excessive copies cause computers to crash

Computer experts known as **hackers** and **crackers** are often the ones responsible for the spread of viruses and worms. The term *hacker* has multiple meanings. On the positive side, hackers are enthusiastic computer programmers who like to expand their knowledge of programming languages and computer systems. Other types of hackers appreciate the challenge of circumventing computer and network security systems. In general, hackers break into computers for fun, such as thrill-seeker hackers, or for work purposes, such as white-hat hackers hired to expose computer system weaknesses.

In contrast, *crackers* break into systems for malicious purposes. Crackers may gather information for monetary gain, steal credit information, destroy data, or attempt to bring extensive harm to multitudes of people, such as cyberterrorists. However, protecting the safety of a computer system can be easily accomplished with a number of security tools:

- **Antivirus software:** programs that scan a computer's hard disk and memory to identify and destroy viruses
- **Firewall:** system of hardware and/or software that shields a computer or network from intruders by analyzing, controlling, and filtering incoming and outgoing packets
- **Password:** unique set of symbols, words, or codes used for restricting access to a computer or network
- **Biometrics:** use of physical attributes like fingerprints, voices, faces, or eyes to confirm an individual's identity
- **Encryption:** process of scrambling or hiding data into an unreadable form to prevent unauthorized access
- **IPS/IDS:** IPS stands for intrusion prevention systems, and it is a control tool, while IDS stands for intrusion defense systems, and it is a visibility tool. They appear similar, and they both increase the network security level; however, IPS can be best compared to a firewall. Rules can be set up and initiated to decide what is allowable and what is not allowable. IPS examines network traffic flows and attempts to detect and prevent vulnerability threats. An IDS manages network threats by monitoring network traffic at specific points—it detects intrusions, logs the attack, and then it alerts the administrator.

Not only is computer security important for individuals but also for businesses and government agencies. With so many organizations going paperless, the security of electronic databases is vital.

MOBILE NETWORKS

A mobile (or cellular) network is a communication network that is distributed over **cells** (land areas served by one or more cell towers, which transmit voice, data, etc.). When combined, these cells provide radio coverage over large geographic areas. Mobile phone signals are transferred to and from the mobile phone via radio waves. To ensure service quality and avoid interference, neighboring cells often use different frequencies. Cellular networks are large networks that need to be able to handle a large number of users or mobile subscribers. Both coverage and capacity are important and are an advantage of cellular networks.

SOFTWARE DEVELOPMENT

Obviously, software does not just magically appear on store shelves. Someone creates the idea and then designs, develops, and tests the software before selling it to consumers. The following section will review the way in which software is developed.

SOFTWARE LIFE CYCLE

The system's development life cycle refers to the steps taken by organizations when analyzing and designing a system. A system is any group of components that work together to accomplish a task. Numerous models exist for developing software and other systems, and some organizations create their own models. In general, all software life cycle models follow a pattern similar to the six-stage process shown in the following table:

Software Life Cycle	
Stage 1: Preliminary investigation	Conduct an initial analysis, propose alternative solutions, indicate costs/benefits, submit preliminary plan in a written report to executives.
Stage 2: System analysis	Gather data from surveys and observations, analyze data using modeling tools to create graphic representations of the software system, and write a report for management.
Stage 3: System design	Create a preliminary design or a prototype of the software system, and then create a detailed design that defines input/output requirements, storage/processing requirements, and system controls and backup; write a report summarizing the preliminary and detail designs.
Stage 4: System development	Develop the software; software is tested in two stages: unit testing of individual parts and then system testing with actual data; system testing may involve using incorrect data or large quantities of data to force the system into failing or crashing. Programmers also need to debug in order to identify and remove errors.
Stage 5: System implementation	Convert hardware, software, and files of old system to new system with direct, parallel, phased, or pilot implementation; direct implementation means user stops using old system and starts using new one; parallel implementation means both old and new systems are used at the same time until the new one seems reliable; phased implementation means parts of the new system are phased in gradually; pilot implementation means a few users test the entire system before everyone else uses it; users are then trained on the new system.
Stage 6: System maintenance	Modify and improve the system with audits and evaluations.

The fourth step of the life cycle involves developing the software program, which is a list of instructions written in programming language understood by the computer. **Programming,** or software engineering, involves following a five-step process to create instructions for a computer:

1. Clarify programming needs regarding input, output, and processing requirements
2. Design a solution with modeling tools
3. Write, or code, the program with the appropriate programming language

4. Test the program to remove errors or bugs

5. Write program documentation about what the program does and how to use it and maintain the program with modifications, repairs, and tests

The second step of the programming process refers to designing a solution with modeling tools. When designing a solution, a programmer needs to create an **algorithm,** which is a formula for solving a specific problem. Algorithms, which are similar to cooking recipes, can be written in a number of ways. There are two steps involved in program design.

Step 1: Determine program logic

- Modularization—develop and test each subprogram or subroutine separately

- Top-down program design—use hierarchy chart to illustrate general purpose of program all the way down to specific purposes of each module

Step 2: Design details

Use pseudocode to generate a summary or outline of the program and/or flowcharts to graphically explain the logical flow of the program

PROGRAMMING METHODOLOGY

Programming languages have changed significantly over the years. In the 1940s, engineers used **machine language,** which is the basic language of any computer as represented by binary digits. By the 1950s, programmers were using assembly language to write programs with abbreviations instead of numbers. Third-generation languages of the late 1950s and early 1960s, such as FORTRAN, COBOL, BASIC, Pascal, and C, were high-level or procedural languages. Such languages enabled programmers to write in human language rather than abbreviations and numbers. Many modern languages, such as C++ and Java, are third-generation languages. The early 1970s brought very high-level, or problem-oriented, languages, such as SQL and NOMAD, which allowed users to write programs with fewer commands. Fifth-generation languages of the 1980s are natural languages that allow programmers to phrase questions and commands in conversational ways. Prolog and Mercury are examples of fifth-generation languages.

Natural languages are associated with **artificial intelligence,** which is the technology geared toward humanizing machines.

In addition to traditional programming languages, **object-oriented programming (OOP)** and **visual programming** are options for software engineers. OOP is a method in which data and processing instructions are combined into **objects**, modules of programming code that can be used in other programs. A visual programming language, such as Visual BASIC, allows users to develop programs by drawing, pointing, or clicking on icons that represent certain programming routines.

Each programming language serves a different purpose, and the following list indicates some of the most commonly used languages for modern programs:

- **C++**—One of the most popular and commonly used languages; combines traditional C programming with object-oriented functions; used in writing systems software, application software, device drivers, and video game software

- **Java**—Object-oriented language used for writing compact programs to be downloaded over the Internet and immediately executed; similar to C++ but simpler to use
- **JavaScript**—Object-oriented scripting language supported in Web browsers that adds interactive functions to HTML pages
- **Perl (Practical Extraction and Report Language)**—General-purpose language used for Web development, network programming, system administration, and GUI development
- **COBOL (Common Business-Oriented Language)**—Oldest programming language; still used in business, finance, and administrative systems

SOFTWARE DEVELOPMENT TOOLS

Computer programs built to support other computer programs and applications are called software development tools. A variety of these tools exist to assist software developers create, maintain, or debug computer programs and applications.

Assemblers are types of computer programs that interpret software programs written in assembly language. They interpret the assembly language into machine language and machine code so that the computer can execute the instructions. Assemblers are also known as assembly language compilers. They allow software and application developers to gain access to the computer's hardware architecture and components. They also allow software and application developers to manage and operate the computer's hardware architecture and components.

Compilers are software programs that take a developer's high-level written source code and convert it into a binary code (low-level object code) in machine language so that the processor can understand it. Once the processor understands it, the processor then executes the object code.

Interpreters translate high-level instructions into an intermediate form prior to execution. An interpreter does not go through the compilation stage where machine instructions are generated. It immediately executes high-level programs.

Profilers use statistical, simulation, event-based, or instrumented methods to monitor or measure program source code or its binary executable form. Profilers measure the time complexity and the space or memory of a program, how certain instructions are used, and/or the duration and frequency of particular function calls.

Debuggers, also referred to as debugging tools, are software programs used to test and find bugs/errors in programs. In the event a program crashes, a debugger will show the location of the error within the program. Some debuggers can modify programs while they are running and some can run programs step-by-step.

Editors, also referred to as text editors, are computer programs that allow users to enter, change, store, and print text. A text editor often displays an empty screen or scrollable page with visible line numbers (at a fixed length). A user is able to fill in the lines with text, scroll forward, scroll backward, save the document, go to a new page, and make global changes. The document can be printed and displayed once it is saved. Program language source statements, technical manuals, and other documents can be created using text editors.

SOCIAL IMPACT AND HISTORY

HISTORY

When they were first invented, computers were so simplistic that it is hard to believe that they were ever considered computers. They were used neither for entertainment purposes nor to communicate with others. They served purposes that were very different from how we use them today. Some of the first computers were created during World War II. In 1939, Clifford Berry and John Atanasoff built one of the first computers—a 700-pound machine that contained 300 vacuum tubes and was the size of a desk. Although such a computer may be considered impractical by today's standards, it was actually considered a major breakthrough at the time. During World War II, engineers designed computers to help calculate missile flights and break enemy codes. By the next decade, computers were assisting large businesses with managing payroll and inventory. However, the computers of the 1940s and 1950s filled up entire rooms and were too costly for individuals or small businesses.

Over the years, engineers developed smaller computer components. Transistors and then integrated circuits replaced the vacuum tubes installed in the early computers. In the 1960s, prototypes for graphical user interfaces (GUIs), the computer mouse, and BASIC computer language (developed by Paul Allen and Bill Gates) were invented. BASIC helped pave the way for Microsoft. By the mid-1970s, Apple was selling personal computers, but a lack of software made most consumers leery of spending roughly $2,400 for the Apple II. The Apple II computer specs were as follows:

- Its cost ranged from 4 kilobytes (4K) of random-access memory (RAM) for $1,298 to 48K of RAM for $2,638.

- Its central processing unit (CPU) was a 1 MHz MOS 6502.

- The display was 280 X 192 (40 X 24 of text).

- It contained up to six colors of composite video output cassette interface with eight internal expansion slots.

- It originally contained a generic cassette drive and later an external 143K floppy drive.

- The operating system was a Woz Integer BASIC in read-only memory (ROM).

These are specifications that no longer exist today.

In the 1980s, IBM introduced its first personal computer, and then Compaq was able to clone IBM's computer. The 8088 processor was introduced, as were 16KB of memory (expandable to 256KB) and MS-DOS. More businesses began using computers, and, although they were still expensive, the number of computers in U.S. homes began to increase. Eventually, software caught up to hardware, and computers replaced typewriters and mechanical calculators in many businesses and homes. In the 1990s, computer use exploded. The **Windows® operating system** revolutionized the way people used computers. Most computers now contained color monitors and one could use a mouse to click icons on the computer instead of using DOS (disk operating system) functions. E-mail and the Internet were invented during this time, further changing the way people used computers. They could now serve as a means to stay in touch with friends and family. As people began to rely more on electronic communications, more people began purchasing desktop computers. By end of the 1990s, many U.S. homes had at least one computer and some homes had two or more. Today airplanes and cars rely heavily on computers and information technology. Many cars have global positioning (GPS) systems, Bluetooth capabilities, satellite radio, and the ability to add other features using Internet capabilities. Airplanes provide the pilot the capability of having the plane self-fly, and all of the controls are computerized to keep the pilot informed about any issues/problems with the plane, including weather conditions.

Since the early 1980s, the number of U.S. households that own computers has increased from 10 percent to over 85 percent today. In addition, more than 75 percent of adults in the United States regularly use the Internet. Computers continue to become smaller and more powerful every year, and their uses are nearly endless. Understanding computer hardware, software, and networks is essential to success in the twenty-first century.

ETHICAL/LEGAL ISSUES

Privacy Concerns

It is important that users manage their privacy when using the computer and surfing the Internet. One thing that is important to remember is that once information is on the Internet, it is there forever. Therefore, users should exercise caution when uploading any personal information (addresses, travel plans, photographs, etc.) on the Internet. Another type of information that can be traced and tracked is a user's browsing history and digital footprint. When users go online to different websites, and particularly when users upload information on the Internet, a digital footprint is created, and this digital footprint allows hackers to learn about the user, his/her personal information, and more.

One way that users can protect their privacy is by password-protecting information with a strong password, for example, using a combination of lowercase and uppercase letters, numbers, and special characters. It is also important to periodically change the password—every 90 days is ideal—and set up a screensaver lock so that a password needs to be entered when accessing the computer. Keep in mind that the password(s) need to be kept in a safe place. Never write them on a piece of paper that is left in the open for anyone to see.

There are a host of privacy concerns that users need to consider, depending on what type of software and system that the user intends to use. One final privacy issue to discuss is making sure users surf the Internet on a secure network. Surfing on a secure network will make it more difficult for hackers to access a user's computer and steal his/her personal information. This also is true when using a work computer issued by an employer. Because of intellectual property rights, the original, private, creative work that the user creates for the organization also needs to be protected so that it is not easily accessible to hackers.

Telecommunications Law refers to the laws and policies that are in place to regulate electronic communications and broadcasting within the United States. These laws are regulated by the federal government, specifically the Federal Communications Commission (FCC). The Internet was included in the Communications Act in 1996 to allow communications businesses to compete with each other. Because there are still some aspects of communications (voice over Internet protocol (VoIP), wireless services, and video conferencing) that are yet to be sorted out in terms of regulation, the telecommunications industry is dealing with increasing legal issues.

SAFETY AND SECURITY

When using the Internet and computers, safety and security issues and considerations may arise. One consideration is to always ensure safety when surfing the Internet. But Internet safety is not only limited to ensuring that there is a firewall and antivirus software installed on the computer to prevent viruses and malware; it also involves being aware of social engineering attacks, avoiding being a victim or initiator of cyberbullying, and guarding oneself (or one's company) from cybercrime.

Social engineering attacks can take on many different forms, ranging from attacking computers to attempting to gain people's personal information in an effort to commit fraudulent acts. One commonly used social engineering attack is **phishing**. With phishing, attackers attempt to obtain others' personal information by using hyperlinks, embedded links, and fraudulent websites. By obtaining personal information, attackers can steal identities and pose as the victims to do harm as well as corrupt computers and networks. One high-profile phishing scam was the 2011 RSA SecurID breach, which cost the company over $66 million to recover from the attack. The attacker sent two different e-mails over a two-day period to a small number of non-key employees with the subject "2011 Recruitment Plan." The e-mail was professionally written as if it came directly from the company, asking employees to open an attached spreadsheet about the recruitment plan. The spreadsheet contained a backdoor vulnerability allowing the attacker to access the network through a popular browser plug-in.

Another social engineering attack that is gaining more momentum is called **quid pro quo**. With quid pro quo attacks, the attacker promises something, usually some type of good or product, in exchange for information. A common quid pro quo attack involves the attacker posing as a help desk representative. These attackers either spam call people indicating that there is a problem with their computer or Internet service, or they set up websites with help desk phone numbers listed to trap unsuspecting victims. The attacker promises the victim that he or she will remedy computer issues by removing a virus. Instead, the attacker gains access to the computer to install malware.

Pretexting is another commonly used social engineering attack. For pretexting to be successful, the attacker has to create a convincing scenario or situation that will allow him or her to steal the victim's personal information. For example, the attacker will make a victim feel as if it is urgent to provide the attacker with some important or personal information. By instilling fear, coupled with attempting to establish a false sense of trust with the victim, an attacker can take advantage of the victim and therefore use the victim's information to partake in cybercriminal activity.

There are more sophisticated pretexting techniques whereby attackers quickly establish a rapport with the victim in an effort to coax the victim to divulge personal information confirming his or her identity. Sophisticated attackers can also persuade company employees to exploit a network's structural weakness so that the attacker can gain access to the network and therefore gain access to other company systems.

Cyberbullying is another ethical issue that is traumatizing for the victim but can also result in grave consequences for the initiator. Cyberbullying occurs when kids threaten and harass other kids through electronic communication, such as social media, e-mail, text messages, websites, chat, pictures, and videos, often by creating fake profiles. Cyberbullying can happen quickly and at any time (24 hours a day, 7 days a week, 365 days a year). It can also occur anywhere, as long as the receiver has a device that can access the Internet. Messages can also be sent anonymously, further complicating the cyberbullying issue. Cyberbullying can have detrimental effects for the victim and can result in the victim turning to substance abuse and suicide. Because of this, there are safeguards in place to protect the victim. Cyberbullying can lead to incarceration. It is not easy to simply delete text, videos, messages, and pictures because once something is posted online, it is there forever.

Cybercrime is another ethical issue that affects both computer users and nonusers. A cracker can hack personal computers as well as company networks and servers to steal passwords, personal identification numbers, and other personal information. With this information, a cracker can steal and assume a person's identity and essentially ruin his or her life. Some of the most common forms of cybercrime are identity theft and fraud. **Identity theft** can take several different forms, such as forging checks, creating fake identification cards, or producing replica credit and debit cards. **Fraud** occurs once the cracker assumes the victim's identify to make purchases or engage in other illegal, unauthorized acts.

Privacy in Online Services

Although there are many mechanisms and features put in place to make users *feel* as if what they are doing online is private, there is no true privacy, and this is particularly true with some of the day-to-day online services that users access. When using an online service, information is usually backed up on the company's server, so even if the user presses the Delete key, the information is not deleted; it is no longer visible to the user but is still stored on the company's server. Also, when individuals use online services and visit websites, companies keep track of their immediate digital footprint in an effort to solicit additional business from you.

CAREERS IN COMPUTER SCIENCE AND INFORMATION SYSTEMS

Nearly every job or career requires a certain level of computer knowledge and skills. In some jobs, computers are tools for accomplishing tasks effectively and efficiently. For example, police officers often have laptops installed in their cruisers, which enable them to quickly find data about stolen cars, arrest warrants, and criminal records. In other jobs, working with computers is the focal point of the position; think database developer, games programmer, robotics engineer, technical writer, graphic designer, and web developer. Advancements in computer technology have not only transformed jobs but have also created new professions and career opportunities.

Careers in computer science and information systems are different from careers in computers. A career in computer science and information systems usually requires one to complete college and obtain at least a bachelor's degree. Some examples of careers in computer science and information systems include the following:

- Computer programmer
- Database administrator
- Computer engineer
- Network architect
- Web developer

The average compensation for jobs in these fields ranges from $51,000 to $110,000, and the median annual wage is $81,500. According to the Bureau of Labor Statistics, computer and information technology jobs are expected to grow 12 percent faster than all other occupations between 2014 and 2024. Computer and information technology jobs are expected to grow from 3.9 million (in 2014) to around 4.4 million (in 2024).

Telecommuting jobs are also growing. Global companies are champions at embracing telecommuting (working from home jobs). There are many domestic companies that also have employees who telecommute, and sometimes this occurs throughout entire departments.

SOCIAL ISSUES

Increased productivity, globalization, and efficient communication methods are only some of the societal benefits of computer technology. However, the technological revolution raises some social concerns as well. One environmental issue is e-waste, which refers to the millions of PCs, cell phones, printers, and other electronic equipment that are discarded when they break or become obsolete. Many technology firms, including Dell and Hewlett-Packard, are responding to environmental concerns by offering to recycle or refurbish unwanted computer devices.

Although technology enables people to connect with others around the world, it is also linked to mental health issues. With computer technology, people are able to work, shop, and play games without speaking to or seeing another person, which may lead to isolation, loneliness, and depression. Online gambling is another mental health concern, since technology makes gambling so accessible. It is illegal to gamble by wire in the United States, but the global nature of the Internet simplifies the process of making bets in the Caribbean and other offshore locations.

SOCIAL MEDIA RESPONSIBILITY

While social media can be a fun way to meet and connect with people, it can also be a potential pitfall if used irresponsibly. Employers are able to view employees' social media pages to learn more about their employees. What you put on your social media page is a reflection of you and your employer. Adding unprofessional pictures and language on a social media page may cause you to lose your job, and if you are looking for a new job, potential employers may view the social media page as a deciding factor to determine if they want you representing the company.

Children and teenagers with computer access face security threats when using social media irresponsibly to meet and communicate with strangers. Daily news reports indicate that sexual predators solicit children online, especially young girls. With the anonymity of cyberspace, predators easily portray themselves as caring peers to unsuspecting children and teenagers. Although parents are becoming increasingly aware of online threats, teenage girls remain the target of many online predators.

ARTIFICIAL INTELLIGENCE

Artificial intelligence (AI) can be described as technology seeking to understand and create a computer-based technology able to simulate human sensory capabilities and characteristics of intelligence. Some would describe it as technology to create machines that think and act rationally. Some would define AI simply as programming machines to behave like humans. Examples of artificial intelligence are self-driving cars; voice-powered digital assistants (such as Siri or Alexa); humanoid robots with the ability to "see," "touch," and "hear," allowing them to respond to their environment; drones; and machines that can compete in strategic games (such as chess) or interpret complex data.

The idea of artificial intelligence dates as far back as the 1600s when mathematician Rene Descartes questioned whether it was possible for machines to think. The question became more relevant in 1950 when Alan Turing published his paper, "Computing Machinery and Intelligence," which Turing began by stating, "I propose to consider the question, 'Can machines think?'" By developing what is now known as the Turing test, he took that question a step further. The question, according to Turing, was if there were imaginable digital computers which would do well in the imitation game? The Turing test is a variation of a party game called the "imitation game," which tasks a person, called the "interrogator," to determine which of the other two players (who are hidden from the interrogator) is a computer by submitting written questions to make the determination based on the answers submitted. If a computer could respond in such a way that a human would believe it too was human, is it displaying human cognition?

AI has come a long way since Turing's imitation game, and as with most technological developments, it raises philosophical issues, such as if general artificial intelligence is truly possible, are there limits to what a machine can do, and are intelligent machines dangerous to humans? It also raises ethical issues, such as if a machine can be sentient, does it have or deserve rights; and how can humans regulate that intelligent machines are used and treated ethically? As the AI technology continues to progress, these and other issues will have to be addressed.

SUMMING IT UP

- The four functions of a computer are as follows:
    1. Accepting input
    2. Processing data
    3. Storing data
    4. Producing output
- **Basic computer terms include:** CPU, file, hardware, input, microprocessor chip, motherboard, output, peripheral device, RAM, software, and storage.
- Computers convert data into signals, marks, or binary digits that electronic circuitry can understand. **Data representation** is the format in which data is stored, processed, and transmitted.
- In the **binary number system** there are only two digits: 0 and 1.
    - A group of **8 binary digits is a byte**, or B.
    - A **kilobyte (KB) equals 1,024 bytes** and refers to small computer files.

- A **megabyte (MB) is approximately 1 million bytes** (size of medium to large computer files).

- A **gigabyte (GB) is approximately 1 billion bytes** (generally refers to a computer's storage capacity).

- **Random-access memory (RAM)** is a temporary holding location for data, software instructions, and the operating system while the computer is running. RAM chips included in most personal computers are DRAM: Dynamic RAM; SDRAM: Synchronous dynamic RAM; SRAM: Static RAM; and DDR-SDRAM: Double-data rate synchronous dynamic RAM. Three other primary types of memory chips in computers are ROM, CMOS, and Flash memory chips.

- The **operating system** controls activities occurring within the computer system and interfaces with software, peripheral devices, and hardware. The operating system controls booting and CPU, file, task, and security management.

- A **system's development life cycle** refers to the steps taken by organizations when analyzing and designing a system. Software life cycle includes preliminary investigation, system analysis, system design, system development, system implementation, and system maintenance.

- **Programming**, or software engineering, involves a **five-step process** to create instructions for a computer:

  1. **Clarify programming needs** regarding input, output, and processing requirements
  2. **Design a solution** with modeling tools
  3. **Write, or code, the program** with the appropriate programming language
  4. **Test the program** to remove errors or bugs
  5. **Write program documentation and maintain the program** with modifications, repairs, and tests

- A brief timeline of programming languages:
  - 1950s–1960s—The programming languages FORTRAN, COBOL, BASIC, Pascal, and C enabled programmers to write in human language rather than abbreviations and numbers.

  - 1970s—languages such as SQL and NOMAD allowed users to write programs with fewer commands.

  - 1980s—Prolog and Mercury, fifth-generation or natural languages, allowed programmers to phrase questions and commands in conversational ways.

  - 1990s–present—Some of the most commonly used languages for today's programs are C++, Java, JavaScript, Perl, and COBOL.

- Certain legal restrictions apply to both purchased and free computer software.
  - A **copyright** gives the software's creator the exclusive right to copy, distribute, sell, and modify the software.

  - A **software license** is a legal contract that defines the way(s) that a program may be used.

- Software licenses include single-user, site, multiple-user, concurrent-user, shrink-wrap, and end-user licenses.

- The two software categories are **public domain** and **proprietary**.
  - Proprietary software includes commercial, shareware, freeware, demoware, and open source.

  - **Pirated software** is illegally obtained.

- In 1969, the U.S. Department of Defense developed **ARPANET**, the starting point for today's Internet. Since then, the World Wide Web has replaced ARPANET, and over 1 billion people use the Internet each day.

- A **network** is a group of interconnected computers, phones, and other communications devices that are able to communicate with each other and share resources.
  - Types of networks include **LAN** (local area network), **MAN** (metropolitan area network), **NAN** (neighborhood area network), **PAN** (personal area network), **WAN** (wide area network), and **HAN** (home area network).

  - **Network components** include the host, node, packet, protocol, hub, switch, bridge, gateway, router, backbone, network interface card, and network operating system.

  - **Networks use either wired or wireless connection systems.** Wireless network methods include infrared transmission, microwave radio, broadcast radio, and communication satellites. Wireless fidelity, or Wi-Fi, transmits data as radio waves.

- **The World Wide Web and the Internet are not the same.** The Internet is a worldwide communication infrastructure that connects computer networks. The Web is a collection of multimedia files linked and accessed through the Internet.

- Browsers enable people to access web pages or websites. Each website has a unique address or **URL** (**Uniform Resource Locator**).

- **Malware**, or malicious software, is any program designed to secretly infiltrate a computer and disrupt normal operations. Security problems include browser hijackers, denial-of-service attacks (DoS), key loggers, pharming, phishing, pop-up generators, search hijackers, spam, spoofing, Trojan horses, viruses, and worms.

- **Spyware** also secretly enters a computer system, but it gathers personal information for advertising purposes.

- In general, **hackers** break into computers for fun or for work purposes. **Crackers** break into systems for malicious purposes.

- Computer security systems include **antivirus software, firewalls, passwords, biometrics, and encryption**.

- The **first digital computers were used in World War II** to help calculate missile flights and break enemy codes. In the 1940s and 1950s, large businesses used computers for payroll and inventory, but they were too big and expensive for small businesses. Smaller computer components, such as transistors and then integrated circuits, replaced the early computers' vacuum tubes.

- While **social media** can be a fun way to meet and connect with people, it can also be a potential pitfall if used irresponsibly.

COMPUTING AND INFORMATION TECHNOLOGY POST-TEST

> **Directions:** Carefully read each of the following 60 questions. Choose the best answer to each question and fill in the corresponding circle on the answer sheet. The Answer Key and Explanations can be found following this post-test.

1. Which application software program is used to create databases and store data?
   A. Microsoft Excel
   B. Microsoft Access
   C. Microsoft Word
   D. Microsoft PowerPoint

2. What term is used for any preformatted style guide in word processing software?
   A. Kernel
   B. Label
   C. Template
   D. Cell

3. What is used to store data for later retrieval?
   A. An operating system
   B. A database
   C. A device driver
   D. A utility program

4. Which of the following refers to a unit of data that is transmitted over a network?
   A. Mail
   B. Node
   C. Packet
   D. Attachment

5. What application software program can be used to create professional presentations?
   A. Microsoft Word
   B. Microsoft PowerPoint
   C. Microsoft Excel
   D. Microsoft Access

6. Which of the following network architectures prevents messages from colliding along transmission lines?
   A. Internet
   B. Ethernet
   C. Intranet
   D. Extranet

7. The structure of which type of database resembles a family tree?
   A. Multidimensional
   B. Relational
   C. Object-oriented
   D. Hierarchical

8. What can be used to prevent cybercriminal activity?
   A. Antivirus software
   B. A modem
   C. Wi-Fi
   D. A router

9. What is the term for the data transmission capacity of a communications channel?
   A. Bitmap
   B. Fidelity
   C. Bandwidth
   D. Frequency

10. Which of the following is the newest and most popular RAM chip?
    A. DRAM
    B. SRAM
    C. SDRAM
    D. DDR-SDRAM

11. Which of the following is an example of a domain name?
    A. .org
    B. http://
    C. home.htm
    D. www.google.com

12. What term is used for a search specification that leads a computer to search for a record in a database?
    A. Field
    B. Query
    C. Phish
    D. Queue

13. Which of the following wireless network methods is used for GPS?
    A. Infrared transmission
    B. Broadcast radio
    C. Microwave radio
    D. Communications satellites

14. Which of the following implementation methods requires all users to stop using an old system completely before beginning to use a new one?
    A. Direct
    B. Parallel
    C. Phased
    D. Pilot

15. Which of the following is most often used by airlines and banks to process and store large amounts of data?
    A. Compiler
    B. Graphics terminal
    C. Mainframe computer
    D. Supercomputer

16. What is a mechanism that scrambles data into an unreadable form to prevent security breaches?
    A. Biometrics
    B. Encryption
    C. Executable
    D. Antivirus software

17. What is the term for the core module of an operating system?
    A. Menu
    B. Buffer
    C. Bootstrap
    D. Kernel

18. Which of the following records characters typed by a computer user and enables strangers to learn passwords?
    A. Key logger
    B. Browser hijacker
    C. Pop-up generator
    D. Search hijacker

19. Which of the following is a holding area in memory used with the Copy command in word processing programs?
    A. Template
    B. Default
    C. Desktop
    D. Clipboard

20. What is the term for a component that expands the input, output, or storage functions of a computer?
    A. Peripheral
    B. Hard drive
    C. Modem
    D. Software

21. In what decade was the first personal computer introduced?
    A. 1960s
    B. 1970s
    C. 1980s
    D. 1990s

22. Which of the following helps users locate information on the Web?
    A. Search engine
    B. Data warehouse
    C. Network router
    D. Local area network

23. Which of the following RAM chips retains its contents without needing to be refreshed by the CPU?
    A. SRAM
    B. DRAM
    C. SDRAM
    D. DDR-SDRAM

24. Which of the following software applications offers sophisticated graphic and design features?
    A. Spreadsheet
    B. Network database
    C. Word processing
    D. Desktop publishing

25. The format in which data is stored, processed, and transmitted by electronic circuitry in a computer is known as data
    A. convergence.
    B. representation.
    C. transfer.
    D. language.

26. What is the term for high-bandwidth communications systems like DSL?
    A. Narrowband
    B. Voiceband
    C. Broadband
    D. Crossband

27. Which company introduced the first computer with a single-circuit board?
    A. Compaq
    B. IBM
    C. Microsoft
    D. Apple

28. What is the final step of the boot process?
    A. Power distributed to circuitry
    B. CPU checks configurations
    C. Diagnostic tests activated
    D. Peripheral devices identified

29. Which invention allowed computers to connect to the Internet without wires?
    A. Wi-Fi
    B. Dial-up
    C. DSL
    D. Local Area Network (LAN)

30. Which of the following describes a kilobyte?
    A. 8 binary digits
    B. 1,024 bytes
    C. 1,048,576 bytes
    D. 1,073,741,824 bytes

31. Which of the following databases may include links to audio and video?
    A. Network database
    B. Relational database
    C. Object-oriented database
    D. Multidimensional database

32. What term describes the action consistent with attacking, harassing, or threatening a person via electronic communication?
    A. Netiquette
    B. Cyberbullying
    C. Flaming
    D. Social engineering

33. What invention allowed the use of graphics and music on PCs?
    A. MS-DOS
    B. COBOL
    C. Motherboard
    D. Pentium® microprocessor

34. What is used to block hackers from accessing a computer or a network?
    A. A firewall
    B. Antivirus software
    C. A modem
    D. An Ethernet cable

35. Which of the following is a central computer that supplies a network with data and storage?
    A. Central processing unit
    B. Supercomputer
    C. Ethernet
    D. Server

36. Which of the following refers to the unique numbers assigned to each computer on a network?
    A. Path
    B. Domain
    C. IP address
    D. Query processor

37. What is the term for disk areas where programs or documents wait?
    A. Directories
    B. Spools
    C. Buffers
    D. Paths

38. What is the term for programs designed to secretly penetrate a computer and disrupt operations?
    A. Freeware
    B. Shareware
    C. Demoware
    D. Malware

39. What type of application software is most often used by architects and engineers?
    A. Computer-aided design
    B. Image editing
    C. Multimedia
    D. Drawing

40. What is the term used to describe data that can only exist with a constant power supply?
    A. Zipped
    B. Portable
    C. Volatile
    D. Unformatted

41. Which of the following is NOT a computer science or information systems career field?
    A. Network architect
    B. Database administrator
    C. Phone support representative
    D. Computer and information research scientist

42. Which programming tool results in an outline or summary of a program?
    A. Flowchart
    B. Pseudocode
    C. JavaScript
    D. Hypertext

43. Which of the following refers to the software and hardware that enable people to communicate with computers?
    A. Operating systems
    B. Utility programs
    C. Architectures
    D. User interfaces

44. Which of the following was used in the first digital computers?
    A. Vacuum tube
    B. Silicon chip
    C. Integrated circuit
    D. Transistor

45. Which of the following chips holds flexible startup instructions, such as time and date?
    A. RAM
    B. ROM
    C. CMOS
    D. DRAM

46. Which of the following is the unit of measurement used by computer circuitry?
    A. Base-1 number system
    B. Base-2 number system
    C. Base-5 number system
    D. Base-10 number system

47. Which of the following is a fourth-generation problem-oriented language?
    A. NOMAD
    B. COBOL
    C. OOP
    D. XML

48. Which of the following utilities rearranges files on a disk to speed up operation?
    A. Data recovery
    B. Backup
    C. Defragmenter
    D. Compression

49. Which of the following is a fifth-generation language?
    A. Prolog
    B. Pascal
    C. Java
    D. C++

50. Which of the following stores flexible programs in MP3 players and cell phones?
    A. CMOS chips
    B. Flash memory
    C. Application software
    D. Shareware

51. Which of the following is unrestricted software?
    A. Open source
    B. Public domain
    C. Commercial
    D. Proprietary

52. Which of the following units of measurement is most often used when referring to a computer system's storage capacity?
    A. B
    B. GB
    C. KB
    D. MB

53. What is the term for a personal computer connected to a network?
    A. Supercomputer
    B. Microcontroller
    C. Workstation
    D. Mainframe

54. Any hardware or software component available for use by a computer processor is a
    A. resource.
    B. device.
    C. packet.
    D. server.

55. What is the term for the area where data remains permanently in files?
    A. Primary storage
    B. Memory
    C. Secondary storage
    D. CPU

56. Which of the following mechanisms enables people to organize files into directories and subdirectories?
    A. Device driver
    B. Application software
    C. Operating system
    D. Utility software

57. What is the term for the most commonly used interface that allows people to choose icons from menus with a mouse?
    A. Natural-language interface
    B. Command-line interface
    C. Motion tracking interface
    D. Graphical user interface

post-test

58. What is the term for a word processing feature that automates the process of creating personalized form letters?
    A. Track changes
    B. Mail merge
    C. Hyperlink
    D. Wizard

59. What is the term for the location where a row and a column intersect in an electronic spreadsheet?
    A. Cell
    B. Label
    C. Range
    D. Value

60. What is the term for a computer that requests information from another computer or a server?
    A. Router
    B. Client
    C. Modem
    D. Bridge

ANSWER KEY AND EXPLANATIONS

1. B	**13.** D	**25.** B	**37.** C	**49.** A
2. C	**14.** A	**26.** C	**38.** D	**50.** B
3. B	**15.** C	**27.** D	**39.** A	**51.** B
4. C	**16.** B	**28.** B	**40.** C	**52.** B
5. B	**17.** D	**29.** A	**41.** C	**53.** C
6. B	**18.** A	**30.** B	**42.** B	**54.** A
7. D	**19.** D	**31.** C	**43.** D	**55.** C
8. A	**20.** A	**32.** B	**44.** A	**56.** C
9. C	**21.** B	**33.** D	**45.** C	**57.** D
10. D	**22.** A	**34.** A	**46.** B	**58.** B
11. D	**23.** A	**35.** D	**47.** A	**59.** A
12. B	**24.** D	**36.** C	**48.** C	**60.** B

1. **The correct answer is B.** Microsoft Access is an application software program used to create databases and store data. Microsoft Excel (choice A) is an application software program that is considered a spreadsheet. Microsoft Word (choice C) is a graphical word processing program. Microsoft PowerPoint (choice D) is a software package designed to create electronic presentations consisting of a series of separate pages or slides.

2. **The correct answer is C.** A template is any preformatted style guide in word processing software. Templates are often used for organizing memos and formal letters. *Label* and *cell* (choices B and D) are terms related to spreadsheets. A kernel (choice A) is the core module of an operating system.

3. **The correct answer is B.** A database is used to store data for later retrieval. An operating system (choice A) is the software that supports a computer's basic functions, such as scheduling tasks, executing applications, and controlling peripherals. A device driver (choice C) is a program that controls a particular type of device that is attached to your computer. A utility program (choice D) is a program for carrying out a routine function.

4. **The correct answer is C.** A packet is a unit of data that is transmitted over a network. E-mails and attachments are broken into packets when sent, so choices A and D are incorrect. A node (choice B) is a device that attaches a device to a network.

5. **The correct answer is B.** Microsoft PowerPoint is an application software program used to create professional presentations. Microsoft Word (choice A) is a graphical word processing program. Microsoft Excel (choice C) is an application software program that is considered a spreadsheet. Microsoft Access (choice D) is an application software program used to create databases and store data.

6. **The correct answer is B.** Ethernets are network architectures that prevent messages from colliding along transmission lines. Ethernet nodes are connected by coaxial cable or twisted pair wire. The Internet, intranets, and extranets (choices A, C, and D) are computer networks differentiated by access limitations.

7. **The correct answer is D.** Hierarchical databases group data in a way that is similar to a family tree with lower-level records subordinate to higher-level records. A multidimensional database (choice A) structures data in more than one dimension. A

relational database (choice B) organizes data into rows and columns. An object-oriented database (choice C) includes graphics, audio, and video.

8. **The correct answer is A.** Antivirus software can be used to prevent cybercriminal activity. A modem (choice B) is a combined device for modulation and demodulation, for example, between the digital data of a computer and the analog signal of a telephone line. Wi-Fi (choice C) is a facility allowing computers, smartphones, or other devices to connect to the Internet or communicate with one another wirelessly within a particular area. A router (choice D) is a networking device that forwards data packets between computer networks.

9. **The correct answer is C.** Bandwidth is the data transmission capacity of a communications channel. Cable TV and DSL provide high bandwidth communications abilities, while dial-up offers less. *Frequency* refers to how often an event occurs in a period, so choice D is incorrect. Choices A and B are incorrect.

10. **The correct answer is D.** Double-data rate synchronous dynamic RAM (DDR-SDRAM) is the newest and most popular RAM chip found in most PCs today. Both SDRAM (choice C) and SRAM (choice B) are faster than DRAM (choice A), which needs to be refreshed constantly by the CPU.

11. **The correct answer is D.** The domain name is the location of a website on the Internet, such as *www.google.com*. Choice A is the domain type, which is a nonprofit organization (.org) in this case. Choice B is the Web protocol (http://). Choice C is the file name and extension (home.htm).

12. **The correct answer is B.** A query is a search specification that leads a computer to search for a record in a database. Information in a database is sorted into records and fields, so choice A is incorrect. *Phishing* refers to an e-mail scam, so choice C is incorrect. *Queue* (choice D) refers to the line in which data and programs wait.

13. **The correct answer is D.** Communications satellites transmit data wirelessly for Global Positioning Systems. Infrared transports data just below the visible light spectrum, so choice A is incorrect. Broadcast radio requires transmitters and receivers, so choice B is incorrect. Microwave radio is used for Bluetooth, so choice C is incorrect.

14. **The correct answer is A.** The direct implementation method requires that all users stop using an old system before they begin using a new one. Parallel implementation (choice B) means both old and new systems are used at the same time. Phased implementation (choice C) means parts of the new system are phased in gradually. Pilot implementation (choice D) means a few users test the entire system before everyone else uses it.

15. **The correct answer is C.** Mainframe computers are large, fast computers capable of processing, storing, and managing great amounts of data. Large organizations, such as banks, airlines, and universities often use mainframes. Supercomputers (choice D) are used for weather forecasting and other processes requiring extensive calculations. A compiler (choice A) is a type of software used for translating computer language. Graphics terminals (choice B) are not used to store data.

16. **The correct answer is B.** Encryption is the process of scrambling data into an unreadable form to prevent security breaches. Only individuals with the necessary key can unscramble the information. Biometrics and antivirus software (choices A and D) are security tools but not ones that scramble data. An executable (choice C) is a file type that contains instructions for a computer.

17. **The correct answer is D.** The kernel is the core module of an operating system, and it manages memory, processes, tasks, and storage devices while the computer is on. The bootstrap program (choice C) initiates the loading of the operating system. A menu (choice A) is the graphical element that communicates commands from the user to

the computer. The buffer (choice B) is the disk area where programs wait.

18. **The correct answer is A.** A key logger records characters that are typed by a computer user and enables strangers to learn passwords and other private information. Browser hijackers (choice B) and search hijackers (choice D) are types of spyware that interfere with browser settings and search requests. A pop-up generator (choice C) is a type of adware that monitors online surfing and spending.

19. **The correct answer is D.** The clipboard is the holding area in memory used with the Copy command of word processing programs. Templates are reformatted style guides, so choice A is incorrect. Choices B and C are incorrect.

20. **The correct answer is A.** Peripheral devices are components that expand the input, output, and storage capabilities of a computer. Printers, scanners, and speakers are types of peripheral devices. A hard drive is a type of peripheral that expands storage functions, so choice B is incorrect. A modem (choice C) is a peripheral device that allows communications between computers. Software (choice D) is not considered a peripheral device.

21. **The correct answer is B.** The first personal computer was introduced in the 1970s. Choice A, C, and D are incorrect.

22. **The correct answer is A.** Search engines, such as Google and Bing, help users locate information on the Web. People find information through keyword indexes, subject directories, and metasearch engines. Network routers and local area networks (choices C and D) are components of a network, but they do not provide help with locating information. A data warehouse (choice B) is a system used for reporting and data analysis.

23. **The correct answer is A.** Static RAM (SRAM) holds on to its contents without needing to be refreshed by the CPU. DRAM, SDRAM, and DDR-SDRAM are all dynamic RAM chips. *Dynamic* means that the chip needs to be refreshed constantly by the CPU or its contents will be lost. Therefore, choices B, C, and D are incorrect.

24. **The correct answer is D.** Desktop publishing programs offer sophisticated graphic and design features. Word processing programs include only limited graphic options, so choice C is incorrect. Spreadsheets and network databases (choices A and B) are not equipped with significant graphic tools.

25. **The correct answer is B.** *Data representation* refers to the format in which data are stored, processed, and transmitted. Computers convert characters, numerals, or audio/visual data into marks, or binary digits, that electronic circuitry is able to manage. Choices A, C, and D are incorrect.

26. **The correct answer is C.** *Broadband* refers to high-bandwidth communications systems like DSL and cable TV. *Narrowband* (choice A), also known as voiceband (choice B), has less capacity than broadband and is associated with dial-up Internet access. *Crossband* (choice D) refers to radio frequencies.

27. **The correct answer is D.** Apple was the first company to introduce a computer with a single-circuit board. Choices A, B, and C are incorrect.

28. **The correct answer is B.** The final step of the boot process is when the microprocessor checks configurations. Power being distributed to circuitry (choice A) is the first step, and diagnostic tests being activated (choice C) is the third step. Peripheral devices are identified (choice D) in the fourth step of the sequence.

29. **The correct answer is A.** Wi-Fi allows computers to connect to the Internet without wires. Dial-up (choice B) is a form of Internet access that uses the facilities of the public switched telephone network (PSTN) to establish a connection to an Internet service provider (ISP) by dialing a telephone number on a conventional telephone line. Digital Subscriber Line, or DSL (choice C), is the way a computer connects to the Internet

at high speeds using telephone lines. A Local Area Network (LAN) is a network that connects computers and other devices in a relatively small area, typically a single building or a group of buildings, so choice D is incorrect.

30. **The correct answer is B.** A kilobyte (KB) equals 1,024 bytes. One byte is a group of 8 binary digits, so choice A is incorrect. A megabyte is 1,048,576 bytes, so choice C is incorrect. A gigabyte is 1,073,741,824 bytes, so choice D is incorrect.

31. **The correct answer is C.** A hypermedia database that includes links to audio, video, and graphics is a type of object-oriented database. Network databases and relational databases include no links, so choices A and B are incorrect. Multidimensional databases (choice D) organize data into two or more dimensions, but they do not include links to text, graphics, video, or audio.

32. **The correct answer is B.** Cyberbullying includes using electronic communication to attack, harass, or threaten others. *Netiquette* and *flaming* refer to communication over the Internet, so choices A and C are incorrect. *Social engineering* (choice D) refers to manipulating others to provide confidential information.

33. **The correct answer is D.** The Pentium® microprocessor allowed the use of graphics and music on PCs. MS-DOS (choice A) is a computer operating system by Microsoft Corporation. COBOL (choice B) is a computer programming language. A motherboard (choice C) is the physical arrangement in a computer that contains the computer's basic circuitry and components.

34. **The correct answer is A.** A firewall is a part of a computer system or network that is designed to block unauthorized access while permitting outward communication. Anti-virus software (choice B) is used to prevent cybercriminal activity. A modem (choice C) is a combined device for modulation and demodulation, for example, between the digital data of a computer and the analog signal of a telephone line. An Ethernet cable (choice D) is used in structured cabling for computer networks.

35. **The correct answer is D.** A server is a central computer that serves the computers on a client/server network by supplying data and storage. A central processing unit (CPU) is the microprocessor inside individual computers, so choice A is incorrect. Supercomputers (choice B) can act as servers if they have been configured as such, but they are not defined as servers. Ethernet is a type of network, so choice C is incorrect.

36. **The correct answer is C.** An IP (Internet Protocol) address consists of the unique numbers assigned to each computer on a network. The IP address enables data to be routed to the correct destination. A path (choice A) is a file's storage location. A domain (choice B) is a website's location on the Internet. A query processor (choice D) is a search engine component.

37. **The correct answer is C.** Buffers are the disk areas where programs or documents wait. *Spooled* refers to being placed in a buffer but not the waiting area itself. Paths and directories refer to where files are located for organizational purposes, so choices A and D are incorrect.

38. **The correct answer is D.** Malware, or malicious software, is designed to secretly penetrate a computer and disrupt operations. Viruses and worms are types of malware. Choices A, B, and C are proprietary software.

39. **The correct answer is A.** Architects and engineers use computer-aided design (CAD) software to create blueprints and product specifications. Image editing and drawing software are used for illustrations and graphics, but they do not provide the accuracy of CAD software that is needed in architecture and engineering.

40. **The correct answer is C.** *Volatile* refers to data that can exist only with a constant power supply. RAM is volatile because it requires electrical power to hold data, unlike ROM,

which cannot be changed. Choices A, B, and D are incorrect.

41. **The correct answer is C.** A phone support representative is not a job/position related to computer science or information systems. Choices A, B, and D are incorrect because they are jobs/positions in either computer science or information systems.

42. **The correct answer is B.** Pseudocode enables software engineers to design a program in narrative form, and it results in an outline or a summary of the program. Flowcharts graphically explain the logical flow of a program. Choices C and D are scripting and markup languages.

43. **The correct answer is D.** A user interface is the hardware and software that enable users and computers to interact. A computer's user interface includes hardware, such as the monitor, mouse, and keyboard, and software mechanisms, such as icons, menus, and toolbars. Operating systems and utility programs help a computer run, but they do not allow users to interact with computers. *Architecture* refers to the computer's design.

44. **The correct answer is A.** Vacuum tubes were used in the first digital computers developed in the 1940s. Vacuum tubes were replaced with transistors (choice D). Transistors were replaced with integrated circuits (choice C), which are also known as silicon chips (choice B).

45. **The correct answer is C.** CMOS chips hold flexible startup instructions that must be kept up to date when the computer is not on, such as time and date. ROM contains fixed startup instructions, so choice B is incorrect. Choices A and D are memory chips that temporarily hold data.

46. **The correct answer is B.** The base-2 number system is the unit of measurement used by computer circuitry. In the binary number system, there are only two digits—0 and 1. Such a system enables computers to represent nearly any number with 0's and 1's. Choices A, C, and D are incorrect.

47. **The correct answer is A.** NOMAD is a problem-oriented language developed along with other fourth-generation languages during the 1970s. COBOL is a third-generation language, so choice B is incorrect. Choices C and D are not fourth-generation languages.

48. **The correct answer is C.** Defragmenter utilities rearrange scattered files on a hard drive to speed up operation. Data recovery utilities restore damaged data, so choice A is incorrect. Backup utilities make duplicate copies of a hard disk, so choice B is incorrect. Data compression utilities help make more storage space available.

49. **The correct answer is A.** Prolog is a fifth-generation programming language associated with artificial intelligence. Choices B, C, and D are third-generation languages that enable programmers to write in human language rather than abbreviations and numbers.

50. **The correct answer is B.** Flash memory chips store flexible programs in computers, cell phones, digital cameras, and MP3 players. CMOS chips hold flexible startup instructions like time and date. Choices C and D are two types of software that do not store information.

51. **The correct answer is B.** Public domain software is available to the public without restrictions or copyrights. Proprietary software has restrictions on the way it may be used. Choices A and C are both copyright protected.

52. **The correct answer is B.** A gigabyte (GB) is approximately 1 billion bytes, and gigabytes are most often used when referring to a computer's storage capacity. Choices A and C are too small for the storage needs of a computer system. Megabytes (choice D) are usually used for describing medium to large files.

53. **The correct answer is C.** A personal computer connected to a network is a workstation. Supercomputers (choice A) are high-capacity, costly machines used for

complicated calculations. Microcontrollers (choice B) are embedded in cars and MP3 players. Mainframes are accessed by workstations, so choice D is incorrect.

54. **The correct answer is A.** Any hardware or software component available for use by a computer processor is a resource. Memory, storage, servers, and peripheral devices are resources, so choices B and D are close but incorrect. Packets are units of data transmitted through a network, so choice C is incorrect.

55. **The correct answer is C.** Secondary storage, or storage, is where files remain permanently when they are not needed for processing. Primary storage, which is known as RAM or memory, is where data is temporarily stored, so choices A and B are incorrect. The CPU is the microprocessor of a computer, so choice D is incorrect.

56. **The correct answer is C.** Through the operating system, users are able to organize files into directories and subdirectories. The operating system software controls the computer's use of memory and disk storage space. Choices A, B, and D are not involved with file organization.

57. **The correct answer is D.** A graphical user interface (GUI) allows users to choose icons or commands from menus with a mouse or a keyboard, and it is used in most modern computers. A command-line interface was the original type of interface that required users to type commands for programs to run. Choices A and C are not common interfaces.

58. **The correct answer is B.** Mail merge automates the process of creating personalized form letters by combining information in a mailing list with a form letter. Tracking changes (choice A) is a useful tool when editing documents. A hyperlink (choice C) is a reference within a document to another piece of information. Wizards (choice D) are interactive utilities programs that lead users through steps in creating documents.

59. **The correct answer is A.** The cell is the location where a row and a column intersect in an electronic spreadsheet. The label (choice B) is the text used to describe data in a spreadsheet. A group of cells adjacent to each other is a range (choice C). The numbers entered into a cell are the values (choice D).

60. **The correct answer is B.** A client is any computer that requests information from another computer or a server. Clients may include PCs, workstations, or other digital devices. Routers, modems, and bridges are various components of a network, so choices A, C, and D are incorrect.

Introduction to Business

OVERVIEW

Chapter 5

The DSST® Introduction to Business exam consists of 100 multiple-choice questions that cover the foundations and functions of business. The exam focuses upon the following topics: economic issues, international business, government and business, business ownership, entrepreneurship and franchise, management process, human resource management, production and operations, marketing management, financial management, risk management and insurance, and management and information systems. Careful reading, critical thinking, and logical analysis will be as important as your knowledge of business practices.

DIAGNOSTIC TEST ANSWER SHEET

1. Ⓐ Ⓑ Ⓒ Ⓓ   5. Ⓐ Ⓑ Ⓒ Ⓓ   9. Ⓐ Ⓑ Ⓒ Ⓓ   13. Ⓐ Ⓑ Ⓒ Ⓓ   17. Ⓐ Ⓑ Ⓒ Ⓓ
2. Ⓐ Ⓑ Ⓒ Ⓓ   6. Ⓐ Ⓑ Ⓒ Ⓓ   10. Ⓐ Ⓑ Ⓒ Ⓓ   14. Ⓐ Ⓑ Ⓒ Ⓓ   18. Ⓐ Ⓑ Ⓒ Ⓓ
3. Ⓐ Ⓑ Ⓒ Ⓓ   7. Ⓐ Ⓑ Ⓒ Ⓓ   11. Ⓐ Ⓑ Ⓒ Ⓓ   15. Ⓐ Ⓑ Ⓒ Ⓓ   19. Ⓐ Ⓑ Ⓒ Ⓓ
4. Ⓐ Ⓑ Ⓒ Ⓓ   8. Ⓐ Ⓑ Ⓒ Ⓓ   12. Ⓐ Ⓑ Ⓒ Ⓓ   16. Ⓐ Ⓑ Ⓒ Ⓓ   20. Ⓐ Ⓑ Ⓒ Ⓓ

POST-TEST ANSWER SHEET

1. Ⓐ Ⓑ Ⓒ Ⓓ   13. Ⓐ Ⓑ Ⓒ Ⓓ   25. Ⓐ Ⓑ Ⓒ Ⓓ   37. Ⓐ Ⓑ Ⓒ Ⓓ   49. Ⓐ Ⓑ Ⓒ Ⓓ
2. Ⓐ Ⓑ Ⓒ Ⓓ   14. Ⓐ Ⓑ Ⓒ Ⓓ   26. Ⓐ Ⓑ Ⓒ Ⓓ   38. Ⓐ Ⓑ Ⓒ Ⓓ   50. Ⓐ Ⓑ Ⓒ Ⓓ
3. Ⓐ Ⓑ Ⓒ Ⓓ   15. Ⓐ Ⓑ Ⓒ Ⓓ   27. Ⓐ Ⓑ Ⓒ Ⓓ   39. Ⓐ Ⓑ Ⓒ Ⓓ   51. Ⓐ Ⓑ Ⓒ Ⓓ
4. Ⓐ Ⓑ Ⓒ Ⓓ   16. Ⓐ Ⓑ Ⓒ Ⓓ   28. Ⓐ Ⓑ Ⓒ Ⓓ   40. Ⓐ Ⓑ Ⓒ Ⓓ   52. Ⓐ Ⓑ Ⓒ Ⓓ
5. Ⓐ Ⓑ Ⓒ Ⓓ   17. Ⓐ Ⓑ Ⓒ Ⓓ   29. Ⓐ Ⓑ Ⓒ Ⓓ   41. Ⓐ Ⓑ Ⓒ Ⓓ   53. Ⓐ Ⓑ Ⓒ Ⓓ
6. Ⓐ Ⓑ Ⓒ Ⓓ   18. Ⓐ Ⓑ Ⓒ Ⓓ   30. Ⓐ Ⓑ Ⓒ Ⓓ   42. Ⓐ Ⓑ Ⓒ Ⓓ   54. Ⓐ Ⓑ Ⓒ Ⓓ
7. Ⓐ Ⓑ Ⓒ Ⓓ   19. Ⓐ Ⓑ Ⓒ Ⓓ   31. Ⓐ Ⓑ Ⓒ Ⓓ   43. Ⓐ Ⓑ Ⓒ Ⓓ   55. Ⓐ Ⓑ Ⓒ Ⓓ
8. Ⓐ Ⓑ Ⓒ Ⓓ   20. Ⓐ Ⓑ Ⓒ Ⓓ   32. Ⓐ Ⓑ Ⓒ Ⓓ   44. Ⓐ Ⓑ Ⓒ Ⓓ   56. Ⓐ Ⓑ Ⓒ Ⓓ
9. Ⓐ Ⓑ Ⓒ Ⓓ   21. Ⓐ Ⓑ Ⓒ Ⓓ   33. Ⓐ Ⓑ Ⓒ Ⓓ   45. Ⓐ Ⓑ Ⓒ Ⓓ   57. Ⓐ Ⓑ Ⓒ Ⓓ
10. Ⓐ Ⓑ Ⓒ Ⓓ   22. Ⓐ Ⓑ Ⓒ Ⓓ   34. Ⓐ Ⓑ Ⓒ Ⓓ   46. Ⓐ Ⓑ Ⓒ Ⓓ   58. Ⓐ Ⓑ Ⓒ Ⓓ
11. Ⓐ Ⓑ Ⓒ Ⓓ   23. Ⓐ Ⓑ Ⓒ Ⓓ   35. Ⓐ Ⓑ Ⓒ Ⓓ   47. Ⓐ Ⓑ Ⓒ Ⓓ   59. Ⓐ Ⓑ Ⓒ Ⓓ
12. Ⓐ Ⓑ Ⓒ Ⓓ   24. Ⓐ Ⓑ Ⓒ Ⓓ   36. Ⓐ Ⓑ Ⓒ Ⓓ   48. Ⓐ Ⓑ Ⓒ Ⓓ   60. Ⓐ Ⓑ Ⓒ Ⓓ

INTRODUCTION TO BUSINESS DIAGNOSTIC TEST

Directions: Carefully read each of the following 20 questions. Choose the best answer to each question and fill in the corresponding circle on the answer sheet. The Answer Key and Explanations can be found following this Diagnostic Test.

1. A cafeteria benefits plan provides employees with
   A. an incentive to work harder.
   B. a set dollar amount to be used to select from a variety of benefits.
   C. reduced price lunches.
   D. the option of either selecting a profit-sharing plan or a merit salary plan.

2. The targeted market segment for the magazine *Popular Science* is probably based on
   A. geographic region.
   B. age.
   C. interest.
   D. income level.

3. Which of the following describes a drop shipper?
   A. It inventories goods, sets up displays in stores, and bills for goods that are sold.
   B. It passes orders on to a manufacturer or another wholesaler and receives a commission.
   C. It inventories goods and sells directly to retailers.
   D. It inventories, sells, and delivers goods.

4. Which of the following is an example of public relations?
   A. Thirty-second ad on a TV show
   B. Personal appearance by an actor to promote a movie
   C. Press release about a new product
   D. Fan website for a TV show

5. What does SWOT stand for?
   A. Sweat equity, weaknesses, opportunities, threats
   B. Strengths, weaknesses, opportunities, threats
   C. Standards, wariness, optimism, threats
   D. Software, web, opportunities, technology

6. Which of the following describes the time value of money concept?
   A. The time value of money is a reason to invest in certificates of deposit.
   B. The value of money increases or decreases depending on inflation.
   C. Through investing, money will grow over time by earning interest.
   D. It is better to pay off debts with future money than with current money because inflation cheapens the value of money over time.

7. Which of the following is the most common form of business ownership in the United States?
   A. Sole proprietorship
   B. Partnership
   C. Limited liability partnership
   D. Corporation

8. Which of the following systems adds value to all businesses involved in producing goods from raw materials to finished product?
   A. Distribution channel
   B. Quality improvement team
   C. Supply chain management
   D. Organizational analysis

9. The second step in effective decision making is to
   A. evaluate alternative solutions.
   B. choose one solution and execute it.
   C. generate alternative solutions.
   D. evaluate how well the solution is working.

10. Insider trading directly violates ethical conduct toward
    A. other employees of the company.
    B. investors in the company.
    C. the company's customers.
    D. the company's creditors.

11. Which of the following measures the market value of goods and services produced within a country during a year?
    A. GDP
    B. GNP
    C. CPI
    D. PPI

12. A U.S. tech company hires a company in Ireland to handle its help line. The U.S. company is
    A. not focused on customer care as a goal.
    B. entering into a partnership with the Irish company.
    C. outsourcing work.
    D. offshoring a part of its business.

13. Which of the following affect the demand for a product?
    I. Changes in consumer preferences
    II. The price of substitute goods
    III. Decrease in the number of suppliers for the raw materials in the product
    A. I only
    B. I and II only
    C. II and III only
    D. I, II, and III

14. A major risk to companies that shift manufacturing to other countries is
    A. the shuttering of their factories domestically.
    B. home country import quotas.
    C. the risk of political instability in host countries.
    D. the high price of foreign labor.

15. Buying a smartphone because everyone in your group has one illustrates what type of influence on consumer behavior?
    A. Personal
    B. Sociocultural
    C. Psychological
    D. Demographic

16. A company's extranet is available to
    A. anyone trolling the Internet.
    B. employees, customers, and vendors.
    C. employees and customers.
    D. employees only.

17. Among other traits, an affiliative leadership style
    A. uses top-down management.
    B. inspires employees.
    C. is collaborative.
    D. encourages goodwill and harmony among employees.

18. An example of direct marketing is a(n)
    A. department store.
    B. electronic storefront.
    C. Tupperware® party.
    D. manufacturer's representative calling on a chain store buyer.

19. Unemployment that is caused by a lack of demand for workers because of conditions in the economy is
    A. seasonal unemployment.
    B. cyclical unemployment.
    C. structural unemployment.
    D. frictional unemployment.

20. eBay® is an example of what type of e-commerce?
    A. Business to business
    B. Consumer to business
    C. Business to consumer
    D. Consumer to consumer

ANSWER KEY AND EXPLANATIONS

1. B	**5.** B	**9.** C	**13.** B	**17.** D
2. C	**6.** C	**10.** B	**14.** C	**18.** B
3. B	**7.** A	**11.** A	**15.** B	**19.** B
4. A	**8.** C	**12.** C	**16.** B	**20.** D

1. **The correct answer is B.** Cafeteria benefits plans are meant to reduce the cost to companies of employee benefits. Choice A is incorrect because benefits don't depend on performance. Choice C is incorrect; reduced price lunches are subsidized lunches. Choice D is incorrect because neither a profit-sharing plan nor a merit salary plan are matters of employee choice; both compensation programs are determined by company policy.

2. **The correct answer is C.** The market segment for *Popular Science* is probably based on an interest in things scientific. Geographic region (choice A), age (choice B), and income level (choice D) are not likely to be influences on a purchase that doesn't depend on living in a certain region, being in a certain age range, or having a certain income level.

3. **The correct answer is B.** A drop shipper doesn't inventory the goods that it sells; it passes the orders that it takes on to the manufacturer or another wholesaler and receives a commission. Choice A is incorrect because it describes a rack jobber. Choice C is incorrect because it describes a cash-and-carry wholesaler. Choice D is incorrect because it describes a truck wholesaler.

4. **The correct answer is A.** Only a prepared ad is an example of public relations. Choices B, C, and D are examples of publicity, where the company has no control over what is said or shown. Even the press release may not be used in the manner in which the company wants.

5. **The correct answer is B.** SWOT stands for strengths, weaknesses, opportunities, threats. Choices A, C, and D are incorrect.

6. **The correct answer is C.** In addition to earning interest, money may yield other returns, such as dividends and stock splits. Choice A is incorrect because the time value of money is a reason to invest in CDs, but that's not a definition of the time value of money, which is what the question is asking. Choices B and D are true about inflation, but they are incorrect answers to the question.

7. **The correct answer is A.** Sole proprietorship is the most common form of business ownership in the United States, making up about three quarters of U.S. businesses, but only about 5 percent of business revenue. Corporations (choice D) make up about 20 percent of U.S. businesses. Partnerships (choice B) and limited liability partnerships (choice C) are also incorrect.

8. **The correct answer is C.** The key word here is *value*. Miss that word and you might select choice A, distribution channel, which moves a product from raw materials to finished good. Choice B is incorrect because a quality improvement team operates within a single company to improve the quality of its processes and products. Choice D is incorrect because organizational analysis is a review of strengths and weaknesses conducted within a single company.

9. **The correct answer is C.** Step 1 is to identify the problem and step 2 is to generate alternatives (choice C). This has to be done before evaluating alternative solutions, which is step 3 and choice A. Step 4 is to choose one of those alternatives and implement it (choice B). Step 5 is to evaluate how well the solution is working (choice D).

10. **The correct answer is B.** Insider trading is buying or selling stock based on confidential information about a company and can directly harm investors, either by driving down the price of the stock through selling or driving up the price of the stock through buying, putting it out of the range of an average investor. The key word here is *directly*. Insider trading may indirectly harm other employees (choice A), customers (choice C), and creditors (choice D) if the stock price dives and investors and lenders lose confidence in the business. However, this represents indirect, not direct, damage.

11. **The correct answer is A.** GDP stands for gross domestic product and is defined as the market value of all goods and services produced within a country during a year. GNP (choice B) stands for gross national product and includes the value of all goods and services produced by facilities owned by domestic companies, but located anywhere in the world. CPI (choice C) stands for consumer price index and refers to a market basket of goods and services that is monitored monthly for changes in its prices. PPI (choice D) is the producer price index and is the industrial equivalent of the CPI.

12. **The correct answer is C.** Outsourcing means giving work that was handled internally to an outside company, typically a company based in another country, whereas offshoring (choice D) is sending part of a company to another country. Choice A is incorrect because hiring a company in another country to provide customer service is not an indication that the company is not interested in offering good follow-up services to its customers post-purchase. Choice B is incorrect because the question states that the U.S. company is hiring another company; there is no mention of any kind of partnership arrangement.

13. **The correct answer is B.** Items I and II are both factors that affect demand, whereas item III is a factor that affects supply, so only items I and II are correct. The only answer choice that includes both of those items and only those items is choice B.

14. **The correct answer is C.** Outsourcing work to other countries or building plants in other countries is risky if the country has a history of political unrest or repressive government. Choice A is not a risk to a company moving production off shore, though it may be a possibility or even a certainty. Choice B is incorrect because products made by or for a home country company on foreign soil don't come under import regulations when the goods are being shipped to the company's home country; import quotas govern goods made by foreign companies with no affiliation to a home country company. Choice D is incorrect because a major reason that companies shift manufacturing offshore is the low cost of labor in other countries.

15. **The correct answer is B.** Buying something because one's peers are buying it illustrates sociocultural influences on consumer behavior. Choice A is incorrect because a personal influence would be buying a cheap phone because the buyer is always losing phones. Choice C is incorrect because psychological influences include perception, motivation, learning, and experience. Choice D, demographic, is a way to segment the market, not an influence on a consumer purchase.

16. **The correct answer is B.** A company's extranet is available to employees and to customers and vendors who are authorized to gain access. Choice A is incorrect and describes public sites on the Internet. Choice C is too narrow an answer because it omits vendors. Choice D describes a company's intranet.

17. **The correct answer is D.** An affiliative leader encourages goodwill and harmony among employees. A leader who is authoritarian uses a commanding style (choice A). A visionary style (choice B) inspires employees. Choice C describes a democratic style. The other leadership styles that have been identified are coaching (counselor, delegator) and pacesetting (micromanager, driven, and driver).

18. **The correct answer is B.** Direct marketing, or direct response marketing, is direct contact between the seller and the buyer. A department store is not an example of direct marketing, so choice A is incorrect. Choices C and D are incorrect because both are examples of direct selling, not direct marketing.

19. **The correct answer is B.** The high unemployment rate during and after the recession of 2007 to 2010 was a result of cyclical unemployment; the unemployed were willing and able to work, but businesses were not hiring because of economic conditions. Seasonal unemployment (choice A) is unemployment tied to changes in season. Structural unemployment (choice C) is unemployment due to changes in an industry that may result from technological changes or changes in market demand. Frictional unemployment (choice D) is temporary unemployment that results when people change jobs or relocate.

20. **The correct answer is D.** eBay® enables consumers to sell to one another. Choices A and C are other types of e-commerce and so are incorrect. Choice B is incorrect.

answers

diagnostic test

DIAGNOSTIC TEST ASSESSMENT GRID

Now that you've completed the diagnostic test and read through the answer explanations, you can use your results to target your studying. Find the question numbers from the diagnostic test that you answered incorrectly and highlight or circle them below. Then focus extra attention on the sections within the chapter dealing with those topics.

Introduction to Business		
Content Area	**Topics Covered**	**Questions**
Foundations of Business	• Forms of business ownership • Government and business • Economics of business	7, 11, 13, 19
Functions of Business	• Management • Marketing • Finance • Accounting • Production and operations • Management information systems • Human resources • Entrepreneurship	1, 2, 3, 4, 5, 8, 9, 10, 15, 16, 17, 18
Contemporary Issues	• Role of technology and e-commerce • Business ethics and social responsibility • Global business environment	6, 12, 14, 20

GET THE FACTS

To see the DSST® Introduction to Business Fact Sheet, go to **http://getcollegecredit.com/ exam_fact_sheets** and click on the **Business** tab. Scroll down and click the **Introduction to Business** link. Here you will find suggestions for further study material and the ACE college credit recommendations for passing the test.

FOUNDATIONS OF BUSINESS

Every business produces a good or a service or both. How it produces its product is determined by a number of factors. Before even those decisions are made, however, a businessperson needs to decide the type of business organization he or she wants to establish. Depending on the answer, the new business owner(s) will need to fill out government forms, pay taxes in a certain way, and obey rules and regulations pertinent to the business. Underpinning all this is the economics of conducting business.

FORMS OF BUSINESS OWNERSHIP

There are five basic forms of business ownership:

1. Sole proprietorship
2. Partnership
3. Co-operative
4. Corporation
5. Nonprofit corporation types

Partnerships and corporations have several different formats.

Sole Proprietorship

The sole proprietorship is the most common form of business ownership in the United States, accounting for almost three quarters of the business organizations in the country. Anyone who runs a business alone is a sole proprietor unless that person has incorporated the business. No paperwork or special reporting to the Internal Revenue Service is required of sole proprietorships. Sole proprietorships are run by one person, but that person may hire employees.

There are a number of advantages to the sole proprietorship form of business ownership: lack of legal requirements for establishing and operating the business, low start-up costs, no separate tax filings so the owner gets all the benefit of any tax loss, no need to divide any profits, and no shared decision making. However, some of these benefits may also be a disadvantage. For example, without a partner, there is no one with whom to share losses. The disadvantages to sole proprietorships are unlimited liability, difficulty in borrowing money, responsibility for all losses, no one to share in making decisions, and the end of the business when the owner retires or dies.

The major disadvantage is **unlimited liability**, that is, the sole proprietor is held responsible for all debts that the business incurs, as well as all liabilities. For example, if a plumber doesn't turn off the water before installing a new toilet and water floods the bathroom and leaks to the first floor, the homeowner could sue the plumber for damages. If the plumber is a sole proprietor and the homeowner wins, the homeowner could go after the plumber's savings and home to satisfy the judgment. A sole proprietor who employs others is responsible for them as well when it comes to liability. It is also difficult to borrow money to set up or expand a sole proprietorship because a bank will only lend based on the owner's assets.

Partnership

In forty-eight of the fifty states, a partnership must file information about the business under the federal **Revised Uniform Limited Partnership Act.** However, partnerships are similar to sole proprietorships in that no separate business tax filings are required. However, an important advantage of a partnership over a sole proprietorship is that the former will find it easier to borrow money for

TIP

All partnership agreements should establish at the beginning the responsibilities of all partners and the guidelines for the addition and departure of partners over time.

the business from banks. In a partnership, the business doesn't rest on the ability of just one person to make it grow. Other advantages include all partners share in contributing to the start-up costs, in any profits, and in decision making.

The most important disadvantage to partnerships is unlimited liability. In a partnership, each partner is responsible not only for his or her own debts and actions in the course of conducting the business but also for whatever the other partners incur in the course of doing business.

There are two types of partnerships: general and limited. The description so far of a partnership describes the general partnership arrangement. In a limited partnership, some partners are investors only and have no decision-making authority over the operations of the business. The liability of limited partners is equal only to the percentage of the business they own. A partnership that has limited partners must have at least one general, or active, partner. This person manages the business on a day-to-day basis and has unlimited liability.

Co-operative

Another form of business ownership is the co-operative. A group of partnerships and/or sole proprietorships join together to benefit their individual businesses. As a group, they have more financial power than as individual businesses and, therefore, have greater bargaining power for things such as reduced rail rates for shipping goods. Co-operatives are more common in agriculture than in other industries.

Corporation

A corporation is formed according to state laws. It is an entity that is separate from its owners, the stockholders, and thus has liability separate from its owners. It must file corporate tax returns annually and has certain legal rights, such as the ability to sue, and certain legal obligations, such as obedience to the law. Unlike the other forms of business ownership, a corporation raises capital by selling shares in its business. The liability of investors, or stockholders, in a corporation is limited; their liability extends only to the amount of their investment in the corporation.

In addition to limited liability for investors, the advantages of a corporate form of business ownership are ease of obtaining capital and continuity of management. The future growth and management of a corporation doesn't depend on one person—unless the corporation is really a one-person operation formed for liability purposes. A major disadvantage of corporations is double taxation. The profits of a corporation are taxed as business income, and when they are paid out as dividends, stockholders must pay tax on them as personal income.

Corporations are owned by their investors. Overall governance falls to a board of directors, but day-to-day operations are overseen by the officers of the corporation, typically a chief executive officer (CEO) and a chief financial officer (CFO). Sometimes, the CEO is a chief operation officer (COO) instead.

There are six types of corporations:

1. *Privately or Closely Held:* The founding family, a group of investors, or the employees of the company may hold the shares. Outsiders cannot buy stock. Profits are taxed as corporate income and shareholders have limited liability.

2. *Public or Publicly Held, Also Known as a C Corp:* Any member of the public and employees can buy stock. Profits are taxed as corporate earnings, and shareholders have limited liability.

3. *Subchapter S, Commonly Called S Corp:* Shareholders pay personal income tax on their share of any profits that the business earns. S corps don't pay corporate taxes, but they must file tax returns annually. Shareholders have limited liability.

4. *Limited Liability (LLC):* Profits are taxed as personal income and shareholders enjoy limited liability.

5. *Professional:* These are formed by professionals such as lawyers and doctors and enjoy limited liability.

6. *Multinational or Transnational:* These corporations have operations in multiple countries and their stock is sold on multiple stock exchanges. Regulations, including taxes, vary from country to country.

Nonprofit Corporation

A nonprofit, or not-for-profit, is set up to support some social or educational mission. A not-for-profit, as the name implies, doesn't make a profit. Any revenue that it generates that isn't required for operations is used to further its mission. Nonprofits are tax-exempt if they qualify under federal regulations, but they must file a tax return and fulfill other reporting requirements for the federal government and for the states under which they operate.

GOVERNMENT AND BUSINESS

Government influences the business climate in two ways: through regulatory policy and through economic policy. Governments—federal, state, and municipal—regulate what businesses can and cannot do. Through their tax policies, all three levels of government affect how much money businesses have to spend and can borrow. The federal government also affects businesses through monetary policy.

Regulatory Policies

State and local governments have a variety of rules and regulations that affect businesses, from requiring licenses for companies to do business to collecting city wage taxes on suburban commuters. These are statutory laws, which are made by state legislatures and, therefore, vary from state to state. For example, some states require that companies of a certain size carry disability insurance on their employees, but other states do not. Some have **right-to-work laws** forbidding closed shops, and other states don't. However, when many think of "government," they think of the federal government and its regulatory reach. Every aspect of business is covered under some department or agency of the federal government. For example:

- **Department of Labor**: The Bureau of Labor Statistics compiles a number of economic indices to aid businesses and workers. The Occupational Safety and Health Administration (OSHA) is the main agency charged with setting and enforcing standards for the workplace and for workforce training and education. The Fair Labor Standards Act regulates the minimum wage.

Other independent
agencies related to
business are the
Consumer Product
Safety Commission
(CPSC), the Environ-
mental Protection
Agency (EPA), and
the National
Transportation
Safety Board (NTSB).

- **Department of Agriculture (USDA)**: In addition to overseeing farm subsidy programs, the USDA supports the Women, Infant, and Children (WIC) food assistance program, as well as other Child Nutrition Programs.

- **Department of Health and Human Services**: The Food and Drug Administration (FDA) oversees food safety programs and approves new drugs before they can be sold in the United States.

- **Department of Commerce**: According to its website, the U.S. Department of Commerce has "a wide range of responsibilities in the areas of trade, economic development, technology, entrepreneurship and business development, environmental stewardship, and statistical research and analysis." Commerce oversees patents and trademarks, imports and exports, and manufacturing standards.

- **Federal Trade Commission (FTC)**: The FTC is a separate agency of the federal government, not affiliated with an executive branch-level department. The agency's mission includes consumer protection as well as the advancement of competition. Deceptive advertising practices come under its jurisdiction, as do the Telemarketing Sales Rule, the Pay-Per-Call Rule, and the Equal Credit Opportunity Act.

Businesses, regardless of their size, are subject to a variety of laws:

- **Contract**: To be valid, a contract must include a stated offer and acceptance, have mutual consent, include a consideration (exchange of item of value, such as a dollar), be legal, and be in the proper form depending on the amount and term of the contract.

- **Tort**: No contract exists: intentional, product liability, or negligent

- **Property**: intellectual, tangible real, tangible personal, or intangible personal

- **Agency**: Governing those who act for another party

- **Commercial**: Uniform Commercial Code: contracts, warranties

- **Bankruptcy**: Federal law: Chapter 7, liquidation, and Chapter 11, reorganization

Fiscal and Monetary Policies

One aspect of federal economic policy is the maintenance of a stable economic environment in which businesses can operate. As you will read below, economies go through fluctuations known as business cycles. The federal government through fiscal and monetary policies seeks to smooth out these ups and downs in output, unemployment, and inflation.

Fiscal policy refers to taxes and government spending. With the exception of some fees, the federal government—like state and local governments—raises revenue through levying taxes on businesses and individuals. When inflation is rising, raising taxes can cool down the economy. The higher the taxes, the less money there is for consumers to buy goods and services and the slower the economy. When the economy is in a downturn, cutting taxes doesn't have the opposite effect. Some people will use the additional money for new spending as the government intends, but some will pay off old debts, and others will save the additional money. Another way to stimulate the economy in a downturn is to increase government spending. Rather than increase taxes, the government borrows money by selling Treasury bonds, notes, and bills for varying periods of time and at competitive market rates.

Monetary policy is the tool of the **Federal Reserve System**, commonly referred to as the Fed, which is an independent agency. The Fed is the nation's central bank, or banker's bank, and as such, operates the twelve district banks of the Federal Reserve System, oversees member banks in those districts, and sets the nation's general money and credit policies. It has three tools that it can use:

1. *Discount Rate:* The rate charged to member banks to borrow money (the higher the discount rate, the less money banks will borrow, the less they will lend, and the slower the economy); a tool to keep inflation in check (the lower the discount rate, the more money banks will borrow, the more they will lend, and the more the economy will grow)

2. *Reserve Requirement:* The percentage of their deposits that member banks must hold as a reserve against their deposits (acts similarly to increases and decreases in the discount rate)

3. *Open-Market Operations:* Mechanism to buy or sell bonds and securities on the open market (buying puts money into the economy to stimulate it and selling takes money out of the economy to contract it)

ECONOMICS OF BUSINESS

Economics, as defined by Webster's dictionary, is "the science that deals with the production, distribution, and consumption of wealth and with the various related problems of labor, finance, taxation, etc." It almost sounds like a definition of business. Businesses try to accurately discern the needs, wants, and desires of the marketplace in order to produce and distribute the right mix of goods, or products, while dealing with labor, financial issues, competition, and the like.

A company may operate in any one of four types of economic systems:

1. *Traditional:* Rural, agrarian economy of which few still exist

2. *Planned:* Control by the government over what is produced, how, and for whom and at what price; complete control under a communist system and a lesser degree of control in a socialist system; in the latter, typically government-run social services and utilities

3. *Market:* Decisions about what to produce, how, for whom, and at what price made by businesses and individuals; free market, free enterprise, capitalist systems

4. *Mixed:* Combination of planned and market systems; economic decisions made by businesses and individuals with some government control and oversight; examples include the United States, Great Britain, and Germany

Regardless of the type of economic system, there are five factors of production in play: labor, natural resources, capital, entrepreneurs, and technology. Capital is divided into real capital, meaning the equipment and facilities used to produce goods and services, and financial capital, the money needed to start up and operate a business.

Economics of Supply and Demand

In a **market economy** or **mixed economy**, such as the United States, market forces set prices through the laws of supply and demand. Demand is the willingness and ability of consumers to buy a good or service, and supply is the willingness and ability of producers to produce a good or service. The law of supply states that producers will offer more of a product/service as the price increases and less of a product/service as the price decreases. The law of demand works in reverse. Consumers will buy more of a product/service as the price decreases and less of a product/service as the price increases.

The point at which a balance between supply and demand is reached is called the **equilibrium point** or, in business terms, the **market price.**

Supply and demand are shown on supply curves and demand curves. A **supply curve** indicates the amount of goods or services offered at different price points, and a **demand curve** shows how many products or services will be bought at different price points. When there is more demand than supply, a shortage occurs. When there is more supply than demand, a surplus occurs.

A variety of factors can affect both supply and demand and thus the availability and price of goods and services. Factors affecting supply, positively or negatively, may be changes in the price of raw materials, forecasts of future prices—either up or down, acceleration of technological change, increase or decrease in the number of competitors, and increase or decrease in the price of substitute goods. Demand may be changed positively or negatively by such factors as increase or decrease in income distribution, changes in consumer preferences, changes in population age and distribution, and increase or decrease in demand for substitute goods.

Competition

Competition is one characteristic of market and mixed economies. The other three are the right to own property, freedom of choice in buying and selling goods and services and one's labor, and profits. There are various degrees of competition from none to complete, or perfect, competition:

- **Monopoly**: Lack of competition; single supplier of a good or service, or one dominant supplier in an industry; controls pricing

- **Monopolistic**: Several producers making similar products that are perceived as slightly differentiated; no perfect substitute goods; each producer can set own price within certain limits of the marketplace; mix of large and small businesses competing for market share

- **Oligopoly**: Few producers, little differentiation of product, little difference in pricing; occurs in industries with high barriers to entrance, such as large initial investment costs, well-established firms, fierce competition

- **Perfect**: Many producers—large and small; no perceived differences by consumers among products; pricing set by the marketplace

Economic Indicators

To be successful, those who run businesses must be aware of the economic environment in which they operate. **Aggregate output** is the total amount of goods and services produced by an economy in a given period. There are a number of indicators that show how well or how poorly the economy is doing. Many of the reports are compiled and published by the federal government. Among the indicators are the following:

- **Gross Domestic Product (GDP)**: Total value of all goods and services produced domestically in a given period; no goods and services produced outside the country are included

- **Gross National Product** (**GNP**): Total value of all goods and services produced by a nation's companies regardless of where the facilities are located in a given period of time; considered a less accurate indicator of an economy's health than GDP

- **Consumer Price Index** (**CPI**): Based on a market basket of goods and services that doesn't vary from month to month in order to show a pattern of monthly expenses for the typical urban household; the eight categories are food, housing, clothing, transportation, medical care, recreation, education, and miscellaneous items, such as haircuts and cigarettes

- **Producer Price Index** (**PPI**): Measurement of selling prices received by domestic producers of goods and services for their products, includes prices for raw materials, component goods, and finished goods

- **Unemployment Rate**: Low rate can translate into difficulty finding qualified workers; high rate can indicate low consumer demand

- **Productivity**: Rate at which goods and services are produced in a given period; output per capita; the higher the productivity, the healthier the economy

Two other important numbers that affect a nation's economy are the national debt and the balance of trade. To raise money to pay its bills, the federal government sells bonds in addition to levying and collecting taxes. The more bonds the government sells, the more money it takes out of the general pool of investor dollars, which makes it more difficult for businesses—large and small—and individuals to borrow. The balance of trade may affect the economy positively or negatively. If a country sells more goods abroad than it imports, the balance of trade is positive. If the opposite is true, the balance of trade runs a trade deficit. The country owes more to other countries than it takes in from exports.

Over time, the economy goes through peaks and valleys—expansions and contractions—that are known as **business cycles.** Expansions are known as booms; severe contractions are called depressions and less severe contractions are called recessions. In addition, the economy can be affected by inflation, when price levels across the economy rise, and deflation, when price levels across the economy decline. The federal government, through its fiscal and monetary tools, attempts to even out these ups and down with stabilization policies. The aim of the polices is (1) to keep prices in check in order to slow inflation and (2) to expand demand in order to lower unemployment.

Unemployment rate can be affected by several factors and categorized into four types:

1. *Cyclical unemployment*, in which the unemployed are willing and able to work, but businesses are not hiring because of economic conditions. The high unemployment rate during and after the recession of 2007 to 2010 was an example of cyclical unemployment.

2. *Seasonal unemployment*, which is unemployment tied to changes in season, such as construction workers who have no work in the winter and ski instructors who are unemployed in the summer.

3. *Structural unemployment*, which is unemployment due to changes in an industry that may result from technological changes or changes in market demand; for example, the loss of jobs by typewriter repairers when computers replaced typewriters.

4. *Frictional unemployment*, which is temporary unemployment resulting from people changing jobs or careers or relocating.

FUNCTIONS OF BUSINESS

What types of organization are used currently in companies? What makes a good manager? How are prices set? What financial controls should a company have? How do information systems make companies more efficient? This section answers these questions and more as it describes the varied functions of business.

MANAGEMENT

As Ebert and Griffin's *Business Essentials* defines management, it "is the process of planning, organizing, leading, and controlling an organization's financial, physical, human, and information resources to achieve its goals." Planning is an essential element of the role of management and includes setting the goals, strategies, and tactics for the business. The function of control includes monitoring the business' performance and making adjustments as needed if goals are not being met.

Management is divided into three levels:

1. *Top managers* run the overall organization.

2. *Middle managers* see that the company's strategies are implemented and goals are being met.

3. *First-line* managers directly oversee employees.

Organizations have a number of functional areas in common: financial, human resources, information, marketing, and operations. Depending on the industry, an organization may have additional functional areas, such as research and development (R&D) or strategic alliances.

Managers need certain skills:

- **Technical**: The specialized skills required for a particular industry and series of jobs within that industry

- **Interpersonal**: The ability to interact with and motivate employees. It's more than the ability to get along with people and includes the ability to communicate effectively and inspire confidence, loyalty, and good work

- **Decision Making**: The ability to identify problems, gather and evaluate information, develop alternative solutions, evaluate alternatives, and select the best one for the problem; the plan is then subjected to further evaluation to determine if it met its goals

- **Conceptual**: The ability to think in the abstract, to see the big picture; extremely useful in SWOT analysis (strengths, weaknesses, opportunities, threats; the first two are internal factors and the last two are external to the organization)

- **Time Management**: Using time for one's self and one's subordinates most efficiently and effectively, includes prioritizing paperwork, establishing agendas for meetings, setting aside a time for phone calls, and organizing and prioritizing e-mails for response and filing

In addition to these skills, many managers today will need to be able to manage in a global environment, which requires understanding of the global business environment and understanding of cultural differences with foreign nationals within their own companies and with strategic partners and competitors. The ability to conceptualize the use of technology for efficient operations and communication is also important.

Planning

Organizations develop five types of plans: strategic, tactical, operational, contingency, and crisis. Contingency planning helps a company deal with unexpected changes, for example, a huge jump in gasoline prices that sends car buyers to smaller, more fuel-efficient foreign cars forced U.S. car makers to change their car designs and produce smaller, more fuel-efficient cars. Crisis management planning describes how an organization will continue to operate during an emergency such as 9/11 or the earthquake and tsunami that hit Japan in 2011.

An extremely important function of managers, especially top management, is **strategic planning** to set the future of the organization. Strategic planning encompasses developing a vision statement, developing a mission statement, conducting a SWOT analysis, establishing goals, developing objectives, and determining tactics to achieve the objectives and goals and ultimately create the vision.

An organization's goals typically fall into long-range, intermediate, and short-range categories. Tactical planning is carried out by middle managers with the oversight of top managers and involves intermediate goals—from one to five years. Middle managers and first-line managers typically develop operational plans based on short-range goals—anywhere from daily to quarterly.

Long-range goals refer to periods longer than five years.

Organizing

Organizing a company is determining how the company will be structured. **Structure** is determined by specialization of tasks, departmentalization of those specialties/tasks, and distribution of decision making. Typically, large businesses have three levels of management: top, middle, and first-line. This structure resembles a pyramid.

Within this structure, there are three types of organizational frameworks possible, based on the distribution of authority: vertical, or flat; horizontal, or tall; and network. The vertical structure flats out the pyramid. This type of structure decentralizes authority among various levels of management within the organization, including line departments, staff, and committees and teams. The horizontal structure centralizes authority in top-line management.

Leading

Part of a manager's job is to motivate, encourage, and influence others. There are a variety of approaches to leadership as identified by researchers: trait, behavioral, situational, transformational, and charismatic. Motivation may be extrinsic or intrinsic. There are three main theories about motivation:

1. *Maslow's Hierarchy of Needs:* From lowest to highest: physiological, safety, belonging, esteem, self-actualization

2. *Herzberg's Motivator-Hygiene Theory or Two Factor Theory: Hygiene* translates into basic features: pay and benefits, company policy and administration, relationships with coworkers, supervision, status, job security, working conditions, personal life; motivators include achievement, recognition, the work, responsibility, promotion, growth

3. *McClelland's Three Needs Theory:* Needs for achievement, affiliation, power

Controlling

Management establishes and oversees the controls necessary to ensure that the business is working toward and achieving its goals. The basic categories of controls are bureaucratic, market, and clan, that is, the mutual sense of benefit that employees gain from working together.

MARKETING

The concept of marketing has evolved through four stages since the earliest product marketing in the Industrial Revolution. These stages are production, sales, marketing, and relationship.

Marketing strategies have two components: target market and marketing mix. Product, price, promotion, and place—the **Four P's of marketing**—comprise the marketing mix. *Place* refers to distribution. An integrated marketing strategy merges the elements of the marketing mix so that the Four P's are presented as a coherent whole to the marketplace.

Marketing Process

The first step in the marketing process may begin before there is even a product to sell: identifying a market need. Market research helps identify the need and how to fulfill it and also identifies the target market. The next step is to develop a marketing plan that includes a SWOT analysis, the target market, the product, and how it will be produced, priced, promoted, and distributed. The groundwork has been laid, so the fifth step is to implement the plan and then assess the effectiveness of the marketing plan.

Market segmentation is an important part of identifying a target market. Market segments may be geographic, demographic, psychographic (lifestyles, personality traits, motives, and values), and behavioral (benefits sought, volume use, brand loyalty, price sensitivity, and product end use).

Consumer and B2B Marketing

A variety of influences affect consumer behavior: psychological, personal, social, cultural, situational, and marketing mix. The process that consumers undertake in making buying decisions includes need/problem recognition, information search, evaluation of alternatives, purchase decision, and post-purchase evaluation.

Business-to-business (**B2B**) marketing is different from marketing to consumers because business buyers are trained professionals who specialize in purchasing, business buyers are few in number compared to the millions of potential consumers in the nonbusiness marketplace, and sellers and buyers in the B2B market develop close relationships over time that facilitate purchasing.

Consumer goods and services are classified as convenience, shopping, specialty, and unsought. B2B goods and services are categorized as equipment; maintenance, repair, and operating (MRO); raw and processed materials; components; and professional services.

Product

Without products—goods or services or both—a company will have nothing to sell, and unless a company is a start-up or sells to a niche, a company will sell a group of products known as its product mix. A product mix is made up of a number of product lines, all the products, including peripherals, which serve a similar need for customers.

Consumer goods and services can be classified as convenience such as milk and bread, shopping (subject of some comparison shopping because of price), and specialty such as a prom dress. Goods for the business-to-business market can be classified as expense or component and capital.

Products go through a life cycle: introduction, growth, maturity, and decline. During the growth phase of a product, competitors begin to introduce their own products to compete. During the maturity stage, the company may look upon the product as a cash cow, putting little money into new developments for the product in return for a higher profit. In doing this, a company is attempting to maximize profits and defend market share at the same time.

Branding and packaging are two important aspects of marketing a product. **Branding** is the use of a name, slogan, symbol, social media strategy, or design to differentiate a company and its products from its competitors. The intent of a company's branding activities is to generate brand recognition, brand preference, and, ultimately, brand insistence. There are several types of brands: generic, manufacturer's or national, private, family, individual, licensed, and co-branding. Licensing takes place when a company or person sells the right to use its name or logo to another company for use on its products, such as the Italian designer Valentino's selling the right to use his name to a French fashion house. Co-branding occurs when two companies put both their names on the same product, such as the Intel logo on Lenovo computers.

Packaging is important because it safeguards the product, is meant to discourage stealing, promotes the product/brand, lists features and benefits, and may add utility. Considering the emphasis on being "green" today, it should also be environmentally friendly to appeal to certain customers.

Price

Product pricing depends on the goal of the company, which may be to maximize profits, build market share, build traffic, maximize sales, and/or foster an image, for example, low prices for value or high prices to denote quality. The major strategies for pricing are:

- **Cost-Based, or Cost-Plus**: Based on the cost of manufacturing/offering the product
- **Demand-Based, or Value-Based**: Based on the demand for or perceived value of the product in the marketplace
- **Competition-Based**: Pricing influenced by what the competition is charging
- **Price Skimming**: For new products; an initial high price to recoup costs associated with development and introduction of the product; high-profit margin
- **Penetration Pricing**: For new products; an initial low price to introduce a product to the market and begin to generate market share

Pricing is also affected by price adjustments like discounts; rebates; product bundling (so that the combined price is lower than the single price of each item); psychological, or fractional pricing, which prices items at less than a whole dollar ($1.99); and loss leaders, which lower the price on one or more sale items to bring customers into the store.

Promotion

Promotion is all the techniques that companies use to get the message to the marketplace about their products. The promotional mix includes advertising; personal selling; sales promotions like cents-off discount coupons, bounce-back coupons, and point-of-sale (POS) displays; and publicity and public relations. To ensure a clear, coherent, and unified message for all contacts with customers, companies use an integrated marketing communication strategy.

Once a target market has been identified and objectives determined, a marketing manager or product manager develops the product's "message," determines the appropriate media mix (including social media networks) to get the message out, develops the budget, launches the campaign, and assesses the effectiveness of the campaign, revising as needed.

Place

Place is actually places; it's the distribution aspect of marketing. **Distribution** is made up of distribution channels that take products from raw materials to buyer. Distribution may involve intermediaries between the producer and end user: wholesalers who buy from producers and resell to other intermediaries or to end users, retailers who sell directly to end users, and agents and brokers.

Unlike wholesalers and retailers, agents and brokers do not purchase the products they sell; they act on behalf of the buyer or seller, depending on the type of agent or broker. Agents and brokers are paid a commission, rather than making a profit on their deals, and may be manufacturer's agents, selling agents, or purchasing agents.

There are four distribution channels:

> *Channel 1:* Direct: producer to consumer or business
>
> *Channel 2:* Retail: producer to retailer to consumer or business
>
> *Channel 3:* Wholesale: producer to wholesaler to retailer to consumer or business
>
> *Channel 4:* Broker or agent: producer to broker or agent to consumer or business

There are a variety of retailers, with both physical and virtual presences:

- **Bricks-and-Mortar Retailers**: department stores, supermarkets, specialty stores, convenience stores, discount/bargain stores, wholesale/warehouse clubs, factory outlets, catalog showrooms
- **Direct Response Retailers**: catalog mail order, telemarketing
- **E-tailers**: e-catalogs, virtual storefronts

FINANCE

A company's financial management is responsible for the planning and budgeting of funding for both its short-term and long-term operations, including research and development and capital investments. Monitoring cash flow is an important part of the job of financial management. Having adequate cash flow ensures that creditors can be paid, but it also means that the company's invoices are being paid in a timely manner. Oversight of receivables and payables falls under the oversight of financial management.

To ensure that short-term needs are met, financial managers in collaboration with department heads prepare an operating budget for the organization. Long-term needs, including capital projects, for example, the purchase of new technologies or large-scale equipment, are provided for in a capital budget. Whereas operating expenses should be paid for out of revenue, capital expenditures may be financed by borrowing money, selling a new block of stock, or issuing corporate bonds.

Using the proceeds from the sale of stock is called equity financing. Issuing bonds to raise capital is called debt financing. There are two types of bonds: unsecured and secured, also known as debenture bonds. An unsecured bond is backed only by the promise to repay the full value of the bond with interest at a stated time in the future.

Even short-term financial needs may require borrowing to balance cash out with cash in. Small businesses may be able to satisfy their needs with a bank line of credit or with a commercial loan; corporations more typically sell unsecured commercial paper. A commercial loan may or may not be secured by a company's assets, which include any cash on hand, investments, equipment, and real estate. The creditworthiness of the business typically determines whether the borrower qualifies for an unsecured loan.

The **gross profit margin** determines the overall profitability of a company's production. It indicates the overall efficiency of the organization in using its resources—both human and material. Gross profit margin equals total revenue minus cost of goods sold divided by total revenue.

TIP

Assets are defined as everything a company owns, including any cash on hand, investments, equipment, and real estate.

ACCOUNTING

Accounting is the recording, analysis, and reporting of the financial transactions of a business, which includes all its income and expense activities—accounts receivable and accounts payable. There are different types of accounting:

- **Managerial**: Tracks the costs of doing business and the resulting income; monitors profitability of various business activities; develops budgets; audience is internal managers

- **Financial**: Prepares documents that show the financial performance of a company; the audience is those outside the company, such as stockholders

- **Auditing**: Reviews a company's financial documents to ensure their accuracy and reliability; may be internal accountants, but also reviewed by outside auditors

- **Tax**: Advises on tax strategies and prepares tax returns

The financial reports that accountants prepare for businesses typically consist of balance sheets, income statements, and cash flow. Each contains different kinds of information about a company's financial health or lack thereof:

- **Balance Sheets**: current assets, fixed assets, short-term liabilities, long-term liabilities, and owner's equity. Assets may also be intangible, like trademarks, patents, and goodwill
- **Income Statements**: revenues, cost of goods sold, gross profit, operating expenses, operating income, and net income
- **Cash Flow Statements**: cash from operations, investments, and financing

Financing cash flow statements includes both inflows of cash from debt and equity financing, as well as outflows in the form of interest and dividend payments and repayment of principle borrowed.

Accountants must follow **GAAP standards** (generally acceptable accounting principles) in preparing and reviewing financial reports. All financial reporting starts with bookkeeping and is based on the accounting equation:

Assets = Liabilities + Owner's Equity

Owner's equity is what the business is worth if the owner chose to sell it. The owner would get whatever was left after the liabilities were deducted from the assets. Assets minus liabilities is the net worth of a business.

PRODUCTION AND OPERATIONS

Operations include all the activities that go into producing products; operations management is the control of those activities. **Products** may be tangible goods or intangible services. **Services** are also "unstorable"; you can't store the cheerful, helpful attention of a waiter in a restaurant. Production results in three types of utility, or value, for customers: form (what customers need), time (when customers need it), and place (where customers need it).

There are a variety of processes that companies use to make goods and services and a variety of ways of classifying them. Three typical processes are mass; flexible, also known as custom; and customer-driven. The first is the traditional assembly-line process instituted by Henry Ford at the beginning of the twentieth century. In a flexible system, a central computer operates a network of machines and can adjust product specifications and output as needed. The first two are typical make-to-stock operations and the last is a make-to-order operation. Service operations are classified as low-contact or high-contact, depending on the amount of involvement of the customer in the process.

Ford's assembly line was among the first uses of technology to speed and improve manufacturing. The most noticeable technology on the manufacturing floor today is the presence of robots. They do many of the manufacturing processes that humans once did; humans still control the type and flow of work, however. Other processes that employ technology are computer-aided design (CAD), computer-aided manufacturing, and computer-integrated manufacturing (CIM).

A number of factors need to be managed in order to establish smooth-running operations. These include determining optimum number, size, and location of facilities; optimum number of employees; proximity of facilities to transportation networks, utility grids, and suppliers; and design of the facility.

Once facilities are up and running, operations managers are responsible for the timely flow of materials through production to final goods and into the distribution channel, so part of the planning for smooth-running operations is scheduling and controls. Controls on the operations side include inventory control and quality control. **Inventory control** consists of all the activities involved in receiving, storing, and tracking whatever the business uses to produce its goods—for example, raw materials—as well as the finished goods. Two popular methods of materials management among large corporations are materials requirement planning (MRP) and enterprise resource planning (ERP). Both use technology for planning/scheduling and inventory control, but ERP integrates them into the overall business. Two methods for tracking production processes are PERT (Program Evaluation and Review Technique) charts and Gantt charts (named after chart designer Henry Gantt).

A business's quality control methods and activities include establishing what "quality" means in its environment and monitoring goods and services to ensure that they provide that quality. It is not simply a matter of maintaining the same level of quality, but of improving that quality over time. With a process known as total quality management (TQM), companies attempt to infuse quality into the entire production process from the first design of a product to follow-up service after the product has been delivered to the customer. With TQM, ensuring quality becomes the mission of every employee in a company.

The **International Organization for Standardization (ISO)** establishes global standards for what constitutes quality. It has two programs worldwide: ISO 9000 certification and ISO 14000 certification. The latter certification attests to the company's development of an environmental management system.

MANAGEMENT INFORMATION SYSTEMS

Management information systems (MIS) is one part of the technology side of a business. Information technology (IT) is the overall umbrella label for a company's technology systems, and it is overseen by the chief information officer (CIO) in large corporations. The IT department designs and implements all computer-based information systems in a company, whereas MIS uses technology to collect and analyze data, and use the resulting information to inform decisions and solve problems.

The shift from data to information occurs when the surveys, statistics, facts—whatever has been collected—are analyzed, arranged, and interpreted. The data that the business collects are stored in what is called a **data warehouse.** Analyzing the data to find trends and patterns is called **data mining**.

There are different kinds of information systems software: decision support systems, executive information systems, knowledge information systems, and business intelligence. Knowledge information systems software is used by knowledge workers to create new types of information based on manipulating data. The other three systems provide data and models to help various levels of management in different departments make informed decisions.

Companies face any number of threats to their information systems because of access to the Internet. Businesses may find themselves and their customers the victims of hackers, intellectual property theft, identity theft, spyware, viruses, Trojan horses, worms, and spam. Firewalls, encryption software that encodes e-mail, spam-filtering software, antivirus protection, and antispyware protection are ways to defend against hackers and malicious attacks on networks.

In addition to doing business over the Internet, large companies have intranets that are closed to all but their own employees and extranets that are available to employees, customers, and vendors who are authorized to gain access. Companies use social media to connect with customers. Some companies are also creating work and process groups on their own social media sites to exchange information.

HUMAN RESOURCES

The human resources department is a vital part of an organization, responsible for recruiting and training employees, developing compensation and benefits packages, and developing a system for evaluating employees. Many companies consider HR a strategic partner in planning future goals and objectives for achieving those goals.

Recruiting and Hiring

HR is responsible for job analysis within an organization and then creating job descriptions and job specifications for open positions. Recruiting to fill those jobs may be external or internal. External sources of candidates are online job sites; networking, both online and offline; career fairs; hiring headhunters to recruit employees away from competitors; newspaper and trade journal ads; employment agencies; and referrals.

A number of federal laws regulate **hiring practices.** Title VII of Civil Rights Act of 1964 prohibits discrimination based on race, color, national origin, gender, religion, and retaliation ("for opposing unlawful employment practices, for filing a complaint, for testifying about violations or possible violations"). In addition, the Age Discrimination Act prohibits age discrimination against anyone over the age of 40 in companies with 20 or more employees. Discrimination against those with disabilities is prohibited by the Americans with Disabilities Act, and discrimination against those who take a leave to serve in a state's National Guard is prohibited by the Uniformed Services Employment and Reemployment Rights Act. As more women have entered the workforce and many of them work in blue collar jobs, sexual harassment has become a more visible problem. Claims of discrimination are handled by the Equal Employment Opportunity Commission (EEOC).

A variety of issues have transformed the workplace in the last two decades. Hiring has been transformed to increase **diversity** in companies so that their workforce mirrors their markets. With each succeeding innovation, from mainframes to desktops to laptops to smartphones, the importance of data has increased, and along with this has emerged a new category of employees—knowledge workers—employees whose jobs are to "think for a living"—such as software engineers and developers, computer programmers, accountants, and financial analysts.

Beginning in the late 1980s, another employee type emerged. Companies began turning to **contingent workers**. These employees fill a need when a project requires increased resources or specialized skills for a limited time period. Contingent workers include part-time, temporary, seasonal, and leased employees. Companies that turn to this employment option save on salaries and benefits that would be extended to permanent full-time employees.

Training and Evaluation

The initial training that employees undergo is typically a half- or full-day orientation on a company's rules and regulations, history, and corporate culture. During the course of employment, workers also receive additional training—on the job, in an apprentice program, at off-site sessions, or through distance learning. Training programs deal with the here and now, whereas development programs take the long view and help employees learn skills that will help them grow in their jobs and the organization.

Performance appraisals assess how employees are doing their jobs. They include a self-assessment as well as an assessment of the employee by his or her managers. The assessment is conducted against a set of standards that includes the goals set by the employee and manager in the previous performance appraisal. Newer forms of employee assessment have reviews on an ongoing basis rather than once a year.

Compensation and Benefits

Wages are paid for hourly work, and salaries are paid for a specific job. Some employees, specifically salespeople, may work on commission only or on a combination of salary and bonus. Workers may be exempt or nonexempt, depending on how jobs are classified under the Fair Labor Standards Act.

Employers of nonexempt workers must abide by the law. These workers must be paid at least the federal minimum wage and receive overtime pay for working more than a regular workweek, which is typically 40 hours.

There are exceptions to the minimum wage law, for example, tipped employees, full-time students, workers under 20 years of age, and workers with disabilities. An employer must follow the guidelines regarding limits on how far below the minimum wage he or she is legally allowed to pay workers, and wages may be subject to increase if the worker's circumstances change.

Companies used to offer employees defined benefit pension plans for retirement, but many have changed in recent decades and now offer defined contribution pension plans. Other forms of retirement plans include 401(k), profit sharing, and employee stock ownership plans (ESOP).

Companies must carry worker's compensation insurance by law, and many also carry disability insurance. Other benefits that companies may offer include medical insurance, health insurance, paid vacation, paid sick leave, tuition reimbursement, scholarships for children of employees, child care, and wellness programs. To reign in the cost of benefits, some companies have introduced a cafeteria benefits plan. With this plan, employees are provided with a set amount of money they can use to select from a list of benefits.

With the entrance of more women into the workforce and the desire of men to spend more time with their families, companies have responded by creating more family-friendly work arrangements. In addition, computers, the Internet, and mobile devices make it possible to do many jobs from remote locations. Having fewer employees deskbound in company cubicles reduces facilities' costs for employers. Companies now offer flextime, flexplace or telecommuting, shared jobs, permanent part-time workers, and compressed workweeks.

Termination

Perhaps the hardest job of an HR professional's job is terminating employees. Sometimes terminations occur because of poor performance, but other times it may be the result of an economic downturn for the company or for the economy as a whole. Employees who lose their jobs through no fault of their own are laid off rather than fired and typically given severance packages that may be based on one or two weeks for each year of employment. They are also eligible for unemployment compensation.

Employees who are fired are not eligible for unemployment and do not receive severance. Terminating an employee for cause requires following a process: a verbal warning and the opportunity to remedy the problem, written warning and the opportunity for remediation, and then termination if performance has not improved. Even though most workers fall under the category of "employment at will," the process is followed.

Labor Unions

Labor union contracts are built on the principle of collective bargaining. Management of a company sits down with representatives of the union to work through a set of compromises to come up with a contract. If agreement cannot be reached, there are several options: work slowdown, sickout, and strike. A strike is accompanied by a picket line and sometimes by a boycott of the company's product by a sympathetic portion of the public. A company may bring in strikebreakers to take over the strikers' work. To end the impasse, the union and the company may agree to the use of a mediator or to binding or nonbinding arbitration.

ENTREPRENEURSHIP

Ford didn't start out as a multinational corporation, neither did Apple®. Both companies began with one or two individuals and an idea, and, from that idea, the founders went on to produce a product and launch a business. They were entrepreneurs, individuals willing to take risks. Various characteristics are ascribed to entrepreneurs, such as being innovative, resourceful, risk-takers, flexible, self-motivated, able to work well with others, good leaders, and able to see the "big picture." The desire to be one's own boss also plays a role in entrepreneurship. Some entrepreneurs start their own businesses because they want to make a comfortable living, want more control over their lives, or want the flexibility that comes with owning their own business, whereas others start their businesses with the intention of making it as large and profitable as possible. The former are the owners of small businesses, the majority of U.S. companies, and the latter are the start-ups looking for sizable infusions of venture capital.

While many entrepreneurs start businesses based on their own idea, some choose instead to buy an existing business. The risks are more or less known, there is an existing base of customers and suppliers, and there is a financial history to use as the basis for projections of future financial performance. For the same reasons, other entrepreneurs choose to buy franchises. The franchiser also provides its expertise in helping the franchisee set up the business and training and marketing, including advertising materials. The downsides to a franchise are the cost of buying the franchise license, the associated start-up costs, the percentage that the franchisee pays the franchiser, the lack of creativity and control over the individual business, and the competition from similar national brands.

The first step for both types of entrepreneurs is creating a business plan that includes goals and objectives, a sales forecast, and a financial plan indicating income, the break-even point, and a budget. Securing funding is the next big hurdle. Typically, a small business is funded with the owner's savings and loans or investments from family and friends. Other forms of funding include venture capital companies, small business investment companies (SBIC), angel investors (individuals rather than companies), and various programs of the Small Business Administration (SBA), including 7(a) loans, special purpose loans, micro loans, and the Certified Development Company (504) loan program.

Reasons for small business success include competent management, commitment to doing whatever it takes to succeed, accurate reading of demand in the marketplace for the product or service, and "being in the right place at the right time with the right product," in other words, good luck.

Some of the reasons for small business failures include (1) lack of planning upfront before the business is set up, (2) inexperienced or incompetent management, (3) lack of commitment to the business, (4) weak financial and inventory controls, and (5) lack of enough capital to support the business until it becomes profitable.

CONTEMPORARY ISSUES

Companies—whether multinationals or sole proprietorships—face a number of issues in today's business environment. Among them are the role of e-commerce, business ethics and social responsibility, and the global business environment.

THE ROLE OF TECHNOLOGY AND E-COMMERCE

E-commerce is the business of buying and selling electronically. The transaction may be with another business, or it may be a direct sale to a consumer. The latter, known as **e-tailing**, is becoming an ever larger share of consumer sales, not only in the United States, but worldwide. E-tailing has several forms: online auctions, e-catalogs, electronic storefronts (websites), electronic or cyber malls (collection of sites), and interactive marketing on blogs and social media sites.

Like bricks-and-mortar sales, the e-tailing transaction involves one buyer and one seller, but in e-commerce, comparison shopping is easy and the product array is considerably larger than what is possible by going from store to store in a local area checking product features and prices. The consumer, therefore, has an advantage. However, the disadvantage is the inability to see and touch the actual product.

Business-to-business e-commerce is in many ways similar to traditional business-to-business selling. There are a few customers for a product, the orders are large, the transaction is formalized, and decisions are made by purchasing agents after internal consultations about product features and pricing among competitors.

With e-commerce, a company no longer has to warehouse goods. It can take orders, process them, and have them drop shipped from the manufacturer to the customer, saving on warehousing costs.

The Internet also makes it possible to do business on a global basis without having a physical presence in other countries. It is not just manufacturing that can be moved offshore but accounting and marketing functions as well.

With the ease of doing business over the Internet, however, comes a number of security risks. Even with what they consider secure sites, credit card companies, banks, and retailers have found their sites hacked and customers' personal information stolen. The result is identity theft and millions of dollars lost through the use of stolen information.

As companies turn more and more to doing business online—whether selling, buying, or exchanging information—their work processes are undergoing changes, known as **business process reengineering.**

BUSINESS ETHICS AND SOCIAL RESPONSIBILITY

Ethics is a set of moral beliefs, a code of conduct based on what is considered right and wrong. Living an ethical life does not stop at the workplace door. Part of an organization's culture is its ethical stance on issues, which can be found in a company's code of ethics, mission statement, and legal compliance. Ethical behavior within a company includes doing right by fellow employees, customers, suppliers, and the organization itself. The organization in turn has a responsibility to treat employees, customers, suppliers, and other business partners ethically.

Social responsibility is the belief that organizations as well as individuals are obligated to act in such a way as to benefit the larger society. Corporate social responsibility (CSR) institutionalizes this belief on a company-wide basis. Areas of concentration for CSR activities include human rights; employees and other stakeholders, including customers, the larger community, and the environment; and ethical business practices related to sourcing, producing, and marketing. The last includes recognizing consumer rights, disavowing deceptive advertising practices, and using fair pricing practices.

The benefits of CSR include:

- **Less government intervention into business practices** because the organization is obeying all applicable legislation and regulations
- **Better financial performance** as a result of efficient use of resources, including people, and an enhanced perception in the marketplace
- **Fewer scandals** related to corruption and fewer accidents, thereby reducing the company's exposure to risk
- **Competitive edge with customers** by advertising CSR programs, including philanthropic endeavors
- **Easier recruitment of employees** because they embrace the company's CSR initiatives
- **Higher rate of employee retention** for the same reason

Some companies may adopt any one of four approaches to CSR, from embracing it wholeheartedly to doing as little as possible:

1. *Obstructionist Stance:* Do as little as possible to solve the problems that it creates, deny or hide any responsibility
2. *Defensive Stance*: Do what is legally required, admit mistakes, remedy the problem to the letter of the law only, defend the stance that the job of the company is to generate profits
3. *Accommodative Stance*: Meet ethical obligations and legal requirements; participate in social programs, but do not seek them out
4. *Proactive Stance*: Seek out opportunities to support social programs, perception as "citizens of society"

How well a company is living up to its CSR can be measured by taking a social audit in which the company's performance is measured against its goals. Some companies choose to make this information public. A **benefit corporation**, or **B corporation**, is a for-profit corporate entity authorized by thirty U.S. states and the District of Columbia that is required to consider the impact of its business decisions both on shareholders and the environment and society.

Some businesses go so far as to become certified for benefiting society. A for-profit company that obtains a **B Corp certification** has met certain standards of social and environmental performance, accountability, and transparency as outlined by B Lab, a global nonprofit organization.

Another public expression of CSR is **corporate philanthropy.** Some corporations set up charitable foundations to donate money to worthy causes, thereby living up to their goals to support the larger community. A number of outside groups such as Boston College's Center for Corporate Citizenship and *Fortune* magazine also rate and rank corporations on their CSR programs.

GLOBAL BUSINESS ENVIRONMENT

Business ethics and CSR extend across borders when doing business. The **globalization** of the world's economies affects workers, consumers, businesses, unions, the environment, and national governments—and even state governments. Some states send trade representatives to other countries in an effort to encourage foreign companies to establish facilities in their states. The increase in the rate of globalization in the last two decades is a result of changes in technology and the lowering of trade barriers.

Globalization impacts both markets and production. A market for a company's products could be consumers in China as well as Chicago. With outsourcing of production, factories producing the components for smartphones could be spread across Asia. **Cultural differences** come into play in conducting market research and developing, advertising, and selling products in multiple markets.

Cultural differences also affect the production process. A cultural difference that can lead to legal difficulties—and ethical ones—is the issue of bribery. Some nations consider it business as usual if a company wants to operate within their borders. However, the U.S. Foreign Corrupt Practices Act of 1977, the Anti-Bribery Convention of the Organization for Economic Cooperation and Development, and the UN Convention Against Corruption all prohibit bribery of foreign officials. In addition to cultural differences, companies doing business across borders must deal with economic, legal, and political environments that vary not only from their home country but also from country to country worldwide.

Trade Policies

Countries seek to have a favorable balance of trade, that is, having the value of exports be greater than the value of imports. This situation results in a favorable balance of payments, which is when a country takes in more revenue than it pays out. When this occurs, the country has a **trade surplus**. The opposite is a **trade deficit**.

One issue that can constrain businesses is **protectionist trade policies**—their own country's and that of countries with which they wish to do business. A protectionist trade policy uses quotas and tariffs to protect domestic industries by making foreign goods more expensive to import. A home country may also use subsidies as a way to protect domestic producers. Instead of limiting imports as a quota does or raising prices as a tariff does, a subsidy is a payment to domestic producers to enable them to keep their prices lower than those charged by importers of the same or similar goods.

Those in favor of protectionist trade policies use the following arguments to support their position:

- **Infant Industry**: Newly emerging domestic industries need to be protected from foreign competition

- **National Security**: Industries vital to the nation's security need to be protected so that foreign competitors do not undercut them on price or the nation will find itself dependent on the foreign companies

- **Foreign Labor**: Companies in developing nations will undercut domestic companies by using cheap labor to produce their goods

- **Bargaining Chip**: A tough trade policy can be used to negotiate with trading partners to get them to relax their trade policies

Dumping is selling goods abroad for less than they cost to make or are sold for domestically. Charges of dumping can be brought to the World Trade Organization for resolution.

Regional and International Organizations

There are a variety of organizations that promote free trade. Among them are the World Trade Organization (WTO), General Agreement on Tariffs and Trade (GATT), European Union (EU), North American Free Trade Agreement (NAFTA), MERCOSUR (Brazil, Argentina, Paraguay, Uruguay), and Association of Southeast Asian Nations (ASEAN).

Absolute and Comparative Advantage

A nation has an **absolute advantage** when it produces more of a product more cheaply than any other country. **Comparative advantage** occurs when a nation can produce a product more efficiently than any other country. Therefore, it should concentrate on producing that product and buying from other countries the products that they have comparative advantage in. Comparative advantage is competitive advantage.

Ways to Enter Foreign Markets

A company wishing to enter a foreign market has a variety of paths to choose from. It can simply hire an import agent who deals with customs, tariffs, and selling the company's goods. A company can enter into a deal with a domestic company by selling a franchise or license. It can enter into a joint venture or strategic alliance, or, depending on the type of company, it can set up a turnkey project for which it will be paid, but will have no ownership stake in when finished. Another arrangement for a manufacturing company is contracting out its manufacturing to a company in the country it wishes to enter. Any type of company could set up a wholly owned subsidiary.

SUMMING IT UP

- The basic forms of business ownership are **sole proprietorship, partnership, and corporation.** There are also **co-operative and nonprofit** corporation forms of businesses.

  - The **sole proprietorship** is the most common form of business ownership in the United States. Advantages include lack of legal requirements for establishing and operating the business, low start-up costs, no separate tax filings, no need to divide any profits, and no shared decision making. The disadvantages are unlimited liability, difficulty in borrowing money, responsibility for all losses, no one to bounce ideas off, and the end of the business when the owner retires or dies.

  - In a **partnership**, no separate business tax filings are required, it is easier to borrow money from banks, all partners contribute to start-up costs, and all partners participate in decision making. A disadvantage is that any profits are divided as well, but the most important disadvantage is unlimited liability. Partnerships may be general or limited.

  - A **corporation** is formed according to state laws; is an entity that is separate from its owners, the stockholders; has liability separate from its owners; must file corporate tax returns annually; and has certain legal rights.

  - In a **co-operative**, a group of partnerships and/or sole proprietorships join together to benefit their individual businesses.

  - A **nonprofit**, or **not-for-profit**, is set up to support some social or educational mission.

- Government influences the business climate in two ways: through **regulatory policy** and through **economic policy**.

- Businesses are subject to **contract, tort, property, agency, commercial, and bankruptcy laws**.

- One aspect of federal economic policy is the **maintenance of a stable economic environment in which businesses can operate**. This is the **goal of the Federal Reserve System's monetary policy**.

- **Entrepreneurs** may start a business based on their own idea, buy an existing business, or buy a franchise.

- A **franchiser** provides expertise, training, and marketing. The disadvantages of buying a franchise are the cost of buying the franchise license, start-up costs, the percentage the franchisee pays the franchiser, lack of creativity and control over the business, and competition from similar national brands.

- There are **five factors of production**:
  1. labor
  2. natural resources
  3. capital (real and financial)
  4. entrepreneurs
  5. technology

- In a **market economy**, or **mixed economy**, market forces set prices through the laws of supply and demand.
  - The **law of supply** states that producers will offer more of a product/service as the price increases and less of a product/service as the price decreases. The **law of demand** states that consumers will buy more of a product/service as the price decreases and less of a product/service as the price increases.
  - The characteristics of market and mixed economies are competition, private property rights, freedom of choice in buying and selling goods and services, and profits.
- Economic indicators are **gross domestic product** (**GDP**), **gross national product** (**GNP**), **consumer price index** (**CPI**), **producer price index** (**PPI**), **unemployment rate**, and **productivity**.
- **Management** plans, organizes, leads, and controls the financial, physical, human, and information resources of an organization.
  - **Planning** is an essential element of management and includes setting the goals, strategies, and tactics for the business.
  - The **function of control** includes monitoring the business's performance and making adjustments as needed if goals are not being met.
  - There are a variety of **approaches to leadership** as identified by researchers: **trait**, **behavioral, situational, transformational, and charismatic**. **Motivation** may be extrinsic or intrinsic.
- Marketing strategies have two components: **target market** and **marketing mix**.
  - **Product, price, promotion, and place**—the **Four P's of marketing**—comprise the marketing mix. The Four P's are presented as a coherent whole to the marketplace.
  - The **promotional mix** includes advertising; personal selling; sales promotions; publicity, including social media campaigns; and public relations.
- A company's **financial management** is responsible for the planning and budgeting of funding for both its short-term and long-term operations.
- **Accounting is the recording, analysis, and reporting of a business's financial transactions**, which includes all its income and expense activities—accounts receivable and accounts payable.
- **Operations include all the activities that go into producing products**; operations management is the control of those activities. **Products** may be tangible goods or intangible services.
- **Management information systems** (**MIS**) use technology to collect and analyze data and use the resulting information to inform decisions and solve problems.
- The **human resources department** is responsible for recruiting and training employees, developing compensation and benefits packages, and developing a system for evaluation employees.
- **E-commerce** is the business of buying and selling electronically where the transaction may be between business and business or business and consumer.

- **Ethics** is a set of moral beliefs, a code of conduct based on what is considered right and wrong. Part of an organization's culture is its ethical stance on issues.

- **Social responsibility** is the belief that organizations as well as individuals are obligated to act in such a way as to benefit the larger society. **Corporate social responsibility (CSR)** institutionalizes this belief on a company-wide basis.

- **Globalization** impacts both markets and production.

- Some countries take a **protectionist approach** to their trade policies with the intent of protecting domestic industries from foreign competitors.

INTRODUCTION TO BUSINESS POST-TEST

Directions: Carefully read each of the following 60 questions. Choose the best answer to each question and fill in the corresponding circle on the answer sheet. The Answer Key and Explanations can be found following this post-test.

1. What is the most common form of business ownership in the United States?
   A. Corporation
   B. Sole proprietorship
   C. Partnership
   D. Co-operative

2. Price skimming is used in which stage of the product life cycle?
   A. Introduction
   B. Growth
   C. Maturity
   D. Decline

3. Which of the following poses a question of social responsibility for a company?
   A. Price fixing
   B. Outsourcing
   C. Harassing a whistleblower
   D. Reporting inflated profits

4. Which of the following illustrates the concept of direct foreign investment?
   A. Opening a sales office in a foreign city
   B. Building a factory in a foreign country
   C. Licensing the use of technology to a foreign company
   D. Selling a business unit to a foreign company

5. The benefits that buyers receive from a product are categorized as what type(s) of utility?
   A. Time, form, and place
   B. Price, promotion, and place
   C. Form, time, place, and ownership
   D. Value

6. Which of the following type of information systems software allows users to create new types of information?
   A. Decision support
   B. Knowledge information
   C. Business intelligence
   D. Executive information

7. Which of the following is an example of corporate philanthropy?
   A. Sponsoring the Great American Cleanup
   B. Refusing to do business with a company that uses sweatshops
   C. Shifting to recycled packaging for a company's products
   D. A network's refusing to allow the product placement of cigarettes in a TV program

8. What is a major disadvantage of buying an existing business?

   A. Buying an existing business takes more time than setting up a new company.

   B. It can be easier to obtain financing for a start-up than to buy an existing business.

   C. There is little opportunity for creating a new look for the business or introducing new products.

   D. An existing business may have a poor reputation for customer service or product quality.

9. In which stage of a product's life cycle do competitors introduce rival products?

   A. Introduction

   B. Growth

   C. Maturity

   D. Decline

10. Which of the following is an accounting function in a company?

    A. Preparing income statements

    B. Investing a company's surplus funds

    C. Providing input for budgeting

    D. Determining whether to borrow money or issue stock to fund capital needs

11. Encryption software protects a company's e-mail by

    A. filtering out spam.

    B. identifying and removing spyware.

    C. encoding messages so they can't be read without a passphrase to unscramble them.

    D. erecting a barrier to block messages unless told to recognize the sender.

12. Which of the following is an example of dumping?

    A. Manufacturers sell goods in a foreign country for less than what it cost to manufacture them.

    B. Clothing manufacturers cut up out-of-season clothes and trash them to clear inventory.

    C. Stores sell goods for less than what they paid in order to clear inventory.

    D. A foreign government offers a subsidy to domestic manufacturers that make and sell goods abroad to offset import duties.

13. Enterprise resource planning program (ERPP) software does which of the following?

    A. Helps entrepreneurs predict the potential for success

    B. Is an online performance appraisal system

    C. Connects all functions of a business operation such as inventory control, scheduling, finance, marketing, and human resources

    D. Is a tool for franchises

14. The Smith Company wants to enter the German market with its product and decides to establish the business with a German company. They are setting up what kind of business?

    A. Licensing

    B. Joint venture

    C. Strategic alliance

    D. Contract manufacturing

15. The airline industry with few competitors could be characterized as

    A. an oligopoly.

    B. an industry with perfect competition.

    C. having monopolistic competition.

    D. a monopoly.

16. Which of the following is an example of a company's exercising its corporate social responsibility?

    A. Returning an overpayment to a customer

    B. Conducting an audit of working conditions in a foreign factory producing components for its smartphones

    C. Turning over e-mails requested by a federal investigation into fraudulent dealings by a CFO

    D. Labeling food packaging with nutrition information

17. According to the principles of financial management, which of the following should be paid for through the issuance of corporate bonds?

    A. Research and development

    B. Operating expenses

    C. Interest payments on loans

    D. Construction of new facilities

18. Which of the following is a conceptual skill that managers need to be effective?

    A. Empathy

    B. Ability to use situation analysis

    C. Ability to implement plans

    D. Ability to fact find

19. Entrepreneurship and technology are increasingly important

    A. capital requirements.

    B. elements in the product mix.

    C. operations units.

    D. factors of production.

20. A flat organizational structure is most often found in a(n)

    A. decentralized organization.

    B. tall organization.

    C. centralized organization.

    D. autocratic organization.

21. Which of the following is an example of a shopping good?

    A. Computer tablet

    B. Wedding gown

    C. Doughnut and coffee

    D. Engagement ring

22. Which of the following is an internal environment that affects how companies do business?

    A. Cross-cultural environment

    B. Economic environment

    C. Corporate culture

    D. Political-legal environment

23. Net income is

    A. gross profit minus operating expenses and income taxes.

    B. gross profit minus operating expenses.

    C. assets minus liabilities.

    D. costs of materials used to produce goods during a given year.

24. An organization would typically write an intermediate goal for something it wished to accomplish

    A. in less than one year.

    B. in one year.

    C. within one to three years.

    D. within one to five years.

25. Currency depreciation causes

    A. imports to rise in price.

    B. imports to become cheaper.

    C. exports to rise in price.

    D. no effect on imports and exports.

26. A Gantt chart shows the
    A. structure of an organization.
    B. sequence of tasks that must be performed in order and the tasks that can be performed simultaneously with those tasks.
    C. steps in a project and time required to perform each step.
    D. products to be produced, their deadlines, and those who will be working on the projects.

27. A characteristic of business-to-business markets is
    A. that purchasing decisions are made by individual agents.
    B. the lack of personal relationships between sellers and buyers.
    C. the small number of customers.
    D. the informal nature of the seller-buyer process.

28. Businesses fail for which of the following reasons?
    I. Ineffective financial controls
    II. Lack of adequate capitalization
    III. Inexperienced management
    A. I only
    B. I and II only
    C. II and III only
    D. I, II, and III

29. The ISO 9000 label indicates that a company's products
    A. adhere to the highest quality.
    B. are environmentally safe.
    C. are manufactured in a socially responsible way.
    D. are organic.

30. In determining where to locate a manufacturing facility, a company needs to consider
    A. inventory management.
    B. the size of the market.
    C. the availability of workers with appropriate skills sets.
    D. creating an efficient layout for the facility.

31. A nation has a comparative advantage in a certain good when that country
    A. can produce the good at a lower cost than other countries.
    B. was the earliest producer of the product.
    C. can produce the good more efficiently than other nations.
    D. can produce a higher quality of the good.

32. Which of the following can be binding on both sides in a labor dispute?
    A. Mediation
    B. Arbitration
    C. Collective bargaining
    D. Boycott

33. A small business selling craft materials and needing money to balance out cash flow would most likely
    A. sell a debenture.
    B. sell unsecured commercial paper.
    C. issue stock.
    D. apply for a bank line of credit.

34. How is B2B e-commerce similar to traditional B2B selling?
    A. The orders are small.
    B. The customer base for a product is small.
    C. There is decentralized purchasing.
    D. Little or no comparison shopping is done among competitors.

35. The goal of U.S. monetary policy is to
    A. issue government debt at a favorable market rate.
    B. collect revenue for the purpose of operating the government.
    C. stabilize the economy.
    D. safeguard money kept in depository institutions.

36. A balance sheet details a company's
    A. profit and loss.
    B. financial status.
    C. receipts and payments.
    D. assets, liabilities, and owner's equity.

37. Which of the following is an intrinsic motivator for employees?
    A. Profit-sharing plan
    B. Employee-of-the-month program
    C. Sense of achievement
    D. Promotion

38. Taking out a bank loan has an advantage over having an angel investor because
    A. a bank will make a loan to a partnership, but angel investors typically prefer to invest in sole proprietorships.
    B. a bank loan is paid off over time, whereas an angel investor is paid a share of the profits for as long as the business exists.
    C. a bank will act in an advisory capacity to the entrepreneur, whereas an angel investor takes a hands-off role.
    D. it means that the entrepreneur will still be eligible for an SBA loan.

39. Using an Internet job site is what type of recruiting for a new hire?
    A. External
    B. Prospecting
    C. Internal
    D. Headhunting

40. Which of the following is a contingent worker?
    A. Call center employee
    B. Lawyer on lease
    C. Truck driver who owns and drives his own truck
    D. Daughter employed as a sales agent for the family construction company

41. An organization that changes and adapts to its environment is referred to as a
    A. continuous improvement organization.
    B. TQM organization.
    C. learning organization.
    D. flexible organization.

42. Statutory law is law
    A. established by administrative agencies.
    B. passed by state legislatures.
    C. developed from court decisions.
    D. based on court precedents.

43. The amount of goods and services that will be bought at all price levels at a given point in time is
    A. the equilibrium point.
    B. aggregate output.
    C. aggregate demand.
    D. real growth rate.

44. Which of the following are reasons that motivate people to become entrepreneurs?
    I. Desire to control what they work at and how they do their work
    II. Desire for flexibility in their lives
    III. Desire to make more money
    A. I and II
    B. II only
    C. I and III
    D. I, II, and III

45. Employees who feel connected to the company and to their fellow employees most likely fall into which category in Maslow's hierarchy of needs?
    A. Safety
    B. Belonging
    C. Esteem
    D. Self-actualization

46. Software that is designed to disrupt a computer's operation is
    A. spyware.
    B. malware.
    C. spam.
    D. cookies.

47. Total revenue minus cost of goods sold divided by revenue equals
    A. operating expenses.
    B. operating profit margin.
    C. gross profit margin.
    D. earning per share.

48. Jack's department is charged with analyzing data to find trends and patterns, which is known as
    A. data mining.
    B. data interpretation.
    C. data collection.
    D. data drilling.

49. Competition from goods manufactured in developing countries is used to support which of the following arguments for a protectionist trade policy?
    A. Bargaining chip
    B. Infant industry
    C. Cheap foreign labor
    D. National security

50. Which of the following is characteristic of a market economy?
    A. Government control of some industries and competition in others
    B. Central planning
    C. Low barriers to entry into industries
    D. The right to own property

51. To help new junior employees learn their jobs and adjust to the company culture, some companies
    A. make them part of a work team.
    B. enroll them in apprenticeships.
    C. assign them a mentor.
    D. give them an orientation program.

52. In backward scheduling, the operations department has to schedule
    A. according to supplier availability.
    B. based on input from the just-in-time inventory control system.
    C. based on when raw materials are due to arrive.
    D. based on when a product needs to be shipped.

53. In terms of assets, brand recognition and a company's reputation are classified as
    A. intellectual property.
    B. liquid assets.
    C. goodwill.
    D. tangible property.

54. Advertising, public relations, sales promotions, and personal selling are the components of which of the following?
    A. Four P's
    B. Promotional mix
    C. Media mix
    D. Product differentiation

55. To calculate net income, an accountant would need what information?

    I. Total revenue

    II. Total assets

    III. Total expenses

    A. I only

    B. I and II only

    C. I and III only

    D. I, II, and III

56. The role of the World Bank in global development is to

    A. rescue failing banks that are too big for their own governments to help.

    B. fund programs to improve conditions and increase productivity in developing nations.

    C. provide advice and technical expertise to nations to avert financial crises.

    D. develop monetary policy to stabilize the economy.

57. Which of the following is a true statement about the minimum wage?

    A. All hourly jobs are covered by the minimum wage.

    B. The Federal Fair Labor Standards Act mandates those jobs that must be paid the minimum wage.

    C. Violations of the minimum wage are investigated by the Employment Opportunity Commision.

    D. Any job that is negotiated by collective bargaining is not covered by the minimum wage.

58. Which of the following is an advantage to a business partnership over a sole proprietorship?

    A. Limited liability

    B. Greater ability than a sole proprietorship to borrow money to expand the business

    C. Less paperwork than a sole proprietorship to start the business

    D. Greater tax advantages to the owners than a sole proprietorship

59. What is a disadvantage to e-tailing for consumers?

    A. Comparison shopping is difficult.

    B. The product array is limited.

    C. The consumer cannot see and touch the product.

    D. Prices are higher than in bricks-and-mortar stores.

60. Point-of-sale displays are an example of

    A. sales promotion.

    B. advertising.

    C. a distribution channel.

    D. an impulse buy.

post-test

ANSWER KEY AND EXPLANATIONS

1. B	**13.** C	**25.** A	**37.** C	**49.** C
2. A	**14.** B	**26.** C	**38.** B	**50.** D
3. B	**15.** A	**27.** C	**39.** A	**51.** A
4. B	**16.** B	**28.** D	**40.** B	**52.** D
5. C	**17.** D	**29.** A	**41.** C	**53.** C
6. B	**18.** B	**30.** C	**42.** B	**54.** B
7. A	**19.** D	**31.** C	**43.** C	**55.** C
8. D	**20.** A	**32.** B	**44.** D	**56.** B
9. B	**21.** A	**33.** D	**45.** B	**57.** B
10. A	**22.** C	**34.** B	**46.** B	**58.** B
11. C	**23.** A	**35.** C	**47.** C	**59.** C
12. A	**24.** D	**36.** D	**48.** A	**60.** A

1. **The correct answer is B.** Sole proprietorship is the most common form of business ownership in the United States, accounting for almost three quarters of the business organizations in the country. Anyone who runs a business alone is a sole proprietor unless that person has incorporated the business. Choices A, C, and D are incorrect.

2. **The correct answer is A.** Price skimming might seem like a pricing strategy for the decline phase, but it's used at a product introduction in an attempt to recoup costs. Choices B, C, and D—growth, maturity, and decline—are incorrect. During growth (choice B), penetrating pricing is used.

3. **The correct answer is B.** Relocating jobs from the home country to another country because the other country has a lower wage scale involves a question of social responsibility if that means laying off workers and possibly closing a factory or offices in the home country. Doing so would take income away from employees and suppliers of goods and services for both the company and the employees as consumers and deprive municipalities, states, and the federal government of revenue. Price fixing (choice A), harassing a whistleblower (choice C), and reporting inflated profits (choice D) are not matters of social responsibility—they are illegal.

4. **The correct answer is B.** There may be some investment in office equipment and supplies, but opening a sales office in a foreign city is not direct foreign investment, so eliminate choice A. Choices C and D also aren't examples of direct foreign investment, so they are incorrect.

5. **The correct answer is C.** The benefits of a product provide form, time, place, and ownership utility to buyers. Choice A is incorrect because it omits ownership. Choice B is incorrect because price, promotion, and place are three of the Four P's of marketing; the first is the product itself. Choice D is incorrect because the four types of utility create the value of a product.

6. **The correct answer is B.** Choices A, C, and D are all systems software that enable managers at different levels in an organization to use data and models to make informed decisions about their departments.

7. **The correct answer is A.** Corporate philanthropy involves donating some of a company's profits for charitable work, such as sponsoring civic projects like the Great American Cleanup. Refusal to do business with sweatshops (choice B) is an example of CSR related to human rights, not corporate philanthropy. Choice C is incorrect because

recycled packaging is an example of CSR related to environmental issues. Choice D is incorrect because refusing to allow cigarettes to be used in a program is an example of CSR related to marketing and health.

8. **The correct answer is D.** Presumably a potential buyer will have done his or her homework ahead of time and discovered what the marketplace thinks about the business, but a poor reputation (choice D) is a risk when buying an existing business. Choice A is incorrect because buying an existing business takes less time than establishing a new business. Choice B is incorrect because the opposite is true; it is easier to get financing for an existing business than a start-up. Choice C is incorrect because the lack of creative control is a disadvantage of buying a new franchise, not an existing business. Once a person owns a non-franchise business, a person can do whatever he or she believes is necessary for the market.

9. **The correct answer is B.** During a product's growth stage, competitors become aware of the product's surge in sales and market share and begin introducing products to compete with it. Choices A, C, and D—introduction, maturity, and decline—are incorrect.

10. **The correct answer is A.** The accounting department of a company prepares income statements and also budgets. However, choice C is incorrect because other departments provide input, which the accounting department then uses to develop budgets. Investing surplus funds (choice B) and determining capitalization strategies (choice D) are functions of financial managers, not accountants.

11. **The correct answer is C.** Encryption software encodes messages so they can't be read without a key, which is "unlocked" with a passphrase. Choice A is incorrect because it describes spam-filtering software. Choice B is incorrect because it describes anti-spyware software. Choice D is incorrect because it describes a firewall.

12. **The correct answer is A.** Selling goods abroad for less than what they cost to produce or less than their domestic price is dumping. Choice B is a practice some manufacturers use, but it is not dumping. Choice C defines a sale. Choice D is incorrect because it is the definition of a subsidy.

13. **The correct answer is C.** All four answers may seem possible, but only choice C describes enterprise resource planning programs (ERPP). Choices A, B, and D are all incorrect because they don't relate to ERPP.

14. **The correct answer is B.** In a joint venture, both companies will enjoy the benefit of shared resources and information. The downside is the potential for the loss of specialized knowledge and technology and the problems that may arise from sharing control. Choice A is incorrect because in licensing, one company sells the right to its name, product, or process to another and has no control over the resulting business, but it provides a quick entry into a foreign market. Choice C is incorrect because a strategic alliance is a working arrangement for a period of time and for some specific purpose; neither company cedes its independence or control to the other. Choice D is incorrect because in contract manufacturing, a company contracts with a foreign company to manufacture its product for that foreign market; it provides quick, low-cost entry into the foreign marketplace.

15. **The correct answer is A.** Unlike an oligopoly, which has few competitors, an industry that exhibits perfect competition (choice B) is one with many sellers and buyers, almost no differentiation among products, and low barriers to entry. The airline industry doesn't fit either multiplicity of buyers nor low barriers to entry, so perfect competition doesn't characterize the airline industry. Monopolistic competition (choice C) characterizes an industry with many buyers and sellers; buyers believe that there are differences among products, though in reality there aren't. The airline industry doesn't have many sellers, and buyers don't

perceive much in the way of differences among those sellers, so eliminate choice C. A monopoly (choice D) has only one seller, and that doesn't describe the airline industry.

16. **The correct answer is B.** Corporate social responsibility is a company's taking responsibility for the ways in which it affects the community—both internally, domestically, and globally. Choice A is incorrect because that is an example of ethical conduct. Choices C and D are incorrect because both are legal issues.

17. **The correct answer is D.** Only capital expenditures such as the construction of new facilities are appropriate reasons for issuing corporate bonds. Research and development (choice A) is paid for normally out of operating expenses (choice B), and issuing corporate bonds to fund operating expenses is not appropriate. Borrowing money to pay interest on borrowed money (choice C) is also not appropriate.

18. **The correct answer is B.** Situation analysis looks at the trends in a company's market and considers the customers, companies, and competitors and considers opportunities. Even if you didn't know this term, you could determine the correct answer by the process of elimination. Choice A is an interpersonal ability, so it can be eliminated. Choices C and D are both steps in the decision-making process, so eliminate them.

19. **The correct answer is D.** The five factors of production are labor, natural resources, capital, entrepreneurs, and technology. Choice A is incorrect because capital is either physical (facilities) or financial (money), and neither technology nor entrepreneurship fits this definition. Choice B is incorrect because a product mix is the products that a company sells. Choice C is incorrect because operations are the activities that produce a company's goods or services.

20. **The correct answer is A.** A flat structure implies a decentralized organization. A tall structure (choice B) implies a centralized

organization (choice C). An autocratic organization is not a recognized term, but autocratic management would come under the category of choice D.

21. **The correct answer is A.** A shopping good is one that is bought infrequently and for which a person does research and comparison shopping. Choices B and D are incorrect because a wedding gown and an engagement ring are classified as specialty goods. Choice C is incorrect because a doughnut and coffee are typically convenience purchases.

22. **The correct answer is C.** The corporate culture is the shared beliefs, values, history, and norms that shape what an organization believes and does. Choice A is incorrect because cross-cultural environments are external and affect how businesses operate in countries other than their own. Choices B and D, economic and political-legal environments, are also external influences that affect companies both domestically and internationally.

23. **The correct answer is A.** Choice B is incorrect because this is operating income. Choice C is incorrect because this is the owner's equity in a business. Choice D is incorrect because this is the cost of goods.

24. **The correct answer is D.** Choices A and B describe short-term goals, so they are incorrect. Choice C is incorrect because intermediate goals are typically intended to be achieved within one to five years, not one to three years.

25. **The correct answer is A.** A depreciating currency is declining in value, so imports cost more and exports cost less. Choice B is the opposite of the effect of currency depreciation on imports. Choice C is the opposite of what happens to exports when currency depreciates. Choice D is incorrect because currency depreciation causes imports to rise in price and exports to decline in price.

26. **The correct answer is C.** A Gantt chart shows steps in a project and time required to perform them. Choice A is incorrect because this describes an organization chart. Choice

B is incorrect because this describes a PERT chart. Choice D is incorrect because this describes a master production schedule.

27. **The correct answer is C.** In relation to the consumer market, the B2B is small. Choices A, B, and D more appropriately characterize the consumer market than the B2B market. In the latter, purchasing decisions are typically group decisions, making choice A incorrect. Buyers and sellers tend to develop personal relationships over time, making choice B incorrect. The buying process is highly formalized in B2B markets, making choice D incorrect.

28. **The correct answer is D.** All three factors—ineffective financial controls, lack of adequate capitalization, and inexperienced management—can lead to the failure of a business. Only choice D includes all three items.

29. **The correct answer is A.** Choice B is incorrect because it is similar to the ISO 14000 certification that a company's products are manufactured in an environmentally friendly way. Choices C and D are incorrect descriptions of the ISO 9000 label.

30. **The correct answer is C.** The question asks about locating a manufacturing facility, and only choice C describes a factor related to deciding where to place a new manufacturing facility. Inventory management (choice A) is part of production management, but is not related to where to locate a new facility, although it may impact the size of the facility. The size of the market (choice B) is a marketing concern, but not one of the factors related to deciding where to locate a manufacturing facility. Choice D is part of laying out a facility, not locating it, so it is incorrect.

31. **The correct answer is C.** Choices A and D both define absolute advantage, not comparative advantage. Whether a country is the earliest producer of a product (choice B) is irrelevant.

32. **The correct answer is B.** Arbitration may be binding or not, depending on whether the sides agreed to its being binding or whether they were ordered by a court to binding arbitration. Choice A is incorrect because mediation is a recommendation by a third party as to how to end a dispute between parties; it is not a mandatory resolution. Choice C is incorrect because collective bargaining is negotiation. Choice D is incorrect because a boycott is a refusal to buy or use certain products.

33. **The correct answer is D.** Of the choices given, a small business needing money for cash flow would most likely apply for a bank line of credit. It could also apply for a commercial loan, depending on the circumstances. Choice A is incorrect because a debenture is a bond and is a financial tool of large companies, as are choices B and C.

34. **The correct answer is B.** In both e-commerce and traditional sales in the B2B marketplace, there are few customers for any given product. Choice A is incorrect because in both types of selling, orders are generally large. Choice C is incorrect because in both cases, purchasing is centralized in a purchasing department. Choice D is incorrect because comparison shopping to see what competitors offer is routine.

35. **The correct answer is C.** Choice A is the task of the U.S. Treasury Department and is part of fiscal policy, as is choice B. Choice D is the job of the Federal Deposit Insurance Corporation, an independent agency of the federal government.

36. **The correct answer is D.** Choice A is incorrect because an income statement shows profit and loss. Choice B is not the best answer because it is not specific. Choice C is incorrect because a cash flow statement shows the receipts and payments.

37. **The correct answer is C.** The sense of achievement at the end of the project comes from within the employee. Choices A, B, and D are extrinsic motivators.

38. **The correct answer is B.** Choice A is incorrect. While it is true that it is easier for a partnership to get a bank loan, there

is no support for the statement that angel investors prefer to invest in sole proprietorships. If part of an answer is incorrect, the entire answer is incorrect. Choice C is incorrect because it is unlikely that a bank will act as an advisor; it is more likely that an angel investor will adopt that role rather than take a hands-off approach. Choice D is irrelevant to a loan status.

39. **The correct answer is A.** Choice B is not a recognized term. Choice C is incorrect; posting the job on the company Intranet would be an internal method. Choice D is incorrect because using a headhunter is employing a company to do one-on-one recruiting for candidates.

40. **The correct answer is B.** Part-time, temporary, and contract workers are contingent workers. While any of the workers listed in choices A, C, and D could be contingent employees depending on the circumstances, a lawyer leased from a company that places lawyers in companies on contract (choice B) definitely refers to a contingent worker.

41. **The correct answer is C.** Choice A may seem like a good choice, but continuous improvement refers to work process engineering. Choice B is incorrect because TQM stands for Total Quality Management, which is not the same as adaptability. Choice D may seem correct, but it is not a recognized term.

42. **The correct answer is B.** Choice A is incorrect because regulatory law is established by administrative agencies, both state and federal. Choices C and D both describe common law.

43. **The correct answer is C.** Choice A is incorrect because the equilibrium point is the point at which supply and demand are equal. Choice B is incorrect because aggregate output is the total amount of goods and services that an economy produces during a given period of time. Choice D is incorrect because the real growth rate is the gross domestic product adjusted for inflation and fluctuations in a country's currency.

44. **The correct answer is D.** All three items are motivators that push people toward becoming entrepreneurs. (Three additional reasons are the desire for financial independence, losing one's job, and the desire to capitalize on a great idea.) Only choice D has all three items.

45. **The correct answer is B.** Belonging is the third level of Maslow's hierarchy and satisfies the human need for social interaction and acceptance. Choice A is incorrect because safety is the second level and refers to feeling safe; while having a safe work environment is part of satisfying this need, the question refers to connectedness, which is more than just feeling safe. Esteem (choice C) is the fourth level and refers to respect, which is more than feeling connected. Self-actualization (choice D) is the highest level and is not dependent on others.

46. **The correct answer is B.** Malware can be a virus, worm, or Trojan horse. Choice A is incorrect because spyware transmits information such as passwords, contacts, and credit card numbers and transmits the data back to the sender of the spyware. Choice C is incorrect because spam is junk e-mail. Choice D is incorrect because cookies are bits of code left in computers when users visit commercial sites that enable the sites to customize pages for viewers.

47. **The correct answer is C.** The formula results in gross profit margin. Choice A is incorrect; operating expenses are the costs of doing business minus income taxes. Choice B is incorrect because operating profit margin is total revenue minus cost of goods sold minus operating expenses divided by total revenue. Choice D is incorrect because net income divided by number of outstanding shares equals earnings per share.

48. **The correct answer is A.** Data interpretation (choice B) may seem like a good answer, but the correct term is "data mining." Choice C is incorrect because the the question asks about analyzing, not collecting, data. Choice D is incorrect, but it may be confusing because it sounds like "drill down," which means "to

look at data in increasingly more detailed levels."

49. **The correct answer is C.** Choice A is incorrect because the bargaining chip argument contends that high tariffs can be useful in negotiating with a trading partner to reduce its tariffs in exchange for a reduction in comparable tariffs. Choice B is incorrect because the infant industry argument contends that a developing industry at home needs to be protected from foreign competition. The national security argument (choice D) is incorrect because it claims that certain industries should be protected from foreign competition in the interests of their vital importance to the nation's defense.

50. **The correct answer is D.** The right to own property is an essential characteristic of a market economy. Some government control and some competition (choice A) describes an economy with some central planning, also known as socialism. Choice B is incorrect because central planning is a characteristic of communist and socialist economies, not market economies. The barrier to entry (choice C) is incorrect because the barrier in any industry may be high or low in a market economy. The answer is too narrow and is, therefore, incorrect.

51. **The correct answer is A.** Choice B is incorrect because an apprenticeship is a specific type of training program for skilled workers; it would not include information on a company's culture. Choice C is incorrect because mentoring is typically a found on the managerial level, not on the junior employee level. Choice D is incorrect because an orientation program describes the company, but not a new employee's job.

52. **The correct answer is D.** Choices A and B are incorrect. Backward scheduling is used with a variety of inventory control systems; policy dictates whether forward or backward scheduling is used by a company. Choice C describes forward scheduling.

53. **The correct answer is C.** Goodwill is a company's intangible asset. Choice A is incorrect because intellectual property describes a person's creative output. Choice B is incorrect because liquid assets are tangible things that can be easily converted to cash. Choice D is incorrect because brand recognition and a company's reputation are not tangible.

54. **The correct answer is B.** The four P's are product, price, promotion, and place, so choice A is incorrect. Choice C is incorrect because the media mix is the combination of media used to advertise a product. Choice D is incorrect because product differentiation refers to the features of a product that distinguish it from its competitors.

55. **The correct answer is C.** Net income is calculated on total revenue (item I) and operating expenses and income taxes (item III), so choice C is correct.

56. **The correct answer is B.** Choice A is incorrect because it is not a policy of the World Bank. Choice C is incorrect because it describes a function of the International Monetary Fund. Choice D is incorrect because it is a function of the U.S. Federal Reserve System.

57. **The correct answer is B.** Choice A is incorrect because the question asks about analyzing, not collecting, data. Choice C is incorrect because unless violations of the minimum wage are related to job discrimination, the Equal Employment Opportunity Commission would not investigate. Choice D is incorrect; unions use collective bargaining to raise wages whether they are minimum wages or not.

58. **The correct answer is B.** Partnerships find it easier to borrow money because the business doesn't rest on one owner. Choice A is incorrect because neither sole proprietorships nor partnerships enjoy limited liability. Choice C is incorrect because partnerships require more paperwork to establish than do sole proprietorships. Choice D is incorrect because sole proprietorships and

partnerships have similar tax benefits; in both, owners pay taxes as personal income.

59. **The correct answer is C.** Like catalog shopping, consumers can't see and touch the products they are interested in buying. Choices A and B are the opposite of what's true about e-tailing—comparison shopping is easier and product array is larger than a consumer would have in local stores. Choice D is incorrect because prices are comparable or even lower than bricks-and-mortar stores.

60. **The correct answer is A.** Like bounce-back coupons and discount coupons, point-of-sale displays are sales promotion strategies. Advertising (choice B) is not a sales promotion technique; product placement in a movie or TV show is an example of advertising a product. A distribution channel is a way to move goods from producer to consumer, so choice C is incorrect. Choice D is incorrect because while a point-of-sale display may prompt an impulse buy, it's not an impulse buy, but a sales promotion technique.

Introduction to World Religions

OVERVIEW

Chapter 6

The DSST® Introduction to World Religions exam consists of 100 multiple-choice questions that cover the historical development, doctrine, and practice of religions throughout the world. The exam focuses upon the following topics: dimensions and approaches to religion, primal religions, Hinduism, Buddhism, Confucianism, Daoism, Judaism, Christianity, Islam, Shintoism, and religious movements and syncretism. Careful reading, critical thinking, and logical analysis will be as important as your knowledge of religious doctrines.

DIAGNOSTIC TEST ANSWER SHEET

1. Ⓐ Ⓑ Ⓒ Ⓓ   5. Ⓐ Ⓑ Ⓒ Ⓓ   9. Ⓐ Ⓑ Ⓒ Ⓓ   13. Ⓐ Ⓑ Ⓒ Ⓓ   17. Ⓐ Ⓑ Ⓒ Ⓓ

2. Ⓐ Ⓑ Ⓒ Ⓓ   6. Ⓐ Ⓑ Ⓒ Ⓓ   10. Ⓐ Ⓑ Ⓒ Ⓓ   14. Ⓐ Ⓑ Ⓒ Ⓓ   18. Ⓐ Ⓑ Ⓒ Ⓓ

3. Ⓐ Ⓑ Ⓒ Ⓓ   7. Ⓐ Ⓑ Ⓒ Ⓓ   11. Ⓐ Ⓑ Ⓒ Ⓓ   15. Ⓐ Ⓑ Ⓒ Ⓓ   19. Ⓐ Ⓑ Ⓒ Ⓓ

4. Ⓐ Ⓑ Ⓒ Ⓓ   8. Ⓐ Ⓑ Ⓒ Ⓓ   12. Ⓐ Ⓑ Ⓒ Ⓓ   16. Ⓐ Ⓑ Ⓒ Ⓓ   20. Ⓐ Ⓑ Ⓒ Ⓓ

POST-TEST ANSWER SHEET

1. Ⓐ Ⓑ Ⓒ Ⓓ   13. Ⓐ Ⓑ Ⓒ Ⓓ   25. Ⓐ Ⓑ Ⓒ Ⓓ   37. Ⓐ Ⓑ Ⓒ Ⓓ   49. Ⓐ Ⓑ Ⓒ Ⓓ

2. Ⓐ Ⓑ Ⓒ Ⓓ   14. Ⓐ Ⓑ Ⓒ Ⓓ   26. Ⓐ Ⓑ Ⓒ Ⓓ   38. Ⓐ Ⓑ Ⓒ Ⓓ   50. Ⓐ Ⓑ Ⓒ Ⓓ

3. Ⓐ Ⓑ Ⓒ Ⓓ   15. Ⓐ Ⓑ Ⓒ Ⓓ   27. Ⓐ Ⓑ Ⓒ Ⓓ   39. Ⓐ Ⓑ Ⓒ Ⓓ   51. Ⓐ Ⓑ Ⓒ Ⓓ

4. Ⓐ Ⓑ Ⓒ Ⓓ   16. Ⓐ Ⓑ Ⓒ Ⓓ   28. Ⓐ Ⓑ Ⓒ Ⓓ   40. Ⓐ Ⓑ Ⓒ Ⓓ   52. Ⓐ Ⓑ Ⓒ Ⓓ

5. Ⓐ Ⓑ Ⓒ Ⓓ   17. Ⓐ Ⓑ Ⓒ Ⓓ   29. Ⓐ Ⓑ Ⓒ Ⓓ   41. Ⓐ Ⓑ Ⓒ Ⓓ   53. Ⓐ Ⓑ Ⓒ Ⓓ

6. Ⓐ Ⓑ Ⓒ Ⓓ   18. Ⓐ Ⓑ Ⓒ Ⓓ   30. Ⓐ Ⓑ Ⓒ Ⓓ   42. Ⓐ Ⓑ Ⓒ Ⓓ   54. Ⓐ Ⓑ Ⓒ Ⓓ

7. Ⓐ Ⓑ Ⓒ Ⓓ   19. Ⓐ Ⓑ Ⓒ Ⓓ   31. Ⓐ Ⓑ Ⓒ Ⓓ   43. Ⓐ Ⓑ Ⓒ Ⓓ   55. Ⓐ Ⓑ Ⓒ Ⓓ

8. Ⓐ Ⓑ Ⓒ Ⓓ   20. Ⓐ Ⓑ Ⓒ Ⓓ   32. Ⓐ Ⓑ Ⓒ Ⓓ   44. Ⓐ Ⓑ Ⓒ Ⓓ   56. Ⓐ Ⓑ Ⓒ Ⓓ

9. Ⓐ Ⓑ Ⓒ Ⓓ   21. Ⓐ Ⓑ Ⓒ Ⓓ   33. Ⓐ Ⓑ Ⓒ Ⓓ   45. Ⓐ Ⓑ Ⓒ Ⓓ   57. Ⓐ Ⓑ Ⓒ Ⓓ

10. Ⓐ Ⓑ Ⓒ Ⓓ   22. Ⓐ Ⓑ Ⓒ Ⓓ   34. Ⓐ Ⓑ Ⓒ Ⓓ   46. Ⓐ Ⓑ Ⓒ Ⓓ   58. Ⓐ Ⓑ Ⓒ Ⓓ

11. Ⓐ Ⓑ Ⓒ Ⓓ   23. Ⓐ Ⓑ Ⓒ Ⓓ   35. Ⓐ Ⓑ Ⓒ Ⓓ   47. Ⓐ Ⓑ Ⓒ Ⓓ   59. Ⓐ Ⓑ Ⓒ Ⓓ

12. Ⓐ Ⓑ Ⓒ Ⓓ   24. Ⓐ Ⓑ Ⓒ Ⓓ   36. Ⓐ Ⓑ Ⓒ Ⓓ   48. Ⓐ Ⓑ Ⓒ Ⓓ   60. Ⓐ Ⓑ Ⓒ Ⓓ

answer sheets

INTRODUCTION TO WORLD RELIGIONS DIAGNOSTIC TEST

Directions: Carefully read each of the following 20 questions. Choose the best answer to each question and fill in the corresponding circle on the answer sheet. The Answer Key and Explanations can be found following this Diagnostic Test.

1. Which of the following accurately describes Ramadan?
   A. It is the Muslim month of fasting.
   B. It is the Jewish day of atonement.
   C. It is the forty days before Easter.
   D. It is the Hindu festival of lights.

2. The Hasidim
   A. is a modern denomination of Judaism that follows a liberal interpretation of Jewish law.
   B. are followers of mystical rabbis who live in their own communities separated from the world.
   C. are descended from Jews who were expelled from Spain and Portugal in the fifteenth century.
   D. is a twentieth-century denomination that keeps traditional historical Jewish customs.

3. The purpose of the Second Vatican Council was to
   A. reassert that Confirmation, Penance, the Eucharist, Extreme Unction, Marriage, and Holy Orders, as well as Baptism, were sacraments.
   B. affirm the basic tenets of the faith by developing what became known as the Nicene Creed.
   C. modernize and revitalize the Catholic Church.
   D. reassert Catholic Church teachings after the Protestant Reformation.

4. The basic sacred text of Hinduism is the
   A. *Law of Manu.*
   B. *Vedas.*
   C. *Analects.*
   D. *Bhagavad Gita.*

5. The basic belief system of Zoroastrianism is based on which of the following?
   A. Five Pillars
   B. Four Books
   C. Three-fold path
   D. Eight-Fold Path

6. Dimensions of basic religions include
   I. rituals.
   II. taboos.
   III. ancestor worship.
   IV. animism.
   A. I and II only
   B. I and III only
   C. I, II, and IV only
   D. I, II, III, and IV

7. A basic tenet of Confucius' teachings is
   A. the renunciation of all desire in order to enter nirvana.
   B. behaving ethically at all times and in all relationships.
   C. making regular sacrifices to the deities in order to have one's transgressions wiped away.
   D. the balance between dark and light, heaven and earth.

8. In Hinduism, *samsara* is
   A. the force generated by actions in this life that set up what the next life will be like.
   B. the breaking free of life.
   C. the wandering of the life force from one body and time to another.
   D. a riddle that will help a believer achieve insight.

9. The Second Pillar of Islam is
   A. daily prayer.
   B. almsgiving.
   C. hajj.
   D. fasting.

10. Daoists believe that human suffering, pain, and violence are eliminated only through a belief in
    A. no action, or inaction, which leads individuals to a state of harmony with their own nature.
    B. a single, all-powerful God who makes ethical demands and places responsibilities on individuals and community.
    C. the practice of ethical relationships that involve reciprocal duties and responsibilities among specific members of society.
    D. the idea that the individual, or essential, self is one with Brahman and everything else in the universe.

11. Which of the following is the body of Islamic law?
    A. Shi'a
    B. Shari'ah
    C. Hadith
    D. Qur'an

12. A practice common to Protestant denominations in general and the Orthodox Churches is
    A. veneration of icons.
    B. married clergy.
    C. belief in the presence of Jesus in the Eucharist.
    D. acceptance of the seven sacraments.

13. Mahavira, who believed that he had found a way to stop the endless cycle of birth, life, and death, is the traditional founder of
    A. Ecumenism.
    B. Buddhism.
    C. Jainism.
    D. Daoism.

14. Right views, right thoughts, and right speech are elements of
    A. the right relationships that Confucius taught.
    B. yin and yang.
    C. Jesus' Sermon on the Mount.
    D. Buddhism's Eight-Fold Path.

15. What was the practice of Shinto as a national Japanese religion called?
    A. Shrine Shinto
    B. Folk Shinto
    C. Sect Shinto
    D. State Shinto

16. Which of the following indigenous groups did NOT practice human sacrifice as a part of their worship?
    A. Aztecs
    B. Yoruban
    C. Maya
    D. Inca

17. Passover celebrates the
    A. exodus of the Jews from Egypt.
    B. retaking of the Temple in Jerusalem.
    C. harvest.
    D. delivery of the Jews from Persia.

18. Which of the following men introduced the concept of predestination into Protestantism?
    A. Henry VIII
    B. Martin Luther
    C. John Calvin
    D. John Wesley

19. What is the Buddhist name for the Three Jewels, a symbol that represents the three core values of Buddhism: Buddha, dharma, and sangha?
    A. Triratna.
    B. Dhammapada
    C. Vedas
    D. Dukkha

20. Two of the important values of the Shinto religion are
    A. poverty and celibacy.
    B. Indra and Agni.
    C. yin and yang.
    D. fertility and family.

ANSWER KEY AND EXPLANATIONS

1. A	**5.** C	**9.** A	**13.** C	**17.** A
2. B	**6.** D	**10.** A	**14.** D	**18.** C
3. C	**7.** B	**11.** B	**15.** D	**19.** A
4. B	**8.** C	**12.** B	**16.** B	**20.** D

1. **The correct answer is A.** During Ramadan, Muslims who are physically able and not pregnant must fast from sunrise to sunset from all food and drink. Choice B is incorrect because it describes Yom Kippur, a Jewish holy day. Choice C is incorrect because the forty days before Easter are known as Lent in the Christian calendar. Choice D is incorrect because the Hindu festival of lights is called Diwali.

2. **The correct answer is B.** Hasidic Judaism was founded in the eighteenth century in Poland and follows a mystical version of Judaism separated from the modern world. Choice A is incorrect because it describes Reform Judaism. Choice C is incorrect because it describes Sephardic Jews who might be of any denomination today. Choice D is incorrect because it describes Reconstructionist Judaism.

3. **The correct answer is C.** The Second Vatican Council was called by Pope John XXIII in 1962. Its purpose was to modernize and revitalize the Catholic Church. Choice A is incorrect because this reaffirmation was one result of the Council of Trent. Choice D also describes the Council of Trent, not the Second Vatican Council. Choice B is incorrect because the Nicene Creed was promulgated after the First Council of Nicaea in 325.

4. **The correct answer is B.** Choice A is incorrect; the *Law of Manu* was written after the *Vedas* and contains ethical and social standards for living, but not all the basic concepts of Hinduism. Choice C is incorrect because the *Analects* collect the teachings of Confucius. Choice D is incorrect; the *Bhagavad Gita* is an epic poem about deities and heroes.

5. **The correct answer is C.** To fulfill the will of their god Ahura-Mazda, Zoroastrians follow the three-fold path: good thoughts, good words, and good deeds. Choice A is incorrect because the Five Pillars are the basic belief system of Islam. Choice B is incorrect because the Four Books are part of the basic writings of Confucianism. Choice D is incorrect because Buddhism centers on the Eight-Fold Path.

6. **The correct answer is D.** All four—(I) ritual, (II) taboos, (III) ancestor worship, and (IV) animism—are features of basic religions. Only choice D includes all four and so is the correct answer.

7. **The correct answer is B.** Choice A is incorrect; renunciation of desire to enter nirvana is a tenet of Buddhism. Choice C is incorrect because Confucius did not teach about deities, sacrifices to them, or forgiveness of sins. Choice D refers to the concepts of yin and yang in Daoism.

8. **The correct answer is C.** Choice A is incorrect because the actions in this life that set up what the next life will be like is called karma. Choice B is incorrect because moksha is the breaking free of the life cycle. Choice D is incorrect because koan is a riddle used in Zen Buddhism to help a person achieve sudden insight.

9. **The correct answer is A.** The first pillar of Islam is "There is no God but Allah; Muhammad is the messenger of Allah." Daily prayer is the second pillar. Almsgiving (choice B) is the third pillar. Fasting (choice D) is the fourth pillar. The hajj, or pilgrimage to Mecca (choice C), is the fifth pillar.

10. **The correct answer is A.** Choice B is incorrect because it describes the views of Judaism. Choice C is incorrect because it

answers diagnostic test

describes the practices of Confucianism. Choice D is one of the basic tenets of Hinduism.

11. **The correct answer is B.** Choice A is incorrect because Shi'a is one of the two major branches of Islam; the other is Sunni. The Hadith (choice C) is a collection of traditions relating to Muhammad and his companions. Choice D is incorrect because the Qur'an is the basic sacred text of Islam.

12. **The correct answer is B.** Protestant denominations don't have celibacy requirements for priests and ministers, and priests in the Orthodox Churches may be married if they were married before ordination. Choice A is incorrect because icons are not venerated in Protestant denominations. Choice C is incorrect because Protestant denominations do not believe in transubstantiation. Choice D is incorrect because Protestant denominations do not accept all seven sacraments.

13. **The correct answer is C.** Mahavira is the traditional founder of Jainism. Choice A is incorrect because Ecumenism was a movement by the Roman Catholic, Eastern Orthodox, and some Protestant churches to heal divisions among themselves. Choice B is incorrect because Siddhartha Gautama was the founder of Buddhism. Choice D is incorrect because Lao-zi was the founder of Daoism.

14. **The correct answer is D.** The Eight-Fold Path of Buddhism contains a series of steps: right views, right thoughts, right speech, right action, right livelihood, right effort, right mindfulness, and right concentration. Choice A is incorrect because the teachings of Confucius on right relationships don't specifically use these terms. Choice B is incorrect because yin and yang are elements of Daoism and refer to opposing yet complementary principles of life. Choice C is incorrect because Jesus' Sermon on the Mount includes the Beatitudes.

15. **The correct answer is D.** State Shinto was the national religion of Japan until after World War II. Choice A describes the type of Shinto practiced at outdoor shrines from prehistoric times in Japan. Choice

B describes the type of Shinto without any formal doctrine or structure based on Japanese folk beliefs. Choice C describes the Shintoism that is made up of thirteen different sects.

16. **The correct answer is B.** The Yoruban of southeast Nigeria practice a polytheistic religion that centers primarily on Ogun, the god of blacksmiths, warriors, and metal workers and which does not involve human sacrifice. The Aztecs (choice A) believed that human sacrifice could forestall the end of the world. The Maya (choice C) sacrificed humans as a ritual offering of nourishment to their gods. The Inca (choice D) sacrificed children to honor their mountain gods in a ceremonial ritual called *capacocha*.

17. **The correct answer is A.** Choice B is incorrect because Chanukah celebrates the retaking of the Temple in Jerusalem. Choice C is incorrect because Sukkoth is a harvest celebration. Choice D is incorrect because Purim celebrates the delivery of the Jews from Persia.

18. **The correct answer is C.** Choice A is incorrect because, other than substituting his power for that of the Pope, Henry VIII made few changes in the Catholic Church in England. Choice B is incorrect because Martin Luther did not introduce predestination into Protestantism. Choice D is incorrect because John Wesley founded Methodism, but he didn't introduce predestination into Protestantism.

19. **The correct answer is A.** Triratna is the Buddhist name for the three Jewels. Dhammapada (choice B) is the name of a collection of Buddhist proverbs and adages. Vedas (choice C) is the name of the Hindu book of hymns, prayers, and myths. Dukkha (choice D) is the idea that all life is suffering as described in the Four Noble Truths of Buddhism.

20. **The correct answer is D.** Fertility and family are two important values in Shintoism. Poverty and celibacy (choice A) are two important aspects of Theravada Buddhism. Indra and Agni (choice B) are two deities of the Aryans. Yin and yang (choice C) are concepts in Daoism that represent balance.

DIAGNOSTIC TEST ASSESSMENT GRID

Now that you've completed the diagnostic test and read through the answer explanations, you can use your results to target your studying. Find the question numbers from the diagnostic test that you answered incorrectly and highlight or circle them below. Then focus extra attention on the sections within the chapter dealing with those topics.

Introduction to World Religions		
Content Area	**Topics Covered**	**Questions**
Definition and Origins of Religion	• Basic dimensions of religion • Approaches to religion	6
Indigenous Religions	• Northern Native American traditions • Southern Native American traditions • West African traditions • Ancient Middle Eastern traditions	16
Hinduism	• The history of Hinduism • Major Hindu traditions • Hindu doctrine and practice	4, 8
Buddhism	• The history of Buddhism • Major Buddhist traditions • Buddist doctrine and practice	14, 19
Confucianism	• The history of Confucianism • Confucian doctrine and practice	7
Daoism	• The history of Daoism • Daoist doctrine and practice	10
Shintoism	• The history of Shintoism • Shinto doctrine and practice	15, 20
Judaism	• The history of Judaism • Denominations • Judaic Doctrine and practice	2, 17

Introduction to World Religions		
Content Area	**Topics Covered**	**Questions**
Christianity	• The history of Christianity • Major Christian traditions • Christian doctrine and practice	3, 12, 18
Islam	• The history of Islam • Major Islamic traditions • Islamic doctrine and practice	1, 9, 11
Religious Movements and Syncretism	• Before 1000 CE • After 1000 CE • Contemporary religious movements	5

GET THE FACTS

To see the DSST® Introduction to World Religions Fact Sheet, go to **http://getcollegecredit.com /pdf/exam_fact_sheets** and click on the **Humanities** tab. Scroll down and click the **Introduction to World Religions** link. Here you will find suggestions for further study material and the ACE college credit recommendations for passing the test.

DEFINITION AND ORIGINS OF RELIGION

Religions—modern and ancient—appear on the surface to be very different, but if you look just a little below the surface, you will find many similarities.

BASIC DIMENSIONS OF RELIGION

The Merriam-Webster dictionary defines religion as "the service and worship of God or the supernatural, a commitment or devotion to religious faith or observance, a personalized set or institutionalized system of religious attitudes, beliefs, and practices." Regardless of the religion, all religions, then, have certain characteristics in common: a supernatural aspect, a belief system, and rituals.

In his 1969 work, *The Religious Experience of Mankind*, Ninian Smart describes six characteristics of religion in terms of ritual, mythical, doctrinal, ethical, social, and experiential dimensions:

1. *Ritual:* Rituals are the practices that members of a religion engage in, such as worship (prayer) and fasting. Ritual includes such rites of passage as baptism and confirmation in Christian churches, bar mitzvah and bat mitzvah in Judaism, and marriage in any given religion.

2. *Mythical:* Myths are the stories that provide information about the supernatural aspects of a religion as well as its human actors. "Creation myths" are good examples. These stories may be collected as oral tradition or written down as holy scripture.

3. *Doctrinal:* Doctrine is the belief system that develops within a religion. Doctrine, or dogma, is a body of teachings that defines the truth, values, rituals, and practices of a religion. Some religions have organized and structured written doctrine and others do not.

4. *Ethical:* A religion's doctrine shapes the code of ethics of a religion, that is, the way that members should behave toward themselves and others based on the religion's teachings.

5. *Social:* Religion is social. Religions have members who make up a community and give witness to their faith by their actions.

6. *Experiential:* According to Smart, "personal religion normally involves the hope of, or realization of, experience of that [invisible world of the particular religion]." Being "born again" is an example.

Other writers on the subject of a definition of religion use other categories, such as experience as revelation (showing the invisible world of the supernatural to humans in some way) and faith as response to revelation.

APPROACHES TO RELIGION

Ancient philosophers and intellectuals have tried since the time of Plato to understand religion and make a rational argument for the existence of God. During the thirteenth century, Thomas Aquinas explored the connections of Christianity to the natural world through the theory of natural theology. Natural theology differed from revealed theology in that it was not based on revelations or knowledge gained from written texts, personal stories, or simple faith. Instead, natural theology attempted to explain God based on the natural world and human reason. Other philosophers later expanded on Aquinas' work. A modern view of natural theology incorporates art, science, history, and morality into a vision where God and religion also fit.

Beginning in the nineteenth century, several different approaches to the study of religion have been popular:

1. *Anthropological:* Anthropologists observe and study the religious elements of a culture, such as its myths, rituals, and taboos. Taboos are those things that adherents of a religion are forbidden to do. For example, Muslims and Jews may not eat pork.

2. *Phenomenological:* Scholars following this school of thought believe that religion is a phenomenon that exists across all cultures and all time. The phenomenological approach has influenced the field of comparative religious studies.

3. *Psychological:* The influence of religion on the thoughts and actions of adherents is the subject of this approach.

4. *Sociological:* This approach considers religion a social rather than a theological phenomenon.

5. *Historical* or *Descriptive:* This approach applies historical methodologies to collect all of the data and evidence available in order to determine what really happened in past events detailed by a religion. The historical approach determines whether the key figures of a religion really did live at one time or if the events actually took place.

All have their supporters and their critics.

INDIGENOUS RELIGIONS

Indigenous religions have certain features in common, namely: animism (the elements of nature have spirits), magic (control of nature by manipulation), divination (predicting the future), totem (family or clan identification with animals), ancestor veneration or worship, sacrifice, taboo (certain people, places, and things considered either too holy or too "unclean" to touch), myth, ritual, and rites of passage.

NORTHERN NATIVE AMERICAN TRADITIONS

There is no single Native American religion, but there are certain characteristics that many of these religions share. They are generally animistic and polytheistic. Followers of these religions believe that nature is alive with spirits and that people must live in harmony with nature. Some religions also have a central Supreme Being and a creation story that involves powers or gods creating the world. But, unlike the God of Christianity, Judaism, or Islam, this Supreme Being is above the things of Earth. The spirits of nature, not the Supreme Being, answer the prayers of the people.

Northern Native American religious traditions include ceremonies, rituals, and taboos. Dance and the use of magic are part of many of these practices. There is no special priesthood or hierarchy in northern Native American religions, though some incorporate medicine men and women, sometimes called shamans. These individuals have the power to heal, but they also have the power to cause illness and death.

Though it was not typical for northern Native Americans to practice human or animal sacrifice, there is history of human sacrifice and cannibalism occurring in some cultures.

Aztec

The Aztec people lived in central Mexico from the fourteenth to sixteenth centuries and were a warrior culture. According to Aztec legend, the god **Huitzilopochtli**, the god of the sun and war, told the Aztec they would be a great people if they did what he said. They were to go in search of land where they could plant corn and beans. When the time was right, that is, when they were strong enough to defeat any opponent, then and only then should they make war. Any captives they took should be sacrificed to the gods. When the wandering Aztec came to an island and saw an eagle sitting on a cactus with a serpent in its beak, the Aztec would know that this was where they should settle.

The Aztec state was a theocracy and a warrior culture, so it is not surprising that Aztec religion was focused on death and the end of the world. Aztecs believed that human sacrifice could forestall the destruction of the world.

Other northern Native American traditions were much less violent than the Aztecs and focused more on pleasing gods through offerings, selfless behavior, and even payment of fines. For example, the Inuit, or first peoples of Artic Canada, revere the spirit gods of all things, living and nonliving. Shamans, powerful religious leaders of the Inuit, wear animal masks and instruct people about what prayers and offerings appease the gods, sometimes even assessing fines. They believe that the well-being of their people depends on the pleasure of gods such as Sedna, the goddess of the sea, who only provides food from the ocean if she is pleased with them. Like many Native American cultures, the Inuit have many rules about what they can and cannot do in order to remain in the good graces of the gods.

The Lakota, another Native American culture, are nomadic hunters located in the western plains of the United States. They also practice polytheism and have strong ties to nature and the spirit world. The Lakota religious beliefs hinge on the Sacred White Buffalo Calf Woman, believed to have come to Earth and provided them with the four winds, or directions, to which the Lakota pray. Every prayer is associated with a compass direction, a corresponding color, and a positive or negative connotation. For example, North, or red, is associated with cold, harsh, but cleansing, winds. South, or yellow, represents the origin of the sun, and is the direction to which Lakota pray for wisdom and understanding. Lakota and other tribes also practice **vision quest**, the rite of passage for the young entering puberty. A young man is sent away from his group to live with no food and little else until his vision appears. Often, the vision includes an animal that becomes the young man's totem. People still go on vision quests, usually when faced with a life-defining decision.

The Hopi, a native American culture of the American southwest desert area, leave their spiritual leadership to the village chiefs. Chiefs lead ceremonies performed in the kivas, or underground adobe buildings, built in each village. The Hopi creation myth involves otherworldly beings who create and destroy worlds based on the behavior of people. The spirits are said to lead men into the world through holes in the grounds of the kivas. Solstice celebrations also feature prominently, as the Hopi try to live in harmony with nature and celebrate all that each season brings.

Probably one of the most famous of the Native American cultures is that of the Cherokee. Located in the American southeast, in the area of Virginia, Tennessee, Georgia, and North and South Carolina, the Cherokee incorporate many elements of nature in their creation stories, traditions, and symbolism. Similar to the Lakota, the four directions of the compass hold special significance for them. The Cherokee believe that the world was created at the new moon, and they worship the sun to ensure good fortune, health, and successful crop yields. Their connection to nature is further solidified in their belief that fire was created by the sun and moon to care for man. Shamans in the Cherokee tradition are identified at birth and often raised separately.

SOUTHERN NATIVE AMERICAN TRADITIONS

Major native cultures of South America were the Mayan, Incan, and Mapuche; each had a distinctive religious tradition.

Mayan

The Mayan culture lived mainly on the Yucatan Peninsula. Predominantly a farming people, their religion centered on deities related to the harvest and included deities associated with rain, soil, sun, moon, and corn. According to the Mayan creation story, all humans were descended from the **Four Fathers** who were created from corn. Maize was the name of the corn god. Human sacrifice was practiced.

Inca

The Inca culture lived in the area that is now Peru, part of Chile, and included northern parts of Argentina. It was a vast expanse ruled by emperors and filled, at its height, with impressive buildings, massive temples, and riches. The Incas' polytheism included numerous gods for nearly every part of nature, including the moon, lake, sea, sun, fire, grain, and so on. Though there are differing versions of the Incan creation story, all integrate nature and aspects of animism. The most popular myth involves two main gods: Inti and Viracocha. This myth tells how Viracocha rose from the water to revive the world, created people from rocks and clay, gave them language and songs, and created the sun, moon, and stars so that he could see. Inti, the sun god, is said to be the father of the first Incan king. Symbols of the links to nature are apparent in architecture that remains today. Incas believed that huacas, or elements of nature that were considered sacred, should be incorporated into niches in buildings so that offerings could be made frequently. Incas also believed that natural elements—caves, mountain peaks, and other objects—all resembled shrines and could be used as places of worship. Inca culture, however, was not without violence. Like the Aztecs, the Inca practiced human and animal sacrifice as a part of their religious tradition.

Mapuche

Another southern Native American culture is that of the indigenous Mapuche people who live in Chile and parts of Argentina. Their culture is a complex one that incorporates polytheism and animism. The Mapuche look to spiritual healers called *machu*, as well as herbalist healers called *ampive*. Their religious beliefs involve Earth's creator, Ñenemapun, a ruler god of Mapuche called Ñenechen, and many gods represented by nature or natural elements, such as the sun, moon, volcanoes, and thunder. The Mapuche hold agriculture and fertility festivals to honor their gods and pray for a good harvest, and their beliefs include an afterlife. In Mapuchen tradition, the forces of evil take the forms of people or of animals, and funeral rites must be performed carefully in order to prevent the evil witches (*kaku*) from capturing the spirit of the deceased and turning him or her into a ghost.

WEST AFRICAN TRADITIONS

Like Native American religions, there is no single African religion, but there are a number of commonalities among them. African religions are typically polytheistic, but have a central **High God** who created the world and withdrew from it. This High God is above all the lesser deities, spirits, and ancestors. The spirits are life forces that inhabit nature.

Animism, ancestor veneration, and divination may be aspects of these religious traditions. Similar to northern Native American traditions, spirits in African religions communicate with humans through dreams and signs, and Africans make offerings and sacrifices to the spirits and ancestors. While these are usually simple—such as an offering of food—animal sacrifices may also be conducted on important occasions. Rites of passage, such as ritual circumcision at puberty, are practiced.

Some traditions, especially in West Africa, have male and female priests and temples, though most do not. They often utilize special curers or healers, similar to medicine men and women. Some African religions also have diviners. In some religions, their powers of foretelling the future are important. In others, diviners are called upon to figure out why people are experiencing various problems.

Yoruban

The Yoruban tradition practiced in southeast Nigeria and Benin offers examples of some commonalities. It includes an all-powerful god called Olorun and a creation story that explains how deities from otherworldly places came to Earth and formed men from clay and rocks. More than 400 lesser gods, or *orisha*, are worshiped by the Yoruban, including one of the most important, Ogun, the god of blacksmiths, warriors, and anyone who works with metal. Due to the nature of oral tradition and the need for enslaved Yorubans to hide their religious tradition from their masters, gods' names and genders as well as the details about the tradition's creation story vary slightly from region to region. The Yoruban god Ifa represents the tradition's belief that gods can foretell the future. Ifa is believed to use nuts, signs, and squares of the number four to predict the future.

Dogon

The religious traditions of the Dogon people who now live in parts of Mali, in West Africa, are an example of the complexities of an oral tradition that dates back, some believe, as far as Ancient Egypt. The Dogon migrated from their ancestral lands to the areas of Mali and worship ancestors as well as spirits they encountered on their journey. Their creation story involves an amphibian-like creature that may or may not have come from outer space. The Dogon tradition is divided into three important cults: Awa, the cult of the dead; Lebe, or Earth god; and Binu, sacred places and shrines used to honor ancestors and make sacrifices.

Similar to many religions in the African tradition, the Dogon believe in the power of divination. The Dogon look to diviners to interpret patterns they have made in the sand as well as footprints made by foxes, animals considered sacred by the Dogon. These diviners are called upon to answer everyday questions as well as life-changing ones.

Bavenda

Another culture that incorporates animism, ritual, and a belief in a supreme, otherworldly being is the Bavenda, or Venda. Located more centrally in Africa, their supreme being is Raluvhimba, a god who created the world and lives in the heavens. The mythical belief system prominently incorporates water at its center. Venda believe that water spirits, or *zwidutwane*, live at the bases of waterfalls and need to be kept happy and fed with offerings of food. These water spirits are half visible in this world and half visible in the spirit world. Venda also revere their ancestors as gods and their king as a living ancestor. Children and elderly are thought to be closest to ancestors, the former because they are so new to this world and the latter because they are so close to leaving this world.

Many of the details of the religious traditions of the Venda are not known to westerners. It is known, however, that Venda incorporate many rituals involving music and dance. Their religious traditions include a coming of age ceremony for young men and women that features a python dance and courtship rituals that involve musical dances with flutes made of bamboo. As with other African religious traditions, the Venda see Raluvhimba and zwidutwane in all aspects of nature, whether it is the rumble of thunder, a flood, or a great harvest. If the gods are not happy, the result is a force of nature.

ANCIENT MIDDLE EASTERN TRADITIONS

The ancient Middle East, or the geographic areas that are now Iran and Egypt, as well as parts of Iraq and Syria, were home to many early religious traditions. Some of the aspects of these early traditions later influenced the major religious traditions of Islam, Christianity, and Judaism that also began in that region of the world and still endure today. Some of these traditions had several important beliefs in common. These included a belief in pleasing god in order to receive benevolent treatment, the belief that god was the source of all existence, mythical stories that explained good and evil, fertility and harvest rituals, and the belief that kings or leaders had some sort of divine lineage. In part due to the difference in climate and geography, the religious traditions of the Mesopotamians, and later the Canaanites, which developed in the area that was Mesopotamia and northern Egypt, varied slightly from the religious traditions that developed in ancient Egypt.

Ancient Egypt

Initially, the sun god **Ra** was the most important Egyptian deity, and all Pharaohs were said to be his sons. He was supplanted by the god **Osiris** who, as god of the afterlife, judged the goodness and evilness of the dead. **Isis**, who was both his wife and sister, was the goddess of magic and familial love. According to the myth, Osiris' brother Set cut Osiris into pieces and scattered him across the earth. Isis brought him back to life. The cult of Isis and Osiris spread across the Middle East and into Greece and the Roman Empire.

In the 1300s BCE, the pharaoh Amenhotep IV introduced worship of a single god, **Aton.** According to Amenhotep, who changed his name to Ikhnaton to honor Aton, Aton was the god of light and truth and had created the world. Ikhnaton became the high priest of the new religion, and worship of Aton became the state religion. After Ikhnaton's death, the worship of Aton ended and Egyptians once again worshiped a variety of deities, including local and regional ones.

Interestingly, the ancient Egyptian religion believed in an afterlife, which was similar to life on Earth and for which pharaohs would need food, clothes, drink, and furniture—to make the afterlife as comfortable as this one. They would also need their bodies, which led to the science of mummification. Initially, Egyptians believed that only pharaohs could journey across the river Styx into the afterlife. By the 1500s BCE, however, belief in the afterlife had expanded to include all Egyptians.

Mesopotamians

Like other early religious traditions around the world, the people of what is today known as modern Iran, as well as parts of Iraq, Syria, and Turkey, also had a polytheistic view, and believed that man's goal was to live in harmony with the gods. This area, called Mesopotamia and bordered by the Tigris and Euphrates Rivers, was the birthplace of many civilizations who all shared a belief in the same gods, though oftentimes the names of these gods changed depending on which city-state one lived in.

The people of Mesopotamia believed in a creation story that, like other ancient religions, explained the existence of the cosmos and everything in it. They believed that before man existed, there was only chaotic, swirling water. It was separated into the female principle Tiamat, or salt water, and male principle Apsu, or fresh water. These gods united; from this union, all other gods were formed.

Apsu was annoyed with the new, younger gods because they were loud and unruly, and so he made plans to kill them. Tiamat heard of these plans and convinced her son Ea, God of Wisdom, to kill Apsu. Ea killed Apsu and created Earth from his body. Angry over Apsu's death, Tiamat conjured the forces of chaos to kill her children, but the great storm god Marduk defeated her and created the sky from her body. He is also said to have created humans as gods' helpers.

Religion played an important part of daily life. Man, it was believed, was created to serve the gods and, in turn, the gods would provide for man through protection, good harvests, and fertility. If man neglected the gods, evil would be inflicted on him. Each town or city-state had a temple that housed a unique patron god, and people believed that the patron god actually resided in the temple. Temple priests were tasked with tending to the patron god, including providing clothing, food, and other human necessities on a daily basis. The temple god was even carried around (in statue form) once a year to visit the city and, on occasion, to visit the temples of other patron gods. In addition to worshiping gods at public temples, individual homes included shrines for personal worship and sacrifice.

Divination was also a large part of the religion of the Mesopotamian cultures. Priests interpreted the will of the gods through the appearances of everyday items, the behavior of birds, dreams, and even the entrails of sacrificial animals. Because the gods had already determined the future, diviners were employed to unravel the messages that described the intent of the gods. Often rulers had personal diviners, while common people had to turn to the services of a local diviner.

Mesopotamians developed intricate legends, stories, and hymns about their gods, some of which later evolved into the stories and hymns of major religions that later developed in this part of the world, such as Zoroastrianism, Judaism, Islam, and Christianity.

Canaanites

Another early civilization of the region, one that developed south of Mesopotamia and north of ancient Egypt, was that of the Canaanites. Like the civilizations of Mesopotamia, they were an agrarian people, and but their religion reflected the importance of fertility and life cycles much more than the religious traditions of Mesopotamia.

The main gods of the Canaanites were Baalot and Baalim, or Asherah when spoken of in the singular. Baalot represented the male gods, or lords, while Baalim represented the female goddesses, or ladies. Both were said to control Earth and the weather. Due to the agrarian nature of the Canaanite civilization, fertility ceremonies, both symbolic and actual, were extremely important. To ensure that the gods would send rain and that harvests would be abundant, temples housed sacred prostitutes. These prostitutes were required to have sexual relations with chosen men who represented Baalot. By impregnating the sacred prostitutes, the community would continue to grow. In addition, the gods would be pleased and send rain and bountiful harvests to the Canaanites.

HINDUISM

There are an estimated one billion Hindus in the world today. The majority live in India and Nepal. They can trace their religion back to the ancient beliefs of the Aryans, a group of nomadic warriors from Central Asia who invaded the Indian subcontinent sometime between 1700 and 1500 BCE.

THE HISTORY OF HINDUISM

The early history of Hinduism is viewed in distinct periods beginning as far back as 2000 BCE. Little is known, however, of the religious practices before the development of the Aryan civilization. The Aryans worshiped deities that represented beauty and the forces of nature. Among them were Indra, the female deity of the storm; Agni, the female deity of fire; Varna, the female deity of the sky; and Soma, the male deity of the moon who ruled the stars. The Aryans practiced ritual sacrifices of animals to invoke the deities.

Aryans left records of their religious beliefs and practices in writings that developed into the sacred books of Hinduism. The **Vedas** written during the Vedic period, from 1500 to 500 BCE, are collections of hymns, prayers, myths, rituals, and beliefs about the creation and the deities. The Vedas are divided into four collections; the oldest is the Rig Veda and contains more than a thousand hymns. The Upanishads are later writings that were added to the earlier writings and contain advice from Hindu mystics; reincarnation is first mentioned in the Upanishads. In all, there are seven books of sacred writings that make up the basic Vedas.

During Hinduism's classical period, from 500 BCE to 500 CE, temple worship grew popular and worship of three of the major sects of Hinduism—Vaishnavism, Shaivism, and Shaktism—developed. More religious writings were produced, resulting in two epic poems of great importance to Hinduism, the *Mahabharata* and the *Ramayana*. The former describes two Indian families who are fighting for control of a kingdom in a bloody war. Within the *Mahabharata* is the poem **Bhagavad Gita**, meaning the "Lord's song." In the poem, the god Krishna and Arjuna, a member of one of the warring families, discuss the meaning of duty. The *Ramayana* tells the story of the wanderings of Prince Rama and his wife Sita who are exiled because of a jealous stepmother.

A later document of importance in the development of Hinduism and written during the classical period is the **Law of Manu**. This ancient text describes *varna*, or the caste system, as already in existence in Hindu society. It is possible that the caste system goes back to the Aryan invaders who considered themselves superior to those they conquered. However the caste system began, it came to divide Hindus into a complex and rigid social system of thousands of different castes, or categories, based on hereditary occupations. The *dalits*, or untouchables, are below the caste system and perform menial manual labor.

The medieval period (500 CE to 1500 CE) saw further development of the Hindu religion, including its assertion over the practices of Buddhism and Jainism as well as the construction of regional temples. The gods Vishnu, Shiva, and Devi (Shakti) rose in popularity during this period of Hinduism.

Hinduism's modern period during the nineteenth and twentieth centuries was marked by its colonization by the British as well as attempts by missionaries to covert Hindus to Christianity. During this same period, Hinduism experienced a renaissance, with spiritual leaders examining their religion closely and undertaking reform efforts. These reformers' views and writings led to the concept of Indian nationalism and the beginning of an effort to export Hinduism to the West.

MAJOR HINDU TRADITIONS

Unlike many religions, Hinduism had no single founder and no single set of revealed dogma. Hinduism has grown and developed internally by incorporating outside influences and is still evolving. It can, however, be organized into four major traditions, or theistic paths, though those paths or sects are loose divisions with much overlap. Many practicing Hindus don't subscribe to any particular theistic path or sect.

Each of the four major theistic paths worships a different god, adheres to a different doctrine about god, and follows a different path to union with god. There are two main doctrines, monoism and inclusive monotheism, and each of these four sects adheres to one of these two beliefs:

- **Monoism:** the belief that there is one impersonal supreme god without qualities or a form and who is represented equally by lesser gods.

- **Inclusive Monotheism:** the belief that there is only one Supreme God who is personal and exhibits qualities and a form, while acknowledging the existence of other, lesser gods.

Each of the four traditions, or sects, is summarized below:

1. *Vaishnavism:* Vaishnavas are personalists and believe in inclusive monotheism, worship Vishnu, and follow the path of devotion, or *bhakti-yoga.*

2. *Shaivism:* Shaivas are impersonalists, or adherents to monoism, who worship Shiva and follow the paths of knowledge (*jnana-yoga*) and meditation (*astanga-yoga*). Asceticism, or self-denial to achieve a spiritual state, is very common among Shaivas.

3. *Shaktism:* This sect is less developed than others and is based on Shaivism. Shaktas are impersonalists, or adherents to monoism, and are most aligned with *karma-yoga*, the path of action. They worship Shakti, or Devi, the female goddess said to be a force of cosmic energy.

4. *Smartism:* Smartas are also monists, believing that god is impersonal. They worship all five deities, whom they treat with the same reverence: Vishnu, Shiva, Shakti (Devi), Ganesh, and Surya. They are impersonalists who adhere to the path of *jnana-yoga*, the path of knowledge. Smartas are liberal and nonsectarian, accepting of all Hindu gods.

HINDU DOCTRINE AND PRACTICE

Hinduism has both a central creator of the world known as Brahma and many other deities. Some are avatars of Brahma. The three major deities, or triad, of Hinduism, are Brahma; Vishnu, the preserver; and Shiva, both destroyer and regenerator. Other important deities are Krishna and Rama, both incarnations of Vishnu, and Shakti, also known as Parvati and Kali, among other names, and the wife of Shiva.

Basic Hindu beliefs involve the following:

- **Nature of Reality:** All reality is one with Brahman, the Ultimate Reality. The individual, or essential, self is called *atman* and is one with Brahman and everything else in the universe. Everything is simply a representation of Brahman, the formless, nameless, changeless reality.

- **Samsara:** Hindus believe that life is a cycle of birth, life, and death, which they call *samsara*.

- **Karma:** In what form a person is reborn depends on the law of karma: the actions that an individual performs while living determines future lives. Each reincarnation is the result of previous lives. Do good now and it will be reflected in future lives; do evil and that, too, will be reflected. Good actions raise the status of future lives and evil actions lower future castes.

- **Moksha:** Moksha is release from samsara, which comes with enlightenment. The purpose of the cycle of reincarnations is spiritual progress to reach moksha. Individuals can choose the path of renunciation and find enlightenment or choose the path of desire and continue the cycle of birth, life, and death.

- **Dharma:** Dharma is the rules and duties for Hindus that provide a guide for living. The goal is to act with detachment; that is, people need to destroy desire if they are to achieve moksha.

- **Stages of Life:** Hinduism sets four stages to progress to enlightenment: *student*; *householder*; *anchorite*, a person living in seclusion to meditate and study; and *sannyasi*, a holy man wandering among the people.

- **Ahimsa:** This is the concept of "do no harm," or acting always in a nonviolent manner.

TIP

Brahman is the Ultimate Reality, Brahma is the creator, and a Brahmin is a member of the priestly caste.

Yoga

The goal of yoga is to free the mind of distractions, so atman can become more open to the Ultimate. There are several schools of yoga, including karma, raja, bhakti, jnana, hatha, and kundalini.

Holy Days

Certain holy days are more prevalent in some areas of India than in others. Major Hindu holy days include:

- **Diwali:** Festival of lights that occurs in autumn and includes a thorough housecleaning to welcome Laksmi, the female deity of wealth

- **Durga Puja:** Celebrates the female deity Durga and the triumph of good over evil; occurs in autumn

- **Krishna Janmashtami:** Celebrates the birth of Krishna and includes fasting for 24 hours; occurs in late summer

- **Ram Navmi:** Celebrates the birth of Rama, an incarnation of Vishnu; occurs in spring

BUGDHISM

Buddhism began as an offshoot of Hinduism. Like Christianity and Islam, Buddhism has a single, historical founder, Siddhartha Gautama.

THE HISTORY OF BUDDHISM

Buddhism was founded by Siddhartha Gautama who lived in the 500s BCE. The son of a wealthy and powerful family, his life changed at the age of 29. Leaving his palace one day, he met an old man, a sick man, a corpse, and a beggar. The misery, sorrow, and decay of life made a great impression on him. In what is known as the **Great Renunciation**, Gautama gave up his riches and left his family to search for an answer to samsara, the Hindu cycle of birth, life, and death. He studied with a variety of teachers but found their teachings unsatisfying. He tried penance and self-mortification, but they, too, seemed lacking to him.

Finally, one night while practicing yoga and meditation, enlightenment came to him. He realized that the answer was choosing a life that took the middle path between asceticism and indulgence, or desire. That night, Gautama became the Buddha, the fully enlightened one. Gautama Buddha, as he was known from then on, spent the next forty-five years of his life on Earth teaching the middle path.

Buddhism expanded across India over the next 200 years. Monasticism as a way of life developed as some disciples built monasteries and became monks and nuns devoted to prayer and meditation. By the third century BCE, the teachings (or *dharma*) of Buddhism were spreading outside India to what are today Sri Lanka, Myanmar, and Nepal; the nations of Southeast Asia, and eventually to Korea and Japan.

MAJOR BUDDHIST TRADITIONS

Buddhism has evolved into several thousand sects. Theravada and Mahayana are the principle sects; Theravada is the more conservative. Vajrayana Buddhism is another form of Buddhism practiced mostly in the country of Tibet. Authorities on the subject disagree whether Vajrayana is a third, distinct sect or a variation that came out of the Mahayanan tradition. Unlike Hinduism, Buddhism does not have multiple deities, nor is there a supreme ultimate being.

- **Theravada Buddhism:** This is the path of poverty and celibacy embraced by those men who choose to live as monks. They believe that individuals must achieve enlightenment on their own through meditation and actions, as Gautama Buddha did. When a man achieves enlightenment, he becomes an *arhat* and is released from samsara at death. However, not all Theravada Buddhists choose monasticism as a way of life. Some men make only a limited commitment to the monastic life. Women may not become monks; however, they can support them with offerings. In this way, they can make merit, that is, influence their karmaic destiny. Theravada Buddhism is practiced today mainly in Thailand, Cambodia, Vietnam, Laos, Myanmar, and Sri Lanka.

- **Mahayana Buddhism:** Most Buddhists belong to this sect. Gautama Buddha's compassion is a central focus. Mahayana Buddhists believe that Gautama Buddha was close to godlike and visited Earth to aid humans. They also believe that he was only one among many Buddhas who are on Earth to help humans. The ideal became bodhisattvas, or Buddhas-in-waiting who, though worthy of nirvana, remain on Earth to help others achieve enlightenment. Unlike Theravada Buddhists who rely on their own efforts, Mahayana Buddhists believe that devotion to Buddhas and bodhisattvas can aid in their efforts to achieve nirvana. Mahayana Buddhism is practiced mainly in China, Tibet, Nepal, Korea, and Japan. Two important forms of Mahayana Buddhism are the following:

1. *Zen Buddhism:* This sect of Mahayana Buddhism became popular among some Japanese after its introduction from China around 400 CE. Adherents of Zen believe that the Buddha-nature is all around, and only through meditation will humans be able to discover and understand it and, thus, reach enlightenment. Zen Buddhists use riddles called *koans* to aid them in finding enlightenment.

2. *Vajrayana Buddhism*, also known as *Tibetan Buddhism* or *Lamaism:* Mahayana Buddhism was originally brought to Tibet in the 600s CE, but over the centuries, it has evolved in unique ways. While many of the practices of Vajrayana Buddhism are similar to those of other forms of Buddhism, it relies heavily on magic; has a priestly class known as lamas; recites the phrase "Om, the jewel of the lotus, hum" to address the Bodhisattva Avalokiteshvara, the patron of Tibet; and uses a prayer wheel to "say" prayers. The chief lama among lamas is the Dalai Lama, who is not only the spiritual leader of Tibetans but also considered the temporal ruler.

BUDDIST DOCTRINE AND PRACTICE

Buddhism centers on the **Four Noble Truths** and the **Eight-Fold Path.** The Four Noble Truths are as follows:

1. All life is suffering, called *dukkha.*
2. The source of all suffering is desire, attachment to self.
3. The cessation of desire is the way to end suffering.
4. The path to the cessation of desire is the Eight-Fold Path.

The Eight-Fold Path is right understanding, right thought, right speech, right action, right livelihood, right effort, right mindfulness, and right concentration. People are doomed to samsara because of desire. If people can eliminate desire, they will achieve *nirvana*, the release from their karma and, thus, from samsara.

Another important concept in Buddhism is compassion for all living things, which is exemplified by Gautama Buddha's life. Like Hindus, Buddhists practice *ahimsa*, or nonviolence to all things. While monasticism became important, Buddhism did not reject those who chose to live in the world. It welcomed anyone who was trying to live up to the standards of Buddhist teachings and was also willing to support Buddhist monks and nuns.

Rituals

All schools of Buddhism incorporate similar rituals. Meditation is the most common form of Buddhist ritual, helping practitioners find enlightenment. In Tibetan Buddhism, mantras, or sacred sounds that help the practitioner focus and commune with deities, are frequently used. Mudras, or symbolic hand gestures, are less common but still used as Buddhist ritual to aid in meditation. Finally, pilgrimages to Buddha's birthplace, the site of his first teaching, the place he received enlightenment, and the site where he achieved Parinirvana are the most sacred rituals in all of Buddhism.

Three Jewels of Buddhism

Imagery from ancient texts shows the symbol of three jewels, or the Triratna, often found in the depiction of Buddha's footprint. This symbol is a metaphor for the three most important aspects of Buddhism: Buddha himself; the dharma, or Buddha's teachings; and the *sangha*, or community of followers. Each of these three aspects of Buddhism is represented by a different colored jewel. Followers, practitioners as well as those taking steps toward ordination, are said to take refuge in these three jewels. Taking refuge can mean following the path to enlightenment, as well as turning to Buddha, his teachings, or the community as a way of dealing with the trials of everyday life.

Sacred Writings

The two main branches of Buddhism have their own sacred writings. The major works of Theravada Buddhism are the Tripitaka (rules and regulations for Buddhist monasteries, life and teachings of Gautama Buddha, and dictionary and teachings) and Dhammapada (collection of proverbs and adages). Among the major works of Mahayana Buddhism are the Lotus Sutra, Heart Sutras, Tibetan Book of the Dead, and Translation of the Word of the Buddha. *Sutra* in Buddhism means "a collection of the stories and teachings of Gautama Buddha." (In Hindu, *sutra* means "a collection of sayings about Vedic doctrine.")

Holy Days

The various sects have their own holy days and celebrations, but common ones are Buddha Day, April 8, honoring the birth of Buddha; Nirvana Day, February 15, observing his death; and Bodhi Day, December 8, celebrating the day he sat down under the Bodhi tree to achieve enlightenment. Days of the month when the moon is full or new are also of great importance to Buddhists.

There are also a number of rites of passage in Buddhism, including marriage, pregnancy, birth, adolescence, and, ultimately, death.

CONFUCIANISM

Confucianism is a philosophy—an ethical code of living—rather than a religion. There is no central supreme being who created the world. However, there is a respect for the past, including ancestors; a focus on humane treatment of one another; and a belief in the duty of the government to provide for the well-being of the governed.

THE HISTORY OF CONFUCIANISM

Confucianism takes its name from **Confucius**, who lived from 551 BCE to 479 BCE. Around that time, China was undergoing what has come to be called the Warring States Period. A group of independent states was vying for control of China. This lasted until the third century BCE when the Han dynasty consolidated its power and ruled China for 400 years. Over the centuries, Confucian principles came to dominate Chinese government regardless of the dynasty in power; Confucian teachings and their evolution by government bureaucrats provided an orderly structure for society and governance.

An especially important concept in this development was the Confucian idea of the state as family; family was the basic element of society in Confucian teaching. The emperor was the father of all Chinese and responsible to an impersonal force known as Heaven for the well-being of his people/children. If he did not live up to his role, the people had a mandate from Heaven to replace him. In this way, dynasties rose and fell in China for centuries. Claiming that the current emperor was not working in the best interests of the people, a rival would depose him, calling on the mandate of Heaven as his authority. In this way, Confucianism was used by various rulers over the centuries to cement their position as supreme earthly rulers.

Another aspect of Confucianism that shaped Chinese society was its influence on the Chinese educational system. In order to advance in the Chinese bureaucracy, a position of prestige and power, a man needed to be educated. Confucianist principles became the focus of this education and centered on learning what constituted right action. The reliance on Confucianism resulted in the development of a conservatism in Chinese society that lasted until the Communist Party came to power in the twentieth century.

CONFUCIAN DOCTRINE AND PRACTICE

Confucius taught that five relationships exist that involve reciprocal duties and responsibilities, or right action, between:

1. Ruler and subject
2. Father and son
3. Elder brother and younger brother
4. Husband and wife
5. Friend and friend

With the exception of the last relationship, each relationship involves a superior and a subordinate, that is, one person is subject to the other. The subordinate owes loving obedience to the superior, and the superior has a loving responsibility to see to the well-being of the subordinate. Friends owe each other the same responsibility. The correct behavior, or conduct, between the individuals in these relationships is known as *li*.

In addition to these ethical relationships, Confucius taught the concept of *jen*, or humaneness, also described as sympathy, benevolence, or love toward others. Unlike many Eastern religions, Confucius did not see the proper role of humans as self-absorbed in meditation and isolated from one another. He felt that people needed to work toward becoming *junzi*, or genteel, superior, humane beings.

Through education and adherence to moral ways, and with much practice, Confucius believed that people could achieve junzi. His goal was to create harmony in society. Other key concepts include *zhong*, or loyalty to one's true nature, and *xiao*, or filial piety.

Filial piety, or respect for one's parents, was part of Chinese culture prior to Confucius' teachings. Families showed respect for their ancestors and family elders, and in that respect filial piety existed. Confucius expanded on the concept. He felt that it was impossible to repay one's parents for the care and love they have provided their children, particularly during the early years when children are helpless. He felt it was impossible to be a virtuous individual without showing filial piety while parents were alive and even after they were dead. Confucius believed that children should take care of their parents, bury them properly when the time came, provide them with a male heir, and never speak ill of them, even years after they had passed on.

Important Works

The **Five Classics** and the **Four Books** make up the basic writings of Confucianism. Three books to remember are the Analects of Confucius, one of the Four Books; Yi jing, the first of the Five Classics; and Book of Mencius (Meng-Zi). The Analects are stories and sayings of Confucius that his followers collected, the Yi jing is a book of divination, and the Book of Mencius is a defense of Confucian teachings by Mencius, a later Confucian scholar. Mencius took the position that human nature is good. Hsun Tzu (Xun-Zi), an even later Confucian scholar, took the opposite position, that human nature is evil.

DAOISM

Daoism developed slightly later in China than Confucianism and is based on a belief in the naturalness of all things. Its spirituality is a complement to the structure and rigid etiquette required in Confucianism rather than a rival belief system.

THE HISTORY OF DAOSIM

The beginnings of Daoism date to the 400s and 300s BCE. The traditional founder is considered to be **Lao-zi**, who is also credited with writing the *Dao de jing*, the basis of Daoism. The word *Dao* means "the way." It is possible, however, that the *Dao de jing* is actually a collection of writings of earlier ancient scholars. A second important work is the slightly later *Zhuang-zi* by a man of the same name; it is a collection of parables and allegories.

Initially, Daoism was a philosophy, but it took on religious elements over the centuries. The majority of Chinese people were farmers who saw a relationship between nature as described in Daoism and the deities who were part of their daily lives. Daoism was also influenced by Mahayana Buddhism and adapted some of its rituals and the concept of priesthood. Daoism, in turn, influenced Zen Buddhism's focus on nature.

DAOIST DOCTRINE AND PRACTICE

What is the Dao? According to Daoists, the Dao cannot be defined. It is without measure, shape, or characteristics; it is infinite and unceasing. It simply flows "without motive and without effort." The Dao gives life to all things, but, more than life, it gives all things their natures. The Dao is why a human is a human and not a dog or a horse.

The central focus of Daoism is **naturalness.** Human suffering, pain, and violence are the result of the opposite of naturalness—unnaturalness. At one time, people lived a natural life, unhampered by the conventions and restrictions of society. They had been "in harmony with their nature and with the Dao." This harmony began to change with the introduction by society of social conventions and notions of right and wrong as well as people's growing desire for things outside themselves—whether the possession of material goods or of knowledge. Knowledge is a problem because it leads to ideas that interfere with the spontaneity of oneness with the Dao.

To free themselves, Daoists believe that people must become one with the Dao, and then they will realize that all is one with the Dao. There is no reason or need to seek possessions or knowledge. Instead of right action, Daoists believe in no action, or inaction, a concept called *wu wei.* Daoists also apply this idea to government. In essence, the government that governs the least, governs best. A ruler who follows the Dao will govern without seeming to govern, ensuring that the people are fed, living in peace, and free of worry.

A basic teaching of Daoism is the concept of yin and yang. The symbol for yin and yang is a circle with two interlocking black and white sections. The white section has a smaller black circle within it, and the black section has a smaller white circle within it. The black represents yin—earth, female, dark, and passive—whereas the white is the yang, the active principle that represents heaven, male, and light. These two basic forces, or things, are not static, as depicted by their symbols, and depend on each other. They must work together in harmony in order to exist.

Meditation is an important vehicle for achieving oneness with the Dao. Unlike Zen Buddhism, which focuses on physical cleansing, Daoism asks adherents to purge their minds of thoughts, thus opening themselves to the Dao. Dao rituals incorporate meditation, along with purification and offerings to deities. Some, such as *jiao,* the ritual of cosmic renewal, are so complex that only Dao priests and their assistants can perform the required chants, music, and prayers. A shorter, less complex jiao ritual still manages to involve every household in a village and has several smaller rituals within it. Temple prayers and chants are also part of the practice of Daoism to honor gods and regulate the balance of yin and yang.

SHINTOISM

The indigenous faith of the Japanese people, Shintoism has no specific founder, religious texts, or gods in the traditional Western sense. It is as old as Japan, and its origin stories explain the existence of Japan and its superiority above all other nations and their peoples. In Shinto teachings, the divine resides in all things in nature from rocks to rainfall, as well as in important ideas or concepts. The word *Shinto* means "the way of the kami," and *kami* are the spirits, or essences, of the natural world. The geography and climate of Japan influenced how the Japanese view the connection among its people, nature, and the divine.

THE HISTORY OF SHINTOISM

The *Kojiko*, or *Records of Ancient Matters*, written in 712 CE, explains the origins of Shintoism. It is a record of the oral traditions handed down over centuries. Shintoists believe that in the chaos of the beginnings of the universe, when heaven and earth were formed, gods emerged and gave birth to two kami, a brother and sister named Izanagi and Izanami, respectively. These two kami used a jeweled spear to stir the ocean, and thus the first landform—the main island of Japan—was formed. Izanagi and Izanami united and formed the remaining islands of Japan as well as many other kami. This mythological beginning substantiates the belief that Japan and its people are chosen above all others.

Shintoism has many kami, some of them everyday objects and others concepts or ideas. The more important kami include:

- **Amaterasu**, the Sun Goddess, believed to be an ancestor of the Imperial family
- **Benten** or **Benzaiten**, a female kami of music and art with Indian origins
- **Ebisu**, a kami who brings prosperity
- **Susanoo**, the kami of wind who can cause, or protect people from, disasters
- **Tenjen**, the kami of education who grants people success in their exams

Buddhism was introduced to Japan in the sixth century CE, and Shintoism and Buddhism began a struggle that would last centuries. Buddhist, and later Confucian, elements and teachings were introduced to Shintoism. Shinto shrines were turned into Buddhist temples, and some were overseen by Buddhist priests. During this period, the idea that rulers should follow the will of the gods when governing become very popular in Japan. Buddhist, Confucian, and Shinto practices were followed by all in order to ensure the kami protected Japan and its people.

During later centuries, the practice of Shintoism continued to be influenced by Buddhism and then later by Christian missionaries. Eventually, during the Mejii period, Shintoism was separated from Buddhism and became the official religion of Japan. This period of Shintoism is referred to as State Shintoism. Though Shinto and Buddhist elements were again separated and temples turned back into Shinto shrines, this separation didn't last. Eventually, Shintoism and Buddhism learned to coexist. Buddhists came to view the kami of Shintoism as manifestations of Buddha. State Shinto fostered nationalism and patriotism among the Japanese, making Shinto priests government officials and supporting tens of thousands of shrines with state funds. However, at the request of Allied Forces following World War II, Japan disbanded its national religion and permanently separated religion and government.

Shintoism can be broken into three categories: Shrine Shinto, Sect Shinto, and Folk Shinto. **Shrine Shinto** is the form of Shinto closest to what was practiced during prehistoric times in Japan and includes State Shinto in its history. Those who practice Shrine Shinto today worship at outdoor public shrines that were funded by the Japanese government during the days of State Shintoism.

Sect Shinto is another form of Shintoism that began in the nineteenth century and is differentiated from other versions of Shintoism by the thirteen different sects that are officially recognized by the Japanese government.

Folk Shinto is Japanese folk belief, without any formal doctrine or organizational structure. It is practiced by rural Japanese at small shrines in the countryside.

SHINTO DOCTRINE AND PRACTICE

Men and women can be Shinto priests and can marry and have children. Priests live on the grounds of the shrines, caring for them and overseeing worship and festivals. Shinto shrines integrate natural surroundings to show respect to the kami, and Shintoists make offerings in an attempt to keep evil away and to remain in the good graces of the kami.

Festivals and Rituals

Shinto practitioners hold festivals and rituals to honor ancestors, pray for bountiful harvests, give thanks, and ward off evil spirits. These include music and dance, as well as offerings of all types of food that participants share in. Shinto festivals reflect the influence of the farming culture in Japan and are held at turning points during the seasons; spring festivals ask deities for a bountiful harvest, while autumn festivals thank deities for a bountiful harvest. The Grand Purification Ritual, performed on December 31, cleanses Shinto practitioners of all sin, impurities, and misfortune. By doing so on the last day of the year, they begin the new year unencumbered.

In addition to worshiping at outdoor public shrines, many Shinto practitioners build shrines in their homes, where, it is believed, their ancestors reside. Having a shrine in the home allows practitioners to make daily offerings to ancestors. Two of the important values of Shinto are fertility and family, including ancestor veneration and social cooperation. Worship of ancestors and the deities in nature is called **matsuri.** Prior to entering shrines, Shintoists perform purification rituals, including washing their hands and rinsing their mouths to cleanse themselves of dirt.

The most revered Shinto shrine in Japan is called the Ise Jingu (Grand Shrine of Ise). Amaterasu-Omikami, the sun goddess, has been worshiped at the Ise Jingu for 2,000 years. Toyouke-Omikami, the guardian of well-being, is also worshiped at Ise Jingu. Here Shintoists make offerings to honor the sun goddess and in hopes of receiving protection for clothing, shelter, and food. More than 1,500 ceremonies are performed at this shrine each year. Every twenty years, the buildings at this shrine are dismantled and put back together, piece by piece. The artifacts are refurbished, and the deities receive new clothing. This process ensures that traditions are passed on to younger generations, while refreshing the minds and faith of Shinto practitioners.

JUDAISM

The Hebrews, or Israelites, were unique in the history of world religions up to that point in time in basing their national identity on a "single, all-powerful God who made ethical demands and placed responsibilities on them as individuals and as a community," according to the authors of *The Heritage of World Civilizations.*

THE HISTORY OF JUDAISM

The Hebrews, under the leadership of Abraham, probably arrived in the area of Mesopotamia sometime between 1900 and 1600 BCE. Some stayed in what was to become known as Palestine, but others moved to Egypt, where they were enslaved. Moses led the Hebrews out of Egypt around the beginning of the thirteenth century BCE, and they settled in Canaan, a region of Palestine, which the Bible calls their Promised Land. The Hebrews built a successful kingdom for some 300 years under rulers such as David and Solomon during what is considered to be the First Temple Period. During this period, Solomon built the Temple to God. In the 800s BCE, the kingdom split into the kingdoms of Judah, formed by ten tribes, and Israel, formed by two tribes.

Over the next centuries, foreign peoples invaded and conquered the two kingdoms. The northern kingdom of Israel disappeared entirely. The southern kingdom, which included the Temple in Jerusalem, was conquered by the Babylonians in the mid-500s BCE. The temple was destroyed and the people taken to Babylon in what is called the **Babylonian Captivity.** They returned to Judah after the defeat of the Babylonians in 539 BCE and rebuilt the Temple more than twenty years after their return from the Babylonian Captivity. This period is referred to the Second Temple Period, and it ended when the Romans, their new captors, destroyed the second temple in 70 CE and again in 132 CE.

The first mention of the Covenant between the Hebrews and the god Yahweh is in the Hebrew Bible's account of Abraham. The reaffirmation of the Covenant came on Mount Sinai, when Moses received the **Ten Commandments.** In exchange for obeying these laws, the Jews would receive Yahweh's protection. Troubles such as foreign conquests were the result of the Jews' failure to abide by their part of the Covenant. Prophets such as Jeremiah and Ezekiel were sent to remind the Jews of their Covenant and of the one true God, Yahweh.

Throughout these periods of subjugation, the Jews retained their religion and their sense of being God's chosen people. The Diaspora, or dispersion of the Jews, began after Assyrians conquered the Kingdom of Israel in 721 BCE, and led to the development of the synagogue as a local center of worship, the position of rabbi as teacher, kosher food laws, and the Sabbath as day of worship.

The Diaspora continued after the Jewish revolt of 66 CE, when the Romans conquered the area, renamed it, and forbade the Jews to enter Jerusalem. Many Jews moved into Western Europe. Over time, they became known as the Sephardim and settled in Spain. Persecuted there during the Inquisition, they fled to Portugal, the Netherlands, North Africa, the Balkans, and the Americas. German Jews became known as Ashkenazi. After persecution there, they moved into Eastern Europe. Ashkenazi and Sephardic Jews have different languages, rituals, and traditions. In the early 1900s, more than a half million Jews lived in Germany. The rise of anti-Semitism and the growing power of the Nazi party led to a systemic and methodical curtailing of the rights of German Jews. Many German Jews fled; those who did not were denied the right to work, subject to quota systems, gathered up and sent to ghettos, and eventually killed in the genocide known today as the Holocaust. By the end of World War II, 6 million Jews had been murdered by the Nazi regime.

DENOMINATIONS

Modern Judaism has four main divisions, or movements: Orthodox, Conservative, Reform, and Reconstruction. The differences revolve around how strictly each interprets the laws and traditions of Judaism, including the place of women. Although the term may be confusing, Conservative Jews are less conservative than Orthodox Jews. The latter, for example, do not allow women to become rabbis and cantors, whereas Conservative, Reform, and Reconstructionist Jews do. Orthodox Jews also require that the sexes be separated in synagogues. While Orthodox Jews eat kosher at home and outside the home, Conservative Jews typically keep kosher at home but may eat nonkosher outside the home, and Reform Jews typically do not observe kosher rules. Reconstructionist Jews and Reform Jews have many practices in common, although Reconstructionist Jews tend to follow more of the traditional historical practices of Judaism. Mordecai M. Kaplan is considered the founder of Reconstructionism in the 1930s.

Orthodox Judaism is the largest group within Judaism and is further divided into Modern Orthodox and Hasidic. Hasidic Judaism was founded in the mid-1700s in Poland by Israel ben Eliezer, who came to be known as Baal Shem Tov. He taught a simple faith that included elements of mysticism; he wanted Jews to maintain their identity and traditions and live within their own enclaves separated from non-Jews. Hasidic Judaism attracted many followers in Eastern Europe. The spiritual leader of a group of Hasidic Jews is known as a *rebbe*, and a rebbe is descended from a line of rebbes.

Another important leader of Judaism was the nineteenth-century German philosopher and writer Moses Mendelssohn. He encouraged Jews to leave their ghettoes and live within the larger society.

JUDAIC DOCTRINE AND PRACTICE

The Hebrews, who were surrounded by neighbors worshiping many gods, were unique in adopting monotheism, the worship of one God. The basic teachings of Judaism are Yahweh (God) is the supreme creator, Yahweh will send a messiah to redeem the world, and the Jews are God's chosen people. Yahweh formed a covenant with the Jews, who, in return for offering obedience to the Law and worshiping only Yahweh, would become a great nation. The sense of Judaism as a community of believers is of central importance.

The Ten Commandments are the ethical code of Judaism—the Law—given by Yahweh to the Hebrews as a guide to moral living. A slightly shortened version of the Decalogue is the following:

1. I am the Lord thy God.
2. Thou shall have no other gods before Me.
3. Thou shall not take the name of the Lord thy God in vain.
4. Remember the Sabbath Day.
5. Honor thy father and thy mother.
6. Thou shall not kill.
7. Thou shall not commit adultery.
8. Thou shall not steal.
9. Thou shall not bear false witness against thy neighbor.
10. Thou shall not covet thy neighbor's goods.

Moses received these commandments on Mount Sinai during the forty years that the Hebrews wandered in the desert after their exodus from Egypt.

Writings

The Jewish sacred writings are the Hebrew Bible and Talmud. The Bible contains the Pentateuch, Prophets, and the Ketuvim. The Pentateuch is also known as the Torah or the Five Books of Moses; these are the first five books of the Bible. The Prophets contain the writing of the major prophets (Jeremiah, Isaiah, and Ezekiel), as well as the twelve minor prophets. The Ketuvim is a collection of twelve other books, including the Psalms, Song of Songs, and the Book of Ruth.

The Mishnah is the collection of all the disputes and commentary on Jewish law up to the 100s CE. It was compiled under the direction of Judah the Prince. Later, the Gemara was added to the Mishnah to make up the Talmud. The Gemara is additional rabbinic teachings on every aspect of Jewish life. The material in the Talmud is divided into two categories: the **Aggadah**, which includes parables, sayings, sermons, and stories and is ethical, inspirational, or explanatory in nature, and the **Halakha**, commentary, discussions, and decisions related to Jewish law and practice.

Another work of note is the Sefer Ha'Zohar, commonly referred to as the Zohar. It is one of the books of the Kabbalah, the mystical aspect of Judaism, and focuses on such themes as angels, demons, charms, the coming of the Messiah, and numerology.

Holy Days

Shabbat, or the Sabbath, takes place from sundown on Friday night to sunset on Saturday. There are services Friday night and Saturday morning. Most Orthodox Jews are prohibited from engaging in work during this period.

Major holy days include:

- **Rosh Hashanah:** The Jewish New Year celebrated sometime between mid-September and early October
- **Yom Kippur:** The Day of Atonement, which includes fasting and contemplation; comes ten days after Rosh Hashanah
- **Sukkot:** Feast of Booths or Tabernacles, which celebrates the harvest and Yahweh's protection of the Jews during their forty years in the wilderness; nine days between late September and the end of October
- **Chanukah:** Festival of the Lights, also the Festival of Dedication, celebrating the victory of the Maccabees over the Greeks and Syrians in the 100s BCE and the rededication of the Temple in Jerusalem
- **Passover:** Celebrates the deliverance, or exodus, of the Hebrews out of Egypt; seders, special dinners, are held the first two and last two days; comes between March and April for eight days
- **Shavuot:** Celebrates the Yahweh's giving of the Ten Commandments to Moses; comes between late May and early June

The **menorah** is an important symbol of Chanukah. It holds nine candles, one for each of the eight nights of Chanukah and a ninth candle to light the others. According to the story of Chanukah, there was only enough oil for one night for the lamps in the Temple, but the oil lasted for eight nights. Each night of Chanukah, an additional candle is lit until all are lit the last night. The Star of

David, probably the most recognized symbol of Judaism today, is a six-pointed star created from two interwoven equilateral triangles. The star, or shield, as it is sometimes called, began to appear during the Middle Ages but was not solely representative of Judaism and appeared in many different places. Later, Kabbalists, or Jewish mystics, used the symbol to protect against evil. It became the official symbol of Judaism during the seventeenth century. Later, in Nazi Germany, Jews were required to wear a yellow Star of David as a method of identification.

Another symbol integral to Judaism is the mezuzah, a small piece of parchment paper containing the prayer Shema from the Bible. Encased in a small ceramic or metal case about three to five inches long, a mezuzah is mounted to the doorpost of the entry to the home and any room inside the home. Mezuzahs identify a home as Jewish and offer the inhabitants God's protection.

Hebrew school teaches Jewish children about their faith. It is typically held on Sundays and one weekday. For older students, it provides preparation for Bar Mitzvah for boys and Bat Mitzvah for girls, their coming-of-age ceremonies.

CHRISTIANITY

The focus of Christians is on the future: the redemptive power in their own lives of Jesus' resurrection. This message has resonated with millions of people since 33 CE, when Jesus was reported to have died for humankind's sins and then risen again. Today, there are over 2 billion Christians in the world belonging to three branches and more than a dozen denominations. Christianity is a continuation of the promise of the Old Testament but with a difference.

THE HISTORY OF CHRISTIANITY

Jesus of Nazareth is a historical figure; he lived and died in the first century CE in Judea. He began preaching around the year 30 and quickly gained a following. His message was one of piety and the abandonment of sin and material things. In the Sermon on the Mount, he laid out a moral code, known as the Beatitudes, for his followers. He was seen as the Messiah promised by Yahweh, the Supreme Being, to the Jews, although they expected a kingdom on earth, whereas Jesus talked about a Day of Judgment when the good would be rewarded and the evil punished. (The word "messiah" translates as "christos" in Greek and Jesus became known as Jesus Christ, that is, Jesus the Messiah.) He proclaimed himself the Son of God. When Jesus attacked the practices of some of the Jewish leaders, and as the crowds following him grew larger, the leaders determined to put a stop to his preaching. They convinced the Roman governor that his preaching was dangerous; the governor arrested Jesus and had him crucified like a common criminal.

After Jesus' death, resurrection, and ascension into heaven, his followers began to preach about Jesus and his mission, initially only among Jews. However, there were two schools of thought about the nature of Christianity: Was it a version of Judaism or a new religion? Some believed that it was a form of Judaism and should be presented only to Jews. Paul of Tarsus was a Jew but believed that it was a new religion that should be preached to everyone. Once a persecutor of Christians, he had converted in 35 CE after a vision and became a zealous missionary among gentiles.

The word of Jesus Christ and his teachings found receptive audiences wherever the new missionaries went, and, by the first century CE, they had attracted the attention of the government. At that time, the emperor was worshiped as a god. Christians mindful of the one God refused to obey and a period of persecution began, which continued more or less until the conversion of the Emperor Constantine to Christianity in 312. By the end of the fourth century, Christianity had become the official religion of the Roman Empire.

In the second century, Christianity had developed a formal organization of bishops and was centered in Rome. Peter had been the first bishop of Rome, and later popes would claim supremacy over the church as successors to Peter, citing Jesus' words: "Thou art Peter, and upon this rock I will build my church." The **Eucharist** as a celebration of the Lord's Supper had also developed as the central ritual. The title "Catholic," meaning "universal," came to identify the body of teachings of this church and included the Old Testament, the Gospels, and the Epistles of St. Paul.

In addition to adopting Christianity, Constantine established a new capital for the Roman Empire at the ancient site of Byzantium and named it Constantinople. Ultimately, his decision would lead to a schism in the Catholic Church in 1054 when the Western and Eastern branches split over doctrinal issues.

After the collapse of the Roman Empire in 476 and during the Middle Ages, the Catholic Church was often the most stable and unifying force in Western Europe as nomadic peoples moving out of Asia and Vikings from northern Europe invaded. By the sixteenth century, the hierarchy of the Roman Catholic Church in the West had amassed large fortunes, lived less than pious lives, and competed with temporal rulers for power. Into this mix, add disputes over doctrinal issues, and the time was ripe for the Protestant Reformation.

It should be noted that the Catholic Church answered the calls for reform generated by the Protestant Reformation with the **Council of Trent** that lasted from 1545 to 1563. Among the changes that the Council made were bishops had to live within their dioceses and preach regularly, seminaries to educate priests were to be erected in every diocese, and parish priests were to be better educated and actively minister to their parishioners. However, the Council reaffirmed a number of doctrines that were at the root of the Protestant reformation, namely:

- **The Role of Good Works in Salvation:** Grace, alone, as taught by several Protestant churches, was not enough for salvation

- **The Seven Sacraments:** Not all Protestant churches accept all seven sacraments

- **Transubstantiation:** The changing of bread and wine into the body and blood of Jesus during the act of consecration at Mass

- **Purgatory:** The place where the souls of sinners are purified after death and before entering heaven

- **Clerical Celibacy:** The belief that some or all members of the clergy are required to be unmarried

- **Veneration of the Saints, Relics, and Sacred Images:** Catholics honor and pray to them to intercede with God for them but do not worship these people and objects

- **Granting of Indulgences:** An indulgence is a remission of the temporal punishment that a priest has given a penitent to perform as a result of sinning. If not performed by the sinner, the sinner would suffer in purgatory. Beginning in the Middle Ages, sinners could give a small amount of money, considered alms, in exchange for an indulgence. By the time of the Reformation, indulgences had been extended to include those who had already died and were presumed to be suffering in purgatory. Indulgences had also become a lucrative way of raising money for the Church and Church leaders by preying on the fears of the faithful that they or their loved ones would languish in purgatory.

MAJOR CHRISTIAN TRADITIONS

Christianity over the centuries has developed three main branches: the Roman Catholic Church, the Eastern Orthodox Church, and more than a dozen Protestant denominations.

Roman Catholic Church

Until the **schism in 1054** between the Catholic Church in the West and the East, the history of Christianity was synonymous with the development of the Catholic Church. As noted above, the organizational structure of what became known as the Roman Catholic Church began as early as the first century CE with positions of priest and bishop. In time, the structure became increasingly hierarchical. The position of bishop of Rome was elevated to supremacy over all other bishops and was called "Pope." The position of cardinal, who oversaw a number of bishoprics, was added.

At various times and as early as the third century CE, the Church called councils of bishops and scholars to debate and affirm church doctrine. Among the results were such statements of dogma as the **Apostles Creed** and the **Nicene Creed**, which established certain precepts that Catholics had to accept. The Vatican Council of 1870 defined the doctrine of papal infallibility, though the concept had been in practice since the beginning of the Church. According to this principle, the Pope speaks infallibly when he proclaims a doctrine of faith and morals. Not all pronouncements of popes bear this weight. The most recent council was the Second Vatican Council held between 1962 and 1965, which sought to modernize Church practices and doctrines, including allowing Mass to be said in vernacular languages rather than Latin and eliminating the requirement that Catholics abstain from eating meat on Fridays.

Orthodox Church

Even before the schism, there were cultural and linguistic differences that evolved between Christian churches in the two parts of the former Roman Empire. The West spoke Latin and was influenced by Roman culture, whereas the Eastern part of the Empire had been deeply influenced by the Greeks and spoke Greek. Among the factors that caused the schism were the claim of the supremacy of the Pope of Rome in matters of faith and morals; the doctrine that raised the Holy Spirit equal to God the Father and God the Son; and an eighth-century controversy over the use of icons, highly ornate depictions of Jesus, Mary, and the saints.

There is no single Orthodox Church in that there are several national churches, for example, the Russian Orthodox Church and the Greek Orthodox Church. The Orthodox churches are overseen by a network of patriarchs, and there are a number of commonalities among them. There are also a number of doctrinal differences and practices that separate these Churches from the Roman Catholic Church:

- The Orthodox Churches do not recognize the primacy of the Pope.

- The Orthodox Churches do not accept the Holy Spirit to be on the same level as God the Father and God the Son, as Catholics do.

- Priests may marry in the Orthodox Churches before ordination, whereas the Roman Catholic Church forbids married priests.

- The Roman Catholic Church does not allow people to receive communion, that is, the Eucharist, before the age of seven, considered the age of reason. The Orthodox Churches allow infants to receive communion.

- The Roman Catholic Mass is said daily, whereas the Orthodox liturgy is not necessarily celebrated daily.

- The Roman Catholic Mass is only sung if it is specifically a High Mass. The Orthodox liturgy is always sung.

- Orthodox churches are highly decorated, especially with icons and gold decorations, whereas the typical Roman Catholic Church is less ornate.

- Orthodox churches accept the seven sacraments as the major sacraments, but believe that whatever the church does is sacramental.

Protestant Denominations

The basic elements that connect the various Protestant denominations are the importance of community and the power of the direct experience of God. In general, Protestants believe that salvation comes through God's gift of grace alone, accept the Bible as revealed and infallible truth, and do not require their priests or ministers to be celibate. Some faiths also accept female and gay clergy, unlike the Catholic Church. Statues and saints are not important and may not even be part of a denomination's theology. The emphasis is on preaching and singing, and services tend not to be daily.

There are two major doctrinal differences between Protestantism and Roman Catholicism: the Protestant belief in grace alone as the source for salvation and Jesus is present only symbolically in the Eucharist. Catholics believe that salvation comes from a combination of grace and good works and that Jesus, through the mystery of transubstantiation, is fully present in the Eucharist. (The Orthodox Churches also believe in transubstantiation and the combination of grace and good works as the path to salvation.)

The major Protestant denominations are:

- **Anglican/Church of England and Episcopalian:** Anglican is the original English church, and the Episcopalian church is the U.S. counterpart. It split from the Roman Catholic Church when the Pope refused to allow King Henry VIII to divorce and remarry. Little changed in hierarchy or practice until the reign of Henry's third child, Elizabeth I. The Anglican Church is still closest in theological doctrine to the Roman Catholic Church.

- **Baptist:** Founded by Separatist John Smyth in Holland; spread to England and then to the American colonies during the First Great Awakening and later to the United States during the Second Great Awakening; agreed-upon theology and practices vary widely.

- **Congregational:** Founded on the ideas of Robert Browne; evolved from the Nonconformist movement in Great Britain that also fostered the Separatist or Puritan reform movement; important in Massachusetts Bay Colony.

- **Lutheran:** Founded by Martin Luther; doctrine of justification: belief that salvation comes through faith alone and the gift of grace; that is, good works are not counted.

- **Methodist:** Founded by John Wesley as a way to reform the Church of England; believes in the Trinity, accepts Baptism and the Eucharist as sacraments.

- **Presbyterian:** Founded on the ideas of John Calvin; emphasizes the doctrine of election: belief that God foreordained who would be saved (the elect) and who would not.

- **Seventh-Day Adventist:** Established in the United States in the mid-nineteenth century; observes Saturday as the Sabbath; believes that the Second Coming of Christ is near; accepts the Trinity and the Bible as infallible.

- **Unitarian:** Developed in the late eighteenth century and spread to the United States in the early nineteenth century; rejects the Trinity, original sin, predestination, and the infallibility of the Bible.

CHRISTIAN DOCTRINE AND PRACTICE

Some denominations support religious, or parochial, school systems, whereas others rely on religious instruction of the young during Sunday School sessions.

Christians believe that Jesus was crucified for humankind's sins and rose from the dead on the third day. He remained with his disciples, teaching them for forty days, and then ascended into heaven. Jesus is seen as God made Man and, depending on the form of Christianity, as part of the Trinity of the Father, Son, and Holy Spirit. At Pentecost, fifty days after Easter (Christianity's most important holy day and the one that celebrates the resurrection of Jesus), the Holy Spirit came down upon the Apostles and they began to preach the message of Jesus.

Doctrines such as transubstantiation, the position of Mary, original sin, and infant baptism vary from religion to religion. For example, Catholics believe in original sin; it is the sin that Adam committed, and, because of it, all humans are born with this sin on their souls, but baptism removes it. For this reason, Catholics are baptized in infancy. (However, infants who die before they can be baptized are thought to be taken into heaven.) On the other hand, the Orthodox churches reject the concept of inherited guilt associated with original sin. The Orthodox churches also practice infant baptism, as do most Protestant churches. Some Protestant churches (e.g., branches of the Baptist denomination) generally practice adult baptism, believing that people are saved through God's gift of grace and baptism.

Sacred Writings

The Christian Bible is made up of the Hebrew Bible or Old Testament and the New Testament. The latter contains the Gospels of Matthew, Mark, Luke, and John and other writings, including the Acts of the Apostles, the Epistles, and the Book of Revelation, as well as thirteen pieces in the Hebrew Apocrypha. The Epistles are of special importance because they were written by Apostles and others to early Christian communities, discussing their issues and problems.

Depending on the branch or denomination of Christianity, the Bible is either considered to be the exact words of God or to have been inspired by God.

Holy Days

The major holy days of Christianity, depending on the branch or denomination, are:

- **Christmas:** Celebrates the birth of Jesus, or "God made Man"
- **Epiphany:** Celebrates the visit of the three Magi to the infant Jesus; twelve days after Christmas
- **Easter:** Celebrates Jesus' rising from the dead three days after being crucified by the Romans
- **Lent:** Forty days of fasting and prayer before Easter; begins on Ash Wednesday when Christians are reminded that "thou art dust and unto dust thou shalt return"
- **Palm Sunday:** Beginning of Holy Week; commemorates Jesus' entry into Jerusalem before his crucifixion
- **Holy Week:** Holy Thursday, which recognizes the Last Supper; Good Friday, which commemorates Jesus' death on the cross
- **Ascension Thursday:** Forty days after Easter Sunday; memorializes Jesus' ascent into heaven
- **Pentecost:** Sunday fifty days after Easter; celebrates the descent of the Holy Spirit on the Apostles and the beginning of the Christian church

In addition to these and depending on the branch of Christianity, there are other special days dedicated to the Virgin Mary and to various other saints. The dates for all of these holy days, as well as specific saints' days and when different parts of Scripture should be featured in religious ceremonies, are determined annually by the liturgical calendar.

ISLAM

Islam is the third monotheistic religion that developed in the Middle East. Muslims believe that Abraham, Jesus, and Muhammad are great prophets, and that Muhammad is the greatest and last prophet, the "Seal of the Prophets," who completes the revelations of God, the Supreme Being, or Allah, to humankind. The word "Islam" means "submission," and "Muslim" means "one who submits." In this case, Muslims submit to Allah.

THE HISTORY OF ISLAM

The historical founder is Muhammad, who lived from around 570 to 632 CE in what is today Saudi Arabia. However, Muslims believe that Muhammad was only a vehicle for Allah. Muhammad was born in Mecca, married, and became a wealthy merchant there. In 610 CE, at about age 40, he received the first of his revelations from Allah through the angel Gabriel. He began to preach the word of the one God, Allah, and to condemn the practice of idolatry among the city's inhabitants. As Muhammad began to gain followers, the authorities of Mecca became concerned and offered him bribes to stop. But Muhammad continued to preach his message of one God and religious piety. Finally, the authorities had had enough and began a campaign of persecution against Muhammad and his followers.

In 622, Muhammad fled Mecca and an assassination plot. His flight is called the Hegira. Muhammad found refuge in Medina, where he was able to bring together warring clans and become the leader of the city. Over the next ten years, his followers grew, and in 632, after years of fighting, they captured Mecca, founding the first Islamic state. Muhammad died shortly after.

After Muhammad's death, Islam continued to grow in numbers and in area, eventually becoming a vast political-religious empire that stretched across much of the Middle East, North Africa, and into Europe. The first four caliphs, as the leaders were known, are called the rightly guided, or orthodox, caliphs. They were relatives of Muhammad or had personally known him and were chosen by other Muslims to lead them. However, in 661, the Umayyad clan seized the caliphate from the fourth caliph, Ali, Muhammad's son-in-law, and shifted the focus of the caliphate to that of a temporal leader rather than a religious leader. The caliphate passed from dynasty to dynasty over the next centuries, and it was during these decades—from the eighth century through the thirteenth century—that Islam had what later came to be referred to as its Golden Age. Arabs and non-Arabs, Muslims and non-Muslims alike, all worked to translate major works of literature into Arabic, engaged in scientific discovery, and made advancements in math. Later, during the 1200s, the Ottoman state was formed by the Turks. It eventually grew into the Ottoman Empire and became a great Islamic empire and seat of Muslim power. The empire and the title of sultan, which had replaced caliph, ended after World War I.

In the early part of the 1500s, a Timurid king called Babur invaded the Indian Subcontinent and established the Mughal Empire. It was later ruled by his grandson, Akbar the Great, and encompassed what is today most of the Indian Subcontinent and Afghanistan. The Mughal Empire was unique in that, under Akbar, it encouraged "Goddism," a melding of Christian, Islamic, and Hindu religions. Later emperors discouraged this practice and instituted Shari'ah law.

Islam as a religion continued to grow. Today, more than a billion people worldwide consider themselves Muslims. Most belong to the Sunni branch, but Shi'a is the state religion of Iran. Other concentrations of Shi'ites can be found in India, Pakistan, and Iraq. Transcending all divisions is the **ummah**, the sense of community of believers. Madrasahs are Muslim educational institutions; they range from schools teaching young children to great universities. Their subjects range from the Qur'an to the Hadith to the law.

MAJOR ISLAMIC TRADITIONS

Islam is divided into two branches: Sunni and Shi'a. The division goes back to the fourth caliph, Ali. Shi'ites believe that Ali should have been the first caliph and that his descendants are the rightful leaders of Islam, whereas the Sunnis believe that no leader was chosen by Muhammad to succeed him. To Sunnis, the four caliphs are the rightful heirs because they were chosen by Muslims themselves. Sunnis, who make up about 85 percent of Muslims, and Shi'ites also have doctrinal differences that divide them.

Sunnis do not have a religious hierarchy, but they do have *imams*, also called *mullahs*, who lead the community in prayer. Sunnis look for guidance in their lives to the Hadith; to Shari'ah, which is Islamic law; and to a consensus of interpretation between the Qur'an and Muslim scholars and leaders of the community. The Sunni form of Islam lends itself to interpretations, and no one set of interpretations is considered definitive. This flexibility has allowed it to embrace a number of cultures as it spread outward from its original location. Sunnis do believe in a Madhi, or Messiah, whose appearance on Earth will signal the beginning of an era of peace that will culminate in the end of the world.

Imams also lead Shi'ites in prayer. However, Shi'ites believe that their imams speak with special authority. They believe that the next Imam after Ali was Zain, Ali's son, who was followed by eleven more Imams. Known as Twelvers, they believe that the Twelfth Imam is still alive and still rules over them—though hidden from them—and that their imams are representatives of this Twelfth Imam.

A distinct part of both Sunni and Shi'ite branches of Islam is the Sufi movement, or the practice of mystical Islam. Sufis believe that the only way to have a relationship with God is through personal and direct experience. Though it is believed that Sufism began out of a practice of asceticism, this eventually became less of a main focus and only one of many tools to reach God. Sufis value kindness, patience, and love and use meditation and dancing to achieve a direct spiritual and mystical connection with God. Sufism developed into different orders, the most famous of which is the Mevlevi, whose founder Rumi is known worldwide for his mystical poetry.

Shi'ites believe that the Madhi will come one day and inaugurate a period of justice before the final end of the world. Shi'ites believe that the Qur'an must be interpreted rather than read literally, because it omits their belief that Muhammad designated Ali as his successor. For Shi'ites, religious and political authority rests not with community but with the imam. Ayatollahs are experts in Islamic law and religion; a Grand Ayatollah is an expert in religious studies and also a religious leader.

Wahhabism is a conservative movement that began on the Arabian Peninsula in 1744. Its founder Abd-al-Wahhab wanted to reform Islam and return it to what he considered the original, strict interpretation as found in the Qur'an. Wahhabism was adopted by the Sa'ud family that gained control of the kingdom in the early 1800s. Today, Wahhabism is the religion of Saudi Arabia and bound up with Saudi nationalism.

> **TIP**
> There is another Shi'ite sect called Seveners who believe that there were seven Imams.

ISLAMIC DOCTRINE AND PRACTICE

According to the Qur'an, there are **Five Pillars**, or duties, that Muslims must perform and these are the foundational principles of Islam. Monotheism, the basic truth of Islam—that Allah is the one God—is revealed in the first pillar.

1. *Repeat the Shahadah*, or *Confession of Faith:* "There is no God but Allah and Muhammad is the Prophet of God."

2. *Perform Ritual Prayer:* Muslims are called to prayer five times a day and must face Mecca when praying. The five times are before sunrise, at noon, in mid-afternoon, at sunset, and at night before going to sleep.

3. *Fast:* Muslims must fast from sunrise to sunset during the month of Ramadan.

4. *Almsgiving:* Muslims contribute alms, known as Zakat, to the poor, typically 2.5 percent of their wealth.

5. *Pilgrimage, Called the Hajj, to Mecca:* This must be done at least once during one's life. The central focus of Mecca is the Ka'bah, which Muslims must circle seven times and then touch or kiss the Black Stone that it houses. Muslims believe that the Black Stone was

given to Adam by Allah and that Abraham and Ishmael, his son, built the Ka'bah to hold the Black Stone.

Muslims believe that each person must face Allah at the end of life and account for the way that he or she lived. While Muslims believe that life is submission, or surrender, to Allah, it is also a test. People have the ability to commit evil and will be held accountable for it. At the time of death, a person's body and soul are separated; on the day of judgment, Resurrection Day, souls and bodies will be reunited and judged by Allah. Those who lived good lives will go to paradise and those who lived evil lives will go to hell. Shari'ah is the term for the Islamic moral code and religious law that guides Muslims in their daily lives. Shari'ah law is derived from the Qur'an, the Haddith, and consensus of Islamic scholars. Together these lead to an understanding, or fiqh, of Islamic law.

Jihad is an important concept in the Muslim religion. *Jihad*, an Arab word that translates to "struggle," can be fought by Muslims in one of four distinct fashions: by the heart, the tongue, the hand, or the sword. The concept, considered a duty by all Muslims, is accomplished by fighting evil in one's heart, doing good through words (tongue) or deeds (hands), or physically fighting (sword) against those who are enemies of Islam and are considered nonbelievers.

Sacred Texts

The Qur'an is the major text of Islam; the word *Qur'an* means "reading" or "recitation." Muslims believe that the Qur'an is the exact words of Allah as revealed to Muhammad. There are 114 chapters, or *surahs*, arranged by length, not topic, and some 6,000 verses.

Hadith is a collection of traditions, analogies, and consensus. The traditions relate to the life and words of Muhammad and those of his companions, and the analogies and consensus are the result of the study of Muslim scholars endeavoring to answer questions, especially ones relating to legal issues and the duties of Muslims. There are thousands of hadith.

Holy Days

The holiest of Muslim celebrations is the month of Ramadan, which occurs in the ninth month of the Muslim calendar (the Muslim calendar has twelve months, but only 354 or 355 days). It honors the giving of the Qur'an to Muhammad. Muslims fast from sunrise to sunset each day for the month. Id al-Fitr, the Feast of Breaking the Fast of Ramadan, is celebrated at the end of the month.

Other holy days include:

- **Al-Hijrah:** The Muslim New Year; celebrates Muhammad's journey from Mecca to Medina
- **Mawlid al-Nabi:** Celebrates Muhammad's birthday
- **Laylat al-Qadr:** The Night of Power; occurs on the twenty-fifth day of Ramadan; honors the first revelation to Muhammad

RELIGIOUS MOVEMENTS AND SYNCRETISM

A religious movement may be defined as "a movement intended to bring about religious reforms." Using that definition, Buddhism and the Sunni branch of Islam can both be considered religious movements, as can any of the Protestant denominations. A number of such movements developed both before and after the beginning of the second millennium. In an attempt to reform religion, people tried to connect different aspects of various religions in ways they felt best served knowing god. This practice, called religious syncretism, can be seen in several of the movements that borrowed aspects of some religions but left behind others in their quest for spirituality.

BEFORE 1000 CE

Mystery Cults

During the time of the Ancient Greeks, all citizens participated in state religious worship, though it did not meet the spiritual needs of some. Those individuals turned to what were known as mystery cults, or private groups open only to those who were initiated. These groups honored a particular god or goddess, oftentimes less popular or well-known gods. Popular figureheads of mystery cults included Dionysus and Demeter and even gods from other cultures, such as Egypt's Isis.

In order to participate in these secret cults, members had to endure a secret initiation. Once initiated, members gathered to dance, drink wine, and, often, have sex. The mystery cult that honored Dionysus, the Greek goddess of fruitfulness and wine, incorporated sexual relations among its activities. The mystery cult of Eleusis, named for the city where important agricultural festivals happened, also incorporated sexual relations into its cult activities during reenactments of the story of Hades and Kore.

At first mystery cults were exclusive and offered citizens a different experience than state religion. Some cults eventually lost their exclusivity, and anyone could decide to participate. Some even lost their religious character and become more like social clubs.

Jainism

Jainism began in the sixth century BCE in India as a reaction to some of the practices of Hinduism. Its traditional founder is **Mahavira**, who believed that he had found a way to stop the endless cycle of birth, life, and death. Like Hinduism, a person's karma determines his or her future lives, so Jains believe that only a person's own actions can end this cycle. Unlike Hindus, Jains believe that deities are of no help, so there is no reason to pray to them. Individuals must find release from the cycle of reincarnations through their own actions, and those actions should use as little effort as possible. Jainism is an ascetic religion. Those who are able to give up their material lives and become monks are closer to ending their cycle than those who remain "in the world."

The basic tenet of Jainism is that all living things have souls. As a result, Jains practice nonviolence. They also vow to speak truthfully and never take anything that they are not given. Jain monks also vow to be celibate and to renounce all attachments. Jains believe that attachment to material things keeps humans tied to the earthly life.

Zoroastrianism

Zoroastrianism is still practiced in parts of Iran and India, where adherents are known as Parsis. The religion began sometime between 1600 BCE and 1400 BCE, when the creator of goodness and life, **Ahura-Mazda**, revealed his truths to the prophet Zarathustra, also called Zoroaster. These truths are collected in the Zend-Avesta.

Zoroastrians believe that good and evil are fighting a battle for control of the universe and humanity. One force is Ahura-Mazda—representing good—and the other is **Ahriman**—the creator of evil and darkness. The battle will end in the final judgment, when the good will receive heaven and immortality and the evil will receive eternal punishment. To fulfill the will of Ahura-Mazda, Zoroastrians follow the threefold path: good thoughts, good words, and good deeds. Their liturgy consists of reciting from the Zend-Avesta and pilgrimages to holy fire-temples.

AFTER 1000 CE

A number of religious movements have occurred in an attempt to bring about change. Lutheranism and other Protestant denominations, the Catholic Counter-Reformation, and Wahhabism all fit the definition of religious movements and were discussed earlier in the chapter.

Fundamentalism

A major movement that transcends religious boundaries is fundamentalism. Fundamentalists wish to return to the basic, or fundamental, tenets of their religion. In general, Christian fundamentalists believe that the Bible is the literal word of God and oppose many trends in modern society, such as abortion, same-sex marriage, and legal protections for women and homosexuals. On the other hand, along with some evangelical Christians, some fundamentalists push for increased environmentalism because they see humans as stewards of God's creation.

Islamic fundamentalists, known as Islamists, wish to strip all modernity from Islamic practices and reinstate theocratic government. The Taliban is an example of an Islamic fundamentalist group.

The Lubavitch, a missionary movement of the Hasidim, is a fundamentalist group within Judaism.

Sikhs

Sikhism began in the 1400s in Punjab, India, as a reaction to Hindu and Muslim practices that involved rituals, priests, and temples. A young Indian religious teacher, or *guru*, named Nanak felt that individuals needn't be a member of a particular caste or need the aid of a priest to have access to God. He believed that actions, more than words or rituals, brought one closer to God. He was the first of ten gurus that Sikhs later turned to for spiritual guidance.

Central to their beliefs is the understanding that there is only one God, with no physical form, and who resides in each individual. Sikhs believe that serving community and living a good, honest life, more so than devotion to the practice of religion, will help people to truly know God.

Baha'i

Baha'i, another movement that valued action over ritual or ceremony, originated in Iran in the mid-1800s. Baha'is believe that Moses, Abraham, Buddha, Muhammed, and Zoroaster were all prophets leading up to the arrival of Bahá'u'lláh, who brought a message of peace and justice. Bahá'is believe in the existence of a soul and the importance of prayer, meditation, and pilgrimages as ways to reinforce the connection between the soul and god. Like the message of Sikhism, Bahá'u'lláh's message stresses the importance of service to others as well behaving in noble and virtuous ways.

CONTEMPORARY RELIGIOUS MOVEMENTS

Evangelical Christians

Evangelical Christianity may seem like a modern phenomenon, but it began in Great Britain and from there was brought to the American colonies. It became the basis of the First Great Awakening, which took place from around 1720 until around 1760, and the Second Great Awakening of the 1790s through much of the nineteenth century. Evangelicals stress the need for personal conversion, known as being born again, and, like fundamentalists, place their trust in the authority of the Bible. They also emphasize the saving grace of Jesus' death and resurrection. Evangelical preachers of the Great Awakenings appealed to emotions and found a receptive audience among people for whom the erudite, emotionless sermons of the educated clergy held little appeal and few answers to the dangers and fears of the people. Modern evangelicals fill a similar need for contemporary people beset with fears and concerns about a world moving quickly and in ways that they may not understand or want.

Mormons

The Church of Jesus Christ of Latter Day Saints, known as the Mormon Church, is another Christian religious movement. Members believe that founder **Joseph Smith** was instructed by the angel Moroni where to find golden tablets containing the Book of Mormon, the history and teachings of the Nephite prophets. The Nephites were descended from one of the tribes of Israel that were scattered after the destruction of their kingdom. They traveled to the North American continent, and Moroni was the last prophet. The Mormons have an active mission to convert others to the original, true Christianity.

Ecumenism

The ecumenical movement was an effort of the Roman Catholic, Eastern Orthodox, and some Protestant churches to heal some of the divisions among them. Little progress was actually made, and the ordination of women and the inclusion of gays in the ministry have widened and hardened some divisions and have created new ones within some denominations, for example, the Anglican and Episcopalian churches.

Jehovah's Witnesses

Jehovah's Witnesses, or Bible Students as they were originally called, are members of a religious movement whose modern-day organization began at the end of the nineteenth century. The movement draws from Christianity but differs in its understanding of the Bible and its beliefs about the Holy Trinity, or God, Jesus Christ, and the Holy Spirit. Jehovah's Witnesses believe that God, or Jehovah, is the only true God. Jesus is the son of Jehovah but not equal to him, and the Trinity is a construct that resulted from pagan influences. In addition to these distinct differences, Jehovah's Witnesses believe that God wrote the Bible through the pens of others and believe it is a historically accurate account of God's word.

Jehovah's Witnesses believe that holidays such as Easter and Christmas have their roots in paganism, and so don't celebrate these or other holidays. They encourage followers to keep their lives simple to allow them as much time as possible for the most important aspect of their faith, witnessing. Witnessing involves walking door to door; sharing their beliefs; distributing copies of Bible-based literature, including the journals *The Watchtower* and *Awake*; and offering home Bible studies. Successful witnessing leads to repeat visits with the ultimate goal of converting individuals to their beliefs.

Jehovah's Witnesses do not believe in hell as a place of eternal torment; they believe that when a person dies, they simply stop existing. However, they do believe in an End Times, and point to passages in the Bible that indicate its coming. They believe that God's Kingdom is the solution to mankind's problems, and, as part of that kingdom arrangement, 144,000 people who are anointed by God will be resurrected to life in heaven to rule with Jesus in God's Kingdom. Those who do not go to heaven will remain in a paradise on Earth.

Scientology

The Church of Scientology was founded in the United States in 1954 by science fiction writer L. Ron Hubbard, following the success of his book *Dianetics: The Modern Science of Mental Health*. While his book dealt with the science of the mind, Scientology, the religion that evolved out of the success of this work, deals with the science of the spirit. Scientologists call this spirit the *thetan*; they believe that the thetan, or a person's true essence, has lived for thousands of years, inhabiting many different human bodies. Because man is a spiritual being, his unwanted emotions and negative thoughts (engrams) interfere with his attempt to reach the highest level of spirituality as a thetan. Specially trained auditors assist Scientologists in releasing engrams and achieving a "clear" state. This process goes on for eight levels, until the thetan reaches the level of All, or Infinity.

Though it doesn't have a sacred text similar to the Bible or the Qur'an, the religion is based on L. Ron Hubbard's extensive writings. Many courses and trainings exist to help practitioners continue to achieve a clear state, and strict adherence to these trainings is of utmost importance. Dedicated Scientologists are asked to sign a billion-year covenant showing that they will continue to spread the word about the religion in each new body their spirit inhabits.

Nature Spirituality

In addition to these movements, Earth-centered spirituality, or nature spirituality, is another movement that can be traced back to early mythology of many cultures and is still popular today. Earth-centered spirituality honors all of nature, offers little judgment, has no temples, and typically holds the view that the life force is female. Forces of nature and natural objects are celebrated, and practitioners thank the Earth goddess for the gifts of nature she has bestowed upon them. Earth-centered spirituality can be seen today as part of the Unitarian Universalist religious tradition.

SUMMING IT UP

- Shared dimensions of world religions include the **ritual, mythical, doctrinal, ethical, social,** and **experiential**. Approaches to the study of religion can be classified as **anthropological, phenomenological, psychological,** and **sociological**.

- **Indigenous religions** have certain characteristics in common: animism, magic, divination, totem, ancestor veneration or worship, sacrifice, taboos, myth, ritual, and rites of passage.

- **Native American religions** share certain characteristics. Generally, they are **animistic** and **polytheistic**; include a Supreme Being who created Earth and withdrew from it; have ceremonies, rituals, and taboos; do not practice human or animal sacrifice; include rites of passage, such as the vision quest; and have no special "priesthood" or hierarchy.

- **African religions typically are polytheistic**; have a central High God who created the world and withdrew from it; practice animism, ancestor veneration, and divination; make offerings and sacrifices of food; have rites of passage; and some have male and female priests and temples.

- **An important aspect of Egyptian religion was the cult of Isis and Osiris,** which spread across the Middle East and into Greece and the Roman Empire.

- **In Shintoism, the divine resides in all things in nature**; the word *Shinto* means "the way of the kami," meaning the spirits of the natural world. There exist three types of Shinto religion: **Shrine Shinto, Folk Shinto,** and **Sect Shinto**.

- **Hinduism is polytheistic; the major deities are the Triad: Brahma, Vishnu, and Shiva**. Hindus believe in Brahman, the Ultimate Reality; samsara; karma; moksha; and the four stages of life on the way to moksha.

- **Four theistic paths exist in Hinduism: Vaishnavism, Shaivism, Shaktism,** and **Smartism**. These paths honor a different god or group of gods and adhere to a particular path of enlightenment, or yoga practice.

- **Buddhism's historical founder is Siddhartha Gautama. Theravada Buddhism** and **Mahayana Buddhism** are its major sects; **Zen Buddhism** is popular in Japan, and Vajrayana, or **Tibetan Buddhism,** is very important in Tibet. Buddhism centers on the Four Noble Truths and the Eight-Fold Path.

- **Confucianism is a philosophy, not a religion.** Confucius taught that five relationships exist that involve reciprocal duties and responsibilities, or right action. The correct behavior, or conduct, is known as li.

- **The traditional founder of Daoism is considered to be Lao-zi,** also credited with writing the Dao De Jing, the basis of Daoism. "Dao" means "the way," and it is infinite and unceasing. It gives life and their nature to all things.

- **Jews believe that Yahweh made a covenant to protect them in exchange for their worship.** They believe that Yahweh gave Moses the Ten Commandments, the basic law, on Mount Sinai.

- **Jesus, worshiped as the Son of God the Father, is the historical founder of Christianity.** The Old and New Testaments are the central sacred writings of Christianity.

- **Muslims believe that Muhammad, the historical founder of Islam, is the greatest and last prophet who completes the revelations of God, or Allah, to humankind.** Islam has two branches: Sunni and Shi'a. The sacred writings of Islam are the Qur'an and the Hadith.

- **The Zoroastrian creator of goodness and life, Ahura-Mazda, revealed his truths to the prophet Zarathustra, also called Zoroaster.** These truths are collected in the Zend-vesta.

- **Greek Mystery Cults offered citizens mysterious religious practices** that differed from state religious worship, required initiation, and involved secret dances and rituals.

- **A number of religious movements have arisen over the centuries,** drawing from existing religious doctrine, in an attempt to reform existing religions or as reactions to the dogma and rituals of existing religions. Some of these movements include Sikhism and Baha'i, as well as Mormonism, Scientology, and Jehovah's Witnesses.

- **Earth-centered spirituality, or nature spirituality, is another movement that can be traced back to early mythology of many cultures;** its central figures are typically female, and worship is conducted in natural settings.

INTRODUCTION TO WORLD RELIGIONS POST-TEST

Directions: Carefully read each of the following 60 questions. Choose the best answer to each question and fill in the corresponding circle on the answer sheet. The Answer Key and Explanations can be found following this post-test.

1. Which religion celebrates Diwali, the Festival of Lights?
   A. Judaism
   B. Islam
   C. Mahayana Buddhism
   D. Hinduism

2. According to Shinto, which of the following are earthly and heavenly spirits?
   A. Kami
   B. Koan
   C. Karma
   D. Li

3. Paul is important in the history of Christianity because he
   A. wrote one of the four Gospels.
   B. was the first bishop of Rome.
   C. believed that Christianity was more than a Jewish sect.
   D. converted the Emperor Constantine to Christianity.

4. The break between the Roman Catholic Church and the Eastern Church in 1054 is called a
   A. heresy.
   B. schism.
   C. sect.
   D. denomination.

5. Which of the following best describes the Dao?
   A. Fundamental presence in all things
   B. Harmony with nature
   C. Self-awareness
   D. Simplicity

6. Two epic poems are of great importance to the Hindu religion: the *Mahabharata*, which describes two Indian families who are fighting for control of a kingdom in a bloody war, and one that describes the wanderings of Prince Rama and his wife Sita. The latter is known as the
   A. *Bhagavad-Gita*.
   B. *Ramayana*.
   C. *Tripitaka*.
   D. Hadith

7. Eating pork is considered taboo in
   A. Islam.
   B. Hinduism.
   C. Buddhism.
   D. Shinto.

8. The Hindu theistic tradition or path that worships all five deities, Vishnu, Shiva, Shakti, Ganesh, and Surya, is called
   A. Vaishnavism.
   B. Smartism.
   C. Shaktism.
   D. Shaivism.

9. Which of the following might a Buddhist do to improve his or her karma?
   A. Remove shoes before entering a mosque to pray
   B. Rinse one's mouth and wash one's hands before entering a shrine to pray
   C. Offer a bowl of food to a monk
   D. Pray to one's ancestors

10. Which of the following is/are reciprocal relationships described by Confucius?

    I. Father and son

    II. Brother and sister

    III. Ruler and subject

    A. I only

    B. I and II only

    C. II and III only

    D. I and III only

11. The angel Moroni appeared to

    A. Moses.

    B. Joseph Smith.

    C. Muhammad.

    D. Abraham.

12. A network of patriarchs is the form of organization in

    A. Lutheranism.

    B. Judaism.

    C. Eastern Orthodox churches.

    D. the Anglican Church.

13. Jains believe that

    A. a life devoted to monasticism is not helpful or necessary in finding release from reincarnation.

    B. praying to the deities will aid humans in their quest for release from reincarnation.

    C. release from the cycle of reincarnation comes through one's own actions.

    D. celibacy is unnatural.

14. Why are Catholics baptized?

    A. As a reminder of Jesus' death and resurrection

    B. To affirm that they are born again in Christ

    C. To remove the stain of original sin

    D. To make amends for the sin of Adam

15. What is the cause of suffering according to Daoism?

    A. Unnaturalness

    B. Desire

    C. Violence

    D. The innate evil in the world

16. Which of the following best describes a bodhisattva in Mahayana Buddhism?

    A. A yogi master

    B. A Buddhist monk

    C. Anyone working toward enlightenment

    D. Someone who has achieved nirvana, but remains in life to help others to enlightenment

17. The Aztec practiced human sacrifice to

    A. ensure a good harvest.

    B. prevent the end of the world.

    C. thank the deities for victory in battle.

    D. instill fear in their enemies.

18. Which of the following describes a way that an anthropologist would study a religion?

    A. Compare taboos across three religions

    B. Question subjects on what a worship service means to them

    C. Observe an initiation rite for an adolescent

    D. Investigate the impact of a church's outreach to the homeless

19. Dharma is the

    A. cycle of birth, death, and rebirth in Buddhism.

    B. release from the cycle of reincarnation in Hinduism.

    C. religious and moral duties of individuals in Hinduism.

    D. name given to Buddhas-in-waiting.

20. Which of the following sacraments removes original sin?

    A. Confirmation

    B. Baptism

    C. Eucharist

    D. Penance, also called Confession

21. At a madrasah, a person would

    A. study the Talmud.

    B. make an offering to the kami.

    C. make an offering to Vishnu.

    D. study the Qur'an.

22. God as the Creator or Supreme Being is a concept found in

        I. Christianity.

        II. Judaism.

        III. Northern Native American religions.

        IV. Islam.

    A. I and II only

    B. I and IV only

    C. I, II, and IV only

    D. I, II, III, and IV

23. In which of the following would you find icons?

    A. Russian Orthodox church

    B. Roman Catholic church

    C. Mosque

    D. Buddhist temple

24. What insight about life, death, and rebirth did Gautama receive that "enlightened" him about how to live one's life?

    A. Monasticism is the proper way to receive enlightenment.

    B. Life must be lived on a middle path between asceticism and desire.

    C. Practicing yoga and meditation are the only way to enlightenment.

    D. All reality is one with Brahman.

25. All of the following are steps in the Eight-Fold Path EXCEPT:

    A. Right understanding

    B. Right speech

    C. Right action

    D. Right loyalty

26. Which of the following statements best describes Islamists?

    A. They preside over religious courts.

    B. Their goal is to reestablish theocratic states.

    C. They are scholars of Islamic law.

    D. They lead the faithful in prayer services at mosques.

27. Which of the following men urged Jews to leave their ghettoes and live within their larger communities in the nineteenth century?

    A. Maimonides

    B. Mordecai Kaplan

    C. Moses Mendelssohn

    D. Baal Shem Tov

28. Islam existed as a vast political-religious empire that stretched across much of the Middle East, North Africa, and into Europe, but ended after

    A. World War I.

    B. World War II.

    C. 661 CE.

    D. the 1500s.

29. The influence of Martin Luther on later Protestant denominations can be seen in their adoption of his doctrine of

    A. salvation through faith alone.

    B. baptism as the only sacrament.

    C. the continuation of the central role of priests/ministers in confession.

    D. the continuation of Latin for services.

post-test

30. What is the Hindu name for the ultimate reality?
    A. Yin and yang
    B. Ahimsa
    C. Brahman
    D. Atman

31. The Ka'bah is sacred to Muslims because
    A. they believe that Abraham and Ishmael built it.
    B. it is where the angel Gabriel appeared to Muhammad.
    C. it houses Muhammad's grave.
    D. it is where Muhammad ascended into heaven.

32. Which of the following believed that human nature is evil?
    A. Confucius
    B. Mencius Meng-Zi
    C. Hsun Tzu Xun-Zi
    D. Lao-zi

33. The Talmud contains the
    I. Mishnah.
    II. Gemara.
    III. Haggadah.
    IV. Torah.
    A. I and II only
    B. I and III only
    C. I, II, and III only
    D. I, II, III, and IV

34. Typically, religions have ceremonies honoring which of the following rites of passage?
    I. Death
    II. Birth
    III. Marriage
    IV. Puberty
    A. I and II only
    B. I, II, and III only
    C. I, II, and IV only
    D. I, II, III, and IV

35. The Bavenda, or Venda, religious tradition of Africa honors a supreme being referred to as
    A. Zwidutwane.
    B. Raluvhimba.
    C. Awa.
    D. Binu.

36. According to Buddhism, what is the cause of suffering?
    A. Desire
    B. Striving after a good reputation
    C. Material goods
    D. Human attachments

37. Social virtue, or *jen*, is a basic concept of
    A. Islam.
    B. Shintoism.
    C. Buddhism.
    D. Confucianism.

38. Kosher laws relate to
    A. whom Jews may marry.
    B. what Jews may and may not do on the Sabbath.
    C. what Jews may wear.
    D. what Jews may and may not eat.

39. The division between Sunni and Shi'ite Muslims has its origins in
    A. the dispute over who was the rightful heir of Muhammad.
    B. how strictly to interpret the Qur'an.
    C. what the proper role of women is in Islam.
    D. disagreements over the position of imams in Islam.

40. Jainism developed over dissatisfaction with aspects of
    A. Buddhism.
    B. Hinduism.
    C. Shinto.
    D. Confucianism.

41. Rosh Hashanah celebrates the
    A. victory of the Maccabees and the rededication of the Temple in Jerusalem.
    B. harvest.
    C. Jewish New Year.
    D. exodus from Egypt.

42. Which of the following is a reason for the schism between the Roman Catholic and Eastern Orthodox churches in 1054?
    A. The Eastern Orthodox Church practices adult baptism, and the Roman Catholic Church practices infant baptism.
    B. The Eastern Orthodox Church does not allow any kind of ornamentation, whereas the Roman Catholic Church does.
    C. The Roman Catholic Church claims that the Pope has supremacy over all other churches in matters of faith and morals.
    D. The Orthodox Church accepts married clergy, as long as they were married before ordination.

43. Ummah is the
    A. niche in the wall of a mosque or a design in a prayer rug pointed in the direction of Mecca during prayer.
    B. call to prayer five times a day.
    C. pilgrimage to Mecca.
    D. community of the faithful.

44. The major divisions of Islam are
    A. Sufi and Shari'ah.
    B. Sunni and Wahhabism.
    C. Shi'a and Sunni.
    D. Twelvers and Shi'a

45. Buddhism differs from Islam in that Buddhism
    A. does not have a historical founder, but Islam does.
    B. practices polytheism, but Islam is monotheistic.
    C. calls its God Buddha and Islam calls its God Allah.
    D. does not have the concept of a single supreme being, but Islam does.

46. All of the following are offshoots of Islam EXCEPT:
    A. Sikhism
    B. Jainism
    C. Wahhabism
    D. Sufism

47. In 622 CE, Muhammad fled Mecca because of an assassination plot; his flight is called the
    A. Umayyad.
    B. Hadith.
    C. Medina.
    D. Hegira.

48. Which of the following is a tenet of Confucianism but NOT Daoism?
    A. Right action
    B. God as creator
    C. Harmony
    D. The less government, the better

49. The Hindu caste system is documented in which of the following?
    A. Law of Manu
    B. Rig Veda
    C. *Ramayana*
    D. Varna

50. Which of the following best describes the outcome of the Council of Trent?
    A. It ignored issues raised by the Reformation.
    B. It reaffirmed Catholic doctrine.
    C. It made significant changes to Catholic doctrine in a conciliatory gesture that was not reciprocated.
    D. It was an attempt to modernize the Catholic Church.

51. Which of the following honors the first revelation to Muhammad by the angel Gabriel?
    A. Id al-Fitr
    B. Al-Hijrah
    C. Laylat al-Qadr
    D. Ramadan

52. Which of the following groups observes the Sabbath most strictly?
    A. Orthodox Jews
    B. Reform Jews
    C. Conservative Jews
    D. Reconstructionist Jews

53. All of the following developed as ways to preserve Judaism through early centuries of persecution EXCEPT:
    A. Synagogues as the center of worship
    B. The development of mystical elements in Jewish teaching
    C. The rabbi as teacher and explicator
    D. Designating Saturday as the Sabbath based on the Book of Genesis

54. Daoism was seen as a complement to, rather than a rival of,
    A. Hinduism.
    B. Shintoism.
    C. Theravada Buddhism.
    D. Confucianism.

55. The basic belief system of Buddhism is/are the
    A. Mishnah.
    B. Four Noble Truths.
    C. Five Pillars.
    D. Analects.

56. In indigenous religions, which religious personage foretells the future?
    A. Animist
    B. Healer
    C. Diviner
    D. Medicine man and woman

57. The triad of Hindu deities is
    A. Brahma, Krishna, and Shakti.
    B. Brahma, Vishnu, and Shiva.
    C. Shiva, Shakti, and Krishna.
    D. Vishnu, Rama, and Kali.

58. In order to know God, Sikhs believe that an individual must
    A. be of the correct caste.
    B. adhere to a specific meditation practice.
    C. worship in a certain temple.
    D. live a good, honest life.

59. The name of which of the following religions means "submission"?
    A. Catholic
    B. Islam
    C. Orthodox
    D. Buddhism

60. Hinduism draws from the beliefs of the Aryans, who worshiped deities that represented beauty and the forces of nature. These deities included
    A. Abraham and Moses.
    B. Matthew, Mark, Luke, and John.
    C. Indra, Agni, Varna, and Soma.
    D. Apsu and Tiamat.

ANSWER KEY AND EXPLANATIONS

1. D	**13.** C	**25.** D	**37.** D	**49.** A
2. A	**14.** C	**26.** B	**38.** D	**50.** B
3. C	**15.** A	**27.** C	**39.** A	**51.** C
4. B	**16.** D	**28.** A	**40.** B	**52.** A
5. A	**17.** B	**29.** A	**41.** C	**53.** B
6. B	**18.** C	**30.** C	**42.** C	**54.** D
7. A	**19.** C	**31.** A	**43.** D	**55.** B
8. B	**20.** B	**32.** C	**44.** C	**56.** C
9. C	**21.** D	**33.** A	**45.** D	**57.** B
10. D	**22.** D	**34.** D	**46.** B	**58.** D
11. B	**23.** A	**35.** B	**47.** D	**59.** B
12. C	**24.** B	**36.** A	**48.** A	**60.** C

1. **The correct answer is D.** Hindus celebrate Diwali, the Festival of Lights, in autumn. The celebration includes a thorough house-cleaning to welcome Laksmi, the female deity of wealth. You might be confused by the term "Festival of Lights" because it's also an English translation for the Jewish celebration, Chanukah, but *Diwali* is the operative word. Choices B and C are incorrect.

2. **The correct answer is A.** In Shintoism, Kami are the spirits or essences of the natural world. Choice B is incorrect because koan are used in Zen Buddhism to help people reach enlightenment. Choice C is incorrect because the law of karma is the determinant in the kind of future lives a person will have, according to Hinduism and Buddhism. Choice D is incorrect because li is the principle of correct behavior between individuals in Confucianism.

3. **The correct answer is C.** Paul is important because he believed that Christianity was a completely new religion. Choice A is incorrect because the Gospels were written by Matthew, Mark, Luke, and John. Peter is believed to have been the first bishop of Rome, so choice B is incorrect. Choice D is incorrect because Paul lived in the first century CE, and Constantine was converted after a vision in 312 CE.

4. **The correct answer is B.** A schism is a split between entities caused by differences in opinion or belief. Doctrinal issues caused the schism in 1054. Choice A is incorrect because a heresy is a belief in conflict with the orthodox, that is, official, teachings of a church. Choice C is incorrect because a sect is a small group that has broken from an established church; the qualifier "small" doesn't fit the size of either the Roman Catholic or Eastern Churches. Choice D is incorrect because a denomination is a type of religious body and is larger than a sect.

5. **The correct answer is A.** The Dao is the fundamental presence or essence in all things. The question asks for a description of the Dao, not a definition of the word. Choices B and D are incorrect, although Daoists seek harmony with nature and simplicity in their lives. Achieving self-awareness (choice C) is not an explicit goal of Daoism.

6. **The correct answer is B.** Choice A is incorrect because the *Bhagavad-Gita* is a poem found within the *Mahabharata*. Choice C is incorrect because the *Tripitaka* is one of the sacred writings of Theravada Buddhism. Choice D is incorrect because the Hadith is one of the sacred writings of Islam.

7. **The correct answer is A.** Islam prohibits Muslims from eating pork; it is taboo in their religion. Judaism, which also originated

in the Middle East, also prohibits the consumption of pork. Choice B is incorrect because pork is not taboo for Hindus, but eating beef is. Choices C and D are incorrect because pork is not taboo for either Buddhists or Shintoists.

8. **The correct answer is B.** Smartists worship all five deities with the same level of reverence. Vaishnavism (choice A) is the theistic path that worships Vishnu. Shaktism (choice C) is the theistic path that worships Shakti. Shaivism (choice D) is the theistic path that worships Shiva.

9. **The correct answer is C.** Actions to improve one's karma, such as providing food to monks, are known as making merit. Choice A is incorrect because the word *mosque* signals that the shoe removal before entering is a practice of Muslims, not Buddhists. Choice B is incorrect because washing before entering a shrine to pray is a ritual of Shinto. Choice D is incorrect because Buddhists do not venerate their ancestors.

10. **The correct answer is D.** The reciprocal relationships taught by Confucius include that of father and son and ruler and subject. Confucius doesn't mention sisters, so statement II is incorrect. Choices B and C are, therefore, incorrect because they both include statement II. Choice A is incorrect because it omits statement III.

11. **The correct answer is B.** Moroni appeared to Joseph Smith, gave him the golden tablets that are the sacred writings of the Church of Jesus Christ of Latter Day Saints, and gave him the ability to translate them into English. Choice A is incorrect because Yahweh appeared to Moses in the form of a burning bush on Mount Sinai. Choice C is incorrect because the angel Gabriel appeared to Muhammad. Choice D is incorrect because Yahweh appeared to Abraham.

12. **The correct answer is C.** The Orthodox churches are overseen by a network of patriarchs. Lutheran churches are organized into synods overseen by ministers, so choice A is incorrect. Judaism (choice B) has no organized structure of overseers. The highest clerical office in the Anglican

Church, or Church of England (choice D), is the Archbishop of Canterbury.

13. **The correct answer is C.** Jains believe that release from the cycle of reincarnation comes only through one's own actions. Choice A is incorrect because Jains believe that monks are closer to release than those who live in the world. Choice B is the opposite of what Jains believe: Prayer is of no help in attaining release. Choice D is incorrect because Jain monks take vows of celibacy.

14. **The correct answer is C.** Catholics believe that all humans are born with Adam's sin on their souls and that baptism removes it. Choice A may seem like a good answer, but it's incorrect. Choice B is incorrect because Catholics believe in infant baptism. This answer hints at being a "born again" Christian, someone who believes in adult baptism. Choice D is incorrect because baptism removes the sin inherited from Adam, but doesn't make amends for it.

15. **The correct answer is A.** According to Daoism, unnaturalness is the cause of suffering, pain, and violence. Violence (choice C) is one result of unnaturalness, so it is not the correct answer. Choice B is incorrect; Buddhists believe that desire is the cause of suffering. Choice D is incorrect because the Daoists don't consider evil as a cause for suffering; evil in the world would be another result of unnaturalness.

16. **The correct answer is D.** In Mahayana Buddhism, a bodhisattva may also be someone who has achieved nirvana, died, and is now prayed to by other Buddhists. Choice A is incorrect because yoga in its various forms is found in Hinduism, not Buddhism. Choice B is incorrect because a Buddhist monk is not yet a bodhisattva. Choice C is incorrect because a bodhisattva has already achieved nirvana.

17. **The correct answer is B.** The Aztec believed that by offering human sacrifices to the gods, they could prevent the end of the world. Choices A, C, and D are plausible but incorrect.

18. **The correct answer is C.** Choice A describes how a follower of the phenomenologist

school of thought would study religion. Choice B is incorrect because a psychologist would study how religion influences thoughts and behavior. Choice D is incorrect because it is an approach that a sociologist might take.

19. **The correct answer is C.** Dharma is the religious and moral duties of individuals in Hinduism. Choice A is incorrect because the cycle of reincarnation is called samsara in both Hinduism and Buddhism. Choice B is incorrect because moksha is the release from the cycle of reincarnation. Choice D is incorrect because Buddhas-in-waiting are called bodhisattvas.

20. **The correct answer is B.** According to the Catholic Church, baptism removes original sin. Choice A is incorrect because Confirmation is the sacrament that initiates the believer into full and mature participation in the Church. Choice C is incorrect because the sacrament of the Eucharist is the body and blood of Jesus. Choice D is incorrect because the sacrament of Penance removes the sins that individuals themselves commit.

21. **The correct answer is D.** A madrasah is an Islamic school, so students would study the Qur'an. Choice A is incorrect because a student would study the Jewish Talmud at a yeshiva. Choice B is incorrect because a person would make an offering to a kami at a Shinto shrine; the names of the shrines vary depending on whom the shrine honors. Choice C is incorrect because a Hindu would make an offering to Vishnu at a mender, a Hindu temple.

22. **The correct answer is D.** A supreme being or creator of all things—whether known as God, Yahweh, the High God, or Allah—is a concept found in Christianity, Judaism, Native North American religions, and Islam. Only choice D has all four answers.

23. **The correct answer is A.** Icons, highly ornate depictions of Jesus, Mary, and saints, decorate Eastern Orthodox churches, so you find icons in Russian Orthodox churches. Roman Catholic churches (choice B) are less ornate. Mosques (choice C), and Buddhist temples (choice D) are incorrect

answers because they are places of worship for non-Christian religions. Choice C is also incorrect for another reason: Muslims believe that representations of Muhammad are blasphemous.

24. **The correct answer is B.** Buddha's enlightenment about a middle path led to the Eight-Fold Path and the Four Noble Truths. Monasticism (choice A) is a practice found in Theravada Buddhism, and the belief that yoga and meditation are the only way to enlightenment (choice C) is taught in Zen Buddhism, but neither was what prompted the Buddha's enlightenment. Worship of Brahma (choice D) is a tenet of Hinduism.

25. **The correct answer is D.** Right understanding (choice A), right speech (choice B), and right action (choice C) are all aspects, of the Eight-Fold Path of Buddhism. Right loyalty, which is not one of the aspects, is the correct answer.

26. **The correct answer is B.** Islamists are Muslim fundamentalists who want to return Islam to what they consider its original teachings. Choice A is incorrect because religious courts are typically presided over by clerics. Choice C is incorrect because those who study Islamic law are called mujtahid. Imams lead the faithful in prayer at mosques, so choice D is incorrect.

27. **The correct answer is C.** Moses Mendelssohn encouraged Jews to move out the ghetto and into the modern European world. Baal Shem Tov (choice D) preached that Jews should maintain their identity and live apart from the secular world. Jewish scholar Maimonides (choice A) lived in the late twelfth and early thirteenth centuries. Mordecai Kaplan (choice B) is credited as a founding thinker of Reconstructionist Judaism, which originated in the United States in the 1920s and 1930s.

28. **The correct answer is A.** The Golden Age of Islam ended after World War I, not World War II (choice B). Choice C is incorrect because the Umayyad clan seized the caliphate from the fourth caliph, Ali, Muhammad's son-in-law, in 661, but this didn't end the power of the empire. Choice D

is incorrect because it was during the 1500s that the Ottoman Turks seized control of the empire. Though they changed the title of the empire's leader from caliph to sultan, the empire continued.

29. **The correct answer is A.** Even if you weren't sure about the other answers, Luther's concept of justification by faith should have stood out as the correct answer. It was a monumental change in Christian theology. Choice B is incorrect because Luther accepted baptism and the Eucharist as sacraments. Choice C is incorrect because Luther didn't accept the rite of confession to a priest. Choice D is incorrect because Luther introduced the use of the vernacular, in his case, German, for services and for scripture.

30. **The correct answer is C.** Hindus believe that Brahman is the ultimate reality. Choice A is incorrect because yin and yang are concepts in Daoism that represent balance. Choice B is incorrect because ahimsa is the Hindu and Buddhist principle of nonviolence. Choice D is incorrect because atman is the self or soul to Hindus.

31. **The correct answer is A.** Muslims believe that Abraham and Ishmael built the Ka'bah as a resting place for the Black Stone given to Adam by Allah. Choice B is incorrect because Gabriel appeared to Muhammad in various places but not in the Ka'bah. Choice C is incorrect because Muhammad ascended into heaven, so there is no grave. Choice D is incorrect because the site of the ascension was the Dome of the Rock in Jerusalem.

32. **The correct answer is C.** Hsun Tzu Xun-Zi was a later Confucian scholar who believed that human nature was inherently evil, in contrast to Mencius Meng-Zi (choice B), who believed that human nature was inherently good. Confucius (choice A) is incorrect because he believed in the natural goodness of people. Choice D is incorrect because Lao-zi is the traditional founder of Daoism.

33. **The correct answer is A.** The Talmud contains the Mishnah, a collection of disputes and commentary on Jewish law up to the

100s CE, and the Gemara, additional rabbinic teachings on Jewish life. Statement III, the Haggadah, is the service for a Seder, and statement IV, the Torah, is the first five books of the Hebrew Bible. Choices B and C are incorrect because they contain the Haggadah. Choice D is incorrect because it contains both the Haggadah and the Torah.

34. **The correct answer is D.** In general, world religions have ritual ceremonies to celebrate or mark death, birth, marriage, and puberty. Only choice D includes all four, so it is the correct answer.

35. **The correct answer is B.** Raluvhimba is the supreme being worshiped by the Bavenda or Venda. Zwidutwane (choice A) is the name that Bavenda call the water spirits. Awa (choice C) is what the Dogon refer to as their cult of the dead. Binu (choice D) is the Dogon name for special places, or shrines, where they honor their ancestors.

36. **The correct answer is A.** The best answer is always the most complete, and while striving after a good reputation (choice B), material goods (choice C), and human attachments (choice D) are all things that can cause suffering, they are specific causes. The best answer for this question is desire, which encompasses the other answers.

37. **The correct answer is D.** *Jen*, translated as social virtue and also as humaneness, is a basic concept of Confucianism. It is not a concept taught in Islam (choice A), Shintoism (choice B), or Buddhism (choice C).

38. **The correct answer is D.** Kosher laws are dietary laws describing what foods and combinations of foods Jews may and may not eat. There are 620 mitzvah, or commandments, plus commentary in Jewish law that relate to marriage (choice A), activities on the Sabbath (choice B), and other elements of Jewish life such as dress and grooming (choice C), but they are not kosher laws.

39. **The correct answer is A.** Interpretation of the Qur'an (choice B), the role of women in Islam (choice C), and the positions of imams (choice D) may be differences that have developed between Sunni and Shi'a Muslims, but the dispute over who was the

rightful heir of Muhammad is the origin of any differences that have developed over the centuries.

40. **The correct answer is B.** Both Jainism and Buddhism developed because of dissatisfaction with aspects of Hinduism. Choice A is incorrect because Buddhism itself developed as a reaction to elements of Hinduism. Choices C and D are incorrect because Jainism is not related to either Shintoism or Confucianism.

41. **The correct answer is C.** Rosh Hashanah celebrates the Jewish New Year. The celebration of the victory of the Maccabees and the rededication of the Temple in Jerusalem (choice A) is Chanukah, known as the Festival of Lights or the Feast of the Dedication. Sukkot, the Feast of the Tabernacle, celebrates the harvest (choice B). Passover (choice D) celebrates the exodus from Egypt.

42. **The correct answer is C.** In contrast to the Roman Catholic Church, the Orthodox Churches do not recognize the primacy of the Pope. Choice A is incorrect because both churches practice infant baptism. Choice B is a misstatement of the controversy over icons that was one of the reasons that precipitated the schism. The emperor in the East in the early 700s came under the influence of Islam and ordered churches to remove their religious imagery. The Pope condemned this iconoclasm, destruction of icons, or representations, as heresy. In time, the Eastern Church returned to the use of icons as symbols. Choice D is a difference between the Roman Catholic and Eastern Orthodox Churches but not a reason that brought about the schism, so it's incorrect.

43. **The correct answer is D.** The ummah is the community of faithful Muslims, which transcends all branch divisions. The wall niche or rug design pointed in the direction of Mecca (choice A) is called the mihrab. The call to prayer (choice B) is the adman. Hajj (choice C) is the pilgrimage to Mecca.

44. **The correct answer is C.** Islam divided into Shi'a and Sunni in a dispute over who was the legitimate successor to Muhammad. Choice A is incorrect because Sufism is a mystical branch of Islam but is not a major division; Shari'ah is Islamic law, not a religious division. Choice B is incorrect because Wahhabism is a conservative movement within Islam that originated on the Arabian Peninsula. It is not a major division of Islam. Choice D is incorrect because Twelvers are another name given to Shi'ites who believe that there have been Twelve Imams and the Twelfth and last is still alive and hidden to them.

45. **The correct answer is D.** There is no ultimate being in Buddhism. Choice A is incorrect because both Buddhism and Islam have historical founders, Gautama Buddha and Muhammad, respectively. Choice B is incorrect because Buddhism is not polytheistic; however, Islam is monotheistic, worshiping only Allah. Choice C is incorrect because, although the God of Islam is Allah, Buddha is not the same as a supreme being.

46. **The correct answer is B.** Jainism was founded as a reaction against Hinduism. Sikhism (choice A) was founded by Guru Nanak in the late 1400s and early 1500s as a reaction to both Islam and Hinduism. It preaches monotheism and includes the concepts of karma, dharma, and reincarnation. Wahhabism (choice C) is a very conservative form of Islam that developed in Saudi Arabia. Sufism (choice D) is the mystical tradition within Islam.

47. **The correct answer is D.** Muhammad's flight from Mecca is called the Hegira. Choice A is incorrect because the Umayyad was a clan that seized the caliphate from the fourth caliph, Ali, Muhammad's son-in-law. Choice B is incorrect because the Hadith is a collection of traditions, analogies, and consensus that relate to the life and words of Muhammad and his companions, as well as the study of Muslim scholars relating to legal issues and the duties of Muslims. Choice C is incorrect as it is the name of the second holiest city in Islam and the place where Muhammad found refuge when he fled Mecca.

48. **The correct answer is A.** Confucianism believes in the need for right action, whereas Daoists believe in the need for inaction. Choice B is incorrect because neither Confucianism nor Daoism includes a supreme being who created the world. Choice C is incorrect because harmony is a basic principle of Daoism, not Confucianism. Choice D is incorrect because the Daoists believe that the less the government governed, the better. On the other hand, Confucianism teaches that it is the duty of the government to provide for the well-being of the governed.

49. **The correct answer is A.** The Hindu caste system is described in the Law of Manu. Choice B is incorrect because the Rig Veda is a collection of more than a thousand hymns. Choice C is incorrect because the *Ramayana* is an epic poem about Prince Rama and his wife. Choice D is incorrect because varna is the name of the caste system.

50. **The correct answer is B.** The Council of Trent made changes to certain abuses of Church practices but reaffirmed all issues of dogma. Choice A is incorrect because the Council of Trent was convened because of the Reformation and took up issues highlighted by the Reformation. Choice C is incorrect because the Council made no changes to doctrine. Choice D describes the Second Vatican Council, so it is incorrect.

51. **The correct answer is C.** Laylat al-Qadr honors the first revelation to Muhammad by the angel Gabriel. Choice A is incorrect because Id al-Fitr is known as the Breaking of the Fast of Ramadan. Choice B is incorrect because al-Hijrah celebrates Muhammad's journey to Medina from Mecca. Choice D is incorrect because Ramadan is the month of fasting.

52. **The correct answer is A.** Orthodox Jews are the strictest in their observance of Jewish traditions and religious doctrines and practices. Therefore, choices B, C, and D are incorrect.

53. **The correct answer is B.** Choice B refers to the Kabbalah, a body of mystical teachings that was collected in several volumes and doesn't relate to efforts of the ancient Jews

to preserve their identity through centuries of persecution. Using synagogues as the centers of worship (choice A), appointing rabbis as teachers and explicators (choice C), and designating Saturday as the Sabbath based on the Book of Genesis (choice D) are traditions that Jews followed to preserve their identity and religion.

54. **The correct answer is D.** Daoism was seen as a complement to the rigid etiquette of Confucianism and flourished in China for several centuries. However, as Theravada Buddhism (choice C) spread in China, a rivalry developed between adherents of the two religions. Over the centuries, rulers influenced by one or the other of the religions persecuted its rival adherents. However, over time, Daoism and Theravada Buddhism, along with Confucianism, became firmly established as major religions among the Chinese. Neither Hinduism (choice A) nor Shintoism (choice B) became forces within Chinese religious life.

55. **The correct answer is B.** Buddhism centers on the Four Noble Truths and the Eight-Fold Path. Choice A is incorrect because the Mishnah is the collection of all the disputes and commentary on Jewish law up to the second century CE. It is one part of the Talmud. Choice C is incorrect because the Five Pillars are the basic belief system of Islam. Choice D is incorrect because the Analects collect the teachings of Confucius.

56. **The correct answer is C.** A diviner has the power to see into the future; among the ancient Greeks, the person able to do this was called an oracle. Choice A is incorrect because an animist believes that the objects of the natural world, such as rocks, are spiritually alive, but an animist doesn't foretell future events. *Healer* (choice B) and *medicine man/woman* (choice D) are different terms for people who cure the sick.

57. **The correct answer is B.** The three major deities, or triad, of Hinduism are Brahma, Vishnu, and Shiva. Choice A is incorrect because although Krishna is an incarnation of Vishnu, it's not the same. Shakti is the wife of Shiva but not one of the triad. Choice C is incorrect in part because it contains Shakti

and also because Krishna is an incarnation of Vishnu, but not the same. Choice D is incorrect because Rama is an incarnation of Vishnu, and Kali is another name for Shakti, the wife of Shiva.

58. **The correct answer is D.** Being of the correct caste (choice A), adhering to a specific meditation practice (choice B), and worshiping in a certain temple (choice C) are all things that other religions, such as Hinduism and Buddhism, ask of followers in order to know God. Sikhs feel that one can know God without those things, as long as one lives an honest and good life.

59. **The correct answer is B.** The word *Islam* means "submission," and *Muslim* means "one who submits." Choice A is incorrect because *Catholic* means "universal." Choice C is incorrect because *Orthodox* means "conforming to established beliefs." Choice D is incorrect because *Buddhism* is derived from a Sanskrit word meaning "the enlightened one."

60. **The correct answer is C.** The Aryans worshiped the deities Indra, Agni, Varna, and Soma. Choice A is incorrect because Abraham and Moses were historical figures in Islam and Judaism. Choice B is incorrect because Matthew, Mark, Luke, and John were authors of the Gospels found in the New Testament. Choice D is incorrect because Apsu and Tiamat are names of the main Mesopotamian gods.

answers post-test

Management Information Systems

OVERVIEW

The DSST® Management Information Systems exam consists of 100 multiple-choice questions that cover the structure and functions of business information systems. The exam focuses upon the following topics: knowledge of communications, network security, systems analysis and design, business decision making, knowledge management, data warehousing, and data mining. Careful reading, critical thinking, and logical analysis will be as important as your knowledge of MIS structure.

Chapter 7

DIAGNOSTIC TEST ANSWER SHEET

1. Ⓐ Ⓑ Ⓒ Ⓓ	5. Ⓐ Ⓑ Ⓒ Ⓓ	9. Ⓐ Ⓑ Ⓒ Ⓓ	13. Ⓐ Ⓑ Ⓒ Ⓓ	17. Ⓐ Ⓑ Ⓒ Ⓓ
2. Ⓐ Ⓑ Ⓒ Ⓓ	6. Ⓐ Ⓑ Ⓒ Ⓓ	10. Ⓐ Ⓑ Ⓒ Ⓓ	14. Ⓐ Ⓑ Ⓒ Ⓓ	18. Ⓐ Ⓑ Ⓒ Ⓓ
3. Ⓐ Ⓑ Ⓒ Ⓓ	7. Ⓐ Ⓑ Ⓒ Ⓓ	11. Ⓐ Ⓑ Ⓒ Ⓓ	15. Ⓐ Ⓑ Ⓒ Ⓓ	19. Ⓐ Ⓑ Ⓒ Ⓓ
4. Ⓐ Ⓑ Ⓒ Ⓓ	8. Ⓐ Ⓑ Ⓒ Ⓓ	12. Ⓐ Ⓑ Ⓒ Ⓓ	16. Ⓐ Ⓑ Ⓒ Ⓓ	20. Ⓐ Ⓑ Ⓒ Ⓓ

POST-TEST ANSWER SHEET

1. Ⓐ Ⓑ Ⓒ Ⓓ	13. Ⓐ Ⓑ Ⓒ Ⓓ	25. Ⓐ Ⓑ Ⓒ Ⓓ	37. Ⓐ Ⓑ Ⓒ Ⓓ	49. Ⓐ Ⓑ Ⓒ Ⓓ
2. Ⓐ Ⓑ Ⓒ Ⓓ	14. Ⓐ Ⓑ Ⓒ Ⓓ	26. Ⓐ Ⓑ Ⓒ Ⓓ	38. Ⓐ Ⓑ Ⓒ Ⓓ	50. Ⓐ Ⓑ Ⓒ Ⓓ
3. Ⓐ Ⓑ Ⓒ Ⓓ	15. Ⓐ Ⓑ Ⓒ Ⓓ	27. Ⓐ Ⓑ Ⓒ Ⓓ	39. Ⓐ Ⓑ Ⓒ Ⓓ	51. Ⓐ Ⓑ Ⓒ Ⓓ
4. Ⓐ Ⓑ Ⓒ Ⓓ	16. Ⓐ Ⓑ Ⓒ Ⓓ	28. Ⓐ Ⓑ Ⓒ Ⓓ	40. Ⓐ Ⓑ Ⓒ Ⓓ	52. Ⓐ Ⓑ Ⓒ Ⓓ
5. Ⓐ Ⓑ Ⓒ Ⓓ	17. Ⓐ Ⓑ Ⓒ Ⓓ	29. Ⓐ Ⓑ Ⓒ Ⓓ	41. Ⓐ Ⓑ Ⓒ Ⓓ	53. Ⓐ Ⓑ Ⓒ Ⓓ
6. Ⓐ Ⓑ Ⓒ Ⓓ	18. Ⓐ Ⓑ Ⓒ Ⓓ	30. Ⓐ Ⓑ Ⓒ Ⓓ	42. Ⓐ Ⓑ Ⓒ Ⓓ	54. Ⓐ Ⓑ Ⓒ Ⓓ
7. Ⓐ Ⓑ Ⓒ Ⓓ	19. Ⓐ Ⓑ Ⓒ Ⓓ	31. Ⓐ Ⓑ Ⓒ Ⓓ	43. Ⓐ Ⓑ Ⓒ Ⓓ	55. Ⓐ Ⓑ Ⓒ Ⓓ
8. Ⓐ Ⓑ Ⓒ Ⓓ	20. Ⓐ Ⓑ Ⓒ Ⓓ	32. Ⓐ Ⓑ Ⓒ Ⓓ	44. Ⓐ Ⓑ Ⓒ Ⓓ	56. Ⓐ Ⓑ Ⓒ Ⓓ
9. Ⓐ Ⓑ Ⓒ Ⓓ	21. Ⓐ Ⓑ Ⓒ Ⓓ	33. Ⓐ Ⓑ Ⓒ Ⓓ	45. Ⓐ Ⓑ Ⓒ Ⓓ	57. Ⓐ Ⓑ Ⓒ Ⓓ
10. Ⓐ Ⓑ Ⓒ Ⓓ	22. Ⓐ Ⓑ Ⓒ Ⓓ	34. Ⓐ Ⓑ Ⓒ Ⓓ	46. Ⓐ Ⓑ Ⓒ Ⓓ	58. Ⓐ Ⓑ Ⓒ Ⓓ
11. Ⓐ Ⓑ Ⓒ Ⓓ	23. Ⓐ Ⓑ Ⓒ Ⓓ	35. Ⓐ Ⓑ Ⓒ Ⓓ	47. Ⓐ Ⓑ Ⓒ Ⓓ	59. Ⓐ Ⓑ Ⓒ Ⓓ
12. Ⓐ Ⓑ Ⓒ Ⓓ	24. Ⓐ Ⓑ Ⓒ Ⓓ	36. Ⓐ Ⓑ Ⓒ Ⓓ	48. Ⓐ Ⓑ Ⓒ Ⓓ	60. Ⓐ Ⓑ Ⓒ Ⓓ

answer sheets

MANAGEMENT INFORMATION SYSTEMS DIAGNOSTIC TEST

> **Directions:** Carefully read each of the following 20 questions. Choose the best answer to each question and fill in the corresponding circle on the answer sheet. The Answer Key and Explanations can be found following this Diagnostic Test.

1. Which of the following is considered the computer's "brain," which enables it to coordinate the instructions of the computer and performs and manages calculations and instructions of the computer?
   A. Register
   B. Central Processing Unit
   C. Arithmetic Control Unit
   D. RAM memory

2. The identifier in databases that gives uniqueness to the record is called a
   A. link list.
   B. master key.
   C. primary key.
   D. merge link.

3. What information system usually has unstructured information, often has *ad hoc* content, and is used for strategic decisions by executives of an organization?
   A. Decision Support System (DSS)
   B. Management Information System (MIS)
   C. Transactional Reporting System (TRS)
   D. Executive Information System (EIS)

4. What software controls the basic functions of the computer and manages and coordinates the interaction between hardware devices and users?
   A. Systems
   B. Applications
   C. Integration
   D. Command

5. A network that resides in a relatively small area and allows computer users to connect and share information within a building or small geographical area is called a
   A. Wide Area Network (WAN).
   B. Virtual Private Network (VPN).
   C. Value-added Network (VAN).
   D. Local Area Network (LAN).

6. Which term refers to data that have been stored in a central location derived from various internal and operational locations, external data locations, and even other internal data centers?
   A. Data warehousing
   B. Data modeling
   C. Database maintenance
   D. Data interrogation

7. Which of the following is the set of rules, generally created to implement a standard for communicating messages, that networks utilize wherever data are formatted, transmitted, secured, and received?
   A. National Radio System
   B. Network System Rules
   C. Protocol
   D. Network Standards

8. Face recognition, finger print recognition, retina scanning, and other personal identifying methods that help identify a unique human characteristic are known as
   A. bioanalysis.
   B. biometrics.
   C. bio-challenge.
   D. biodiversity.

9. Which of the following is used to describe the overall diagram of a network?
   A. Communications mapping
   B. Network geography
   C. Network morphology
   D. Network topology

10. What information system enhances the strategies and processes an organization uses to build and maintain relationships with its current and prospective users?
    A. Customer relationship management
    B. Enterprise resource planning systems
    C. Human capital management
    D. Customer analytics

11. Cache, random access memory (RAM), and read-only memory (ROM) are examples of what kind of storage?
    A. Hard drive storage
    B. USB storage
    C. Primary storage
    D. Secondary storage

12. What stage in the systems development life cycle contains hardware and software acquisitions and undergoes testing to ensure that it is operational?
    A. The investigation stage
    B. The implementation stage
    C. The analysis stage
    D. The maintenance stage

13. Which is the most common model in today's Data Base Management System?
    A. Object-Oriented
    B. Hierarchical
    C. Relational
    D. System

14. What is the process of taking data input and encoding the data into algorithms that only authorized parties can transform into usable information?
    A. Hacking
    B. Encapsulation
    C. Encryption
    D. Enlightenment

15. What is the concept of analyzing data to seek patterns and trends in order to discover information useful in strategic decisions?
    A. Data warehousing
    B. Data mining
    C. Database manipulation
    D. Data interrogation

16. Which of the following is not a component of Porter's five forces?
    A. Information influence
    B. Threats of substitutes
    C. Threats of new market
    D. Rivalry among competitors

17. What is the e-commerce relationship in which organizations buy and sell products or services online from or to one another?
    A. Consumer to consumer (C2C)
    B. Business to consumer (B2C)
    C. Business to business (B2B)
    D. Consumer to business (C2B)

18. In order for a system to be successful, it must have which of the following fundamental implications?

I. The system must be designed to accomplish a defined and predetermined objective.

II. The system must have interdependency and collaboration among its components.

III. The strategy must compliment the system.

IV. The strategic objective must have higher priority over the system than the subsets of the system.

A. I, II, III

B. II, III, IV

C. I, III, IV

D. I, II, IV

19. What is the term for a group of activities that have a clear objective in mind, with a defined beginning and a defined completion?

A. Execution

B. Closing

C. Project

D. Phase

20. Actions by countries and terrorist organizations that penetrate, disrupt, and potentially cause damage to network systems and/or computer systems is called

A. hacking.

B. cyberwarfare.

C. cyberspam.

D. cyberfirewall.

diagnostic test

ANSWER KEY AND EXPLANATIONS

1. B	5. D	9. D	13. C	17. C
2. C	6. A	10. A	14. C	18. D
3. D	7. C	11. C	15. B	19. C
4. A	8. B	12. B	16. A	20. B

1. **The correct answer is B.** The Central Processing Unit is the "brain" that enables the coordination and management of instructions. Choice A is incorrect because registers are only storage and calculation points within the CPU. Choice C is incorrect because it is a subcomponent of the CPU. It does not coordinate instructions. Choice D is incorrect because RAM is only used in active software applications.

2. **The correct answer is C.** Primary keys are the unique identifiers of a table within the database. Choices A, B, and D are incorrect because they are not real networking terms.

3. **The correct answer is D.** Executive Information Systems usually consist of DSS and MIS components. They also are mostly unstructured and *ad hoc* in nature. Choice A is incorrect because it is a subset of the EIS and usually contains more analysis of the structured data used by managers. Choice B has semi-structured data and is often a subset of the EIS used by managers. Choice C is not correct because it is the operational, short-term reports of front-line management.

4. **The correct answer is A.** Systems software controls all the basic functions of the computer. Choice B is incorrect because application software programs perform common information processing jobs. Choice C is incorrect because it is not a real software choice. Choice D is incorrect because command is an action given to the computer, not a type of software.

5. **The correct answer is D.** A LAN operates in a relatively small area and allows computer users to connect and share information within a building or small geographic area. Choice A is incorrect because WANs operate in a large geographic area. Choice

B is incorrect because VPNs can be used in a large geographic area. Choice C is not a real network.

6. **The correct answer is A.** Data warehousing is when data are collected in a central repository for analysis and use. Choice B is not correct; it is the identification of relationships of the data. Choice C is not correct because it is the activity of adding, editing, or changing data in a database. Choice D is not correct because it allows users to query databases.

7. **The correct answer is C.** Protocols are the set of rules and standards for networks. Choice A is incorrect because it has no relationship to network rules. Choice B is incorrect because even though network systems have rules, protocols institute a standardization of communicating in the network. Choice D is incorrect because it represents standards without the format and rules of telecommunication.

8. **The correct answer is B.** Biometrics is the line of security that employs human physical characteristics as well as other personal identifying methods. Choices A, C, and D are incorrect because they are unrelated to information systems.

9. **The correct answer is D.** Topology provides the shape of the network. Choice A is incorrect because maps are not an item used in networking. Choice B is incorrect because geography implies location, rather than a model. Choice C is incorrect because it is not a real networking term.

10. **The correct answer is A.** Customer relationship management is the embodiment of an information system to enhance relationships with customers. Choice B is incorrect because it contains a more enterprise view of

the enterprise's information requirements. Choices C and D are incorrect because they are not information systems.

11. **The correct answer is C.** Cache, RAM, and ROM are all primary storage devices. Choice A is incorrect because hard drive storage is a secondary storage device. Choice B is incorrect because USB storage devices are secondary storage devices. Choice D is incorrect because Cache, RAM, and ROM are not secondary storage devices.

12. **The correct answer is B.** The implementation stage is where acquisitions occur as well as testing the network and ensuring the information system is operable. Choice A is incorrect because it is the first stage of the SDLC and asks questions more about the enterprise need of a new system. Choice C is incorrect, because it primarily analyzes the current system and evaluates future need. Choice D is incorrect because it is the post-implementation phase AFTER acquisitions have occurred.

13. **The correct answer is C.** Relational models are the most common DBMS model in use today. The object-oriented model (Choice A) is incorrect because it is used with complex data types. The hierarchical model (choice B) is incorrect because it was the first and oldest method of database management; however, it is not being used as much today. A system (choice D) is not a DBMS model.

14. **The correct answer is C.** Encryption is the process of taking inputs and, through the use of algorithms, transforming the data into unusable information to parties without authorization. Choice A is incorrect because hacking employs deciphering data without authorization. Choice B is incorrect because encapsulation is the process that binds the data and functions that manipulate the data and that keeps both safe from outside interference and misuse. Choice D is incorrect because it is unrelated to information systems.

15. **The correct answer is B.** Data mining uses data analysis to uncover "nuggets" of information, mostly through trends and data patterns. Choice A is not correct because

data warehousing is combining data from numerous data centers. Often, extracts used for data mining come from data warehouses. Choice C is not correct because it is the activity of adding, editing, or changing data in a database. Choice D is not correct because it allows users to query databases.

16. **The correct answer is A.** Porter's Five Forces are: rivalry among competitors, threats of new market entrants, threats of substitutes, customer influence, and supplier influence. Information influence is not one of the five forces.

17. **The correct answer is C.** B2B is business-to-business commerce where goods and services are exchanged among businesses. Choice A is incorrect because it is consumer to consumer. Choice B is incorrect because it is e-commerce from a business to the average consumer. Choice D is incorrect because it is e-commerce from a consumer to business exchange.

18. **The correct answer is D.** Choice III is not a good implication because the MIS system must be built around the strategy, not vice versa. Otherwise, you have a large expensive MIS system that is unusable for the business strategically.

19. **The correct answer is C.** This is the definition of a project. Choice A is not correct, because it is a phase of the project. Choice B is not correct because it is a phase of the project. Choice D is not correct because a project contains numerous phases.

20. **The correct answer is B.** Cyberwarfare is a weapon used by terrorist organizations and countries that is designed to cripple information infrastructures and disrupt normal activity. Choice A is incorrect because hacking is just one method used by cyberwarfare agents. Choice C is incorrect because spam is unwanted e-mail; however, much of it is just annoying rather than used for the purpose of destroying information infrastructures. Choice D is incorrect because it is not a feasible product used to disrupt or destroy.

DIAGNOSTIC TEST ASSESSMENT GRID

Now that you've completed the diagnostic test and read through the answer explanations, you can use your results to target your studying. Find the question numbers from the diagnostic test that you answered incorrectly and highlight or circle them below. Then focus extra attention to the sections within the chapter dealing with those topics.

Management Information Systems		
Content Area	Topic	Question #
Computer Hardware	• History and evolution • Terminology • Hardware components • Hardware devices • Classification	1, 11
Computer Software	• History and evolution of computer software and programming • Terminology • Types of software	4
Telecommunications and Networks	• Terminology • Strategic importance to the enterprise • Components of telecommunications and networks • Information systems security • Topology and protocols	5, 7, 9
Business Information Systems	• Electronic commerce • Types of information systems • Enterprise resource planning, customer relationship management, supply chain management systems, and knowledge management systems	10, 17
Systems Analysis and Design	• Characteristics of a system • Systems architecture • Systems development life cycle	12, 18

Management Information Systems		
Content Area	**Topic**	**Question #**
Managing Data Resources	• Data models • Database management systems • Data query and update	2, 13
Business Decision Making	• Knowledge management • Data warehousing • Data mining • Project management	6, 15, 19
MIS and the Organization	• Organization of MIS • Relationships of MIS to the enterprise • Value of the MIS function	3, 16
MIS Issues	• Security • Ethics/Legal/Social • Privacy • Global Issues	8, 14, 20

GET THE FACTS

To see the DSST® Management Information Systems Fact Sheet, go to **http://getcollegecredit.com/assets/pdf/dsst_fact_sheets** and click on the **Business** tab. Scroll down and click on the **Management Information Systems** link. Here you will find suggestions for further study material and the ACE college credit recommendations for passing the test.

WHAT IS MIS?

A **management information system (MIS)** is a comprehensive organizational management structure in business where e-commerce, data management, and decisional influence from information systems reside. A basic MIS course provides a historical evolution and general study of important MIS topics business professionals should understand. This chapter features an overview of all key topics presented on the DSST exam.

COMPUTER HARDWARE

HISTORY AND EVOLUTION OF COMPUTER HARDWARE

Humans have been computing since the beginning of recorded history. From the conception of trade, the use of fingers, stones, and sticks were the simple means of human counting and numerical interactivity. Calculating using mechanical devices has been a human activity for thousands of years—we can trace the usage of the abacus in trade as far back as 2400 BCE.

The Roots of Computing

Numerical calculating derives from Egyptian, Persian, Chinese, and Arabic civilizations, but the **binary system** (the system used for computer calculations) comes from the Indian mathematician Pingala. While the counting system we are most familiar with in modern calculations is the decimal system, where we use the numerical values of 0 through 9, the system Pingala formulated was based on the use of only two numbers: 1 and 0. This is useful because modern computing systems only have two states: "on" and "off," which equate to "1" and "0," electronically.

Computing mathematics mechanically evolved in 1642, when French prodigy Blaise Pascal is credited with inventing an adding machine at the age of 16. This simple machine became the foundation of other calculating machines created by other inventors. Charles Babbage, an English inventor, expanded on Pascal's invention in 1837. His ingenious device, named the **Analytical Engine,** is extremely important to the modern computing world because it actually incorporated an **arithmetic logic unit** (**ALU**) for calculations, a control mechanism to send instructions to mechanical registers, and a system to store the computations.

Development During World War II

During the height of World War II, the German military created and used a device called the **enigma,** which sent encrypted military messages via telegraph to other military stations and to the most lethal weapons the German military had at the time, their U-boat submarines. The enigma provided U-boats with targeting information and gave them information that the Allied Forces could not decipher. As the war between the Germans and Allied Forces expanded, it became crucial to the success of the Allied Forces to find a means of deciphering and overcoming the usage of the enigma. Through great necessity, mathematician and inventor Alan Turing expanded Babbage's use of mechanics using electric energy. He created a new electrical and mechanically operated device that is credited for deciphering the enigma but, more important, is seen as a primary contributor of the modern computer.

In the same time period, American teams were collaborating on a device similar to Turing's. The Americans were devising a computing system to calculate ballistics and artillery-firing tables and to analyze thermonuclear weapons. This totally electronic computing machine was known as **Electronic Numerical Integrator and Computer** (**ENIAC**).

TIP

ENIAC contained over 17,000 vacuum tubes, nearly 100,000 electronic components, and over 5,000,000 million hand-soldered joints. It weighed over 30 tons and consumed an enormous amount of electricity. It could calculate a mathematical equation of 10 digits, using multiplication, at a rate of 357 calculations per second. It was quite an accomplishment for its time. In comparison, today's computers have the capacity to calculate billions of 64-digit calculations per second.

Today's devices have more computing power than all the NASA Johnson Space Center computers that monitored *Apollo 11* in 1969!

Computing in the Mid-to-Late Twentieth Century

The large, electronic computer systems became a common tool in larger businesses and for research and military purposes during the 1950s, 1960s, and 1970s. However, vacuum tubes were large, consumed high levels of electrical energy, and were often subject to failure. A small switching device called the **transistor** came to fruition. Arguably one of the most significant inventions of modern technology, this small device consumed a small level of electricity and was easily made from one of Earth's most abundant elements: silicon. This device could replace vacuum tubes and decrease the size of computers.

Meanwhile, a method of exchanging data between computers was established, called American Standard Code for Information Interchange, or **ASCII**. Computers were already calculating "on" and "off" electrical states as 1s and 0s (**bits**). ASCII captured the use of 1s and 0s and standardized a way to combine the series of eight 1s and 0s into what is known today as **bytes**.

Expansion of transistor use enabled manufacturer Texas Instruments to create devices for consumer use, including the hand-held calculator. It was through the hand-held calculator that the **integrated circuit** (**IC**) became a significant contributor to the development of the modern personal computer when developers realized several transistors and components could be "integrated" onto a single device.

Numerous IC manufacturers expanded on the complex circuitry as technology began to explode. Entrepreneur and engineer Gordon Moore created the company Intel and increased development and production output simultaneously. With this new demand on ICs, Moore observed ICs were doubling the amount of transistors in the same amount of space every two years. Known as **"Moore's law,"** this trend is the foundation that many businesses use to justify of expenditures for technology.

Think of Moore's law this way. Consider the computing power of the average American cellular phone. The technology is literally in the palm of your hand. No matter what operating system, it has more computing power than *Apollo 11's* computer—the spacecraft that put the first man on the moon.

Today, our computers are small enough to put in your pocket. We communicate freely across the globe with them. We can personally do calculations engineers of the past only dreamed of. We watch whatever movie we want. We can go to college online. We can create incredible presentations. The size and power of hardware has evolved immensely from the abacus.

HARDWARE COMPONENTS AND DEVICES

Computer hardware can be described as any physical device that resides in the computer and is essential for its operation. Hardware can be mechanical, magnetic, electrical, electronic, or optical, as long as it physically occupies a space in the computer.

A modern computer system must have four essential hardware components to operate. Most often, these devices are mounted on a main circuit board known as the motherboard. Let's go into the details of all of them.

Input

Input devices convert the movement or click of a mouse, the touch of a keyboard, the scan of an optical device, or the touch on a touch screen to electronic data for processing. Input devices include keyboards, mice, optical scanners, touch screens, pens, and voice and midi inputs, among many other mechanical and electrical input devices.

Central Processing Unit

The **Central Processing Unit** (**CPU**) is the "brain" of a computer. Also known as the microprocessor, it is the fundamental calculator and control mechanism of the computer system. There are two fundamental circuit systems in the CPU:

- The **control unit** has registers that interpret software instructions and transmit directions and controlling activities of the other components within the computer.

- The **arithmetic logic unit** (**ALU**) performs the calculations and logic functions necessary to execute software instructions.

Storage

Storage devices are circuits that electronically, physically, or magnetically store the 1s and 0s in the computer, which are converted to words and instructions held within the computer for use. There are two types of memory in computer systems: primary and secondary storage.

Primary Storage

Primary storage is typically mounted within the computer's main circuit system on the motherboard. It most often contains both **Read-Only Memory** (**ROM**) and **Random Access Memory** (**RAM**). ROM is a non-volatile memory, because it maintains all instructions as storage even when the computer is turned off. Because it will not lose its memory contents when powered off, computer operating and algorithmic software instructions are stored in these areas. However, RAM is volatile. When you turn your computer off, all memory registers typically assume an "off" condition (all 0s). RAM is used most often as the user opens multiple applications on a computer system. As the user opens each program, the RAM acts as the memory storage area of the user's input for those open programs. Computers may also have a memory circuitry known as **cache memory**. This circuitry most often is volatile; however, it can be non-volatile in nature. Its usage is for high-speed, temporary storage of commonly used instruction and highly used data elements. Cache memory is often used when you access an often-visited website or use numerous computer applications simultaneously.

Secondary Storage

Secondary storage refers to hardware devices that are most often not mounted on the motherboard: think the "hard drive," flash drive, or USB drive. Other secondary storage devices include magnetic tape, magnetic disks, optical disks, DVDs, or CDs.

TIP

We see outputs in television screens, monitors, printers, 3D printers, automation and robotics, and even as human movement via prosthetics.

Output

Output of a computer system can only be limited by the imagination. It converts the electronic information delivered by the CPU into a human-interpreted format. It could be in a visual or audible format. It could be a robotic movement. It could be a printed document. It could deliver controlling mechanisms to an automation system. Output devices can even create and deliver 3D objects via 3D printers!

Miscellaneous hardware devices that are not essential for computer operation but are significant to networking are often included inside the computer system. Some of the most common devices are **Network Interface Cards (NICs)** and modems, which we will discuss later in the chapter.

COMPUTER SOFTWARE

HISTORY AND EVOLUTION OF COMPUTER SOFTWARE AND PROGRAMMING

Software is defined as the instructions, programs, and procedures that integrate with a computer to enable the designed operation to function. It has no physical properties, but is essential in instructing the computer "what" to do, the sequence of "when" to do it, and "how" the instructions are to be performed in each hardware component.

TIP

Due to the success of instructional input, many consider Ada Lovelace to be the "first programmer."

The Birth of Programming

The algorithms for calculating those instructions are often credited to mathematician Ada Lovelace. Her mathematical prowess allowed her to "instruct" Charles Babbage's Analytical Engine to perform mathematical computations. She directed the Engine on what to do, when to do it, and how to incorporate the instructions into the mechanical system.

The algorithmic work of both Alan Turing and U.S. Army scientists during World War II to simply perform calculations via electromechanical and electronic means was very simple in nature; however, in that time period, calculations at that speed and depth were very necessary for scientific and wartime advancement. With the standardization of ASCII and bytes, computers could be instructed to perform algorithms and a machine language could be developed. The algorithms were the calculations, and the machine language was the manner in which circuits could be controlled.

Software in the Mid-Twentieth Century

In the 1950s, two computer languages were introduced:

- The programming language FORTRAN was introduced in 1956. FORTRAN was used in engineering programs that enabled robotics and automation to grow. FORTRAN was very suited for complex calculations and was frequently used for scientific applications using a system of punch cards. These punch cards were typically made of cardboard index cards with holes in them that queued the input devices of where the 1s and 0s were placed algorithmically. It was critical that they were punched in sequence, as well.

- Common Business-Oriented Language (COBOL) was developed in 1959 as a business calculation software. This language became popular in use and was widely supported as late as 1997. COBOL enabled businesses to store and calculate complex algorithms utilized in a growing data-rich environment.

The mid-1970s brought the foundation of computer languages and a more robust use of databases.

- In 1973, the programming language C came to the market. C could be used across several unique computer platforms, which allowed a more dynamic use of one single programming language.

- In 1974, Structured Query Language (SQL) allowed databases to be managed through relationships of common and unique data identities. It was robust in that it allowed a collection of small tabular data to have connectivity for a larger analytical use.

- In 1975, the programming language Beginner's All-purpose Symbolic Instruction Code (BASIC) changed the computer language dynamics into what we know today. Its simplicity and power were the foundation of Disk Operating System (DOS) and the launch of Microsoft Corporation.

Today's software roots evolved from the basic mathematic algorithms of the abacus and Babbage's Analytical Engine. We use Java, Perl, HTML, Mac OS, Windows, Linux, and various other systems in our daily lives. Truly, software is only limited by the imagination.

TYPES OF COMPUTER SOFTWARE

Software has two major categories and functions: system software and application software. Let's look at each in more detail.

System Software

System software is the software that manages, controls, and supports the computer system and controls the basic functions of the computer. Without this software, the computer has no real use or method of operating. It can be subdivided into the system management programs and the system development programs.

- **System management programs** manage the hardware, software, network, and data resources of a computer system. It has the ability to manage network interfaces and how the instructions are interpreted.

- **System development programs** enable language translators and program editing and give IT professionals the ability to create specific programs for specific business processes.

The system software is maintained in the primary memory (ROM) due to the nature and volatility of electrical connectivity. Computer operating software is maintained even when electricity is turned off.

Programming Languages

Programming languages are a major category of system software. Because of the complexity and constant advancement and changes in technology, operating systems contain several levels of instructions and code.

TIP

Database management is performed from system software. Other functions include system utilities, security monitoring, task management, file management, operating systems management, and maintenance of the system's performance through resource management.

There are five levels of programming languages:

1. *Machine language* is the most basic level of programming. It is here where the binary codes are written for the CPU. Machine language also enables processing tasks.

2. *Assembler language* was developed to reduce difficulties in writing machine language. It allows computers to convert symbolic languages, via a translator, into the machine language.

3. *High-level language* uses instructions, called statements, for programming mathematic computations. Most often, high-level language programming includes arithmetic instructions similar to X = Y + Z. Examples of high-level languages are BASIC, COBOL, and FORTRAN.

4. *Fourth-generation languages* were devised to enable programmers to program in a nonprocedural or nonsequential manner. The user is encouraged to program for results and allow the computer to determine the sequences.

5. *Object-oriented languages* tie data elements to the procedures in an "object." Most often, this language provides a graphic user interface GUI that supports a point-click mechanism for operation. From this language, we get software that allows web-based applications and services.

Application Software

The second primary category is application software, which has the most variety of uses. Application software includes programs that perform common information processing jobs such as productivity programs that allow business management, word processing, tabular analytics, graphics programs, web management, e-mail, and groupware. Application software also includes entertainment programs that allow people to view movies and pictures, play games, and listen to music. It is here that custom software developed for business, art, or scientific needs can be created.

TELECOMMUNICATIONS AND NETWORKS

THE STRATEGIC IMPORTANCE OF TELECOMMUNICATIONS AND NETWORKS

The strategic value of networks in an organization is very important in today's business world, as well as for the future. Within an organization, enterprises are using the Internet, intranets, virtual private networks, and other networks to provide support for business operations and collaboration among business partners within the supply chain and with their customers. The Internet provides strategic business value because it enables organizations to disburse information on a global scale by allowing communication and interactive trade with individuals and other businesses. The Internet decreases costs and increases profit by enhancing customer service and interactivity on a 24-hour, 7-day basis—the customer has immediate access to the business products, services, and information on an almost "always open" basis.

TIP

Today's users of smartphones might not realize they are using a very appropriate term when they talk about "apps," a term that technically describing the software system they're using to interface.

Telecommunication has become an extremely competitive environment with multiple vendors, carriers, and service providers. Due to the explosion of telecommunication technology and network expansions, a major trend of network communications is toward a more open inter-network of voice, video, data, and multimedia services in the Internet environment, which drives costs down even further.

A major trend is using the Internet and its technology to interconnect global enterprises and networks, especially enterprises seeking total connectivity among multiple locations with multiple local area networks. This allows easy and secure access among business partners and even the enterprise's customers. With this interconnectivity among business stakeholders, an enterprise can offer electronic collaboration, e-commerce, and other e-business systems, yielding smooth, fast, and efficient methods of business activity. **E-Commerce** is key for today's business model. It provides electronic business between customers and suppliers with little or no human interface.

COMPONENTS OF TELECOMMUNICATIONS AND NETWORKS

Interfacing with a computer requires an input. In a telecommunication system, the most common method of transmitting information is called **analog format**. This format is similar to the physical events that occur when you speak. The modulation and tones of your voice are reflected in highs and lows of pressure waves. By converting pressure waves into electronic waves, these modulated tones can be transmitted on telecommunication media.

However, there is a dilemma. A computer requires digital information, and telecommunication devices require analog signals. The two don't work very well together without assistance. This is where a necessary hardware/software interface comes into place. A device known as a **modulator-demodulator (modem)** takes digital signals (1s and 0s) and converts them into an analog signal that can be sent over telecommunication channels. Furthermore, that modulated signal can be converted from the analog signal to a digital format easily used by the computer.

Telecommunication Media

Telecommunication media make up the variety of channels by which the analog (and now digital) signals are transmitted. The most commonly used physical media include twisted pair, coaxial cable, and fiber optic cables.

- **Twisted pair cables** are often referred to as telephone wires, because they were widely used before the Internet as the media for household telephones. They were the most widely used cable system before advancements in media technologies occurred.

- **Coaxial cables** are similar to the twisted pair in usage. However, instead of twisting the wires together, coaxial cables have a center copper wire wrapped in insulation and allow a higher frequency bandwidth.

- **Fiber optic cables** consist of a hair-thin fiber made of glass material. Instead of electronic signals, very small pulses of light are transmitted in the fiber and can be refracted along the path of the fiber. This allows multiple light beams to travel on the same fiber, which creates a channel for multiple signals to be transmitted at an increased speed. Other advantages of fiber optics are less electronic interference from natural phenomena and a lower error rate.

TIP

The biggest limitation of the twisted pair and the coaxial cable is that only one signal can pass through the cable at one time.

Wireless technologies make up the nonphysical media that allow communication between devices. These technologies rely on radio waves, microwaves, infrared light, and other lighted methods of energy transfer. Wireless technologies include terrestrial microwave, satellites, cellular systems, and Bluetooth.

- **Terrestrial microwave systems** transmit radio signals at very high frequencies. Most often, these have a line-of-sight path where the signals are passed through microwave relay stations and are usually seen on top of hills, towers, and mountain peaks. These are very popular for long-distance and metropolitan area networks.

- **Satellites** also use microwave energy as their telecommunication medium. They orbit the Earth in stationary zones to enable communication between large volume voice and data centers.

- **Cellular technology** uses numerous radio signals and technologies as a transmission medium. The technology uses small, integrated geographic areas called cells to pass signals. Because they are small in scope, as the user moves between cells the integrated signal is coordinated and controlled from one cell to another by the service provider. This allows the user to have mobility in usage as long as the coordinated and controlled cells are within the area of the user. This technology is becoming more and more popular because of the ability of users to have access to communications and data almost anywhere services are available.

- **Bluetooth technology** is another wireless technology that allows a very short-range signal to be used to interface with computers and other devices.

Because of the higher demand on telecommunications, one of the greatest concerns is the use of bandwidth. **Bandwidth** is the frequency range allowed in a communication channel. It is determined by physical properties and also distances allowed. It is also the determining factor in how fast data and the signals can be transferred. The speed and capacity of data transmission is typically measured in bits (1s and 0s) per second, or bps. As the usage goes up, the amount of bandwidth being used is also being depleted.

COMPUTER INFORMATION SYSTEMS SECURITY

Because of the expanded use of the Internet, e-mail, and general e-commerce, a new generation of fraud and theft has emerged. One of the most common issues facing the average person is identity theft. Savvy computer users identify means to "hack," or invade, business computers where sensitive identity and financial information of businesses and individuals reside. Because they gain access, they can then use credit card or social security information to purchase goods online. Interestingly, these hackers often obtain goods and services without any means to identify the source of who, where, and how they obtained the access.

Viruses such as a **distributed denial-of-service** (**DDOS**) attack impede the use of business websites by creating thousands of "phantom" users. After the phantom users are created, they attack a business's website bandwidth by denying access to customers. This is similar to thousands of people trying to crowd through a door at one time. One method of determining whether a human is really interacting with a system is through the use of Completely Automated Public Turing test to tell Computers and Humans Apart, better known as **CAPTCHA**. CAPTCHA requires a human to look at a picture and identify the characters.

The best network security is human. While automatic systems are in place and complex algorithms may try to invade computers, the best defense mechanism is the user, because humans have random uniqueness and complexity.

Network security is a very serious issue in the growth of the Internet and the globally connected world. Each time you open a website, an e-mail containing **spam** (unsolicited, unwanted email), or any item from a network that is unfamiliar, users should be aware of the potential hazards and security breaches that are possible.

TIP

Usernames and passwords, both generated by people, create two different patterns necessary for network access.

TOPOLOGY AND PROTOCOLS

Many types of telecommunication networks serve enterprises; however, there are three basic types of networks. The identity of each is mostly determined by the geographic area it operates within.

- A **local area network** (**LAN**) allows computer users to connect and share information within a building or small geographic area.

- Expanding geographically, **metropolitan area networks** (**MANs**) operate in a geographic area taking up several blocks to an entire city. MANs are used in corporations where campuses might be in several locations within a city.

- Networks that cover a large geographic area are known as **wide area networks** (**WANs**). These networks allow enterprises to operate in large cities, regions, or even on a global scale.

Within a network environment, enterprises often need to centralize their data for operation, creating a business environment where information is easily controlled and readily shared among employees. This environment has allowed network architecture to deliver what is known as a **client/server network**. Within this environment, clients (PCs or workstations) have access to applications and data provided by a server (a higher-capacity, higher-speed computing system).

Network topology is the overall shape of a network in a diagram. Fundamentally, there are three basic topologies of a network:

- The **ring network** ties the local processors in a ring on a semi-equal basis.

- The **star network** ties end users to a central computer.

- The **bus network** ties the processors that share the same bus system or communication channel. *Figure 1* illustrates the basic topologies:

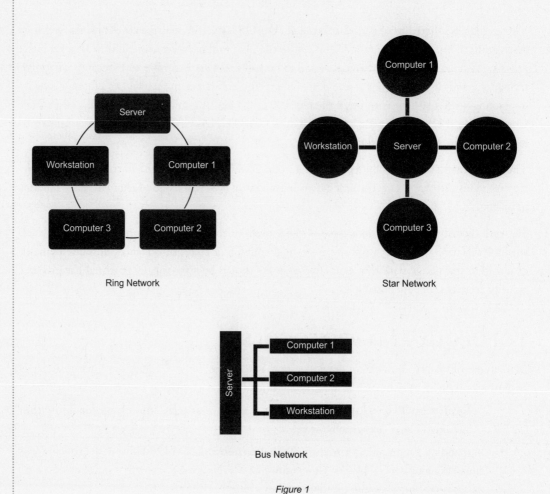

Ring Network

Star Network

Bus Network

Figure 1

Networks in the past had a very diverse system of communicating. Depending upon the manufacturer and the type of network, the interfaces between computers and networks were quite unique and serviced only those who had similar languages for communication. Toward the end of the twentieth century, a set of standards were created regarding how networks transmit data and where the data are formatted, transmitted, secured, and received. Known as **protocol**, these rules were created to implement a standard whereby dissimilar manufacturers and networks could easily "handshake" across the dissimilarity to send messages and data. Examples include **Transmission Control Protocol/Internet Protocol** (**TCP/IP**), where the Internet rules of data transmission are standardized, and Simple Mail Transfer Protocol (SMTP), used in the transmission of e-mail. We are now seeing expansions of other protocols, such as **Voice over Internet Protocol** (**VoIP**), which allows voice data to be transmitted across the Internet connections.

BUSINESS INFORMATION SYSTEMS

ELECTRONIC COMMERCE

With the expansion of the Internet and the explosive growth of business and personal use on the Internet, the concept of **e-commerce**, or electronic commerce, has become more popular in today's business. E-commerce consists of developing, marketing, selling, delivering, servicing, and paying for products and services entirely online.

In years past, the most common method of exchanging goods and services was through the brick-and-mortar business, the model where the goods and services are strictly sold through a storefront where the customer had to physically enter the "brick-and-mortar" building. As businesses came to value the use and marketing potential of the Internet, many adopted a growth strategy where they could market their products outside their geographical operating areas. The business model is called **clicks-and-bricks**, where the business operates storefronts in physical buildings but also has an online presence. Businesses such as Amazon have provided consumers with a concept of acquiring goods without any storefront, where the exchange happens totally online through the company's website. This business model is known as **click-only**.

E-commerce was initially rejected due to consumer fear of communicating personal and business credit information across unfamiliar channels. Because of this initial rejection, e-commerce needed to create and implement procedures to protect its customer credit information. The minimum requirements e-commerce needed to implement were access control and security, personalization and profiling, search management and optimization, content management, catalog management, secured payment options and systems, workflow management processes, event notification, and collaboration of the trade. As these processes and procedures were implemented, comfort level of consumers and businesses greatly increased. This comfort provided the catalyst that enabled e-commerce to expand globally and grow exponentially in use. Businesses are no longer inhibited by geographic limitations; business owners now have the world to sell their goods and services to.

The expansion of **intranets** (company internal-use networks) and **extranets** (external-use networks) allowed greater connectivity of businesses to the World Wide Web. Because of the greater connectivity, e-commerce technology provided the platform for three primary e-commerce business strategies: business-to-consumer (B2C), business-to-business (B2B), and consumer-to-consumer (C2C).

- **B2C businesses** sell their goods and services mostly through e-commerce websites to the general population for personal consumption. They develop attractive websites that contain catalogs full of multimedia, an interactive method for shopping and order processing, secure payment methods, and the ability to interact with customer support. Successful B2C businesses maintain customer satisfaction and loyalty by providing customers greater selection and value, performance and service efficiency, incentives, personal attention, security, and reliability. The competitive advantage of B2C businesses is that exposure to global markets, coupled with an ability to leverage other marketing processes, is significant in a growing global economy.

- **B2B businesses** sell their goods and services mostly through e-commerce websites to other businesses. They are very similar to the B2C business models; however, many of these businesses utilize a system known as **Electronic Data Interchange** (**EDI**). EDI is a means by which business transactions are transmitted by network links between the businesses in a standardized electronic format. A great example of this is when Ford Motor Company is building one of its automobiles. Ford needs access to multiple parts vendors in order to build the automobile. As the inventory of a part is depleted, the computer system automatically utilizes the EDI to order the part from the vendor. The B2B system efficiently allows transactions to occur automatically.

- In **C2C businesses**, consumers interface with a website to purchase goods and services from other consumers. The C2C business facilitates the transaction by taking a percentage of the total sale. Ideal examples are the transactions that occur on popular websites like eBay and Etsy.

TYPES OF INFORMATION SYSTEMS

The structure of the Information System in business is designed around the needs of an organization. Fundamentally, there are three categories of information systems in an organization. Let's explore each of them.

Transaction Processing and Reporting Systems

These systems are designed in order to meet the needs of the day-to-day operational level of business. For example, the Transaction Processing System processes business transactions and creates reports for the enterprise. Most often, this system helps maintain the operational processes of business, including recordkeeping, data storage, and data retrieval. This level of interactivity is typically the fastest and most accurate because most of the data input is highly structured at this level. The main function of **management reporting systems** is to provide printed or electronic reports to lower- and middle-level managers and to give them inquiry capabilities in order to help sustain operations and managerial control of the business.

Management Information Systems

Management information systems assist lower-level managers with decisions and problem solving. Within the system, data are semistructured and often collaborated and combined transactional data used for analysis. Most often, this level of information is tactical in nature, which provides decisional information in support of the overall strategy of the business.

Decision Support Systems

Decision support systems (**DSS**) are the highest level of information systems providing an unstructured/semistructured approach to decision making. At this level, flexibility is necessary to enable change and to enable strategic developments. Most often at this level, the reports are *ad hoc* in nature, are less structured than the MIS level, and provide fact-based content that executives use in support of strategic evaluations. *Figure 2* illustrates how information systems are categorized:

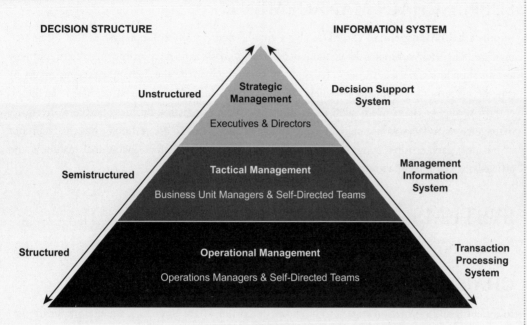

Figure 2

ENTERPRISE RESOURCE PLANNING

Enterprise Resource Planning (ERP) is a cross-functional, organization-wide information system. Most often, this software system consists of "modules" that support the internal business processes of an enterprise or firm by providing a real-time view of the business and its core processes. For example, the view may be of production, order processing, sales and inventory, shipping status, and financial and human resource requirements. ERP is the most robust information system, and it is often the vital backbone of the enterprise. Because of its dynamic cross-functionality, it helps the firm achieve both efficient and effective goals by being responsive to the informational needs in a very accessible manner.

CUSTOMER RELATIONSHIP MANAGEMENT

Customer relationship management (CRM) is a cross-functional information system that automates and integrates the customer relationships of an enterprise. It enhances the strategies, processes, and information systems an organization uses to build and maintain relationships with its current and prospective users. By using information systems to facilitate sales processes and data, marketing programs, and the customer interface, it provides a consistent interactive presence for the customer.

As the use of information systems grows, many businesses are realizing the importance of the customer and are developing new ways in which they can leverage CRMs to be more customer-focused. Most of the applications CRMs are providing include contact and account management, sales, marketing, order fulfillment, customer service and support, retention and loyalty management, and any other program that will enhance the relationship between the enterprise and the customer. The primary goal of a CRM is helping the enterprise acquire, enhance, and retain profitable relationships with its customers.

SUPPLY CHAIN MANAGEMENT

Supply Chain Management (SCM) is also a cross-functional information system that integrates, manages, and often automates the network of business processes and relationships between a company and its suppliers and its customers. It helps the company manage the demand of its customers by integrating responses from the suppliers. The design of the SCM is crucial because it facilitates enterprise supply chain needs such as demand forecasting, logistics, business partners, inventory management, and warehouse management. The goal of SCM is to use technology as the facilitator of business partnerships along the supply chain to improve enterprise operational readiness and efficiencies in a full collaborative environment.

SYSTEMS ANALYSIS AND DESIGN

CHARACTERISTICS OF A SYSTEM

In order for an information system to be successful, it must have three fundamental implications:

1. The system must be designed to accomplish a defined and predetermined objective.
2. The system must have interdependency and collaboration among its components.
3. The strategic objective must have higher priority over the system than the subsets of the system.

Systems must have five general characteristics in order to function in a complete and successful manner.

1. *Organization.* Organization is valuable to the system because the system needs consistency. Structure and order are necessary to achieve organization.
2. *Interaction.* Interaction is necessary for system success. If the components of the system do not collaborate or function with the other components, failure is almost a certainty.
3. *Central Objective.* It is important for all system components to have a common purpose and for the system users to have a common goal. This ensures that all facets of the objective are understood and the team collaborates for the same end result.
4. *Interdependency.* Each part of the organization and the system must be able to rely on the other parts of the organization. This implies a coordinated effort that enhances the dependency of one part of the system upon the other.
5. *Integration.* This is the holism of the system. Most often, integration is achieved when the system ties all the unique and collaborated parts together as a single functioning unit.

The **systems approach** is a problem-solving methodology most often used in information systems development. It uses a systems orientation to define problems, opportunities, and needs in order to develop an appropriate, feasible solution. The process involves five sequential steps that assist in systems development:

1. Understand and define the problem or opportunity with as much detail as possible.
2. Develop and evaluate alternative systems and solutions.
3. Select the system that meets the need the best.
4. Design the solution.

5. Implement and evaluate the successes and failures of the system in order to refine the system in place.

As these systems are created, it is important to evaluate all avenues with a paradigm-shift mentality—that is, keep an open mind for opportunities that are in a dynamic business environment.

SYSTEMS ARCHITECTURE

Systems architecture is the blueprint, the conceptual design, or the model created to provide a visual representation of the proposed/planned system. It has three primary components.

- The first component is the **technology platform**. The technology platform provides a set of multiple items that integrate the hardware, the software, and the network items associated with "what is available and what is needed" for the system to be complete.

- The second component is the **data resources**. Data that are operational and specialized are often a vital component of a business and its ability to function properly. Data resources are often found internally and externally to the enterprise; however, the necessity of decision support and business processes is important to the overall system. These are the "eyes and ears" of an information system.

- The final component is **applications architecture**. Business information systems are designed today to host a variety of business applications, also known as the portfolio. It is essential that the applications architecture supports each component in a cross-functional means. Thus, applications architecture facilitates and coordinates the integration of the software systems.

SYSTEMS DEVELOPMENT LIFE CYCLE

In the systems approach for modeling information systems, one of the most prevalent methods to create an organizational system is the use of a multistep, iterative process known as the **systems development life cycle** (SDLC). Within this model, interdependency and highly relational activities can actually overlap and mingle with each other. There may be activities that are refined and repeated to obtain optimum results as well.

The SDLC occurs in five interactive stages: investigation, analysis, design, implementation, and maintenance.

Investigation Stage

The **investigation stage** starts the systems development process. The function of this stage is to ask questions and, most important, to address the question of feasibility. For example: "Is there a business opportunity?" "What are the priorities of the business?" "Will this system address our business priorities?" Organizations conduct feasibility studies on operational, economic, technical, and human factors and legal/political feasibility.

Analysis Stage

The second stage in the SDLC is the **analysis stage,** which includes activities analyzing "who" needs the information—such as employees, customers, and other business stakeholders. It also defines the functional requirements that meet the priorities of the business and all stakeholders. It would also provide the logical models of the *current* system and define the specifications of all the associated systems architecture and whether or not it would satisfy the business needs of the proposed system.

Design Stage

The third stage in the SDLC is the **design stage**. This stage creates the minimum specifications of the proposed system, including the processes, the hardware, software, and the integrated network. In this stage, the *new* system would be developed.

Implementation Stage

The fourth stage of the SDLC is the **implementation stage**, where the hardware and software are acquired and implemented. This stage also requires that the hardware, software, and network undergo testing to ensure they are operational. There are numerous implementation methods; however, at this stage, it is crucial that change management is established to evaluate the effects on end users. Finally, this is the stage where the conversion to the new system takes place.

Maintenance Stage

The final stage of the SDLC is the **maintenance stage**. This stage is the post-implementation stage where the processes and equipment are refined and maintained. This is the costliest stage because it has the longest period of activity. Furthermore, it is at this stage where consistent refining and evaluations occur over that longer period.

Figure 3 provides an illustration showing how each of these activities interacts and flows.

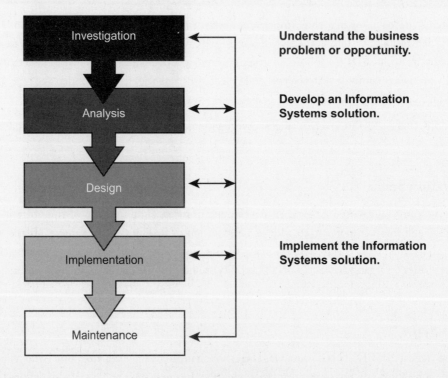

Figure 3

MANAGING DATA RESOURCES

Data are as vital an organizational resource as any other business asset. In today's business environment, it would be extremely difficult to survive and succeed without quality data for internal operations and external customer interface needs. Because of this multifaceted need, organizations and their managers should consider **data resource management** a vital part of the business. Data resource management is an activity where information technology incorporates database management, data warehousing, and other tasks that allow the organization to meet the informational needs of the enterprise. It includes all the information technology and software tools necessary for managing the organization's resources.

During the early years of databases, individual files were kept in a specialized file approach where the entire file was maintained, rather than filed by a record. This was too cumbersome, costly, and inflexible and highly inefficient for accessing data. As the database management approach evolved, it solved many of the file processing system shortfalls.

DATA MODELS

Data modeling is an essential part of the database management approach. It defines the elements of the data, how they are identified, and the logical relationships it also has among the other elements. Relationships can be structured for the business process and integrated through logical frameworks, or **schema**, which provide an overall view of each relationship within the databases and whether or not it makes logical sense. As we create a logic design of the database, there must be a place to store this information. The **physical design** determines where the data are stored and where they are accessed.

When creating a database model, it is important to understand the elements of the data. The most fundamental and basic logic element is the **character**, which can be a letter of the alphabet, a number, or a simple symbol. When several characters are combined, they create the next highest element that typically contains a group of characters. This single item, or group of characters contained in a single area, is called the **field**. As a field is formulated, a commonality should be evident. The common characteristic of the data within the common field is known as the **attribute**. Combining the characters within the field and having an attribute creates an entity, which is an object, person, place, or event. When the fields are combined collectively, they become a **record**. When creating a record in today's database management system, it is necessary to create an identifier, called a **primary key** that gives uniqueness to that record.

Once records are designed, they can be combined with other records that have similar structure and equivalent attributes to create what is known as a **file**. A file is merely a group of related records that have been combined because of their similarity and use. Then, groups of files are collected for storage. When an integrated collection of logically related elements is created, it forms a **database**.

> **TIP**
>
> Examples of primary keys include a driver's license number, a social security number, or an account number. It is something unique and nonduplicable in other records.

DATABASE MANAGEMENT SYSTEMS

While databases are created, a management system provides users with an easy-to-use and efficient way to extract information. A **database management system** (**DBMS**) is a software tool used for creating, maintaining, and using databases in an organization for the purposes of extracting data, manipulating data, and creating information from that data. There are five fundamental database structures in use today: the hierarchical, network, relational, object-oriented, and multidimensional models.

1. In the early years of DBMS packaging, the **hierarchical structure** was the most common. The relationships were developed and combined in a manner similar to a tree or hierarchy. The problem with this structure was that it always represented a "one-to-many" structure because the relationship was built so that a set of multiple records related only to the one above it.

2. A more complex data structure is the **network DBMS model**. It allows relationships to be built on a "many-to-many" relationship. In other words, it allows access through one or more paths of relational connectivity.

3. The most commonly used DBMS model today is the **relational model**. This DBMS is built by using what is known as two-dimensional tables, or flat files. With each flat file, the primary key represents the unique attribute of each record. Then, as each flat file is developed, it can have a relationship with another flat file by connecting the primary keys of each table. Because of the nature of each flat file, the database can be maintained and edited with a mere correction of that particular flat file. This is advantageous comparative to other DBMS structures.

4. The **object-oriented DBMS** model is a newer generation of DBMS. The "object" consists of descriptive data values that describe the attributes of entities. This is known also as data encapsulation. This type of structure is most commonly used with much more complex data types, such as graphics, video, audio, and other web-based data.

5. The **multidimensional DBMS** model is similar to the relational model; however, the data can be structured into data cubes that have more than two dimensions. This allows for deeper data analysis on a three-dimensional scale. For example, a single cell could show data elements such as total sales, by region, for a specific channel. This structure, which is becoming very popular for analysts, supports online analytical processing (OLAP).

DATA QUERY AND UPDATE

Data are inherently static; they don't change until they are acted upon. However, as databases evolve, the conditions for dynamic abilities are increasing rapidly. For example, inventory availability for an online product might show online as having many available, yet numerous customers have depleted the inventory of the product to an actual count of zero. If the database retains the numerical value (static) of that field and shows many products available, then there will be many customers upset that their order is not available. Because of scenarios like this, update mechanisms in the DBMS system must have efficient and easy methods of updating data through queries and updates.

Database interrogation allows end users to query for information from the DBMS. The query language enables the user to interface with the data and obtain nearly immediate responses under *ad hoc* requests. Other queries that are generated on a regular basis are typically captured through report generators.

The most common query language used to interface and query the DBMS is **Structured Query Language** (SQL)—the language to "ask a question." For example, a common and basic form of SQL is: SELECT…FROM…WHERE, which allows the user to define the table to be selected, the files or tables to be retrieved, and the conditions where filters should extract and limit the selected data for query. In addition to the SELECT…FROM… WHERE statement, it is highly beneficial that a user understands and uses Boolean logic within an SQL statement. This logic allows the user to interface and collect *only* the desired output of data using one of three operators: AND, OR, and NOT.

Database maintenance is the activity of keeping a database up to date by adding, deleting, or changing data within it. This is where data become more dynamic. By interfacing with Transaction Processing Systems, the data can be manipulated and changed during business transactions. Furthermore, when data appear to have redundancy and duplication, databases should be scrutinized for accuracy.

Organizations depend upon easy access, dynamic content, and accuracy of data. With the DBMS in place, organizations can utilize the information to analyze and report information that is useful for decision making at all levels in the organization.

BUSINESS DECISION MAKING

Good business decisions are delivered from solid and proven processes. The two primary issues a decision should consider are (1) business impact and (2) recovery time in case the decision is costly. The higher the business impact, the more immediate a decision should be and the closer it should be analyzed. If it has a lower impact, the decision should be scrutinized for disposal.

Figure 4 is a model of business decisions based upon impact and recovery time.

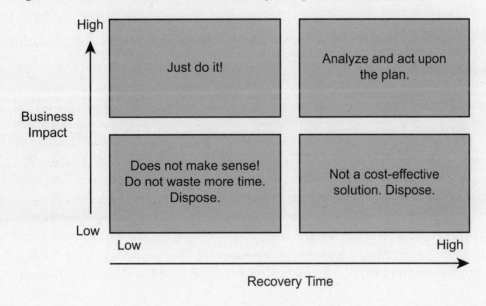

Figure 4

A rational decision-making model used to rationalize decisions associated with information systems contains eight steps:

1. Identify the problem.
2. Establish the decision criteria.
3. Weigh the decision criteria.
4. Generate alternatives.
5. Evaluate the alternatives.
6. Choose the best alternative.
7. Implement the decision.
8. Evaluate the decision.

Each step defines an objective. However, as each objective is achieved, there may be a call of action to stop depending upon the results of each step. Then, as you finalize Step 8 in the decision-making model, return to Step 1. Why? Because this is a model of perpetuation—it assists an organization in maintaining competitive advantage through the use of information systems. The value of the decision helps executives to achieve greater strategic results.

KNOWLEDGE MANAGEMENT

As an organization obtains more and more data, the data within the organization become extremely valuable, as they enable managers and executives to retrieve prior decision information and allow the organization to freely access important shared information. The means of using information technology to gather, organize, disburse, control, and share knowledge within an organization's intranet is called a **knowledge management system**. Strategies, corporate culture and policies, best practices, business solutions, technology management, and prior analysis are stored for access within that knowledge management system. Most often, the knowledge accessed is at the project, team, business unit, and even the enterprise levels of the company.

DATA WAREHOUSING

A physical warehouse is a place where goods from numerous locations are collected and housed. Goods are stored in the warehouse until there is a need for those goods to be shipped to their next destination. This is the concept of warehousing data as well. In **data warehousing**, data derived from various internal and operational locations and external data locations are stored in a central location. Most often, this information has been extracted (cleaned), transformed, and loaded so it can be used by managers, executives, and other professionals for the purpose of data mining, online analytical processing (OLAP), and other forms of analysis. Business intelligence, operational intelligence, marketing intelligence, and other intelligence needs can be extracted from this data center for decisional support. In these data repositories, a more useful form of data called **metadata** takes form. Simply put, metadata define the data in the data warehouse. For example, when an analyst is seeking "profit" as a data point, it is not a data point in itself; it is dependent upon other variable data points. We know that "profit" is the result of revenue minus cost of goods sold. Therefore, the data warehouse combines the data from revenue and cost of goods sold to retrieve the metadata data point of "profit."

DATA MINING

Data mining is the concept of discovering "nuggets" of information yet to be revealed or discovered. By utilizing data warehouses, most analysts that data mine seek patterns and trends in historical data to discover something that can be strategic in nature for the organization. Analysts use pattern recognition software, statistical analysis software, and other unique methods of capturing that "nugget" in the vast field of data.

More and more, data mining is becoming a valuable staple in corporate organizations. Because analysis is becoming more prevalent, executives can scrutinize the most miniscule strengths and weakness within their own organizations and seek out the threats of the competition. This is known as a **SWOT (strengths, weaknesses, opportunities, and threats) analysis**. Data mining is an excellent method of capturing the most effective means of developing an organizational competitive advantage. In turn, that competitive advantage can be exploited for taking customer relationships to the next level.

PROJECT MANAGEMENT

Information systems implementation requires a human interface to manage the overall process of completing a task. Therefore, an organization must understand the concept of what a project is. A **project** is any group of activities with a clear objective and a defined beginning and end. Projects also all contain limitations and constraints.

The project management approach to implementation contains five identifiable phases:

1. *Initiating and defining* is the phase where the goals are established and the objectives are defined. In addition, resources must be secured and a cost/benefit study for feasibility must be completed.

2. *Planning* identifies the sequence of activities and the "critical paths." Critical paths are those places in a plan where the most time is engaged on a project to complete tasks on schedule. It also accounts for time and resource allocation for completing the project. In the planning phase, the project plan is written in detail.

3. *Executing* begins by committing resources to specific tasks and evaluating whether or not additional resources should be acquired. Here, the actual project work begins.

4. The *controlling* phase evaluates and creates reporting obligations and reporting tools. As the reports are created, progress is evaluated and compared with baseline objectives. If there is any disparity between the progress and baseline, intervention may take place.

5. At the final *closing* phase, all deliverables have been installed and tested. All obligations are completed, and all resources are released. At this point, the stakeholders have had a meeting to discuss the closure and the final report is delivered.

MIS AND THE ORGANIZATION

In the **business growth cycle**, a business goes through four cycles of growth:

1. The **introductory phase**, where businesses may or may not see growth dependent upon information and the market.

2. If good decisions are made in the introductory phase, it enters the phase of rapid growth, known as the **growth phase**.

3. As people become familiar with the business, growth apexes, then plateaus, and begins a small decrease. This is known as the **maturity phase**.

4. Finally, business sees a steady decline. This is known as the **decline phase**.

Each phase of business growth has its challenges. With a solid MIS in place, as the business enters the maturity phase, information can be leveraged to maintain competitive advantage for the organization in the marketplace.

ORGANIZATION OF MIS

If you look back at *Figure 2*, (see page 359) you can see that organizations define information systems in correlation to the needs based upon the level and structure of decision-making. MIS needs can be based upon that model as well. The organization of MIS is based upon the level and structure of management decision-making. Levels of management are still used, though the dissemination of information is very dynamic in nature.

Information technology has three distinct decision-making levels. Let's look at each in more depth.

Strategic Management

Most often, this level consists of the board of directors and the executives of the organization. Their information needs are typically unstructured and most often are *ad hoc* in nature. Within this management level, organizations create **executive information systems (EIS)**, which usually contain management information system and the decision support system information. Many EIS systems also contain what is known as a dashboard: a real-time interface on business metrics. Usually, these metrics are tailored for the unique needs of the executive.

Tactical Management

This level contains directors and teams that create short-, medium-, and long-term plans that direct the energy of the firm toward strategic initiatives. At this level, organizations often use two types of information systems: the DSS (decision support system) and the MIS. The DSS supports modeling and analytical routines to capture data for decision making at the tactical level for the longer-term decisions. Managers use the MIS to enable mechanisms from the operational data to assist them in decision-making processes on a more short-term need.

Operational Management

This level of management typically initiates short-term plans that help achieve operational tasks and objectives. This is the **transactional reporting** level. Within this level of management, the reporting mechanisms offer very short-term information based upon transactional data. These data are very structured in order to capture business operations on a day-to-day basis. They help front-line managers make daily decisions on the performance of the organization.

RELATIONSHIP OF MIS TO THE ENTERPRISE

The relationship of MIS to the enterprise is a two-way relationship. They influence each other and need each other to successfully operate. The influence of the organization upon the MIS can be seen through corporate culture, the organization's structure, the business processes, the business environment, the influential internal and external politics, and management decisions. For example, organizations that utilize MIS to its fullest capability tend to have more data-driven decision-making processes in place, rather than decisions made from human "hunches." They depend upon the data and have great influence on what data are stored.

Similar to information systems, organizations have a hierarchical structure, accountability for decision-making, rules and routines, and a need to be efficient and effective. No wonder the need for identifying the scope of implementing an information system is so crucial and strategic. It embodies the organization in both intangible benefits and tangible outcomes.

THE VALUE OF THE MIS FUNCTION

The most valuable impact of the MIS function to an organization is its economic impact. The MIS changes and influences the cost of capital and reduces decisional errors of management. It influences the cost, quality, and speed of delivering information. It also reduces the amount of manpower required to deliver information. Furthermore, it reduces transaction costs, by decreasing errors and human interface and allows greater market operability through e-commerce.

In addition, MIS allows businesses to take advantage of Porter's five forces:

1. *Rivalry among competitors:* As a business evaluates its own strategy and those of the competitors, it can take advantage of its competitive advantage.

2. *Threats of new market entrants:* Because of MIS, businesses can exploit the weaknesses of the new entrant and increase customer value propositions of the organization through knowledge.

3. *Threats of substitutes:* Business leaders should understand that its competitive advantage is not permanent. As substitutes arise, the MIS should enable an organization to understand how to counter and modify its business to meet the demands of the customer in order to make the substitute irrelevant.

4. *Customer influence:* Through the CRM, organizations should be able to develop relationships with customers, become intimate with customer needs, and meet the demands of the changing customer.

5. *Supplier influence:* Through SCM, organizations should have solid communication processes

and protocols that allow a fully integrated supply chain. By utilizing the SCM, suppliers have a better understanding of the organizational need and can strategically influence the needs of the organization.

MIS ISSUES

MIS has advantages. However, it does have issues that need to be closely guarded and protected: security (both personal and corporate-wide); ethics, especially in a global environment in which the ethical behavior of one society clashes with another; privacy and how enterprises respond to personal identity protection; and issues facing companies that operate in the global network.

SECURITY

Security management of MIS is a rapidly growing requirement in today's global organization. It is the function of security management to ensure an organization is minimizing the risks associated with information threats that cause loss of data and with information vulnerabilities that allow data breaches to occur. It should also minimize the risks associated with the impact of operations should disaster occur.

The strongest line of defense in securing a network is **biometric**, a human characteristic that provides access control and identification. There are numerous technologies for biometrics available, including face recognition, fingerprint recognition, retina scanning, and other personal identifying methods. However, the most common methods used are personal identifications and passwords.

When these identification and authorization methods are used, data input is then encrypted before transmission. Data **encryption** is the process of taking the input and encoding that data into algorithms that only the authorized parties can decipher. Complex algorithms and layers of encryption are used. What this means is that the encryption doesn't occur just once, but through numerous dynamic encryption algorithms. Some organizations are even using CAPTCHA as a means to ensure that a human interface is trying to access the data, rather than a hacker's algorithm.

Most large organizations that maintain their own e-mail servers and organizations that provide e-mail service utilize a firewall system. The **firewall** may be hardware, software, or a combination of both. Its purpose is to catch and block unwanted e-mails and e-mails that are deemed to have suspicious intent.

Another great concern in the security of data is disaster preparedness. **Disaster controls** are the processes and measures that reduce the risk of damage, whether natural or man-made, on the information systems and their operational abilities. These controls are designed to initiate a quicker and more effective recovery. Often, information systems have redundancy systems that enable data to be quickly restored through what is known as backup systems. These systems have layers of redundancy and are prioritized and maintained based upon the organization's critical needs.

ETHICS

Organizational culture and ethics define the norms of what is right or wrong in business interactivity. Yet information systems also virtually bring the world to your organization. While the organization's ethics may be of higher standards, the world that interacts with your information system may not have the same values and ethics. This makes it necessary to have an information system "police force" protecting your network activities. **Network security** is a means of protecting information systems through policies and procedures. The security should be designed to curb any unauthorized access and any misuse of the computer system internally and to ensure network-accessible resources are managed properly.

The World Wide Web has become a haven for professional computer crimes that make network security necessary. Some crimes involve hacking or malicious behavior. The term *hacker* has multiple meanings. On the positive side, hackers are enthusiastic computer programmers who like to expand their knowledge of programming languages and computer systems. Other types of hackers appreciate the challenge of circumventing computer and network security systems. In general, hackers break into computers for fun, such as thrill-seeker hackers, or for work purposes, such as white-hat hackers hired to expose computer system weaknesses.

In contrast, *crackers* break into systems for malicious purposes. Crackers may gather information for monetary gain, steal credit information, destroy data, or attempt to bring extensive harm to multitudes of people, as cyberterrorists do. However, protecting the safety of a computer system can be easily accomplished with a number of security tools:

- **Antivirus software:** programs that scan a computer's hard disk and memory to identify and destroy viruses
- **Firewall:** system of hardware and/or software that shields a computer or network from intruders by analyzing, controlling, and filtering incoming and outgoing packets
- **Password:** unique set of symbols, words, or codes used for restricting access to a computer or network
- **Biometrics:** use of physical attributes like fingerprints, voice, face, or eyes to confirm an individual's identity
- **Encryption:** process of scrambling or hiding data into an unreadable form to prevent unauthorized access

Not only is computer security important for individuals but also for businesses and government agencies. With so many organizations going paperless, the security of electronic databases is vital.

Hacking involves numerous activities; the most common are a breach of network security systems to access corporate or personal information illegally. Theft is also a common activity, where personal and sensitive information may be stolen—even intellectual property, such as video games, software, movies, and music. Hacking has become more than just a nuisance in today's growing networks; it is extremely dangerous if left unchecked.

One of the activities hackers employ is the use of malicious software and Trojan software. While someone is encouraged to visit a website, that website has a code designed by the hackers to deploy a computer virus onto the user's computer. A **computer virus** is a complex computer code that embeds itself within the computer memory and/or the operating system to disrupt the operation or to steal valuable personal information. **Antivirus software** is a program designed to search, detect, remove, and prevent virus invasions on computer systems. Most often, antivirus software detects and removes virus invasions before they are allowed to penetrate the system. Good network security and human awareness are the most effective antivirus mechanisms to prevent unwanted activity.

PRIVACY

Because of the issues associated with networking, corporate and individual privacy is of great concern. Most organizations utilize personal identifications and passwords, along with strict personal use policies and authorization mechanisms on how the information system can be used by employees within the organization. **Personal use policies** define how the computer can be used on the network and what activities are permitted.

GLOBAL ISSUES

While the issues of war and terrorism generate the visuals of injury and death, a more threatening issue called **cyberwarfare** looms. Cyberwarfare is the actions by countries and terrorist groups that aim to penetrate, disrupt, and potentially cause damage to network systems and/or computers. For many years, nuclear proliferation was the greatest global threat. It is now cyberwarfare. Why? Networks are now controlling electric grids, nuclear power plants, drones, stock markets, hospital records, and many other applications. It is feasible that any intrusion left unchecked could cause immeasurable damage to a country's information infrastructure and disrupt vital operations. Imagine a total shutdown of the American electric grid: food would spoil from lack of refrigeration, business would not be able to fully function, transportation corridors would be upset, and many other vital uses of electricity would be disrupted. This is why cyberwarfare is a growing global concern of information professionals and leaders of nations.

SUMMING IT UP

- The **binary system** comes from the Indian mathematician Pingala and is based on 0's and 1's. Blaise Pascal invented the **adding machine** in 1642; in 1837 Charles Babbage used it to create the **Analytical Engine**, which incorporated an **arithmetic logic unit** (ALU) **for calculations**, a **control mechanism**, and a **storage system**.

- During World War II, the German military created the **enigma** to send encrypted military messages. Alan Turing expanded Babbage's use of mechanics using electric energy to create a device that deciphered the enigma and birthed the idea of the modern computer.

- The mid-twentieth century saw the birth of the **transistor**, a small silicon device that could replace vacuum tubes to decrease the size of computers. Its development led to the hand-held calculator, through which the integrated circuit arose—developers realized several transistors and components could be "integrated" onto a single device.

- A modern computer system must have four essential hardware components to operate: **input**, a **Central Processing Unit** (made up of the control unit and the arithmetic logic unit), **storage** (made up of primary storage—ROM and RAM—and secondary storage), and **output**.

- Two computer languages were introduced in the 1950s: **FORTRAN** and **COBOL**. The 1970s brought about a more robust use of databases with the languages **C**, **SQL**, and **BASIC**.

- **System software** controls a computer's basic functions and is contained in a computer's ROM. **Programming languages** are a major category of system software and exist in five levels: machine language, assembler language, high-level language, fourth-generation language, and object-oriented language. **Application software** (think "apps") includes programs that perform common information processing jobs: productivity programs for business management, word processing, tabular analytics, graphics programs, web management, e-mail, entertainment programs, and groupware.

- **Telecommunications** has become an extremely competitive environment. Due to technology and network expansions, a trend of network communications is toward a more open inter-network of voice, video, data, and multimedia services in the Internet environment. In a telecommunication system, the most common method of transmitting information is called **analog format**. A **modulator-demodulator** (**modem**) converts digital signals into an analog signal to communicate over telecommunication channels.

- Telecommunication media can be **physical** (twisted pair, coaxial, or fiber optic cables) or **wireless** (terrestrial microwave systems, satellites, Bluetooth).

- There are three basic types of networks: a **local area network** (**LAN**), a **metropolitan area network** (**MAN**), and a **wide area network** (**WAN**).
  - There are three basic topologies, or shapes, of a network: ring, star, and bus.

- The expansion of **intranets** and **extranets** allows businesses to connect to the World Wide Web. There are three primary e-commerce business strategies: **business-to-consumer** (**B2C**), **business-to-business** (**B2B**), and **consumer-to-consumer** (**C2C**).

- There are three basic categories of information systems in an organization: **transaction and reporting systems** (to meet the needs of the day-to-day operational level of business), **management information systems** (to assist lower-level managers with decisions and problem solving), and **decision support systems** (to provide fact-based content executives use in support of strategic evaluations).

- A **rational decision-making model** used to rationalize decisions associated with information systems contains eight steps: **identify** the problem; **establish** the decision criteria; **weigh** the decision criteria; **generate** alternatives; **evaluate** the alternatives; choose the best alternative; **implement** the decision; **evaluate** the decision.

- In order for an information system to be successful, it must be designed to accomplish an objective and have collaboration among its components. Its objective must have the highest priority over the system. Systems must have five general characteristics:

  1. **organization**
  2. **interaction**
  3. **a central objective**
  4. **interdependency**
  5. **integration**

- **Systems architecture** is the blueprint of a proposed system. It has three components: a **technology platform**, **data resources**, and **applications architecture**.

- The **systems development life cycle** is a multistep process by which companies can create an organization system. Its stages are **investigation**, **analysis**, **design**, **implementation**, and **maintenance**.

- Through **data resource management**, information technology incorporates database management, data warehousing, and other tasks that allow the organization to meet the informational needs of the enterprise. **Data modeling** defines the elements of the data, how they are identified, and the logical relationships they also have among the other elements. A **database management system** (**DBMS**) is used to create, maintain, and use databases to extract and manipulate data to find relevant information. There are five fundamental database structures in use today: the hierarchical, network, relational, object-oriented, and multidimensional models. To interface and query the DBMS systems, the most common query language used is **Structured Query Language** (**SQL**).

- In **data warehousing**, data derived from various internal and operational locations and external data locations are stored in a central location. **Metadata** define the data in the data warehouse. Through data warehouses, analysts **data mine** to seek patterns and trends in order to discover something that can be strategic in nature for the organization.

- The project management approach contains five phases: **initiating and defining**, **planning**, **executing**, **controlling**, and **closing**.

- In the **business growth cycle**, a business goes through four cycles of growth: the **introductory** phase, the **growth** phase, the **maturity** phase, and the **decline** phase.

- Information technology has three distinct decision-making levels: **strategic management** (usually a board of directors and executives), **tactical management** (directors and assembled teams making key, long-term business decisions), and **operational management** (groups initiating short-term decisions, usually on a day-to-day basis).

- **Economic impact** is the most valuable impact of the MIS function to an organization. The MIS changes and influences the cost of capital and reduces decisional errors of management, while positively affecting the cost, quality, and speed of delivering information.

- Problems that come along with MIS advancements include major security, ethics, and privacy issues.
  - **Network security** protects a company's information systems via policies and procedures designed to halt unauthorized access and any misuse of the computer system internally.
    - The strongest line of defense in securing a network from intrusion is **biometric**, or entering a system via a human characteristic.
  - **Personal use policies** define how a computer can be used on a company's network and what activities are allowed.
  - **Cyberwarfare** is actions taken to penetrate network systems and/or computers to cause major damage, which is a major and growing global concern.

MANAGEMENT INFORMATION SYSTEMS POST-TEST

Directions: Carefully read each of the following 60 questions. Choose the best answer to each question and fill in the corresponding circle on the answer sheet. The Answer Key and Explanations can be found following this post-test.

1. Who is credited with inventing the analytical engine in 1837?
   - **A.** Blaise Pascal
   - **B.** Charles Babbage
   - **C.** Alan Turing
   - **D.** Gordon Moore

2. What telecommunication media consists of copper wires, which are often referred to as telephone wires?
   - **A.** Twisted pair
   - **B.** Coaxial cables
   - **C.** Modulator cables
   - **D.** USB cables

3. What computer language allowed databases to be managed through relationships of common and unique data identities?
   - **A.** SQL
   - **B.** FORTRAN
   - **C.** BASIC
   - **D.** COBOL

4. Which of the following is a network that is used internally by an organization?
   - **A.** Internet
   - **B.** World Wide Web
   - **C.** Intranet
   - **D.** Extranet

5. What is the purpose of a firewall?
   - **A.** To catch and block unwanted e-mails and e-mails that are deemed as having suspicious intent
   - **B.** To prevent fires from entering a computer room
   - **C.** To create a wall of firing viruses to counter-attack cyberterrorism
   - **D.** To prevent users in an organization from accessing the Internet

6. Why does the decision-making model used to rationalize decisions associated with information systems contain eight steps that are perpetual in nature?
   - **A.** Perpetuation assists an organization in maintaining database security through the use of information systems.
   - **B.** Perpetuation assists an organization in maintaining competitive advantage through the use of information systems.
   - **C.** Perpetuation assists an organization in maintaining decisional content through the use of information systems.
   - **D.** Perpetuation assists an organization in upgrading database systems through the use of information systems.

7. What device converts digital information into analog signals that can be sent over communication channels?
   - **A.** Amplitude modulator
   - **B.** Frequency modulator
   - **C.** Modem
   - **D.** Network interface card

8. What is the language interface used to query DBMS systems in which the language is fundamentally written to "ask a question," such as SELECT...FROM...WHERE?

   A. Database Management System (DBMS)

   B. Database Relational Model (DRM)

   C. Database Query and Update (DQU)

   D. Standard Query Language (SQL)

9. What software was developed in 1959 as a business-specific, calculation software and enabled businesses to store and calculate complex algorithms in a growing data-rich environment?

   A. SQL

   B. FORTRAN

   C. BASIC

   D. COBOL

10. When two businesses interact with each other in an e-commerce environment, transactions are transmitted by network links between the businesses in a standardized electronic format. What is this standardization known as?

    A. Electronic Data Interchange (EDI)

    B. Protocol

    C. e-Market

    D. C2C

11. Why is cyberwarfare a concern in today's world?

    A. Cyberwarfare involves too many high-level employees in playing war games online during business hours.

    B. It is feasible that any intrusion left unchecked could cause immeasurable damage to a country's information infrastructure and disrupt vital operations.

    C. Cyberwarfare between countries enables terrorists to acquire nuclear weapons.

    D. Cyberwarfare causes businesses to gain competitive advantage.

12. What program manages the hardware, software, network, and data resources of a computer system and has the ability to manage network interfaces and how the instructions are interpreted?

    A. Applications control program

    B. Systems development program

    C. Systems management program

    D. Machine language program

13. What telecommunication media has the lowest electronic interference from natural phenomena and a lower error rate than most?

    A. Twisted pair cables

    B. Fiber optic cables

    C. Coaxial cables

    D. USB cables

14. Which virus impedes the use of business websites by creating thousands of "phantom" users that attack a business's website bandwidth by denying access to customers?

    A. Spyware

    B. Trojan virus

    C. Malware

    D. Distributed denial of service

15. What software programs are associated with information processing jobs, productivity programs that allow business management, word processing, tabular analytics, graphics programs, web management, e-mail, and groupware?

    A. Systems software

    B. Machine language software

    C. Operating systems software

    D. Applications software

16. What is/are the most effective antivirus mechanisms to prevent unwanted computer activity?

    A. Network security and firewalls

    B. Network security and human awareness

    C. Antivirus software and firewalls

    D. Antivirus software only

17. Which of the following devices is NOT considered a secondary storage device in a computer?

    A. Optical disk

    B. USB drive

    C. Random Access Memory (RAM)

    D. Hard drive

18. What devices convert the movement or click of a mouse, the touch of a keyboard, the scan of an optical device, or the touch on a touchscreen to electronic data for processing?

    A. Analytical devices

    B. Input devices

    C. Processing devices

    D. Output devices

19. What is the business strategy of having both an online presence and a storefront in a building?

    A. Clicks store

    B. Clicks-and-bricks

    C. Brick-and-mortar

    D. Electronic Data Interchange (EDI)

20. What level in an organization contains directors and teams that create short-, medium-, and long-term plans that direct the energy of the firm toward strategic initiatives?

    A. Organizational level

    B. Tactical management level

    C. Executive management level

    D. Strategic management level

21. What is a method of determining whether interactivity online is really being done by a human?

    A. Spam

    B. CAPTCHA

    C. DDOS

    D. Visual Basic

22. What are the five general characteristics a system must have in order for it to function in a complete and successful manner?

    A. Organization, assessment, central objective, interdependency, and integration

    B. Organization, interaction, customer's opinion, interdependency, and integration

    C. Organization, interaction, central objective, intradependency, and integration

    D. Organization, interaction, central objective, interdependency, and integration

23. When considering Porter's Five Forces and the threat of substitutes, what should business leaders understand about competitive advantage?

    A. It is permanent.

    B. It is not permanent.

    C. It is consistent.

    D. It is useful only during the product life cycle.

24. What is the frequency range allowed in a communication channel that is the determining factor in how fast data and the signals can be transferred?

    A. Bandwidth

    B. Protocol

    C. Microwave

    D. UHF

25. What is an activity where information technology incorporates database management, data warehousing, and other tasks that allow the organization to meet the informational needs of the enterprise?

    A. Data design

    B. Data delivery

    C. Database management system

    D. Data resource management

26. In the systems approach for modeling information systems, one of the most prevalent methods to creating an organizational system is the use of a multistep, iterative process known as
    A. Systems topology process
    B. Systems architecture creation steps
    C. Systems organization process
    D. Systems development life cycle

27. In which of the following systems are strategies, corporate culture and policies, best practices, business solutions, technology management, and prior analysis stored for access?
    A. Transaction processing system
    B. Executive information system
    C. Knowledge management system
    D. Decision support system

28. There are three primary components of systems architecture. Which of the following is not a component?
    A. Technology platform
    B. Applications platform
    C. Business design
    D. Data resources

29. Which of the following consists of developing, marketing, selling, delivering, servicing, and paying for products and services entirely online?
    A. E-marketing
    B. E-commerce
    C. E-mail
    D. Internet Service Provider

30. When considering Porter's Five Forces and supplier influence, what information system is best suited for an organization with built-in communication processes and protocols that allow a fully integrated supply chain?
    A. CRM
    B. MIS
    C. DSS
    D. SCM

31. Which of the following is the term for an object, person, place, or event in a database?
    A. Record
    B. Entity
    C. Character
    D. Field

32. What is the phase in project management that evaluates and creates reporting obligations and reporting tools?
    A. Initiating and defining
    B. Planning
    C. Executing
    D. Controlling

33. What telecommunications technology uses radio signals and small, integrated geographic areas to pass signals?
    A. Terrestrial microwave technology
    B. Fiber optic technology
    C. Cellular technology
    D. Bluetooth technology

34. What performs the calculations and logic functions necessary to execute software instructions in a CPU?
    A. ASCII
    B. BASIC
    C. ENIAC
    D. ALU

35. Which of the following is NOT a biometric method of security?
    A. Face recognition
    B. Fingerprint recognition
    C. Encryption recognition
    D. Retina scanning

36. In the early years of database development, what structural database model in which the data relationships were developed and combined in a manner similar to a tree was most widely used?
    A. Network DBMS model
    B. Relational model
    C. Hierarchical model
    D. Object-oriented DBMS model

37. Which of the following refers to places in a plan where the most time is engaged to complete tasks on schedule?

A. Critical objectives

B. Critical initiatives

C. Critical paths

D. Critical needs

38. What is a complex computer code that embeds itself within the computer memory and/or the operating system to disrupt the operation or to steal valuable personal information?

A. Computer inference

B. Computer disease

C. Computer biometric

D. Computer virus

39. Of the five stages of the Systems Development Life Cycle, at which stage are questions of feasibility asked, such as: "Is there a business opportunity?" "What are the priorities of the business?" "Will this system address our business priorities?"

A. Investigation stage

B. Implementation stage

C. Analysis stage

D. Maintenance stage

40. Which of the following represent the four cycles of growth businesses typically go through?

A. Introductory, growth, maturity, decline

B. Creation, development, plateau, decline

C. Introductory, development, plateau, decline

D. Introductory, growth, plateau, decline

41. Which of the following provides an overall view of each relationship within the databases and determines whether or not the relationship makes logical sense?

A. Data design

B. Data relationship

C. Schema

D. Data logic

42. Which of the following statements is true when considering business needs from a decision-making process?

A. The higher the business impact, the more immediate a decision should be and the closer it should be analyzed.

B. The lower the business impact, the more immediate a decision should be and the closer it should be analyzed.

C. The higher the business impact, the closer a decision should be scrutinized for disposal.

D. The higher the business impact, the more appropriate it is to scrutinize for disposal, allowing a significant time for decision making.

43. Which of the following is the software tool used for creating, maintaining, and using databases in an organization for the purposes of extracting data, manipulating data, and creating information from that data?

A. Database Management System (DBMS)

B. Database Relational Model (DRM)

C. Database Query and Update (DQU)

D. Standard Query Language (SQL)

44. Which of the following are the two most commonly used methods of biometric entry used by organizations?

A. Personal identification and fingerprints

B. Personal identification and passwords

C. Personal identification and social security numbers

D. Personal identification and face recognition

45. By which analysis do executives seek the most miniscule strengths and weaknesses within their own organization and the opportunities and threats of the competition?

A. Competitive analysis

B. Strategy analysis

C. TWOS analysis

D. SWOT analysis

46. What is the activity of keeping a database up-to-date by adding, deleting, or changing data within it?

    A. Database management

    B. Database maintenance

    C. Database development

    D. Database interrogation

47. What is the correct order of the five phases of the project management approach to implementation?

    A. Initiating and defining, planning, executing, controlling, and closing

    B. Planning, initiating and defining, executing, controlling, and closing

    C. Planning, initiating and defining, controlling, executing, and closing

    D. Initiating and defining, planning, controlling, executing, and closing

48. What is the problem-solving methodology most often used in information systems development that uses an orientation to define problems, opportunities, and needs in order to develop an appropriate, feasible solution?

    A. Systems approach

    B. Objectives approach

    C. Synthesis approach

    D. Developmental approach

49. Which of the following is not a decision-making level typical of an organization?

    A. Tactical

    B. Operational

    C. Strategic

    D. Transferal

50. When an individual does business with another individual online, such as using Ebay or Etsy, this individual is conducting business in what e-commerce strategy?

    A. Peer-to-peer (P2P)

    B. Business-to-Consumer (B2C)

    C. Consumer-to-Consumer (C2C)

    D. Business-to-Business (B2B)

51. What level in an organization supports short-term plans that help achieve day-to-day level tasks and objectives?

    A. Organizational level

    B. Tactical management level

    C. Executive management level

    D. Strategic management level

52. Which of the following refers to data received from other data sources, such as revenues and costs, that are combined to create other data points (often referred to as "defining the data in a data warehouse")?

    A. Megadata

    B. Metadata

    C. Waredata

    D. Teradata

53. Of the five stages of the Systems Development Life Cycle, which is the most costly and time-consuming stage?

    A. Investigation stage

    B. Implementation stage

    C. Analysis stage

    D. Maintenance stage

54. What data are very structured in order to capture business operations on a day-to-day basis and help front-line managers make daily decisions?

    A. DSS data

    B. MIS data

    C. Transactional data

    D. EIS data

55. What is the management function that ensures an organization is minimizing the risks associated with information threats that cause loss of data, information vulnerabilities that allow data breaches to occur, and risks associated with the impact of operations should disaster occur?

    A. Security management

    B. Information management

    C. Organization management

    D. Data management

56. What is the standardization of a combined series of eight 1's and 0's into what is known today as bytes?

A. ASCII

B. BASIC

C. ENIAC

D. ALU

57. What is the concept of collecting data to a single location where they have been extracted, transformed, and loaded so they can be used by managers, executives, and other professionals for the purpose of data mining, online analytical processing (OLAP), and other forms of analysis?

A. Data warehousing

B. Data diving

C. Data analysis

D. Data exporting

58. Which of the following statements is true regarding ethics and computer usage?

A. While an organization's ethics may be of higher standards, the world that interacts with its information system may not have the same values and ethics.

B. While an organization's ethics may be of higher standards, the world that interacts with its information system never has the same values and ethics.

C. While an organization's ethics may be of higher standards, the world that interacts with its information system always has the same values and ethics.

D. While an organization's ethics may be of higher standards, the ethics of other organizations cannot be trusted.

59. What is the blueprint, the conceptual design, or the model created to provide a visual representation of a proposed/planned system?

A. Systems topology

B. Systems architecture

C. Systems archaeology

D. Systems development life cycle

60. What is a computer program designed to search, detect, remove, and prevent virus invasions on computer systems?

A. Malware software

B. Spyware software

C. Antivirus software

D. Antitheft software

post-test

ANSWER KEY AND EXPLANATIONS

1. B	13. B	25. D	37. C	49. D
2. A	14. D	26. D	38. D	50. C
3. A	15. D	27. C	39. A	51. A
4. C	16. B	28. C	40. A	52. B
5. A	17. C	29. B	41. C	53. D
6. B	18. B	30. D	42. A	54. C
7. C	19. B	31. B	43. A	55. A
8. D	20. B	32. D	44. B	56. A
9. D	21. B	33. C	45. D	57. A
10. A	22. D	34. D	46. B	58. A
11. B	23. B	35. C	47. A	59. B
12. C	24. A	36. C	48. A	60. C

1. **The correct answer is B.** Charles Babbage invented the Analytic Engine. Choice A is incorrect because Blaise Pascal is credited with creating the binary adding machine. Choice C is incorrect because Alan Turing created the electrical/mechanical decipher machine during World War II. Choice D is incorrect because Gordon Moore co-created Intel.

2. **The correct answer is A.** This is the definition of twisted pair. Choice B is incorrect because coaxial cables contain a center copper wire wrapped in insulation and allow a higher frequency bandwidth. Choice C is incorrect this is a made-up choice. Choice D is incorrect because USB cables are universal serial bus cables.

3. **The correct answer is A.** This is the definition of SQL. Choice B is incorrect because FORTRAN is used mostly for scientific and engineering applications. Choice C is incorrect because BASIC changed the computer language dynamics into what we know today. Choice D is incorrect because COBOL is a business-specific, calculation software and enables businesses to store and calculate complex algorithms.

4. **The correct answer is C.** This is the definition of an intranet. Choice A is incorrect because this is the interconnectivity of intranets. Choice B is incorrect because the

World Wide Web is the entirety of networks across the globe. Choice D is incorrect because extranets allow activity outside the organization.

5. **The correct answer is A.** A firewall's purpose is to block unwanted spam and unwanted e-mails from entering a server. Choice B is incorrect because a firewall is not a physical device that prevents fires in an information system application. Choice C is incorrect because firewalls do not act as counter-attack device. Choice D is incorrect because a firewall is not used to block users' access.

6. **The correct answer is B.** Information systems are an integral part of competitive advantage, and a perpetual evaluation of information systems is always required. Choice A is incorrect because perpetuation doesn't help with database security. Choice C is incorrect because this is database maintenance. Choice D is incorrect because perpetuation doesn't upgrade a database system.

7. **The correct answer is C.** Choice A is incorrect because this is a radio device for AM radio. Choice B is incorrect because this is a radio device for FM radio. Choice D is incorrect because a network interface card is a computer network device that allows

computers to interface with a network. It is not a modulator-demodulator.

8. **The correct answer is D.** This is the definition of SQL. Choice A is incorrect because a DBMS is the whole database system. Choice B is incorrect because relational models are a component of DBMS, but not a query. Choice C is incorrect because there is no such thing as DQU.

9. **The correct answer is D.** Choice A is incorrect because is SQL is Structured Query Language for querying databases. Choice B is incorrect because FORTRAN is mostly used for scientific and engineering applications. Choice C is incorrect because BASIC changed the computer language dynamics into what we know today.

10. **The correct answer is A.** The defining component of this answer regards the standardization of the transactions between businesses in e-commerce. Choice B is incorrect because protocols are rules of the network itself. Choice C is incorrect because this is not the standardization of the format. Choice D is incorrect because C2C is the business model of consumer to consumer.

11. **The correct answer is B.** The intrusion into any infrastructure is a very dangerous activity and leaves a system vulnerable. Choice A is incorrect because although gaming online by employees is a time-wasting activity for businesses, it is not the main concern. Choice C is incorrect because cyberwarfare is intended to disrupt operations rather than acquire weapons. Choice D is incorrect because cyberwarfare is intended to disrupt activity rather than acquire a nontangible product like competitive advantage.

12. **The correct answer is C.** This is the definition of a systems management program. Choice A is incorrect because applications control is maintained by the systems management program. Choice B is incorrect because systems development enables language translators, facilitates programming editing, and gives IT professionals the ability to create specific programs for specific business processes. Choice D is incorrect because machine languages are the most

basic level of programming where the binary codes are written for the CPU.

13. **The correct answer is B.** Electronic phenomena have very little impact on the light beams traveling in a fiber. Choice A is incorrect because twisted pair cables are subject to electronic and natural phenomena interference. Choice C is incorrect because coaxial cables have similar characteristics to the twisted pair but with a bit more isolation. Choice D is incorrect because universal serial bus (USB) cables are usually used in smaller distance applications and can have high levels of electronic interference.

14. **The correct answer is D.** This is the definition of a DDOS virus. Choice A is incorrect because this virus spies on the computer user for capturing personal information. Choice B is incorrect because Trojan viruses are disguised as a legitimate website to obtain access to a user's computer. Choice C is incorrect because this is a virus intended to cause harm to a computer for the purpose of fraud.

15. **The correct answer is D.** Choice A is incorrect because systems software manages, controls, and supports the computer system and controls the basic functions of the computer. Choice B is incorrect because machine language is the most basic level of programming where the binary codes are written for the CPU. Choice C is incorrect because it is the same answer as choice A.

16. **The correct answer is B.** Network security and human awareness are the most effective antivirus mechanisms—especially human awareness. Choices A, B, and C are incorrect because human awareness is the real key to network security.

17. **The correct answer is C.** RAM is considered a primary storage device. Choice A is incorrect because Optical Disks are considered secondary storage devices. Choice B is incorrect because USB drives are considered secondary storage devices. Choice D is incorrect because hard drives are considered secondary storage devices.

18. **The correct answer is B.** This is the definition of input devices. Choice A is incorrect

because analytical devices are part of the processor. Choice C is incorrect because input is a conversion instrument. Choice D is incorrect because output devices convert electronic information delivered by the CPU into a human-interpreted format.

19. **The correct answer is B.** This is the definition of a clicks-and-bricks strategy. Choice A is not a real type of store. Choice C is incorrect because this is a strategy of physical presence only. Choice D is incorrect because EDI is a means where business transactions are transmitted by network links between the businesses in a standardized electronic format.

20. **The correct answer is B.** Tactical management level is the managerial and director level of an organization. Choice A is the lowest decision-making level in an organization. Choice C is the highest decision-making level in an organization. Choice D is the same level as executive management in an organization.

21. **The correct answer is B.** This is the definition of Completely Automated Public Turing test to tell Computers and Humans Apart (CAPTCHA). Choice A is incorrect because this is simply unwanted, unsolicited e-mail. Choice C is incorrect because this is a virus intended to block computer access. Choice D is incorrect because Visual Basic is a programming language.

22. **The correct answer is D.** These five general characteristics comprise a system. Choice A is incorrect because assessment is not a general characteristic of a system. Choice B is incorrect because customer's opinion is irrelevant to a system. Choice C is incorrect because a system should be interdependent, not intradependent, within an organization.

23. **The correct answer is B.** Competitive advantage can be overwhelmed with substitutes in the market. Choice A is incorrect because competitive advantage is *not* permanent with the threat of substitutes. Choice C is incorrect because competitive advantage never remains consistent in any market. It fluctuates depending upon the

market. Choice D is incorrect because the product life cycle is associated with the threat of new entrants.

24. **The correct answer is A.** This is the definition of computer bandwidth. Choice B is incorrect because a protocol is a set of rules or standards created to regulate how a network is used in transmitting data and where the data are formatted, transmitted, secured, and received. Choice C is incorrect because microwave is a communication range only. Choice D is incorrect because UHF is a communication range only.

25. **The correct answer is D.** This is the definition of data resource management. Choice A is incorrect because design is not a component of warehousing. Choice B is incorrect because delivery only delivers information from warehouses. Choice C is incorrect because a database management system is used to maintain a database.

26. **The correct answer is D.** This is the definition of the SDLC. Choice A is incorrect because topology is associated with network design. Choice B is incorrect because systems architecture is created through the SDLC. Choice C is incorrect because organization is not associated with systems design.

27. **The correct answer is C.** This is the definition of a knowledge management system. Choice A is incorrect because transaction processing systems are fundamentally the operational interactivities of a database system. Choice B is incorrect because executive information systems provide executives information primarily on an *ad hoc* basis. Choice D is incorrect because decision support systems are managerial systems and semistructured databases for decisional query.

28. **The correct answer is C.** Business design is not a primary component of systems architecture. Choices A, B, and D are incorrect because they are components of systems architecture.

29. **The correct answer is B.** This is the definition of e-commerce. Choice A is incorrect because this is not the exchange of goods that takes place totally online. Choice C is

incorrect because this is not the full exchange of goods online. Choice D is incorrect because this is the organization that provides Internet services to a company or individual.

30. **The correct answer is D.** SCM is a supply-chain management tool. Choice A is incorrect because CRMs are customer focused, not supply-chain focused. Choice B is incorrect because MIS is a tactical level system for tactical decision making rather than supply chain. Choice C is incorrect because DSSs are similar to MIS-level decisions that are used for managerial decisions, not supply chain.

31. **The correct answer is B.** Choice A is incorrect because records are collectives of field contents. Choice C is incorrect because a character is the most fundamental and basic logic element of an entity. Choice D is incorrect because a field is a group of characters contained in a single area.

32. **The correct answer is D.** This is where the reports are created and progress is evaluated and compared with baseline objectives. If there is any disparity between the progress and baseline, intervention may take place. Choice A is incorrect because this is the phase where the goals are established and the objectives are defined. Choice B is incorrect because this is the phase that identifies the sequence of activities and the "critical paths." Choice C is incorrect because this is the phase where actual work begins.

33. **The correct answer is C.** This is a partial definition of cellular technology. Choice A is incorrect because microwaves have a line-of-sight path where the signals are passed through microwave relay stations that are usually seen on top of hills, towers, and mountain peaks. Choice B is incorrect because fiber optic passes light signals, not radio signals. Choice D is incorrect because this is a wireless technology that allows a very short-range signal to be used to interface with computers and other devices.

34. **The correct answer is D.** ALU is the arithmetic logic unit inside a CPU. It performs the calculations and logic functions necessary to execute software instructions. Choice A is

incorrect because ASCII captured the use of 1's and 0's and standardized a way to combine the series of eight 1's and 0's into what is known today as bytes. Choice B is incorrect because BASIC is a software program. Choice C is incorrect because ENIAC is the first electrical computing system used to calculate ballistics and artillery-firing tables and analyze thermonuclear weapons.

35. **The correct answer is C.** Encryption is the only choice presented that is not a biometric.

36. **The correct answer is C.** The hierarchical model was used in the early years of database development. Choice A is incorrect because this model is relationships built on a "many-to-many" manner. Choice B is incorrect because relational models are built by using what is known as two-dimensional tables or flat files. Choice D is incorrect because it consists of descriptive data values that describe the attributes of entities.

37. **The correct answer is C.** This is the definition of a critical path. Choices A, B, and D are not real MIS terms.

38. **The correct answer is D.** This is the definition of a computer virus. Choice A is not a computer code. Choice B is incorrect because it is not a real term. Choice C is incorrect because biometrics are human characteristics.

39. **The correct answer is A.** The investigation stage primarily involves an extensive feasibility study. Choice B is incorrect because this is the stage of delivery. Choice C is incorrect because the analysis stage includes, in part, activities that analyze "who" needs the information. Choice D is incorrect because this stage comes after a system is delivered and there is much "tweaking" and maintenance.

40. **The correct answer is A.** Only choice A lists the four cycles of growth.

41. **The correct answer is C.** This is the definition of schema. Choice A is incorrect because data design initiates the data content in a field. Choice B is incorrect because relationships only define the interconnectivity

of databases. Choice D is incorrect because data logic is not a real term.

42. **The correct answer is A.** Choice A is correct because the higher the impact upon the organization, the more immediate a decision should be. Choice B is incorrect because a lower business impact does not need an immediate decision. Choice C is incorrect because you do not want to dispose of a decision that has an immediate impact. Choice D is incorrect because high-impact decisions should not be scrutinized for disposal, and an immediate need for a decision is required.

43. **The correct answer is A.** This is the definition of a DBMS. Choice B is incorrect because relational models are a component of DBMS but not the management system. Choice C is not a real tool. Choice D is incorrect because SQL is a query language of databases.

44. **The correct answer is B.** Personal identification and password entry are the most commonly used methods of biometric entry. Choice A is incorrect because fingerprints are not common for computer entry. Choice C is incorrect because social security information is never a security measure. Choice D is incorrect because face recognition is not as common as passwords.

45. **The correct answer is D.** This is the definition of a SWOT analysis. Choices A, B, and C are not real forms of analysis.

46. **The correct answer is B.** This is the definition of database maintenance. "Database management" (choice A) refers to the system used to create, use, and maintain databases. Choice C is incorrect; this is the initial stage of database creation. Choice D is correct because this is extracting data and information only.

47. **The correct answer is A.** Only choice A lists the correct order of the five identifiable phases.

48. **The correct answer is A.** This is the definition of a systems approach to problem solving. Choice B is incorrect because objectives are only a small part of systems

development. Choice C is incorrect because synthesis is a creational activity not associated with systems approach. Choice D is incorrect because this is one of the components of the systems approach.

49. **The correct answer is D.** Transferal is not a level in an organization. Choice A is the second decision-making level in an organization. Choice B is the first decision-making level in an organization. Choice C is the highest decision-making level in an organization.

50. **The correct answer is C.** This is the definition of C2C. Choice A is incorrect because this is a network connection. Choice B is incorrect because B2C is from a business to a consumer. Choice D is incorrect because this type of transaction does not involve individuals.

51. **The correct answer is A.** At the organizational level, the lowest decision-making level in an organization, day-to-day activities occur. Choice B is incorrect because this is the managerial and director level of an organization. Choice C is incorrect because it is the highest decision-making level in an organization. Choice D is incorrect because it is the same level as executive management in an organization.

52. **The correct answer is B.** This is the definition of metadata. Choices A, C, and D are not real terms.

53. **The correct answer is D.** Once a system is delivered, there is much "tweaking," and debugging and repair takes a good amount of time. Choice A is incorrect because the investigation stage primarily involves just a feasibility study. Choice B is incorrect because although implementation is expensive, it is not the most expensive and time-consuming. The analysis stage (choice C) analyzes the current system and evaluates future needs and is not the most time-consuming stage.

54. **The correct answer is C.** This is the definition of transactional data. Choice A is incorrect because this is the decision support level of data. Choice B is incorrect because this is the management information systems

level. Choice D is incorrect because this is the executive information systems level.

55. **The correct answer is A.** This is the definition of security management. Choices B, C, and D are incorrect because none is associated with vulnerability management.

56. **The correct answer is A.** ASCII captured the use of 1's and 0's and standardized a way to combine the series of eight 1's and 0's into what is known today as bytes. Choice B is incorrect because BASIC is a software program. Choice C is incorrect because ENIAC is the first electrical computing system used to calculate ballistics and artillery-firing tables and to analyze thermonuclear weapons. Choice D is incorrect because the ALU is the arithmetic logic unit inside a CPU. It performs the calculations and logic functions necessary to execute software instructions.

57. **The correct answer is A.** This is the definition of data warehousing. Choice B is incorrect because data diving is a concept of data analysis. Choice C is incorrect because this is just analyzing data content. Choice D is incorrect because data exporting is moving data to another location.

58. **The correct answer is A.** Choice A is correct because other people *may* not have the same ethics as an organization. Choice B is incorrect because other people *may* have higher ethics than an organization. Choice C is incorrect because it is not always true that all organizations have equivalent ethics. Choice D is incorrect because this is an irrational judgment.

59. **The correct answer is B.** This is the definition of systems architecture. Choice A is incorrect because topology is associated with network design. Choice C is incorrect because archaeology is not associated with systems design. Choice D is incorrect because a systems development life cycle is a multistep, iterative process used to create an organizational system.

60. **The correct answer is C.** This is the definition of antivirus software. Choice A incorrect because malware is a software hackers use to invade other computers. Choice B is incorrect because spyware is similar to malware. Its intent is to spy on unsuspecting users. Choice D is not a type of software.

Money and Banking

OVERVIEW

Chapter 8

The DSST® Money and Banking exam consists of 100 multiple-choice questions that cover material commonly found in a college-level money and banking course, including the role of money, types of money, commercial banks, the Federal Reserve System, macroeconomics, U.S. monetary policy, and the international monetary system.

This chapter gives you a comprehensive overview of all topics covered on the exam.

DIAGNOSTIC TEST ANSWER SHEET

1. Ⓐ Ⓑ Ⓒ Ⓓ   5. Ⓐ Ⓑ Ⓒ Ⓓ   9. Ⓐ Ⓑ Ⓒ Ⓓ   13. Ⓐ Ⓑ Ⓒ Ⓓ   17. Ⓐ Ⓑ Ⓒ Ⓓ
2. Ⓐ Ⓑ Ⓒ Ⓓ   6. Ⓐ Ⓑ Ⓒ Ⓓ   10. Ⓐ Ⓑ Ⓒ Ⓓ   14. Ⓐ Ⓑ Ⓒ Ⓓ   18. Ⓐ Ⓑ Ⓒ Ⓓ
3. Ⓐ Ⓑ Ⓒ Ⓓ   7. Ⓐ Ⓑ Ⓒ Ⓓ   11. Ⓐ Ⓑ Ⓒ Ⓓ   15. Ⓐ Ⓑ Ⓒ Ⓓ   19. Ⓐ Ⓑ Ⓒ Ⓓ
4. Ⓐ Ⓑ Ⓒ Ⓓ   8. Ⓐ Ⓑ Ⓒ Ⓓ   12. Ⓐ Ⓑ Ⓒ Ⓓ   16. Ⓐ Ⓑ Ⓒ Ⓓ   20. Ⓐ Ⓑ Ⓒ Ⓓ

POST-TEST ANSWER SHEET

1. Ⓐ Ⓑ Ⓒ Ⓓ   13. Ⓐ Ⓑ Ⓒ Ⓓ   25. Ⓐ Ⓑ Ⓒ Ⓓ   37. Ⓐ Ⓑ Ⓒ Ⓓ   49. Ⓐ Ⓑ Ⓒ Ⓓ
2. Ⓐ Ⓑ Ⓒ Ⓓ   14. Ⓐ Ⓑ Ⓒ Ⓓ   26. Ⓐ Ⓑ Ⓒ Ⓓ   38. Ⓐ Ⓑ Ⓒ Ⓓ   50. Ⓐ Ⓑ Ⓒ Ⓓ
3. Ⓐ Ⓑ Ⓒ Ⓓ   15. Ⓐ Ⓑ Ⓒ Ⓓ   27. Ⓐ Ⓑ Ⓒ Ⓓ   39. Ⓐ Ⓑ Ⓒ Ⓓ   51. Ⓐ Ⓑ Ⓒ Ⓓ
4. Ⓐ Ⓑ Ⓒ Ⓓ   16. Ⓐ Ⓑ Ⓒ Ⓓ   28. Ⓐ Ⓑ Ⓒ Ⓓ   40. Ⓐ Ⓑ Ⓒ Ⓓ   52. Ⓐ Ⓑ Ⓒ Ⓓ
5. Ⓐ Ⓑ Ⓒ Ⓓ   17. Ⓐ Ⓑ Ⓒ Ⓓ   29. Ⓐ Ⓑ Ⓒ Ⓓ   41. Ⓐ Ⓑ Ⓒ Ⓓ   53. Ⓐ Ⓑ Ⓒ Ⓓ
6. Ⓐ Ⓑ Ⓒ Ⓓ   18. Ⓐ Ⓑ Ⓒ Ⓓ   30. Ⓐ Ⓑ Ⓒ Ⓓ   42. Ⓐ Ⓑ Ⓒ Ⓓ   54. Ⓐ Ⓑ Ⓒ Ⓓ
7. Ⓐ Ⓑ Ⓒ Ⓓ   19. Ⓐ Ⓑ Ⓒ Ⓓ   31. Ⓐ Ⓑ Ⓒ Ⓓ   43. Ⓐ Ⓑ Ⓒ Ⓓ   55. Ⓐ Ⓑ Ⓒ Ⓓ
8. Ⓐ Ⓑ Ⓒ Ⓓ   20. Ⓐ Ⓑ Ⓒ Ⓓ   32. Ⓐ Ⓑ Ⓒ Ⓓ   44. Ⓐ Ⓑ Ⓒ Ⓓ   56. Ⓐ Ⓑ Ⓒ Ⓓ
9. Ⓐ Ⓑ Ⓒ Ⓓ   21. Ⓐ Ⓑ Ⓒ Ⓓ   33. Ⓐ Ⓑ Ⓒ Ⓓ   45. Ⓐ Ⓑ Ⓒ Ⓓ   57. Ⓐ Ⓑ Ⓒ Ⓓ
10. Ⓐ Ⓑ Ⓒ Ⓓ   22. Ⓐ Ⓑ Ⓒ Ⓓ   34. Ⓐ Ⓑ Ⓒ Ⓓ   46. Ⓐ Ⓑ Ⓒ Ⓓ   58. Ⓐ Ⓑ Ⓒ Ⓓ
11. Ⓐ Ⓑ Ⓒ Ⓓ   23. Ⓐ Ⓑ Ⓒ Ⓓ   35. Ⓐ Ⓑ Ⓒ Ⓓ   47. Ⓐ Ⓑ Ⓒ Ⓓ   59. Ⓐ Ⓑ Ⓒ Ⓓ
12. Ⓐ Ⓑ Ⓒ Ⓓ   24. Ⓐ Ⓑ Ⓒ Ⓓ   36. Ⓐ Ⓑ Ⓒ Ⓓ   48. Ⓐ Ⓑ Ⓒ Ⓓ   60. Ⓐ Ⓑ Ⓒ Ⓓ

MONEY AND BANKING DIAGNOSTIC TEST

Directions: Carefully read each of the following 20 questions. Choose the best answer to each question and fill in the corresponding circle on the answer sheet. The Answer Key and Explanations can be found following this Diagnostic Test.

1. *Fiat money* is the term used for a means of payment that
   A. can be converted into gold at any time.
   B. is widely accepted because it's made of precious metals like silver or gold.
   C. cannot be accepted as repayment of a debt.
   D. is not backed by any commodity.

2. Up until 1994, nationwide branch banking was prohibited by
   A. Regulation Q and the Glass-Steagall Act.
   B. the McFadden Act.
   C. the Depository Institutions Deregulation and Monetary Control Act.
   D. the Riegle-Neal Interstate Banking Act.

3. When an American money market mutual fund purchases U.S. Treasury notes from an American bank, the transaction is
   A. not counted in the Gross Domestic Product for the current period.
   B. counted in the Gross Domestic Product in the financial account.
   C. counted in the Gross Domestic Product under Gross Private Investment.
   D. counted in the Balance of Payment in the financial account.

4. The Federal Reserve Bank was created primarily to
   A. maintain the stability of the financial system by providing liquidity and acting as lender of last resort to member banks.
   B. maintain the stability of the banking sector by providing insurance to depositors' accounts.
   C. prevent any form of discrimination toward women and minorities in all aspects of credit transactions.
   D. enforce macro-prudential regulation that would help contain systemic risk.

5. A financial intermediary has a liquidity problem when
   A. its liabilities exceed the bank's assets.
   B. its asset portfolio is predominantly composed of Treasury securities that the intermediary can easily sell to other financial institutions.
   C. it has cash assets in excess of its required reserves.
   D. its current obligations exceed the institution's current liquid resources.

6. Central banks do not have complete control over the money supply because
   A. they do not fully control the money multiplier.
   B. they do not have the legal authority to set reserve requirements.
   C. they prefer controlling the monetary base.
   D. the policy interest rate does not influence the money supply.

7. A downside of having the FDIC insure deposit accounts up to $250,000 is the
   A. increase in financial contagion.
   B. increase in banks' holdings of excess reserves.
   C. decrease in market discipline.
   D. decrease in bank failures.

8. One difference between classical economists and Keynesian economists is that Keynesian economists believe that
   A. prices are flexible and absorb all shocks in demand and supply.
   B. higher investment spending can raise the level of output.
   C. the economy is always at full employment and any worker out of job is voluntarily unemployed.
   D. lower interest rates and a higher money supply tend to reduce the price level.

9. Unlike an expansionary fiscal policy, an expansionary monetary policy lowers
   A. total spending.
   B. taxes.
   C. interest rates.
   D. government purchases.

10. According to the quantity theory of money, a continual increase of the money supply leads to inflation because
    A. real GDP is below potential output.
    B. interest rates are sticky.
    C. the foreign exchange rate is overvalued.
    D. the velocity of money is constant.

11. Each year, the Federal Open Market Committee (FOMC) has eight regular meetings. Which of the following is decided at the regular meetings of the FOMC?
    A. The reserve requirement imposed on member banks
    B. The target level of the Federal Funds Rate
    C. The discount rate charged in each of the twelve Reserve districts
    D. The target level of the monetary aggregate M2

12. Monetarists believe that firms, workers, and investors have rational expectations and that
    A. the price level they expect is not sensitive to the money supply.
    B. they suffer from monetary illusion.
    C. monetizing the public deficits would lower inflation.
    D. only monetary policy can contain inflation.

13. An advantage of requiring borrowers to post collateral when they apply for a loan is that it
    A. helps bank reach a wider public and better meet the Equal Credit Opportunity Act requirements.
    B. increases borrowers' incentive to apply for loans.
    C. lowers borrowers' incentive to take up excessive risk.
    D. attracts borrowers with a poorer credit history who are willing to pay higher interest rates.

14. The different channels through which monetary policy influences economic activity are called the
    A. transmission mechanism.
    B. equation of exchange.
    C. automatic stabilizers.
    D. monetary lags.

15. A distinctive feature of the banking sector of the United States is the

    A. even geographical distribution of commercial banks and Savings and Loans Associations.

    B. prevalence among depository institutions of member owned credit unions.

    C. existence of a limited number of very large bank holdings among thousands of relatively small commercial banks.

    D. highly restricted range of bank activities allowed to Savings and Loans Associations.

16. Which of the following is a function of the International Monetary Fund (IMF)?

    A. Promoting international cooperation among monetary authorities and financial supervisory officials

    B. Providing development loans so as to end extreme poverty

    C. Promoting smooth and free international trade flows

    D. Providing loans to countries with balance of payment difficulties or facing debt crises

17. When the Federal Reserve lowers the federal funds rate, banks

    A. would rather borrow from the Federal Reserve at the discount rate than from each other at the lower federal funds rate.

    B. can borrow reserves more cheaply than before and are more likely to extend new loans so that the money supply increases.

    C. find it harder to meet reserve requirements and increase their holdings of excess reserves.

    D. become aware of the new policy only if it is clearly announced at the end of the FOMC meeting.

18. A Certificate of Deposit differs from a Money Market Deposit Account in that a

    A. money market deposit account is not FDIC insured.

    B. certificate of deposit will give you access to your funds at a specified time in the future.

    C. certificate of deposit does not pay interest.

    D. money market deposit account is a bank liability, while a CD is a bank asset.

19. Which of the following statements best characterizes the Federal Reserve's response to the financial crisis of 2008/2009?

    A. Concerned that injecting liquidity in the largest banks could worsen existing problems of moral hazard, the Federal Reserve took a hands-off approach and allowed these institutions to fail.

    B. According to the principle that acute crises can have a cleansing effect on financial markets, the Federal Reserve allowed larger commercial banks to fail; however, to contain systemic risk, it supported smaller banks.

    C. The Federal Reserve lowered the federal funds rate down to the zero lower bound and found itself with no other tools it could use to inject liquidity in the banking sector and in money markets.

    D. The Federal Reserve lowered the federal funds rate and used unconventional monetary tools like large purchases of Mortgage Back Securities from Government Sponsored Entities to stimulate the housing market.

20. After President Kennedy created the United States Agency for International Development (USAID), U.S. foreign aid to other countries sharply increased,

A. raising debits in the U.S. current account of the Balance of Payment.

B. raising credits in the U.S. current account of the Balance of Payment.

C. raising debits in the U.S. financial account of the Balance of Payment.

D. raising credits in the U.S. financial account of the Balance of Payment.

ANSWER KEY AND EXPLANATIONS

1. D	5. D	9. C	13. C	17. B
2. B	6. A	10. D	14. A	18. B
3. A	7. C	11. B	15. C	19. D
4. A	8. B	12. D	16. D	20. A

1. **The correct answer is D.** Unlike commodity money, fiat money is not backed by anything. Fiat money has value because people trust that it will be widely accepted as a means of payment now and in the future. Choice A is incorrect because money that can be converted into gold is called commodity-backed money. Choice B is incorrect because money made of precious metal is called commodity money. Choice C is incorrect because fiat money is currency that the government has declared legal tender.

2. **The correct answer is B.** The McFadden Act of 1927 required national banks to open branches only according to the laws of the state where they were located, effectively prohibiting national branching. Choice A is incorrect because Regulation Q imposed limits on interest paid on various deposits and prohibited paying interest on demand deposits. Choice C is incorrect because the DIDMCA did not prohibit nationwide branching, but, among other things, it lifted restrictions on interest paid on deposits. Choice D is incorrect because the Riegle-Neal Interstate Banking Act removed the restrictions on nationwide branching.

3. **The correct answer is A.** Gross Domestic Product only counts transactions of final goods and services. Choice B is incorrect because the financial account is not a component of Gross Domestic Product. Choice C is incorrect because purchases of U.S. Treasury notes are a form of financial investment, not of Gross Private Investment. Choice D is incorrect because the purchase is a domestic transaction.

4. **The correct answer is A.** The Federal Reserve System was created to provide elastic liquidity to the banking sector and act as a lender of last resort to member banks so as to maintain financial stability. Choice B is incorrect because bank deposits are insured by the FDIC and other agencies, not by the Federal Reserve Bank. Choice C is incorrect because discrimination in lending was outlawed by the Equal Credit Opportunity Act in 1974. Choice D is incorrect because the Federal Reserve Bank has started enforcing macro-prudential regulation in response to the financial crises of 2008.

5. **The correct answer is D.** A financial intermediary has a liquidity problem if it does not hold enough liquid resources like cash or Treasury securities to meet its current obligation, like short-term debt or depositors' withdrawals. Choice A is incorrect because when a financial intermediary's liabilities exceed its assets the intermediary is insolvent. Choice B is incorrect because assets that can be easily sold are very liquid. Choice C is incorrect because not all financial intermediaries are subject to reserve requirements.

6. **The correct answer is A.** Money supply is sensitive to changes in the monetary base and the money multiplier and central banks do not fully control the money multiplier. Choice B is incorrect because central banks set reserve requirements. Choice C is incorrect because central banks want to influence money supply while the monetary base is an intermediate target. Choice D is incorrect because the money supply is sensitive to the policy interest rate.

7. **The correct answer is C.** Deposit insurance reduces depositors' incentive to monitor the sound management of their banks, reducing market discipline. Choice A is incorrect because deposit insurance prevents financial contagion. Choice B is incorrect because deposit insurance reduces

the chances of a bank run and banks' incentive to hold excess reserves. Choice D is incorrect because a decrease in bank failures is an upside of deposit insurance.

8. **The correct answer is B.** Keynesian economists believe that prices are sticky and output follows total spending so that higher investment spending can raise output. Choice A is incorrect because it's classical economists who believe that prices are flexible. Choice C is incorrect because Keynesian economists believe that when total spending drops because of sticky prices and wages many workers become involuntarily unemployed. Choice D is incorrect because both theories support that a higher money supply increases the price level.

9. **The correct answer is C.** An expansionary monetary policy lowers interest rates to stimulate investment and consumption while an expansionary fiscal policy increases the public deficit leading to higher interest rates. Choice A is incorrect because an expansionary monetary policy aims at increasing total spending. Choice B is incorrect because taxes are a tool of fiscal policy. Choice D is incorrect because government purchases are a tool of fiscal policy.

10. **The correct answer is D.** The quantity theory of money states that money and prices are linked by the equation of exchange $P \times Y = M \times V$ and assumes that V and Y are constant so that changes in the money supply lead to equal changes in the price level. Choice A is incorrect because the quantity theory of money assumes that the economy is always at full employment. Choice B is incorrect because the quantity theory of money is silent on interest rates. Choice C is incorrect because the quantity theory of money does not take into account the foreign exchange market.

11. **The correct answer is B.** At its regular meetings, the FOMC discusses the current economic outlook and decides the target level of the Federal Funds Rate. Choice A is incorrect because reserve requirements are decided by the Board of Governors. Choice C is incorrect because the discount rates

charged by the Reserve banks are decided by the individual banks under the control of the Board of Governors. Choice D is incorrect because the U.S. monetary policy uses the Federal Funds Rate as its policy target, not the monetary aggregate M2.

12. **The correct answer is D.** Monetarists believe that, because market participants have rational expectations, fiscal policy is ineffective in controlling inflation, which is a monetary phenomenon. Choice A is incorrect because according to the rational expectation hypothesis the money supply influences the price level people expect. Choice B is incorrect because when people have rational expectations, they do not suffer from monetary illusion. Choice C is incorrect because monetarists believe that printing money to pay for the public deficit increases inflation.

13. **The correct answer is C.** With collateralized loans, in the case of default, the borrower loses the collateral, leading the borrower to be more cautious when choosing how to use the funds. Choice A is incorrect because many families and small businesses do not have assets they can post as collateral, and collateral requirements reduce a bank's reach. Choice B is incorrect because posting collateral lowers a borrower's incentive to apply for a loan. Choice D is incorrect because borrowers with a poorer credit history are less likely to own assets they can post as collateral.

14. **The correct answer is A.** The transmission mechanism describes the ways in which monetary policy influences total spending and the level of economic activity. Choice B is incorrect because the equation of exchange illustrates only the relationship between the money supply and the price level. Choice C is incorrect because automatic stabilizers are tools of fiscal policy. Choice D is incorrect because the monetary lags describe different reasons why it takes about two years for monetary policy to influence the economy.

15. **The correct answer is C.** In the United States, most commercial banks are rather

small and the eighty-four largest bank holdings hold more than 70 percent of all deposits. Choice A is incorrect because the geographical distribution of commercial banks is not geographically even. Choice B is incorrect because most depository institutions are commercial banks. Choice D is incorrect because, thanks to recent regulatory changes, Savings and Loans Associations can perform most of the same activities as commercial banks.

16. **The correct answer is D.** The IMF was founded to help countries with balance of payments difficulties under the Bretton Woods regime of fixed exchange rates. More recently it acts as a lender of last resort for countries with external debt crises. Choice A is incorrect because promoting international cooperation among monetary authorities and financial supervisory officials is the key function of the Bank of International Settlements (BIS). Choice B is incorrect because providing development loans to end extreme poverty is a key function of the World Bank. Choice C is incorrect because promoting smooth and free trade flows is the key function of the World Trade Organization (WTO).

17. **The correct answer is B.** Banks extend loans when they have a cheap source of funding. A lower federal funds rate lowers banks' cost of money. Choice A is incorrect if the federal funds rate is lower than the discount rate banks would borrow in the federal funds market instead of borrowing from the Fed. Choice C is incorrect because if banks can borrow from each other more cheaply than before, they find it easier, not harder, to meet reserve requirements. Choice D is incorrect because the federal funds rate is the interest rate that banks charge each other on overnight loans of federal funds so they are directly aware of changes in the rate.

18. **The correct answer is B.** Certificates of deposit are one type of time deposits, deposits that give you access to your funds only at a specified time in the future. Choice A is incorrect because money market deposit accounts are FDIC insured up to $250,000 per account. Choice C is incorrect because certificates of deposit pay a fixed pre-specified interest. Choice D is incorrect because both money market deposit accounts and certificate of deposits are types of deposits and are a bank's liabilities.

19. **The correct answer is D.** After lowering the federal funds rate to its zero lower bound, the Fed introduced new liquidity provisions and started large purchases of mortgage back securities and long-term Treasury securities; these are unconventional tools of monetary policy. Choice A is incorrect because the Federal Reserve did not take a hands-off approach. Choice B is incorrect because during the financial crises more than 400 banks failed, most of them smaller banks. Choice C is incorrect because the Federal Reserve used several unconventional tools to inject liquidity in the banking sector and in specific segments of the U.S. financial markets.

20. **The correct answer is A.** In the Balance of Payment, foreign aid is tallied as a debit in the current account. Choice B is incorrect because in the Balance of Payment, foreign aid is tallied as a debit, not a credit. Choice C is incorrect because in the Balance of Payment, foreign aid is tallied in the current account, not the financial account. Choice D is incorrect because in the Balance of Payment, foreign aid is tallied as a debit, not a credit.

answers diagnostic test

DIAGNOSTIC TEST ASSESSMENT GRID

Now that you've completed the diagnostic test and read through the answer explanations, you can use your results to target your studying. Find the question numbers from the diagnostic test that you answered incorrectly and highlight or circle them below. Then focus extra attention on the sections within the chapter dealing with those topics.

Money and Banking		
Content Area	**Topics Covered**	**Questions**
The Roles and Kinds of Money	• Alternative definitions of money • Money and other assets	1
Commercial Banks and Other Financial Intermediaries	• Regulation of the banking industry • Structure of the banking industry • Operation and management of financial markets and intermediaries • Deposit insurance	2, 5, 7, 13, 15, 18
Money and Macro-economic Activity	• Basic classical and Keynesian economics • Monetarism and rational expectations • Money and inflation	3, 8, 10, 12
Central Banking and the Federal Reserve	• Historical and philosophical framework • Structure and organization • Current monetary management	4, 6, 11
Monetary Policy in the United States	• Policy effectiveness • Conducting monetary policy • Interest rates and the impact on money supply • Monetary vs. fiscal policy • The financial crisis of 2008/2009	9, 14, 17, 19
The International Monetary System	• International banking • International monetary institutions and debt crisis • International payments and exchange rates • Monetary policy in conjunction with exchange rate	16, 20

GET THE FACTS

To see the DSST® Money and Banking Fact Sheet, go to **http://getcollegecredit.com/exam_fact_sheets** and click on the **Business** tab. Scroll down and click the **Money and Banking** link. Here you will find suggestions for further study material and the ACE college credit recommendations for passing the test.

THE ROLES AND KINDS OF MONEY

ALTERNATIVE DEFINITIONS OF MONEY

Let's start by defining the concept of money. Money is an **asset**—a durable item with value that is widely accepted as means of payment.

Only some valuables or assets can be used as money. Assets that can be used as money are:

- **Durable:** They last over time.
- **Acceptable:** People do not find them repulsive or inconvenient to carry.
- **Divisible:** They can be divided into smaller units
- **Fungible:** Each unit is similar to every other unit so that they can be easily interchanged.

The Four Key Roles of Money

Economists find that money has four key roles:

1. *Means of payment:* Money makes it easier for buyers and sellers to come together and trade. Without money, people would have to barter, that is exchange one good for another. However, bartering requires a double coincidence of wants: If Joe wants to trade his Netflix subscription for a DSST study guide, he has to meet someone willing to trade a DSST study guide for a Netflix subscription. Because money is widely accepted as a means of payment, when Joe wants to trade money for a DSST study guide, he can easily find a bookstore willing to trade a DSST study guide for money.

2. *Store of value:* An important feature of money is that people can save it for future purchases. If snowballs were used as money, our wages would melt before we could spend them.

3. *Standard of deferred payment:* Money is the unit we use to agree on the future repayment of a debt. In the United States, the Coinage Act of 1965 states that the dollar is legal tender and must be accepted as repayment for all debts. This is the main reason we use dollars as our money.

4. *Unit of Account:* Money is the reference measure to set prices and to evaluate important economic indicators.

Kinds of Money

Through history, societies have used three kinds of money.

Commodity Money

In past centuries, people have used various commodities like gold and silver as money. Commodity money is inconvenient because it is heavy to carry, it is easy to debunk, and its value swings with changes in the demand and supply of the commodity.

Commodity-Backed Money

In more recent times, private and central banks started issuing paper certificates backed by gold that proved a more convenient means of payment. Under the **gold standard,** the dollar was backed by gold. At any time, the carrier of a dollar bill could visit the central bank and have the dollar bill converted into gold.

Fiat Money

Nowadays, most money is in the form of paper certificates that are not backed by gold or any other commodity. This is called **fiat money** because its value comes from people's trust that now and in the future the certificates will be accepted as a means of payment.

How Money Is Defined and Measured

The quantity of money in an economy is called the **money stock** or the **money supply.** Central banks use different definitions of the money stock. These are labeled with the capital letter M and a number. A lower number indicates a narrow definition of money that includes only very liquid assets.

Transaction deposits (for example, deposits in a checkable account) that can be withdrawn without limits are as liquid as cash and are considered money. Other forms of deposits that impose restrictions on withdrawals like NOW accounts, savings accounts, or time deposits are less liquid and are considered near money.

In the United States, the Federal Reserve Bank uses two monetary aggregates:

1. *M1*, which includes cash in circulation, checking accounts, and travelers' checks.
2. *M2*, which includes M1 and savings accounts, small time deposits, and retail money-market mutual funds.

TIP

An asset is liquid when it can be quickly and cheaply converted into cash. Assets that are highly liquid are also called near-money. The most liquid asset is cash itself.

MONEY AND OTHER ASSETS

Money is a type of **financial asset**—an asset that derives value from a contractual claim. A **loan** is a type of financial asset that derives value from a contract that states that the borrower will pay money to the lender at some point in the future.

Another important class of financial assets is represented by **securities.** These are financial assets that can be traded. There are three classes of securities:

1. *Debt securities:* tradable *I Owe Yous*, like bank notes and bonds
2. *Equity securities*: standardized ownership shares like common stock
3. *Derivatives:* contracts where flows of money depend on the realization of uncertain events like futures, options, and swaps

Securities are traded in three types of markets: the primary market, the secondary market, and the open market. In the **primary market**, the issuer (the company that issues the security) sells the securities to the public and receives funds. In the **secondary market**, previously issued securities are exchanged between investors. Securities exchanged between the monetary authority (a.k.a. the central bank) and banks are traded in the **open market.**

Interest Rates

Unlike cash, other financial assets often pay interest. In a credit transaction, the money lent out at the start is called the **principal,** while the **interest** is all the extra payments the lender receives from the borrower over the duration of the transaction. The **interest rate** is the ratio of interest to principal. Interest rates are measured in basis points. A basis point is one hundredth of one percent.

The interest rate is easy to compute in the case of a simple loan where a person lends M dollars to another and receives N dollars back at maturity. In this case, the interest is $I = (N - M)$ and the interest rate is $I = \dfrac{N - M}{M}$.

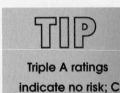

TIP

Triple A ratings indicate no risk; C or D ratings indicate very high risk.

In the case of **fixed payment loans** (for example, a home mortgage loan or a coupon bond), computing the interest rate is more difficult. A common approach is to compute the yield to maturity. The yield to maturity is the interest rate that equates the current price of a debt security or loan to the present discounted value of all payments the lender will receive from the security or loan if he holds it until its maturity. The present discounted value of a future payment is the highest price at which you are willing to sell your claim to that payment.

There is a negative relationship between the price of a debt security, say a bond, and the interest rate. Bond prices increase when the demand for bonds increases and decline when the supply of bonds increases. Therefore, a higher demand for bonds leads to higher bond prices and lower interest rates; a higher supply of bonds leads to lower bond prices and higher interest rates.

Debt securities can be more or less risky depending on the probability that the issuer might default, or not repay. Riskier securities are cheaper and pay a higher interest than safe securities. **Credit rating agencies** are firms that research the likelihood that different issuers might default and rate issuers' bonds accordingly.

A **yield curve** is a graph that shows the interest rate on similar securities with different terms to maturity (the time remaining before the principal is repaid), for example, a three-month Treasury bill versus a 10-year Treasury bond. People are impatient—the interest rate on short-term securities (securities near maturity) is lower than the interest rate on long-term securities (securities far from maturity). Hence, the yield curve tends to be slightly upward sloping.

There is also a relationship between the slope of the yield curve and investors' expectations on the future behavior of short-term interest rates. If investors believe that short-term interest rates will soon rise, the yield curve becomes steeper. If investors believe that short-term interest rates will soon decline, the yield curve becomes flatter or even downward sloping.

COMMERCIAL BANKS AND OTHER FINANCIAL INTERMEDIARIES

Now that you have a better understanding of what money is, let's discuss **financial intermediaries**—institutions that move money from those who want to save it to those who want to borrow it.

Most financial intermediaries are depository institutions, normally called **banks**. Depository institutions are financial intermediaries that, by law, can accept deposits in transaction accounts and that together make up the banking sector.

In a nutshell, depository institutions accept funds from depositors and loan these funds out to families and businesses. A bank loan is called a **tool of indirect finance** as the bank intermediates between lenders (the depositors) and borrowers (loan applicants).

The banking sector of the United States has three distinguishing characteristics:

- An unusually large number of small banks
- A dual nature where some banks are chartered at the state level while others are nationally chartered
- One of the most heavily regulated banking sectors in the world

The U.S. banking sector was greatly shaped by the nation's history. American historical wariness for centralized power led to the unusually large number of small banks that still operate in the country, as, up until 1927, banks could be chartered only at the state level. Starting in 1927, with the passage of the **McFadden Act,** banks could be chartered at the national level. However, the Act subjected national banks to their home-state branching rules, effectively prohibiting interstate branching and severely limiting interstate banking. The limits on interstate banking were later lifted by the **Riegle-Neal Interstate Banking Act of 1994,** which relaxed branching rules and started an era of bank mergers.

The heavy regulatory environment typical of the U.S. banking sector is a consequence of the duality of the system, as well as an inheritance of the stock market crash of 1929 and the wave of bank panics and bank failures that followed in the 1930s. In response to the financial upheaval, Congress passed the Banking Act of 1933, often called the **Glass-Steagall Act,** which imposed limitations on the type of activities that banks could engage in and on the interest rates they could pay on deposit accounts.

Also, since the banking sector is dual, most banks are regulated both at the state and at the national level, and they are subject to supervision from state and federal agencies. Starting in the 1980s, the U.S. banking sector witnessed a process of deregulation. In 1980, the **Depository Institutions Deregulation and Monetary Control Act (DIDMCA)** allowed banks to pay interest on special demand deposits called NOW accounts. Starting from the mid 1990s, the reinterpretation and then complete repeal of the Glass-Steagall Act (Gramm-Bleach-Bliley Act of 1999) allowed banks to engage in a wide array of non-bank financial activities.

STRUCTURE OF THE U.S. BANKING INDUSTRY

In the United States, there are three types of depository institutions: **commercial banks**, **thrifts**, and **credit unions**.

Commercial Banks

Commercial banks are the largest category of financial intermediaries by value of assets. In the United States, commercial banks can be chartered and supervised by states (state banks) or by the Office of the Comptroller of the Currency (OCC), a branch of the Federal Treasury (national banks). All national banks and some state banks are members of the **Federal Reserve System.**

Most commercial banks have assets between $100 million and $500 million. However, the largest commercial banks have assets of more than $10 billion each, which means the largest 1 percent of banks holds more than 70 percent of all banking assets. Commercial banks are stock owned and earn profit by accepting deposits, extending loans, investing in securities, and offering various financial services for a fee. Deposits at commercial banks are insured by the **Federal Deposit Insurance Corporation (FDIC)** for up to $250,000 per account.

"Thrifts": Savings Associations and Savings and Loans Associations (S&Ls)

More than 1,000 U.S. banks are Saving Associations (SAs) and Savings and Loans Associations (S&Ls). These primarily extend residential loans. They started as mutual institutions that collected members' funds through savings (thrift) deposits and financed residential developments for their members. Nowadays, many such associations are stock owned, accept demand deposits, and extend a wider variety of loans.

SAs and S&Ls can be chartered at the state or national level and are regulated by the Office of Thrift Supervision (OTS), which is now merged with the OCC. Deposits at SAs and S&Ls are insured by the FDIC. In the 1980s, a spike in interest rates led to a severe crisis of the S&Ls system, which was then overhauled. Nowadays, thanks to a number of regulatory changes, S&Ls perform many of the same activities as commercial banks.

Credit Unions

Credit unions are mutual institutions where members with a common bond deposit saving shares and apply for consumer loans. Because of the common bond, these institutions are quite small and, like other types of clubs, benefit from tax advantages and are not subject to antitrust regulation. They can be chartered by states or at the national level. The National Credit Union Administration regulates and oversees federally chartered credit unions and the National Credit Union Share Insurance Fund (NCUSIF) insures deposits at all credit unions for up to $250,000 per account. In time of crisis, credit unions can borrow funds from the Central Liquidity Facility (CLF).

TIP

The number of commercial banks has been steadily declining over the past decades. But today, the number of bank branches is twice as high as in the early 1970s— banks realized that proximity to home or the workplace was a key factor in people's decision about where to bank.

Other Financial Intermediaries

Banks are just one type of financial intermediary. Several other types of firms offer different services of financial intermediation. With the deregulation of the banking sector, today's bank holding companies are often made up of various financial intermediaries.

The other most important types of financial companies are:

- **Investment banks:** Investment banks help companies issue securities like stocks and bonds to raise funds directly from the public (unlike commercial banks that offer borrowers indirect finance). They also assist companies with mergers and acquisitions and risk management.

- **Insurance companies:** Insurance companies are financial intermediaries that help people better manage the risks in their lives and protect themselves from financial losses. Typically, insurance companies offer contracts in which, for the payment of a fixed premium, they promise to reimburse certain expenses, such as medical expenses or car repairs after an accident.

- **Mutual funds/pensions funds:** Mutual funds are professionally managed pools of funds invested in various securities like stocks and bonds. The funds' owners are called shareholders. Funds that are used to pay pensions are called **pension funds**.

- **Bank Holding Company (BHC):** These are financial companies that own one or more banks.

In the past couple of decades, the importance of these financial intermediaries has significantly grown. They often lend funds just like commercial banks would do; however, instead of doing so by extending loans, they channel funds through the various securities markets. Often, these institutions are referred to as the **shadow banking system**.

OPERATION AND MANAGEMENT OF FINANCIAL MARKETS AND INTERMEDIARIES

Commercial banks and other financial intermediaries are for-profit enterprises. Banks earn profit by charging fees (credit card fees, for example) and by borrowing funds at a low interest rate and lending those funds at a higher interest rate. Economists call this activity **asset transformation.**

Here is an example of asset transformation. When an individual deposits $1,000 in a checkable account at First Bank, the deposit increases the First Bank's reserves by $1,000. By law, the bank must keep a share of the deposit as required reserves. (In the United States, the required reserve ratio varies depending on the size of the bank, with higher ratios imposed on larger banks.) However, the bank can loan out up to the full amount of its excess reserves.

Suppose the required reserve ratio is 10 percent. After a deposit of $1,000, First Bank can loan out up to $1,000 − (10% × $1,000) = $900. If First Bank pays an interest rate of 0.5% on its checkable deposit and charges an interest rate of 5% on its loans, at the end of the year, the Bank has (5% × $900) − (0.5% × $1,000) = $45 − $5 = $40 of income it can use to pay for nonfinancial expenses and to distribute a dividend to its stockholders.

The Balance Sheet of a Commercial Bank

To fully understand the different activities performed by financial intermediaries, it is important to understand how these organizations raise funds and use them. We can do so in an organized way by taking a quick look at the typical balance sheet of a commercial bank.

The **balance sheet** is an accounting tool with two columns, one listing a firm's **liabilities** (money owed) and **capital** (net worth) and the other listing the firm's **assets**. At all times, the two sides balance:

assets = liabilities + capital

A bank's liabilities and capital show how the bank raises money, while the bank's assets show how the bank uses that money.

Liabilities

Liabilities are funds the bank owes to some person or business. The larger share of a commercial bank's liabilities is in the form of deposits. These come in three types:

1. *Demand deposits:* Deposits that can be withdrawn without limits like checkable accounts (18 percent of all deposits). Until 2011, they were not allowed to pay interest in accordance with Regulation Q, the regulation that in accordance with the Banking Act of 1933 (Glass-Steagall Act) prohibited paying interest on deposits payable on demand.

   - *Negotiable Orders of Withdrawal (NOW) accounts:* Introduced by the Depository Institutions Deregulation and Monetary Control Act (DIDMCA) in 1980, these are deposits that, while structured similarly to checking accounts, were not considered demand deposits and hence were allowed to pay interest in compliance with Regulation Q.

2. *Savings deposits* (61 percent of all deposits) There are two main types of saving deposits:

   - *Savings accounts:* Accounts that pay interest but that do not allow writing checks (20 percent)

   - *Money market deposit accounts:* Similar to money market mutual funds shares; however, they are federally insured and pay interest. The law limits transfers to third parties to six per month (47 percent).

3. *Time deposits:* (15 percent of all deposits) The funds in time deposits are available only at a specified time in the future (maturity date). The two most important types of time deposits are:

   - *Certificates of Deposit (CDs):* Certificates issued in specific amounts that pay a fixed-interest rate.

   - *Negotiable Certificates of Deposit:* These have larger denominations than regular CDs ($100,000 or more) and are negotiable.

Other important liabilities on a commercial bank's balance sheets are:

- **Borrowed funds:** Funds borrowed from wholesale money markets. Their importance increased as demand for loans outpaced banks' ability to attract new deposits.

- **Federal funds:** Funds held at the Federal Reserve as required or excess reserves.

- **Repurchase agreements (repos):** A form of loan where the bank sells a security to a lender with the promise to repurchase the same security for a specified price at a specified date.

- **Eurodollars:** These are deposits denominated in dollars but held in foreign branches of U.S. banks (or at foreign banks). The interest rate banks charge each other in the Eurodollar market is called the London Interbank Offer Rate (LIBOR).

- **Fed loans:** These are funds the bank has borrowed from the discount window of the Federal Reserve. The term is typically 15 days.

- **Trading liabilities:** Funds owed due to losses on derivative contracts or due to short positions (when the bank sells securities it does not own).

Bank Capital

A bank's equity capital is also called **net worth**. Banks have lower capital than most other firms. The smaller the ratio of a bank's capital to its assets, the more leveraged the bank is. There are two types of bank capital:

1. *Capital stock:* The funds stockholders have directly invested in the bank
2. *Undivided profits:* Profit that has not yet been paid out as dividend

Assets

Under assets, we find the different uses of the deposited or borrowed funds. The majority of assets comes from money that others owe to the bank. Here are some of the main examples of assets:

- **Cash assets:** Very liquid assets the bank holds as cash in vault or funds deposited at the Federal Reserve Bank

- **Fed funds sold and reverse repos:** The reverse of a repurchase; in this case, the bank is lending funds by purchasing securities from the borrower, who agrees to repurchase them at a future date for a specified price

- **Investments:** Highly liquid portfolios of bonds issued by the U.S. government or a U.S. government agency or a municipality; they can be easily sold when the bank is in need of reserves, and they give tax benefits. Bonds are standardized contracts that provide the issuer financing but no other service

- **Loans:** More than 55 percent of commercial banks' assets are represented by loans; loans are not as liquid as investment assets and are contracts specifically designed to address each customer's needs. Most bank loans are secured with some form of collateral. If the lender defaults on the loan, the bank acquires ownership of the collateral. A mortgage, for example, is a secured (or collateralized) loan. Some loans charge a fixed interest rate, while others charge a floating interest rate that moves following a benchmark rate (like the LIBOR or the prime rate). Banks extend commercial loans to businesses, real estate loans (mortgages) to individuals and businesses for the purchase or remodeling of buildings and structures, agricultural loans to farmers, and consumer loans to individuals. Bank credit cards are a growing type of consumer loan. The first credit cards offered only local credit, but, starting in 1966 with changes in bank regulations, they have become a national phenomenon.

A cardholder has access to funds up to a set limit and each billing cycle must pay a minimum installment. Interest is charged on any purchase not covered within the monthly billing cycle.

- **Leases:** Starting in the mid 60s, banks could purchase items that they lease to individuals or businesses; this type of contract has tax advantages.

Key Management Activities

Let's have a closer look at these important facets of bank management.

Liquidity Management

When a bank has to meet an unusually high volume of withdrawals, it can generate the necessary reserves in several ways. The bank could borrow funds in the federal funds market, sell some liquid securities, borrow funds from the Federal Reserve through the discount window, or reduce the stock of loans—either by not renewing some of the short-term loans that reach maturity that day (that is, by calling in loans) or by selling some loans to other financial intermediaries.

Each of these actions comes at a different opportunity cost. For example, the bank has to pay the federal funds rate on funds borrowed in the federal funds market and the discount rate on funds borrowed from the Federal Reserve. Calling in loans can spoil the relationship with a valuable client. The bank manager has to decide which option is the most profitable and in the end might decide that the bank should hold a large volume of excess reserves instead.

Asset Management

Bank managers purchase and sell assets and liabilities to reach three goals: earn the highest returns, avoid risk, and guarantee liquidity. There are four strategies bank managers can follow to reach their goals. They can seek borrowers who are willing to pay high interest even if they have a limited risk of default, they can buy securities that pay high returns even if their risk is low, they can diversify the bank portfolio, and they can hold some very liquid securities even if these pay low interest.

Liability Management

After the 1960s, checkable deposits ceased to be the main source of funds at commercial banks. Now, when a commercial bank wants to raise funds, it can sell a negotiable CD or borrow funds in the federal funds market. Banks can increase their profit by paying attention to the composition of their liabilities.

Capital Adequacy Management

Banks face a tradeoff when choosing an adequate level of bank capital. On the one hand, banks must keep a minimum amount of capital to avoid failure and to meet regulatory requirements. On the other hand, the capital stock affects the rate of return the bank can pay to its investors. Economists use two measures to assess a bank's profitability:

$$\text{The Return on Average Assets (ROAA): ROAA} = \frac{\text{Net income (i.e., returns after taxes)}}{\text{Assets}}$$

$$\text{The Return on Average Equity (ROAE): ROAE} = \frac{\text{Net income (i.e., returns after taxes)}}{\text{Equity Capital}}$$

For a given return on assets, the lower the capital stock, the higher the return on average equity.

Risk Management

Banks face two sources of risk that could rock their operations and push them in the red: credit risk and interest-rate risk. **Credit risk** refers to the possibility that borrowers default on their loans, while **interest-rate risk** refers to the possibility of sudden changes in the interest rate the bank charges its debtors or pays to its creditors.

Managing Credit Risk

Information asymmetries on borrowers' creditworthiness lead to a problem called **adverse selection**, where charging higher interest rates attracts riskier borrowers—in effect, selecting an adverse outcome for the bank. Information asymmetries on borrowers' choices and actions lead to a problem called **moral hazard**, in which, since banks cannot monitor borrowers' use of funds, borrowers have an incentive to take up more risk than they can handle, consequently raising the hazard of default.

There are several strategies bank managers can follow to reduce moral hazard and adverse selection:

- They can collect detailed information on loan applicants, screening out borrowers with higher chances of default.
- They can visit commercial borrowers to monitor how they are employing the borrowed funds.
- They can specialize in specific types of loans or in specific geographical areas to gain higher expertise and reduce the cost of screening and monitoring.

The tool banks most commonly use to reduce moral hazard is collateral requirements. **Collateral** is any asset that by contract the bank acquires in case of default. Vehicles, real estate, or financial assets are used often as collateral. **Compensating balances**, funds the borrower must keep deposited at the lending bank for the duration of the loan, are another form of collateral.

To limit moral hazard, banks develop long-term bank relationships with their clients, who then find it more costly to choose projects that raise their risk of default on a loan. Long-term relationships also lower the cost of screening and monitoring future loan applications from the same client. Adverse selection and moral hazard can lead banks to ration credit by either refusing to lend any amount of funds to some borrowers or by limiting the amount of funds a borrower can obtain at the offered interest rate.

Managing Interest-Rate Risk

Interest-rate volatility raises a bank's earnings volatility, exposing the bank to undesired risk. There are two approaches economists use to analyze interest rate risk: **gap analysis,** which focuses on the difference between interest rate-sensitive liabilities and interest rate-sensitive assets, and **duration analysis,** which evaluates how changes in interest rates affect the value of assets and liabilities in the bank's balance sheet. The name of this approach comes from the relationship between a security's market value, the interest rate, and the number of years during which the security will produce a stream of payments, called the security's **duration**.

Off-Balance Sheet Banking

Over the last two decades, as banks have become more reliant on fee-based activities instead of interest-based activities, a larger share of banks' activities are not reflected in changes of the balance sheet. These are the so-called off-balance sheet activities. Banks charge fees on a variety of financial services from foreign exchange trades to the creation of structured investment vehicles and securitization.

Banks also earn income (or incur losses) on trades of derivative securities like forwards, futures, and swaps.

More traditional off-balance sheet activities, however, are loan commitments, promises to lend money according to agreed rules. Credit card limits, lines of credit, and revolving credit are three kinds of loan commitments. Banks are also more likely to engage in loan sales and loan brokerage. If they have specific expertise in a geographic area or a type of client, banks earn profit by cheaply originating loans they resell at a higher price to other financial intermediaries. The practice has become so widespread that the loan-related data in call reports are becoming less and less informative of the overall volume of loan origination.

REGULATION OF THE BANKING INDUSTRY

Governments that wish to mitigate adverse selection and moral hazard in credit markets heavily regulate the banking sector to protect consumers from abuses and to enhance the stability of the financial system.

As we mentioned earlier, in the United States, several agencies charter, regulate, and supervise commercial banks and other depository institutions, and it is possible for the same financial institution to be regulated and supervised by up to four different state or federal agencies.

Banking regulation and supervision is very complex. So here we will break it down into its most relevant categories:

Capital Requirements

Capital requirements are regulations that force banks to keep a sound amount of capital. Banks with more capital are less likely to fail.

Equity capital is an effective buffer when a bank must absorb losses. Also, more capital means the bank has more to lose from poor management and risky activities significantly reducing problems of moral hazard. Until the mid 1980s, capital requirements were set in terms of the leverage ratio, the ratio between core capital and total assets. In 1988, however, the central bankers of the United States and eleven other high-income countries signed an accord known as Basel 1 that introduced the idea of tying capital requirements to a bank's risk exposure.

In the United States, current regulation now divides capital in two categories, called **Tier 1 capital** (or core capital) and **Tier 2 capital** (or supplemental capital) and requires a bank's leverage ratio be higher than 3 percent and that the ratio of Tier 1 plus Tier 2 capital to risk-weighted assets be at least 8 percent. When computing risk-weighted assets, assets are divided into four categories from less risky to more risky and assigned different weights. Off-balance sheet activities are also factored in after they are converted into on-balance sheet equivalents and assigned to the different risk categories.

Implementation of the original Basel accord highlighted how banks can increase their effective risk exposure without affecting their measured exposure by holding riskier assets within each asset category, an activity economists call **regulatory arbitrage**. The guidelines of the original Basel accord were revised in 1999 to strengthen the link between capital requirements and risk for large international banks. However, the suggested capital requirements proved too low to protect large banks from the financial crisis of 2008.

Financial Supervision and Bank Examinations

To protect the public from scams, banks are chartered after a long review process. Charter applicants must provide extensive information on the bank's business plan, suggested senior management, and financial viability. Once operating, banks must file quarterly call reports describing the bank''operations and financial conditions. Banks are also subject to periodic unannounced safety and soundness examinations. Bank examiners review the bank's records for possible fraud, analyze assets (loans in particular) and liabilities to assess the bank's creditworthiness, and verify management's ability to identify and monitor risk. Regulators use information from the call reports and the on-site examinations to rate each bank on a scale from 1 (highest) to 5 (lowest) according to the **CAMELS rating system**, which stands for **C**apital, **A**sset quality, **M**anagement, **E**arnings, **L**iquidity, and **S**ensitivity to market risk. Starting in the mid 90s, regulators raised their emphasis on supervising banks' risk management, and large banks must pass **stress tests,** simulations that assess how the bank would weather severe economic shocks and whether the bank needs to raise more capital.

Disclosure Requirements

To alleviate problems of asymmetric information, regulators require banks to disclose information on the composition of their assets and risk exposure. Disclosure requirements allow investors, stockholders, and depositors to gain all the information they need about the financial condition of a bank to make good decisions. Indirectly, this nudges bank managers to steer away from excessively risky activities. Disclosure requirements were first introduced in the 1930s and were greatly tightened by the Sarbanes-Oxley Act of 2002.

Consumer Protection

Another goal of bank regulation and supervision is to protect consumers from scams, discrimination, and predatory lending practices. Starting in 1969, the Truth in Lending Act (Consumer Credit Protection Act, CCPA) requires that lenders (including banks) give borrowers clear and correct information on the interest rate they pay. For each loan, creditors must clearly indicate the **annual percentage rate** (**APR**) and total finance charges. The Fair Credit Billing Act (FCBA) requires that credit card issuers clearly state how they will assess finance charges and that they resolve billing disputes quickly. The Fair and Accurate Credit Transaction (FACT) act regulates credit-reporting agencies, protecting them from state-level over-regulation and requiring that each year consumers are entitled to a free credit report.

The Equal Credit Opportunity Act (ECOA) forbids banks from discriminating according to race, age, gender, marital status, and national origin, while the Community Reinvestment Act (CRA) of 1977 requires that banks offer credit to individuals and firms from all neighborhoods in their market area and refrain from **redlining,** the practice of using a red marker to highlight on a map neighborhoods where the bank does not extend loans.

Compliance with the CRA regulation is heavy in documentation and costly. What's worse, by requiring banks to offer loans in all areas, including economically depressed neighborhoods, the CRA has the unintended consequence of leading banks to extend risky loans to financially weak families that are unable to repay and end up bankrupt.

DEPOSIT INSURANCE

In this section, we will explore the regulations and the agency that help keep the banking sector stable and stop bank failures from becoming bank panics.

Bank Failures and Lender of Last Resort

As we mentioned earlier, when a bank can no longer meet its obligations to depositors and creditors, it fails. A bank failure can be triggered by **illiquidity** or **insolvency.** During a bank crisis, depositors withdraw their funds all at once, and even a sound bank can find itself illiquid and unable to meet its obligations. In such a time, even sound banks are forced to sell security investments at a loss, losing assets and risking bankruptcy. Central banks prevent this type of failure by acting as **lenders of last resort.** Since 1914, the Federal Reserve offers liquidity to distressed member banks through its discount window or through open market operations, acting as a lender of last resort to these intermediaries.

Excessive risk-taking lies behind failures triggered by **insolvency.** As we mentioned before, bank managers tend to extend loans and buy securities that are risky, as these pay higher interest. However, if creditors default on their loans and security prices drop, the bank can suddenly lose assets and, unless it has an adequate amount of equity capital, it quickly finds itself unable to repay short-term debt or meet depositors' cash withdrawals. Capital requirements help prevent failures due to insolvency.

Before new regulation was introduced in the 1930s, bank failures would spread like a contagious disease. One single bank failure would make all depositors nervous. Because of asymmetric information, depositors could not tell if their bank was sound or on the brink of collapse, and they would all rush to withdraw their funds at the same time, triggering bank runs and bank panics. Economists call this phenomenon the **financial contagion effect**.

The Federal Deposit Insurance Corporation

From the late 1800s through the 1930s, bank failures were a serious problem, and bank panics were frequent. Between 1920 and 1933, more than 10,000 banks failed. By statute, only member banks could borrow from the Federal Reserve as lender of last resort, and fewer than 10 percent of depository institutions were members. The number of bank failures, however, dropped precipitously after the establishment of the **Federal Deposit Insurance Corporation** (FDIC) by the Glass-Steagall Act in 1933.

The FDIC insures deposit accounts and prevents bank runs and panics very effectively. Today, the FDIC insures depositors at commercial banks and S&L associations for up to $250,000 per account. The National Credit Union Share Insurance Fund insures accounts at credit unions. While all types of deposit accounts (checking accounts, savings accounts, money market accounts, and certificates of deposit) are insured, the FDIC does not cover other financial products, like investment accounts, shares in mutual funds, or life insurance.

Let's discuss how the FDIC handles failed banks. Typically, insolvent banks are shut down by their chartering authority; in rare cases, however, after a negative examination, the FDIC makes the decision to resolve a failing bank. Once the decision to shut down a bank has been made, there are two methods the FDIC can use to resolve the failed business: the payoff and liquidate method and the purchase and assumption method. By law, the FDIC must use the method with lowest cost.

Under the **payoff and liquidate method,** the FDIC pays off depositors up to $250,000 per account, and then liquidates all the bank's assets to pay off all other debts. Creditors have different levels of precedence: depositors and the FDIC are paid off first, then general creditors, and last, if any money is left, it pays shareholders. Under the **purchase and assumption method,** the FDIC brokers the sale or merger of the failing bank with a willing and financially stable institution. The FDIC often facilitates the deal by extending subsidized loans or by assuming some of the bad loans and investments of the failing bank. Under a **clean bank purchase and assumption,** the assuming bank keeps only the failing bank's insured deposits and purchases only few of the bank's assets. On the other hand, under a **whole bank agreement,** the assuming bank receives all assets and liabilities for a one-time payment.

Deposit Insurance and Moral Hazard

Deposit insurance reduces the risk of financial contagion and the likelihood of bank panics; however, it creates several types of moral hazard. Deposit insurance reduces depositors' need to monitor their banks worsening market discipline. Because insured depositors do not bear any of the bank's risk, managers are able to attract deposits at low interest even while extending risky loans. Even if these loans fail, the bank can still look profitable by propping up earnings with origination fees, since it can still attract cheap deposits to raise loanable funds.

Too Big to Fail (TBTF)

The FDIC has always shied away from liquidating large failing banks, creating an incentive for shareholders, uninsured depositors, and creditors to own or do business with large banks instead of smaller banks.

In 1984, when one of the largest American banks called Continental Illinois almost failed, the FDIC went a step further and announced that a number of very large American banks were "too big to fail" and would never be liquidated. The policy wanted to prevent instability in the banking sector. One bank's liability is another bank's asset, and the liquidation of one very large bank could drastically reduce the value of other banks' assets, triggering bank runs and bank panic. However, the too big to fail policy exacerbates the problems of moral hazard we mentioned earlier, and it gives large banks an unfair advantage in attracting depositors at low interest rates, as all deposits at TBTF banks are effectively insured.

However, in September 2008, the failure of Lehman Brothers, an investment bank, had dramatic consequences on the financial system, highlighting that indeed some financial institutions are too big to fail and heightening regulators' emphasis on what economists call **systemic risk**—events that would rock the whole banking and financial system instead of just one financial intermediary.

MONEY AND MACROECONOMIC ACTIVITY

In this section, we'll outline different theories that explain how the economy works and how money supply and interest rates influence economic activity and our everyday lives. This knowledge will help you better understand when and how central banks can influence inflation and employment with their tools of monetary policy.

BASIC CLASSICAL AND KEYNESIAN ECONOMICS

Before diving into the theories, let's review some common economic terminology.

Economists call **total output** the amount of goods and services an economy produces in a year, and they track total output using an economic indicator called **Gross Domestic Product** (**GDP**). **Potential output** is the level of output the economy produces when inputs, labor in particular, are fully employed and the economy operates efficiently.

Gross domestic product is the value of all final goods and services produced for the market over a period of time in the country. A **final good** is an item that is not used and totally transformed in production over the same period. GDP has four components: **consumption, investment, government spending**, and **net exports** (the difference between exports to other nations and imports from other nations). Consumption counts families' expenditures in durable and non-durable goods. Investment has two components: **fixed investment**, which counts expenditures on residential and non-residential structures and firms' purchases of new equipment and machinery, and **inventory expenditure**, which counts changes in firms' holdings of materials, parts, and final products.

The payment people receive for their work or financial investment is called **income**. Economists track income using the economic indicator **net national income** (**NNI**). Net national income has four components: wages and salaries, rents, interest, and profit.

Economists call **disposable income** (**DI**) the difference of **net national income** and **net taxes**. Every year, families pay a portion of their income in taxes and receive a portion of their income as transfers from government social security pension. Net taxes are the difference between taxes and transfers.

Families spend a portion of their **disposable income** (after-taxes income) in consumption (just like the GDP component) and the save the rest. Hence, disposable income is the sum of consumption and saving.

The **price level** is an average of all prices and is tracked using several indicators, for example the Consumer Price Index (CPI) or the Personal Consumption Expenditures (PCE) deflator.

Inflation is a continual and generalized increase in the price level. The inflation rate measures how fast prices are increasing.

Unemployment is the number of jobless workers in search of work. **Employment** is the number of workers who have jobs. The **unemployment rate** is the ratio of unemployment to the labor force, the sum of unemployment and employment. When people are out work because they don't have skills in demand, they are deemed *structurally unemployed*. When people are out of work due to a low level of economic activity, they are deemed *cyclically unemployed*. The economy is called at full employment when there is no cyclical unemployment.

The **interest rate** is the proportion of a loan or of the value of a debt security that is charged as interest. The **real interest rate** is the difference between the interest rate and the rate of inflation people feel will prevail in the future.

Theories

This section focuses on two economic approaches: the classical approach and the Keynesian approach (after British economist John Maynard Keynes).

Classical economists believe the economy is self-regulating and advocate for a **laissez-faire** (let it be) approach to economic policy. According to the classical model, total output follows the amount of labor input and capital input used in production. These amounts are determined in highly competitive markets where flexible prices absorb any change in demand or supply.

In the labor market, workers' and firms' decisions are driven by the **real wage**, the amount of goods the monetary wage can buy. The **supply of labor** is an upward sloping line illustrating that at higher wages, more people are willing to work. The **demand for labor is** a downward sloping line illustrating that at higher wages, firms have lower profit margins and hire fewer workers. The market is in **equilibrium** when firms pay the wage rate where the demand for labor is equal to the supply of labor. Flexible real wages that move in response to changes in demand and supply maintain the market in equilibrium at all times; when the labor market is in equilibrium, all people willing to accept the current wage have found a job, and the only people out of work are those who don't wish to work for the current wage. There is no involuntary unemployment.

The key idea of the classical model is that the market for goods and services is in equilibrium at all times because *supply creates its own demand*, a statement that is often referred to as **Say's law.** Classical economists noted that for every $10 of output a firm produces, $10 of income is paid to workers and entrepreneurs. If in one way or another all of this income is spent to buy goods and services, the very act of producing an item creates the demand for that item.

In the classical model, the market for capital makes sure savings would equate investment, so all income distributed would come back to firms in the form of demand—some as consumption and some as investment. In the classical model's view, in the market for capital families loan out funds to firms that wish to finance their investment spending.

Families and firms base their saving and investment decisions primarily on the real interest rate. The supply of funds is upward sloping, as families are more willing to postpone consumption and save when the interest rate is higher. The demand for funds is downward sloping, as a decline in the interest rate lowers borrowing costs and increases the number of investment projects that are profitable. In equilibrium, the demand for loanable funds equals the supply of loanable funds and investment equates saving.

TIP

All these relationships can be summarized in the following way: GDP ≈ NNI and NNI = Net Taxes = Disposable Income = Consumption + Saving

Early economists believed flexible interest rates adjusted to movements of demand and supply and maintained investment equal to saving and the demand for goods and services equal to the supply of goods and services at all times.

Keynesian economists believe the economy fails to self-adjust at times and that economic policy—in particular, higher government spending—can help maintain the economy at full employment.

According to these economists, prices and wages are sticky and total output follows aggregate expenditures. **Aggregate expenditures** are the sum of four components: consumption, planned investment, government purchases, and net exports.

- **Consumption expenditure** is the largest of the four components and, according to the Keynesian model, it's positively related to current disposable income. Consumption sensitivity to disposable income is called the Marginal Propensity to Consume (MPC): C = Autonomous consumption + MPC × Disposable Income.

- **Planned investment** is the sum of planned fixed investment and planned inventory investment. Keynes agreed with the classical economists that it is negatively sensitive to changes in the cost of borrowing and the real interest rate: I = autonomous investment − d × real interest rate.

- **Government purchases** add directly to total spending, while taxes reduce total spending indirectly reducing disposable income and lowering consumption.

- **Net exports** are sensitive to changes in the foreign exchange rate, to the relative price of domestic and foreign goods and to global economic conditions. A higher interest rate influences the foreign exchange rate and leads to an appreciation of the domestic currency. As a result, net exports are negatively sensitive to the interest rate.

In the Keynesian model, the market for goods and services can be in equilibrium with the economy operating below its potential level and workers being involuntarily out of jobs. Also, since consumption is sensitive to disposable income, changes in aggregate expenditure are amplified by a **multiplier effect.**

According to Keynesian economists, a decline in investment lowers aggregate expenditure and increases inventory investment above its planned level. Firms that see their finite product pile up in their warehouses cut production and let some workers go. As prices and wages are sticky, the real wage does not decline when labor demand drops, and unemployment rises as the economy slows down. Many workers out of jobs are involuntarily unemployed at the current monetary wage at which they would accept work. In modern terminology, they are cyclically unemployed since weak spending is behind their joblessness.

Keynesian economists believed that public policy is effective at stimulating the economy during a recession or cooling it off during inflationary times. Because the banking sector was weak and in upheaval when Keynes wrote most of his theory in the 1930s, early Keynesians tended to favor fiscal policy (in the form of actions taken by the central government like higher public spending) as particularly effective at supporting the economy in times of depression. Keynesian economists pointed out that higher government purchases would increase total spending, creating demand for private businesses and triggering a positive income/consumption multiplier effect.

Classical economists, on the contrary, believed fiscal policy could never stimulate the economy. Classical economists stressed that higher government spending must be financed either by higher taxes today or by higher taxes in the future; and that in both cases, families anticipating the tax hike would lower consumption, neutralizing the positive effects of the fiscal policy.

After WWII, Keynesian economists believed that the government could run public deficits during economic downturns and surpluses during expansions to fine tune the economy, that is, to preempt possible swings in economic activity. They also thought that the central bank could stimulate the economy with little consequence for the inflation rate. A study of empirical data had found a negative relationship between the inflation rate and the unemployment rate, called the **Phillips curve**, and some Keynesian economists believed this relationship to be structural and immutable, providing the central bank with a policy trade-off.

MONETARISM AND RATIONAL EXPECTATIONS

During the 1960s and 1970s, however, the yearly inflation rate increased from 1.2 percent in 1964 to 11.8 percent in 1974, and economists' focus shifted from maintaining the economy at full employment to understanding and fighting inflation. It is in these years that a new theory called **monetarism** came to the fore.

Monetarists believed that fiscal policy is ineffective at stimulating the economy and that monetary policy can affect economic activity in the short run, while it affects only prices and inflation in the long run. These economists believed that due to long policy lags, monetary policy would disrupt the economy instead of stabilize it and suggested a fixed rate of growth of the money supply as the optimal policy.

Monetarists believed that inflation is always a monetary phenomenon and stressed the importance of expectations during inflationary times. Milton Friedman, the most prominent of the monetarists, pointed out that the inflation/unemployment trade-off, or the Phillips curve, was not stable, but shifted up along the inflation dimension as people adjusted their inflation expectations. Friedman believed that people had adaptive expectations and would adjust their inflation expectations rather slowly.

In the early '80s, a new group of economists stressed that not only did inflation expectations adjust rather quickly, but also that people used all their knowledge of the economy and the monetary policy when forming expectations. They believed that people have rational expectations; they thought that the economy works the way people expect and that people form expectations using all available information without making systematic mistakes. If people have rational expectations, monetary policy is neutral also in the short run.

MONEY AND INFLATION

Economists have shown that a faster money supply can lead to inflation. There are three theories of inflation.

The Quantity Theory of Inflation

The quantity theory of inflation states that a higher rate of growth of the money supply leads to faster inflation. At the heart of this theory is the **equation of exchange** that states that income at current prices is equal to the money supply times the velocity of money: $P \times Y = M \times V$. The velocity of money is the number of times that each dollar note must change hands over the year so that all transactions are paid for.

The quantity theory of inflation makes the assumption that the velocity of money does not change through time and that the economy is always at potential output, so that changes in the money supply M translate into changes in the level of prices P—in other words, inflation.

Demand-Pull Inflation

The demand-pull inflation theory is a more sophisticated version of the quantity theory of inflation. In this theory, it is recognized that higher money supply lowers interest rates and stimulates investment and consumption, raising total spending. If total spending increases faster than total output, however, the result is a continual increase in the price level, in other words inflation. Many economists believe that the increasing inflation of the 1960s and 1970s was an example of demand-pull inflation.

Cost-Push Inflation

Inflation could also arise from increases in the cost of production. This is what economists call cost-push inflation. For example, a sudden increase in the cost of imported materials like petroleum or copper would force firms to raise their prices and could trigger a wage/price spiral where workers demand higher wages to protect their purchasing power and firms agree to the wage increases just to increase prices even further.

CENTRAL BANKING AND THE FEDERAL RESERVE

The central bank of the United States is called the Federal Reserve System. A central bank is the institution that supervises a nation's banking sector and is in charge of the money supply.

HISTORICAL AND PHILOSOPHICAL FRAMEWORK

The Federal Reserve System was created in 1913, when Congress passed the **Federal Reserve Act.**

In the early years of the Union, at the urgency of Alexander Hamilton, who believed a national bank could improve credit conditions and spur economic development, Congress established a First Bank of the United States as a repository of federal funds. However, in 1811, the bank's charter was allowed to expire. The second attempt at creating a central bank failed in 1836. The predominantly agrarian society of the early Union, represented by Andrew Jackson, was wary of concentrated power and feared that a central bank would represent only the interests of bankers and industrialists.

Between 1836 and 1865, the so-called **free banking era,** the United States had thousands of state chartered banks that extended loans funded via the issuance of bank notes. The country had no centralized currency and people used these thousands of different bank notes as money. Each bank's note carried the issuer's risk of failure and notes issued by well-run banks were exchanged at their face value, while notes issued by poorly managed banks were exchanged at a discount.

During the years of the Civil War, Congress passed the **National Bank Acts,** which led to the current dual nature of the U.S. banking system. The Acts empowered the Comptroller of the Currency to

TIP

Before 1913, the United States had no central bank.

charter national banks that could issue tax-exempt national notes backed by government securities. State bank notes were subject to a 10 percent tax and the Act reduced the number of currencies in circulation but increased state banks' reliance on demand deposits as their main source of liquidity. Demand deposits were not insured, and state banks kept scant reserves, often reinvested at other depository institutions; as a result, bank runs and bank panics were very frequent. At the time, most banks extended call loans, loans that borrowers had to repay the moment the bank needed the money back.

During panics, banks in dire need of liquidity would call their loans in, pushing cash strapped farmers and businesses into bankruptcy and plunging entire regions into deep economic depressions. The worst of these came in 1907 when a severe financial crisis in the New York Stock Exchange spread to the banking sector and then engulfed the whole economy. The joint intervention of some of the richest men in America saved the economy, but time was ripe for the creation of a central bank to bring some stability to the U.S. financial system.

Between 1908 and 1912, a national monetary commission chaired by Senator Nelson Aldrich worked at the design of a decentralized, banker-controlled monetary authority. However, in 1912, the newly elected Woodrow Wilson abandoned Aldrich's proposal and instructed Carter Glass and Parker Willis to craft an alternative plan for a government-controlled central bank. With several compromises on the way, Glass' and Willis' proposal evolved into the Federal Reserve Act of 1913.

The Act established a central bank that would bring stability to the financial system, streamline check collection and clearing, and provide strong supervision to the banking sector. The bank was authorized to issue Federal Reserve notes convertible into gold that it would use to maintain an "elastic currency" accommodating businesses' needs for liquidity as prescribed by the real bills doctrine. Reflecting the current fears of concentration of power, the Reserve System was organized in twelve regional districts, each with a Federal Bank owned by local member banks.

Surprisingly, even if the Federal Reserve's main mandate was preserving financial stability, the Federal Reserve Bank was not given the full authority to act as a lender of last resort; the Bank could lend to institutions in financial distress only if they were member banks, and these were always a minority of all depository institutions.

STRUCTURE AND ORGANIZATION

The structure and organization of the Federal Reserve System clearly reflects the institution's history and a clear desire for compromise between stability and decentralization.

The Federal Reserve System is composed of a Board of Governors located in Washington, DC, that supervises the system, twelve regional banks, and a Federal Open Market Committee that is responsible for monetary policy.

The Board of Governors of the Federal Reserve System

The federal agency that supervises the Fed system, the **Board of Governors,** is located in Washington, DC. It is composed of 7 members appointed by the President of the United States and confirmed by the senate for fourteen-year terms. The Chair of the Federal Reserve System is chosen from the members of the Board.

The Board of Governors has several functions and is directly involved in designing and directing the U.S. monetary policy. All 7 members of the Board are voting members of the Federal Open Market Committee, the committee that sets the monetary policy target. The Board is also responsible for setting the reserve requirements and for controlling the discount rate, the interest rate the Fed charges member banks as lender of last resort. The Board has other responsibilities unrelated to monetary policy. For example, it designs bank supervision policies and publishes information and data on the economy and the financial sector.

The Federal Reserve Banks

Each Federal Reserve Bank serves a district and provides services to local banks and the Treasury. Federal Reserve Banks have 9 directors, 6 chosen by member banks and 3 chosen by the Board of Governors. Six of the 9 directors appoint the bank president. The local Reserve Banks have several functions: they extend discount loans to banks in the district, supervise and examine bank holdings and state-chartered member banks, verify that local banks offer fair and equitable services, clear checks, and destroy and substitute damaged currency. The largest district Fed banks in terms of assets held are the New York Fed, the Chicago Fed, and the San Francisco Fed.

The Federal Open Market Committee (FOMC)

The FOMC is the committee that decides the monetary policy target (currently the Federal Funds Rate) and is responsible for open market operations. It is composed of 12 members: the 7 members of the Board of Governors, the president of the New York Fed, and 4 of the other Reserve Banks presidents on a rotating basis. The FOMC meets about every six weeks. During its regular meetings, the FOMC discusses current economic conditions and makes policy decisions. At the end of each meeting, the committee issues a statement on the economic outlook and choices of monetary policy.

CURRENT MONETARY MANAGEMENT

Central banks can take actions that influence interest rates and the money supply. These actions are called the tools of monetary management and policy. As mentioned earlier, interest rates and the money supply influence many facets of the national economy, such as inflation, output, and employment.

Central banks have no direct control over interest rates and the money supply; however, they have a set of tools they use to control one or more policy instruments that in time can influence interest rates and the money supply.

Tools ➔ Policy Instruments ➔ Money Supply & Interest Rates

The Federal Reserve's current policy instrument of choice is an interbank rate called the **federal funds rate**. The federal funds rate is the interest rate depository institutions (and few other financial intermediaries) charge each other on uncollateralized overnight loans of reserves deposited at the Fed. Between 1979 and 1993, when inflation was the main concern of monetary policy, the Federal Reserve used a monetary aggregate called the **monetary base** as its key policy instrument.

TIP

The New York Fed is the only Reserve Bank with a trading floor and it performs the open market operations necessary to implement monetary policy.

Conventional Tools of Monetary Management and Policy

Historically, the Federal Reserve had three tools it could use to influence interest rates and the money supply: open market operations, the discount rate, and the reserve requirement ratio. In response to the financial crisis of 2008/2009, the bank introduced a fourth conventional tool, the interest on reserves, and temporarily started unconventional actions. The four conventional tools of monetary management and policy are:

- **Open market operations:** Open market operations (OMOs) are purchases or sales of securities on the open market. The Federal Reserve uses dynamic OMOs to change the intermediate target level and defensive OMOs to off-set market driven changes in the intermediate target. Permanent (dynamic) OMOs are outright purchases or sales of securities. To perform temporary (defensive) OMOs, the Federal Reserve uses repurchase agreements (repos) or inverse-repurchase agreements (reverse repos). A repo stipulates that the Fed buys a set of securities from a financial intermediary with the agreement that the seller will buy them back at a set time in the future. In a reverse repo, the roles of the Fed and the financial intermediaries are reversed. The Federal Reserve trades securities with a selected group of large financial intermediaries called the primary dealers.

- **Discount window policies:** The Federal Reserve lends funds to financial intermediaries through its discount window. Healthy banks can borrow any amount of funds at the discount rate (primary credit). Distressed member banks can also borrow funds from the Fed as a lender of last resort (secondary credit), paying a premium of 50 basis points over the discount rate.

- **Reserve requirements:** In the U.S., all depository institutions must hold reserves for a portion of the funds in their demand deposits. The reserve requirements are designed so that smaller banks have a lower reserve ratio than larger banks. Deposits are divided into a lower tranche (currently up to $110.2 million) with a reserve ratio of 3 percent and a higher tranche with a reserve ratio of 10 percent. The first $11.5 million of deposits are exempt. The tranches amounts are updated yearly to respond to the natural expansion of deposits as the economy grows.

- **Interest on Excess Reserves:** Starting in 2008, the Federal Reserve is paying interest on banks' required and excess reserves. The interest on excess reserves (IOER) is an incentive for banks to hold reserves and as such can be used as a monetary policy tool.

CURRENT MANAGEMENT: MANAGING THE FEDERAL FUNDS RATE

To manage credit conditions and money supply, the Federal Reserve uses the federal funds rate. A higher federal funds rate tightens credit conditions and lowers money supply; a lower federal funds rate eases credit conditions and raises the money supply. The federal funds rate is a market interest rate, and it is driven by changes in banks' demand for reserves and the Federal Reserve's supply of reserves.

The Demand for Reserves

The demand for reserves illustrates the amount of reserves banks wish to hold at different federal funds rates. The demand for reserves is downward sloping in the federal funds rate down to the interest on reserves, where it flattens out. When the federal funds rate is higher than the interest on reserves, a higher federal funds rate raises the opportunity cost of holding reserves and lowers the amount of reserves banks wish to hold. If the federal funds rate drops just below the interest rate on reserves, banks have an arbitrage opportunity as they can borrow funds at the lower federal funds rate and deposit them at the Federal Reserve, which pays the higher interest rate on reserves. So, once the federal funds rate declines all the way down to the interest rate on reserves, banks are happy to hold trillions of dollars in reserves.

Supply of Reserves

The supply of reserves illustrates the amount of reserves the Fed supplies at different levels of the federal funds rates. The Federal Reserve has full control of the supply of reserves when the federal funds rate is below the discount rate. In this scenario, banks find it cheaper to borrow in the federal funds market than directly from the Federal Reserve, and the Fed can use open market operations to control the supply of reserves. However, if the federal funds rate rises above the discount rate, banks find it cheaper to borrow from the discount window, and the Federal Reserve cannot push the federal funds rate any higher.

How the Federal Reserve Controls the Federal Funds Rate

The Federal Reserve has great control over the federal funds rate. However, the tools the Federal Reserve can use to control it depend on the federal funds' current level and the current amount of bank reserves.

If the federal funds rate is above the interest on reserves and below the discount rate: If reserves are scarce, the federal funds rate hovers between the interest on reserves and the discount rate. When the federal funds rate is between the interest on reserve and the discount rate, the Federal Reserve uses open market operations to keep the rate to its desired target level or to move it up or down:

- An **open market purchase** of securities lowers the federal funds rate. A purchase of securities increases the supply of reserves, shifts the supply of reserves curve to the right, and lowers the federal funds rate.

- An **open market sale** of securities decreases the supply of reserves, shifts the supply curve to the left and raises the federal funds rate.

As an alternative, the Federal Reserve could use changes in the reserve requirement ratio to move the federal funds rate. This tool, however, influences banks' demand for reserves and is less precise. A higher reserve ratio increases the demand for reserves, shifts the demand for reserves to the right, and raises the federal funds rate. A lower reserve ratio lowers the demand for reserves, shifts the demand for reserves to the left, and lowers the federal funds rate.

If the federal funds rate is at the discount rate: When the federal funds rate is very close to the discount rate, it loses its sensitivity to open market operations. However, the Fed can still control the federal funds rate by raising or lowering the discount rate. A higher discount rate raises the horizontal portion of the supply of reserves and raises the federal funds rate. A lower discount rate lowers the horizontal portion of the supply of reserves and lowers the federal funds rate.

If the federal funds rate is at the interest on reserves: In response to the financial crisis of 2008/09, the Federal Reserve expanded its balance sheet and the supply of reserves. When the supply of reserves is very abundant, the federal funds rate falls just below the interest on reserves. When the federal funds rate is close to the interest on reserves or lower, it also loses sensitivity to open market operations (unless these are massive). This is the current scenario where banks are holding an unusually large amount of excess reserves. However, the Federal Reserve can still control the federal funds rate by raising or lowering the interest on reserves. A higher interest on reserves raises the demand for reserves, shifts the horizontal portion of the demand for reserves up, and raises the federal funds rate. A lower interest on reserves lowers the demand for reserves, shifts the horizontal portion of the demand for reserves down, and lowers the federal funds rate.

Money Creation

New money is created when a bank uses excess reserves to extend a new loan. Through a multiplicative effect, a $1 loan creates more than $1 in extra money. This multiplicative effect is called the **money multiplier.** The size of the money multiplier depends positively on the reserve ratio and negatively on the excess reserve ratio (excess reserves/deposits) and the currency ratio (desired currency holdings/deposits). Hence, the more excess reserves banks wish to hold and the more currency the public wishes to hold, the smaller the money multiplier and the amount of new money created when an extra $1 of reserves is loaned out.

The Fed, the Monetary Base, and Money Creation

The central bank can influence money supply by injecting or draining reserves from the banking system and by influencing the size of the money multiplier. Between 1979 and 1993, the Federal Reserve tried to tightly control the money supply through changes in the monetary base. The monetary base (also called high-powered money) is the sum of the Fed's liabilities and the U.S. Treasury monetary liabilities. Because Treasury liabilities are a small share of the monetary base and are not actively managed, changes in the Fed's liabilities move the monetary base dollar per dollar.

The Fed's liabilities come in two forms: currency in circulation and banks' reserves. Remember: Currency in circulation is cash in the hands of the public. Also, it is important to remember that some banks hold reserves to meet the Fed's reserve requirements (required reserves) but also to meet depositors' withdrawals and to maintain a sound level of liquidity (excess reserves).

On the asset's side of the Fed's balance sheet, securities (generally bonds issued by the U.S. Treasury, but, after the 2008 financial crises, also other securities) and loans to financial institutions play an important role in money creation.

To raise or lower the monetary base, the Fed uses open market operations. An open market purchase raises the monetary base dollar per dollar, while an open market sale lowers the monetary base dollar per dollar. When the Fed buys (or sells) securities to banks, it also raises (or lowers) banks' reserves dollar per dollar. If the Fed buys or sells securities to a non-bank, the effect of the open market operation on reserves is uncertain as it depends on whether the counterpart deposits (or withdraws) the funds at (from) a bank. Discount loans also raise the borrowed portion of the monetary base. The Fed can use the discount rate to influence the volume of these loans; however, it can't perfectly control this component of the monetary base.

The Fed can also control money supply by influencing the money multiplier.

The Fed can influence the money multiplier because, on the one hand, it sets the reserve ratio and, on the other hand, it sets the discount rate and the interest on reserves that in turn influence the excess reserve ratio. A higher reserve ratio lowers the money multiplier. A higher discount rate and/or IOER rate raise the amount of excess reserves banks wish to hold and lower the money multiplier. However, the Fed cannot perfectly control the money multiplier, as economic conditions also affect the excess reserve ratio and the currency ratio—for example, in the early 1930s, the repeated banking crises pushed people to hold more currency and banks to hold larger excess reserves reducing the size of the money multiplier so severely that the money supply dropped even though the Federal Reserve had expanded the monetary base.

The instability of the money multiplier in periods of banking crisis and in times of swift financial innovation is one of the reasons why the Fed decreased its focus on monetary aggregates when implementing monetary policy.

MONETARY POLICY IN THE UNITED STATES

Monetary policies are actions taken by the monetary authority to reach specific macroeconomic goals, like price stability and stability of financial markets.

POLICY EFFECTIVENESS

The key idea behind monetary policy is that monetary authorities can influence interest rates and credit availability that, in turn, influence **consumption** and **investment expenditures**, the two largest components of total spending. Since prices and wages are sticky and adjust rather slowly, higher total spending results in higher economic activity and slightly higher inflation, while lower total spending results in slower economic activity and lower inflation.

Monetary policy is very effective when the central bank has good control over interest rates and credit conditions and when private investment and consumption are very sensitive to changes in interest rates or the ease with which families and businesses find financing for their purchases and investment projects.

Because central banks cannot influence total spending directly, it takes time for monetary policy to affect output, employment, and inflation. The time it takes for a change in policy to influence the economy is called the **effectiveness lag**.

CONDUCTING MONETARY POLICY

In the United States, as stated in the 1977 amendment to the Federal Reserve Act, the goals of monetary policy are **price stability, maximum sustainable employment,** and moderate long-term interest rates. These two goals are often referred to as the "dual mandate."

The Federal Reserve pursues its dual mandate of price stability and maximum sustainable employment using two sets of tools called conventional and unconventional tools of monetary policy.

The **conventional tools** of monetary policy are:

- Open market operations
- Reserve requirements
- Discount window policy
- Interest on reserves

The **unconventional tools** of monetary policy were developed by the Federal Reserve in response to the challenges posed by the financial crisis of 2008/2009. The unconventional tools of monetary policy are:

- **The expansion of the Federal Reserve balance sheet.** This tool is often referred to as Quantitative Easing. Once changes in regular tools had lowered short-term interest rates down to zero, the Federal Reserve started using very large purchases of specific types of securities to directly lower long-term interest rates by altering the overall market demand/supply. The goal of this tool is to stimulate lending.

- **Changes in the composition of the Federal Reserve's balance sheet.** While traditionally the Federal Reserve had always traded short-term Treasury securities, in order to lower long-term interest rates and mortgage rates, the Federal Reserve focused its new purchases on mortgage backed securities and long-term Treasury securities.

- **Forward guidance.** The Federal Reserve significantly increased the information it would provide to the public about its future intentions hoping to help investors form accurate expectations for the future.

Policy Instruments

In regular times, the Federal Reserve uses its conventional tools to influence its policy instrument, the federal funds rate. An operating target is a variable the Federal Reserve can fully control and that can influence short-term interest rates and money supply.

The choice of the federal funds rate has consequences for the money supply. If the Federal Reserve wishes to maintain the federal funds rate at its target level for a while, it must inject reserves when the federal funds rate tends to increase and drain reserves when the federal funds rate tends to decline losing control over the monetary base. Hence, either the Federal Reserve targets the federal funds rate or it targets reserves and the monetary base.

Transmission Channels

In the United States, it takes about one year for monetary policy to influence the level of economic activity and about two years to influence the inflation rate. Monetary policy affects the economy through several channels.

- **Interest rate channel:** Monetary policy affects the real interest rate and fixed investment and consumption of durable goods.

- **Asset prices channels:** Monetary policy affects the value of the currency and asset prices influencing net exports, investment, and consumption.

- **Credit channels:** Monetary policy affects bank deposits and banks' willingness to lend as well as asset prices and firms' and families' ability to post collateral and borrow influencing investment and consumption.

Targets and Strategy

In the United States, the Federal Reserve performs monetary policy with a clear attention to controlling inflation in the long run, however, not with an officially stated inflation rate target. Inflation targeting—setting and communicating an explicit target for inflation and performing monetary policy so as to reach the inflation target at all times—would not allow the Federal Reserve to pursue its dual mandate of price stability and maximum sustainable employment during periods of cost-pushed inflation.

Because of the long time lags between monetary policy actions and the inflation rate response, the Federal Reserve tries to be forward-looking. This strategy has been very successful at containing inflation and allowed the Federal Reserve some flexibility during recessions. This strategy, however, relies very heavily on the prestige and credibility of the central bankers.

INTEREST RATES AND THE IMPACT ON MONEY SUPPLY

As discussed, if the central bank targets interest rates it must adjust the money supply in response to fluctuations in what economists call the money demand—the amount of cash and liquidity the public wishes to hold at every interest rate.

According to the Keynesian "liquidity preference theory," people wish to hold cash and deposits in the bank because they need cash to pay for transactions. However, every dollar kept in the bank is a dollar not invested in stocks and bonds, securities that pay a much higher interest rate than any bank deposit. In economic parlance, the interest rate paid by bonds is an opportunity cost of holding money. Hence, according to the theory, at every interest rate people wish to hold more cash when they need to cover more transactions and at every level of transactions they wish to hold less cash when interest rates are higher.

When the economy is doing well and people have more transactions to pay for, they wish to hold more cash at every interest rate, and money demand increases. If people cannot borrow the extra cash from commercial banks, they get the cash from selling securities like stocks and bonds. As the supply of stocks and bonds increases, asset prices decline. Because there is a negative relationship between asset prices and interest rates (or yields), as asset prices decline, interest rates increase. Hence, more transactions lead to a higher money demand and higher interest rates and fewer transactions lead to a lower money demand and lower interest rates.

If the central bank wishes to keep interest rates somewhat stable, it must inject reserves and increase money supply when money demand increases and drain reserves and lower money supply when money demand declines.

MONETARY VS. FISCAL POLICY

Monetary policies are actions central banks (or other monetary authorities) take to reach some macroeconomic goals. In the United States, the Federal Reserve has a dual goal of price stability and maximum sustainable employment.

Fiscal policies are discretionary actions a central government—in the United States, the Federal Government—takes to reach certain macroeconomic goals and influence the macroeconomic outlook.

There are three tools of discretionary fiscal policy:

1. *Government purchases:* The federal government can directly influence total spending by increasing or cutting its consumption and investment expenditures or the grants it pays to states.

2. *Public transfers:* public transfers are direct payments to families and businesses like social security pensions or unemployment insurance benefits. Transfers influence disposable income and consumption expenditures, the largest component of total spending.

3. *Taxes:* during economic downturns, the federal government can introduce temporary tax credits or tax cuts that can boost disposable income and consumption.

Governments can reduce economic fluctuations through the use of automatic stabilizers, properties of the tax system and the organization of public expenditures that automatically raise public expenditures and lower taxes during economic downturns and lower public expenditures and raise taxes during inflationary periods. Progressive taxation and generous welfare programs would act as automatic stabilizers. Compared to most European nations, the United States has weaker automatic stabilizers.

When evaluating the relative merits of employing monetary instead of fiscal policy, economists make three considerations:

1. The first consideration is **public policy and the real interest rate**. While an expansionary monetary policy tends to lower the real interest rate stimulating private investment, an expansionary fiscal policy tends to increase the real interest rate depressing private investment an important phenomenon called the **"crowding out"** effect. Typically, government pays for its expansionary fiscal policies by issuing new debt. As government increases its borrowing the supply of loanable funds declines and the real interest rate increases "crowding out" private investment.

2. The second factor to consider: **is fiscal policy at all effective?** Some economists believe that fiscal policy is quite ineffective at stimulating the economy. They believe that when government purchases increase, even if the increase is paid by issuing new debt, families anticipate that some time in the future they will have to pay higher taxes to lower the national debt and therefore decide to increase their saving and reduce consumption.

3. The third consideration is **time lags**. Fiscal policy and monetary policy suffer from different time lags. Monetary policy is fast to decide and implement, but has long effectiveness
lags, while fiscal policy has long implementation lags but once implemented it reaches the
economy faster than monetary policy.

THE FINANCIAL CRISIS OF 2008/2009

In 2008/2009, the world financial sector experienced a severe financial crisis that triggered a deep
economic downturn that economists and commentators have labeled the **Great Recession.** A housing
market boom and bust, financial innovation, and problems of moral hazard at loan originators and
at credit rating companies all contributed to the crisis.

In the 2000s, financial innovation had channeled trillions of dollars into the market for mortgage
loans, increasing the demand for new and existing homes and inflating home prices. Financial
intermediaries had found a way to bundle individual mortgage loans into a new type of bond
called a mortgage-backed security. This process, called securitization, was meant to lower risk; but
instead, it reduced mortgage originators' incentive to carefully screen mortgage applicants so that
mortgage-backed securities ended up being backed by shaky and risky mortgages. Soon, financial
intermediaries started using mortgage-backed securities to build other complex collateralized debt
obligations (CDOs). As more and more complex securities hit the market, credit-rating agencies
that were earning huge fees advising financial firms on the most profitable way to structure these
new financial instruments found themselves in a conflict of interest and their ratings lost all accuracy.

Investors and financial intermediaries who saw mortgage-backed securities receive high ratings
thought that CDOs carried little risk and invested heavily in these new obligations. When home
prices started falling in 2006, many homeowners could not afford their monthly payments any more
and started defaulting on their mortgages, bringing down the value of mortgage-backed securities.
Financial intermediaries were heavily invested in these types of securities, which they commonly used
as collateral to borrow short-term. As the market for mortgage-backed securities collapsed, some
investment banks saw their assets vaporize, as they had to engage in fire sales of assets to keep liquid.

In the United States, the first sign of serious stress came in January 2008 when **Countrywide** financial
corp, the largest mortgage bank in the country, failed and was sold to Bank of America. Then in
March 2008, **Bear Stearns**, an investment bank and brokerage firm, collapsed and had to be sold
to JP Morgan at a tenth of its value. The most dramatic events, however, took place in September
2008 when within a few days 1) the investment bank **Lehman Brothers** failed, 2) two large Government Sponsored Enterprises (GSEs)—**Fannie Mae and Freddie Mac**—that provided credit to
the housing market repurchasing mortgage loans, were taken over by the Treasury, and 3) America's
largest insurance company, **AIG**, had to be rescued by the Federal Reserve.

The Federal Reserve and the Treasury took exceptional steps in response to the crisis to prevent
financial contagion and to support liquidity. Starting in 2007, the Federal Reserve injected liquidity
lowering the discount rate and opened several lending facilities where non-bank financial intermediaries could borrow funds or swap securities and where foreign banks could swap domestic currency for
dollars. In 2008, The Bush administration passed the **Economic Recovery Act** that authorized the
Treasury to spend $700 billion to get troubled mortgage-backed securities off financial intermediaries'
balance sheets or to support their capital in other ways through the **Troubled Assets Relief Plan**

(TARP). In 2009, the Obama administration passed the **American Recovery and Reconstruction Act** a $750 billion stimulus package to be disbursed over three years.

THE INTERNATIONAL MONETARY SYSTEM

INTERNATIONAL BANKING

Although the Federal Reserve Act of 1913 allowed American banks to open branches abroad and in 1919 the passage of the Edge Act allowed the creation of special corporations that could own portions of foreign financial institutions, American banks started expanding their global activities only in the 1960s.

Banks' interest in foreign operations followed 1) an intensification of U.S. firms' trade with the rest of the world, 2) the expansion of U.S. companies abroad and the rising number of multinational corporations, 3) a desire to escape the stricter regulatory environment typical of the U.S. banking system—in particular, the restrictions on capital outflows imposed in the mid-60s, the old Regulation Q that limited the interest banks could charge on demand deposits, and the limits the Glass-Steagall Act imposed on commercial banks' activities.

U.S. banks can opt for a variety of organizational forms to expand their foreign reach, from representative offices that offer minimal information and assistance services to foreign branches, integral parts of the parent bank, that offer a full range of services. To assist with interbank transactions, an American bank might open a shell branch. These branches do not offer services to the public and are generally located in countries with simple banking regulation, no taxes, a stable political regime, and no currency controls.

Nowadays, foreign bank operations are subject to the larger share of domestic banking regulations. For example, unless they are set up as international banking facilities (IFBs), they must keep required reserves, they can only offer services allowed to domestic banks, and, starting in 2010 with the passage of the Dodd-Frank Act, they can engage in limited trading or speculative activities.

Just like their domestic parents, international branches earn most of their income from extending loans. These are often funded and priced differently from domestic loans. Very large loans are often extended by groups of banks called banks syndicates. Foreign loans expose banks to additional risks. Like all other loans, they expose the bank to interest risk and credit risk; however, unlike domestic loans, they also expose the bank to **currency risk** and **country risk.** If the loan is extended in a foreign currency, the value of the loan is sensitive to changes in the value of the currency. The country risk stems from possible political turmoil in the foreign country where a change in the governing elite could lead to restrictions on foreign loans repayment.

As U.S. banks have expanded their operations abroad, foreign banks have entered the United States banking system. Currently, about 100 foreign banks have offices in the United States; however, the larger ones dominate the market.

TIP

Foreign banks in the United States are subject to very strict oversight from the Federal Reserve and are more limited than U.S. banks in their geographical reach and range of activities.

INTERNATIONAL MONETARY INSTITUTIONS AND DEBT CRISIS

In July 1944, representatives of the allied forces met at a resort in Bretton Woods, NH, to design the post-war international system of payments. The delegates agreed that all countries would keep their currencies in a fixed exchange rate regime backed by gold: the **Bretton Woods system**.

To guarantee stability to the new system, the international community agreed to create an organization called the **International Monetary Fund** (**IMF**). Under a fixed exchange regime, countries with a balance of payment deficit (in other words, countries that buy abroad more than they sell abroad) lose foreign reserves. As they work to correct the trade and investment imbalances, they need injections of foreign reserves to prop up the value of their currency and maintain the fixed exchange rate. The key role of the IMF was loaning foreign currency to member countries with this type of problem. In the 1970s, increasing inflation in the United States put an end to the fixed exchange rate system and significantly reduced the relevance of the IMF.

However, starting in the mid-1980s, the Fund found a new role as a lender of last resort to countries facing an external debt crisis. In the 1980s, the IMF gave assistance to Latin American countries that in the 1960s and 1970s had accumulated large and unsustainable external debt to pay for development investments. Again, in the mid and late 90s, the IMF provided loans to Mexico and a number of Asian countries that found themselves in a similar position.

Most recently, the Fund helped more than fifty countries respond to the financial crisis of 2008/2009, including a number of European countries whose governments were unable to repay their debt to foreign investors and foreign banks. The IMF raises funds through a quota system. Each member country deposits a quota proportional to the nation's contribution to global GDP that is paid in a mix of hard currencies (U.S. dollar, Euro, Yen, etc.), domestic currency, and **Special Drawing Rights**, a fiat currency used solely to extend IMF loans. After the financial crisis of 2008/2009, the IMF significantly modified and expanded the types of loans offered to member countries.

Other Important International Monetary System Institutions

- **The World Bank:** The World Bank is one of the organizations created at the Bretton Woods conference in 1944. The original goal of the bank was financing the European reconstruction efforts at the end of WWII. Today, the bank is a group of organizations that offers loans and other assistance for development projects in low-income and middle-income countries with the overarching goal of ending extreme poverty in the world.

- **The Bank for International Settlements (BIS):** Created in 1930 and based in Basel, Switzerland, the Bank for International Settlements fosters cooperation among monetary authorities with the overarching goal of pursuing the stability of domestic and global financial markets.

- **The World Trade Organization:** The World Trade Organization is an organization of governments that negotiates and renegotiates international trade agreements. It was created in 1995 and substitutes the General Agreement on Tariffs and Trade (GATT) negotiation rounds. The overarching goal is to reduce barriers to international trade.

- **The Euro zone and the ECB:** The Euro zone is a monetary union of nineteen European countries that share a common currency called the Euro. While each country maintains a separate central bank, a central authority called the European Central Bank (ECB) decides and implements the zone's monetary policy.

INTERNATIONAL PAYMENTS AND EXCHANGE RATES

Foreign exchange markets are trades of deposits denominated in different currencies. The price of one currency in terms of another is called the **foreign exchange rate**. Trades between individuals or firms and domestic banks are called the retail foreign exchange market while interbank trades of very large deposits are called the interbank or wholesale foreign exchange market. Unlike stocks that are traded in exchanges (for example, the New York Stock Exchange), currencies are traded directly over-the-counter among hundreds of dealers and each transaction is generally for more than $1 million.

Currencies can be traded in spot markets where bank deposits are exchanged immediately or in forward markets where deposits are exchanged at a chosen date in the future.

When the price of the domestic currency in terms of a foreign currency increases, economists use the term domestic currency appreciation. When the price of the domestic currency in terms of a foreign currency declines, the domestic currency is depreciating.

The foreign exchange rate is very important to an economy as it influences net exports and sales and purchases of securities. When the domestic currency appreciates, domestic goods become relatively more expensive than foreign goods and exports of domestic goods decline while imports of foreign goods rise.

Forces That Drive the Foreign Exchange Rate

The foreign exchange rate is a price, and, like all prices, it fluctuates in response to changes in demand and supply. Other things staying the same, when the demand for domestic currency increases, the domestic currency appreciates and the price of the domestic currency in terms of the foreign currency rises. For example, a higher demand for dollars paid in Euros appreciates the dollar; it depreciates the Euro and raises the number of Euros one must pay to buy one dollar. When the supply of the domestic currency increases, the domestic currency depreciates and the price of the domestic currency in terms of the foreign currency declines.

The forces behind long-term movements in the foreign exchange rate are different from those that shape day-to-day fluctuations. In the long run, the foreign exchange rate is driven by changes in international trade. Economists track the long run behavior of the foreign exchange rate using the **purchasing power parity theory.** According to this theory, people must be indifferent to buying the same item domestically or internationally, as changes in imports and exports triggered by a mis-alignment of domestic and foreign prices would move the exchange rate in a equilibrating direction.

According to the purchasing power theory, in the long run, the foreign exchange rate is driven by:

- **The domestic price level:** If the domestic price level increases, domestic goods become less competitive compared to foreign goods and the demand for dollars declines, leading to a depreciation of the dollar.

TIP

In a formula, suppose P is the domestic price level, P* is the foreign price level, and E is the price of domestic currency in foreign currency. Then, according to the purchasing power parity theory: $P = E \times P^*$.

- **The foreign price level:** If the foreign price level increases, domestic goods become more competitive compared to foreign goods and the demand for dollars rises, leading to an appreciation of the dollar.

- **Relative productivity:** If productivity in the U.S. grows faster than abroad, U.S. items become cheaper than foreign items and the demand for dollars increases, so that the dollar appreciates.

- **Tariffs and other trade barriers:** The introduction or increase of tariffs and other trade barriers raise the demand for domestic goods compared to foreign goods, so that the domestic currency appreciates.

In the short run, the demand and the supply of domestic currency is driven by the relative return of investing in domestic assets compared to investing in foreign assets. Financial investors compare the domestic interest rate to the foreign interest rate controlling for the effect of a possible appreciation of the domestic currency.

- **The domestic interest rate:** A higher domestic interest rate increases the relative demand for domestic assets and the demand for the domestic currency leading to an appreciation of the domestic currency.

- **The foreign interest rate:** A higher foreign interest rate decreases the relative demand for domestic assets and the demand for the domestic currency leading to a depreciation of the domestic currency.

- **Changes in the expected appreciation of the domestic currency:** An appreciation of the domestic currency lowers the rate of return in domestic currency paid by securities denominated in foreign currency. If investors now expect a faster appreciation of the domestic currency, they demand relatively more domestic assets, raising the demand for the domestic currency and leading the domestic currency to appreciate.

The Balance of Payments (BoP)

The balance of payments is an accounting tool that tallies a country's transactions with the rest of the world. Transactions that create an inflow of payments (e.g., exports of domestic goods) are called **credits**, while transactions that create an outflow of payments (e.g., imports of foreign goods) are called **debits**.

Transactions are divided into three accounts:

- **The current account** tallies flows of payments from 1) the purchase or sale of goods and services, 2) earnings on financial investment and from labor earnings, and 3) unilateral payments like remittances and direct foreign aid. The value of exports minus the value of imports is called the trade balance.

- **The financial account** tallies payments from the purchase and sale of investment assets like securities or real estate. Flows of government-owned reserves, including special drawing rights (SDRs), are also tallied here. The financial account measures a country's net borrowing from abroad as the difference between the net sale of domestic assets abroad. A positive net sale indicates an inflow of payments and an increase in net borrowing, and so it's a BoP credit—and the net repayment of liabilities abroad. A positive net repayment of liabilities indicates an outflow of payments and a decline in net borrowing, and so it's a BoP debit.

- **The capital account** tallies payments from the purchase or sale of non-financial assets or non-produced items, for example land or intellectual property rights.

Aside from statistical discrepancies (that at times can be significant), the balance of payment is equal to zero, as the name suggests. The capital account is very small, and deficits of the current account are compensated by surpluses of the financial account. If a country runs a current account deficit, perhaps because it imports more than it exports, it can pay for the difference by selling domestic assets and increasing net borrowing, by drawing down on foreign reserves, or by selling domestic currency for foreign currency. All of these actions lead to a surplus in the financial account that keeps the BoP balanced.

MONETARY POLICY IN CONJUNCTION WITH THE EXCHANGE RATE

The effectiveness of monetary policy depends on a country's foreign exchange regime.

The Fixed Exchange Rate Policy Trilemma

A country that wants to maintain a fixed parity against one or more other currencies faces a fixed exchange rates policy trilemma: the three policies of fixed exchange rates, open capital markets, and control over monetary policy cannot coexist.

Monetary policy is effective only when it can influence the real interest rate. However, if a country has open financial capital markets, movements of the real interest rate change the inflow and outflow of financial securities shifting the demand and the supply of the domestic currency. So either the central bank allows the foreign exchange rate to fluctuate in response to these movements in demand and supply, or it buys domestic currency when there is a surplus and sells domestic currency when there is a shortage, actions that influence the size and direction of monetary policy. With open financial capital markets, the central bank must choose between fixed exchange rates and control over its monetary policy.

Monetary Policy with a Foreign Exchange Rate Float

A country that allows its currency to fluctuate against other currencies enjoys a particularly effective monetary policy.

In a closed economy, that is an economy that does not trade goods or securities with the rest of the world, monetary policy influences the economy only through changes in investment and consumption.

In an open economy with a fluctuating foreign exchange rate, monetary policy influences the economy also through changes in net exports triggered by movements in the foreign exchange. For example, if the central bank wants to raise output and employment and lowers the real interest rate, in an open economy, the resulting outflow of financial capital depreciates the domestic currency stimulating net exports, adding an extra channel to the transmission mechanism.

SUMMING IT UP

- Money is an **asset,** or a durable item with value that is accepted as a means of payment.

- Assets that can be used as money include **durable assets** (which last over time), **acceptable assets** (which are convenient for people to use), **divisible assets** (which can be divided into smaller units), and **fungible assets** (which are similar to every other unit so that they can be used interchangeably).

- The four key roles of money are as **a means of payment**, as **a store of value**, as a **standard of deferred payment**, and as **a unit of accounting**.

- The three types of money are **commodity money** (like gold and silver), **commodity backed money** (money aligned to the gold standard), and **fiat money** (paper certificates not backed by gold or any other commodity), which makes up most money today.

- **Financial assets include money** (assets that derive value from a contract), **loans** (financial assets that derive value from a repayment contract), **and securities** (financial assets that can be traded).
  - **Securities are traded in primary markets, secondary markets, and open markets,** and have three classes:
    1. Debt securities (bank notes and bonds)
    2. Equity securities (common stocks)
    3. Derivatives (event-based money flow which includes futures, options, and stocks)

- Financial assets often pay **interest,** or additional payments made on top of the principal amount loaned at the start $(I = (N - M))$. The interest rate is the ratio of interest to principal, or $I = \dfrac{N - M}{M}$. Interest can be difficult to calculate in the case of fixed payment loans, like mortgage loans or coupon bonds, so the yield to maturity method is used. This is the interest rate that equates the current price of a debt security or loan to the present discounted value of all payments the lender will receive from the security or loan at maturity.

- The **U.S. banking sector** is characterized by three things: a **large number of small banks, banks chartered at two levels** (state and national), and **heavy regulation**. These regulations included the Glass-Steagall Act of 1933 (which limited banks' activities and interest rate charges) and the Gramm-Bleach-Bliley Act of 1999 (which replaced Glass-Steagall and enabled banks to participate in non-bank financial activities).

- The three main types of banks in the U.S. are **commercial banks, Saving Associations/ Savings and Loans Associations,** and **credit unions**. Deposits at these banks are insured for up to $250,000 per account by the Federal Deposit Insurance Corporation (FDIC) or the National Credit Union Share Insurance Fund (NCUSIF). In addition to banks, the most important types of financial companies are investment banks (which raise funds via securities); insurance companies (which help protect people from potential losses in exchange for a fixed premium payment); mutual funds/pension funds (which are pools of funds invested in securities); and bank holding companies (which own other banks).

- **Banks' assets are their liabilities plus their capital.** Liabilities include: demand deposits, savings deposits, time deposits, borrowed funds, federal funds, repurchase agreements (repos), Eurodollars, Federal Reserve (Fed) loans, and trading liabilities. A bank's capital (a.k.a. "net worth") includes capital stock invested by stockholders and undivided profits that haven't yet been paid out as dividends. Assets are measured by cash assets, Fed funds/reverse repos, investments, loans, and leases.

- **Bank management is made up of liquidity management** (where a bank must have enough reserves to meet a minimum requirement and be able to pay out any customer withdrawals), **asset management** (where the bank monitors its asset portfolio to minimize the risk of default), **liability management** (attracting new funds at low cost/low risk), **capital adequacy management** (ensuring the bank has enough capital), and **risk management** (adjusting assets, liabilities, and capital to be able to minimize losses and risk without endangering profits).

- **Banks are regulated in four main areas.** **Capital requirements** (minimum amounts of capital on hand) are a buffer that help ensure banks won't fail. **Charters** (licenses) are legally required to ensure that banks meet industry requirements, and banks are inspected and rated on an ongoing basis to make sure they're in compliance with that charter. **Disclosure requirements** ensure transparency about the health and activities of a bank. **Regulations** like the Consumer Credit Protection Act and the Fair Credit Billing Act (FCBA) are designed to protect consumers from scams, discrimination, and predatory lending practices.

- The value of all final goods and services produced for the market over a period of time is the **Gross Domestic Product** (**GDP**), which is made up of **consumption** (money spent on goods), **Investment** (money spent on residential and non-residential structures**), Government spending**, and **Net Exports** (the difference between exports to other nations and imports from other nations). Income is tracked via Net National Income (NNI) (wages and salaries, rents, interest and profit), and is further refined into disposable income (DI), which is the difference between NNI and taxes.

- Price levels, or the average of all prices, are tracked using the **Consumer Price Index** (**CPI**) or the **Personal Consumption Expenditures deflator** (**PCE deflator**). Inflation is continual and generalized increase in the price level, and inflation rate measures how fast the prices are increasing.

Remember the three theories of economics:

  - In **classical economics,** the economy is seen as self-regulating and calls for a laissez-faire approach, because supply creates its own demand and eliminates the need for government involvement.

  - In **Keynesian economics**, the economy can't self-adjust and calls for government spending and public policy to maintain economic equilibrium.

  - In **monetarist economics**, fiscal policy affects the economy in the short term, while affecting prices and inflation in the long term.

- **Inflation can be broken down into three theories.** In the **quantity theory of inflation**, high money growth leads to faster inflation. In **demand-pull inflation**, higher money supply lowers interest rates, thus stimulating investment and consumption (total spending). In **cost push inflation**, increased production costs lead to inflation.

- **The U.S.'s central bank is the Federal Reserve**, which was created in 1913, bringing stability to the country's banking system, streamlining check collection, and supervising the banking industry. The Fed now had the power to issue Federal Reserve notes that could be converted into gold and used to maintain elastic currency. The Federal Reserve System is made up of twelve regional banks, a Board of Governors, and a Federal Open Market Committee and is overseen by a Chair appointed by the President and approved by Congress.

  The **Federal Reserve** uses three tools to influence interest rates and money supply:
  1. *Open market operations* (sales or purchases of securities on the open market)
  2. *Discount window policies* (funds lent by the Federal Reserve to banks at a discount)
  3. *The reserve requirement ratio* (the percentage of deposits that banks must keep on hand in order to cover withdrawals)

- The Fed also uses the **federal funds rate** (a market interest rate driven by the supply and demand for reserves) to manage credit and money supply. If this rate is above the interest on reserves and below the discount rate, it is lowered by open market purchases of securities and raised by open market sales of securities. If the rate is at the discount rate or is at the interest on reserves, it is not affected by open market operations.

- **Money supply** is the sum of currency in circulation and checkable deposits (M1). New money is created when a bank uses excess reserves to extend a new loan, resulting in the money multiplier effect, where a $1 loan creates more than $1 in new money. Money supply is also affected by the Fed's actions to inject or drain reserves from the banking system and influence the size of the money multiplier.

- Per the 1977 amendment to the Federal Reserve Act, the **goals of monetary policy** are **price stability**, **maximum sustainable employment**, and **moderate long-term interest rates**.

- The **conventional tools of monetary policy** are **open market operations, reserve requirements**, **discount window policy**, and **interest on reserves**.

- **Unconventional tools of monetary policy** (developed in response to the 2008/2009 financial crisis) are **expansion of the Federal Reserve's balance sheet, changing the composition of the Federal Reserve's balance sheet**, and **forward guidance/information** from the Federal Reserve to the public.

- **Fiscal policy** (government spending and taxation) consists of government purchases, public transfers (payments like Social Security or unemployment benefits), and taxes (including tax credits or cuts).

- The **Great Recession of 2008–2009** came on the heels of a severe financial crisis caused by a housing boom and bust, financial innovation leading to risky mortgage loans, and the collapse of major mortgage, investment, and credit companies.

- Emergency measures included relief and stimulus bills to help stabilize at-risk banks and companies:
  - The Economic Recovery Act
  - Troubled Assets Relief Plan (TARP)
  - The American Recovery and Reconstruction Act

- **American banks began expanding global banking activities in the 1960s**, following increased global trade, the expansion of U.S. companies abroad, and companies' desire to escape the U.S.'s strict regulations. As a result of the expansion, foreign banks began entering the U.S. as well.

- After World War II, the **International Monetary Fund** (**IMF**) was established to ensure that all countries kept their currencies in a fixed exchange rate regime backed by gold. The IMF ensures economic stability throughout the world by raising funds through a quota system.

- Other international monetary institutions include the **World Bank** (which offers loans and assistance for projects in developing countries), the **Bank for International Settlements** (BIS) (which fosters cooperation between monetary authorities to maintain market stability), the **World Trade Organization** (**WTO**) (which negotiates international trade agreements), and the **Euro Zone/ECB** (which provides a common currency for nineteen European nations).

- The **foreign exchange rate** (price of one currency in terms of another currency) is an essential piece of a national economy, as it influences net exports and the sale/purchase of securities. The rate is driven by changes in international trade (domestic price level, foreign price level, relative productivity, and tariffs/trade considerations) in the long run. In the short run, the rate is driven by the relative return of investing in domestic assets compared to investing in foreign assets (domestic interest rate, foreign interest rate, and shifts in domestic currency).

MONEY AND BANKING POST-TEST

> **Directions:** Carefully read each of the following 60 questions. Choose the best answer to each question and fill in the corresponding circle on the answer sheet. The Answer Key and Explanations can be found following this post-test.

1. In many countries, central authorities impose reserve requirements to influence money supply and help prevent bank runs. In the United States, reserve requirements are decided by the
   A. Board of Governors of the Federal Reserve System.
   B. Federal Open Market Committee (FOMC).
   C. Office of the Comptroller of the Currency (OCC).
   D. Federal Deposit Insurance Corporation (FDIC).

2. In the United States, the central authorities that provide liquidity guarantees and credit guarantees are the
   A. OCC and the state regulatory agencies.
   B. OCC and the FDIC.
   C. Federal Reserve Bank and the OCC.
   D. Federal Reserve Bank and the FDIC.

3. When a central bank implements monetary policy so as to target the interest rate,
   A. implicitly, it also targets the monetary aggregate M1.
   B. the money supply becomes pro-cyclical.
   C. the money supply becomes anti-cyclical.
   D. banks are more reluctant to lend funds to families and small businesses.

4. Which of the following is an example of "asset transformation"?
   A. A bank signs a repurchase agreement with another financial intermediary.
   B. A financial intermediary chooses the stocks and bonds to include in a new growth-oriented mutual fund.
   C. A commercial bank accepts a new NOW deposit and uses the funds to offer a mortgage to a homeowner.
   D. A bank sells $100 million of mortgage-backed securities and uses the proceeds of the sale to buy $100 million of Treasury notes.

5. What does the term "quantitative easing" refer to?
   A. When the Federal Reserve buys bonds from the Treasury to ease government's budget problems
   B. When the Federal Reserve injects reserves when interest rates are rising and lowers reserves when interest rates are low
   C. When the Federal Reserve eases credit by increasing the quantity of funds that intermediaries can borrow through its primary credit facility
   D. When the Federal Reserve buys large amounts of securities from financial institutions to increase liquidity in the financial system and stimulate lending

6. Which of the following products offered by commercial banks is NOT covered by FDIC insurance?

   A. A money market mutual fund

   B. A money market deposit account

   C. A certificate of deposit

   D. A savings account

7. According to monetarist and Keynesian economists, monetary policy is more effective at stimulating total output

   A. when private investment spending is more sensitive to credit conditions and the interest rate.

   B. when consumption spending is less sensitive to total output and net taxes.

   C. when the central bank has little control over interest rates.

   D. in the longer run than in the shorter run.

8. The Board of Governors is the key player in monetary policy decisions because

   A. it's the branch of the Federal Reserve System with banking supervision authority.

   B. it creates and publishes statistics on current economic conditions.

   C. its 7 members have voting rights in the Federal Open Market Committee (FOMC).

   D. it chooses the target level for the Federal Funds Rate.

9. On September 25, 2008, when the FDIC transferred all of the failing Washington Mutual's assets and liabilities to JP Morgan Chase, it was following which approach to failing banks' resolutions?

   A. Payoff and dissolve

   B. Liquidate and resolve

   C. Whole bank purchase and assumption

   D. Clean bank purchase and assumption

10. Before 2008, which of the following actions would the Federal Reserve take in order to increase the money supply?

    A. It would increase the interest paid on reserves.

    B. It would purchase Treasury securities on the open market.

    C. It would increase the discount rate.

    D. It would increase the required reserve ratio.

11. In the U.S. Balance of Payment, interest on German Treasury securities paid to an American mutual fund is recorded as a

    A. credit in the financial account.

    B. debit in the capital account.

    C. credit in the current account.

    D. debit in the financial account.

12. Which of the following is an action taken by the U.S. Treasury in response to the financial crisis of 2008/2009?

    A. Capital injections under the Troubled Asset Relief Plan

    B. The institution of a new Term Auction Facility that lent funds to financial intermediaries in trouble

    C. The extension of loans to the American International Group (AIG) to avoid the company's failure

    D. The sale of the investment bank Bear Stearns to J.P. Morgan

13. Why did monetarists like Milton Friedman favor strict rules of monetary policy?

    A. They believed that fiscal policy was a better tool for discretionary actions.

    B. They believed that monetary policy affected the economy with long lags.

    C. They believed that monetary policy had no effect on total spending or total output.

    D. They believed that discretionary monetary policy would lead to deflation.

14. The Federal Reserve System is made up of _____ regional Reserve Banks, the Board of Governors, and the _____.
    A. twelve; FOMC
    B. twelve; FDIC
    C. twenty; FOMC
    D. twenty; FDIC

15. When you agree with your employer that at the end of the week he will pay you $1,000 for your work, you use money as a
    A. store of value.
    B. standard of deferred payment.
    C. unit of account.
    D. means of payment.

16. Which of the following lifted limits on interstate banking?
    A. Regulation Q and the Glass-Steagall Act
    B. The McFadden Act
    C. The Depository Institutions Deregulation and Monetary Control Act
    D. The Riegle-Neal Interstate Banking Act

17. If a central bank lowers the primary credit rate, we should expect the money supply to
    A. increase as banks will borrow more funds from the Federal Reserve, raising the borrowed monetary base.
    B. increase as banks will buy more securities from the Federal Reserve, raising the unborrowed monetary base.
    C. decrease as banks will now hold more excess reserves for precautionary purposes, and the money multiplier will decline.
    D. decrease as the public will now want to hold less currency, and the money multiplier will decline.

18. Which of the following is the most liquid asset?
    A. A plot of land
    B. A deposit in a checkable account
    C. Shares in a retail money-market mutual fund
    D. A deposit in a savings account

19. How does an increase of the required reserve ratio influence the money supply?
    A. After the Federal Reserve increases the required reserve ratio to achieve compliance, banks reduce the amount of demand deposits, and the money supply declines.
    B. A higher required reserve ratio increases banks' incentive to hold reserves, and the money supply increases.
    C. A higher required reserve ratio raises banks' leverage ratio and the public's trust in the stability of the banking sector, reducing the public's currency holding ratio and increasing the money supply.
    D. A higher required reserve ratio reduces the share of reserves that banks can loan out, slowing the money creation process and lowering the money supply.

20. In the CAMELS rating system, the C stands for
    A. capital adequacy.
    B. credit availability.
    C. currency holdings.
    D. consumer protection enforcement.

21. The problem with a bank crisis is that as more and more people withdraw cash from their bank deposits,
    A. the volume of currency in circulation rises and the money supply expands.
    B. the volume of required reserves declines and banks, to avoid accumulating too many excess reserves, start offering riskier loans.
    C. the balance sheet of the Federal Reserve shrinks and monetary base declines.
    D. unless the Federal Reserve increases the monetary base, banks start calling in loans and the money supply drops.

22. The idea that people adjust their price and inflation expectations slowly is called
    A. rational expectations.
    B. hyperbolic expectations.
    C. slow-response expectations.
    D. adaptive expectations.

23. In the past century, the number of commercial banks in the United States has
    A. steadily increased, even if the number of bank branches has remained the same.
    B. remained stable at around 6,000 institutions.
    C. declined up to the mid-seventies and increased ever since.
    D. steadily declined, although the number of bank branches has increased.

24. The equation of exchange states that
    A. in the Balance of Payment the current account and the financial account always sum to zero.
    B. when trading with the rest of the world, the price of a domestic item must equal the price in domestic currency of a foreign item.
    C. the stock of money in the economy times the velocity of money is equal to income at current prices.
    D. in an exchange, different units of the same product must be traded at the same price.

25. When Joanna withdraws $1,000 from her money market mutual fund and deposits them in her checking account,
    A. M1 increases and M2 decreases.
    B. M1 increases and M2 stays the same.
    C. M1 and M2 decrease.
    D. M1 and M2 stay the same.

26. A difference between commercial banks and credit unions is that commercial banks are
    A. allowed to accept deposits, while credit unions are not.
    B. stock-owned, while credit unions are mutual institutions.
    C. generally quite small with deposits of less than $100 million, while credit unions are very large financial intermediaries.
    D. chartered by states, while credit unions are regulated by the Comptroller of the Currency.

27. Gross domestic product is the sum of which of the following components?
    A. Consumption and savings
    B. Disposable income and net taxes
    C. Consumption, investment, net taxes, and net exports
    D. Consumption, investment, government purchases, and net exports

28. The larger share of commercial banks' assets is in the form of
    A. equity capital.
    B. loans.
    C. security investments.
    D. deposits.

29. Both classical economists and the Keynesian economists believe that
    A. all markets are competitive and that prices are flexible and fluctuate to maintain demand equal to supply in every market.
    B. fiscal policy is ineffective in reducing the level of unemployment.
    C. monetary policy is ineffective in maintaining price stability.
    D. in the long run, the economy operates at its potential level where all resources are fully employed.

30. Current capital adequacy regulation requires that a bank's
    A. ratio of Tier 1 and Tier 2 capital to risk-weighted assets be at least 8 percent.
    B leverage ratio be at least 8 percent.
    C. Tier 1 capital be at least 3 percent.
    D. ratio of Tier 1 to Tier 2 capital be at least 3 percent.

31. A higher inflation rate leads to a lower level of total spending because when inflation increases,
    A. the purchase power of real wages declines and firms lower output.
    B. the central bank raises the interest rate dampening investment spending and consumption spending.
    C. business confidence declines and firms drop all investment projects.
    D. firms find it harder to finance research and development projects slowing the pace of technological change.

32. What is an unintended consequence of the regulation introduced by the CRA?
    A. Banks cannot pay interest on demand deposits and find it hard to compete with money market mutual funds.
    B. Financially weak families are offered mortgages they cannot repay and end up losing their homes.
    C. Insured depositors do not feel the need to closely monitor banks' manager behavior, and banks end up taking too much risk.
    D. During a financial crisis, the mark-to-market accounting requirements force financial intermediaries to mark down their assets, exposing them to bank runs.

33. If economic agents have rational expectations,
    A. anticipated monetary policy has no effect on prices and inflation.
    B. the economy cannot suffer from demand pull inflation.
    C. the economy cannot suffer from cost push inflation.
    D. anticipated fiscal policy has no effect on GDP and employment.

34. A reason why a monetary policy might not be fully effective in stabilizing the economy is that
    A. the central bank has no control over short-term interest rates.
    B. monetary policy has a long effectiveness lag.
    C. monetary policy has a long implementation lag.
    D. total spending is not sensitive to the interest rate.

35. Which of the following statements best explains an unintended consequence of the National Bank Acts?

    A. State banks started relying very heavily on demand deposits as their primary source of liquidity.

    B. The number of state banks quickly declined, so that nowadays, all U.S. banks are nationally chartered.

    C. The number of different currencies used for payments declined significantly.

    D. The Federal Reserve Bank lost control over state banks.

36. The Federal Deposit Insurance Corporation was established in _____ by the _____.

    A. 1933; Glass-Steagall Act

    B. 1933; Federal Reserve Act

    C. 1913; Federal Reserve Act

    D. 1980; McFadden Act

37. Which of the following men championed the creation of the First Bank of the United States?

    A. Andrew Jackson

    B. Alexander Hamilton

    C. John Maynard Keynes

    D. Milton Friedman

38. Which of the following would be an example of banks' increasing reliance on off-balance sheet activities?

    A. Banks have increased the number and type of loans they extend each year.

    B. Since the financial crisis, banks have expanded their holdings of excess reserves deposited at the Fed.

    C. Banks are more likely to resell loans right after origination instead of holding them until maturity

    D. Banks are expanding their holdings of mortgage-backed securities.

39. What do economists refer to when they talk about the "policy trilemma"?

    A. The impossibility of having floating exchange rates, a democratic political system, and a deficit in the trade balance

    B. The impossibility of having a trade balance deficit when running a public budget deficit

    C. That in an open economy, the monetary authority can only use one of the three tools of monetary policy

    D. That a country cannot have a fixed exchange rate, open capital markets, and control of monetary policy

40. The Board of Governors influences who is appointed President at each regional Reserve Banks by

    A. directly appointing the President of each regional Reserve Bank.

    B. making a recommendation to the President of the United States, who then appoints the President of each regional Reserve Bank.

    C. appointing three members of the regional Reserve Banks' Board of Directors, which then appoints the Bank's President.

    D. making recommendations to the Bank's Board of Directors, which then appoints the Bank's President.

41. Which of the following is NOT a tool of monetary policy?

    A. Large-scale asset purchases

    B. The interbank rate

    C. The interest on reserves

    D. The discount rate

42. Which of the following statements best describes the concept of real interest rate?
    A. The difference between the market interest rate and the rate of inflation borrowers and lenders believe will prevail over the duration of the loan
    B. The difference between the market interest rate and banks' cost of money
    C. The interest rate that banks charge on loans collateralized by a piece of real estate
    D. The difference between the domestic interest rate and the foreign interest rate after adjusting for the expected appreciation of the currency

43. An open market purchase of treasury securities
    A. increases the monetary base but decreases the money supply.
    B. increases the monetary base and increases the money supply.
    C. decreases the monetary base and decreases the money supply.
    D. decreases the monetary base but increases the money supply.

44. After 2009, if the FOMC announced its intention to raise the federal funds rate target by 25 basis points, the next day, the
    A. trading floor of the New York Federal Reserve Bank would perform a sale of Treasury securities on the open market.
    B. Board of Governors would raise the interest on reserves by 25 basis points.
    C. Board of Governors would lower the required reserve ratio applied to the first tranche of funds from 3 percent to 0 percent.
    D. FOMC would raise the primary discount rate by 25 basis points.

45. Which of the following is NOT an example of a fiscal policy?
    A. During recessions, unemployment benefits expenditure increases, driven by higher unemployment.
    B. The administration temporarily cuts income taxes.
    C. The federal government temporarily increases grants to states.
    D. The Federal Reserve purchases Treasury securities.

46. What is the main point of the purchase power parity theory of the foreign exchange rate?
    A. In reality, the law of one price rarely holds.
    B. When the depreciation of the currency raises, prices and wages also increase, so that workers' purchase power remains unaffected.
    C. The foreign exchange rate moves to maintain the parity between the domestic interest rate, the foreign interest rate, and the expected appreciation of the currency.
    D. The foreign exchange moves so as to maintain the parity between an item's domestic price and its foreign price in domestic currency.

47. Which of the following statements best describes how the FDIC contributes to the stability of the financial sector?
    A. The FDIC has the authority to act as *lender of last resort* to member banks and inject liquidity when money markets dry up.
    B. The FDIC reduces the chances that a bank's failure could trigger a bank run by insuring bank deposits.
    C. The FDIC reduces uncertainty in financial markets by resolving all bank failures following a payoff and liquidate approach.
    D. The FDIC regulates commercial banks' capital requirements so as to minimize systemic risk.

48. Which of the following statements best explains the "crowding out" effect?
    A. Higher public spending creates fears of higher taxes that depress business confidence, and so firms cut investment.
    B. Higher public spending forces the central bank to print more money, creating inflation that reduces real investment.
    C. Higher public spending does not raise total output in the short run.
    D. Higher public spending leads to more public borrowing, depressing the supply of loanable funds and increasing the real interest rate, pushing firms to lower investment.

49. Which of the following is a tool of indirect finance?
    A. Crowd-funding
    B. A newly issued corporate bond
    C. A bank loan
    D. A stock

50. A reason why the Federal Reserve decided to abandon the use of monetary aggregates as intermediate targets is that the money multiplier
    A. is stable through time.
    B. is not responsive to the Federal Reserve's actions.
    C. can sharply drop in periods of banking and financial crises.
    D. is sensitive to changes of the U.S. Treasury monetary liabilities.

51. Which of the following best describes demand-pull inflation?
    A. A continual increase of the price level due to misguided expansionary policies
    B. Inflation that is due to a decline in the rate of growth of money supply
    C. Inflation that is due to a temporary increase in the cost of material or cost of labor
    D. A once and for all increase in the price level due to a new collective bargaining contract

52. Which of the following actions would help a mutual fund maintain its liquidity when faced with an unusually high volume of withdrawals?
    A. Purchase Treasury securities on the open market.
    B. Sell assets at a distressed or fire sale price.
    C. Apply for primary credit at the Federal Reserve Bank.
    D. Ask its liquidity managers to focus on capital adequacy management until the crisis is over.

53. Which of the following events were NOT among the factors behind the financial crisis of 2008/2009?
    A. Financial innovations like the securitization of sub-prime mortgages
    B. Tight monetary policy in the 2003–2006 period
    C. Declining business standards in mortgage loans origination
    D. Conflict of interest at credit-rating agencies

54. Which of the following economic indicators can be used to measure the inflation rate?

   A. The Personal Consumption Expenditures deflator

   B. Labor force

   C. Employment

   D. Gross domestic product

55. Which of the following was NOT a reason for the expansion of U.S. banking operations abroad?

   A. The expansion of multinational corporations

   B. The narrow focus of banking activities in foreign countries

   C. The expansion of U.S. firms' involvement with global trade

   D. The stricter regulatory environment of the United States

56. According to the Keynesian "liquidity preference theory" of money demand, an increase in nominal income would

   A. increase the demand for money, lowering the interest rate.

   B. leave the demand for money unaltered but increase the interest rate.

   C. decrease the demand for money but leave the interest rate unaltered.

   D. increase the demand for money, raising the interest rate.

57. Which of the following statements best describes how the International Monetary Fund finances its loans during sovereign debt crises?

   A. Member countries are assigned quotas proportional to the size of their economy and, in times of crises, the Fund can also borrow from member countries' accounts.

   B. The Fund collects voluntary contributions in hard currency or gold from member countries.

   C. The central banks of the largest industrialized countries contribute 20 percent of their foreign reserves.

   D. Monthly, the Fund borrows on the open market the funds needed, with a majority of the funds borrowed being denominated in dollars, euros, or yens.

58. In which of the following cases does targeting inflation prevent the central bank from achieving its dual goal of price stability and maximum sustainable employment?

   A. When the economy is subject to a sustained increase in total spending

   B. When the economy is subject to a sustained decrease in total spending

   C. When the economy suffers from a permanent decline in potential output

   D. When the economy is subject to a temporary increase in the price of oil or the cost of labor

59. The Glass-Steagall Act, also known as the Banking Act of 1933, imposed several types of regulations on the banking sector. For example, it
    A. prohibited commercial banks from engaging in non-bank activities like underwriting insurance.
    B. allowed banks to pay interest to holders of checkable deposits.
    C. prohibited gender and racial discrimination in credit transactions.
    D. allowed the Comptroller of the Currency to charter national banks.

60. If an accommodating monetary policy of the central bank successfully lowers interest rates, we should expect a
    A. depreciation of the domestic currency.
    B. decline in consumption expenditures.
    C. decline in asset prices.
    D. decline in inflation expectations

ANSWER KEY AND EXPLANATIONS

1. A	13. B	25. B	37. B	49. C
2. D	14. A	26. B	38. C	50. C
3. B	15. B	27. D	39. D	51. A
4. C	16. D	28. B	40. C	52. B
5. D	17. A	29. D	41. B	53. B
6. A	18. B	30. A	42. A	54. A
7. A	19. D	31. B	43. B	55. B
8. C	20. A	32. B	44. B	56. D
9. C	21. D	33. D	45. D	57. A
10. B	22. D	34. B	46. D	58. D
11. C	23. D	35. A	47. B	59. A
12. A	24. C	36. A	48. D	60. A

1. **The correct answer is A.** Setting reserve requirements is one of the responsibilities of the Board of Governors of the Federal Reserve System. Choice B is incorrect because the FOMC decides the target level for the Federal Funds Rate, not reserve requirements. Choice C is incorrect because the Office of the Comptroller of the Currency charters and regulates national banks but does not set reserve requirements. Choice D is incorrect because the FDIC helps prevent bank runs by insuring bank depositors up to $250,000 per insured bank.

2. **The correct answer is D.** An authority provides liquidity guarantee if it can inject liquidity and act as a lender of last resort; an authority provides credit guarantees if it insures deposit accounts. In the United States, these functions belong to the Federal Reserve Bank and the FDIC. Choice A is incorrect because the OCC and state agencies charter and regulate commercial banks but do not provide liquidity or credit guarantees. Choice B is incorrect because the OCC does not provide liquidity guarantees. Choice C is incorrect because the OCC does not provide credit guarantees.

3. **The correct answer is B.** If the central bank wants to maintain the interest rate stability, it must inject reserves when the economy is strong and family and businesses want to borrow and drain resources when the economy is weak. Choice A is incorrect because the central bank can target the money supply or the interest rate but not both. Choice C is incorrect because if the central bank drains resources when there is a higher demand for credit, the interest rate increases. Choice D is incorrect because banks' willingness to lend is not sensitive to the central bank's choice of target.

4. **The correct answer is C.** Asset transformation is the activity of transforming a bank's liabilities into assets, for example, transforming deposited funds into a loan. Choice A is incorrect because a repo affects liabilities only. Choice B is incorrect because the choosing of stocks to include in a mutual fund does not transform liabilities into assets. Choice D is incorrect because selling one type of assets to purchase another is called asset management, not asset transformation.

5. **The correct answer is D.** When central banks cannot influence bank lending by lowering the policy rate, they try to obtain the same result with massive injections of reserves. Choice A is incorrect because buying securities from the Treasury does not stimulate lending. Choice B is incorrect because this is the practice of supplying "easy credit." Choice C is incorrect because this is

answers post-test

a different unconventional tool of monetary policy.

6. **The correct answer is A.** The FDIC does not cover investment accounts, life insurance products, securities, stocks, bonds, and other products offered by banks. Choice B is incorrect because the FDIC insures all deposit accounts, including money market deposit accounts. Choice C is incorrect because the FDIC insures all deposit accounts, including certificates of deposit. Choice D is incorrect because the FDIC insures all deposit accounts, including savings accounts.

7. **The correct answer is A.** Monetarists and Keynesians agree that monetary policy can stimulate the economy by affecting credit conditions and the interest rate if investment is sensitive to credit conditions and interest rates. Choice B is incorrect because Keynesians believe that expansionary policy is less effective when consumption is not sensitive to current disposable income. Choice C is incorrect because if the central bank has little control over interest rates, it finds it hard to stimulate investment and total spending. Choice D is incorrect because, in the long run, monetary policy is neutral, and it has no effect on total output.

8. **The correct answer is C.** The U.S. monetary policy is decided by the FOMC, and the 7 members of the Board of Governors are voting members of the FOMC. Choice A is incorrect because banking supervision is not an activity related to monetary policy. Choice B is incorrect because the Board of Governors creates and publishes economic data; however, this activity is not one aspect of monetary policy. Choice D is incorrect because the FOMC chooses the target level for the Federal Funds Rate.

9. **The correct answer is C.** Under a whole bank purchase and assumption agreement, all assets and liabilities of the failing bank are transferred to the assuming bank for a one-time payment. Choice A is incorrect because under a payoff and dissolve approach, the FDIC pays off depositors and then liquidates all assets and uses the sale's proceeds to pay off other creditors. Choice B is incorrect

because no approach to the resolution of a failing bank is called liquidate and resolve. Choice D is incorrect because under a clean bank purchase and assumption approach, the assuming bank acquires only insured deposits and few assets or, in other words, a clean bank.

10. **The correct answer is B.** An open market purchase of Treasury securities injects reserves in the banking system and increases the monetary base, leading to a higher money supply. Choice A is incorrect because a higher interest on reserves would reduce the amount of reserves banks wish to loan out, reducing the money multiplier and the money supply. Choice C is incorrect because a higher discount rate raises the amount of excess reserve banks wish to hold, reducing the money multiplier and the money supply. Choice D is incorrect because a higher required reserve ratio would lower the money multiplier and money supply.

11. **The correct answer is C.** In the Balance of Payment, inflows of payments are recorded as credits and earnings payments are tallied in the current account. Choice A is incorrect because the financial account tallies payments from the purchase and sale of financial assets. Choice B is incorrect because the capital account tallies payments from the purchase and sale of non-financial assets. Choice D is incorrect because an inflow of payments is tallied as a credit.

12. **The correct answer is A.** The Economic Recovery Act of October 2008 authorized the Treasury to inject $700 billion into the shadow banking system to prop up its capitalization. Choice B is incorrect because the Federal Reserve set up the Term Auction Facilities to lower the stigma associated with borrowing funds from the Fed. Choice C is incorrect because the Federal Reserve extended loans to AIG. Choice D is incorrect because the Bear Stearns deal was brokered by the Federal Reserve.

13. **The correct answer is B.** Monetarists believed that only monetary policy could sway total spending. They also believed it did so with long lags, hence discretionary policy could destabilize the economy and

they favored strict rules. Choice A is incorrect because monetarists believed fiscal policy had no effect on total spending. Choice C is incorrect because they believed that monetary policy was the only policy that could influence total spending. Choice D is incorrect because they feared that discretionary monetary policy would lead to higher inflation.

14. **The correct answer is A.** The Federal Reserve System is composed of twelve regional Reserve Banks, the Board of Governors, and the Federal Open Market Committee (FOMC). Choice B is incorrect because the Federal Deposit Insurance Corporation (FDIC) is not part of the Federal Reserve System. Choice C is incorrect because there are twelve regional Reserve Banks in the Federal Reserve System. Choice D is incorrect because there are twelve regional Reserve Banks in the Federal Reserve System and the FDIC is not part of the system.

15. **The correct answer is B.** You use money as a standard of deferred payment when you agree money can be used to settle a debt. Choice A is incorrect because you use money as a store of value when you store money for future purchases. Choice C is incorrect because you use money as a unit of account when you measure prices in cash units. Choice D is incorrect because you use money as a means of payment when you use money for a current purchase.

16. **The correct answer is D.** The Riegle-Neal Interstate Banking Act of 1994 removed the restrictions on nationwide branching. Choice A is incorrect because Regulation Q, introduced by the Glass-Steagall Act, imposed limits on interest paid on various deposits and prohibited paying interest on demand deposits. Choice B is incorrect because The McFadden Act of 1927 required national banks to open branches only according to the laws of the state where they were located, effectively prohibiting national branching. Choice C is incorrect because the DIDMCA did not prohibit nationwide branching but, among other things, it lifted restrictions on interest paid on deposits.

17. **The correct answer is A.** A lower primary credit rate reduces banks' cost of using Fed loans to raise liquidity, leading to an increase in Fed loans and the borrowed monetary base. Choice B is incorrect because banks would buy more securities from the Fed if the Fed performed an open market purchase of securities. Choice C is incorrect because a lower discount rate leads banks to hold fewer excess resources, increasing the size of the money multiplier. Choice D is incorrect because when the public holds less currency, the money multiplier increases.

18. **The correct answer is B.** An asset is liquid when it can be easily turned into cash. Checkable deposits can be turned into cash with no limits and restrictions. Choice A is incorrect because it takes time to cash in a plot of land. Choice C is incorrect because, while shares in money market mutual funds can be cashed in without penalties, it takes time to do so. Choice D is incorrect because banks impose restrictions on withdrawals from savings accounts.

19. **The correct answer is D.** A higher required reserve ratio lowers the money supply, as it forces banks to keep a larger share of deposits as reserves, reducing the amount of excess reserves banks can loan out. Choice A is incorrect because banks do not close depositors' accounts to comply with reserve requirements. Choice B is incorrect because a higher required reserve ratio lowers the money supply. Choice C is incorrect because a higher required reserve ratio lowers the money supply.

20. **The correct answer is A.** Bank examiners rate banks according to the soundness and adequacy of their capital, assets, management, earnings, liquidity, and sensitivity to risk. Choices B, C, and D are incorrect because none of them is a dimension of the CAMELS rating system.

21. **The correct answer is D.** During a bank crisis, depositors' withdrawals drastically increase banks' obligations, forcing banks to stop renewing expiring loans (they call

in loans) to create some liquidity. As a result, money supply sharply declines. The Federal Reserve can prevent this outcome by injecting liquidity and raising the monetary base. Choice A is incorrect because the increase in currency in circulation less than compensates the decline in deposits and money supply declines. Choice B is incorrect because when depositors withdraw funds total reserves decline and so do excess reserves. Choice C is incorrect because depositor's withdrawals do not affect the Fed's balance sheet or the monetary base.

22. **The correct answer is D.** When investors adapt their expectations slowly, they have adaptive expectations. Choice A is incorrect because when investors have rational expectations, they use all information efficiently and adapt their expectations very fast. Choice B is incorrect because hyperbolic expectations are not relevant economic concepts. Choice C is incorrect because even if investors are slow in responding to changes in economic variable, the name is adaptive expectations.

23. **The correct answer is D.** Through bank failures and mergers, the overall number of commercial banks has declined from more than 30,000 in 1920 to around 6,000 today. However, the number of branches has increased. Choice A is incorrect because the number of commercial banks has not increased. Choice B is incorrect because while today there are about 6,000 commercial banks, the number of banks has declined over the last century. Choice C is incorrect because the number of banks has been declining over the entire century.

24. **The correct answer is C.** The equation of exchange is at the heart of the quantity theory of money, and it states that the stock of money in the economy times the velocity of money is equal to income at current prices or, in economic parlance, to the nominal value of output. Choice A is incorrect because the current account and the financial account sum to the negative of the capital account. Choice B is incorrect because the statement describes the purchase power parity theory, not the equation

of exchange. Choice D is incorrect because the statement describes the law of one price, not the equation of exchange.

25. **The correct answer is B.** Checkable deposits are counted in M1 and in M2, while shares in money market mutual funds are counted in M2 only. Moving $1,000 from a mutual fund to a checkable deposit raises M1 and leaves M2 the same. Choice A is incorrect because both shares in money market mutual funds and checkable deposits are counted in M2. Choice C is incorrect because both shares in money market mutual funds and checkable deposits are counted in M2. Choice D is incorrect because the deposit raises M1 and leaves M2 the same.

26. **The correct answer is B.** Commercial banks are stock-owned, while credit unions are mutual institutions. Choice A is incorrect because both commercial banks and credit unions are depository institutions allowed to accept deposits; deposits at credit unions are called shares. Choice C is incorrect because credit unions are rather small because depositors must share a common bond. Choice D is incorrect because commercial banks are supervised by states and the Comptroller of the Currency, while credit unions are supervised by the National Credit Union Association.

27. **The correct answer is D.** Gross domestic product is a measure of total output and is the sum of consumption, investment, government purchases, and net exports. Choice A is incorrect because the sum of consumption and saving is disposable income, which is total income minus net taxes. Choice B is incorrect because disposable income and net taxes sum up to net national income that, unlike GDP, doesn't count capital depreciation. Choice C is incorrect because net taxes are not a component of GDP.

28. **The correct answer is B.** Loans represent about 55 percent of commercial banks' total assets. Choice A is incorrect because equity capital is the bank's net worth, which is the difference between the bank's assets and the bank's liabilities. Choice C is incorrect because security investments represent less

than 20 percent of commercial banks' total assets. Choice D is incorrect because deposits are the larger share of commercial banks' liabilities.

29. **The correct answer is D.** Classical economists believe that prices and the economy operate at full employment all the time. Keynesian economists believe that prices are sticky, but the economy readjusts to potential output over time. Choice A is incorrect because Keynesian economists believe that prices are sticky in the short run. Choice B is incorrect because Keynesian economists believe that higher government spending can help maintain the economy at full employment. Choice C is incorrect because both classical and Keynesian economists believe that monetary policy can help maintain price stability.

30. **The correct answer is A.** The Basel 1 agreement made capital requirements sensitive to risk exposure, so that currently banks must have a leverage ratio of more than 3 percent and a ratio of Tier 1 and Tier 2 capital to risk-weighted assets of at least 8 percent. Choice B is incorrect because regulation requires a leverage ratio higher than 3 percent. Choice C is incorrect because capital regulation focuses on the ratio of capital to assets. Choice D is incorrect because capital regulation focuses on the ratio of capital to assets.

31. **The correct answer is B.** When inflation increases, the central bank responds by increasing the real interest rate, which dampens investment and total spending. Choice A is incorrect because when real wages decline, firms hire more workers. Choice C is incorrect because inflation does not necessarily lower business confidence. Choice D is incorrect because a slower pace of technological change does not lead to lower spending.

32. **The correct answer is B.** The CRA is the Community Reinvestment Act that requires banks to extend loans to customers from all neighborhoods in their market and pushes banks to extend loans to families that have a high risk of default. Choice A is incorrect because banks are now allowed to pay

interest on demand deposits. Choice C is incorrect because the type of moral hazard described is an unintended consequence of insuring deposit accounts. Choice D is incorrect because the SEC is responsible for accounting rules.

33. **The correct answer is D.** If economic agents have rational expectations, they anticipate the long-term effects of fiscal policy on prices and inflation and act accordingly, thereby keeping the GDP and employment levels at an equilibrium for both the long- and short-run. Choice A is incorrect because rational expectations agents correctly anticipate the policy's effect on prices and inflation speeding up the policy lag of monetary policy. Choice B is incorrect because if economic agents have rational expectations expansionary policies are more likely to create demand pull inflation. Choice C is incorrect because if economic agents have rational expectations, a misguided expansionary policy or an increase in the cost of material can easily trigger cost push inflation.

34. **The correct answer is B.** It takes about two years for a change in the federal funds rate to fully affect total spending. Choice A is incorrect because the central bank has significant control over short-term interest rates. Choice C is incorrect because the central bank can immediately change the federal funds rate. Choice D is incorrect because investment and consumption, two key components of total spending, are sensitive to the interest rate.

35. **The correct answer is A.** The Acts allowed national banks to issue tax-free notes, and it increased state banks' reliance on demand deposits. With no reserve requirements or deposit insurance, bank runs and bank panics became very frequent. Choice B is incorrect because the U.S. banking system is still a dual system with state and national banks. Choice C is incorrect because the number of currencies declined and soon only notes issued by national banks and backed by Treasury securities were used as money, but this was a positive consequence of the Acts. Choice D is incorrect because

the National Bank Acts were passed in the 1860s, while the Federal Reserve Bank was created pursuant the Federal Reserve Act of 1913.

36. **The correct answer is A.** The FDIC was established by the Banking Act of 1933, also known as the Glass-Steagall Act. Choice B is incorrect because the Federal Reserve Act was signed in 1913. Choice C is incorrect because the Federal Reserve Act of 1913 established the Federal Reserve Bank. Choice D is incorrect because the McFadden Act was signed in 1927 and did not establish the FDIC.

37. **The correct answer is B.** The First Bank of the United States was established by Congress in 1781 at the urgency of Alexander Hamilton, who believed a national bank could improve credit, tax collection, and business in the Union. Choice A is incorrect because Andrew Jackson, who represented the interests of the agrarian states, was opposed to the idea of a National Bank. Choice C is incorrect because John Maynard Keynes, a British economist, lived in the twentieth century. Choice D is incorrect because Milton Friedman was the most important monetarist who lived in the twentieth century.

38. **The correct answer is C.** Banks engage in interest-based activities, like lending, and in fee-based activities of pure intermediation; these activities have no influence on the banks' balance sheet and hence are called off-balance sheet activities. Originating loans for resale is one such activity. Choice A is incorrect because loans held to maturity are assets recorded in banks' balance sheets. Choice B is incorrect because excess reserves are assets recorded in the banks' balance sheet. Choice D is incorrect because, while securitization is an off-balance sheet activity, holding mortgage-backed securities is an on-balance sheet activity.

39. **The correct answer is D.** A country that allows inflows and outflows of financial capital can maintain the foreign exchange rate at a chosen parity only by forcing its interest rate to follow the interest rate in the rest of the world, effectively losing control

of its monetary policy. Choice A is incorrect because the United States is a democratic country with a trade balance deficit that allows its currency to float against foreign currencies. Choice B is incorrect because countries that run a public deficit generally also suffer from a balance of trade deficit. Choice C is incorrect because the U.S. can have an open economy and the Federal Reserve can use any of the tools of monetary policy.

40. **The correct answer is C.** The President of each Regional Reserve Bank is elected by 6 of the 9 members of the Bank's Board of Directors. The Board of Governors chooses 3 of these 6 voting members. Choice A is incorrect because the Board of Governors does not directly appoint the regional Reserve Banks' Presidents. Choice B is incorrect because the President of the United States appoints the members of the Board of Governors, not the Presidents of the regional Feds. Choice D is incorrect because the Board of Governors does not make recommendations to the Board of Directors.

41. **The correct answer is B.** The interbank rate, the interest rate banks charge each other on short-term loans, is not a tool of monetary policy but a policy instrument and an operational target. Choice A is incorrect because large-scale asset purchases, also known as quantitative easing, are unconventional tools of monetary policy. Choice C is incorrect because the interest on reserves is a tool of monetary policy. Choice D is incorrect because the discount rate is a tool of monetary policy.

42. **The correct answer is A.** Real variables focus on the purchase power of their nominal counterparts, hence the real interest rate is the difference between the market rate and the change in price people expect. Choice B is incorrect because the difference between the market rate and the cost of money is an indicator of banks' profitability. Choice C is incorrect because the interest rate on mortgages or auto loans is a nominal variable. Choice D is incorrect because the difference between the domestic and foreign rates is

an indicator of future movements of the foreign exchange rates.

43. **The correct answer is B.** An open market purchase of securities injects reserves into the banking system, raising the monetary base and the money supply. Choice A is incorrect because an increase in the monetary base leads to higher money supply. Choice C is incorrect because an open market purchase of securities increases the monetary base. Choice D is incorrect because an open market purchase of securities increases the monetary base, which increases the money supply.

44. **The correct answer is B.** Starting in 2009, banks are holding trillions in excess reserves and the equilibrium federal funds rate is close to or lower than the interest on reserves. To raise the federal funds rate, the Federal Reserve can rely on changes in the interest on reserves. Choice A is incorrect because after 2009 an outright sale of Treasury security could not raise the federal funds rate. Choice C is incorrect because lowering the required reserve ratio depresses the federal funds rate. Choice D is incorrect because the FOMC has no authority over the primary discount rate.

45. **The correct answer is D.** Purchases of Treasury securities on the open market are a tool of monetary policy. Choice A is incorrect because unemployment benefits are one type of transfer, and their automatic increase during downturns is an example of an automatic stabilizer. Choice B is incorrect because a temporary reduction in taxes is a tool of fiscal policy. Choice C is incorrect because grants to states to finance government purchases are a tool of fiscal policy.

46. **The correct answer is D.** The purchase power parity theory applies the law of one price to international trade. If it's cheaper to buy an item domestically than import it from abroad, then exports will increase, imports will drop, and the foreign exchange will adjust, returning parity to the domestic and international price. Choice A is incorrect because the purchase power parity theory applies the law of one price to international trade. Choice B is incorrect because

the depreciation of the currency does not necessarily lead to higher wages. Choice C is incorrect because it states the main point of the interest rate parity theory.

47. **The correct answer is B.** In the 1930s, the frequency of bank panics and bank runs fell only after the FDIC was created and started insuring bank deposits. Choice A is incorrect because in a bank crisis it is the Federal Reserve that can inject liquidity and act as lender of last resort. Choice C is incorrect because the FDIC uses several methods to resolve failing banks. Choice D is incorrect because the FDIC does not regulate capital requirements.

48. **The correct answer is D.** The key idea of crowding out is that government and the private sector compete for funds so that when government absorbs more funds, fewer are available to finance private investment. Choice A is incorrect because higher public spending creates expectations of a stronger economy, boosting business confidence. Choice B is incorrect because if the central bank increases money supply, the interest rate declines, boosting investment. Choice C is incorrect because the "crowding out" effect is a long-run phenomenon.

49. **The correct answer is C.** Indirect finance channels funds from investors to users through financial intermediaries. A bank loan is a tool of indirect finance as it is intermediated by a bank. Choice A is incorrect because in crowd-funding the funds move directly from holders to users. Choice B is incorrect because when an investor buys a newly issued corporate bond, the funds flow directly to their user. Choice D is incorrect because when a corporation issues new stock, the funds flow directly to their user.

50. **The correct answer is C.** The money multiplier is sensitive to the currency ratio and the excess reserve ratio that are not stable through time. Choice A is incorrect because evidence from the years following the financial crises shows a decline of the money multiplier. Choice B is incorrect because a change in the discount rate or the interest paid on reserves can influence the excess reserve ratio and the money

multiplier. Choice D is incorrect because changes in the U.S. Treasury monetary liabilities affect the monetary base but do not affect the money multiplier.

51. **The correct answer is A.** If policy makers unwittingly try to keep the unemployment rate below its natural level, they repeatedly stimulate spending, triggering demand-pull inflation. Choice B is incorrect because a decline in the rate of growth of money supply slows inflation. Choice C is incorrect because inflation that is due to a temporary increase in the cost of material or in the cost of labor is called cost-push inflation. Choice D is incorrect because inflation is a continual increase of the price level.

52. **The correct answer is B.** In a liquidity crisis, a mutual fund can sell some of its assets at a price below its intrinsic value (fire sale) to increase cash at hand. Choice A is incorrect because buying securities exacerbates the fund's liquidity problem. Choice C is incorrect because only depository institutions can apply for primary credit at the Fed. Choice D is incorrect because the fund has a liquidity problem and should not divert resources away from the liquidity management division into the capital management division.

53. **The correct answer is B.** In the 2003–2006 period, monetary policy was accommodating. In fact, some economists believe that this accommodating stance fueled the housing bubble at the heart of the financial crisis. Choice A is incorrect because financial innovation like securitization dramatically increased funds availability in the housing market fueling the market bubble. Choice C is incorrect because declining business standards at mortgage originators lowered the quality and raised the risk of the mortgages backing the new securities, injecting risk in the financial sector. Choice D is incorrect because credit agencies' new practice of advising firms on how to structure new complex financial instruments created a conflict of interest that led them to give these instruments inaccurately high ratings.

54. **The correct answer is A.** Inflation is a continual increase of the price level. To

measure inflation, economists use a price indicator like the Personal Consumption Expenditures deflator. Choice B is incorrect because the labor force counts employed and unemployed workers. Choice C is incorrect because employment counts all workers who hold a job. Choice D is incorrect because gross domestic product is a measure of total output.

55. **The correct answer is B.** In foreign countries, commercial banks have always been allowed to engage in a broader range of financial activities, such as offering life insurance. Choice A is incorrect because U.S. banks expanded their operations abroad in response to the expansion of multinational corporations. Choice C is incorrect because U.S. banks expanded their operations abroad to help their business clients import supplies and parts from abroad and sell their final product to foreign countries. Choice D is incorrect because U.S. banks expanded their operations abroad to evade some of the strict regulations that characterize the U.S. banking sector, such as the separation between commercial and investment banking.

56. **The correct answer is D.** People hold money to pay for transactions and as a store of values. An increase in nominal income raises the demand for money held for transaction purposes, and the interest rate must increase to keep the money market in equilibrium. Choice A is incorrect because a higher money demand leads to higher interest rates. Choice B is incorrect because a higher nominal income raises the money demand. Choice C is incorrect because a higher income leads to a higher demand for money and because a decline in the demand for money would lower the interest rate.

57. **The correct answer is A.** During debt crises, the IMF can expand its ability to act as a lender of last resort by borrowing from member countries. Choice B is incorrect because membership is contingent on the payment of fixed quotas. Choice C is incorrect because all member countries must contribute. Choice D is incorrect because the

funds are not borrowed on the open market, but deposited by member countries.

58. **The correct answer is D.** A temporary increase in the cost of production lowers output below potential and triggers cost-pushed inflation. If the central bank raises interest rates to prevent higher inflation, it depresses investment and consumption, deepening the recession and creating higher unemployment. Choice A is incorrect because higher total spending leads to higher inflation and output above potential. If the central bank raises interest rates to prevent higher inflation, it depresses total spending, cooling off the economy. Choice B is incorrect because lower total spending leads to lower inflation and lower output. If the central bank lowers interest rates to prevent higher inflation, it stimulates total spending, closing the output gap. Choice C is incorrect because a permanent decline in potential output triggers higher inflation but does not create an output gap.

59. **The correct answer is A.** The Glass-Steagall Act limited commercial banks securities and insurance activities. Choice B is incorrect because the Glass-Steagall Act prohibited paying interest on demand deposits. Choice C is incorrect because discrimination in lending is outlawed by the Equal Credit Opportunity Act. Choice D is incorrect because national banks were introduced by the National Bank Acts of the mid-1800s.

60. **The correct answer is A.** A decline in the domestic interest rate lowers the relative demand for domestic securities and the relative demand for the domestic currency, leading to a depreciation of the domestic currency. Choice B is incorrect because lower interest rates stimulate consumption spending. Choice C is incorrect because an accommodating monetary policy raises asset prices. Choice D is incorrect because an accommodating monetary policy raises inflation expectations.

Personal Finance

OVERVIEW

Chapter 9

The DSST® Personal Finance exam consists of 100 multiple-choice questions that cover debit and credit, major purchases, taxes, insurance, investments, and retirement and estate planning. Careful reading, critical thinking, and logical analysis will be as important as your knowledge of finance-related topics.

You are allowed to use a nonprogrammable calculator on this exam.

DIAGNOSTIC TEST ANSWER SHEET

1. Ⓐ Ⓑ Ⓒ Ⓓ	5. Ⓐ Ⓑ Ⓒ Ⓓ	9. Ⓐ Ⓑ Ⓒ Ⓓ	13. Ⓐ Ⓑ Ⓒ Ⓓ	17. Ⓐ Ⓑ Ⓒ Ⓓ
2. Ⓐ Ⓑ Ⓒ Ⓓ	6. Ⓐ Ⓑ Ⓒ Ⓓ	10. Ⓐ Ⓑ Ⓒ Ⓓ	14. Ⓐ Ⓑ Ⓒ Ⓓ	18. Ⓐ Ⓑ Ⓒ Ⓓ
3. Ⓐ Ⓑ Ⓒ Ⓓ	7. Ⓐ Ⓑ Ⓒ Ⓓ	11. Ⓐ Ⓑ Ⓒ Ⓓ	15. Ⓐ Ⓑ Ⓒ Ⓓ	19. Ⓐ Ⓑ Ⓒ Ⓓ
4. Ⓐ Ⓑ Ⓒ Ⓓ	8. Ⓐ Ⓑ Ⓒ Ⓓ	12. Ⓐ Ⓑ Ⓒ Ⓓ	16. Ⓐ Ⓑ Ⓒ Ⓓ	20. Ⓐ Ⓑ Ⓒ Ⓓ

POST-TEST ANSWER SHEET

1. Ⓐ Ⓑ Ⓒ Ⓓ	13. Ⓐ Ⓑ Ⓒ Ⓓ	25. Ⓐ Ⓑ Ⓒ Ⓓ	37. Ⓐ Ⓑ Ⓒ Ⓓ	49. Ⓐ Ⓑ Ⓒ Ⓓ
2. Ⓐ Ⓑ Ⓒ Ⓓ	14. Ⓐ Ⓑ Ⓒ Ⓓ	26. Ⓐ Ⓑ Ⓒ Ⓓ	38. Ⓐ Ⓑ Ⓒ Ⓓ	50. Ⓐ Ⓑ Ⓒ Ⓓ
3. Ⓐ Ⓑ Ⓒ Ⓓ	15. Ⓐ Ⓑ Ⓒ Ⓓ	27. Ⓐ Ⓑ Ⓒ Ⓓ	39. Ⓐ Ⓑ Ⓒ Ⓓ	51. Ⓐ Ⓑ Ⓒ Ⓓ
4. Ⓐ Ⓑ Ⓒ Ⓓ	16. Ⓐ Ⓑ Ⓒ Ⓓ	28. Ⓐ Ⓑ Ⓒ Ⓓ	40. Ⓐ Ⓑ Ⓒ Ⓓ	52. Ⓐ Ⓑ Ⓒ Ⓓ
5. Ⓐ Ⓑ Ⓒ Ⓓ	17. Ⓐ Ⓑ Ⓒ Ⓓ	29. Ⓐ Ⓑ Ⓒ Ⓓ	41. Ⓐ Ⓑ Ⓒ Ⓓ	53. Ⓐ Ⓑ Ⓒ Ⓓ
6. Ⓐ Ⓑ Ⓒ Ⓓ	18. Ⓐ Ⓑ Ⓒ Ⓓ	30. Ⓐ Ⓑ Ⓒ Ⓓ	42. Ⓐ Ⓑ Ⓒ Ⓓ	54. Ⓐ Ⓑ Ⓒ Ⓓ
7. Ⓐ Ⓑ Ⓒ Ⓓ	19. Ⓐ Ⓑ Ⓒ Ⓓ	31. Ⓐ Ⓑ Ⓒ Ⓓ	43. Ⓐ Ⓑ Ⓒ Ⓓ	55. Ⓐ Ⓑ Ⓒ Ⓓ
8. Ⓐ Ⓑ Ⓒ Ⓓ	20. Ⓐ Ⓑ Ⓒ Ⓓ	32. Ⓐ Ⓑ Ⓒ Ⓓ	44. Ⓐ Ⓑ Ⓒ Ⓓ	56. Ⓐ Ⓑ Ⓒ Ⓓ
9. Ⓐ Ⓑ Ⓒ Ⓓ	21. Ⓐ Ⓑ Ⓒ Ⓓ	33. Ⓐ Ⓑ Ⓒ Ⓓ	45. Ⓐ Ⓑ Ⓒ Ⓓ	57. Ⓐ Ⓑ Ⓒ Ⓓ
10. Ⓐ Ⓑ Ⓒ Ⓓ	22. Ⓐ Ⓑ Ⓒ Ⓓ	34. Ⓐ Ⓑ Ⓒ Ⓓ	46. Ⓐ Ⓑ Ⓒ Ⓓ	58. Ⓐ Ⓑ Ⓒ Ⓓ
11. Ⓐ Ⓑ Ⓒ Ⓓ	23. Ⓐ Ⓑ Ⓒ Ⓓ	35. Ⓐ Ⓑ Ⓒ Ⓓ	47. Ⓐ Ⓑ Ⓒ Ⓓ	59. Ⓐ Ⓑ Ⓒ Ⓓ
12. Ⓐ Ⓑ Ⓒ Ⓓ	24. Ⓐ Ⓑ Ⓒ Ⓓ	36. Ⓐ Ⓑ Ⓒ Ⓓ	48. Ⓐ Ⓑ Ⓒ Ⓓ	60. Ⓐ Ⓑ Ⓒ Ⓓ

answer sheets

PERSONAL FINANCE DIAGNOSTIC TEST

Directions: Carefully read each of the following 20 questions. Choose the best answer to each question and fill in the corresponding circle on the answer sheet. The Answer Key and Explanations can be found following this Diagnostic Test.

1. Who is responsible for paying for credit counseling for debtors filing for bankruptcy?
   - **A.** The debtors
   - **B.** Federal government through a debt reduction program
   - **C.** State government through a debt reduction program
   - **D.** Debtors' creditors

2. Which of the following is subtracted from income to arrive at a person's adjusted gross income?
   - **A.** Tax credit
   - **B.** IRA contribution
   - **C.** Real estate taxes
   - **D.** Medical expenses

3. Homeowner's insurance typically does NOT cover
   - **A.** damage from a lightning strike.
   - **B.** equipment used to run a business from home.
   - **C.** theft.
   - **D.** damage from the weight of snow on a roof.

4. Mary retired after thirty years. She will receive $4,000 a month before taxes in pension benefits from her former employer for the rest of her life. What type of pension plan does her former employer have?
   - **A.** Defined-contribution plan
   - **B.** Defined-benefit plan
   - **C.** Guaranteed plan
   - **D.** Simplified employee pension plan

5. The asset that a borrower puts up as repayment for a loan should the borrower default is known as
   - **A.** capital.
   - **B.** credit.
   - **C.** conditions.
   - **D.** collateral.

6. Which of the following is taxable income?
   - **A.** Child support payments
   - **B.** Interest from municipal bonds
   - **C.** Tips
   - **D.** Damages received as a result of a lawsuit against a convicted drunk driver

7. Which of the following types of life insurance has no cash value?
   - **A.** Variable life
   - **B.** Universal life
   - **C.** Whole life
   - **D.** Term life

8. Using the rule of 72, approximately how long will it take to double $4,000 invested at 3 percent?
   - **A.** 8 years
   - **B.** 12 years
   - **C.** 18 years
   - **D.** 24 years

9. If a person is concerned about inflation during retirement, that person would invest in
   A. deferred annuity.
   B. fixed annuity.
   C. variable annuity.
   D. life income annuity.

10. A broker lends securities to a client who wishes to sell them now and buy them back later. This is known as a
    A. margin call.
    B. market order.
    C. short position.
    D. maintenance margin requirement.

11. Which of the following is an example of closed-end credit?
    A. Buying a pair of shoes at a shoe store
    B. A mortgage
    C. Buying a piece of furniture at a department store
    D. Paying for a doctor's services with a check

12. Which of the following provisions of health insurance policies is the most beneficial for policy holders?
    A. Internal benefits
    B. Service benefit
    C. Fixed dollar benefit
    D. Assigned benefits

13. The time value of money refers to
    A. the amount of risk versus the amount of return.
    B. buying or selling assets within a single day.
    C. buying and holding assets in anticipation of income.
    D. the increase in an amount of money as a result of interest earned.

14. Self-employed persons may lower their income tax by deducting which of the following expenses?
    A. Self-employment tax
    B. Health insurance
    C. Contribution to a Roth IRA
    D. Their state's excise tax

15. When is it better to return a leased vehicle rather than buy it when the lease is up?
    A. When the market value is less than the residual value
    B. When the car has reached its capitalized cost
    C. When the lease rate increases more than 5 percent
    D. When the end-of-lease payment is higher than the appraisal

16. Which of the following is classified as a long-term financial strategy?
    A. Saving for a down payment on a house
    B. Saving for a child's college education
    C. Buying a new car
    D. Paying off the $11,000 balance on a credit card

17. Which of the following is NOT a cost of ownership of a vehicle?
    A. Taxes on the vehicle
    B. Vehicle insurance
    C. Depreciation
    D. Buying gas

18. An example of a current liability is a(n)
    A. electric utility bill.
    B. home mortgage.
    C. car loan.
    D. eighteen-month installment loan for a new washer and dryer.

19. The cost of operation of a vehicle includes
   A. depreciation.
   B. registration.
   C. sales tax.
   D. maintenance.

20. Joint tenancy with right of survivorship is a way to
   A. avoid paying federal inheritance tax.
   B. avoid probate.
   C. ensure that property is not part of an estate for tax purposes.
   D. divide an estate equally among heirs

ANSWER KEY AND EXPLANATIONS

1. A	**5.** D	**9.** C	**13.** D	**17.** D
2. B	**6.** C	**10.** C	**14.** B	**18.** A
3. B	**7.** D	**11.** B	**15.** A	**19.** D
4. B	**8.** D	**12.** B	**16.** B	**20.** B

1. **The correct answer is A.** Under the Bankruptcy Abuse Prevention and Consumer Protection Act of 2005, those who file for bankruptcy must enroll in credit counseling before filing for bankruptcy and in a credit education course after filing for bankruptcy. The debtor pays for both. It's a federal law, but the federal government doesn't pay for the programs, so choice B is incorrect. A state program (choice C) and debtor's creditors (choice D) are both incorrect.

2. **The correct answer is B.** Adjusted gross income is income after certain deductions have been subtracted. A contribution to a filer's IRA is one of the items that is used. Real estate taxes and medical expenses (choices C and D) are subtracted from adjusted gross income after it has been determined. Tax credit (choice A) is subtracted directly from the amount of tax owed.

3. **The correct answer is B.** Lightning (choice A), theft (choice C), and damage from the weight of snow (choice D) are typically covered by homeowner's insurance policies. Equipment used in a business operated out of a residence is not covered by a homeowner's policy, so choice B is the correct answer.

4. **The correct answer is B.** The scenario describes a defined-benefit plan (choice B). A defined-contribution plan (choice A) specifies the contribution of the employer but not the level of benefits the employee will receive at or during retirement. A guaranteed plan (choice C) is in essence what a defined-benefit plan is, but that's not the correct term. A simplified employee pension plan, known as a SEP (choice D), is set up by someone who is self-employed.

5. **The correct answer is D.** Collateral is an asset that backs a borrower's promise to repay a loan. Capital (choice A) is the net worth of a borrower. Credit (choice B) is an agreement under which a person receives money, goods, or services in exchange for a promise to repay the money or pay for the good or service at a later date. Conditions (choice C) refers to economic conditions that affect a person's ability to repay a loan. Capital, collateral, and conditions, along with character and capacity, make up what is known as the "five C's of credit."

6. **The correct answer is C.** Tips are taxable income, but child support (choice A), municipal bond interest (choice B), and damages from a lawsuit for personal injury or illness (choice D) are not taxed.

7. **The correct answer is D.** Term life insurance has no cash value; it pays only death benefits. Variable life and universal life insurance (choices A and B) are types of whole life policies (choice C), and all have cash values; the savings feature is a major advantage of whole life policies. With variable life (choice A), the cash value, as well as the death benefits, varies depending on the interest earned in the fund in which it is invested; there is, however, a floor for the death benefits below which they cannot fall. The cash value of universal life (choice B) also depends on the value of its investments.

8. **The correct answer is D.** The rule of 72 is:

$$\text{Doubling Time(DT)} = \frac{72}{\text{interest rate}}$$

so $\frac{72}{3} = 24$ years.

9. **The correct answer is C.** A hedge against inflation is an advantage of variable annuities. Both variable and fixed are investment options of any type of annuity. Variable annuities are invested in equities, which, theoretically, increase their returns over time. A fixed annuity (choice B) is invested in bonds and mortgages; the rate of return is fixed, so increasing inflation will eat into the income. Deferred and life income (choices A and D) are types of annuities rather than investment options.

10. **The correct answer is C.** The question prompt describes taking a short position. A margin call (choice A) is a call from a broker to a client asking the client to increase the amount of money in his or her account for stock bought on margin; a margin call occurs when the price of the stock falls below the initial margin requirement, or percentage of the stock price invested by the client. The amount of the additional money fulfills the maintenance margin requirement (choice D). A market order (choice B) is an order to buy or sell a stock at the best available price.

11. **The correct answer is B.** Buying store merchandise (choices A and C) or paying for a doctor's services with a check (choice D) are all examples of open-end credit, which is a line of credit used for a series of purchases over time and for which the borrower is billed regularly; amounts of repayment vary depending on charges. Closed-end credit is a loan used for a single purchase, such as a mortgage, and must be repaid within a certain period; payments are made regularly and in equal payments.

12. **The correct answer is B.** A service benefit states the services that the insured will receive, whereas fixed dollar benefit (choice C) states the amount of money paid by the insurance company for each service or procedure. A service benefit is better because if a procedure costs more than the fixed dollar amount, the patient has to pay the difference. Internal benefits (choice A) is a distracter meant to seem like a possibility, but it is nonexistent. Assigned benefits (choice D)

gives the insurance company the authority to pay the doctor, lab, or hospital directly.

13. **The correct answer is D.** The time value of money refers to the increase in an amount of money as a result of interest earned. The amount of risk an investor is willing to take versus the amount of return (choice A) refers to opportunity costs. Buying or selling assets within a single day (choice B) is the practice of day trading. Investing in equities involves buying and holding assets in anticipation of income (choice C).

14. **The correct answer is B.** A self-employed person can take a deduction for health insurance. Choice A is Social Security. Every worker must pay this tax, and it is not deductible; a self-employed person pays at a rate of 13.3 percent in Social Security and Medicare taxes. A Roth IRA (choice C) is tax-deferred and has no impact on income tax. An excise tax (choice D) is paid on certain goods, such as gas, tires, and communication services; it is a state and federal tax and is not deductible (but a sales tax is deductible).

15. **The correct answer is A.** There is no profit to be made on a car that you'll pay more to the dealer to buy than you'll be able to sell in the marketplace, so choice A is the best answer. Choice B is incorrect because the capitalized cost is the price that the dealer puts on the car to lease it; it is typically 96 percent of the list price. Choice C is also incorrect because according to the question, the lease is over; also, the lease rate is set when the lease is signed, so it doesn't go up or down over the life of the lease. The end-of-lease payment (choice D) has to be paid regardless of whether the lessee buys the car at the end of the lease; this is a provision of an open-end lease, not a closed-end lease.

16. **The correct answer is B.** Saving for a child's college education is considered a long-term financial strategy. Saving for a down payment (choice A) and possibly paying off a large credit card debt (choice D) are medium-term strategies. A medium-term strategy typically takes more than a year but fewer than five. Buying a new car (choice C) is a short-term strategy.

17. **The correct answer is D.** Choices A, B, and C are all incorrect because taxes on the vehicle, vehicle insurance, and depreciation are costs of ownership of a vehicle. Buying gas is a cost of operation.

18. **The correct answer is A.** A current liability is one that must be paid off within a year. Typically, an electric bill (choice A) must be paid immediately. Choices B, C, and D are noncurrent liabilities, though the installment payments due this year for the mortgage, car loan, and new appliances are current liabilities.

19. **The correct answer is D.** All the answer choices relate to vehicles, but choices A, B, and C—depreciation, registration, and sales tax—are part of the cost of ownership. Maintenance is part of the cost of operation of a vehicle.

20. **The correct answer is B.** Property owned as a joint tenancy with right of survivorship passes to the surviving owner or owners without having to pass through probate court. Choice A is incorrect because there is no federal inheritance tax, though some states do levy an inheritance tax. Choice C describes an irrevocable trust, and choice D describes the per capita division of an estate.

answers diagnostic test

DIAGNOSTIC TEST ASSESSMENT GRID

Now that you've completed the diagnostic test and read through the answer explanations, you can use your results to target your studying. Find the question numbers from the diagnostic test that you answered incorrectly and highlight or circle them below. Then focus extra attention on the sections within the chapter dealing with those topics.

Personal Finance		
Content Area	**Topic**	**Question #**
Foundations of Financial Planning	• Economic terminology • Financial goals and values • Budgeting and financial statements • Cash management • Institutional aspects of financial planning	16, 18
Credit and Debt	• Credit and debit cards • Installment loans • Interest calculations • Federal credit laws • Creditworthiness, credit scoring and reporting • Bankruptcy	1, 5, 11
Major Purchases	• Auto, furniture, appliances • Housing	15, 17, 19
Taxes	• Payroll • Income • IRS and audits • Estate and gift • Tax planning/estimating • Progressive vs. regressive • Other (excise, property, sales, gas) • Tax professionals	2, 6, 14

Personal Finance		
Content Area	**Topic**	**Question #**
Insurance	• Risk management • Life policies • Property and liability policies • Health, disability, and long-term care policies • Specialty insurance (e.g., professional, malpractice, antiques) • Insurance analysis and sources of information	3, 7, 12
Investments	• Liquid assets • Bonds • Equities • Mutual funds and exchange traded funds • Other (e.g., commodities, precious metals, real estate, derivatives) • Sources of information • Time value of money • Asset/portfolio allocation	8, 10, 13
Retirement and Estate Planning	• Terminology (vesting, maturity, rollovers) • Qualified retirement accounts (e.g., IRA, Roth IRA, SEP, Keogh, 401(k), 403(b)) • Social security benefits • Wills, trusts, and estate planning • Tax-deferred annuities	4, 9, 20

GET THE FACTS

To see the DSST® Personal Finance Fact Sheet, go to **http://getcollegecredit.com/exam_fact_sheets** and click on the **Business** tab. Scroll down and click the **Personal Finance** link. Here you will find suggestions for further study material and the ACE college credit recommendations for passing the test.

FOUNDATIONS OF FINANCIAL PLANNING

A person's life typically intertwines nonfinancial and financial goals. In order to achieve nonfinancial goals, such as having a satisfying career, a happy marriage, and a family, a person typically needs a certain amount of money. The amount depends on what satisfies a person. One person may be satisfied only with a twenty-room mansion, while another may be perfectly happy in a studio apartment. Financial planning is managing one's money in order to achieve economic satisfaction.

ECONOMIC TERMINOLOGY

Personal finance refers to how you manage your money, including your income, expenses, and savings. When you focus on managing your personal finances, you have a better grasp on where your money is going and what changes you can make to meet your future financial goals. Here are some common terms related to personal finance:

- **Economics:** The study of how we make use of our financial resources
- **Long-term Goal:** A goal you hope to achieve over a period of years
- **Financial Planning:** Setting short-, medium-, and long-range goals and then collecting and analyzing income and expenditure information to determine how to meet these goals
- **Financial Risk:** The chance that an individual, business, or government will not be able to return the money invested with them.
- **Retirement Accounts:** Accounts such as IRAs (Individual Retirement Accounts), SEPs (Simplified Employee Pension Plans), and Keogh Plans that allow individuals to save money toward retirement on a tax-deferred basis
- **Risk:** The chance of losing your invested money

FINANCIAL GOALS AND VALUES

Financial goals involve **consumption** and **savings;** consumption may be current or future, i.e., what you need/want now versus what you will need/want at some later time. The ability to obtain those needs/wants depends on earnings, savings, and investments. Therefore, financial goals can be categorized based on timeframe as **short-term**, **medium-term**, and **long-term**.

- **Short-term goals** should take no longer than about one year to reach. For example, you may plan to pay off the $2,500 balance on your credit card.
- **Medium-term goals** should be attainable within one to five years. An example of this type of goal would be planning to save $20,000 in the next five years for a down payment on a house.
- **Long-term goals** will take more than five years to reach. Saving for retirement or for a child's education are examples of long-term goals.

Goals may also be categorized by type as follows:

- **Consumable-product goals:** purchasing food, clothing, entertainment
- **Durable-product goals:** buying "big-ticket" items such as a home, cars, and appliances
- **Intangible-product goals:** paying for education (such as earning a degree), leisure, digitized content

Financial goals change in importance as a person moves through each stage of the life cycle. Areas that require people to set financial goals include debt, insurance, investing, retirement, estate, and career.

Facets of Financial Planning	
Financial Goals	Evaluate and plan major outlays Manage credit Secure adequate insurance coverage Establish savings/investment programs Manage employee benefits Reduce taxes Implement retirement program Minimize estate taxes
Budgets	Monitor and control income, living expenses, purchases, and savings on a monthly basis
Financial Statements	Actual financial results: • Balance sheet • Income and expense statement

BUDGETING AND FINANCIAL STATEMENTS

Once the goals are set, a person needs a plan to achieve them, that is, a budget that allocates money to different items, such as rent or mortgage payments, food, utilities, and savings. The budgeting process is typically done on a monthly basis and includes the following steps: estimating income; allocating for fixed expenses; allocating for variable expenses, such as car repairs; allocating for savings, and allocating for an emergency fund. The next two steps are ongoing: entering the actual amounts next to the estimated amounts in order to see variances between budgeted and actual, and then analyzing the monthly results to determine how accurate the original budget was and what needs to be changed in order to stay on track to achieve the financial goals.

The Budgeting Process	
Assess Your Current Situation	In this preliminary phase, your main tasks are to:
	• Measure your current financial position • Determine your personal needs, values, and life situation
Plan Your Financial Direction	The actual budgeting activities occur in this phase:
	Step 1: Set financial goals **Step 2:** Estimate income **Step 3:** Budget an emergency fund and savings **Step 4:** Budget fixed expenses **Step 5:** Budget variable expenses
Implement Your Budget	As you select and use your budgeting system:
	Step 6: Record spending amounts
Execute Your Budget Program	In the final phase of the process, you need to:
	Step 7: Review spending and saving patterns With the completion of the process, possible revisions of financial goals and budget allocations should be considered.

Corporations have financial statements, and individuals, couples, and families can have financial statements as well. The first item should be a **balance sheet**, which lists assets minus liabilities (debt) to show net worth. Assets include **liquid assets**—cash and anything that can be quickly turned into cash—real estate, personal property, and investments. Liabilities are both short-term, that is, less than one year, and long-term, also called noncurrent liabilities.

The second type of statement is a **cash flow statement**; it shows inflows and outflows of money, or what came in and what went out. Inflows include salaries, interest, and dividends. A cash flow statement is a useful tool for planning a household budget.

CASH MANAGEMENT

Should savings be kept in a savings account or a CD? Should they be deposited in a commercial bank, online, or at a credit union? These are questions that are part of creating a **cash management system**, a way to have cash, or the equivalent, handy for regular purchases and for emergencies.

The typical places to hold cash are regular checking accounts, interest-bearing checking accounts, savings accounts, money market deposit/demand accounts, money market mutual funds, certificates of deposit (CD), and Series EE and Series I U.S. government savings bonds. The first four have no restrictions on withdrawals. Mutual funds typically have restrictions on the number of checks that may be written each month, and CDs carry a penalty for early withdrawal. Series I U.S. government savings bonds are interest-bearing bonds intended to be long-term investments. They can be cashed in after one year but doing so before five years will forfeit the last three months of interest accrued.

Banks and other financial institutions offer services to meet a variety of needs. These fall into four primary categories:

1. *Savings*: Savings involves safe storage of funds for future use.

2. *Cash availability and payment services:* Payment services give you the ability to transfer money to others for conducting business. Checking accounts and other payment methods are commonly called **demand deposits**.

3. *Borrowing*: Borrowing refers to credit alternatives available for short- and long-term needs.

4. *Investments and other financial services:* These include insurance protection, investments, real estate purchases, tax assistance, and financial planning.

Institutional Aspects of Financial Planning

Deciding on the institutions, that is, financial services organizations and professionals, that a person will need is also part of financial planning. The choices of depository institutions include commercial banks, both bricks-and-mortar and online; savings and loan associations; mutual savings banks; and credit unions. Other companies that provide financial services include life insurance companies, mutual funds, finance companies, mortgage companies, brokerage houses, and financial planners and investment advisors.

Financial planners are licensed and regulated by the Certified Financial Planner Board of Standards, Inc. Not all individuals who call themselves financial planners are licensed, so a person looking for a financial planner should be aware of this. An **investment adviser** is a legal term, and investment advisers are regulated by either the Securities and Exchange Commission (SEC) or a state securities regulator, depending on the amount of assets the person manages. Stock and bond brokers are regulated by the SEC. They must register with the SEC and also be members of the Financial Industry Regulatory Authority (FINRA).

There are a number of laws that regulate the securities industry. Federal laws such as the Dodd-Frank Act of 2010 resulted from abuses by financial institutions during the first decade of the twenty-first century, which caused the Great Recession.

Financial Institutions Services	
Cash Availabilty	**Payment Services**
Check cashing	Checking account
ATM/debit cards	Online payments
Traveler's checks	Cashier's checks
Foreign currency exchange	Money orders
Savings Services	**Credit Services**
Regular savings account	Credit cards, cash advances
Money market account	Auto loans, education loans
Certificates of deposit	Mortgages
U.S. savings bond	Home equity loans
Investment Services	**Other Services**
Individual retirement accounts (IRA)	Insurance, trust services
Brokerage service	Tax preparations
Investment advice	Safe deposit boxes
Mutual funds	Budget counseling

CREDIT AND DEBT

The world—at least the United States—seems to run on credit today. Mailing a package at the post office? Use a credit card. Buying tickets to the movies? Use a debit card. Buying furniture at a department store? Use the store's charge card and be eligible for one-year deferred payment. From paying for a fast-food meal to buying a new car, a person never needs to have cash on hand, just a credit or debit card. With all the ease of using credit, it may take something as disastrous as bankruptcy to bring home the fact that credit comes with a price.

CREDIT AND DEBIT CARDS

Types of Credit

Consumer credit is use of credit by individuals, that is, an individual's promise to pay later for the use of a good or service now. The reasons for using credit are many: convenience, the ability to consume more than could be afforded based solely on income, as a hedge against inflation, and for emergencies. The disadvantages of using credit are also many: the temptation to spend more than a person has, the consequences of overspending, the cost of credit, and limitation on future spending power because of the cost of credit for past purchases.

Closed-end credit is credit used for a specific purchase for a specific period and for a specific amount of money, such as purchasing a vehicle on a three-year loan. Closed-end credit may be in the form of installment sales credit, installment cash credit, and single lump-sum credit. Repayment for the first two is in regular amounts over a period of time.

Open-end credit is a line of credit that enables a consumer to make a series of purchases over a period of time as long as the consumer doesn't go over the amount of the line of credit. The consumer must repay the amount in regular payments, but the payments may be of varying amounts as long as the payments meet the minimum amount stated by the card issuer. This is also known as a *revolving credit* account. Some stores, such as a cleaner, for example, may offer customers regular charge accounts: the customer charges purchases during the month and then is sent a bill at the end of the month that is due in full.

Open-end credit instruments include credit/smart cards, a debit card, and a home equity line of credit. A travel and entertainment card must be paid in full each month, unlike credit cards, which can be paid in installments.

It's important to research any extra perks or protections a credit card may offer. Some of the most attractive bonuses can help the cardholder save money or protect them from certain losses. Among the most valuable perks include those that offer protection if the card is used to purchase something that breaks or fails to perform as promised or for which the merchant doesn't provide the promised goods or services.

Another important consideration when researching a credit card is the grace period. This is the amount of time (if any) after a purchase in which you can pay off the balance without incurring an interest charge. If a credit card does offer a grace period, it must be at least twenty-one days, as required by the Credit CARD Act of 2009 (a federal law governing many rules related to credit cards and often referred to as the credit cardholder's bill of rights).

There are some important distinctions between credit cards and debit cards. Among the most significant differences: with a debit card purchase, the transaction amount is immediately deducted from your account and there is no grace period or "float" (if there aren't sufficient funds in the account, the transaction may be declined or may result in overdraft charges). Also, losses from a stolen credit card are capped at $50, whereas losses with a stolen debit card are only capped at that amount if the card holder notifies the bank within two days. The cap can rise to $500 for losses incurred if the bank is notified within two and sixty days.

INSTALLMENT LOANS

An installment loan is a loan in which there are a set number of scheduled payments over time. Many different types of loans are installment loans. These include the following:

- **Student Loans:** Student loans are a type of installment loan. With student loans, you receive a set amount of money for your educational costs, and then, once out of school, you pay back the loans by paying a set amount each month. Student loans also allow you the option of deferring your payments when you are unemployed for a period of time, but you will have to resume your payments once you are employed again.

- **Mortgage Loans:** When you take out a mortgage loan, you are able to finance the purchase of your home and pay back the loan over a set number of years. It is important that you stay current with your payments or you risk losing your home and damaging your credit.

- **Car Loans:** When you need a car but do not have enough money to pay up front, taking out a car loan can be ideal. However, similar to mortgage loans, if you do not pay back the money as scheduled, your car can be repossessed and your credit would be damaged.

INTEREST CALCULATIONS

Interest is what you pay to borrow money using a loan, credit card, or line of credit. It is calculated at either a fixed or variable rate that is expressed as a percentage of the amount you borrow, tied to a specific time period. This can be classified as simple interest or compound interest. Simple interest is calculated only on the principal amount of a loan. Compound interest is calculated on the principal amount and also on the accumulated interest of previous periods and thus is regarded as "interest on interest." This compounding effect can make a big difference in the amount of interest payable on a loan as interest is calculated on a compound rather than simple basis.

Simple Interest

The formula for calculating simple interest is:

Simple Interest = Principal × Interest Rate × Term of the Loan

$$I = P \times i \times n$$

If simple interest is charged at 3 percent on a $15,000 loan that is taken out for a three-year period, the total amount of interest payable by the borrower is calculated as:

Simple Interest = 15,000 × 0.03 × 3 = $1,350.

Interest on this loan is payable at $450 annually or $1,350 over the three-year loan term.

Compound Interest

The formula for calculating compound interest is:

Compound Interest = Total amount of Principal and Interest in future
(or Future Value) less Principal amount at present (or Present Value)

$$= [P\,(1 + i)^n] - P$$

$$= P\,[(1 + i)^{n-1}]$$

where P = Principal, i = annual interest rate in percentage terms,
and n = number of compounding periods.

Continuing with the values of the simple interest example, what would be the amount of interest if it is charged on a compound basis? In this case it would be:

$15,000 [(1 + 0.03)^3] − 1 = $15,000 [1.092727 − 1] = $1,390.91.

While the total interest payable over the three-year period of this loan is $1,390.91, unlike simple interest, the interest amount is not the same for all three years because compound interest also takes into consideration accumulated interest of previous periods. Interest payable at the end of each year is shown in the table below:

Year	Opening Balance (P)	Interest @ 3 %	Closing Balance ($P + i$)
1	$15,000	$450	$15,450
2	$15,450	$463.50	$15,913.50
3	$15,913.50	$477.41	$16,390.91
	Total Interest	**$1,390.91**	

Compounding Periods

When calculating compound interest, the number of compounding periods makes a significant difference. The basic rule is that the higher the number of compounding periods, the greater the amount of compound interest. So, for every $100 of a loan over a certain period, the amount of interest accrued at 10 percent annually will be lower than interest accrued at 5 percent semiannually, which will, in turn, be lower than interest accrued at 2.5 percent quarterly.

In the formula for calculating compound interest, the variables i and n have to be adjusted if the number of compounding periods is more than one a year. That is, i has to be divided by the number of compounding periods per year, and n has to be multiplied by the number of compounding periods. Therefore, for a 10-year loan at 10 percent where interest is compounded semiannually (number of compounding periods = 2), $i = 5\%$(i.e., 10% / 2) and $n = 20$ (i.e., 10 × 2).

The following table demonstrates the difference that the number of compounding periods can make over time for a $10,000 loan taken for a 10-year period.

Compounding Frequency	Number of Compounding Periods	Values of i and n	Total Interest
Annually	1	$i = 10\%$, $n = 10$	$15,937.42
Semiannually	2	$i = 5\%$, $n = 20$	$16,532.98
Quarterly	4	$i = 2.5\%$, $n = 40$	$16,850.64
Monthly	12	$i = 0.833\%$, $n = 120$	$17,070.41

FEDERAL CREDIT LAWS

Enacted in 1971, the Fair Credit Reporting Act (FCRA) was the first federal law to regulate how your personal information is used by a private business. This act safeguards your credit by requiring consumer reporting agencies to follow certain standards. It gives you the right to a free credit report annually, protected access, and accurate reporting. This act gives you the right to have inaccuracies fixed in a timely manner, as well as the right to sue and seek damages for violations.

The Fair Credit Reporting Act contains three smaller acts: The Credit CARD Act, the Dodd-Frank Act, and the Fair and Accurate Credit Transactions Act. These deal with the accountability of credit card companies and your rights if someone steals your identity.

The Credit CARD Act

The Credit CARD Act is often called the Credit Cardholders Bill of Rights. President Barack Obama signed the bill into law in May 2009. Many of the most significant provisions of the law took effect in February 2010. The law has two main purposes:

1. *Fairness*: Prohibit certain practices that are unfair or abusive, such as hiking up the rate on an existing balance or allowing a consumer to go over limit and then imposing an over-limit fee.

2. *Transparency*: Make the rates and fees on credit cards more transparent so consumers can understand how much they are paying for their credit card and can compare the costs of different cards.

The Dodd-Frank Act

Dodd-Frank is a law that places major regulations on the financial industry. It grew out of the Great Recession with the intention of preventing another collapse of a major financial institution like Lehman Brothers. Dodd-Frank is also geared toward protecting consumers with rules such as keeping borrowers from abusive lending and mortgage practices by banks. It became a law in 2010 and was named after Senator Christopher J. Dodd (D-CT) and U.S. Representative Barney Frank (D-MA), who were the sponsors of the legislation.

The Fair and Accurate Credit Transactions Act

The Fair and Accurate Credit Transaction Act of 2003 (FACTA) added sections to the federal Fair Credit Reporting Act intended primarily to help consumers fight identity theft. Accuracy, privacy, limits on information sharing, and new consumer rights to disclosure are included in FACTA.

CREDITWORTHINESS, CREDIT SCORING AND REPORTING

Credit comes in many different shapes and sizes, including mortgages, loans, overdrafts, and credit cards. In most cases you will have to pay an agreed amount back every month with interest. Your **credit report** is a history of your credit accounts and payment activity. It also includes your basic personal information and certain types of public data, such as whether you have declared bankruptcy or are involved in a lawsuit. Your **credit score** is a rating that quantifies the potential risk you pose to a lender or merchant.

A **FICO score** is a credit score developed by the Fair Isaac Corporation (FICO), a company that specializes in what is known as "predictive analytics," which means they take information and analyze it to predict what is likely to happen. The FICO score range is 300–850, with the higher number representing less risk to the lender or insurer. To create credit scores, FICO uses information provided by one of the three major credit-reporting agencies:

1. Equifax
2. Experian
3. TransUnion

You are legally entitled to obtain a copy of your credit report from each of the three nationwide credit agencies once a year by visiting **www.annualcreditreport.com**, a site authorized by the federal government to provide the information free of charge.

Consumers with high FICO scores (usually around 760 or higher, though every lender is different) are likely to get the best rates when they borrow, as well as the best discounts on insurance. When qualifying a person for credit, a creditor looks for the five C's of creditworthiness:

1. Character
2. Capacity
3. Capital
4. Collateral
5. Conditions

Character

When lenders evaluate character, they look at stability: how long you have lived at your current address, how long you have been in your current job, and whether you have a good record of paying your bills on time and in full. If you want a loan for your business, the lender may consider your experience and track record in your business and industry to evaluate how trustworthy you are to repay a loan.

Capacity

Capacity refers to considering your other debts and expenses when determining your ability to repay the loan. Creditors evaluate your debt-to-income ratio, that is, how much you owe compared to how much you earn. The lower your ratio, the more confident creditors will be in your capacity to repay the money you borrow. Your monthly obligations related to pay-off debt—such as payments for mortgages, auto loans, student loans, or other debt—are all taken into consideration when calculating your debt-to-income ratio.

Capital

Capital refers to your net worth—the value of your assets minus your liabilities. In simple terms, how much you own (for example, car, real estate, cash, and investments) minus how much you owe.

Collateral

Collateral refers to any asset of a borrower, for example, a home, that a lender has a right to take ownership of and use to pay the debt if the borrower is unable to make the loan payments as agreed. Some lenders may require a guarantee in addition to collateral; a guarantee means that another person signs a document promising to repay the loan if you cannot.

Conditions

Lenders consider a number of outside circumstances that may affect the borrower's financial situation and ability to repay, such as what is happening in the local economy. If the borrower is a business, the lender may evaluate the financial health of the borrower's industry, their local market, and their competition.

This last *C* is outside the control of the consumer applying for credit; "conditions" refers to the stability of the person's job and employer. A creditor checks an applicant's FICO score, which considers length of credit history, on-time payment history, current amounts owed, types of credit in the credit history, and inquiries from new credit sources. If a person has a low score, there are ways to improve creditworthiness: pay bills on time, increase capital, don't move debt from one creditor to another, don't open new credit accounts, and reduce credit card balances. It's also important for consumers to check their credit scores several times per year to correct any mistakes.

BANKRUPTCY

The Bankruptcy Code was established in 1978 and underwent a major overhaul in 2005. At that time, the Bankruptcy Abuse Prevention and Consumer Protection Act of 2005 was hailed as an important measure to ensure that people do not use bankruptcy court as a revolving door that allows them to spend without a thought to the future, go into overwhelming debt, file for bankruptcy to escape paying off their debts, and then do it all over again.

There are two forms of personal bankruptcy: straight bankruptcy and the wage-earner plan. Straight bankruptcy is filed under **Chapter 7** of the Bankruptcy Code, and wage-earner bankruptcy is filed under **Chapter 13.**

Chapter 7—Straight Bankruptcy

As part of Chapter 7 bankruptcy, a debtor must enumerate for the court his or her assets as well as list creditors with the amounts owed and the debtor's income, property, and monthly expenses. In Chapter 7, the debtor must sell most of his or her assets. Exceptions allow the debtor to keep part of his or her equity in a home or personal property such as a car or truck. In addition, Social Security payments and unemployment compensation may be exempted, as well as equipment used in skilled work.

Most debts are wiped clean, but the price is more than losing many or most of one's assets. Credit reports carry notice of Chapter 7 bankruptcies for ten years. A Chapter 7 bankruptcy can be used only once every eight years.

Chapter 13—Wage-Earner Plan

As part of Chapter 13 bankruptcy, the debtor does not have to sell his or her assets to pay debts. Instead, the debtor works out a plan with court approval to pay off current debts with future earnings over a five-year period. This form of bankruptcy is used only for debtors with a regular income. Credit reports carry Chapter 13 bankruptcies for seven years.

Additional Provisions of the 2005 Act
- Debtors must undergo credit counseling before filing for bankruptcy.
- Debtors must take a financial education course after entering bankruptcy. The debtor is required to pay for both. Other costs involved in filing for bankruptcy include court costs, trustees' fees and costs, and attorneys' fees.

In general, certain debts and payments survive a bankruptcy:

- Income taxes

- Alimony payments

- Child support payments

- Student loans

- Any debts deliberately contracted with the idea of filing for bankruptcy

- Court awards, such as restitution of embezzled funds or damages awarded as a result of driving while under the influence of alcohol. Court awards may be discharged in a Chapter 13 filing, but not in Chapter 7.

As noted above, the consequences of filing for bankruptcy are far more than losing one's material assets. Bankruptcy records follow the filer around for seven or ten years. This can affect a person's ability to qualify for credit or a job and to buy insurance.

MAJOR PURCHASES

The largest purchase that consumers typically make is a home. The next largest is a vehicle, but consumer durable goods also have hefty price tags. Comparison shopping involves a trade-off in time versus money, but it is a smart strategy when thousands of dollars are involved. Buying decisions— whether for cars or stocks—involve the same basic steps: gathering information, evaluating alternatives, determining what a person is willing to pay, and financing/paying for the purchase.

PURCHASING AN AUTOMOBILE

As part of gathering information for the purchase of a vehicle, the buyer needs to identify the reasons that he or she wants or needs a car. The next big questions to consider are whether to buy or lease a car and, if buying, whether to buy a new or used car. In signing a lease, the lessee agrees to pay a small upfront fee—the security deposit—and monthly payments for use of the vehicle over a period of time. Vehicle leases usually run for three, four, or five years, and at the end of the lease, the lessee may buy the car. Otherwise, the car must be returned to the lessor.

Evaluating Leasing Versus Buying

Leasing a car rather than buying a car on credit reduces the initial outlay and also incurs smaller periodic payments. An additional benefit to leasing a car is intangible. The lessee may be able to lease a car that is more expensive than what the lessee could afford to buy. However, this can be a negative because a more expensive car depreciates more, and finance charges may be higher. A lessee also has no equity in the vehicle. However, the lessee is required to pay for maintenance, mileage over the amount stated in the leasing agreement, some types of repairs, and a penalty for breaking the lease, that is, turning the car in early.

To determine whether to buy or lease, a comparison can be made based on three basic pieces of information: initial costs, monthly payments, and final expenses to pay off the lease. Even considering the time value of money, that is, the interest earned on the difference between the smaller amount of the periodic payments on the lease and the larger amount of payments on the car loan, the buyer typically comes out better.

Determining Purchase Price

If a buyer decides to buy rather than lease, the question becomes whether to get a new or a used vehicle. Some buyers purchase only used cars because of the depreciation factor. The greatest depreciation occurs in the first two or three years of ownership, so these buyers prefer to purchase cars that are two or three years old. The price of a used car is determined by mileage, condition, features and options, and demand in the marketplace for the make and model. To determine the price that a buyer is willing to pay, he or she may check the prices in car ads and online dealers as well as *Edmund's Used Cars* and *Kelly Blue Book*. On the lot, a buyer should also check the "Buyers Guide" sticker on the car.

One item to look for is whether the car is sold "as is" or is still under warranty. If there is no warranty stated but the car isn't explicitly being sold "as is," there may still be some protections provided under implied warranties. Buyers should be leery of purchasing a used car "as is," because they can be taking a risk that they will incur repair expenses for existing issues. Some states prohibit dealers from selling cars "as is," and a few states also have lemon laws (federal lemon laws generally only apply to new car sales) so buyers should research applicable laws in their area.

Any used car should be checked by the buyer's mechanic to ensure that it is in good working condition.

If the decision is to buy a new car, a buyer should become familiar with the following information:

- **Monroney Sticker Price:** Price that includes the base price, manufacturer's installed options with manufacturer's suggested retail price, transportation charge from the manufacturer to the dealer, fuel economy
- **Base Price:** Price without the options
- **Invoice Price:** Cost to the dealer, which is less than the sticker price

TIP

The difference between the sticker price and the invoice price is the amount available for negotiation.

Financing

In analyzing financing options, a buyer should consider down payment, annual percentage rate (APR), finance charge, and length of the loan. The larger the down payment, the less the risk of paying off a loan on a car that is worth less than what is owed.

Cost of Ownership and Cost of Operation

The cost of ownership includes taxes on the vehicle, vehicle insurance, vehicle registration with the state, depreciation, and the finance charges associated with buying on credit, if the vehicle is not bought with cash.

The cost of operation includes buying gas, doing regular maintenance, and replacing brakes, tires, and other major parts as needed. There may also be other charges, such as renting a garage or space in a parking lot.

Car Warranties

Manufacturers provide warranties on new cars. The warranties are limited by miles driven, number of years, and the parts covered. A typical warranty is three years or 36,000 miles. In terms of parts covered, the drive train, engine, and transmission, as well as basic parts, are covered. Used cars may or may not have warranties, but this information must be stated in the "Buyers Guide."

HOUSING

Like buying or leasing a vehicle, housing has its own question: rent or buy? Each has its advantages and disadvantages, and each requires identifying needs and wants as well as opportunity costs and trade-offs. Factors that come into play in the decision are assumptions about whether housing prices will increase or decrease; whether returns on financial investments will remain steady, fall, or rise in the future; and what potential tax advantages will be. Because of the costs involved in buying and selling housing, the time that the buyer expects to remain in the home is also a factor.

Renting: Advantages and Disadvantages

The advantages of renting a home are mobility, little or no personal or financial responsibility for maintenance or repairs, and the lower initial cost of paying only a security deposit. The disadvantages are inability to derive financial benefits from ownership (tax deductions, increasing equity stake), the likelihood of rent increases over time, and lease restrictions on use of the rental property.

Home Ownership: Advantages and Disadvantages

Advantages of buying a home include tax deductions for mortgage interest and property taxes, capital gain that is probably not taxable because of tax adjustments, and fewer restrictions on how the property can be used. Disadvantages are limited mobility, costs associated with maintenance and repairs, high initial costs, and loss of potential interest earned on the money used for the down payment and closing costs. Buying makes better economic sense in the long term, though renting in the short term means lower initial costs.

In choosing the type of housing to buy, a buyer should consider two sets of factors. One set is the property's size, condition, location, and potential for an increase in value over time. Balanced against these factors are the price, current mortgage rates, amount possible for a down payment, and cost of mortgage payments, insurance, and property taxes on a monthly basis.

The Buying Process

Purchasing a home includes a number of steps, some of which are undertaken simultaneously: determining an amount to spend, determining the down payment, identifying a location in which to begin the housing search, choosing a real estate agent, identifying a property, making an offer and negotiating the price, signing the contract, employing a home inspector, choosing a lender, providing the fee and documentation for a mortgage application, title search by the buyer's attorney, property appraisal by the lender, mortgage approval, choosing title insurance, and the closing.

One issue for buyers in determining the mortgage amount is whether to prepay points, which are a lender's discount on the mortgage. Each point is equal to one percent of the amount of the loan. The more points that are prepaid, the lower the mortgage amount and payments. Prepaying points makes more sense the longer the buyer intends to own a property.

Types of Mortgages

Longer-term mortgages have smaller monthly payments. Also, larger down payments result in smaller monthly payments. An overriding factor may be the interest rate. Rates on long-term mortgages such as the 30-year fixed will be higher than a 5/1 adjustable rate mortgage (a fixed rate for 5 years that then adjusts every year). The lender assumes the risk that rates will rise over 30 years and the lender will be out the increase in the value of the money that he or she would otherwise receive from lending at the higher rates.

Depending on the amount of money that the buyer has to put down, the mortgage lender may require that the buyer take out mortgage insurance. Mortgage insurance is a guarantee that the lender will not lose money if the buyer defaults on the loan. **Private mortgage insurance (PMI)** is required if a buyer has less than 20 percent to put down on a home. Once the equity reaches 20 percent, the PMI is discontinued.

Most mortgages are referred to as **conventional mortgages**, and the terms typically run 30, 20, or 15 years. The mortgaged property serves as collateral. Fannie Mae and Freddie Mac are government-sponsored entities (GSE) that buy mortgages from mortgage lenders in order to return money to the mortgage market and encourage homeownership. A conforming conventional mortgage is one that is guaranteed by Freddie Mac or Fannie Mae. A nonconforming mortgage is one that cannot be sold to Freddie or Fannie because it doesn't meet the organization's requirements, for example, it is over the loan threshold.

The major formats for mortgages are **fixed rate** and adjustable, or **variable rate**, but there are a variety of other types of mortgages as can be seen in the following chart:

Mortgage Types		
Mortgage	**Advantage**	**Disadvantage**
Fixed Rate: 30-, 20-, 15-year Term; Conventional	• Same monthly payment over the life of the mortgage • Amount of the payment that goes to the principal increases and the amount paid toward interest decreases over time; known as *amortization* • Ability to prepay the balance in order to refinance	• Locked into a rate when mortgage rates are falling • Cost of refinancing to take advantage of falling rates • May have prepayment penalty
Adjustable Rate (ARM): 3/1, 5/1, 7/1; Two-Step; Hybrid	• Fluctuation of monthly payments annually after a set number of years at a fixed rate, though some types of ARMs may reset monthly or semiannually: interest rate adjustment period • Initially lower rate than fixed mortgages • Protection against huge increases in interest rate from one adjustment period to another: rate cap • Limit on increases in monthly payments	• Need to re-budget with each rate adjustment • Payment cap: may result in lower monthly payments than needed to repay the loan by the end of the loan term; may require large payment at end of loan term, longer term, or higher monthly payments later: negative amortization • Cost of refinancing if mortgagor chooses to prepay and refinance
Balloon ARM: 3-, 5-, 7-Year Term	• Fluctuation of monthly payments after each interest rate adjustment • Payment of interest only so the payments are lower	• Entire principal owed at the end of the loan term
Interest-Only	• Initial period when interest only is paid on the loan	• Repayment period begins and mortgage is amortized over the new shorter period; increase in monthly payments

Mortgage Types		
Mortgage	**Advantage**	**Disadvantage**
Convertible ARM	• Allows conversion of ARM to fixed rate after a certain time • Rate set in original ARM mortgage	• Requires fee • Refinancing may be better deal depending on interest rate and fee
Balloon Loan: 5-, 7-year Term	• Fixed monthly payments over the life of the loan	• Large payment required at the end of the term of the loan
Graduated Payment Mortgage; Graduated Equity Mortgage (GEM)	• Fixed rate • GEM: increases applied to principal only • Useful for young homebuyers who expect to see their incomes increase	• Amount of payments increases over time
Shared Equity; Shared Appreciation	• Large personal down payment unnecessary • Part of the down payment is borrowed in return for giving a share in the property to the lender	• At end of term, lender gets a share of the profit on the property in proportion to the amount lent—regardless of whether the borrower sells the house

In reviewing ARMs, it's important to check the rate cap and the payment cap. The annual **rate cap** limits the amount that an interest rate may increase, and it may also put a floor on how far a rate may decrease. Typically, an annual cap is no more than 2 percentage points per adjustment period. An aggregate rate cap, or life-of-loan cap, is the limit that a rate may rise during the life of the mortgage. Typically, this is no more than 6 percentage points overall. A **payment cap** limits how much the monthly payment can be increased.

Additional Financing Options

There are a variety of financing possibilities in addition to mortgages, such as the buy-down, which is a form of financing that builders of a newly constructed house offer to buyers. The builder pays a percentage of monthly mortgage payments for the first year or two.

When a buyer is also a seller and hasn't closed on the sale of his or her current home but must close on the new home, the person will use a **bridge loan**, also called a swing loan or temporary loan. Many homeowners use the equity in their homes to pay for other large-ticket items such as a new car or a kitchen renovation. These lines of credit are in essence a second mortgage on their homes and add a monthly payment to their budgets.

Reverse mortgages take money out of the equity in a home. They are available only to homeowners over 62 years of age. The money is repaid at the time of the sale of the home.

Over the course of a 30-year mortgage, interest rates may fluctuate wildly depending on the state of the economy. Refinancing may be a good option if a new mortgage can reduce the interest rate by at least 1 percentage point. In calculating whether to refinance, a homeowner should consider the cost of refinancing, which may be $2,500, versus the amount of savings in monthly payments to determine how long it will take to make up the refinancing costs.

Selling a Home

Up to this point, we've been talking about buying housing, but selling housing also requires information gathering and a series of decisions. The first decision, of course, is to sell and the next is at what price. The local government assessment for tax purposes is one indicator and another is the recent sale prices of comparable homes, known as comps, in your immediate area.

Sellers typically use real estate agents, though about 13 percent choose to save the real estate commission and sell their homes themselves. An advantage of using an agent who belongs to the Multiple Listing Service (MLS) is that the property can be shown by a number of different agencies. Using an agent also means that a property will be showcased on the agency's website.

There are a variety of agencies for selling real estate. A buyer agency represents buyers only. A dual agency may represent both buyers and sellers. To avoid conflicts of interest in a dual agency, an agent may use a designated agent in the same office to represent either the buyer or seller in the transaction. A transaction brokerage or facilitative brokerage does not represent the interests of either a seller or a buyer but simply shows properties to a buyer and assists in the general real estate process.

OTHER MAJOR PURCHASES

Other than housing, a vehicle is probably the most expensive single item a consumer will buy. Vehicles are part of a category known as consumer durables that includes such large-ticket items as washers, refrigerators, dishwashers, large-screen TVs, and home surround-sound systems. If these are paid for out of savings, they represent a loss of interest income. If they are paid for on credit, they represent a limitation on future spending. Their operation, maintenance, and repair represent additional expense and ultimately future cost of replacement.

In considering the purchase of a consumer durable, a buyer should consider timing—certain items go on sale at certain times of the year—store, brand, rebates or other deals, and product information such as energy efficiency or safety.

Comparison shopping is an important aspect of getting a good deal on consumer durables. The Internet makes it easy and cost-effective. It is also a convenient way to make purchases—as long as the buyer is dealing with a reputable site. The federal Mail Order Merchandise Rule applies to online merchants as well as catalog companies and requires that a merchant ship ordered goods within thirty days unless the buyer agrees to a delay. One important issue for consumers to check when considering an online purchase is the site's return policy if the good is unacceptable.

The features of major appliances go beyond matters of convenience. Some features can also offer financial benefits—such as those that help reduce energy usage or eliminate the need for additional appliances or other accessories.

Service contracts offered with the purchase of large items such as appliances or electronics may initially seem appealing to a consumer as a way to help minimize expenses related to future repairs, but in reality they are often a waste of money since most breakdowns tend to happen relatively soon after the purchase when a warranty would still be in effect.

Warranties

A warranty is a guarantee made by the manufacturer or distributor of a good that the good is as represented and will be replaced or repaired if defective. There are implied and express warranties and full and limited warranties. Goods sold "as is" carry neither an implied nor an express warranty, but all other goods carry an implied warranty and may also carry an express warranty. An **implied warranty** generally warrants the merchantability and/or fitness for purpose of a good. The former guarantees that the product is of a quality, grade, and value similar to the quality, grade, and value of similar goods, and the latter guarantees that the good is suitable for the ordinary purpose for which the seller sells it and the buyer will use it.

An **express warranty** is generally in writing and is either a full warranty or a limited warranty. A **full warranty** includes the following provisions:

- If a reasonable number of attempts at resolving the defect have not succeeded, the consumer is eligible for a replacement or a full refund.
- During the period of the warranty, the consumer cannot be charged for parts, labor, or charges to ship the good for repair.
- Whether the registration card was submitted or not does not affect the full warranty.
- The full warranty applies to subsequent owners after the original owner.
- The full warranty in no way affects the scope of the implied warranty.

A **limited warranty** is any warranty that does not include all these provisions. Extended warranties and service contracts are usually not a good buy.

TAXES

Everyone loves to hate taxes, but they pave the highways, pay air traffic controllers, provide scholarships, repair bridges, fund cancer research, offer seed money to alternative energy companies, provide security at home and abroad, construct a social safety net, and so on. Not only the federal government but also state and local governments fund their services through direct taxation. The federal government taxes earnings and wealth (and some purchases such as tires and gasoline, for example, through excise taxes); states and many municipalities tax purchases as well as earnings and property; and most states also tax wealth through an estate tax.

PAYROLL DEDUCTIONS

Payroll deductions may be mandatory or voluntary.

Mandatory deductions include:

- Social Security Taxes, known as FICA (Federal Insurance Contributions Act):
    - *FICA-O:* Old Age Survivors Benefit
    - *FICA-M*: Medicare
- Federal income tax
- State income tax if applicable
- County/city wage tax if applicable
- State workers' compensation insurance fund if applicable

Voluntary non-tax deductions may include payment for or contributions to:

- Health insurance
- Dental insurance
- Life insurance
- Long-term care insurance
- 401(k) or 403(b) pension plans

INCOME TAX

When you say "income tax," most people think of the federal income tax, but forty-three states tax personal income, and some cities also tax income under a city wage tax provision. The types of income that are taxed are as follows:

- **Earned:** Salary, commissions, tips, bonuses
- **Investment:** Dividends from stock, interest from bonds, rent from properties
- **Passive:** Income from limited partnership or forms of limited participation in a company

Among additional types of income that are taxed are the following:

- Alimony (which is added to the payee's income and subtracted from the payer's income)
- Capital gains or losses on investments
- Jury duty pay
- Lottery and gambling winnings
- Monetary prizes and awards
- Social Security benefits (partial)
- Pensions
- Rent
- Royalties
- Travel allowance
- Unemployment compensation

While the previous list makes up a person's **gross income,** there are also certain amounts that are not included in gross income. These include exclusions such as veterans' benefits and military allowances, tax-deferred income such as contributions to traditional IRAs and Keoghs, and tax-exempt income such as the income from state and municipal bonds. These, plus such things as alimony payments, result in a person's **adjusted gross income**. This is the base amount on which people pay their federal income taxes minus further deductions. The adjusted gross income is the amount used to compute these additional deductions such as mileage for medical visits and contributions to charity.

Deductions

Taxpayers may take the standard deduction if the amount of their deductions is less than the amount of the standard deduction for any given year. The amount of the standard deduction is computed each year by the federal government. If their deductions will be greater than the amount listed as standard for any given year, taxpayers itemize.

The categories of deductions that taxpayers can itemize are:

- **State and local taxes** (typically income, real estate, and personal property, but taxpayers may deduct their state's sales tax if it is greater than their income tax)
- **Interest** (investment, mortgage, home equity line of credit)
- **Non-reimbursed medical and dental expenses**, including mileage to and from appointments
- **Charitable contributions**
- **Non-reimbursed moving expenses** related to a job relocation (if it is at least 50 miles from the current location)
- **Non-reimbursed business expenses** (such as uniforms)
- **Losses from casualty and theft**

Tax credits may also reduce a person's tax bill. These are subtracted from the taxes owed rather than subtracted from the amount on which taxes are computed. The filer computes the tax owed and then subtracts the full amount of the tax credit.

Withholding

Employees of companies receive a **W-2** form at the end of the year to verify their earned income and to file their income tax returns. The W-2 indicates the amount of taxes withheld from each paycheck. The amount of the withholding is based on the employee's **W-4** form, which indicates the number of exemptions. Exemptions result in deductions of a certain amount per person from adjusted gross income.

The more exemptions, the less tax is withheld. A single person may take more than one exemption if the person expects to have a large tax payment when the return is filed.

Self-employed persons do not fill out W-4s nor do they receive W-2s. Instead, they file and pay estimated taxes each quarter. If they work for a number of other self-employed people or for companies, they receive **1099** forms at the end of the year from each person or company with the amount of income they received.

IRS AND AUDITS

The Internal Revenue Service (IRS) is a bureau of the Department of the Treasury and is one of the world's most efficient tax administrators. In fiscal year 2015, the IRS collected almost $3.3 trillion in revenue and processed almost 240 million tax returns. The purpose of the IRS is to collect the proper amount of tax revenue at the least cost, serve the public by continually improving the quality of its products and services, and perform in a manner warranting the highest degree of public confidence in its integrity, efficiency, and fairness.

The Internal Revenue Service is organized around divisions that focus on particular constituents. There are four divisions that deal with individual taxpayers, small businesses, mid-to-large businesses, and nonprofits. These operational divisions focus on routine activities of processing tax returns, communicating with taxpayers, conducting audits, and collecting taxes.

A tax return audit is a review/examination of an organization's or individual's accounts and financial information to ensure information is being reported correctly, according to the tax laws, to verify the amount reported is accurate.

When returns are filed, they are compared against "norms" for similar returns. The norms are developed from audits of a statistically valid random sample of returns. These returns are selected as part of the National Research Program, which the IRS conducts to update return-selection information. Following this, the return is reviewed by an experienced auditor. At this point, the return may be accepted as filed, or if, based on the auditor's experience, questionable items are noted, the auditor will identify the items noted and the return is forwarded for assignment to an examining group.

Upon examining the return, it is then reviewed by the manager. Items considered in assigning a case are factors particular to the area, such as issues pertaining to construction, farming, timber industry, etc., that have specific factors and rules that apply. Based on the review, the manager can accept the return or assign the return to an auditor. The assigned auditor again reviews the return for questionable items and either accepts it as filed or contacts the taxpayer to schedule an appointment to review the filing.

ESTATE AND GIFT TAXES

When someone in your family dies and the property of the deceased transfers to you, the federal government imposes an **estate tax** on the value of the property.

A **gift tax** is a tax imposed on the transfer of ownership of property. The federal gift tax exists for one reason: to prevent citizens from avoiding the federal estate tax by giving away their money before they die.

The gift tax is perhaps the most misunderstood of all taxes. When it comes into play, this tax is owed by the giver of the gift, not the recipient—you probably have never paid it and probably will never have to. The law ignores gifts of up to $14,000 per person, per year, that you give to any number of individuals. You and your spouse together can give up to $28,000 per person, per year, to any number of individuals.

For the year 2016, the estate and gift tax exemption is $5.45 million per individual, up from $5.43 million in 2015. This means an individual can leave $5.45 million to heirs and pay no federal estate or gift tax. A married couple will be able to shield $10.9 million from federal estate and gift taxes. The annual gift exclusion remains the same at $14,000. The federal estate and gift tax exemptions rise with inflation.

Here are some gifts that are not considered "taxable gifts" and, therefore, do not count as part of your $5.43 million lifetime total.

- **Present-interest gifts of $14,000 in 2015.** "Present interest" means that the person receiving the gift has an unrestricted right to use or enjoy the gift immediately. In 2015, you could give amounts up to $14,000 to each person, gifting as many different people as you want without triggering the gift tax.

- **Charitable gifts**

- **Gifts to a spouse who is a U.S. citizen.** Gifts to foreign spouses are subject to an annual limit of $143,000 in 2015. This amount is indexed for inflation and can change each year.

- **Gifts for educational expenses.** To qualify for the unlimited exclusion for qualified education expenses, you must make a direct payment to the educational institution for tuition only. Books, supplies, and living expenses do not qualify. If you want to pay for books, supplies, and living expenses in addition to the unlimited education exclusion, you can make a 2015 gift of $14,000 to the student under the annual gift exclusion.

TAX PLANNING/ESTIMATING

In addition to self-employed persons, those who have income other than salaries and wages may also have to file and pay estimated taxes. There are ways to minimize a person's tax bill.

Paying Estimated Taxes

Because the federal government needs revenue to function, it requires that taxpayers with passive income estimate their whole year tax bill and pay it in quarterly installments. These include taxpayers who receive interest on bonds and savings accounts, stock dividends, royalty payments, and retirement or pension plans that are paid out as a lump sum rather than as an annuity. The government allows some leeway in figuring the tax each year. A filer isn't charged a penalty and interest if he or she makes estimated payments that total more than the previous year's tax even though the estimated payments are less than the actual tax for the current year. Also, a taxpayer will not be penalized if he or she pays estimated taxes that are 90 percent or more, but less than 100 percent, of the current year's income tax.

Tax Planning

There are a variety of legal ways that can be used to reduce taxes. Among them are the following:

- **Municipal Bond:** Tax-exempt interest under state and federal governments

- **State Bond:** Tax-exempt interest under the federal government and many states (capital gains may be taxed in certain states)

- **Primary Residence:** Tax-deductible property taxes and mortgage interest

- **Home Equity Line of Credit:** Tax-deductible interest on the loan

- **Real Estate as an Investment:** Depreciation
- **Traditional IRA, Keogh, 401(k), Tax-Deferred Annuity:** Tax-deferred investment vehicles for retirement that reduce current adjusted gross income on which taxes are computed
- **529 Savings Plan for Children's Education:** Tax-deferred investment that provides a tax credit
- **Flexible Spending Account for Health Care or Child Care:** Reduction of current adjusted gross income
- **Self-employment:** Advantages in expensing certain costs that owners would otherwise have to pay themselves, such as health insurance premiums and non-reimbursed medical bills
- **Gift Program:** Up to $14,000 per donor per recipient
- **Trust:** Provides income for a beneficiary who is usually at a lower tax rate than the person who used his or her own money to set up the trust
- **Tax Credits:** Variety of such credits, e.g., earned income, child care, home energy

PROGRESSIVE AND REGRESSIVE TAXATION

A **progressive tax structure** is one in which an individual's or family's tax liability as a fraction of income rises with income. If, for example, taxes for a family with an income of $20,000 are 20 percent of income and taxes for a family with an income of $200,000 are 30 percent of income, then the tax structure over that range of incomes is progressive. It is important to note that progressive tax can come in other forms, such as estate taxes or luxury taxes on goods. Estate taxes require higher net worth individuals to pay an additional tax on their property when they die. If the value of all the property is over a certain amount, then they most likely will be taxed.

Pros	Cons
It helps to provide a buffer against income inequality.	Those who barely break into a new tax bracket may lose their additional earnings.
It provides higher overall levels of revenue.	It creates a complicated system of bureaucracy.

Under a **regressive tax structure**, individuals and entities with low incomes pay a higher amount of that income in taxes compared to high-income earners. Rather than implementing a tax liability based on the individual's or entity's ability to pay, the government assesses tax as a percentage of the assets that the taxpayer purchases or owns. An example is state sales tax, where everyone pays the same tax rate regardless of his/her income. The most apparent advantage of this system is that it provides a positive incentive to work harder. The issue of trying to fall into a lower tax bracket is not part of the equation with the regressive system.

OTHER TAXES

Excise Tax

Excise taxes are taxes paid when specific purchases are made, such as gasoline. Excise taxes are often included in the price of the product. Excise taxes may be imposed by both federal and state authorities. An excise is considered an indirect tax, meaning that the producer or seller who pays the tax to the government is expected to try to recover or shift the tax by raising the price paid by the buyer.

Excise taxes usually fall into one of two types:

- Ad Valorem, meaning that a fixed percentage is charged on a particular good or product; this administration of the tax is less common.
- Specific, meaning that a fixed currency amount may be imposed depending on the quantity of the goods or products that are purchased; specific is the most common type.

Property Tax

Property tax is a tax that local governments impose on real estate. It is known as an ad valorem tax, which means that it is based on the value of the property. Individuals with a home or land that has a higher value pay more in property taxes, although everyone within a given municipality pays property tax at the same flat-percentage rate. Local governments use the money collected from property taxes for a number of programs. The majority of property tax revenue goes toward funding city and county governments, including meeting payroll for city employees. Property taxes also fund public schools, including local school districts and community colleges.

Sales Tax

A **sales tax** is a tax paid to a governing body for the sale of certain goods and services. Usually laws allow (or require) the seller to collect funds for the tax from the consumer at the point of purchase. When a tax on goods or services is paid to a governing body directly by a consumer, it is usually called a use tax. Often laws provide for the exemption of certain goods or services from sales and use taxes.

Gas Tax

A **fuel tax** (also known as a petrol or gasoline or gas tax or as a fuel duty) is an excise tax imposed on the sale of fuel. The United States federal excise tax on gasoline is 18.4 cents per gallon and 24.4 cents per gallon for diesel fuel. On average, as of July 2016, state and local taxes and fees add 29.78 cents to gasoline and 29.81 cents to diesel, for a total U.S. average fuel tax of 48.18 cents per gallon for gas and 54.21 cents per gallon for diesel.

TAX PROFESSIONALS

Any tax professional with an IRS Preparer Tax Identification Number (PTIN) is authorized to prepare federal tax returns; however, tax professionals have differing levels of skills, education, and expertise. Tax return preparers who have PTINs but are not listed in the IRS *Directory of Federal Tax Return*

Preparers with Credentials and Select Qualifications may provide quality return preparation services, but, as with any decision that will affect your financial health, be sure to choose your return preparer wisely. Professional tax services range from straightforward filing to strategic long-term advice. Always ask about the preparer's education and training; it pays to know your preparer's specialty.

- **Chain or local outlet preparers** (e.g., H&R Block, Jackson Hewitt) are trained to fill out tax forms, but their experience and expertise can vary widely, and many are not full-time tax professionals; this route is best for those with uncomplicated tax issues.

- An **enrolled agent** (EA) must pass an IRS exam or have at least five years of work experience at the IRS to be licensed by the federal government; many have areas of specialty. If needed, the agent can represent taxpayers in IRS disputes.

- **Certified public accountants** (CPAs) are trained in maintaining business and financial records, but not all of them prepare tax returns. To earn the CPA designation, one must pass a four-part accounting exam. They, like EAs, are qualified to face the IRS on a taxpayer's behalf. CPAs are best for those seeking a holistic tax strategy to deal with the financial issues from personal businesses, retirement, divorce, etc.

- **Certified financial planners** (CFPs) provide overall financial planning advice on savings, investments, insurance, and big-picture tax issues. Fees can be hourly, flat, or based on a percentage of your assets. Some, not all, offer tax-prep services to clients.

- **Accredited tax accountants** (ATAs) and **accredited tax preparers** (ATPs) specialize in preparing personal and business returns, as well as providing tax-planning services.

- **Tax attorneys** tend to specialize in the minutiae of the IRS tax code, particularly in the areas of trusts, estate planning, tax disputes, and business tax law. They must have a JD degree and must be admitted to the state bar. Some will prepare returns but usually at a premium cost. They also can represent clients in audit, collection, and appeals before the IRS.

INSURANCE

Insurance is about protecting against possible financial loss. Different kinds of insurance protect against different kinds of financial-related loss such as loss of life, loss of income, and loss of property. Insurance is a way to pool risk over a large number of people so that it becomes predictable. There are four strategies for risk management:

1. Risk reduction (taking preventive actions)
2. Risk avoidance (eliminating the risk)
3. Risk retention (agreeing to have some exposure to a risk)
4. Risk transfer (purchasing insurance)

RISK MANAGEMENT

Risk management is the continuing process to identify, analyze, evaluate, and treat loss exposures and monitor risk control and financial resources to mitigate the adverse effects of loss.

Loss may result from the following:

- Financial risks, such as cost of claims and liability judgments
- Operational risks, such as labor strikes
- Perimeter risks, including weather or political change
- Strategic risks, including management changes or loss of reputation

You face risks every day. *Risk*, *peril*, and *hazard* are terms used to indicate the possibility of loss, and they are often used interchangeably, but the insurance industry distinguishes these terms. A **risk** is simply the possibility of a loss, but a **peril** is a cause of loss. A **hazard** is a condition that increases the possibility of loss. For instance, fire is a peril because it causes losses, while a fireplace is a hazard because it increases the probability of loss from fire. Some things can be both a peril and a hazard. Smoking, for instance, causes cancer and other health ailments, while also increasing the probability of such ailments. Many fundamental risks, such as hurricanes, earthquakes, or unemployment, that affect many people are generally insured by society or by the government, while particular risks that affect individuals or specific organizations, such as losses from fire or vandalism, are considered the particular responsibilities of those affected. Risk management is concerned with all loss exposures, not only the ones that can be insured. Insurance is a technique to finance some loss exposures and, therefore, a part of the broader concept of managing risk.

LIFE POLICIES

Buying life insurance has two benefits: it is a way to put aside money in savings and it provides financial security for dependents when the insured dies. In estimating whether a person needs life insurance and if so, how much, it's important to consider the person's life circumstances. A single working person in her mid-twenties probably doesn't need life insurance, whereas a married father in his forties with a wife who doesn't work outside the home and 3 children needs life insurance.

There are four general ways to determine life insurance needs. The **easy method** is seven years (the amount of time it is estimated to take for a family's finances to adjust after the death of a breadwinner) times 70 percent of that person's income equals the amount of life insurance required for a typical family. The **DINK method** estimates life insurance for a "dual income, no kids" couple by including funeral expenses and halving expenses like a mortgage. The **nonworking spouse method** multiplies ten years by $10,000 a year for child-related costs such as child care on the assumption that the nonworking spouse will need to go to work. The **family need method** itemizes a family's actual costs.

Types of Life Insurance

A life insurance policy may be a term policy, meaning "temporary," or a permanent policy. A term policy is bought for a certain number of years. For beneficiaries to collect, the insured must die within that period; there is no savings buildup with a term policy. There are a variety of permanent policies and each accrues cash: whole life, straight life, ordinary life, and cash value life.

Type	Format and Characteristics
Term: No Savings Buildup	**Renewable** • Renewable at the end of the term • Increased premiums as the insured ages **Multiyear Level/Straight** • Same premium for the life of the term **Convertible** • Provision that enables the insured to convert a term to a whole life policy **Decreasing: Group Mortgage Life and Credit Life** • Same premium for the life of the policy but decreasing coverage
Permanent: Savings Buildup	**Whole Life/Straight Life/Ordinary Life/Cash Value** • Same premium for the life of the policy • In comparison to term policies, higher rate in the early years of a whole life policy (term policies increase premiums with each renewal) • Increasing cash and decreasing death benefits over the life of the policy **Limited Payment Life** • Payment of premiums over a certain period, such as twenty years • Insured covered until he or she dies • Payment of death benefits on death of insured • High premium **Adjustable Life** • Premiums and coverage adjustable as the circumstances of the insured change **Universal Life** • Flexible premium payments and flexible payment schedule, that is, the insured may pay any amount at any time as well as skip payments • Policyholder receives a report identifying cost of the protection, management costs, and interest on the cash value of the policy (rate of return)

Type	Format and Characteristics
Permanent: Savings Buildup (continued)	**Variable and Variable-Universal** • Fixed premium • Investment of cash value in a selected portfolio of stocks, bond, money market funds • Cash value may decrease if portfolio loses value • Policyholder receives report similar to universal life • Variable-universal: flexible premiums, investment of cash value in portfolio of stocks, bonds, money market funds
Term	**Group Life** • Employer-sponsored life insurance • High premiums

Payment of death benefits may come as a lump-sum payment, limited installment payment, life income option, or payment of interest on the value. For the latter, the insurance company serves as trustee.

The face amount of a policy is its amount of death benefits. The policyholder indicates the beneficiary or beneficiaries. Other things a consumer should consider are the cash value, surrender value, premium, and dividend. Special provisions, or **riders**, can also be added to life insurance policies. These may include accelerated death benefits, accidental death benefits, cost-of-living adjustment, disability waiver of premium, grace period, guaranteed insurability option, settlement option, and survivorship life.

PROPERTY AND LIABILITY POLICIES

Property insurance shields people from risks to their homes, vehicles, and personal property such as furniture, electronics, and jewelry. Liability insurance protects people from losses as a result of damage done to other persons or to the property of others. Liability is responsibility under the law for the financial cost of another person's losses or injuries. The cause is usually negligence. Both homeowner's insurance and automobile insurance carry liability coverage.

Homeowner's Insurance

Homeowner's insurance covers:

- The main dwelling and any associated buildings on a property and also typically landscaping
- Additional living expenses for temporary housing should the property be uninhabitable for a period of time due to damage
- Personal property, such as jewelry and electronics, both at home and while the insured is traveling with the items
- Liability for injuries sustained by a guest or for damage done to property by the insured.

Personal property insurance typically places a limit on the amount of the replacement value for items. However, a personal property floater can be added to increase replacement limits; the additional coverage increases the premium.

Liability coverage includes payment for medical care for injured parties as well as legal costs for the insured should that person be sued by the injured party or the person's estate.

Typically, losses from natural disasters such as floods and earthquakes are not covered by standard homeowner's insurance, but consumers can buy **endorsements** to cover these potential risks. Endorsements are changes to the basic policy.

In determining how much insurance is needed, a homeowner needs to consider whether to purchase a policy that pays actual cash value or replacement value. The former pays out the current cost of an item minus depreciation, and the latter pays the current cost of an item without factoring in depreciation and is, therefore, more expensive to purchase.

Auto Insurance

All states require drivers to carry some minimum level of auto insurance and more than half of the states have what is called a no-fault insurance system. With no-fault insurance, an injured motorist is paid by his or her own insurance company through a personal injury protection (PIP) policy regardless of who caused the accident. Payments include medical costs, lost income, and other expenses related to the accident. Depending on the state, a motorist may also need to carry residual bodily liability coverage and property damage coverage.

Three factors affect the cost of auto insurance:

1.   Make and model of the vehicle

2.   Rate base, also known as the rating territory

3.   Driver classification

The newer and more expensive the vehicle, the higher the premium. A person who lives in a city, parks on the street, and drives 50 miles to work every day pays more than a person who lives in the suburbs, parks in her own garage, and only drives around town on the weekends. The risk for theft, damage, or an accident is greater for the first driver than the second one, so the premium is higher. A person's driving record, age, gender, and whether he or she is married or single also affect how much the person pays for car insurance.

Umbrella Policies

Homeowners' and auto insurance policies generally have limits on the amount of damages they will cover in the event of accident, injury or damage. If something happens that results in damages or losses beyond these limits, the property owner is often responsible for the difference—which could be a significant expense. This is why an umbrella policy can be a smart choice. An umbrella policy is an additional type of coverage that kicks in where your standard policy ends and can provide additional coverage for excess losses or expenses beyond the limits of your basic home or auto insurance policy.

TIP

Renters don't buy homeowner's insurance; they purchase renter's insurance, which covers their personal property, additional living expenses, and liability.

HEALTH, DISABILITY, AND LONG-TERM CARE POLICIES

The goal of health, disability, and long-term care insurance is to lessen the financial burdens of providing healthcare for one's self and family.

The **Patient Protection and Affordable Care Act** (**PPACA**), commonly called the **Affordable Care Act** (**ACA**) is a United States federal statute signed into law in 2010. The law was enacted to increase the affordability of health insurance, lower the uninsured rate in the U.S. by expanding public and private insurance coverage, and reduce the costs of healthcare. It introduced mandates, tax subsidies, and insurance exchanges for the purchase of individual and family policies.

Health Insurance

Basic health insurance provides protection for hospital stays, surgery, and medical care. In addition to hospital expense, surgical expense, and physician expense insurance, all of which are typically bought as part of a single insurance policy, a consumer may buy major medical insurance, which pays expenses over and above the basic insurance coverage, typically up to $1 million. Major medical policies have a **deductible**—an amount that the insured must reach before benefits kick in—and a co-payment provision through which the insured pays some of the cost of care after the deductible has been reached. Other types of medical coverage include prescription drug coverage and dental and vision insurance.

Health insurance policies may include the following components:

- **Exclusions:** Those conditions that are not covered under a policy
- **Guaranteed Renewability:** Renewal year after year as long the premium is paid
- **Internal Limits:** Restricts the amount of payments regardless of the costs
- **Co-payment:** Insurance pays most of the charges, but the insured pays some even after the deductible has been met for the year
- **Benefit Limit:** A ceiling on the amount of costs the insurer will pay
- **Assigned Benefit:** Ability of the insured to sign payment over directly to the doctor or hospital
- **Fixed-dollar Benefit:** Pays a predetermined amount based on a per-incident or per-period basis, regardless of the actual cost of services rendered
- **Service Benefit:** Pays by services rather than by cost of services
- **Coordination of Benefits:** Enables the insured to receive benefits from primary and secondary insurance up to the total cost of the procedure or hospital stay but no more than the total

An **indemnity health insurance plan**—sometimes also called a "fee for service" plan—can be appealing to those who like freedom over their choice of health care providers and who don't want to deal with hassles related to referrals. This type of plan doesn't require you to be committed to one primary care doctor and also allows you to "self-refer" when you want to see a specialist. The insurance company pays you directly, paying a set amount according to their predetermined list of standard charges for specific procedures or services. You are often required to pay the healthcare provider yourself at the time services are rendered and then submit a claim for reimbursement from the insurance company.

As with other types of policies, the exact details can vary from one plan to another. Some plans place limits on pre-existing conditions, while others have no such restrictions. These plans cover a wide range of services performed by doctors, hospitals and other healthcare providers.

Health insurers include private insurance companies and health maintenance organizations (HMOs), which are also health services providers, and health services providers, such as preferred provider organizations (PPOs). The latter may be an exclusive provider organization (EPO) or a point-of-service (POS) organization. Medicare with its Medigap, Medicare Advantage, and drug prescription plans provides health coverage to those over 65 and people with certain disabilities.

HIPAA, the Health Insurance Portability and Accountability Act of 1996, ensures that workers cannot be required to requalify for health insurance when they change jobs or be charged more for health insurance than current employees. (This act is perhaps most well-known due to its sections protecting patient privacy and the security of sensitive or personal information.)

Many people receive health insurance through their employer, which can create problems if the insured person leaves that job. Individuals can then continue their health insurance coverage under the provisions of COBRA, the Consolidated Omnibus Budget Reconciliation Act of 1986. Under this law, many employers are required to offer terminated and laid-off workers the opportunity to continue their health insurance under the employer's plan. However, the former employee must now pay the full cost of the monthly premiums—including the portion that was previously paid by the employer. This can result in a significant increase in the out-of-pocket cost, which often comes as a surprise to many people who plan to take advantage of the ability to continue coverage as allowed via COBRA.

Disability Insurance

Disability insurance provides income for workers who are unable to work because of a disability. What constitutes a disability depends on the insurance policy. Some policies consider a worker to be disabled if the worker cannot perform any type of work, whereas other policies consider a worker disabled if the worker cannot perform the duties of a specific job, and other policies consider a worker disabled if the worker cannot perform work-related duties or duties similar to the work for which the person was trained.

Long-Term Care Insurance

Long-term care insurance is intended to provide custodial care for those who cannot take care of themselves. Typically, policies are sold to those 60 and over who are concerned about becoming ill and disabled as they age. The benefits of a long-term care policy typically kick in when a person cannot perform some of the activities of daily living, which are bathing, dressing, being continent, eating, and being able to get around alone.

SPECIALTY INSURANCE

Specialty insurance is necessary for items not covered by your ordinary homeowner's or automobile insurance. This can include, but is not limited to, flood coverage, identity theft insurance, mobile home coverage, motorcycle insurance, personal watercraft coverage, boat insurance, pet insurance, private mortgage insurance, travel insurance, title insurance, or renter's insurance.

Other types of specialty insurance include liability insurance. **Professional liability insurance** is a form of insurance designed to protect professionals and professional organizations from financial loss from their negligence. Professional liability insurance is made up of many segments and is also called "errors and omissions," "E&O," or "malpractice" insurance. Professional liability insurance is designed to protect the professional from the significant financial loss that can result from a lawsuit. Regardless of fault, litigation is costly, time consuming, and damaging to a reputation. **Malpractice insurance** is liability insurance that all physicians and most other medical providers must carry in the event that they are sued for medical malpractice. Malpractice is a medical error that results in a bad outcome and is proven to have been caused by gross negligence or deviation from the standard of care.

Specialty insurance is also available for such items as antiques and collectibles, fine art, musical instruments, and jewelry. These items may not be sufficiently covered by an individual's homeowner policy, either because of their monetary or sentimental value.

INSURANCE ANALYSIS AND SOURCES OF INFORMATION

Insurance is a means of protection from financial loss. The insurance transaction involves the insured assuming a guaranteed and known relatively small loss in the form of payment to the insurer in exchange for the insurer's promise to compensate the insured in the event of a covered loss. The best way for consumers to analyze various insurance products is to conduct their own SWOT (strengths, weaknesses, opportunities, threats) analysis for a given product. The SWOT analysis is useful for consumers to gather information to determine the products that best suit their needs. This is created by taking a single piece of paper and dividing it into four quadrants using a single vertical and horizontal line. The top two quadrants are Strengths and Weaknesses. The bottom two quadrants are Opportunities and Threats.

Strengths	Weaknesses
The strength must be unique. If most competitors offer quality service, then that is a necessity not a strength. One of the strengths that a business owner may take for granted might be something that customers would value and that the competition does not have or do.	In the top right box list weaknesses—things that are not included or cannot do at all or does poorly. This is the time for brutal honesty but also a time for realism. Consider this from an internal and external basis. Do outsiders perceive weaknesses that the firm does not see? Are competitors doing anything better? It is best to be realistic now, and face any unpleasant truths as soon as possible.
Opportunities	**Threats**
The lower left box is for opportunities. Look at the strengths and weakness, and evaluate if they can be leveraged into opportunities. List what the marketplace is not doing. Add items that the marketplace seems to need and which the business could perhaps provide. Think in terms of what would benefit clients—cheaper, easier, more convenient, and/or faster.	No one is immune to threats. These could be internal, such as falling productivity. Or they could be external, such as changes in the direction of the insurance companies. What obstacles currently exist? Is changing technology threatening one's position? Carrying out this analysis will often be illuminating, both in terms of pointing out what needs to be done and in putting problems into perspective.

INVESTMENTS

Every type of investment involves some amount of risk—and hopefully reward. Before beginning an investment program, it's important that a person be aware of his or her **risk tolerance**—the ability to endure losses in savings and investments during downturns in the economy. The lower one's risk tolerance, the safer the savings and investment vehicles should be. The higher one's risk tolerance, the riskier the savings instruments and investments can be. However, there is a **risk-return trade-off.** The lower the risk, the lower the returns, and the higher the risk, the greater the returns.

What constitutes risk? Risk factors typically are inflation, changes in interest rates, bankruptcy of a business that a person has invested in—either directly or through stocks and/or bonds—and market risk, either because of changes in the economy (systematic risk) or the behavior of investors (unsystematic). Similar risk factors can affect investments made in foreign countries.

As part of developing an investment plan, it's important to consider **asset allocation,** that is, where to save and invest one's money, and diversification within asset classes. The goal of both asset allocation and diversification is to lesson risk.

LIQUID ASSETS

When talking about investment and risk, it's always good to consider one's liquid assets. As mentioned previously in this chapter, a **liquid asset** is cash or any asset that can be quickly turned into cash—personal property, stocks, short-term bonds and notes, life insurance policies with cash surrender values, and investments. A liquid asset is readily convertible to cash with little impact on its value.

Savings and Money Market Accounts and CDs

A **savings account** is one of the safest places to put money—as long as the account has less than $250,000 and the savings institution is insured by the Federal Deposit Insurance Corporation (FDIC). However, savings accounts and similar savings instruments—**certificates of deposit (CDs)**, **money market deposit accounts**, and **money market demand accounts**—offer low interest rates because of this safety factor. Interest rates on money market accounts are slightly higher than on savings accounts and about the same as short-term CDs, which are lower than the rates for longer-term CDs. Brick-and-mortar and online commercial banks, credit unions, and savings and loans associations offer these savings vehicles. A person may add any amount at any time to both savings accounts and money market accounts and withdraw money at any time by using an ATM or a withdrawal slip. However, a depositor may be limited in the number of checks that can be written in any one month on a money market account. Savings accounts don't have a check-writing feature.

CDs are purchased at a set minimum deposit amount (there may not be a maximum deposit limit, depending on the financial institution) for a fixed length of time and generally at a fixed interest rate. A person cannot add to the amount in a CD, and, if the CD is redeemed before the specified period, the buyer pays a penalty.

Money market deposit and demand accounts should not be confused with money market funds, which are another form of savings and investing for people with low risk tolerance but more risk tolerance than those who invest in the other four investment vehicles. Money market funds are sold by securities brokers and mutual fund companies for $1 a share. The funds are not FDIC-insured, but the funds are principal protected, so that the value of a share does not drop below a dollar. Investors make money on the interest that their shares earn.

Rule of 72

A simple way to determine how long an investment will take to double given a fixed rate of interest is to use the **Rule of 72:** Simply divide 72 by the annual rate of return to get an estimate of the number of years it will take for the initial investment to double:

$$\text{Doubling Time(DT)} = \frac{72}{\text{interest rate}}$$

The Rule of 72 is more precise with lower rates of return such as those offered for savings accounts, CDs, and money market accounts.

STOCKS, BONDS, AND STOCK MUTUAL FUNDS

When buying and selling stocks, bonds, and stock mutual funds, a consideration is the amount of capital gains or capital losses that the investor will have. Both will affect the investor's income taxes: losses positively and gains negatively for the investor. The exceptions are tax-exempt federal and municipal bonds.

Before venturing further into the different types of investments available, look at a few investment-related terms.

Investment Terminology	
Short position (or selling short)	Occurs when an investor borrows stock from a broker with the intention of selling it at a higher price and then buying it back when the value decreases, thus making money on the difference between the price sold on the borrowed stock and the price paid to replace the stock
Call option	An agreement giving an investor the right to buy a stock, bond, or commodity for a specific price within a specified time period, made in anticipation that the asset will rise in value and the investor will make money on it
Market order	An order an investor makes to buy or sell an investment at the best available price
Buying on margin	Buying an asset by paying only a percentage of its value and borrowing the balance of the asset's cost from a broker or bank. The percentage the investor puts down is called the **margin**.
Maintenance margin requirement	The amount an investor must keep in a margin account equal to the value of assets in the account minus what the investor borrowed from the broker or bank.
Margin call	A call from a broker to a client asking the client to increase the amount of money in his or her account for an asset bought on margin; a margin call occurs when the price of the stock falls below the initial margin requirement or percentage of the stock price invested by the client.
Day Trading	Buying or selling assets within a single trading day

Stocks and Stock Mutual Funds

A **stock** is a form of equity, or ownership, in a corporation, and a stock mutual fund is a collection, or portfolio, of stocks from a number of companies. Stocks are classified as common or preferred; both convey voting rights on those who buy them, but preferred stockholders receive their dividends before common stockholders.

The price of a share of stock is the value of the stock. Value can rise and fall as a result of a number of factors including downturns in the economy; natural disasters and hostilities that affect production; changes in government policies, even fear of policy changes; and the financial performance of the individual company. While stocks are a risky investment, they produce higher returns than the previously discussed investment vehicles. However, some stocks are riskier than others. For example, a blue chip company like IBM® that produces quarter after quarter of strong financial results is less risky than a start-up company selling geothermal power or a tablet to compete with Apple®.

When an investor buys shares in a stock mutual fund, the person is buying shares in the company's portfolio of stocks. Buying into a stock mutual fund rather than buying individual stocks diversifies a person's risk because the person has less exposure to any one company. Mutual funds, like individual stocks, are not government insured.

Both individual stocks and stock mutual funds may pay dividends. There are two major strategies for buying and selling stocks: long-term and short-term. Long-term investing strategies include buy-and-hold, dollar-cost averaging, dividend reinvestment, and direct investment. Short-term strategies include day trading, buying on margin, selling short, trading in options, and market timing.

In determining what stocks to buy, a person should consider earning per share, price to earnings (P/E) ratio, whether or not there is a dividend, dividend yield, total return, and annualized holding per yield.

Bonds and Bond Mutual Funds

Bonds are investments in debt, not equity, and are sold by corporations and the federal and municipal governments. The company or government entity that issues the bond must pay bondholders annual interest payments for the term of the bond. At its maturity, the face value of the bond must be repaid to bondholders. The **annual rate of return** on a bond is its yield and is fixed when the bond is sold. Bonds are considered safer investments than stocks, and there are also tax advantages to owning government bonds. U.S. Treasury bonds are exempt from state and local taxes, and municipal bonds are generally exempt from state and local taxes for residents of the state.

Like stocks, the price of bonds may rise or fall, depending on a number of factors similar to those affecting the price of stock. However, the most important factor is the credit quality of the entity that issues the bond. The stronger the company is perceived to be by a bond-rating agency—the more likely that it will make interest payments and repay the face value of the bond—the lower the interest rate. The risk is considered less. The lower the credit rating is, the riskier the investment and the higher the rate. Bond rating agencies like Moody's Investors Services rate the quality of bonds as high-grade, medium-grade, speculative, and default.

Governments—federal, state, local, and agencies—issue bonds to fund operations. Federal issues may be Treasury bills, Treasury bonds, Treasury notes, Treasury STRIPS, and Treasury inflation-indexed bonds. State and local government and agencies, such as transit authorities, secure a common type of municipal bond called a general obligation bond.

Unlike bonds, bond mutual funds don't promise a fixed rate of interest nor is the investor's money repaid. However, buying a bond mutual fund is safer than buying individual bonds because an investor's risk is spread across a number of corporations or government entities. It is also cheaper to buy into a bond fund than to buy individual bonds because they are typically very expensive. Bond mutual funds specialize in a category of bonds: corporate, federal government, or municipal government.

Think of mutual funds as baskets that may contain bonds, stocks, and cash equivalents. With thousands to choose from, mutual funds come in a variety of styles. They may hold a single type of asset, such as only domestic large-cap stocks, or a blend of investments, such as a balanced fund with a mix of stocks and bonds.

EQUITIES

Equity investments involve buying and holding shares of stock in anticipation of income (in the form of dividends) and capital gains (through an increase in the price of a stock).

Equities come in many different flavors. They represent all industries, with some based in the U.S. and others overseas; they also come in all sizes. There are large-cap, mid-cap, and small-cap stocks. The term *cap* is short for "market capitalization," which is found by multiplying a stock's share price by the number of a company's outstanding shares.

In comparison, bonds are considered safer investments than equities. But this is not always true—it depends on the quality of the bond you buy. The riskier the bond, that is, the lower the borrower's credit quality or "rating," the higher the interest rate and the more an investor potentially has to gain, unless, of course, the borrower defaults on the bond.

It's important to become an informed investor, and there are many sources that can be consulted for price-to-earnings ratios, past performance, factors that may affect future performance, and similar information:

- Corporate annual, quarterly, and K-10 reports
- Investment advisers licensed by the SEC who provide guidance for a fee
- Business magazines, newspapers, and newsletters
- Financial news programs on TV and cable
- Investor subscription services accessed on the Internet
- Free Internet sites
- Stock exchange sites

MUTUAL FUNDS AND EXCHANGE TRADED FUNDS

A **mutual fund** pools the assets of its investors and invests the money on behalf of the investors. The rise of mutual funds has given individual investors the chance to participate in the stock market in a way not previously possible. The largest segment of the fund industry focuses on stocks, and just under half of the assets held by the industry are stocks. Within this area, investors have an extensive number of options: index funds, growth funds, sector funds, and many more. Mutual funds have costs, not just in terms of investment risk, but also in terms of fees. Like any investment, these funds have operating costs. Fees are disclosed in a fund's prospectus under the heading "Shareholder Fees."

Exchange Traded Funds (ETFs) are funds that track indexes like the NASDAQ-100 Index, S&P 500, and Dow Jones. When you buy shares of an ETF, you are buying shares of a portfolio that tracks the yield and return of its related index. The main difference between ETFs and other types of index funds is that ETFs do not try to outperform their corresponding index but simply replicate its performance. ETFs have been around since the early 1980s, but they've come into their own within the past 10 years.

ETFs combine the range of a diversified portfolio with the simplicity of trading a single stock. Investors can purchase ETF shares on margin, short sell shares, or hold them for the long term. The purpose of an ETF is to match a particular market index, leading to a fund management style known as passive management. Passive management is the chief distinguishing feature of ETFs, and it brings a number of advantages for investors in index funds.

OTHER INVESTMENT OPTIONS

Commodities, whether they are related to food, energy, or metals, are an important part of everyday life. Commodities can be an important way for investors to diversify beyond traditional stocks and bonds or to profit from commodity price movements.

It used to be that the average investor did not invest in commodities because doing so required significant amounts of time, money, and investing expertise. Today, there are a number of different routes to the commodity markets, and some of these routes make it easy for even the average investor to participate. Commodities contracts require different minimum deposits depending on the broker, and the value of an account will increase or decrease with the value of the contract. If the value of the contract goes down, the investor will be subject to a **margin call** and will be required to place more money into an account to keep the position open. Small price movements can mean huge returns or losses, and a futures account can be wiped out or doubled in a matter of minutes. Most futures contracts also have options associated with them. Options on futures contracts still allow one to invest in the futures contract, but they limit one's loss to the cost of the option. Options are derivatives and usually do not move point-for-point with the futures contract.

Historically, gold and silver have been popular investments for individual investors. For thousands of years, gold and silver have been used as a basis for currency value, either minted into coins or used to back currency value. When a currency is backed by gold, for example, or is "on the gold standard," there should be a direct relationship between the value of the currency and the value of the gold. In times of inflation or deflation, investors worry that the value or purchasing power of currency will change. They may invest in gold or silver as a more stable store of wealth than the currency that is supposed to represent the metal; in other words, if investors lose faith in the currency that represents the gold, they may trade their money for the gold. Most currencies used today are not backed by a precious metal but by the productivity and soundness of the economy that issues them. For example, the value of the U.S. dollar is not related to the value of an ounce of gold but to the value of the U.S. economy.

Investors who want to add a real estate investment to their portfolio more often make an **indirect investment**. That is, they buy shares in an entity or group that owns and manages property. For example, they may become limited partners in a real estate syndicate. A **syndicate** is a group created to buy and manage commercial property such as an apartment, office building, or shopping mall. The syndicate may be structured as a corporation or, more commonly, as a limited partnership. In a limited partnership, there is a general partner and limited partners. The general partner manages the entity, while the limited partners invest in partnership shares.

SOURCES OF INFORMATION

In many financial decisions, identifying and evaluating risk is difficult. The best ways to consider risk are to gather information based on your experience and the experiences of others and to use financial planning information sources. Despite heavy regulation, the finance industry has its share of unethical, and sometimes illegal, operators. Investors must learn to identify a source they can understand and trust before they invest.

The media, including newspapers and other publications, provide current news on financial events that an investor can use to research market trends and opportunities. Financial institutions provide advice on investments that they offer. If you shop around and ask questions, you can compare different products from a range of providers. Institutions with this information include any company that provides these investment products, such as banks, building societies, credit unions, and insurance companies.

A number of people who work in the industry can also help you make informed investment decisions. In addition to investment advisers who work for financial institutions, you can obtain advice about shares from stockbrokers and other kinds of advice from independent financial planners. A responsible adviser will gather as much information about you as possible in order to ascertain which investment may suit you and your situation. They should determine your financial position by taking into account your income, assets, debts, and financial commitments and then speak to you directly about your investment objectives. They should also take into account your personality and assess your risk tolerance.

TIME VALUE OF MONEY

Time value of money is the increase in an amount of money as a result of interest earned on it. It is the future value of money calculated at a certain rate of interest over a certain period of time. Analyzing yield—percentage return on investment—and time period is important in determining where to save and invest. The formula for annual compounding is $FV = PV(1 + i)$, where i equals interest and n equals the number of years.

What if a person has a certain goal in mind, such as having $20,000 for a down payment for a condominium in four years? To determine how much to invest to achieve a certain amount, the person needs to work backwards to find the present value of money; that is, the current value for a future amount based on a certain rate of interest and certain period of time. The process is called **discounting**, and the formula is $PV = FV/(1 + i)$, where i equals interest and n equals the number of years.

Annual Percentage Rate (APR) is an attempt to standardize the calculation of the cost of borrowing to make meaningful comparisons. APR is an annualized rate that can also include other costs of borrowing in addition to the interest charges. APR does NOT reflect compounding of interest within each year. It's easy to confuse APR and the interest rate, but each element has a distinct role.

- **Nominal interest rate:** The amount that is charged on your balance in a given period of time
- **Nominal APR:** The nominal interest rate multiplied by the number of periods in a year
- **Effective interest rate:** Expressed annually, it accounts for compounding, but not fees.
- **Effective APR:** This typically accounts for both compounding interest and any fees charged on the loan.

The interest rate is the rate used to calculate the amount of interest charged each period. When multiplied by the number of periods in the year, you get the nominal APR. The effective interest rate includes compounding, while the effective APR includes both compounding and fees.

Weighing **opportunity cost** is also part of determining how much to save and invest and where. Opportunity cost is the answer to the question: What will a person give up now in order to have more later? In terms of investments, opportunity cost may also be gauged as amount of risk versus amount of return.

ASSET/PORTFOLIO ALLOCATION

Asset allocation involves dividing an investment portfolio among different asset categories, such as stocks, bonds, and cash. The process of determining which mix of assets to hold in a portfolio is a personal one. The asset allocation that works best for an investor at any given point in his/her life will depend largely on time horizon and ability to tolerate risk.

There is no one-size-fits-all asset allocation model. What is good for one investor might not be good for another due to the current size of one's nest egg, risk tolerance, years until retirement, and other considerations. However, one thing that every investor should do is rebalance his/her portfolio to maintain the desired allocation; this is because over time an allocation will likely change.

Ultimately, the objective of a good asset allocation plan is to develop an investment portfolio that will help an investor reach his/her financial objectives with a comfortable degree of risk. A well-diversified plan will not outperform the top asset class in any given year, but over time it may be one of the most effective ways to realize one's long-term goals. Asset allocation helps investors stay in control of their financial plan by tailoring investments to fit individual goals and tolerance for risk.

The most common reason for an asset allocation is a change in an investor's time horizon; as an investor gets closer to his/her investment goal, changes to asset allocation will likely be needed. For example, most people investing for retirement hold fewer stocks and more bonds and cash equivalents as they get closer to their retirement age.

RETIREMENT AND ESTATE PLANNING

Retirement planning involves reviewing assets and living expenses. The increasing average life expectancy, the declining power of the dollar over time because of inflation, and the inadequacy of Social Security and pensions to cover living expenses are three major reasons to begin planning and saving for retirement early. Among the assets to consider in retirement planning are housing and investments, including life insurance and annuities. Downsizing living space and housing expenses has become a goal of many baby-boomers as they move into retirement.

TERMINOLOGY

Before we discuss the options and strategies for retirement planning, let's define a few key terms:

Vesting

The term *vesting* refers to whether or not the money that has been set aside for an individual contributor in a retirement plan can be kept by the individual if employment is terminated. Vested benefits are those to which the investor has an absolute right even if he/she resigns or is terminated. *Vesting* is a term used in the Employee Retirement Income Security Act (ERISA). ERISA protects the rights of employees to receive certain promised benefits, including pension benefits and income from profit-sharing plans, once they have worked at a job for a certain period of time.

Maturity

Maturity is the date on which the life of a transaction or financial instrument ends, after which it must either be renewed or it will cease to exist.

Rollovers

A **rollover** is a method of moving money from one account to another account. Typically, the term rollover is used to describe what happens with retirement accounts when they are moved from one account to another account that falls under the same tax category, all without incurring IRS penalties or taxes. A tax-deferred rollover occurs when one withdraws cash or assets from one eligible retirement plan and contributes them to another eligible retirement plan within sixty days. When handled correctly, completing a rollover is the best way to move money among retirement accounts.

An investor generally cannot make more than one rollover from the same IRA within a one-year period. Also, an investor cannot make a rollover during this one-year period from the IRA to which the distribution was rolled over. Beginning January 1, 2015, an investor can make only one rollover from an IRA to another (or the same) IRA in any twelve-month period, regardless of the number of IRAs the investor owns.

The one-per-year limit does not apply to:
- Rollovers from traditional IRAs to Roth IRAs (conversions)
- Trustee-to-trustee transfers to another IRA

- IRA-to-plan rollovers
- Plan-to-IRA rollovers
- Plan-to-plan rollovers

QUALIFIED RETIREMENT ACCOUNTS

There are a variety of ways to fund retirement. A person has no control over some, that is, whether the companies he or she works for during a career have pension plans and what type. There are other methods of retirement funding that a person can choose to invest in, such as a 401(k) plan and an IRA.

Company Pension Plans

Company pension plans are either **defined benefit** or **defined contribution** plans. With a defined benefit plan, the company states the monthly benefit that retirees will receive. An amount of money is invested annually for each employee to generate enough dividends and interest to pay the stipulated benefits when the employee retires. The Pension Benefit Guaranty Corporation (PBGC) insures defined benefit plans in case the company goes bankrupt.

With a defined contribution plan, a company does not specify the amount of monthly benefits. The company contributes a certain amount of money into each employee's investment account with a brokerage firm. The amount of benefits depends on how well the investments perform. When employees retire, they can convert the amount in the account to an annuity.

To receive benefits, an employee must vest in the pension plan, that is, work for the company for a certain period of time in order to be eligible for pension benefits. However, under the Employee Retirement Income Security Act (ERISA), an employee is vested in his or her own contributions immediately. The Pension Protection Act of 2006 set up a schedule of vesting for employer contributions. Retirement age for company plans is typically 65; however, employees typically can retire with "55 and 10," that is, at age 55 with 10 years of service.

In addition to monetary benefits, company pension plans may also include medical and disability benefits. Some have a survivorship benefit as well.

Additional Company Retirement Plans

Pension plans are becoming more rare. Instead, companies are offering:

- **401(k) for Private Companies, 403(b) for Nonprofits, and 457 for Public Institutions:** Contributions taken from salary/wages; tax-deferred; employers may contribute depending on how the plan is set up
- **Profit-Sharing:** Similar to a defined contribution plan, though the company only contributes in years when there is a profit
- **Employee Stock Option Plan (ESOP):** Employer's contributions in company stock
- **Simplified Employee Pension Plan (SEP):** Immediate vesting; may be set up as a pension plan or a tax-deferred IRA; also used by self-employed persons

- **Savings Incentive Match Plan for Employees (SIMPLE):** Either an IRA or 401(K); company matches employees' contributions

An ESOP is problematic if employees tie up all or most of their retirement funding in their company's stock. If the company's stock value and earnings fall either because of issues with the company or because of a decline in its market sector or in the general economy, retirees can find their income severely curtailed.

Individual Retirement Plans (IRAs)

In addition to company-sponsored retirement plans, there are ways that individuals may save and invest for retirement.

- **Individual Retirement Account (IRA):** Tax deferred until the income is withdrawn; penalties for early withdrawal, that is, prior to age 59½, except for large medical expenses, higher education costs, and first-time homebuyers; certain income and contribution restrictions apply
- **Roth IRA:** Contribution dollars are post-tax; income at the time of withdrawal is not taxed as long as the account has been in existence for at least five years and the person is 59½; certain contribution restrictions
- **Rollover IRA:** Consolidated contributions from several retirement plans; may occur as a person moves from company to company
- **Spousal IRA:** IRA for a spouse who is not employed outside of the home
- **Keogh (HR-10) Plan:** For contributions from self-employment income only
- **Annuity:** Plan purchased from an insurance company to provide income during retirement; ends only with the person's death

There are several types of annuities: **fixed**, although the insurance company may change the rate annually, and **variable**, for which the rate of return varies with the performance of the funds in which the insurance company invests. An annuity may also be **immediate**, which begins to pay income immediately, or **deferred**, which begins paying at some later date. Income is tax-deferred until an annuity begins to pay it out.

SOCIAL SECURITY BENEFITS

Social Security covers almost 100 percent of U.S. workers. Exceptions are federal government employees, survivors of those killed during active military duty who are covered under the Department of Veterans Administration, and employees covered under the Railroad Retirement System. To be eligible for Social Security, a worker must work forty quarters and earn a minimum amount, which is adjusted upward each year to keep pace with increases in wages nationwide. A person's actual amount of benefits is based on the person's actual earnings up to the contribution ceiling for each year.

A person can begin collecting Social Security at age 62, but benefits are reduced by about 25 percent. Beginning with those born between 1943 and 1954, full retirement age is 66. After 1954, full retirement age edges up incrementally (2 months for each year) to 67 for those born in 1960 and later. In addition to the retiree, the person's family may also be eligible to receive Social Security benefits under certain conditions: a spouse if 62 or older, a spouse if under 62 but taking care of the retiree's child under age 16, a former spouse age 62 or older and children up to age 18, children ages 18 and 19 if they are full-time high school students, and children over 18 with disabilities. Whether a spouse opts to take his or her own benefits or the benefits of the retiree should depend on which spouse will receive the greater benefit.

If a person begins receiving Social Security benefits before full-retirement age and continues to work, benefits are reduced by $1 for every $2 that the person receives over a certain amount. Once a person attains full-retirement age, there is no retirement test of earnings. Up to 85 percent of Social Security benefits can be taxed, depending on a recipient's other income. Depending on the rate of inflation, the government calculates an annual cost-of-living adjustment.

WILLS, TRUSTS, AND ESTATE PLANNING

Estate planning isn't just a matter of making sure that a person leaves directions for disposition of his or her assets after death. It's also a matter of building up those assets during one's lifetime. Financial planning is part of a life plan, and planning for the transfer of those assets is part of a death plan.

Wills

Whether a person is part of a married or nontraditional couple or single, everyone needs a written will. Dying without a valid will is called dying intestate. There are various formats for wills, but in some states, a person may be required to leave one half of his or her assets to the spouse:

- **Simple Will:** Leaves everything to a spouse
- **Traditional Marital Share Will:** Leaves half the adjusted gross estate to a spouse and the other half in trust to the spouse or to children or others
- **Exemption Trust Will:** Leaves all but a small amount to a spouse; the remainder is put in trust for the spouse
- **Stated Dollar Amount Will:** Leaves certain amounts to a spouse and to other heirs (leaving a percentage rather than an amount is a safer strategy because the value of an estate may rise or fall depending on economic factors)

Under a simple will, estate taxes are paid at the time of the death of the person whose will is being probated. Under a traditional marital share, half the taxes are paid on the death of the person and half at the death of the spouse. The exemption trust results in almost no tax payment for the estate or at the time of the death of spouse. Taxes may vary under a stated dollar amount depending on how much is left to a spouse.

If there is no requirement to leave half an estate to the spouse or the spouse has predeceased, there are two ways that an estate may be divided: **per capita** and **per stirpes**. The former divides the assets into equal shares, and the latter divides everything equally among the branches of a family. An important part of writing a will is selecting the executor who will see that the terms of the will are carried out and also that all debts are paid and taxes are filed and paid, if required. If a person dies intestate, the court appoints an executor. Those with children or spouses unable to care for themselves or anyone else who is a dependent would also have to name a guardian to handle affairs for the person or persons.

Trusts and Estates

A **trust** is a legal arrangement by which one party holds the rights to property for the benefit of another party or parties. A **testamentary trust** is one that comes into existence upon the death of the owner of the property and is typically used for the support of dependent children; minor children cannot inherit property directly. A **living trust,** formally known as an *inter vivos* trust, is set up during the lifetime of the owner of the assets and, as a result, does not require probate. Living trusts are subject to estate taxes if they are revocable trusts but not if they are irrevocable. A **life insurance trust** is a type of living trust that is funded by the proceeds of a person's life insurance upon the person's death. A trust can also be established by a person for the person's own benefit during his or her lifetime. It is a way to ensure that a person will be taken care of should he or she no longer be able to do so. Trusts can also be set up to provide for the support of a spouse or other dependents, transfer assets without going through probate, reduce estate taxes, and pay estate taxes.

An **estate** is the sum total of all of a person's assets. How an estate is taxed depends on whether the decedent was married and lived in a community-property state or not. In a community-property state, each spouse owns half of the assets. In a noncommunity-state, individual ownership is recognized, though joint ownership is typical. **Joint ownership** may be classified as joint ownership with a right of survivorship, tenants in common, and tenancy by entirety. Each has its own tax consequences. Joint ownership with right of survivorship and tenancy by entirety result in no estate tax at the death of the first spouse (and no need to pass through probate court). Tenancy in common also results in no estate tax for a spouse, but if the joint owners are not married, for example, a parent and child, there would be a tax liability. Upon the death of a tenant in common, the estate must pass through probate court.

Life insurance proceeds are not included in an estate if the policy has been assigned to a beneficiary or a trust. Any death benefits from company pensions, profit-sharing, and Keogh plans are not part of a person's taxable estate unless the estate is the payee.

TAX-DEFERRED ANNUITIES

An **annuity** is a contract between an individual and an insurance company that provides the individual with tax-deferred accumulation and an option to receive a lump sum or fixed-periodic payments starting on a specific date.

An annuity can offer benefits such as:

- Control over when the individual pays taxes by timing distributions
- Unlimited contributions
- Option of guaranteed income for life
- A cost of living adjustment (COLA) that ensures payouts increase in order to offset the effects of inflation
- A death benefit that passes account value to beneficiaries, which may avoid probate but is not tax-free

The federal government levies a federal estate tax, sometimes called a "death tax," on estates in excess of a certain amount. That amount has varied over the last decade from $1.5 million to $5.45 million depending on certain temporary tax provisions. Gifting children $14,000 a year ($28,000 for a married couple) is one way to transfer wealth from one generation to the next without incurring taxes. In addition to federal estate taxes, states also levy estate taxes. Rates vary from state to state. States also levy inheritance taxes on the heirs of a decedent's estate. Tax rates, exemptions, and other provisions vary from state to state. In general, the larger the estate and the greater the distance between decedent and heir, the higher the inheritance tax rate. Gifting during one's lifetime is one way to avoid having an heir pay an inheritance tax. The federal government doesn't levy an inheritance tax.

SUMMING IT UP

- Financial goals may be **short-term**, **medium-term**, or **long-term**. They can also be categorized as **consumable-product**, **durable-product**, and **intangible-product goals**. Financial goals change in importance as a person moves through each stage of the life cycle.
    - ○ Once financial goals are set, it's important to establish a **budget** to achieve those goals.

- A **cash flow statement** shows inflow and outflow of money and is useful in planning a household budget. A **balance sheet** lists assets minus liabilities to show an individual's or family's net worth.

- **Cash management** is a way to have cash, or the equivalent, handy for regular purchases and emergencies.

- The **time value of money** is the increase in the amount of money as a result of interest earned on it. It is, in other words, the future value of money calculated at a certain rate of interest over a certain period of time.
    - ○ Two other important concepts are the **present value of money** and **opportunity cost**. The former is the current value of money needed to generate a future amount based on a certain rate of interest and a certain period of time. The latter is what a person gives up in order to gain something else.

- **Credit** is the promise to pay later for the use of something now.
    - ○ **Advantages of using credit** include convenience, the ability to consume more than possible based on income, as a hedge against inflation, and for emergencies.

    - ○ **Disadvantages of using credit** are the temptation to spend more than a person has, the consequences of overspending, the cost of credit, and limitations on future spending power because of the cost of credit for past purchases.

    - ○ There are three types of credit: **installment sales credit**, **installment cash credit**, and **single lump-sum credit**. Repayment for the first two is in regular amounts over a period of time.

- The five C's of creditworthiness: **character**, **capacity**, **capital**, **collateral**, and **conditions**. A creditor checks an applicant's credit score, known as a **FICO score**, which considers length of credit history, on-time payment history, current amounts owed, types of credit in the credit history, and inquiries from new credit sources.

- There are two forms of personal bankruptcy: **Chapter 7**, **known as straight bankruptcy**, and **Chapter 13, known as the wage-earner plan**. Filing for bankruptcy stays on a personal financial record for seven or ten years and can affect the ability to qualify for credit or a job and to buy insurance.

- A basic question for many when faced with obtaining a car is whether to buy or lease. A comparison can be made based on initial costs, monthly payments, and final expenses to pay off the lease.

- In **evaluating leases**, a consumer should note the capitalized cost, interest rate, amount of monthly payments, number of monthly payments, residual value of the vehicle at turn-in time, and early lease-termination fee.

- If **deciding to buy**, a consumer faces the choice: new or used. The price of a used car is determined by mileage, condition, features and options, and demand in the marketplace for the make and model.

- Whether new or used, a car owner must be able to finance costs of ownership and costs of operation.

- The **advantages of renting housing** are mobility, little or no personal or financial responsibility for maintenance or repairs, and the lower initial cost of paying only a security deposit. The disadvantages are inability to derive financial benefits from ownership (tax deductions, increasing equity stake), the likelihood of rent increases over time, and lease restrictions on use of the rental property.

- The **advantages of buying housing** include tax deductions for mortgage interest and property taxes, capital gain that is probably not taxable because of tax adjustments, and fewer restrictions on how the property can be used. Disadvantages are limited mobility, maintenance and repair costs, high initial costs, and loss of potential interest earned on money used for the down payment and closing costs.

- The larger the down payment on a home, the lower the monthly payments. The longer the term of the mortgage, the higher the interest rate. Depending on the down payment, a lender may require private mortgage insurance.

- Most mortgages are **conventional mortgages** and are for terms of thirty, twenty, or fifteen years. There are also a variety of other types of mortgage, including **adjustable rate mortgages**, **interest-only**, and **convertible**.

- **Payroll deductions** may be mandatory or voluntary, depending on whether they are tax or non-tax deductions from wages.

- Taxpayers may take the **standard deduction** when reporting their income or itemize their deductions if they are higher than the standard deduction in any given year.
    - There are a variety of legal ways to reduce taxes, which is known as **tax avoidance**.

- **Life insurance policies** may be **term policies** or **whole life**. The latter includes a savings component and has a number of formats. Life insurance policies have a face value, which is the amount of death benefits.

- **Property insurance** shields people from risks to their homes, vehicles, and personal property such as furniture, electronics, and jewelry. **Liability insurance** protects people from losses as a result of damage done to other persons or to the property of others. Both homeowner's and auto insurance may include both components.

- **Basic health insurance** provides protection for hospital stays, surgery, and medical care. **Major medical insurance** pays expenses over and above the basic insurance coverage, typically up to $1 million. The Affordable Care Act, which became law in 2010, affects the rules and requirements surrounding health insurance in the United States.

- **Disability insurance** provides income for workers who are unable to work because of a disability. What constitutes a disability depends on the insurance policy.

- **Investments** involve risk, but the least risky are savings accounts, money market deposit/money market demand accounts, money market funds, and certificates of deposit. Individual stocks and bonds are riskier than stock mutual funds and bond mutual funds, because with the latter two, risk is spread over more companies.

- There are a variety of ways to fund retirement through **employer-sponsored plans**:
    - Company pension plans, which may be defined benefit or defined contribution plans: 401(k), 403 (b), and 457 plans

    - Profit-sharing plan

    - Employee Stock Option Plan (ESOP)

    - Simplified Employee Pension Plan (SEP)

    - Savings Incentive Match Plan for Employees (SIMPLE)

- Individuals can also establish retirement plans through **Individual Retirement Account (IRA), Roth IRA, rollover IRA, spousal IRA, Keogh (HR-10) Plan**, and **annuity**, which may be fixed or variable and immediate or deferred.

- **Estate planning** involves writing a will. Depending on the state, a person may be required to leave at least half of his or her estate to the spouse.
    - **Trusts** may be testamentary or living, also known as *inter vivos*. A living trust may be revocable or irrevocable.

    - The federal government levies a **federal estate tax** on estates in excess of a certain amount. States also levy estate taxes and some also tax the heirs.

PERSONAL FINANCE POST-TEST

Directions: Carefully read each of the following 60 questions. Choose the best answer to each question and fill in the corresponding circle on the answer sheet. The Answer Key and Explanations can be found following this post-test.

1. If a homebuyer has less than 20 percent for a down payment, the homebuyer will
   A. need to buy mortgage insurance.
   B. have to apply for an FHA mortgage.
   C. be turned down by the VA.
   D. need to come up with 5 percent more of the down payment.

2. One difference between CDs and savings accounts and money markets is that
   A. the interest rate on a CD varies over time, whereas the interest rate on a savings account or a money market does not.
   B. money cannot be added to a CD over time, whereas money can be added to a savings account or money market.
   C. a CD is not FDIC-insured, but the other two are.
   D. a CD is a good savings vehicle for someone with a low tolerance for risk, but the other two are not.

3. The future value of money is
   A. the amount a given amount of money will be worth in the future when adjusted for inflation
   B. the increase in an amount of money including interest earned over time.
   C. the value of money in today's marketplace.
   D. money earned as profit on an investment.

4. Which of the following does not impact vested benefits?
   A. Length of time worked for an employer
   B. Regulations outlined in Employee Retirement Income Security Act
   C. Amount of notice an employee gives when resigning position
   D. Specific type of benefit involved

5. Which of the following does NOT reduce current tax obligations?
   A. Roth IRA
   B. Traditional IRA
   C. Spousal IRA
   D. SEP

6. A Chapter 13 bankruptcy remains on a person's credit report for
   A. five years.
   B. seven years.
   C. eight years.
   D. ten years.

7. Jason graduated from college in June. He started a job later that month that is paying him an average salary for a new employee in his field. He's sharing an apartment with three roommates and has $30,000 in student loans to pay off. What should his immediate financial goal be?
   A. Paying off his student loans as fast possible
   B. Setting up a retirement plan
   C. Buying life insurance
   D. Setting up a six-month emergency fund

8. In calculating income tax, when are tax credits applied in the process?
   A. Before calculating adjusted gross income
   B. When calculating gross income
   C. After calculating the income tax owed
   D. Before standard deductions and any exemptions are taken

9. Renting a home instead of buying would generally be a wise financial move for someone who
   A is seeking a long-term investment.
   B. wants the freedom to use the property however they wish, including leasing it for income.
   C. is interested in tax deductions.
   D. is likely to move within a year or two.

10. In terms of benefits, a term life policy provides
    A. death benefits, can be borrowed against, and cash if it is a policy that pays dividends.
    B. death benefits and cash if it is a policy that pays dividends.
    C. death benefits and can be borrowed against.
    D. death benefits only.

11. A disadvantage for homebuyers to owning any type of housing is the potential
    A. for disagreements over association rules.
    B. decline in housing prices.
    C. lack of privacy.
    D. assessment fees.

12. The full retirement age for the purpose of receiving Social Security for those born in 1945 is
    A. $62\frac{1}{2}$.
    B. 65.
    C. 66.
    D. 67.

13. The benefit from a resource that a person gives up in choosing one option over another is called its
    A. opportunity cost.
    B. lost opportunity.
    C. alternative.
    D. trade-off.

14. In buying a refrigerator, a consumer might consider which of the following?
    A. Volume discount
    B. Features
    C. Trade-in value
    D. Service contract

15. A liquid asset is one that
    A. can be quickly converted to cash.
    B. guarantees an attractive profit potential.
    C. involves significant red tape or a cumbersome management process.
    D. cannot be accessed or withdrawn for a year or more.

16. Which of the following allows the fastest access to cash with no penalty for withdrawal?
    A. Regular checking account
    B. Certificate of deposit
    C. Series EE bond
    D. Stocks

17. Jake wants to improve his credit score. Which of the following will help him to do this?
    A. Take out several new credit cards
    B. Buy several major appliances using store credit
    C. Open a savings account and make regular deposits each time he is paid
    D. Check his credit score regularly

18. Which of these is a mandatory payroll deduction?
    A. Social Security taxes
    B. 401(k) or 403(b) pension plans
    C. Long-term care insurance
    D. Health insurance

19. Which of the following is both a health insurer and a health services provider?

    A. Health maintenance organization

    B. Preferred provider organization

    C. Point-of-service plan

    D. Fee-for-service

20. Which of the following is a typical rider to a life insurance policy?

    A. Grace period

    B. Automatic premium clause

    C. Cost-of-living protection

    D. Policy loan provision

21. Nadja was comparing credit cards and decided not to take the card from Acme Bank. Which of the following features signaled to Nadja that Acme's card was not a good choice?

    A. The grace period was 21 days.

    B. Interest was charged from the day that a purchase was made.

    C. The card offered buyer protection for purchases.

    D. The annual fee was waived because it was a special offer.

22. Reduction of the principal borrowed over the life of a mortgage is called

    A. RESPA.

    B. rate cap.

    C. escrow accounting.

    D. amortization.

23. Which of the following is an accurate statement about payroll deductions?

    A. All payroll deductions are mandatory.

    B. FICA taxes include Old Age Survivors Benefit and Medicare.

    C. IRA contributions are taken directly as payroll deductions.

    D. A worker can have the premium for a non-company–sponsored life insurance policy deducted from his or her paycheck.

24. Under which of the following programs can an employee who has been terminated or laid off continue health insurance for a period of time?

    A. HIPAA

    B. Medigap

    C. COBRA

    D. COB

25. Any debt that must be paid within a year is a

    A. current liability.

    B. noncurrent liability.

    C. flexible expense.

    D. dissavings.

26. When making a major purchase such as a computer or appliance, you can benefit financially by

    A. buying on credit.

    B. comparison shopping.

    C. paying for the purchase with money withdrawn from a CD or interest-bearing savings account.

    D. opting for the extra service plan.

27. Which of the following is a reason that a person may withdraw money from an IRA before age $59\frac{1}{2}$ without incurring a penalty?

    A. To buy a car

    B. To pay for a college education

    C. To purchase a vacation home

    D. For a large-scale home renovation

28. An indemnity health insurance policy is NOT ideal because it

    A. pays only a specified amount regardless of actual costs.

    B. does not cover preexisting conditions.

    C. will not pay you directly, only the health-care provider.

    D. pays only for regular nonsurgical doctors' services.

29. Sal and Joanna decided against taking out an umbrella policy. This was an unwise decision because an umbrella policy
    A. covers a home office, and Joanna runs a business out of their house.
    B. protects against flood damage, and they live in a floodplain.
    C. would have provided minimal health insurance as well as homeowner's and auto insurance.
    D. extends liability coverage over and above the limits in homeowner's and auto insurance policies.

30. A disadvantage of a regressive tax structure is that
    A. it is complicated to calculate and implement.
    B. those who move up just slightly into a higher tax bracket can suffer a financial penalty.
    C. lower-income people pay a proportionally higher amount of taxes than those with a higher income.
    D. it offers little motivation to work hard or increase one's income.

31. Asset allocation involves
    A. working toward financial goals with a comfortable level of risk.
    B. a standard formula that dictates how assets should always be divided.
    C. committing to a specific plan indefinitely without deviations or changes.
    D. dividing up valuables and giving them away to friends and family.

32. Estimated taxes are paid
    A. weekly.
    B. monthly.
    C. quarterly.
    D. twice a year.

33. Stock mutual funds can be a smart investment choice because
    A. they can help minimize overall risk.
    B. they are insured by the federal government.
    C. you know exactly what your profit will be since they have a fixed rate of return.
    D. you can invest in specific companies you select.

34. An agency like Moody's Investors Services can
    A. guide an entity in repairing or improving their credit score.
    B. help investors determine bonds with the least amount of risk.
    C. set the price of stocks and bonds.
    D. provide individual investors with financial management or accounting services.

35. Alexis believes that buying used cars makes more financial sense than buying new cars. He bases his belief on the fact that
    A. most depreciation of new cars occurs in the first two to three years.
    B. used cars have better warranties than new cars.
    C. used cars cost less to operate than new cars because they've been broken in.
    D. registration costs less for older cars than newer cars.

36. What is one disadvantage of a travel and entertainment card?
    A. The balance must be paid in full each month.
    B. A person can withhold payment regardless of the amount of the disputed charge.
    C. If the store issuing the card goes bankrupt, the cardholder is out the money he or she spent to buy the card.
    D. If a card is stolen, the person has two days to notify the issuer without penalty.

37. Which of the following may be deducted in calculating personal income taxes?

   A. Health savings account contributions for the fiscal year

   B. Life insurance premiums

   C. Expenses related to moving to assisted living

   D. Support for an elderly parent

38. Which of the following is true about annuities?

   A. They involve a deal between several individuals.

   B. They involve risk because the payouts can be random and unpredictable.

   C. They can be part of a smart retirement planning strategy.

   D. As the money accumulates, you will always be required to pay tax on that balance every year.

39. When are taxes paid on an estate that was left under a traditional marital share will?

   A. At the time of the death of the spouse whose will is bring probated

   B. At the time of the death of the spouse who survived

   C. No taxes required

   D. Half when the first spouse dies and half when the surviving spouse dies

40. Which of the following is true about equities?

   A. They only involve companies from certain industries that meet minimum revenue thresholds.

   B. They always involve a greater degree of risk than bonds.

   C. Investors hope to profit via a drop in the stock prices.

   D. Doing your research by consulting a variety of available sources can greatly increase your odds of financial profits.

41. Which of the following forms does a worker complete to indicate the number of exemptions he or she has for tax purposes?

   A. W-2

   B. W-4

   C. 1040

   D. 1099

42. Stan bought a used car with no express warranties. He may still have certain protections under

   A. an implied warranty.

   B. an extended warranty

   C. federal lemon laws

   D. judicial warranties

43. Achieving financial goals depends on how

   A. much a person earns and saves.

   B. much a person earns, saves, and invests.

   C. well the stock market performs.

   D. well the economy performs.

44. A qualified pension plan is

   A. a defined contribution plan.

   B. taxable at the time that contributions are made.

   C. guaranteed by the Pension Benefit Guaranty Corporation.

   D. available only to industries with unions.

45. Which of the following is a retirement plan for self-employed persons?

   A. SEP

   B. SIMPLE

   C. 403(b)

   D. Keogh

46. The limit on the amount a monthly mortgage payment may be increased on an adjustable rate mortgage is the

   A. rate cap.

   B. buy-down.

   C. payment cap.

   D. loan cap.

47. In a no-fault auto insurance plan state, which of the following is typically required?
    A. Only property damage insurance
    B. Only insurance to cover medical expenses
    C. Only insurance to cover damage and medical expenses of the victim(s) of the accident, not the person who caused it
    D. Uninsured motorist coverage

48. Paul buys the right to purchase from his broker 100 shares of a stock at $43 a share within thirty days. This is known as
    A. selling short.
    B. trading in a call option.
    C. buying on margin.
    D. day trading.

49. Which of the following is NOT included when calculating debt-to-income ratio?
    A. Car loan payment
    B. Student loan payment
    C. Mortgage payment
    D. Payments for utilities

50. Which of the following is an example of an open-end credit instrument?
    A. A mortgage
    B. A three-year vehicle loan
    C. A home equity line of credit
    D. An installment cash credit

51. A flexible spending account can be used to
    A. pay for health care.
    B. pay for adult day care for an elderly relative.
    C. put aside money to pay estimated taxes.
    D. pay for retirement expenses.

52. Which of the following is not one of the "five Cs of credit worthiness" considered by creditors?
    A. Capacity
    B. Cash on hand
    C. Capital
    D. Conditions

53. Which of the following is a difference between a credit card and a debit card?
    A. The bank will certify that a person has sufficient funds to cover a purchase with a debit card but not a credit card.
    B. A debit card is preloaded with a certain amount, whereas the credit card can be used up to the credit limit on the card.
    C. Losses from a stolen credit card are capped at $500, whereas with a debit card, losses are capped at $50.
    D. With a credit card, there is float between the time a person charges a purchase and the person is billed, whereas with a debit card, the amount of the purchase is withdrawn from the account immediately.

54. Which of the following is NOT taxed as part of an estate?
    A. Traditional IRA
    B. Roth IRA
    C. Irrevocable trust
    D. Testamentary trust

55. Which of the following is true about income tax?
    A. It always involves the federal government.
    B. Salary is the only type of income considered.
    C. Passive types of income can be taxable
    D. Withholding refers to an amount an individual sets aside in their savings account to pay their tax bill.

56. Reverse mortgages are a good idea for people who
    A. seek a way to obtain more cash or lower/eliminate some monthly payments.
    B. are at least 45 years of age.
    C. have no equity in their home.
    D. do not own a home.

57. Which of the following investments is the best choice for someone with low risk-tolerance?
    A. Individual stocks
    B. Bond mutual funds
    C. Stock mutual funds
    D. Money market funds

58. A will that divides an estate per stirpes divides assets
    A. equally among branches of a family.
    B. into equal shares for distribution.
    C. according to stated amounts in the will.
    D. equally between spouse and children.

59. Manjeet invests in a municipal bond fund for its tax benefit. What is the benefit that he derives from this investment?
    A. The fund enables him to evade paying taxes.
    B. The fund provides him with a tax credit.
    C. The interest earned is tax-exempt.
    D. The interest earned is tax-deferred.

60. Which of the following regulates investment advisers?
    A. State securities regulator
    B. Sarbanes-Oxley
    C. Certified Financial Planner Board of Standards, Inc.
    D. FINRA

post-test

ANSWER KEY AND EXPLANATIONS

1. A	13. A	25. A	37. A	49. D
2. B	14. B	26. B	38. C	50. C
3. A	15. A	27. B	39. D	51. A
4. C	16. A	28. A	40. D	52. B
5. A	17. C	29. D	41. B	53. D
6. B	18. A	30. C	42. A	54. C
7. D	19. A	31. A	43. B	55. C
8. C	20. C	32. C	44. C	56. A
9. D	21. B	33. A	45. D	57. D
10. D	22. D	34. B	46. C	58. A
11. B	23. B	35. A	47. B	59. C
12. C	24. C	36. A	48. B	60. A

1. **The correct answer is A.** Choice B is incorrect because the Federal Housing Administration (FHA) doesn't offer mortgages; it insures mortgages. Choice C is incorrect because, like the FHA, the Department of Veterans Affairs (VA) doesn't offer mortgages; it insures them. In addition, the VA doesn't require mortgage insurance. Choice D is incorrect because there is no requirement for such a down payment related to mortgage insurance.

2. **The correct answer is B.** CDs are purchased for a specified amount of money at a specified interest rate for a specified period. Choice A is incorrect because the interest rate doesn't vary for CDs, but it does vary over time for savings accounts and money market accounts. Choice C is incorrect because all three are FDIC-insured as long as they are less than $250,000. Choice D is incorrect because all three are good savings vehicles for people with low risk-tolerance.

3. **The correct answer is A.** Future value is the value of an asset or cash at a specific date in the future. Choice B defines time value of money, not future value of money. Choice C misstates the definition of the present value of money: the current value for a future amount of money calculated with a specific interest rate for a specific period of time. Choice D is the definition of a return.

4. **The correct answer is C.** Vested benefits are those to which an individual is entitled after they resign, regardless of how they terminated their employment or notified the employer. Vesting often does not go into effect until a minimum length of service has been completed (choice A). An employee's rights to vested benefits are protected under the Employee Retirement Income Security Act (choice B), but only certain types of benefits are considered legally protected vested benefits (choice D).

5. **The correct answer is A.** A person pays taxes on contributions to a Roth IRA, whereas contributions to traditional IRAs (choice B) and spousal IRAs (choice C) are tax-deductible, and the withdrawals are taxed. Contributions to SEPs (choice D) are made with pretax income, but earnings are taxed when withdrawn.

6. **The correct answer is B.** A Chapter 13 bankruptcy filing remains on a person's credit report for seven years. Five years (choice A) is the number of years in which a person with regular income must pay off debts current at the time of Chapter 13 bankruptcy filing. A person may file for Chapter 7 bankruptcy only once in eight years (choice C), and a record of a Chapter 7 bankruptcy filing remains on a person's credit report for ten years (choice D).

7. **The correct answer is D.** Jason needs some cash to fall back on in case he loses his job, has an accident, or is sick for a prolonged period. Paying off his student loan, setting up a retirement plan, and buying life insurance (choices A, B, and C) are important, but financial planning involves a series of staged goals. However, he should take advantage of any retirement plan that his employer offers because the employer's contribution is in effect "free" money; it doesn't cost Jason.

8. **The correct answer is C.** Tax credits are applied after the income tax is calculated, which is after the standard deductions and any exemptions are taken, not before (choice D). Choices A and B are actually the same answer and are both incorrect; they are the first step in calculating income tax.

9. **The correct answer is D.** Because of the initial upfront expenses, such as closing costs, purchasing a home may not be worth the initial costs for those who plan to be in the property for a short time. Buying a home does offer financial advantages, such as tax deductions (choice C) and the potential to use the property as a source of rental income (choice B). Investing in real estate can also be a strategy to attain future financial profits (choice A).

10. **The correct answer is D.** Term life pays death benefits only. Whole life provides death benefits, can be borrowed against, and cash if it is a policy that pays dividends (choice A). Choices B and C are incomplete descriptions of whole life.

11. **The correct answer is B.** A decline in property values is a risk of buying any type of home. Association rules (choice A) refers to planned unit developments, condominiums, and co-operatives, not stand-alone homes. Lack of privacy (choice C) may occur in condos and co-ops, but not stand-alone homes. Assessment fees (choice D) again apply to forms of ownership other than stand-alone homes that are not part of planned unit developments.

12. **The correct answer is C.** For the purpose of receiving Social Security, full retirement age for those born between 1943 and 1954 is 66. The age at which people may begin taking partial Social Security is 62½ (choice A). Full retirement age for those born prior to 1943 was 65 (choice B). The age at which those born after 1960 may begin receiving full benefits under Social Security is 67 (choice D).

13. **The correct answer is A.** The opportunity cost of choosing one thing over another is the loss of the benefit of what was not chosen. Choosing one item over another may be a lost opportunity (choice B), but that's not an economic concept, so eliminate it. Alternative (choice C) also is not an economic concept, so eliminate it. Choice D is simply the exchange of one thing for another; there is no value placed on the items, so it doesn't match the definition.

14. **The correct answer is B.** Volume discount (choice A) doesn't make sense because consumers typically buy only one refrigerator at a time. Choice C also wouldn't be relevant since trade-in value generally applies to cars or other large purchases with extended lifespans. Choice D, service contract, is usually not a good buy for consumers because products tend to fail within the first year when they are still under warranty.

15. **The correct answer is A.** Liquidity refers to the ability to quickly access money or turn an asset into cash. Generally, liquid assets involve low interest rates and aren't considered highly profitable in the short term (choice B). Accounts that require a lot of bureaucratic back-and-forth or time-consuming paperwork to adjust or cash out wouldn't usually be considered desirable as a liquid asset (choice C). Assets or accounts that cannot be touched for a long period of time aren't considered highly liquid (choice D).

16. **The correct answer is A.** When a person needs cash, a regular checking account is the fastest way to get it—whether by ATM or check. There is no penalty involved—assuming there is no overdraft. Choices B and C are incorrect because there is a penalty for early withdrawal of both CDs and Series EE bonds. The former is typically a month's interest, and the latter is three

months' interest. A person may be able to sell stocks (choice D) quickly, assuming it's a day when the stock market is open, but there could be a "penalty" if the stock is sold below the price the person paid for it.

17. **The correct answer is C.** Although checking a credit score (choice D) is important to ensure that it is accurate, it won't help that credit score if a person doesn't use credit wisely. Opening a savings account and making regular deposits provides a way to show that a person can be disciplined when it comes to money. Overusing credit doesn't demonstrate that; both choices A and B can send up red flags to potential creditors. The more inquiries for new credit that show up, the less responsible the person seems.

18. **The correct answer is A.** Social Security taxes, known as FICA (Federal Insurance Contributions Act) consist of Medicare and Old Age Survivors Benefit. Pension plans and insurance coverage (choices B, C, and D) are all voluntary non-tax payroll deductions.

19. **The correct answer is A.** Health maintenance organizations (HMOs) are both insurers and care providers. Choice B, a preferred provider organization (PPO), is a provider, not an insurer, as is choice C, a point-of-service plan (POS). Choice D, the full name of which is fee-for-service health insurance (FFS), is an insurer only.

20. **The correct answer is C.** The cost-of-living protection is a rider that is typically added to a life insurance policy because of the effects of inflation in the long term. The grace period (choice A), the automatic premium clause (choice B), and the policy loan provision (choice D) are common parts of a life insurance policy. The first provides a window to pay the premium on a policy without incurring a penalty; the second enables the insurance company to pay the premium from the cash value of the policy should the policyholder not pay the premium within the grace period; and the third enables the policyholder to borrow against the cash value of the policy.

21. **The correct answer is B.** Choices A and B can't both be correct. Choice A, a grace period of 21 days, contradicts choice B, which is a reason not to take a particular card, all else being equal. Choices A and C are reasons to take a particular card, all else being equal. However, choice D, while a good deal for the first year, might not be a good deal in the long term if an annual fee is added after the first year. Nadja should keep this in mind and check to see if an annual fee is added at the beginning of the second year.

22. **The correct answer is D.** Reduction of the principal borrowed over the life of a loan is called amortization. Choice A is incorrect because RESPA stands for Real Estate Settlement Procedures Act and refers to closing costs and the closing process for buying a home. Choice B is incorrect because a rate cap is the amount by which the interest rate can increase or decrease over the life of an adjustable rate mortgage. Choice C seems correct because of the word *escrow*, but an escrow account holds money to pay property taxes and sometimes homeowner's insurance. The lender sets up the account and deposits part of each month's mortgage payment from the homeowner into the account.

23. **The correct answer is B.** FICA payroll deductions are the Social Security and Medicare contributions that workers make. Choice A is incorrect because some payroll deductions are voluntary. Choice C confuses IRAs with 401(k) and 403 (b) pension plans; deductions for the last two are taken, but contributions to IRAs are not. Choice D is incorrect; an employee can opt into a company-sponsored life insurance program and have the premium deducted, but this is not true for a non-company–sponsored policy.

24. **The correct answer is C.** COBRA stands for the Consolidated Omnibus Budget Reconciliation Act of 1986. Under this law, many employers are required to offer terminated and laid-off workers the opportunity to continue their health insurance under the employer's plan. HIPAA (choice A) stands for Health Insurance Portability and Accountability Act of 1996, which ensures that workers cannot be required to requalify for health insurance when they change jobs

or be charged more for health insurance than current employees. Medigap (choice B) refers to supplemental health insurance for people covered under Medicare. COB (choice D) stands for coordination of benefits, a provision of health insurance policies that enables a policyholder to receive reimbursement from several health insurance policies up to 100 percent of allowable medical costs that the person paid.

25. **The correct answer is A.** A current liability is one that must be paid within a year. A non-current liability (choice B) is one that does not have to be paid within a year. Flexible expense (choice C) refers to an expense that is controllable; that is, a person can choose to take on the expense or not. Dissavings (choice D) occurs when a person's expenses are greater than his or her income, resulting in a decrease in net worth.

26. **The correct answer is B.** Comparing prices and deals among various retailers—which can be done quickly and easily online—helps ensure you are getting the best deal. Buying with credit (choice A) means you may incur interest charges (although you may be able to avoid this if you pay off the balance within the grace period or use a card that offers a no-interest introductory rate). Withdrawing money from savings, CDs, or other accounts (choice C) means losing out on potential future interest earnings. In general, optional service plans (choice D) don't tend to offer a good return on investment.

27. **The correct answer is B.** A person may withdraw money from a traditional IRA for three reasons, namely, to pay large medical expenses, for higher education, or for a first home. Choices A, C, and D are incorrect.

28. **The correct answer is A.** Indemnity insurance limits payments to a specified amount regardless of actual costs; expense insurance is a better deal. Choice B is incorrect because the type of indemnity insurance may or may not cover preexisting conditions; that is not why it is indemnity insurance. Choice C is incorrect because indemnity insurance pays the patient directly, not the health-care provider. Choice D is incorrect because it describes physicians' expense insurance.

29. **The correct answer is D.** An umbrella policy adds liability coverage over and above regular homeowner's and auto insurance policies. Choice A is incorrect because an umbrella policy would only cover a home office if the underlying homeowner's policy had an endorsement covering it. Choice B is incorrect because flood insurance is a separate policy. Choice C is incorrect because an umbrella policy doesn't include health insurance, and it doesn't provide homeowner's and auto insurance as such, but increases liability coverage.

30. **The correct answer is C.** Because this structure doesn't increase with one's income or ability to pay, a lower-income person will end up paying a larger portion of their income than someone who is wealthier, if they are both charged the same amount. Since this type of tax often includes a flat fee or standard percentage rate, it is fairly easy to calculate (choice A), and isn't negatively impacted by moving to a higher tax bracket (choice B). Regressive income can offer motivation to earn more (choice D), as you will have more disposable income since your tax rate will not increase.

31. **The correct answer is A.** Smart asset allocation involves developing a strategy that helps you achieve your long-term goals with a level of risk you deem tolerable. There is no one-size-fits-all formula (choice B), as this is an individual decision determined by specific financial circumstances and objectives. The details of your asset allocation plan will likely change regularly (choice C) as your needs and goals dictate. The allocation in this term refers to dividing your investments into specific categories, not physically separating them and giving them away (choice D).

32. **The correct answer is C.** Estimated tax payments are due quarterly: April 15, June 15, September 15, and the following January 15. Choices A and B are incorrect, but may be confusing because Social Security—Federal Income Contributions Act tax (FICA)—is paid weekly, every two weeks, or monthly, depending on how often a person is paid. Choice D is incorrect.

33. **The correct answer is A.** Mutual funds involve stock in a variety of companies, so your portfolio is diversified and you have less risk since you aren't depending on the performance of one individual company. Like other types of stocks, mutual funds aren't federally insured (choice B) and the profit or loss can fluctuate and may be unpredictable (choice C). These stocks are invested in a mix of a number of companies, but the investor does not make the selection (choice D).

34. **The correct answer is B.** Moody's Investors Services is a bond credit-rating organization that also provides research and analysis related to investments. It rates bonds depending on the strength and credit worthiness of the company behind them, but doesn't provide credit repair services to businesses (choice A). It also doesn't set prices for stock or bonds, whose prices can go up and down depending on a range of factors (choice C). This company also doesn't provide accounting service or serve as a personal financial adviser (choice D).

35. **The correct answer is A.** New cars depreciate more rapidly than older cars, so buying a used car can make financial sense. Choice B is incorrect; many used cars come with no express warranties. Choice C is incorrect because the older a car is, the more maintenance is typically required. Choice D confuses registration with insurance. Typically, the older the car, the less reason to have property damage insurance on it.

36. **The correct answer is A.** The balance on travel and entertainment (T&E) cards must be paid in full each month. Choice B is incorrect because a person can withhold payment on a T&E card only if the amount is over $50. Choice C is incorrect because this describes a store gift card. Choice D is incorrect because a person is still liable for charges under $50 regardless of the type of charge card.

37. **The correct answer is A.** Contributions to a health savings account (HSA) are tax deductible up to certain IRS limits. Life insurance premiums (choice B) are not deductible, nor are expenses related to moving to assisted living (choice C).

(Moving expenses related to a job change are tax-deductible, if the move is more than 50 miles from the current home.) Choice D is incorrect.

38. **The correct answer is C.** Because you can anticipate a specific payout at some future point (either in a lump sum or yearly increments), this can be a great retirement planning tool. Choice A is incorrect because an annuity involves an agreement between an individual and a company. The payout of an annuity is always fixed and predetermined, which makes Choice B incorrect. Money that accumulates is tax-deferred (choice D).

39. **The correct answer is D.** Under a traditional marital share will, half the taxes are paid when the first spouse dies and half when the surviving spouse dies. Choice A describes tax payment under a simple will. Choices B and C are incorrect.

40. **The correct answer is D.** There are a wide range of resources available to help you become a smart investor in equities, including corporate reports and financial news programs. Equities can involve a range of companies of all sizes from many industries (choice A is incorrect), and don't necessarily have a greater or lesser degree of risk than bonds (choice B is incorrect)—it depends on the quality of the bonds you buy. An investor would hope to profit via capital gains realized when the stock rises (choice C is incorrect).

41. **The correct answer is B.** The W-4 lists exemptions. The W-2 (choice A) is an employer's form listing an employee's income for the year. A 1040 (choice C) is the income tax long form. A 1099 (choice D) is the form that self-employed people receive from all the companies that employed them during the year.

42. **The correct answer is A.** Even if a used car dealership doesn't specifically mention a warranty, there are certain warranty protections that may be assumed unless otherwise stated. This would not be the case if the car is sold "as is," although certain states have laws that prohibit dealers from selling "as is" cars with no warranties. Choice B is incorrect; it is often the term used for a service contract

that "extends" the protection of express warranties. Federal lemon laws (choice C) only apply to the purchase of new vehicles, although a handful of states do have some type of lemon laws for purchases involving used cars. Choice D doesn't exist.

43. **The correct answer is B.** While it is true that a person will probably do better in a good economy (choice D) or if the stock market performs well (choice C)—assuming the person owns stocks or shares in stock funds—the major factors are how much a person earns, saves, and invests. Choice A is incorrect because it omits the concept of investing.

44. **The correct answer is C.** A qualified pension plan is one that meets all the requirements under the Employee Retirement Income Security Act of 1974 (ERISA) and is guaranteed by the Pension Benefit Guaranty Corporation. Choice A is incorrect because it is only part of what is true about qualified pension plans; a qualified pension plan may be a defined contribution or a defined benefit plan. Choice B is incorrect because in terms of taxation, whether a plan is qualified or not is irrelevant. Taxes are paid at the time that contributions are made if the plan is a Roth IRA, not if it is a 401(k). Taxes on the latter are paid when withdrawals are made. Choice D is incorrect because a qualified pension plan is open to any company in any industry.

45. **The correct answer is D.** Keoghs, also known as HR-10 plans, are retirement plans for self-employed persons. A SEP or Simple Employee Pension Plan (choice A) is set up by an employer. A SIMPLE or Savings Incentive Match Plans for Employees (choice B) was created for small employers to use. Choice C, 403(b), is an employer-sponsored pension plan for non-profits, similar to 401(k) plans for for-profit companies.

46. **The correct answer is C.** The payment cap limits how much a monthly payment on an adjustable rate mortgage may be increased. An annual rate cap (choice A) limits the amount that an interest rate may increase, and it may also put a floor on how far a rate

may decrease. A buy-down (choice B) is a form of financing that builders of a newly constructed house offer to buyers. Choice D is incorrect.

47. **The correct answer is B.** Personal injury protection (PIP) insurance is required in no-fault insurance states to cover medical expenses and accident-related expenses such as loss of income. No-fault insurance policies typically don't cover damage to property (choice A); therefore, buying insurance to cover property damage in the event of an accident is important. Choice C is incorrect for two reasons: (1) property insurance is not required, and (2) PIP covers the policyholder regardless of whether he or she caused the accident. Uninsured motorist coverage (choice D) is not required under a no-fault insurance system.

48. **The correct answer is B.** A call option is based on the assumption or wish that the stock will rise in value and the investor will make money on it. Selling short (choice A) occurs when an investor borrows stock from a broker with the intention of selling it at a higher price and then buying it back when the value decreases, thus making money on the difference between the price sold on the borrowed stock and the price paid to replace the stock. Buying on margin (choice C) is buying stock in part with borrowed money. Day trading (choice D) is a method of buying and selling stocks constantly rather than holding them for any period of time.

49. **The correct answer is D.** In calculating the debt-to-income ratio, payments for debts and other liabilities are factored into the equation, so that would include a car loan (choice A), a student loan (choice B), and the mortgage payment (choice C). Costs for utilities, maintenance, and other household expenses are not considered.

50. **The correct answer is C.** A home equity line of credit is an open-end credit instrument because it enables a consumer to make a series of purchases over a period of time, as long as the consumer doesn't go over the amount of the line of credit. The consumer must repay the amount in regular payments, but the payments may be of varying amounts.

Choices A, B, and D are all examples of closed-end credit, used for a specific purchase for a specific period and for a specific amount of money.

51. **The correct answer is A.** A flexible spending account can be used to pay for health care and for child care. Choice B is meant to confuse, but the correct answer would be child care, not adult day care. Choices C and D are incorrect.

52. **The correct answer is B.** The amount of cash you have on hand can of course impact your ability to pay bills, but creditors have no way of monitoring or tracking that. However, they do evaluate your ability to take on more debt (choice A), your net worth (choice C), and outside factors that may impact your financial situation (choice D).

53. **The correct answer is D.** A person using a credit card has time between charging a purchase and when the money for it is due, unlike a person using a debit card, which immediately subtracts the purchase price from the user's bank account. Choice A is confusing a certified check with a debit card, so the answer is incorrect. Choice B confuses a smart card with a debit card; smart cards are preloaded with an amount. Neither a debit card nor a credit card is preloaded. Choice C is incorrect; losses from a stolen credit card are capped at $50, but losses from a stolen debit card are capped at $50 only if the person notifies the bank in fewer than two days. If it's between two and sixty days before the bank is notified, losses are capped at $500.

54. **The correct answer is C.** An irrevocable trust is not part of an estate for probate and estate taxation purposes. Traditional and Roth IRAs and testamentary trusts (choices A, B, and D), which are trusts set up by a will, are subject to probate and estate taxes.

55. **The correct answer is C.** Passive income can refer to amounts you receive from things like royalties, partnerships, or ongoing payouts. Income tax can also be owed to state or local governments (choice A), and you may owe taxes on other types of wages, in addition to self-employment, business profits, and other

sources of income (choice B). Withholding refers to the amount your employer takes out of your paycheck each pay period to go toward your taxes (choice D).

56. **The correct answer is A.** Reverse mortgages allow homeowners to "cash out" on some of their home's equity, without owing any monthly payments. In order to quality, they must be at least age 62 (choice B) and have some equity (choice C) in a property they own (choice D).

57. **The correct answer is D.** Money market funds are sold by securities brokers for $1 per share, and, even though the funds are not FDIC insured, they are principal protected, so the value of a share does not drop below a dollar. Individual stocks, bond mutual funds, and stock mutual funds (choices A, B, and C) are not good choices for individuals with low risk-tolerance because they are not insured or principal protected, which means they can lose value.

58. **The correct answer is A.** *Per stirpes* means that assets are divided equally among the branches of a family. Choice B describes a per capita distribution. Choice C refers to a stated dollar amount will. Choice D is incorrect.

59. **The correct answer is C.** The interest earned on municipal bonds is tax-exempt. Choice A is incorrect because Manjeet is avoiding paying taxes, which is legal; he is not evading taxes, which is illegal. Choice B is incorrect because a tax credit is deducted directly from taxable income and has nothing to do with municipal bonds. Choice D is incorrect because he will not have to pay taxes later.

60. **The correct answer is A.** Investment advisers may be regulated by their state's securities regulator or by the SEC, depending on the size of the assets the person manages. Choice B is incorrect because Sarbanes-Oxley regulates the financial disclosure of corporations. Choice C is incorrect because the Certified Financial Planner Board of Standards, Inc., licenses financial planners, which is different from an investment adviser. Choice D is incorrect because FINRA is a self-policing association of securities firms.

Principles of Supervision

OVERVIEW

Chapter 10

The DSST® Principles of Supervision exam consists of 100 multiple-choice questions that cover the basics of managerial and supervisory skills, challenges, and responsibilities. The exam focuses upon the following topics: the roles and responsibilities of the supervisor; planning; organization and staffing; directing at the supervisory level; legal issues; stress management; union environments; and quality concerns. Careful reading, critical thinking, and logical analysis will be as important as your knowledge of management and supervision.

DIAGNOSTIC TEST ANSWER SHEET

1. Ⓐ Ⓑ Ⓒ Ⓓ   5. Ⓐ Ⓑ Ⓒ Ⓓ   9. Ⓐ Ⓑ Ⓒ Ⓓ   13. Ⓐ Ⓑ Ⓒ Ⓓ   17. Ⓐ Ⓑ Ⓒ Ⓓ
2. Ⓐ Ⓑ Ⓒ Ⓓ   6. Ⓐ Ⓑ Ⓒ Ⓓ   10. Ⓐ Ⓑ Ⓒ Ⓓ   14. Ⓐ Ⓑ Ⓒ Ⓓ   18. Ⓐ Ⓑ Ⓒ Ⓓ
3. Ⓐ Ⓑ Ⓒ Ⓓ   7. Ⓐ Ⓑ Ⓒ Ⓓ   11. Ⓐ Ⓑ Ⓒ Ⓓ   15. Ⓐ Ⓑ Ⓒ Ⓓ   19. Ⓐ Ⓑ Ⓒ Ⓓ
4. Ⓐ Ⓑ Ⓒ Ⓓ   8. Ⓐ Ⓑ Ⓒ Ⓓ   12. Ⓐ Ⓑ Ⓒ Ⓓ   16. Ⓐ Ⓑ Ⓒ Ⓓ   20. Ⓐ Ⓑ Ⓒ Ⓓ

POST-TEST ANSWER SHEET

1. Ⓐ Ⓑ Ⓒ Ⓓ   13. Ⓐ Ⓑ Ⓒ Ⓓ   25. Ⓐ Ⓑ Ⓒ Ⓓ   37. Ⓐ Ⓑ Ⓒ Ⓓ   49. Ⓐ Ⓑ Ⓒ Ⓓ
2. Ⓐ Ⓑ Ⓒ Ⓓ   14. Ⓐ Ⓑ Ⓒ Ⓓ   26. Ⓐ Ⓑ Ⓒ Ⓓ   38. Ⓐ Ⓑ Ⓒ Ⓓ   50. Ⓐ Ⓑ Ⓒ Ⓓ
3. Ⓐ Ⓑ Ⓒ Ⓓ   15. Ⓐ Ⓑ Ⓒ Ⓓ   27. Ⓐ Ⓑ Ⓒ Ⓓ   39. Ⓐ Ⓑ Ⓒ Ⓓ   51. Ⓐ Ⓑ Ⓒ Ⓓ
4. Ⓐ Ⓑ Ⓒ Ⓓ   16. Ⓐ Ⓑ Ⓒ Ⓓ   28. Ⓐ Ⓑ Ⓒ Ⓓ   40. Ⓐ Ⓑ Ⓒ Ⓓ   52. Ⓐ Ⓑ Ⓒ Ⓓ
5. Ⓐ Ⓑ Ⓒ Ⓓ   17. Ⓐ Ⓑ Ⓒ Ⓓ   29. Ⓐ Ⓑ Ⓒ Ⓓ   41. Ⓐ Ⓑ Ⓒ Ⓓ   53. Ⓐ Ⓑ Ⓒ Ⓓ
6. Ⓐ Ⓑ Ⓒ Ⓓ   18. Ⓐ Ⓑ Ⓒ Ⓓ   30. Ⓐ Ⓑ Ⓒ Ⓓ   42. Ⓐ Ⓑ Ⓒ Ⓓ   54. Ⓐ Ⓑ Ⓒ Ⓓ
7. Ⓐ Ⓑ Ⓒ Ⓓ   19. Ⓐ Ⓑ Ⓒ Ⓓ   31. Ⓐ Ⓑ Ⓒ Ⓓ   43. Ⓐ Ⓑ Ⓒ Ⓓ   55. Ⓐ Ⓑ Ⓒ Ⓓ
8. Ⓐ Ⓑ Ⓒ Ⓓ   20. Ⓐ Ⓑ Ⓒ Ⓓ   32. Ⓐ Ⓑ Ⓒ Ⓓ   44. Ⓐ Ⓑ Ⓒ Ⓓ   56. Ⓐ Ⓑ Ⓒ Ⓓ
9. Ⓐ Ⓑ Ⓒ Ⓓ   21. Ⓐ Ⓑ Ⓒ Ⓓ   33. Ⓐ Ⓑ Ⓒ Ⓓ   45. Ⓐ Ⓑ Ⓒ Ⓓ   57. Ⓐ Ⓑ Ⓒ Ⓓ
10. Ⓐ Ⓑ Ⓒ Ⓓ   22. Ⓐ Ⓑ Ⓒ Ⓓ   34. Ⓐ Ⓑ Ⓒ Ⓓ   46. Ⓐ Ⓑ Ⓒ Ⓓ   58. Ⓐ Ⓑ Ⓒ Ⓓ
11. Ⓐ Ⓑ Ⓒ Ⓓ   23. Ⓐ Ⓑ Ⓒ Ⓓ   35. Ⓐ Ⓑ Ⓒ Ⓓ   47. Ⓐ Ⓑ Ⓒ Ⓓ   59. Ⓐ Ⓑ Ⓒ Ⓓ
12. Ⓐ Ⓑ Ⓒ Ⓓ   24. Ⓐ Ⓑ Ⓒ Ⓓ   36. Ⓐ Ⓑ Ⓒ Ⓓ   48. Ⓐ Ⓑ Ⓒ Ⓓ   60. Ⓐ Ⓑ Ⓒ Ⓓ

PRINCIPLES OF SUPERVISION DIAGNOSTIC TEST

Directions: Carefully read each of the following 20 questions. Choose the best answer to each question and fill in the corresponding circle on the answer sheet. The Answer Key and Explanations can be found following this Diagnostic Test.

1. Which of the following is not a twenty-first century global challenge faced by business management?
   A. International trade agreements
   B. Exchange rates
   C. Cultural environments
   D. Organizational size

2. Who of the following is in daily contact with blue-collar workers in an organization?
   A. Middle-level manager
   B. Tactical manager
   C. Operational manager
   D. Strategic manager

3. Which of the following is on the highest level of Maslow's hierarchy of needs?
   A. Shelter
   B. Achievement
   C. Security
   D. Friendship

4. The management process used to compare actual performance to organizational goals is known as
   A. produce.
   B. inspect.
   C. control.
   D. plan.

5. Which of the following terms is commonly used to refer to the system of behavior and rituals that distinguishes one company from another in the same industry?
   A. Organization
   B. Environment
   C. Society
   D. Culture

6. Which of the following focuses on short-term goals of an organization?
   A. Strategic planning
   B. Control planning
   C. Operational planning
   D. Tactical planning

7. Internal environmental factors that affect how a medical device company functions include all of the following EXCEPT:
   A. Company profit sharing policies
   B. A change in the company's upper management
   C. Changes by the FDA to certain medical device regulations
   D. Relocation of the company to new offices

8. The ability of a manager to diagnose and solve problems is a function of
   A. people skills.
   B. computer skills.
   C. analytical skills.
   D. conceptual skills.

9. Which of the following terms is commonly used to refer to the process of assigning tasks to subordinates?
   A. Delegation
   B. Accountability
   C. Authority
   D. Responsibility

10. All of the following exert a direct and immediate influence upon the daily activities of a business EXCEPT:
    A. Competitor pricing
    B. Customer spending
    C. Raw material quality
    D. Population shifts

11. Setting goals for employees and closely supervising quality and accuracy are behaviors that describe
    A. transformational leadership.
    B. charismatic leadership.
    C. group maintenance leadership.
    D. task performance leadership.

12. The ten roles of managers were first identified by
    A. Carly Fiorina.
    B. Henry Mintzberg.
    C. Rensis Likert.
    D. Abraham Maslow.

13. Directing and monitoring ongoing activities during production at a factory are typical of
    A. clan control.
    B. feedback control.
    C. concurrent control.
    D. feedforward control.

14. A person who buys four pairs of shoes at an outlet mall is best described as a(n)
    A. intermediate consumer.
    B. wholesale consumer.
    C. mass consumer.
    D. final consumer.

15. Which of the following methods of departmentalization is most likely to trigger confusion regarding authority?
    A. Product organization
    B. Matrix organization
    C. Customer organization
    D. Functional organization

16. The Sarbanes-Oxley Act was enacted in response to
    A. corporate accounting scandals.
    B. age discrimination lawsuits.
    C. sexual harassment complaints.
    D. hazardous waste disposal.

17. Which of the following serves as a benchmark for performance assessment?
    A. Reward
    B. Standard
    C. Vision
    D. Expectancy

18. General influences on a business, such as regulatory agencies and global markets, are known as the
    A. competitive environment.
    B. macro environment.
    C. internal environment.
    D. microenvironment.

19. Which of the following is NOT one of the four established functions of management?
    A. Evaluating
    B. Leading
    C. Planning
    D. Controlling

20. A leader who has a personality that employees find admirable is most likely using
    A. expert power.
    B. coercive power.
    C. referent power.
    D. legitimate power.

ANSWER KEY AND EXPLANATIONS

1. D	**5.** D	**9.** A	**13.** C	**17.** B
2. C	**6.** C	**10.** D	**14.** D	**18.** B
3. B	**7.** C	**11.** D	**15.** B	**19.** A
4. C	**8.** C	**12.** B	**16.** A	**20.** C

1. **The correct answer is D.** Organizational size was at one time a challenge faced by business management striving to stay competitive, but global factors have changed the business landscape. Technology has made competition fiercer, and choices A, B, and C are all factors that impact a business's ability to compete globally.

2. **The correct answer is C.** Frontline or operational managers are in daily contact with the workers in an organization. Middle-level managers (choice A) and tactical managers (choice B) are synonymous, and they are the link between top-level managers and frontline managers. Strategic managers, or top-level managers (choice D), are responsible for long-term planning rather than daily operations.

3. **The correct answer is B.** Achievement falls in the category of esteem, which is near the top of Maslow's hierarchy of needs. Shelter (choice A) is a physiological need at the bottom, followed by security (choice C). Friendship (choice D) is an element of social needs, which are beneath esteem and self-actualization.

4. **The correct answer is C.** The control process is a management function used to compare actual performance with organizational goals and standards. Controlling and planning are two closely connected management functions. Choices A, B, and D are incorrect.

5. **The correct answer is D.** *Organizational culture* is the term used to refer to the system of behavior and rituals that distinguish one company from another. Managers define the culture of a business through employee training, motivational methods, and behavioral expectations. Choices A, B, and C

are not terms that describe the goals and practices shared by employees of a company.

6. **The correct answer is C.** Operational planning focuses on the short-term plans of an organization, which are typically less than two years. Strategic planning relates to long-term goals, and tactical planning involves intermediate-term goals.

7. **The correct answer is C.** Changes by a regulatory agency are considered external environmental factors. Changes to company profit sharing, changes to upper management, or relocating company offices are all internal environmental factors, making choices A, B, and D incorrect.

8. **The correct answer is C.** Analytical skills refer to a manager's ability to diagnose and solve problems. A manager with good people skills works well with others, so choice A is incorrect. Computer skills refer to a manager's ability to use business software to maximize job performance, so choice B is incorrect. Conceptual skills involve seeing the big picture and developing long-range plans.

9. **The correct answer is A.** Delegation involves assigning tasks or responsibilities to subordinates. Accountability is the expectation that a worker will complete a task or face consequences. Authority is the power to make a decision.

10. **The correct answer is D.** A population shift is an indirect force on a business that has long-term effects. Competitors, customers, and suppliers are direct forces on an organization that have immediate and daily effects. The price of a competitor's product influences consumer spending, and the quality of raw materials provided by a supplier affects the quality of a product made by a business.

11. **The correct answer is D.** Goal setting and close supervision characterize task performance leadership. Transformational leaders (choice A) motivate others to focus on the good of the group. Charismatic leaders (choice B) arouse excitement in followers. Group maintenance leaders (choice C) focus on group stability and harmony.

12. **The correct answer is B.** Henry Mintzberg is an academic who conducted research about management roles. Carly Fiorina (choice A) is the former CEO of Hewlett-Packard. Rensis Likert (choice C) researched management styles and developed the linking pin model. Abraham Maslow (choice D) developed the theory of a hierarchy of needs.

13. **The correct answer is C.** Concurrent control focuses on directing, monitoring, and modifying ongoing activities related to any type of business operation. Clan control (choice A) is not typically used to manage specific tasks like manufacturing. Feedback control (choice B) takes place before activities begin. Feedforward control (choice D) evaluates results.

14. **The correct answer is D.** Final consumers purchase products or services in their completed form. Intermediate consumers buy raw materials from wholesalers to make products to sell to final consumers, so choice A is incorrect. Choices B and C are not terms related to consumer types that are a direct environmental force on organizations.

15. **The correct answer is B.** The Matrix organization is most likely to cause employees confusion regarding who is in charge because of its dual line of command. Matrix organization is a blending of functional and product organization. Choices A, C, and D are incorrect.

16. **The correct answer is A.** The Sarbanes-Oxley Act was enacted in 2002 in response to corporate accounting scandals at Enron and WorldCom. The law established strict accounting rules that make top-level managers more responsible for violations. The Sarbanes-Oxley Act does not address age discrimination lawsuits (choice B), sexual harassment complaints (choice C), or hazardous waste disposal (choice D).

17. **The correct answer is B.** Standards serve as benchmarks for performance assessments and clarify desired performance levels. In the control function, the first step involves setting performance standards based on quantity, quality, time, and cost. Choices A, C, and D are incorrect.

18. **The correct answer is B.** *Macro environment* refers to general influences on a business, which are also known as indirect forces. Indirect forces include laws, economies, technological advancements, and global markets. Choice A refers to direct forces, such as suppliers and customers. The internal environment of an organization is employees, management style, and organizational culture.

19. **The correct answer is A.** The four functions of management as developed by Henri Fayol are planning, organizing, leading, and controlling. Evaluating is not one of the specified functions, although evaluation occurs in the organizing stage. Choices B, C, and D are incorrect.

20. **The correct answer is C.** A leader with a personality that employees find admirable is using referent power. Expert power (choice A) refers to a leader's experience. A leader with coercive power (choice B) controls punishments that employees want to avoid. Legitimate power is the authority to tell subordinates what to do.

DIAGNOSTIC TEST ASSESSMENT GRID

Now that you've completed the diagnostic test and read through the answer explanations, you can use your results to target your studying. Find the question numbers from the diagnostic test that you answered incorrectly and highlight or circle them below. Then focus extra attention on the sections within the chapter dealing with those topics.

Principles of Supervision		
Content Area	**Topics Covered**	**Questions**
Roles and Responsibilities of Managers and Supervisors	• Evolution of management/supervision • Knowledge and skill requirements • Managerial roles • Levels of management • Business ethics and corporate social responsibility	2, 8, 12, 16
Management Functions	• Planning • Organizing and staffing • Leading • Controlling	3, 4, 6, 9, 11, 13, 15, 17, 19, 20
Organizational Environment	• Legal, political, economic, and social • Labor-management relations (e.g., union vs. non-union, exempt vs. non-exempt) • Organizational culture • Diversity and inclusion • Global • Sustainable environments • Organizational change • Workplace safety and security	1, 5, 7, 10, 14, 18

GET THE FACTS

To see the DSST® ® Principles of Supervision Fact Sheet, go to **http://getcollegecredit.com/exam_fact_sheets** and click on the **Business** tab. Scroll down and click the **Principles of Supervision** link. Here you will find suggestions for further study material and the ACE college credit recommendations for passing the test.

ROLES AND RESPONSIBILITIES OF THE SUPERVISOR

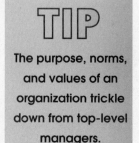

Effective managers facilitate the activities within organizations through planning, organizing, leading, and controlling. Managers use the **principles of supervision** to guide the work of others and to help an organization meet its short-term needs and accomplish its long-term goals.

THE EVOLUTION OF MANAGEMENT AND SUPERVISION

Modern management could be said to have begun with the **industrial revolution**. Prior to that, there were only a few entities large and sophisticated enough to require the kinds of planning, control, and resource allocation associated with management: the Church; armies and navies, and the governments which sponsored them; and large agricultural enterprises requiring that someone manage the workers and processes peculiar to agriculture. But prior to the industrial revolution--which would come to directly influence agricultural practices, including planting, harvesting, and the division of labor responsible for those—not even the largest of farms and plantations were home to anything resembling modern management.

The Industrial Revolution & Scientific Management

The industrial revolution allowed production at a scale never seen before, and the owners of the new, larger enterprises were no longer able to efficiently oversee large operations that required layers of control in order to efficiently mass produce goods. Production at that scale required unheard of levels of quality control, specialization of labor, standardized processes, accounting, and workflow planning.

The industrial revolution made almost inevitable the idea that organizations themselves could be considered machines in their own right: the idea that management was itself a discipline that could be studied, measured, and improved upon naturally followed.

The best known proponent of this sort of "**scientific management**" was Frederick Taylor, who argued in the early 1900s that businesses should be run in a scientific, efficient manner. Taylor felt that the scientific method, applied to the management of business, would result in businesses that outperformed earlier institutions run by brilliant (but unscientific) "captains of industry." Taylor sought the one "best" practice that would lead to optimum performance, and to arrive at that optimum, Taylor sought to break down complex tasks into easily repeatable subtasks the performance (and output) of which could be accurately measured.

Taylor's scientific management was in effect a **mechanistic** view that tended to regard employees as replaceable cogs in the business "machine," and critics have charged that, while the approach did increase production, it also resulted in the dehumanization of workers.

Social Science & Bureaucratic Management

By the 1950s, social scientists, including sociologist and economist **Max Weber**, showed that insights from such disciplines as psychology and sociology could be brought to bear on theories of management. At the same time, writers such as Peter Drucker, in *Concept of the Corporation* (1946), began exploring the idea that *knowledge* was itself a valuable commodity. Information was of value not only in and of itself, said Drucker, but also because information--and tools that allowed workers to acquire and share information--made workers and managers more effective and efficient. Information, noted Drucker and others, creates value over and above the exchange of goods and services that were traditionally a company's products. Also, it became obvious that information itself could in fact *be* a product, and what came to be called "knowledge work" quickly became a much larger proportion of the economy.

Weber is often thought of as a fan of large, impersonal bureaucracies, which is an oversimplification. He felt that a well-organized bureaucracy could indeed be efficient, but cautioned against excessively large bureaucracies, noting that in one, a worker begins to feel like a little cog in a machine, and thus becomes overly preoccupied with the idea of becoming, as Weber put it, "a bigger cog."

Theory X and Theory Y: The Human Relations Movement

Much valuable information resides in the heads of employees, so a great deal of value or potential value walks out of the door every evening--and may never return. This realization led to a school of thought that began to treat employees as important assets; a great deal of a company's capital is invested in hardware, machinery, raw materials, and plant, but much capital also resides in the minds of its employees. Some researchers began to think about how important it might be for a company to *engage* its employees rather than to control them. Sometimes called the **Human Relations Movement**, the new approach was characterized by companies beginning to pay more attention to individuals and their motivational needs, reflecting a growing belief that if the employees prospered, the company would also benefit.

The Human Relations Movement really had its roots in Elton Mayo's famous **Hawthorne Works experiments** during the 1920s. (The experiments took place at the Hawthorne, Illinois, plant of the Western Electric Company.) During those experiments, Mayo studied the effects of various sorts of lighting on worker productivity. The results indicated that there *were* no discernable effects that one could ascribe to lighting, so Mayo began looking at other variables, including meals, rest breaks, the number of hours worked, etc. Unexpectedly, productivity went up at *every* change, and when everyone was returned to their original hours and conditions, productivity went up again. This seemed to indicate that the **social dynamic** (the workers had begun to think of themselves as a team) had more to do with increasing productivity than did finding what Taylor would have called the "one best way" to accomplish their tasks.

Douglas McGregor, of the MIT Sloan School of Management, described **Theory Y,** an optimistic approach that was opposed to the more pessimistic **Theory X** that he felt was often employed. While Theory X stressed strict supervision, direct managerial control, and external motivators, Theory Y was more optimistic: it presumed that providing job satisfaction, self-determination, and autonomy actually yielded better results.

Contemporary Management Theories

In the mid-60s and beyond, Blake & Mouton employed a **management grid** to describe management styles by placing those styles on a matrix that plotted "concern for people" along one axis, and "concern for production (or tasks)" along the other. Leaders were placed in one or more quadrants, based on how they scored on a questionnaire. The idea was that there was a "sweet spot" on the grid; the most desirable place for a leader would be to score highly on both the Task and People measures, but with the understanding that certain situations may call for the other quadrants to be used. For instance, there are times when being authoritarian might serve a manager (and the team) well by instilling a sense of discipline.

In the 1990s, Peter Senge wrote (in *The Fifth Discipline: The Art and Practice of the Learning Organization*) that managers need to think of businesses as complex, growing systems—i.e., as organic entities that constantly respond to various feedback mechanisms. Gone were the days of the staid, stable company that could operate in the same way 20 years after its founding as it did when first established.

Also in the 1990s, **BPM** (business process management) emerged as a tool to help improve company efficiency and responsiveness. BPM focuses on improving a company's business processes, in some ways recalling Taylor's mechanistic views of "the one best way" to accomplish and optimize tasks. But central to the modern interpretation is the idea that managers should concentrate on *processes* used to complete tasks, rather than just on the tasks themselves. In fact, one key to the success of BPM is that it forces businesses (i.e., managers) to realize that processes are in fact necessary in the first place, and that these processes should be thoughtfully, purposely, and purposefully designed, rather than simply having evolved.

Daniel Pink, in his 2011 book, *Drive*, examines motivation, and argues that the old reward/punishment paradigm is no longer an effective approach to employee motivation. Instead, he proposes that three things motivate people: **autonomy** (control over one's life), **mastery** (the need to achieve and to improve), and **purpose** (the desire to be a part of something larger than ourselves, and to act in service of that larger something).

In the 2000s, management approaches continue to evolve, with companies facing new challenges in data management and security, and also attempting to address new technologies and legal requirements. As a result, companies continue to seek new management techniques and tools to help them deal with this dynamic new environment.

KNOWLEDGE AND SKILL REQUIREMENTS

The global and technical nature of modern organizations calls for managers with a range of skills:

- Technical
- Analytical
- Decision making
- Conceptual
- Computer
- Communication
- Interpersonal

Technical skills refer to the ability to perform a specific task that requires knowledge of certain techniques, processes, and resources. Engineering directors, sales managers, and construction supervisors must have technical skills in their field to manage workers and to solve problems. For example, a director of an accounting department needs to understand accounting practices, while a nursing director needs the skills to perform medical procedures. Frontline managers require more technical skills than middle- and top-level managers do because frontline managers deal with daily operations and problems.

Analytical skills refer to a manager's ability to identify problems and develop solutions. Reasoning capabilities are necessary to understand a complex issue, but computer software is available to assist in analyzing data. Supervisors use software to monitor inventory, oversee budgets, and manage staff assignments. Such analytical tools assist managers in diagnosing, evaluating, and solving problems in the workplace.

Managers at every level of an organization use **decision-making skills** on a daily basis. Effective managers separate themselves from ineffective managers by the quality of their decisions. Analytical skills influence decision-making skills, and inadequate reasoning leads to poor decisions. In some instances, supervisors seek advice from a group before making a choice that involves several options, but some problems require quick decisions.

In conjunction with analyzing situations and making decisions is the capacity to understand the big picture. **Conceptual skills** refer to a supervisor's ability to perceive the objectives and strategies of an organization, to realize the interconnections within an organization, and to comprehend the role of the firm in the outside world. Top-level managers utilize their conceptual skills frequently as they make decisions regarding a firm's long-term strategy. For example, the CEO of a corporation attempts to forecast the future when considering mergers, acquisitions, and investments.

Computer skills are necessary for the success of today's managers. Managers do not necessarily need to know how to write programs, but they do need to know how to use business software. Supervisors must be proficient with software in order to generate spreadsheets, create presentations, schedule meetings, and manipulate data. Web-based businesses require supervisors who have the computer skills to monitor digital sales, manage international supply chains, and oversee website development. Quickly changing technology calls for supervisors who have both the technical knowledge and the desire to advance their computer skills.

Communication and interpersonal skills are closely connected concepts in management. The ability to convey ideas clearly is essential for success because managers communicate with employees and executives constantly. Communication skills refer to the ability to explain ideas orally or in writing to others. Effective managers encourage questions from employees to make certain everyone is on the same page. Managers who need results from their employees must clearly communicate what is required or everyone fails. Supervisors need **interpersonal skills**, or **people skills**, to develop strong relationships with other members of the organization. Managers spend the bulk of their days interacting with people, so the ability to lead, motivate, understand, and work with others is critical to success. Often supervisors fail due to a lack of people skills rather than a lack of technical or analytical skills. Showing appreciation, listening actively, resolving conflicts, expressing empathy, and creating a positive work environment are skills not often taught in school, but they are the characteristics of excellent supervisors.

Managers at every level actively work to acquire and develop the skills needed for efficient supervision in the workplace. Frontline, middle-level, and top-level managers need computer skills, interpersonal skills, decision-making skills, and communication skills. Frontline managers use technical skills often because they are close to employees who are performing specific technical tasks. Middle management and top management positions call for analytical skills, while top executives in an organization require conceptual skills.

MANAGERIAL ROLES

A **role** is a job-related behavioral expectation. **Henry Mintzberg**, a Canadian academic, has conducted research and written books about management. Mintzberg's most often cited study involved observing and interviewing five CEOs from different industries over a two-week period. Upon reviewing the information he collected, Mintzberg identified ten roles of managers:

1. Figurehead
2. Leader
3. Liaison
4. Monitor
5. Disseminator
6. Spokesperson
7. Entrepreneur
8. Disturbance Handler
9. Resource Allocator
10. Negotiator

Since many of the roles are closely related, Mintzberg sorted them into three general categories: interpersonal, informational, and decisional. The interpersonal roles—figurehead, leader, and liaison—stem from the formal authority of a supervisor and the interpersonal skills used in the position. Most managers are required to serve as figureheads when they perform ceremonial duties or receive visitors. Examples include a high school principal handing out diplomas to graduates and a manufacturing manager giving a tour of a new facility to stockholders. In the leadership role, a manager directs and coordinates the duties of subordinates. As a leader, a manager hires and fires personnel and ensures that tasks are progressing properly. The liaison role requires managers to maintain communication with individuals inside and outside of an organization. In general, the interpersonal roles of a manager relate to providing information to others and developing interpersonal relationships.

As a monitor, disseminator, and spokesperson, a manager processes information. In the informational role, a manager receives and sends information. As a monitor, a manager assesses the successes, problems, and opportunities that may affect a unit, such as trends or sales. Managers act as disseminators by relaying confidential information to subordinates, such as when a CEO learns about quality concerns from a large customer and instructs a vice president to handle the problem personally. The role of disseminator often requires a manager to filter information and to delegate responsibilities. A manager represents a unit or a group of people when acting as a spokesperson internally or externally.

For example, a sales manager may attempt to persuade executives to pay bonuses to the sales team when acting as an internal spokesperson. When serving as an external spokesperson, a manager serves in a public relations capacity by representing the views of the organization to outsiders, such as civic organizations or the media.

Entrepreneur, disturbance handler, resource allocator, and negotiator are elements of the decisional role. Many people consider the decisional role more important than a manager's interpersonal or informational roles. Making improvements to the unit is the objective of the entrepreneurial role. For example, a restaurant manager is constantly planning changes to the menu and the service to meet customer needs. Taking quick measures to control immediate problems and to create stability is an aspect of the disturbance handler role. A frontline manager who responds to broken equipment or striking workers is acting as a disturbance handler attempting to return the work environment to normal. The resource allocator determines how to distribute limited resources, such as money, people, time, and equipment. Decisions regarding how many workers to assign to a project and how much money to allocate for upgrading office equipment are related to a manager's role as resource allocator. As negotiators, managers bargain with others to acquire benefits for their unit. Executives negotiate salaries and benefits with labor union representatives, and office managers negotiate work schedules with employees.

The ten roles of a manager illustrate three general ideas:

1. The roles explain what management entails and illustrate how the roles are connected.

2. Neglecting one or more of the roles prevents subordinates from working effectively.

3. The significance of each role illustrates the need for supervisors to manage their time well.

According to Mintzberg, managers need to be both specialists and generalists for success in any organization. A specialist is an expert at a specific discipline, such as marketing, accounting, or sales. A generalist has a broad understanding of a variety of business elements that provides managerial perspective. The numerous roles expected of managers call for varied skills to handle complex situations.

LEVELS OF MANAGEMENT

Most large organizations have three different levels of management: frontline (also referred to as first-level or first-line), middle-level, and top-level. A **frontline manager** is a lower-level manager within an organization. Depending on the organization, a frontline manager may be referred to as a supervisor, office manager, foreman, or operational manager. Whatever the title, a frontline manager oversees daily operational activities and serves as the connection between management and employees. Frontline managers supervise the work of various units within an organization, such as sales, marketing, accounting, production, and information technology.

Middle-level managers oversee frontline managers and report to top-level managers. Tactical manager, department manager, plant manager, and director of operations are other titles for middle-level managers. Middle-level managers translate the ideas and objectives developed by top-level executives into specific goals and activities for frontline managers. A middle-level manager interprets corporate objectives into plans for the different units within an organization. Beginning in the early 1990s, corporate reorganizations no longer affected only blue-collar workers. In addition, reorganizations began eliminating many middle-level management positions, a trend that has continued though the financial crisis of the early 2000s and into the current business climate. Flatter, leaner organizations are more desirable; these theoretically have the flexibility to adapt quickly.

Top-level managers, or strategic managers, are the smallest and highest tier of management. The senior executives in an organization, such as the chief executive officer, chief operating officer, president, and vice president, constitute top-level management. Responsible for the performance and effectiveness of an organization, a top-level manager reports to the board of directors, owners, and stockholders of a corporation. Top-level managers concentrate on the long-term issues and growth strategies that middle-level managers broadcast to frontline managers for implementation

BUSINESS ETHICS

Ethics are a system of rules that distinguishes between right and wrong. Business ethics refer to the moral principles that dictate behavior in the business realm. In most cases, customers, society, competitors, and special interest groups judge whether a business acts ethically. However, attempts have been made to institute **universal business ethics.** Swiss executives initiated the **Caux Principles** in conjunction with business leaders from Europe, Japan, and the United States. The two main concepts of the Caux Principles include showing concern for human dignity and working for the common good, a concept known as *kyosei*.

Although universal ethical principles are useful, laws are often required to ensure ethical business practices. In response to corporate scandals, such as those at Enron and WorldCom, the U.S. Congress enacted the **Sarbanes-Oxley Act** in 2002. The law sets strict accounting and reporting rules that make top-level managers more accountable in an attempt to promote ethical behavior within public companies. In addition to laws, business ethics are influenced by ethical standards established within organizations. A company's code of ethics typically addresses conduct of employees, shareholders, customers, and suppliers.

Some organizations develop corporate ethics programs. In addition to an ethics code, an ethics program establishes committees to investigate ethics violations, communication systems to help employees report violations, and disciplinary procedures for employees found guilty of unethical activities. Ethics programs are either compliance-based, integrity-based, or somewhere in between.

- **Compliance-based ethics programs** are designed by an organization's lawyers to prevent, expose, and discipline violations; these programs involve establishing legal procedures and having top-level managers monitor compliance.

- **Integrity-based ethics programs** are designed to instill personal and ethical responsibility among employees; organizations and workers self-govern based on established guidelines with which they concur.

CORPORATE SOCIAL RESPONSIBILITY

Corporate social responsibility refers to the obligations that a business has toward society. A socially responsible company attempts to increase the positive impact it has on society and decrease its negative impact. Social responsibilities are divided into four major categories:

1. *Economic responsibility:* produce goods and services that society desires and that are profitable
2. *Legal responsibility:* obey local, state, federal, and international laws
3. *Ethical responsibility:* meet society's moral expectations
4. *Philanthropic responsibility:* participate in desirable behaviors and activities, such as contributing to charities

In recent years, many businesses have combined the concepts of social responsibility and capitalism: socio-capitalism. Once considered divergent philosophies, profit and social responsibility have been blended in many for-profit businesses, such as those that provide services to the poor or the physically impaired.

MANAGEMENT FUNCTIONS

In the early 1900s, **Henri Fayol,** a French business owner, developed the first general theory of management. Fayol wrote a book about his management experiences in the mining industry. He expressed the idea that professional management involves five primary functions: planning, organizing, leading, coordinating, and controlling. Despite the numerous books that have been written in the last century about management, Fayolism remains the most influential theory. However, Fayol's original five functions have been reduced to four, which are discussed in the next sections:

1. Plan
2. Organize
3. Lead
4. Control

PLANNING

Planning is the first function of management and directs the way in which managers organize, lead, and control. Planning requires managers to create proactive plans to accomplish the goals and objectives of an organization. Managers consider a number of factors when developing plans:

- **Resources:** organizational, human, financial, and physical
- **Opportunities and risks:** innovations, competition, and demand

TIP

Although planning is difficult due to the fluctuating nature of direct and indirect forces, effective and efficient managers develop plans to handle future changes in the business environment.

Planning is a process of making decisions. The following table outlines the six basic steps involved in the planning process.

Step 1: Situational analysis	Process used by planners to gather, analyze, and summarize relevant data; process reviews past events, identifies current conditions, anticipates future trends, and considers internal and external forces; results in identification of decisions that need to be made and helps managers decide whether to move to next step in process
Step 2: Alternative goals and plans	Generate alternate goals (desired targets) and plans (actions to achieve goals); stress creativity and open minds of managers and employees
Step 3: Goal and plan evaluation	Evaluate pros, cons, and possible outcomes of each alternative goal and plan; prioritize and eliminate goals and plans
Step 4: Goal and plan selection	Select plan and goal that is most practical and possible; requires experienced judgment
Step 5: Implementation	Implement the chosen plan once managers and employees understand the plan and the necessary resources become available
Step 6: Monitor and control	Monitor subordinates regarding implementation of the plan; create control systems to measure performance and take corrective actions when necessary

It should be noted that in Step 2, there are three different types of plans that may be developed. **Single-use plans** are intended to accomplish a set of goals one time only. An example of a single-use plan is a grand opening celebration for the opening of a new hospital wing. **Standing plans** are established for ongoing activities that accomplish constant goals, such as a corporation's plan to recruit minorities. Standing plans often develop into corporate policies. **Contingency plans** are established when an initial plan fails or events call for immediate changes. Many organizations have contingency plans for dealing with major disasters to make sure that both data and employees stay safe.

Levels of Planning

Just as there are three levels of management—frontline, middle-level, and top-level—there are three levels of planning that vary in scope and activities.

1. *Strategic planning* focuses on an organization's long-term (more than five years) goals and strategies in general terms. Strategic plans clarify the company's mission and goals for the future, and they are developed by top-level managers. For example, a firm's strategic plan may involve penetrating a new market.

2. *Tactical planning* involves developing specific and intermediate-term (two to five years) goals and plans for implementing elements of the strategic plan. For example, tactical plans, which are implemented by middle management, may include designing and testing equipment needed for a new product.

3. *Operational planning* involves translating tactical plans into specific steps in the short-term (less than two years). Frontline managers implement operational plans, which may require scheduling production runs and staffing.

Strategic Management

In the past, strategic plans filtered downward from the top of an organization, but, in recent years, tactical and operational managers have participated in the strategic planning process. Top executives have learned through experience that middle-level and frontline managers offer valuable input and ideas. **Strategic management** is the term used to describe the process of multi-level managers working together to develop and implement a firm's goals and strategies. The strategic management process is composed of six steps:

1. Establish mission, vision, and goals
2. Analyze external opportunities and threats
3. Analyze internal strengths and weaknesses
4. Perform a SWOT analysis and formulate strategy
5. Implement strategy
6. Implement strategic control system

In the first step of the strategic management process, managers develop a mission statement that conveys the purpose of the organization. Effective mission statements focus on the customer, and they are attainable, inspirational, and specific. A strategic vision is the desired future direction of an organization, while strategic goals are the primary targets.

The mission, vision, and goals of an organization drive the second step of the process, which is analyzing the external environment. Managers study industry growth rates, market segments, and consumer purchasing power. Managers also analyze competitors, political activity related to the industry, social issues, labor issues, macroeconomic conditions, and technological factors.

During the third step, managers conduct an analysis of the strengths and weaknesses of significant internal components, such as finances, human resources, marketing activities, and manufacturing capabilities. Management also assesses the resources of the organization to determine its core competencies. **Core competencies** refer to the special skills or knowledge held by organizations that are especially valuable and rare. The core competence of a company is what it does better than the competition. For example, the core competence of Intel is complex chip design, while the core competence of Honda is small engine manufacturing.

After managers have gathered the information regarding the external and internal environment, they perform a SWOT analysis. A **SWOT analysis** is a comparison of the organization's strengths, weaknesses, opportunities, and threats, and it provides managers with a helpful way to summarize the relevant information gathered in the environmental analysis. Managers then formulate three levels of strategy based on the SWOT analysis.

Levels of Strategy	
Corporate-level strategy	Focuses on the big picture and how to accomplish the organization's goal; may involve concentration on a single business, diversification, or vertical integration
Business-level strategy	Focuses on the way in which a business competes in a specific industry or market for competitive advantage; may implement a low-cost strategy to make basic, inexpensive products or a differentiation strategy to make unique, high-quality products
Functional-level strategy	Implemented by functional units in an organization, such as production, human resources, marketing, finance, and distribution; creates value for the consumer

In the fifth step of strategic planning, managers monitor whether strategies are being implemented appropriately. **Strategy implementation** requires middle-level and frontline managers to define strategic tasks, evaluate the organization's ability to complete the tasks, create an agenda for implementation, and develop an implementation plan. Implementation is followed by **strategic control**, which is a system that helps managers evaluate the organization's progress and correct problems when necessary.

ORGANIZING AND STAFFING

Structuring a company's human and physical resources in a way that achieves organizational objectives is the process of organizing. Tasks, people, and departments all require organization to accomplish a company's goals. One of the initial steps in organizing is determining the organizational structure, which is the configuration of tasks and departments in a business. Organization charts visually clarify the reporting structure and levels of management. Differentiation and integration form the basis of organizational structure.

- **Differentiation:** an organization consists of different units that work on different tasks with different work methods and skills. Differentiation occurs through the division of labor and task specialization.

- **Integration:** the extent that different units in an organization coordinate their efforts to create a product or service.

Organizations with numerous specialized tasks and units are highly differentiated. In such businesses, there is a greater need for integration to ensure that all areas of an organization are working toward accomplishing the same goal.

Authority in Organizations

Authority in an organization refers to the sanctioned right to make a decision or tell others what to do. For example, the vice president of sales has the authority to give an order to a sales representative. Hierarchy establishes authority in an organization. In private businesses, the owners hold the greatest authority, but in publicly owned businesses, stockholders are the owners. Since stockholders lack the most current information needed to make wise decisions, a board of directors oversees an organization.

A board of directors serves four primary duties:

1. Choosing, evaluating, rewarding, and, when necessary, replacing the CEO
2. Assessing an organization's financial performance
3. Deciding an organization's strategic direction
4. Monitoring an organization's ethical, legal, and socially responsible activities

A board of directors is also responsible for reporting to stockholders, protecting the rights of stockholders, and advising management. As the senior member of top-level management, a CEO reports to the board of directors and is responsible for a firm's performance.

An important aspect of an organization's structure is its **span of control**, which is the number of subordinates who report to one manager. Wide spans form flat organizations with many workers reporting to one manager. A narrow span creates a tall organization with numerous reporting levels and fewer workers reporting to one manager. The ideal span of control depends on a number of variables:

- Competence of manager and workers
- Similarity or dissimilarity of tasks
- Amount of interaction required
- Degree to which tasks are standardized

Authority in an organization is dispersed over management levels and spans of control, so delegation is important. Delegation refers to assigning responsibilities to subordinates, and it occurs at every level of an organization as a method of accomplishing tasks through other people. Delegating authority forms a chain of command that defines the line of authority from the top of an organization to the bottom.

Managers who delegate assignments must consider the ideas of responsibility, authority, and accountability. **Responsibility** refers to an employee's obligation to carry out an assigned task. Managers must ensure that a subordinate who has a specific responsibility has the necessary authority. Does the worker have the power to make decisions and give orders? Is the worker able to use necessary resources to fulfill the responsibility? In many cases, subordinates are given responsibilities for which they have no authority. The effective use of delegation saves managers time, and it raises the quality of subordinates.

The delegation of **authority** in an organization is either centralized or decentralized. In centralized businesses, high-level managers make major decisions. Authority is distributed throughout a decentralized organization. Decentralization benefits an organization by helping managers at all levels develop decision-making skills. Moreover, the managers who are the most knowledgeable about a problem are the most qualified to make a decision.

In conjunction with responsibility and the delegation of authority is the concept of accountability. **Accountability** refers to the expectation that a worker will perform a job and that failure to do so will result in corrective measures. One method of accountability involves requiring status reports from subordinates regarding assigned tasks.

Horizontal Structure

The concepts of authority, span of control, and decentralization relate to the vertical nature of an organization, but the horizontal structure is equally important. **Departmentalization** refers to the process of subdividing a business into smaller units or departments. One of the primary methods of subdividing work is by distinguishing line departments from staff departments. **Line departments** are responsible for the primary activities of the organization, which may be making things, selling things, or providing customer service. At Ford Motor Company, line departments include product design, assembly, and distribution. **Staff departments** support line departments with people who have specialized or professional skills. Types of line departments at Ford include accounting, legal, public relations, and human resources.

TIP

A chain of command specifies a reporting relationship for communicating both upward and downward in an organization.

Organizations vary in the way they departmentalize, as indicated by the following table.

Functional organization	Units grouped according to specific activities like production, marketing, finance, and human resources; common in large and small businesses but best in stable environments; efficient use of resources; discourages communication across departments
Product organization	Units grouped around a specific product or product line; clear task responsibilities; flexibility makes it suitable for unstable environments; costly duplication of effort
Customer organization	Units grouped to serve customer needs, such as commercial or consumer accounts at a bank; costly duplication of activities
Geographic organization	Units grouped by defined territories, districts, regions, or countries; useful for firms with varying customer needs and characteristics; used most by multinational corporations; requires large and costly staff at headquarters
Matrix organization	Blending of functional and product organizations; originated in aerospace industry; dual line of command; workers placed in teams for specific tasks; decentralized decision making; vast communications network; can cause confusion regarding authority

Staffing

Skilled individuals are the most important element of any organization, so staffing is a critical part of any manager's job. Recruitment, selection, and outplacement are the three primary staffing functions in organizations. **Recruitment** refers to attracting a pool of job candidates with the skills and attitudes beneficial to an organization. Advertising, visiting universities, and using private employment agencies are some of the ways in which businesses recruit employees.

During the selection process, an organization chooses the best candidate for a position. Selection tools may include applications, résumés, interviews, background checks, drug tests, and performance tests. Whatever the screening method, managers should be aware of legal and illegal activities during staff selection.

| Legal and Illegal Screening Activities ||
Legal	Illegal
Ask if a person is authorized to work in the United States	Ask for proof of citizenship
Ask if a person has been convicted of a crime	Ask if a person has been arrested
Ask for proof of age after hiring	Require a birth certificate
Keep records for recording purposes about racial and ethnic identity	Ask for race, creed, or national origin on application or during interview

Staffing decisions involve more than recruiting and screening. Difficult economic times often force companies to downsize by laying off many employees at once. At such times, many firms offer outplacement services. **Outplacement** refers to the process of assisting dismissed workers find new jobs.

LEADING

Management positions in an organization offer the opportunity to exhibit leadership, which involves making changes and creating a vision for a firm. Successful leaders motivate others to overcome obstacles and accomplish organizational goals. At the core of effective leadership is **power**, the ability to influence other people to do something that they might not otherwise do. In a business setting, managers have five potential power sources.

Reward power	Leader controls valued rewards, such as pay raises, promotions, and bonuses.
Coercive power	Leader controls punishments that people want to avoid, such as below-average performance evaluations.
Expert power	Leader has expertise or knowledge that people trust or believe.
Referent power	Leader has personal characteristics that trigger loyalty and admiration in others.
Legitimate power	Leader has the authority to tell others what to do, so people are obligated to comply.

Classic Approaches to Understanding Leadership

Leadership with regard to management has been studied and researched over the years. The three most widely accepted classic approaches for understanding leadership are the trait approach, the behavioral approach, and the situational approach.

Trait theory was the earliest attempt to define leadership qualities. The study occurred between 1904 and 1948 and focused on more than 100 leadership traits. The trait approach attempted to uncover the personal characteristics shared by exceptional leaders. The trait theory assumes that leaders are born with characteristics such as self-assurance, intelligence, sociability, and aggressiveness. However, upon completion of the study, scholars determined that no specific characteristics were essential for someone to become a great leader. The modern perspective regarding trait theory is that some personality attributes appear to separate successful leaders from other people. Drive, integrity, self-confidence, and business knowledge distinguish leaders from followers.

The **behavioral theory of leadership** attempts to identify the behaviors of effective leaders. Experts have identified three general leadership behavior categories: task-oriented, people-oriented, and directive/participative leadership.

Leader Behaviors		
Category	**Definition**	**Example Behaviors**
Task oriented	Task-oriented leaders focus their behaviors on the organizational structure and operating procedures and they tend to seek to control staff while focusing on the task at hand.	Initiating, setting goals, praising good work, supervising work quality.
People oriented	People oriented leaders attempt to ensure that the inner needs of people are satisfied, so they seek to motivate people by emphasizing the needs of staff members.	Showing concern for people's feelings, expressing appreciation, initiating, organizing, and clarifying.

Leader Behaviors		
Category	**Definition**	**Example Behaviors**
Directive or Participative Leadership	**Directive (Autocratic):** This approach leaves all decisions in the hands of management and gives instructions with the full expectation of having them followed; sometimes referred to as the "my way or the highway" approach.	Not soliciting input from employees, making all company decisions, mandating methods, procedures and policies; exhibiting little or no trust in the decision-making, ideas, suggestions, or advice of employees
	Participative (Democratic): This approach involves all team members in identifying goals, developing strategies, and in arriving at ways to achieve those goals. Actions are taken to involve employees in decision-making.	Soliciting input from employees, encouraging employees to identify performance gaps, using employee *satisfaction* surveys, rewarding employees for innovative ideas, and allowing employees to identify their own strengths and weaknesses.

The **Leader-Member Exchange (LMX) theory** relates to group maintenance behaviors. According to the LMX theory, group maintenance behaviors such as trust, mutual respect, mutual loyalty, and open communication form the basis of satisfying personal relationships with group members.

Situational theorists assert that universal leadership traits and behaviors are nonexistent and that effective leadership varies from one situation to another. Effective leaders analyze a situation before making a decision. The **Vroom model** for decision making and the **path-goal theory** are the primary situational models considered valid for modern management.

- **Vroom model:** a situational model proposed by Victor H. Vroom that helps leaders decide how much participation to use in decision making. The model works like a funnel, asking the leader questions until reaching a recommended decision style. Decide, consult individually, consult the group, facilitate, and delegate are the five possible decision styles.

- **Path-goal theory:** a theory developed by Robert House that assesses characteristics of the followers and environmental factors before determining the appropriate leadership behavior. The four leadership behaviors are directive leadership, supportive leadership, participative leadership, and achievement-oriented leadership. Appropriate leader behaviors lead to effective performance from the followers.

Modern Theories on Leadership

While the historical views on leadership remain relevant today, contemporary experts have developed their own ideas about different leadership styles:

- **Charismatic leader:** Arouses excitement, holds strong moral convictions, and conveys extreme self-confidence
- **Transformational leader:** Motivates people to focus on good of the group rather than personal interests
- **Transactional leader:** Uses legitimate, reward, and coercive powers to give orders in exchange for benefits to followers
- **Level 5 leader:** Combines determination and humility to build long-term leadership
- **Authentic leader:** Uses honesty, genuineness, reliability, and integrity to lead others; willing to sacrifice own interests
- **Pseudo transformational leader:** Speaks about positive change for followers but power, control, wealth, and fame take priority

Motivation

An important aspect of leading is **motivation**, which refers to the set of forces that energize, guide, and maintain a person's efforts. Managers are responsible for motivating employees to be punctual, work well with others, and perform quality work. Setting goals for employees is a valuable motivational tool. For goals to be effective, they should be acceptable to workers, challenging, and achievable. Some of today's large organizations set stretch goals for employees. Stretch goals are especially difficult, but they are attainable. Firms have found that stretch goals push employees out of mediocrity and toward excellence.

Reinforcement is another method of encouraging or discouraging employee behavior. Organizational behavior modification attempts to change worker behavior and improve job performance by managing work conditions and applying consequences for specific actions.

- **Positive reinforcement:** give a consequence that will encourage the behavior to be repeated, such as a letter of commendation, pay raise, or positive performance evaluation
- **Negative reinforcement:** stop, remove, or avoid an unpleasant consequence, such as taking a worker off probation due to improved job performance
- **Punishment:** give an unpleasant consequence, such as criticizing an employee or assigning a worker to an undesirable task or shift
- **Extinction:** fail to give a reinforcing consequence by not complimenting an employee for doing a good job or setting unachievable performance goals

Positive reinforcement is utilized the most in business settings. Effective managers find creative ways to motivate employees by both monetary and nonmonetary means.

While reinforcement theory focuses on how the work environment motivates people's behavior, expectancy theory focuses on how people make behavioral decisions based on expected outcomes. Vroom's expectancy theory is one of the most widely accepted motivation theories, and it is based on three variables.

1. *Expectancy:* an employee's belief that increased efforts will lead to achieving performance goals

2. *Instrumentality:* an employee's belief that good job performance will lead to a specific outcome

3. *Valence:* the value that an employee places on a specific outcome

Expectancy theory proposes that employee motivation is a function of all three variables working together. The theory offers a general method of understanding the complex nature of employee motivation.

Content theories of motivation stem from the idea that people want to satisfy basic needs. The three main content theories are Maslow's hierarchy of needs, Alderfer's ERG theory, and McClelland's needs.

Content Theories of Motivation	
Maslow's hierarchy of needs	People satisfy needs in a specific order; the needs in ascending order are physiological, safety, social, esteem, and self-actualization
Alderfer's ERG theory	People have three basic sets of needs: existence, relatedness, and growth
McClelland's needs	People have three dominant needs: achievement, affiliation, and power

CONTROLLING

Control is the fourth and final function of management. A control process directs employees toward achieving organizational goals and takes corrective measures when plans go unfulfilled. A lack of controls in an organization leads to any number of problems, such as poor product quality and employee theft. Three general methods exist for achieving organizational control.

1. *Bureaucratic control:* guides activities with formal rules, regulations, and authority, such as budgets and performance appraisals; best used for well-defined tasks and independent workers.

2. *Market control:* guides activities with pricing mechanisms and economic information, such as evaluation based on profits and losses; best used where output can be clearly identified.

3. *Clan control:* guides activities with norms, values, and trust with the assumption that the organization and the employee share the same interests; best used in environments where employees are empowered in decision making and where there is no explicit way to complete a task.

The bureaucratic, or formal, control system is the one most commonly used in organizations, although market and clan controls are valid methods for regulating employee performance. However, for the purpose of this review, the focus will be on bureaucratic control systems.

Control systems usually consist of four steps:

1. Setting performance standards
2. Measuring performance
3. Comparing performance with the standard
4. Taking corrective action

A standard is a performance target for an organizational goal. Standards clarify the desired performance level, motivate employee performance, and act as benchmarks for performance assessment. Any activity or unit within an organization—financial, legal, ethical—can have a set of expected standards. Performance standards are based on quantity, quality, time used, and cost.

Measuring performance is the second stage of the control process. Managers measure employee or unit performance by counting the number of dollars earned, products sold, and items manufactured. Written reports, oral reports, and personal observations provide management with the data needed to measure performance.

The third step in the control process involves **comparing performance with the established standards**. Managers analyze and evaluate performance results. According to the principle of exception, managers should focus attention on the cases that deviate significantly from the expected standard. For example, if five computer components out of every 1,000 produced on an assembly line are defective, a manager should investigate the five exceptions rather than the 995 other components. In addition, managers should not focus much time or effort on performance that is equal to or close to the standard. With the principle of exception, managers focus on the exceptions and not the norm to save valuable time.

The final step in the control process involves **taking corrective action** when significant deviations occur. During this step of control, adjustments are made to ensure that the planned results and goals are met. Corrective measures may be taken immediately by the manager or by subordinates involved directly with the problem. In the case of computerized manufacturing, two types of control may occur:

- **Specialist control:** employees who operate computer-numerical-control (CNC) machines notify engineering specialists about equipment problems, and the specialist corrects the issue.

- **Operator control:** trained operators repair problems as they occur, which can be more efficient than specialist control.

In addition to equipment malfunctions, corrective action may require altering a marketing approach, disciplining an employee, or providing specialized training for workers.

Managers choose from three approaches to bureaucratic control: **feedforward**, **concurrent**, and **feedback**.

1. *Feedforward control:* Focuses on preventing problems before they occur; enacted before operations start; involves policies, procedures, and rules that limit certain activities; also known as preliminary control

2. *Concurrent control:* Focuses on directing, monitoring, and modifying ongoing activities

3. *Feedback control:* Focuses on end results; uses performance data to correct deviations and guide future actions; Six Sigma is a feedback control tool used in manufacturing that aims to reduce defects

Auditing and Budgeting

A **management audit** is a type of control used to evaluate the effectiveness and efficiency of an organization. External audits are performed by an outside organization, such as an accounting firm. Internal audits are performed in-house to assess various elements of a firm, such as financial stability, public relations, social responsibility, and manufacturing efficiency.

Budgeting, or **budgetary controlling**, is a widely used control process that involves investigating what a firm has done. Results are compared with budget information for the purpose of verification and correction. Budgets connect feedforward, concurrent, and feedback controls. A budget guides the allocation of resources before an operation begins, which is a feedforward control. During the ongoing activities of an operation, budgets are monitored, which is a concurrent control. Feedback control occurs when sales and expenses are compared.

ORGANIZATIONAL ENVIRONMENT

The environment in which an organization functions influences many decisions, such as whether to expand, contract, build a new plant, or launch a new product. Many factors—both internal and external—make up the organizational environment.

ORGANIZATIONAL CULTURE

One particularly important aspect of an organization's internal environment is the company culture. **Culture** refers to the shared system of behavior, rituals, and practices of an organization's members. It should be inextricably linked to an organization's goals, strategies, and beliefs. The culture of one corporation differs from that of another, and it gives employees behavioral expectations to follow. For example, the culture at Walt Disney Company promotes dedication to customer satisfaction, while the culture at Southwest Airlines encourages customer fun.

Culture is built through the organizational socialization process, which occurs when managers and co-workers help newcomers develop the skills needed for acceptance into the corporate team. A strong organizational culture benefits a business by encouraging employee loyalty and cooperation.

Consider the field of advertising. The work requires long hours and a dedication to customers that asks a great deal of employees. Many agencies pay low entry-level salaries and still expect this level of effort. As a reward, they provide an atmosphere filled with perks and play that goes beyond the typical company picnic. Tech companies fall into this category as well. The rewards rise to such a level that employees are willing to work sixty hours a week, meet unrealistic deadlines, all with a positive attitude. By creating a culture that rewards this dedication, organizations keep employees happy enough to work at a breakneck pace and deliver for their clients.

However, sometimes corporate culture can become problematic. When it becomes unbending and stifling, it prevents change and growth. For many decades, IBM exerted a strong organizational culture, which later became counterproductive. The IBM culture resisted change and hindered the company's ability to compete against new computer firms like Apple and Compaq, which eventually grabbed a significant portion of IBM's market.

LEGAL, POLITICAL, AND ECONOMIC FORCES

Legal and political factors are two components of an organization's **macro environment**. Laws and political decisions play an important part in the success or failure of a business and are areas that management must pay attention to in order to respond quickly to changes. Laws, trade agreements, and rules are reflective of the political party in control as well as the social mores and values of the time and can help or hinder an organization. If an organization produces a product that society deems harmful, it can be subject to taxes and regulations that hinder success. For example, tobacco products, once considered harmless, are now subject to health warnings and increased taxes due to findings regarding tobacco's health hazards. On the other hand, if an organization produces goods or services more in line with the areas popular with legislators and voters, it may have a competitive edge. Similarly, the political decisions determine whether mergers are considered anticompetitive or harmless to the current business climate. Political decisions also determine whether the tax environment is friendly to organizations or whether it is more profitable to find an offshore location to expand business. Antitrust laws, trade regulations, and investment tax credits are legal forces that have an impact on businesses. While organizations can't control the laws passed, rules put in place, or tax codes, they must pay attention to these variables and be ready to shift focus when necessary in order to stay competitive.

In addition to the federal laws, local and state laws factor into this category of an organization's macro environment. Local and state governments have the power to write ordinances that provide advantages to organizations. They can offer tax incentives or make road improvements that are inviting for organizations looking for a place to set up headquarters or build a new plant. Alternatively, they can write ordinances that hinder building or create zoning that doesn't allow a particular type of manufacturing. Local and state government factors are yet another layer of the macro environment that managers must stay abreast of to remain competitive.

Regulators are an additional component of the legal factors involved in an organization's macro environment. Regulators are government agencies with the power to investigate and monitor businesses to ensure compliance with laws regarding workplace, product, and environmental safety. They are responsible for fining organizations guilty of illegal business practices. The Occupational Safety and Health Administration (OSHA), the Federal Aviation Administration (FAA), and the Environmental Protection Agency (EPA) are examples of regulatory agencies. In addition, the Securities and Exchange Commission (SEC) monitors U.S. financial markets, and the Food and Drug Administration (FDA) oversees medical devices, pharmaceuticals, cosmetics, and food.

The economy is another environmental component that shapes management decisions and consumer demand. Economic factors include trade or import restrictions or arrangements in the country where an organization does business, any economic cycles such as recessions or downturns, monetary policies, and income distribution. Management considers all of these factors and expands production when the economy is strong and reduces production and cuts jobs during difficult economic times. Managers adjust staffing, operations, and prices based on inflation rates, interest rates, productivity, and unemployment rates. High interest and inflation rates affect the costs associated with borrowing money to expand a business and reduce consumer demand for products and services. Unemployment rates influence labor availability and wages. Energy sources and costs also have an impact on business by increasing or decreasing the expenses associated with running a business.

Another indirect environmental force on the economy is technology, which businesses use to meet consumer needs. Technological innovations in communication devices, television, software, medical devices, energy, robotics, and transportation change the way in which people live. Advancements in technology create new businesses and increase competition. Effective managers utilize technology to lower costs, increase production, and improve services and products.

Social forces also impact businesses. These can include workers' and customers' values, traditions, and behaviors; all are constantly changing, and businesses must change with them. The growing popularity of social media, for example, has changed how businesses operate: younger consumers, especially, are more often apt to shop more online; their lifestyles and buying habits may be different than those of the company's earlier customers, so companies much adapt in order to reflect—and take advantage of—those changes.

Other social factors that can impact a business can include customers' education levels and disposable income, as well as family size and structure, life expectancy, and cultural diversity. In addition, changing attitudes toward career aspirations and leisure time can affect customers' behavior and expectations.

LABOR-MANAGEMENT RELATIONS

Each day, managers face the direct forces on an organization: competitors, suppliers, and customers. A **competitor** is any rival firm competing for the same group of customers. Colgate and Crest are rivals in the toothpaste market, while Mercedes and Lexus are rivals for luxury car buyers. Businesses attempt to distinguish themselves in the marketplace and to stay ahead of rival firms. Because of this, managers must monitor the competition to determine if rivals are making significant product adjustments or launching sales promotions.

Suppliers provide businesses with capital, office supplies, information, parts, and raw materials, so they directly affect product quality. A motorcycle is composed of parts and materials from suppliers, so low-quality parts will result in a low-quality motorcycle. In addition to quality issues, the price of supplies affects the price of a product or service, which is why some businesses rely on multiple suppliers rather than only one. **Supply chain management** has become increasingly important to businesses wanting to stay competitive and profitable. Supply chain management refers to managing an extensive network of facilities and people involved in the process of acquiring raw materials, creating products, and distributing products to customers.

In some industries, such as auto, steel, and transportation, labor unions act as suppliers of workers. Although only about 10 percent of the U.S. labor force belongs to a union, unions still wield significant power. Labor unions represent the interests of their members in issues related to hiring, salaries, working conditions, and job security. In the past, labor unions and managers were on opposite sides, but the relationship has improved over the years. Managers and labor unions realize the need to work collaboratively to increase productivity and to stay competitive in the marketplace. Labor-management committees are one method of bringing labor and management together to negotiate contracts. Representatives from both sides meet to discuss solutions to problems, which often leads to mutual benefits and trust.

Unionized businesses often operate differently than non-unionized businesses. For instance, in most non-unionized companies, recruiting and staffing are handled by the company's HR (Human

Resources) department. In a union environment, the union itself may recruit and staff positions within the company. Administration may also differ: In a unionized company, *seniority* is often the most important criterion when it comes to promotions or layoffs, and the demotion or laying off of employees may be subject to stipulations laid out in the contract between the company and the union.

Labor-management relations can also be affected by the classification of employees as either **exempt** or **non-exempt**. The former are generally salaried staff, and are "exempt" in the sense that they are excluded from overtime, minimum wage, and other regulations. Exempt staff are often considered "white collar" employees. Non-exempt employees are paid an hourly wage and are entitled to overtime pay under the Fair Labor Standards Act.

Customers, or **consumers**, make or break a business, so they are the most critical direct environmental force. There are two types of consumers—final and intermediate. **Final consumers** purchase products in their completed form, such as a Wendy's hamburger or a pair of Nike running shoes. An **intermediate consumer** buys raw materials or wholesale products and then sells the product to final consumers. For example, Macy's department store is an intermediate consumer that buys clothing from manufacturers and wholesalers. Similar to suppliers, consumers affect the price of products and services by demanding higher quality, better service, and lower prices. The Internet has forced businesses to be more competitive because savvy consumers easily search for low prices.

GLOBAL FORCES AND WORKPLACE DIVERSITY

Global forces, or the actions of countries around the world, are part of the indirect forces of an organization's macro environment. Managers face the challenge of competing with global firms in addition to local ones. As technology increases, it is becoming more common for businesses to compete on an international level. In the past, the size of an organization and its level of experience were the most important qualities to consumers. Today, speed and efficiency are qualities that count.

Foreign governments may subsidize certain industries or pass laws that protect certain types of businesses, creating a less than friendly business climate for organizations. International trade agreements, exchange rates, and multi-country economic associations, such as the Organization of Petroleum Exporting Countries (OPEC), also affect the viability of foreign markets. **Trade relationships** are another piece of an organization's macro environment. Trade relationships—positive or negative—can impact organizations. For example, the decision to thaw relations between the United States and Cuba in 2016 has created economic opportunities for organizations in a variety of industries; those organizations are looking for ways to gain an advantage over their competitors.

Cultural considerations are an additional piece of the global factors of an organization's macro environment of the twenty-first century. For example, as large numbers of older, experienced people retire, managers must find new employees to replace them. Improved education and skill levels overseas have led many managers to outsource telemarketing and manufacturing jobs to India and other countries with low labor costs. This integration of different cultures requires managers to address the challenges arising from culturally based yet differing styles of leadership, motivation, and attitudes toward work. Additionally, an increasing number of immigrants and women in the workforce has created more diversity in businesses; their presence has helped to bring women's issues to the forefront of politics. Laws having to do with paid family leave are being discussed and considered by state and federal legislatures, with some states moving to passing family leave requirements. Managers are increasingly aware of the importance of providing equitable pay for men and women doing the same work, as well as equal opportunities for advancement up through the ranks of management. Health and social issues are also factors of concern. Many businesses are implementing programs that address employee concerns such as mental stress, substance abuse, health care, career planning, and skills training.

SUSTAINABLE ENVIRONMENTS

Businesses have always been expected to exhibit a certain level of social responsibility, but in recent decades that expectation has been expanded to include a responsibility to create a **sustainable** environment in more than one sense. Of course, companies must by definition be sustainable in order to last, and are thus able to continue creating jobs, in addition to the goods and services they sell.

In one sense, then, a sustainable business environment is one in which the business itself can thrive, because it is resilient, it creates economic value, and it contributes to strong communities. A business survives over the long term not simply because it delivers valuable products or services, but because it is part of a healthy system. Sustainability has become an increasingly important part of doing business.

That sustainability is also part of—and the result of—an organizational culture that encourages it. It is a culture in which employees share assumptions and beliefs about how the business should be run and about how it can contribute to social equity and a healthy environment.

The Environmental Component

More recently, the idea of a sustainable business has included doing as little harm to the environment as possible. Thus, the idea of sustainability has acquired an ecological component.

Many businesses now seek to operate in an environmentally responsible fashion, utilizing natural and green energy to the extent possible; the objective is for the businesses to act as a *steward* of natural resources, rather than merely as a consumer of them. One indicator of this new awareness is the popularity of **LEED certification**. LEED (Leadership in Energy and Environmental Design) is a program developed by the nonprofit U.S. Green Building Council that rates the design, construction, and operation of buildings in terms of energy consumption and overall environmental safety. LEED-certified companies may qualify for tax breaks or other rewards, and may ultimately recoup extra costs simply because LEED-certified facilities are, in the long run, less expensive to operate.

ORGANIZATIONAL CHANGE

No organization can remain static and still thrive. It must respond to market forces, economic and cultural change, new technologies, and changes in the competitive arena. The secret to benefitting from organizational change is to *manage* those changes, rather than simply *respond* to them. In fact, an entirely new aspect of management, **organizational change management (OCM)**, has become prevalent as managers come to realize that change is inevitable, and that managed change can be beneficial (even profitable) while unmanaged or unplanned change is too often disruptive and confusing.

Not only is change guaranteed to occur, it appears to be occurring ever more rapidly, due to globalization (which provides more diverse markets for goods and services, but also more diverse sources of raw materials and labor), technological innovation, and other factors.

One of the most challenging tasks a supervisor will face occurs when a business undergoes organizational change. Reasons for organizational change can vary, from the relocation of office space within a building to the release of a new product, to the acquisition of another company. Because each of these changes can affect how employees do their jobs, it is imperative to the company's continued success that the employees continue to work as a team. Management will rely on the supervisors to lead the team while instilling confidence that the company will continue to maintain its identity and core values throughout whatever change occurs. By doing so, they can cultivate a culture of commitment and performance.

Human Factors

The key to successful organizational change is to acknowledge the human factor. When organizations change, people have to adjust. New leaders will be put in place, jobs and responsibilities will change, and new skills may be need to be developed. As a result, employees will be uncertain and may be resistant. To ensure success, a formal approach for managing change that involves all levels of the organization needs to be developed early and adapted often as change moves through the organization. Communication is vital. Management should take three important steps when organizational change is about to occur:

1. State the need or reason for the change.
2. Demonstrate its confidence in the company's future and leadership.
3. Provide a plan to direct decision-making and behavior.

Supervisors then must customize that information to apply to their workforce members, detailing the upcoming changes in terms of how it affects those individuals. In this way, a sense of ownership can develop throughout the organization early in the process of change.

Types of Change

There are four types of organizational change a business may undergo:

1. Organization-wide change vs. subsystem change
2. Transformational vs. incremental change
3. Remedial vs. developmental change
4. Unplanned vs. planned change

An **organization-wide change** involves the entire company. It could include such things as a major restructuring, significant layoffs, or equally significant staff additions. **Subsystem changes** might include department reorganization or the addition or removal of a product to or from a company's product line.

A **transformational** (or **quantum**) **change** is a radical one: perhaps the company's entire management and reporting hierarchy is being reorganized. **Incremental changes**, in contrast, are small—sometimes continuous—improvements to processes or new computer systems brought online to work within the existing business framework.

Organizational change can be thought of in terms of the *goals* of the change. A **remedial change** is intended to remedy an issue, perhaps to rectify poor product performance or to encourage the company to become more proactive. **Developmental change**, on the other hand, may be aimed at making something that's already successful even *more* successful: perhaps looking at ways to duplicate the success of one product by creating similar products.

Finally, **unplanned change** is usually in reaction to some unexpected, significant event—a sudden loss of a high-ranking executive, or a natural disaster that adversely affects production, or an inferior product performance that results in a rapid loss of customers—resulting in a rapid and usually disorganized response. These changes are often implemented on a short-term basis until a more permanent solution can be put in place. **Planned change** is the result of organizational leaders recognizing the need for major changes and being proactive and organized in their implementation. Planned changes are designed to be long-term solutions.

WORKPLACE SAFETY AND SECURITY

A modern business cannot thrive without protecting its property and its people. In many cases, certain safety practices are *mandated* by government agencies, such as OSHA—the **Occupational Safety and Health Administration**, which enforces the **Occupational Safety and Health Act of 1970**. OSHA requires that businesses carry out certain safety, hazard prevention, and training activities, and it provides guidelines and checklists for doing so.

Workplace safety can include everything from employee training to requiring the use of certain protective equipment, such as earplugs and protective eyewear.

Shared Responsibility

In a business, everyone shares responsibility for workplace safety. The employer is responsible for leading the program and for providing safe working conditions. Managers are charged with developing appropriate attitudes and procedures to ensure that operations are carried out with due regard for safety. The employees are expected to comply with all safety-related rules and regulations.

OSHA Requirements

OSHA requires businesses to provide safety information to employees (in the form of Safety Data Sheets, for instance) and to keep records of work-related injuries or illnesses. Under certain circumstances, businesses are also required to put in place certain processes designed to protect employees. These can include, for example, lockout/tag out procedures (meant to immobilize or shield equipment currently undergoing maintenance or repair) and requirements governing who is allowed into dangerous or confined spaces.

In general, employers must abide by provisions of the Act that are meant to protect the company's employees. Among other requirements, companies must do the following:

1. Provide a workplace free from serious recognized hazards.

2. Comply with standards, rules and regulations issued under the Act.

3. Ensure that workplace conditions conform to applicable OSHA standards.

4. Provide safe and properly maintained tools and equipment.

5. Use color coded, posters, labels, or signs to warn employees of potential hazards.

6. Provide safety training in a language and vocabulary workers can understand.

7. Provide medical examinations and training when required by OSHA standards.

8. Post, at a prominent location within the workplace, the OSHA poster (or the state plan equivalent) informing employees of their rights and responsibilities.

Keep in mind that the above is not a complete list of requirements. See **https://www.osha.gov/as/ opa/worker/employer-responsibility.html** for a more thorough explanation of the Occupational Safety and Health Act requirements.

SUMMING IT UP

- Effective managers facilitate the activities within organizations through **planning**, **organizing**, **leading**, and **controlling**. Managers use the **principles of supervision** to guide the work of others and to help an organization accomplish its short-term needs and long-term goals.

- Most large organizations have **three different levels of management**: **frontline**, **middle-level**, and **top-level or (strategic) managers**.

- The global and technical nature of modern organizations requires that managers possess a wide range of skills: **technical**, **analytical**, **decision-making**, **conceptual**, **computer**, **communication**, and **interpersonal**.

- The **ten roles of managers** identified by Canadian academic **Henry Mintzberg** are **figure-head**, **leader**, **liaison**, **monitor**, **disseminator**, **spokesperson**, **entrepreneur**, **disturbance handler**, **resource allocator**, and **negotiator**.

- **Ethics** are a system of rules that distinguish between right and wrong. **Business ethics** refer to the moral principles that dictate behavior in the business realm. **Ethics programs are compliance-based**, **integrity-based**, or somewhere in between.

- **Corporate social responsibility** refers to a business's obligations to society. Social responsibilities are divided into four major categories: **economic**, **legal**, **ethical**, **and philanthropic**.

- **Internal** and **external environmental factors** affect how an organization functions.
  - ○ The **internal environment** includes employees, office layout, management style, and bonus systems.
  - ○ The **external, or macro, environment** comprises "outside" factors that have direct effects (suppliers, competitors, customers) and indirect effects (legal, political, economic, technological, social-cultural, global) on daily operations.

- In the early 1900s, **Henri Fayol**, a French business owner, developed the first general theory of management. **Fayol's Four Functions are Plan, Organize, Lead, and Control.**

- The **three levels of planning** are **strategic, tactical, and operational**.

- A **SWOT analysis** is a comparison of the organization's **strengths, weaknesses, opportunities**, and **threats**; it enables managers to formulate three levels of strategy: **corporate, business**, and **functional**.

- A **board of directors** serves four primary duties: **choosing, evaluating, rewarding**, and, when necessary, **replacing the CEO; assessing** an organization's financial performance; **deciding** an organization's strategic direction; and **monitoring** an organization's ethical, legal, and socially responsible activities.

- It is important to be aware of the difference between **legal screening activities** and **illegal screening activities** during a job interview.

- The three most widely accepted classic approaches for understanding leadership are the **trait approach**, the **behavioral approach**, and the **situational approach**.

- **Vroom's expectancy theory**, one of the most widely accepted motivation theories, is based on three variables: **expectancy; instrumentality**; and **valence**.

- Contemporary **theories of leadership styles** include **charismatic; transformational; transactional; level 5; authentic**; and **pseudo transformational**.

- The three main **content theories** are **Maslow's hierarchy of needs**, **Alderfer's ERG theory**, and **McClelland's needs**.

- The three general methods for achieving organizational control are **bureaucratic control; market control**; and **clan control**.

- A **management audit** is a type of control used to evaluate the effectiveness and efficiency of an organization; it involves external and internal audits. **Budgeting**, or **budgetary controlling**, is a widely used control process that involves investigating what a firm has done.

PRINCIPLES OF SUPERVISION POST-TEST

Directions: Carefully read each of the following 60 questions. Choose the best answer to each question and fill in the corresponding circle on the answer sheet. The Answer Key and Explanations can be found following this post-test.

1. A frontline manager is responsible for
   A. translating the ideas and objectives developed by top-level executives into specific goals and activities.
   B. overseeing daily operational activities and serving as the connection between management and employees.
   C. interpreting corporate objectives into plans for the different units within an organization.
   D. concentrating on the long-term issues and growth strategies that an organization faces.

2. Which of the following persons developed the first theory regarding management functions?
   A. Winslow Taylor
   B. Henri Fayol
   C. Max Weber
   D. Henry Mintzberg

3. The process of teaching new employees the appropriate roles and behaviors needed to become effective members of a business is
   A. organizational socialization.
   B. cultural diagnosis.
   C. interpersonal development.
   D. managerial training.

4. Which of the following is a factor of an organization's macro environment, in addition to legal, political, economic, technological, and sociocultural factors?
   A. Ethical
   B. Local government
   C. Global
   D. Regulatory

5. A primary skill necessary at every level of management is
   A. training.
   B. technical.
   C. conceptual.
   D. decision making.

6. Which of the following is characteristic of feedforward control?
   A. Implementing transfer pricing
   B. Monitoring ongoing data flow
   C. Establishing rules and procedures
   D. Evaluating performance results

7. Which theory is based on the idea that great leaders are born with self-assurance, integrity, and assertiveness?
   A. Content theory
   B. Path-goal theory
   C. Trait theory
   D. Behavioral theory

8. Labor unions traditionally focus on issues related to
   A. salaries.
   B. competitors.
   C. managerial levels.
   D. regulatory agencies.

9. Which of the following questions may legally be asked of a job candidate?
   A. "How old are you?"
   B. "What is your nationality?"
   C. "May I see your proof of citizenship?"
   D. "Have you ever been convicted of a crime?"

10. The process of different levels of managers working together to develop and implement organizational goals and strategies is
    A. systematic management.
    B. tactical management.
    C. administrative management.
    D. strategic management.

11. All of the following are informational roles of managers EXCEPT:
    A. Monitor
    B. Spokesperson
    C. Disseminator
    D. Figurehead

12. Which of the following control systems is most commonly used by firms?
    A. Clan
    B. Market
    C. Bureaucratic
    D. Organizational

13. An employee's belief that increased efforts at work will lead to accomplishing performance goals is known as
    A. equity.
    B. expectancy.
    C. task identity.
    D. instrumentality.

14. Which of the following has the power to regulate X-ray machines and blood glucose meters?
    A. Occupational Safety and Health Administration
    B. Environmental Protection Agency
    C. Food and Drug Administration
    D. Centers for Disease Control and Prevention

15. An increase in the cost of petroleum would affect a manufacturing company that used petroleum-based raw materials by
    A. increasing employment costs.
    B. decreasing transportation costs.
    C. increasing manufacturing costs.
    D. decreasing manufacturing costs.

16. Which of the following is developed to create consistency in situations repeatedly faced by an organization?
    A. Single-use plans
    B. Objectives
    C. Standing plans
    D. Scenarios

17. A sales manager who tries to make improvements in the sales department is functioning as a(n)
    A. entrepreneur.
    B. negotiator.
    C. monitor.
    D. liaison.

18. According to David McClelland, all of the following are people's primary needs EXCEPT:
    A. Achievement
    B. Power
    C. Affiliation
    D. Growth

19. Indirect external forces that influence decisions of whether to borrow money to expand a business include
    A. material costs.
    B. labor costs.
    C. interest and inflation rates.
    D. the end-of-year bonus payouts.

20. An intermediate consumer most likely purchases items from
    A. retailers.
    B. big box stores.
    C. e-businesses.
    D. wholesalers.

21. Which of the following combines aspects of feedforward, concurrent, and feedback control?
    A. Auditing
    B. Marketing
    C. Budgeting
    D. Financing

22. The extent that different work units work together to coordinate efforts is known as
    A. integration.
    B. organization.
    C. configuration.
    D. differentiation.

23. According to expectancy theory, the importance that an employee places on a specific outcome is known as
    A. valence.
    B. motivation.
    C. legitimacy.
    D. instrumentality.

24. Which of the following is the most likely managerial benefit of technological advancements implemented in a manufacturing facility?
    A. Improved labor relations
    B. Increased production
    C. Lower energy costs
    D. Diverse workforce

25. As women and immigrants have entered the workforce, businesses have been forced to provide all of the following EXCEPT:
    A. More equitable compensation packages for men and women
    B. Jobs with pay scales dependent on an employee's gender
    C. Working environments that are respectful of the diverse backgrounds of all employees
    D. Equitable opportunities for promotion for both men and women

26. Which of the following best describes operational planning?
    A. Short-term time frame and low level of details
    B. Short-term time frame and high level of details
    C. Long-term time frame and low level of details
    D. Medium-term time frame and medium level of details

27. The Caux Principles were primarily developed to address
    A. business ethics.
    B. global commerce.
    C. accounting standards.
    D. environmental awareness.

28. Which of the following is established and implemented to help employees behave in the best interests of a business?
    A. Customer organization
    B. Mission statement
    C. Control system
    D. Tactical plan

29. Group maintenance behaviors can lead to the development of personal relationships with group members according to
    A. LMX theory.
    B. LPC theory.
    C. Vroom theory.
    D. Hersey-Blanchard theory.

30. One of the potential benefits of developing a strong organizational culture is
    A. customer satisfaction.
    B. economic stability.
    C. ethics enforcement.
    D. employee loyalty.

31. Which of the following is characterized by high-level managers making the majority of decisions?
    A. Centralized organization
    B. High-involvement organization
    C. Decentralized organization
    D. Learning organization

32. Compliance-based ethics programs are designed to
    A. encourage ethical behavior through rewards.
    B. create interest in social responsibility efforts.
    C. impose punishments upon ethics violators.
    D. comply with global business guidelines.

33. The first step in the strategic management process is
    A. analyzing potential opportunities.
    B. formulating a functional strategy.
    C. assessing strengths and weaknesses.
    D. establishing a mission statement.

34. Stretch goals are best described as
    A. straightforward.
    B. prolonged.
    C. impossible.
    D. demanding.

35. Factors outside of an organization that affect a business are known as the
    A. supply-chain force.
    B. external environment.
    C. global marketplace.
    D. peripheral culture.

36. The concept that a business should obey laws, perform ethically, and contribute positively to a community's quality of life is known as
    A. environmental scanning.
    B. sustainable growth.
    C. internal strategies.
    D. social responsibility.

37. In an automobile manufacturing corporation, the accounting department is known as a
    A. line department.
    B. regional department.
    C. staff department.
    D. product department.

38. A company's culture can become problematic when it
    A. creates a sense of belonging that causes employees to display loyalty to the organization.
    B. is so well known that it creates an influx of applications for employment.
    C. stifles new ideas, the ability to change, and growth.
    D. enables staff to respond quickly to changes in the market.

39. Management reductions in recent years have mostly affected
    A. supervisors.
    B. middle management.
    C. chief executive officers.
    D. top management.

40. Which type of consequence is exemplified when a manager fails to show appreciation to an especially helpful subordinate?
    A. Positive reinforcement
    B. Punishment
    C. Negative reinforcement
    D. Extinction

41. Overseeing the interconnected network of facilities and people that take a product from the raw material stage to distribution is known as
    A. supply chain management.
    B. flexible manufacturing.
    C. egocentric management.
    D. strategic planning.

42. Which of the following is the result of a wide span of control?
    A. Few workers reporting to one supervisor
    B. Few workers reporting to multiple supervisors
    C. Many workers reporting to one supervisor
    D. Many workers reporting to multiple supervisors

43. All of the following are types of corporate-level strategies EXCEPT:
    A. Vertical integration
    B. Implementation
    C. Diversification
    D. Concentration

44. Task-specific knowledge refers to
    A. communication skills.
    B. analytical skills.
    C. computer skills.
    D. technical skills.

45. What is the most critical direct environmental force an organization faces?
    A. Regulatory agencies
    B. Technological innovations
    C. Competitors
    D. Customers

46. Which of the following methods of departmentalization is most commonly used by multinational corporations?
    A. Product
    B. Geographic
    C. Matrix
    D. Functional

47. Management decisions to outsource manufacturing jobs to foreign countries have primarily been influenced by
    A. trade agreements.
    B. immigration.
    C. labor costs.
    D. tax laws.

48. Which of the following developed a situational model of leadership that leads to five possible decision styles?
    A. Henri Fayol
    B. Fred Fiedler
    C. Abraham Maslow
    D. Victor Vroom

49. Which of the following has most likely used a differentiation strategy in pursuit of competitive advantage?
    A. Walmart
    B. Toshiba
    C. Porsche
    D. Hoover

50. A manager's ability to understand the strategies and objectives of a business is an aspect of
    A. decision-making skills.
    B. conceptual skills.
    C. interpersonal skills.
    D. analytical skills.

51. Managers who concentrate on significant deviations from anticipated standards are most likely using the principle of
    A. control.
    B. accountability.
    C. standardization.
    D. exception.

52. Government agencies that have the power to investigate business practices are known as
    A. prospectors.
    B. supervisors.
    C. regulators.
    D. defenders.

53. All of the following are primary duties of an organization's board of directors EXCEPT:
    A. Selecting the chief executive officer
    B. Making daily operational decisions
    C. Monitoring financial performance
    D. Determining strategic direction

54. Management activities such as hiring, training, and motivating workers are part of the
    A. figurehead role.
    B. leadership role.
    C. monitor role.
    D. resource allocator role.

55. Which of the following summarizes information gathered in an environmental analysis during the strategic planning process?
    A. ABC
    B. CRM
    C. LCA
    D. SWOT

56. All of the following are societal factors that indirectly influence businesses EXCEPT:
    A. Birth rate
    B. Productivity
    C. Immigration
    D. Life expectancy

57. A sales manager who reaches a deal with the CEO about implementing flexible scheduling for the sales unit is acting as a
    A. negotiator.
    B. liaison.
    C. figurehead.
    D. disseminator.

58. Exchange rates and trade agreements are examples of
    A. cooperative strategies.
    B. direct forces.
    C. entry barriers.
    D. indirect forces.

59. Studying the ten roles of a manager is important to realizing that
    A. all the roles are interconnected.
    B. technical and general skills are both essential.
    C. some roles are significantly more important.
    D. levels of management are complex.

60. Which of the following is a situational factor in the path-goal theory?
    A. Motivational methods
    B. Characteristics of leaders
    C. Leadership style
    D. Characteristics of followers

ANSWER KEY AND EXPLANATIONS

1. B	**13.** B	**25.** B	**37.** C	**49.** C
2. B	**14.** C	**26.** B	**38.** C	**50.** B
3. A	**15.** C	**27.** A	**39.** B	**51.** D
4. C	**16.** C	**28.** C	**40.** D	**52.** C
5. D	**17.** A	**29.** A	**41.** A	**53.** B
6. C	**18.** D	**30.** D	**42.** C	**54.** B
7. C	**19.** C	**31.** A	**43.** B	**55.** D
8. A	**20.** D	**32.** C	**44.** D	**56.** B
9. D	**21.** C	**33.** D	**45.** D	**57.** A
10. D	**22.** A	**34.** D	**46.** B	**58.** D
11. D	**23.** A	**35.** B	**47.** C	**59.** A
12. C	**24.** B	**36.** D	**48.** D	**60.** D

1. **The correct answer is B.** Choices A and C are incorrect; these are both responsibilities of a middle level manager. Choice D is also incorrect, as it describes the responsibilities of a top-level manager.

2. **The correct answer is B.** Henri Fayol developed the first theory of professional management functions, which include planning, organizing, leading, and controlling. Taylor (choice A) is regarded for improving industrial efficiency. Weber (choice C) was one of the leading founders of sociology. Mintzberg (choice D) identified the ten roles of managers.

3. **The correct answer is A.** Organizational socialization is the process of teaching new employees the appropriate roles and behaviors needed to become effective members of a business. Managers and co-workers help new workers develop the skills necessary for acceptance into an organization. Choices B, C, and D are incorrect.

4. **The correct answer is C.** Global factors are a part of an organization's macro environment. Choice A is incorrect, and choices B and D are both categories within the legal component of the macro environment, making them incorrect also.

5. **The correct answer is D.** Decision-making skills are necessary at every level of management. Training workers and having technical skills are most important for frontline managers who deal with blue-collar workers. Top-level managers must have conceptual skills for making long-range goals, so choice C is incorrect.

6. **The correct answer is C.** Establishing rules and procedures before an activity begins is characteristic of feedforward control. Monitoring ongoing data (choice B) is an aspect of concurrent control. Feedback control involves evaluating performance results (choice D).

7. **The correct answer is C.** Trait theory is based on the idea that great leaders are born with characteristics such as self-assurance, integrity, and assertiveness. Content theory (choice A) is a motivational theory. Choices B and D are leadership theories that do not assert that people are born with leadership qualities.

8. **The correct answer is A.** Salaries, working conditions, hiring practices, and job security are the focus of most labor unions. Labor unions remain a significant direct force in industries such as auto and steel, although only about 10 percent of U.S. workers are members. Choices B, C, and D are less important issues to labor unions.

9. **The correct answer is D.** It is legal to ask a job candidate if he or she has been convicted of a crime; however, it is illegal to ask about arrests. Asking a person's age (choice A) can be done only after hiring. It is illegal to ask about a person's nationality (choice B) and for proof of citizenship (choice C).

10. **The correct answer is D.** *Strategic management* is the term for the process that brings together different levels of managers to develop and implement organizational goals and strategies. Systematic management (choice A) and administrative management (choice C) were two classical approaches toward management that did not involve different managerial levels. Middle-level managers are sometimes referred to as tactical managers (choice B).

11. **The correct answer is D.** The roles of monitor, spokesperson, and disseminator are informational roles performed by managers according to Mintzberg's research study. Interpersonal roles include figurehead, leader, and liaison. Therefore, choice D is the best answer.

12. **The correct answer is C.** Bureaucratic control, which is also known as formal control, is the most commonly used control system within organizations. Market control systems (choice B) are appropriate in situations where output can be clearly identified. Clan control (choice A) is appropriate in flexible settings that allow employees to make decisions.

13. **The correct answer is B.** According to expectancy theory, expectancy is a person's belief that increased efforts at work will lead to accomplishing performance goals. Instrumentality (choice D) is the employee's belief that good job performance will lead to certain outcomes. Choices A and C are not variables in expectancy theory.

14. **The correct answer is C.** The Food and Drug Administration (FDA) monitors medical devices, such as X-ray machines and blood glucose meters, to ensure compliance with safety standards. Choices A and B are both regulatory agencies, but neither oversees medical devices. The CDC is an agency of the U.S. Department of Health and Human Services that provides information related to disease prevention and health improvement.

15. **The correct answer is C.** An increase in raw material costs impacts a business by increasing the costs of manufacturing, making choice D incorrect. Choice A is incorrect because unemployment rates, not raw material costs, influence labor rates. Choice B is incorrect because an increase in petroleum costs would likely increase transportation costs.

16. **The correct answer is C.** Standing plans are established for dealing with ongoing activities so that decisions can be made quickly, easily, and consistently. Standing plans often develop into company policies. Single-use plans (choice A) are developed for one-time situations. Choices B and D are used in the planning process but are not developed for the sake of consistency.

17. **The correct answer is A.** According to Mintzberg, the entrepreneurial role of a manager involves making improvements to a unit. The negotiator (choice B) bargains with others to gain benefits, and the monitor (choice C) observes successes, failures, and problems that may affect the unit. As a liaison (choice D), a manager communicates with people inside and outside the organization.

18. **The correct answer is D.** According to McClelland, people's three main needs are achievement, affiliation, and power. Growth, existence, and relatedness are people's needs according to Alderfer's theory.

19. **The correct answer is C.** Interest and inflation rates are indirect external forces acting on an organization. Choices A, B, and D are incorrect because material costs, labor costs, and bonus payouts are all direct forces that act on an organization.

20. **The correct answer is D.** An intermediate consumer purchases items from wholesalers and manufacturers to make a finished product that will be sold to final consumers. Choices A, B, and C are incorrect because final consumers purchase goods from

retailers, which include big box stores like Walmart and e-businesses.

21. **The correct answer is C.** Budgeting combines aspects of feedforward, concurrent, and feedback control. Budgets are established before a project begins, and they are monitored during a project. At the end of a project or activity, sales and expenses are compared for feedback.

22. **The correct answer is A.** Integration refers to the extent to which different units in an organization coordinate their efforts to create a product or service. Organizations that are highly differentiated need integration to make sure that all units work together to meet goals.

23. **The correct answer is A.** According to expectancy theory, valence refers to the importance that an employee places on a specific outcome. Vroom's expectancy theory analyzes what motivates people, so choice B is incorrect. Instrumentality (choice D) is a variable in the theory that refers to an employee's belief that good work leads to a specific outcome. Choice C is incorrect.

24. **The correct answer is B.** Increased production is the most likely benefit of technological advancements utilized in the workplace. Some technology may improve energy efficiency but not necessarily. Technology will have less effect on labor relations and workforce diversity.

25. **The correct answer is B.** Increasing numbers of women in the workforce have brought pay inequity to light and have helped to eliminate jobs that pay men and women differing wages for the same work. The importance of parity in the workforce makes choices A and D incorrect. An increase in the number of immigrants in the workforce has required companies to become more sensitive to diverse backgrounds in their practices and planning, making choice C incorrect.

26. **The correct answer is B.** A short-term time frame and high level of details best describe operational planning. Choice C describes the characteristics of strategic planning. Choice D describes tactical planning.

27. **The correct answer is A.** An international group of business leaders developed the Caux Principles to address universal business ethics. The main premise of the Caux Principles is showing concern for human dignity and working toward the common good. Choices B, C, and D are not the focus of the Caux Principles.

28. **The correct answer is C.** Control systems are established and implemented to help employees behave in the best interests of a business. Control systems, such as performance appraisals and raises, regulate employee performance. A mission statement (choice B) is an organization's basic purpose, but it does not guide employee behavior. Choices A and D are not specifically geared toward directing the activities of employees.

29. **The correct answer is A.** The Leader-Member Exchange LMX theory asserts that group maintenance behaviors, such as trust, mutual respect, mutual loyalty, and open communication, can lead to the development of personal relationships with group members. LPC theory (choice B) and Hersey-Blanchard theory (choice D) are situational rather than behavioral leadership theories.

30. **The correct answer is D.** Employee loyalty and cooperation are both potential benefits of a strong organizational culture. Employees who feel like they are members of a team are more likely to remain at a job and work hard. Choices A, B, and C are less likely benefits of a strong culture within an organization.

31. **The correct answer is A.** Top executives make most decisions in centralized organizations. In decentralized organizations, decision making is dispersed throughout the company. In high-involvement organizations, upper management seeks a consensus from all levels of the company. An organization especially skilled at problem solving and creativity is known as a learning organization.

32. **The correct answer is C.** Compliance-based ethics programs are designed to impose punishments upon ethics violators. Such programs usually involve increased monitoring of employees and the establishment of legal

answers post-test

standards and procedures regarding ethics. In contrast, integrity-based ethics programs attempt to instill a sense of personal responsibility into employees. Choices A, B, and D do not describe compliance-based ethics programs.

33. **The correct answer is D.** Establishing the mission, vision, and goals of the organization is the first step in the strategic planning process. Choice A is the second stage of the process, and choice C is the third stage. Formulating a strategy (choice B) occurs after performing a SWOT analysis in the fourth stage.

34. **The correct answer is D.** Stretch goals are attainable but demanding goals used by firms to motivate employees to be excellent at their jobs. While stretch goals are challenging and may seem impossible, they are achievable.

35. **The correct answer is B.** The external environment includes the direct and indirect forces that affect an organization. Direct forces include suppliers, competitors, and customers. Indirect forces include the legal system, the economy, and the global marketplace. Choices A, C, and D are incorrect.

36. **The correct answer is D.** Social responsibility refers to the idea that corporations have economic, legal, ethical, and philanthropic responsibilities to society. Environmental scanning (choice A) refers to collecting data about various forces in the management environment. Sustainable growth (choice B) refers to economic growth that addresses current needs without negatively affecting the needs of people in the future. Internal strategies (choice C) are actions taken by businesses to avoid threats and benefit from opportunities.

37. **The correct answer is C.** The accounting department in an automobile manufacturing corporation is a staff department. Staff departments support line departments (choice A), which are the ones responsible for the main activities of a business. Choices B and D are incorrect.

38. **The correct answer is C.** When a company's culture creates an environment that hinders its ability to respond to competition or adapt to market changes, it has become problematic. Choices A, B, and D represent the positive effects of a strong corporate culture.

39. **The correct answer is B.** Middle management has been primarily affected by corporate reductions in management staff. Supervisors are needed to directly oversee workers, while CEOs and other top-level managers are needed to guide a company into the future with long-term plans. Middle managers are more expendable in large corporations, such as IBM and Sears, where efficiency and cost effectiveness are becoming extremely important.

40. **The correct answer is D.** Failing to show appreciation for help or failing to compliment employees for working hard are examples of extinction. Negative reinforcement involves removing an undesirable consequence.

41. **The correct answer is A.** Supply chain management refers to managing an extensive network of facilities and people involved in the process of acquiring raw materials, creating products, and distributing products to customers. Tough competition has increased the need for managers to monitor costs closely at every stage of production and distribution. Choices B, C, and D are incorrect.

42. **The correct answer is C.** With a wide span of control, many workers report to one supervisor. A narrow span of control results in a small number of workers reporting to one supervisor. In most organizations, workers should report to only one supervisor, so choices B and D are incorrect.

43. **The correct answer is B.** The three types of corporate-level strategies include vertical integration, diversification, and concentration on a single business. Implementation is not a type of strategy. Choices A, C, and D are incorrect.

44. **The correct answer is D.** Technical skills are task-specific. Frontline managers must have strong technical skills because they are directly supervising workers, and problems associated with a task, such as nursing or

accounting, arise on a daily basis. Choices A, B, and C are not task-specific knowledge.

45. **The correct answer is D.** Customers make or break a business. Choice A is incorrect because regulatory agencies are an indirect environmental force. Choice B is also incorrect because technological innovations are an indirect environmental force on the economy in which an organization exists. Competitors (choice C) are a direct environmental force, but not the most critical one, making it incorrect.

46. **The correct answer is B.** Geographic organization is the most common method of departmentalization used by multinational corporations. A geographic organization groups units by geographic areas, such as territories, regions, or countries. The structure is useful when customer needs vary greatly from place to place. Choices A, C, and D are less commonly used by multinational corporations.

47. **The correct answer is C.** The decision by many organizations to outsource jobs to other countries has been driven by low labor costs overseas, as well as an educated work force. For example, firms needing telemarketers often outsource to India where low wages pay for a skilled labor force. Choices A, B, and D have less influence on outsourcing than labor costs.

48. **The correct answer is D.** Vroom developed a situational model of leadership that leads to five possible decision styles. Vroom's model works like a funnel with questions that lead to a recommended decision style. Fayol (choice A) wrote the first theory of management. Fiedler (choice B) developed the least preferred co-worker LPC theory that asserts that a leader's style must match a situation. Maslow (choice C) is known for a hierarchy of motivational needs.

49. **The correct answer is C.** Porsche has used a differentiation strategy in seeking competitive advantage. Differentiation strategies involve being unique in an industry either through quality, marketing, or service. Walmart is an example of an organization

that has used low-cost strategies to gain competitive advantage.

50. **The correct answer is B.** Conceptual skills are needed by top-level managers to understand the objectives and strategies of a business. Determining long-term plans and predicting the benefits or problems associated with mergers, acquisitions, and investments require conceptual skills. A manager needs decision-making, interpersonal, and analytical skills, but they do not relate to long-term strategic planning, so choices A, C, and D are incorrect.

51. **The correct answer is D.** The principle of exception indicates that managers should concentrate on deviations from a standard. Managers save time by paying less attention to cases that are close to an established standard and more attention to exceptions. The principle of exception is an important element of the control process.

52. **The correct answer is C.** Regulators, or regulatory agencies, have the power to investigate business practices. Such agencies include the FAA, EPA, SEC, and OSHA. They monitor business compliance with workplace, product, and environmental safety laws. Choices A, B, and D are incorrect.

53. **The correct answer is B.** Making daily operational decisions is not one of the duties of a board of directors. A board's duties include selecting and evaluating the CEO, assessing a firm's financial performance, and deciding a firm's strategic direction. Choices A, C, and D are incorrect.

54. **The correct answer is B.** The leadership role of a manager involves coordinating and directing the activities of workers. Staffing, motivating, and controlling employees and their work are elements of the leadership role. Choice A refers to a manager's symbolic or ceremonial duties. Choice C refers to gathering information that may affect a unit. As a resource allocator (choice D), a manager determines how to distribute money, budget, time, and equipment.

55. **The correct answer is D.** A SWOT analysis is a comparison of the strengths, weaknesses,

opportunities, and threats that managers use to formulate strategies. It summarizes the relevant information gathered in the environmental analysis during strategic planning. ABC (choice A) stands for activity-based costing, and CRM (choice B) stands for customer relationship management. An LCA (choice C) is a life-cycle analysis that helps determine the environmental impact of a product.

56. **The correct answer is B.** Societal factors such as birth rate, life expectancy, and immigration affect businesses indirectly. Changes in society affect the work force, which influences how businesses function. Productivity is more closely related to technology issues than societal ones.

57. **The correct answer is A.** The negotiator role involves bargaining with others in an organization to obtain advantages. Managers who negotiate for flexible scheduling or increased salaries are working as negotiators for the benefit of their unit. Choices B and C are both interpersonal roles that involve developing and maintaining good relationships with people. The disseminator role relates to providing information to subordinates, so choice D is incorrect.

58. **The correct answer is D.** Exchange rates and trade agreements are indirect forces within the global environment. Direct forces, such as suppliers, have an immediate impact on a business, while indirect forces influence a business but not its daily operations. Barriers to entry are conditions that prevent new firms from entering an industry, such as distribution channels and government policies.

59. **The correct answer is A.** Recognizing the existence of ten management roles helps with understanding that every role is connected to another. Neglecting one or more roles hinders employees from working effectively because each role is equally important. Choices B and D may be true, but they are not related to the ten roles identified by Mintzberg.

60. **The correct answer is D.** Characteristics of followers and environmental factors are the two situational factors in the path-goal theory. These two factors determine the type of leadership behavior that is most appropriate given the followers and the situation. Choices A, B, and C are incorrect.

History of the Soviet Union

OVERVIEW

Chapter 11

The DSST® History of the Soviet Union exam consists of 100 multiple-choice questions that cover the history of the Soviet Union (the Union of Soviet Socialist Republics, or USSR) from its beginning in 1917, when the Bolshevik Party led by Vladimir Lenin overthrew Russia's Provisional Government, to its end in 1991, when the leaders of the three key constituent Soviet republics—Russia, Ukraine, and Belarus—signed an agreement to dissolve the USSR and induced its last president, Mikhail Gorbachev, to resign. The exam focuses upon the following topics: life under the Old Regime, the revolutionary period (1914–1921), prewar Stalinism, World War II, postwar Stalinism, the Khrushchev years, the Brezhnev era, and the Soviet Union's reform and collapse. Careful reading, critical thinking, and logical analysis will be as important as your knowledge of Soviet Union history.

DIAGNOSTIC TEST ANSWER SHEET

1. Ⓐ Ⓑ Ⓒ Ⓓ   5. Ⓐ Ⓑ Ⓒ Ⓓ   9. Ⓐ Ⓑ Ⓒ Ⓓ   13. Ⓐ Ⓑ Ⓒ Ⓓ   17. Ⓐ Ⓑ Ⓒ Ⓓ
2. Ⓐ Ⓑ Ⓒ Ⓓ   6. Ⓐ Ⓑ Ⓒ Ⓓ   10. Ⓐ Ⓑ Ⓒ Ⓓ   14. Ⓐ Ⓑ Ⓒ Ⓓ   18. Ⓐ Ⓑ Ⓒ Ⓓ
3. Ⓐ Ⓑ Ⓒ Ⓓ   7. Ⓐ Ⓑ Ⓒ Ⓓ   11. Ⓐ Ⓑ Ⓒ Ⓓ   15. Ⓐ Ⓑ Ⓒ Ⓓ   19. Ⓐ Ⓑ Ⓒ Ⓓ
4. Ⓐ Ⓑ Ⓒ Ⓓ   8. Ⓐ Ⓑ Ⓒ Ⓓ   12. Ⓐ Ⓑ Ⓒ Ⓓ   16. Ⓐ Ⓑ Ⓒ Ⓓ   20. Ⓐ Ⓑ Ⓒ Ⓓ

POST-TEST ANSWER SHEET

1. Ⓐ Ⓑ Ⓒ Ⓓ   13. Ⓐ Ⓑ Ⓒ Ⓓ   25. Ⓐ Ⓑ Ⓒ Ⓓ   37. Ⓐ Ⓑ Ⓒ Ⓓ   49. Ⓐ Ⓑ Ⓒ Ⓓ
2. Ⓐ Ⓑ Ⓒ Ⓓ   14. Ⓐ Ⓑ Ⓒ Ⓓ   26. Ⓐ Ⓑ Ⓒ Ⓓ   38. Ⓐ Ⓑ Ⓒ Ⓓ   50. Ⓐ Ⓑ Ⓒ Ⓓ
3. Ⓐ Ⓑ Ⓒ Ⓓ   15. Ⓐ Ⓑ Ⓒ Ⓓ   27. Ⓐ Ⓑ Ⓒ Ⓓ   39. Ⓐ Ⓑ Ⓒ Ⓓ   51. Ⓐ Ⓑ Ⓒ Ⓓ
4. Ⓐ Ⓑ Ⓒ Ⓓ   16. Ⓐ Ⓑ Ⓒ Ⓓ   28. Ⓐ Ⓑ Ⓒ Ⓓ   40. Ⓐ Ⓑ Ⓒ Ⓓ   52. Ⓐ Ⓑ Ⓒ Ⓓ
5. Ⓐ Ⓑ Ⓒ Ⓓ   17. Ⓐ Ⓑ Ⓒ Ⓓ   29. Ⓐ Ⓑ Ⓒ Ⓓ   41. Ⓐ Ⓑ Ⓒ Ⓓ   53. Ⓐ Ⓑ Ⓒ Ⓓ
6. Ⓐ Ⓑ Ⓒ Ⓓ   18. Ⓐ Ⓑ Ⓒ Ⓓ   30. Ⓐ Ⓑ Ⓒ Ⓓ   42. Ⓐ Ⓑ Ⓒ Ⓓ   54. Ⓐ Ⓑ Ⓒ Ⓓ
7. Ⓐ Ⓑ Ⓒ Ⓓ   19. Ⓐ Ⓑ Ⓒ Ⓓ   31. Ⓐ Ⓑ Ⓒ Ⓓ   43. Ⓐ Ⓑ Ⓒ Ⓓ   55. Ⓐ Ⓑ Ⓒ Ⓓ
8. Ⓐ Ⓑ Ⓒ Ⓓ   20. Ⓐ Ⓑ Ⓒ Ⓓ   32. Ⓐ Ⓑ Ⓒ Ⓓ   44. Ⓐ Ⓑ Ⓒ Ⓓ   56. Ⓐ Ⓑ Ⓒ Ⓓ
9. Ⓐ Ⓑ Ⓒ Ⓓ   21. Ⓐ Ⓑ Ⓒ Ⓓ   33. Ⓐ Ⓑ Ⓒ Ⓓ   45. Ⓐ Ⓑ Ⓒ Ⓓ   57. Ⓐ Ⓑ Ⓒ Ⓓ
10. Ⓐ Ⓑ Ⓒ Ⓓ   22. Ⓐ Ⓑ Ⓒ Ⓓ   34. Ⓐ Ⓑ Ⓒ Ⓓ   46. Ⓐ Ⓑ Ⓒ Ⓓ   58. Ⓐ Ⓑ Ⓒ Ⓓ
11. Ⓐ Ⓑ Ⓒ Ⓓ   23. Ⓐ Ⓑ Ⓒ Ⓓ   35. Ⓐ Ⓑ Ⓒ Ⓓ   47. Ⓐ Ⓑ Ⓒ Ⓓ   59. Ⓐ Ⓑ Ⓒ Ⓓ
12. Ⓐ Ⓑ Ⓒ Ⓓ   24. Ⓐ Ⓑ Ⓒ Ⓓ   36. Ⓐ Ⓑ Ⓒ Ⓓ   48. Ⓐ Ⓑ Ⓒ Ⓓ   60. Ⓐ Ⓑ Ⓒ Ⓓ

HISTORY OF THE SOVIET UNION
DIAGNOSTIC TEST

Directions: Carefully read each of the following 20 questions. Choose the best answer to each question and fill in the corresponding circle on the answer sheet. The Answer Key and Explanations can be found following this Diagnostic Test.

1. The imperial Russian army during the First World War
   A. was encircled and largely destroyed by the Germans in Eastern Ukraine.
   B. came close to capturing Berlin but stopped on the Oder River and was then routed.
   C. won all the major battles until crippled by Bolshevik agitation in 1917.
   D. retreated from Poland and Lithuania, but defeated Austria-Hungary in Galicia.

2. The Pale of Settlement imposed restrictions on which ethnic group?
   A. Finns
   B. Germans
   C. Jews
   D. Poles

3. One of the major decisions at the Yalta Conference in 1944 was that
   A. Poland would become a Communist republic.
   B. the USSR would stay out of the war against Japan.
   C. Communist war criminals would be amnestied.
   D. Germany would be subjected to demilitarization.

4. The Soviet collective farm system created in the late 1920s required villagers to
   A. surrender most of their harvest to meet state procurement quotas.
   B. grow only those crops that had military use, such as cotton or flax.
   C. serve as a collective militia force to defend against enemy invasions.
   D. engage in factory work for two months each year in addition to farming.

5. As the result of the 1941 Operation Barbarossa, the German military
   A. completely cut off Allied supply routes into the Soviet Union.
   B. caused the United States to enter the war on the Allied side.
   C. inflicted huge losses on the Red Army but failed to defeat the Soviet Union.
   D. captured Moscow and Leningrad and murdered most of their populations.

6. During the October Revolution of 1917, the Bolsheviks
   A. forced Tsar Nicholas II to abdicate the throne.
   B. overthrew the Provisional Government.
   C. overthrew Kornilov's military dictatorship.
   D. seized the leadership of the Petrograd Soviet.

7. The ultimate objective of the Five-Year Plans was to
   A. create a modern industrial economy and make the USSR militarily competitive.
   B. create an economy unhindered by post-WWI reparation payments.
   C. create a large domestic market well supplied with food and consumer goods.
   D. maximize the extraction of oil and coal to get cash for buying weapons.

8. The Revolution of 1905–1907 changed Russia's political system by
   A. depriving the tsar of all real power, now given to the Soviets.
   B. extending full political and civil rights to women and peasants.
   C. abolishing the State Duma and the Imperial Council of State.
   D. introducing a limited parliamentary system and basic civil rights.

9. Stalin's policy toward Yugoslavia in 1948 involved
   A. a conflict with Tito that effectively banished Yugoslavia from the Soviet bloc.
   B. tacitly supporting Tito's open invasion of Southern Greece.
   C. close alliance with Tito and a purge of anti-Stalin politicians in Yugoslavia.
   D. the removal of Tito by pro-Stalin politicians angered by his liberalism.

10. Gorbachev's policy of *glasnost* (openness) sought to
    A. open the Soviet Union's borders to tourism and commercial visitors.
    B. open up forced-labor camps in order to start relying on free labor.
    C. strengthen Communism through the public discussion of problems.
    D. expose Communist ideology for the failure that it really was.

11. The secret protocol to the Molotov-Ribbentrop Pact of 1939
    A. promised the Black Sea Straits to Stalin after victory over Britain.
    B. turned Czechoslovakia over to Hitler over British and French objections.
    C. negotiated the end of the Spanish Civil War of 1936–1939.
    D. divided much of Eastern Europe into Soviet and German spheres.

12. The Cuban missile crisis of 1962 broke out because
    A. Cubans stole missile technology from the Soviet Union to threaten the United States.
    B. the United States installed ballistic missiles in Guantanamo Bay to threaten Cuba.
    C. the United States Navy took over a ship with defecting Soviet and Cuban missile scientists.
    D. Soviet ballistic missiles, combat aircraft, and troops were deployed to Cuba.

13. The conflict between Armenia and Azerbaijan in 1988–1994 was over
    A. Nagorno-Karabakh.
    B. South Ossetia.
    C. the Donbass.
    D. Western Transnistria.

14. Stalin's nationality policies after 1945
    A. decided that Russian and Ukrainian languages should be merged.
    B. declared that victory had been achieved by all national groups working together.
    C. emphasized the leading role played by ethnic Russians in defeating Hitler's Germany.
    D. blamed Jews and Americans for causing Hitler's invasion.

15. What was the objective of the Soviet invasion of Afghanistan in 1979?
    - **A.** To remove Hafizullah Amin from power and bolster the pro-Soviet regime
    - **B.** To prevent an imminent Islamist coup by Nur Muhammad Taraki
    - **C.** To install a Communist government that would be friendly to the USSR
    - **D.** To gain access to a warm-water port on the Indian Ocean for the Soviet Navy

16. The objective of the attempted coup in August 1991 was to
    - **A.** remove Communists from power.
    - **B.** save the Soviet Union from collapse.
    - **C.** turn the Soviet Union into a federation.
    - **D.** expel Central Asian republics from the Soviet Union.

17. Khrushchev's "secret speech" of 1956 denounced
    - **A.** Stalin's purges of loyal Bolsheviks.
    - **B.** Stalin's forced collectivization of the late 1920s.
    - **C.** deportations of ethnic Germans during the Second World War.
    - **D.** his own incompetence during the Second World War.

18. The Cultural Revolution of the 1920s involved all of the following EXCEPT:
    - **A.** Purging "bourgeois" academics, artists, and professionals
    - **B.** Ensuring that Communist writers only used the Russian language
    - **C.** Creative experimentation with form in all areas of the arts
    - **D.** Creating the ideal of a "new" Communist individual

19. Brezhnev's leadership style as the General Secretary was to
    - **A.** emulate Stalin's strong-man tactics.
    - **B.** share power with his fellow Politburo members.
    - **C.** delegate power to other ex-KGB men.
    - **D.** give major positions to non-Party bureaucrats.

20. The Soviet leaders' initial reaction to Reagan's increase in military spending in the early 1980s was to become
    - **A.** convinced that a major purge was required to uncover Reagan's spies.
    - **B.** resigned to opening the Soviet Union up to capitalism and democracy.
    - **C.** committed to providing Communist China with nuclear weapons.
    - **D.** alarmed and determined to develop an adequate military response.

ANSWER KEY AND EXPLANATIONS

1. D	5. C	9. A	13. A	17. A
2. C	6. B	10. C	14. C	18. B
3. D	7. A	11. D	15. A	19. B
4. A	8. D	12. D	16. B	20. D

1. **The correct answer is D.** The Russian army retreated from Poland and Lithuania in 1915, but defeated Austria-Hungary in Galicia in 1914 and 1916. Choice A is incorrect because the Russian army was not fighting Germany in Eastern Ukraine. Choice B is incorrect because the Russian army did not come close to capturing Berlin. Choice C is incorrect because the Russian army did not win all the major battles.

2. **The correct answer is C.** The Pale of Settlement imposed civil and legal restrictions upon the Jews. Choices A, B, and D are incorrect because the Pale of Settlement did not apply to these groups.

3. **The correct answer is D.** Allies originally agreed that Germany would be deprived of its military forces and defense industry, though eventually both Eastern and Western Germany were rearmed. Choice A is incorrect because though Poland did soon become Communist, the agreement at Yalta was to hold free elections. Choice B is incorrect because the agreement was for the USSR to attack Japan after Hitler's defeat. Choice C is incorrect because Communist war criminals were not discussed at Yalta.

4. **The correct answer is A.** Collective farms were required to meet harsh grain procurement quotas. They could sell surplus product (if any). Choice B is incorrect because collective farms grew the entire range of agricultural crops cultivated in the Soviet Union. Choice C is incorrect because no military force was raised on collective farms. Choice D is incorrect because, although many villagers left to work in factories, this was not a required feature of collective farms.

5. **The correct answer is C.** The German army captured large amounts of territory and prisoners in the summer and fall of 1941 but failed to inflict a decisive defeat on the Red Army. Choice A is incorrect because Allied supply routes were not a major concern to Germany until 1942 and were never completely cut off. Choice B is incorrect because it was actually Germany that declared war on the United States and not directly as a result of Operation Barbarossa. Choice D is incorrect because Germany's military did kill large numbers of Soviet civilians but never captured Moscow or Leningrad.

6. **The correct answer is B.** In October 1917, Lenin's Bolsheviks overthrew the Provisional Government and seized power in the name of the Soviets. Choice A is incorrect because Nicholas II abdicated earlier, in February 1917. Choice C is incorrect because General Kornilov never became a military dictator. Choice D is incorrect because the Bolsheviks already controlled Petrograd's Soviet by October 1917.

7. **The correct answer is A.** Five-Year Plans were intended to catch up with the most advanced Western countries in industrial output and thus create the industrial capacity needed to upgrade the Soviet military. Choice B is incorrect because reparation payments were not imposed on the Soviet Union. Choice C is incorrect because developing a domestic market, including food and consumer goods, was not considered to be as important as infrastructure and heavy industry. Choice D is incorrect because oil exports were important in the 1930s but not the ultimate objective of Soviet industrialization; moreover, the USSR did not import large numbers of weapons.

8. **The correct answer is D.** The October Manifesto of 1905 granted basic civil rights, such as freedom of speech, religion, and assembly, and established a parliament consisting of the State Duma and the Council of State, which did not, however, have any control over the cabinet. Choice A is incorrect because the tsar retained control over the executive branch and Soviets were not officially recognized government organs. Choice B is incorrect because women and peasants did not receive full political and civil rights in 1905. Choice C is incorrect because the State Duma and the Council of State were not abolished.

9. **The correct answer is A.** Stalin's break with Tito turned Yugoslavia into a "nonaligned" nation equally distant from the West and the Soviet Union. Choice B is incorrect because Yugoslavia supported Communist guerillas in Greece but never openly invaded it. Choice C is incorrect because the Soviet Union's close alliance with Tito ended, rather than began, in 1948, and there was no Stalinist purge. Choice D is incorrect because while Tito's removal or even assassination was contemplated in Moscow, it was never carried out.

10. **The correct answer is C.** Gorbachev initially sought to revive Communism through more active public discussion and public participation in government. Choice A is incorrect because "openness" did not refer to open borders. Choice B is incorrect because Gorbachev's policies did not focus on the USSR's large (nonpolitical) prison inmate population. Choice D is incorrect because Gorbachev did not intend to undermine Communism itself.

11. **The correct answer is D.** The Pact recognized various parts of Eastern Europe as predominantly Soviet or German spheres of influence. Choice A is incorrect because the 1939 Pact did not promise the Black Sea Straits to Stalin. Choice B is incorrect because Czechoslovakia was turned over to Hitler as a consequence of the Munich Agreement of 1938, which was also signed by Britain and France. Choice C is incorrect because the Spanish Civil War ended in a Nationalist military victory and not a negotiated peace.

12. **The correct answer is D.** The 1962 crisis began after the United States found out that Soviet missiles and other forces were deployed to Cuba. Choice A is incorrect because Cuba did not steal missile technology from the Soviet Union. Choice B is incorrect because the United States did not install ballistic missiles in Guantanamo Bay. Choice C is incorrect.

13. **The correct answer is A.** The Armenian-Azeri war involved the region of Nagorno-Karabakh, which belonged to the Soviet republic of Azerbaijan but was largely populated by ethnic Armenians. Choices B, C, and D are incorrect because ethnic tensions in these regions did not involve the Armenians and the Azeri.

14. **The correct answer is C.** While recognizing other national groups and cultures, Stalinist propaganda immediately after the end of the Second World War claimed that the victory was primarily due to the efforts and sacrifices of the Russian nation. Choice A is incorrect because there was never any attempt to merge Russian and Ukrainian languages. Choice B is incorrect because Stalinist policies targeted several ethnic groups, such as the Chechens and the Crimean Tatars, for repression for their alleged collaboration with the Nazis. Choice D is incorrect because although Jews and Americans were indeed portrayed as opponents of the Soviet Union after 1945, they were not blamed for Hitler's invasion.

15. **The correct answer is A.** The Soviet invasion intended to bolster Soviet influence in Afghanistan by placing Soviet garrisons there and by removing Amin because he was thought to be plotting against the Soviet Union. Choice B is incorrect because Taraki was not pro-Iranian and was killed by Amin shortly before the Soviet invasion. Choice C is incorrect because Afghanistan already had a Communist government in 1979. Choice D is incorrect because Afghanistan did not have access to the Indian Ocean, and the Soviet government did not intend to invade Pakistan to obtain such access.

16. **The correct answer is B.** The members of Gorbachev's government who participated in the attempted coup intended to prevent the impending dissolution of the Soviet Union. Choice A is incorrect because the coup was not directed against Communists. Choice C is incorrect because it did not intend to turn the Soviet Union into a federation. Choice D is incorrect because the coup was attempted to save the Soviet Union, not to expel any of its constituent republics.

17. **The correct answer is A.** Khrushchev's "secret speech" condemned Stalin's purges of Bolsheviks who had been loyal to Stalin but did not apply to the purges of numerous other categories of victims. Choices B, C, and D are incorrect because Khrushchev did not address any of these issues in his speech.

18. **The correct answer is B.** New communist literature could be written in languages other than Russian, as long as it was socialist in content. Choices A, C, and D are incorrect because all of these items were part of the Cultural Revolution.

19. **The correct answer is B.** Brezhnev exercised his power through consensus with several other top Party members. Choice A is incorrect because although the cult of Stalin made a limited reappearance under Brezhnev, the latter did not imitate his ruling style. Choice C is incorrect because while the KGB and its chairman Yurii Andropov were important under Brezhnev, he himself was not a KGB man. Choice D is incorrect because membership in the Communist Party was required to hold any important position in the Soviet government.

20. **The correct answer is D.** Soviet leaders were alarmed by U.S. military spending and decided that more advanced military systems had to be designed to counter the latest U.S. weapons. Choice A is incorrect because some Soviet leaders believed that stricter discipline was needed but none of them wanted a major purge. Choice B is incorrect because Soviet leaders did not at any point think that changing the USSR's ideology or socioeconomic system was a proper response to U.S. military pressure. Choice C is incorrect because China already possessed nuclear weapons.

answers diagnostic test

DIAGNOSTIC TEST ASSESSMENT GRID

Now that you've completed the diagnostic test and read through the answer explanations, you can use your results to target your studying. Find the question numbers from the diagnostic test that you answered incorrectly and highlight or circle them below. Then focus extra attention to the sections within the chapter dealing with those topics.

History of the Soviet Union		
Content Area	**Topic**	**Question #**
Russia Under the Old Regime	• Governing Institutions • Economics • Culture and Society • Foreign Affairs • Revolutionary Movements	2, 8
The Revolutionary Period: 1914–1921	• The First World War • February/March Revolution • Interim • Bolshevik Revolution • Civil War • New Economic Policy (NEP)	1, 6
Prewar Stalinism	• Collectivization • Industrialization • Reign of Terror • Stalinist Culture • Nationalities	4, 7, 18
The Second World War	• Prewar Foreign Relations • The Course of the War • The Impact of the War • Settlements of WWII and the Origins of the Cold War	3, 5, 11
Postwar Stalinism	• Reconstruction • Nationalism • The Arms Race • Cold War in Europe • Cold War in Asia	9, 14

History of the Soviet Union		
Content Area	**Topic**	**Question #**
The Khrushchev Years	• Succession Struggle • De-Stalinization • Soviet Relations with the U.S. Under Khrushchev • Proxy Wars • Rift with China	12, 17
The Brezhnev Era	• Growth and Stagnation • Ideological Dissent • Détente • Proxy Wars in the Third World • War in Afghanistan	15, 19
Reform and Collapse	• Global Challengers • External Factors (Afghanistan, Islam) • Perestroika and Glasnost • Reemergence of the Nationalities Issues • Revolutions in Eastern Europe • End of the Union of Soviet Socialist Republics • Gorbachev's Legacy	10, 13, 16, 20

GET THE FACTS

To see the DSST® History of the Soviet Union Fact Sheet, go to **http://getcollegecredit.com/ exam_fact_sheets** and click on the **Social Sciences** tab. Scroll down and click the **History of the Soviet Union** link. Here you will find suggestions for further study material and the ACE college credit recommendations for passing the test.

RUSSIA UNDER THE OLD REGIME

GOVERNING INSTITUTIONS

The country known today as Russia first became powerful in the late fifteenth century, when the Grand Duchy of Moscow (also known as Muscovy) rose to prominence among dozens of small East Slavic states, known collectively as Rus'. Compared to its neighbors, such as Poland or the Mongol Empire, Muscovy was small, poor, and thinly populated. Yet, within a few generations, it became the largest state in Europe and eventually in the world. Traditionally referred to as "tsars," the rulers of Moscow claimed to be overlords of all the lands of medieval Rus', which today comprise European Russia, Ukraine, and Belarus (Belorussia). Tsar Peter the Great (r. 1682–1725) changed much of Russia's politics and culture in accordance with contemporary Western European models. He moved his capital from **Moscow** to the newly founded city of **St. Petersburg** on the Baltic Sea and in 1721 adopted the title of "emperor," intended to assert his equality with the grandest European rulers.

In the 1860s, Alexander II began his trailblazing reign as tsar as he completely overhauled the court system and the process of legal proceedings in an attempt to unify the judicial system, emancipated serfs, and allowed some localized self-government.

In the early twentieth century, Russia was the only major European state headed by a monarch who was not formally limited by an elected parliament or by any law that he could not change at will. The term for this type of rule is **autocracy**.) Russia's last tsar, **Nicholas II** (r. 1894-1917), was brought up believing that he had a divine mission to maintain his autocratic power.

The Revolution of 1905–1907 and the Duma Monarchy

Only in 1905, facing massive labor strikes, urban riots, and military mutinies—the Revolution of 1905–1907—was Nicholas II persuaded to establish an elected legislature, the **State Duma,** with the power to control the budget and to grant his subjects' basic civil rights, including freedom of speech, worship, and assembly. Nonetheless, Nicholas retained important powers, which included control over all cabinet appointments, foreign policy, and provincial governors, thus limiting the parliamentary system. The **Russian Orthodox Church,** closely tied to the monarchy, remained Russia's state religion, although other faiths were tolerated even before 1905. Russia's judiciary was technically independent after the court reform of 1864 and, on the whole, managed to resist political pressure, except for cases involving revolutionary terrorism and propaganda, which were thought to be too sensitive to be tried by regular juries.

ECONOMICS

Russia's economy in the early twentieth century was one of the largest in the world, its GDP inferior only to the United States, Germany, and Great Britain and approximately equal to that of France. It was a leading exporter of agricultural products, for example, holding almost 40 percent of the export market for wheat. It was growing at a rate that was above average for Western countries and it was an attractive market for foreign investment. However, per capita incomes remained among the lowest in Europe.

Agriculture

The reason for the disparity between the size of Russia's economy and its small per-capita income was its mass of small-scale peasant farmers (over 85 percent of the population), whose labor productivity was much lower than that of Western European and American farmers. In central Russia, Ukraine, and Belorussia, peasants typically lived in **village communes,** whose leaders periodically redistributed plots of agricultural land among peasant families to ensure that they would be able to pay their share of taxes. In the **black-earth** regions of South Russia and Ukraine, agriculture was far more profitable than in the north, and huge capitalistic estates worked by hired laborers and owned by aristocrats or wealthy businessmen were common. In Central and Northern Russia, soils were poor, and peasants had to supplement their income by engaging in crafts and trade, finding factory work, or moving to cities.

In the late nineteenth century, peasants' productivity, prosperity, and health were gradually improving, and the population of the Russian empire skyrocketed from 129 million in 1897 to 175 million in 1914.

Nonetheless, the **"peasant question"** was one of the most pressing social problems in late imperial Russia, owing to the fact that rural areas were overpopulated and family land allotments were shrinking. The government attempted to solve this by promoting peasant migration and settlements of fertile lands in Siberia, the Far East, and today's Kazakhstan, but this strategy was only partially successful.

Industry and Trade

The first industrial enterprises appeared in Russia in the seventeenth century, and Peter the Great made an effort to establish a metalworking industry in the resource-rich **Ural Mountains.** In the nineteenth century, new economic centers had emerged:

- **St. Petersburg**, with its heavy and machine-building industry
- The **Moscow** area, with its textile and food-processing plants
- **Ukraine** and South **Russia**, with their rich natural resources and proximity to Black Sea ports

Not surprisingly, given Russia's size, its rail network was the largest in Europe in 1914. The **Trans-Siberian Railroad** connected European Russia to the Pacific Ocean, although it mostly had military, rather than economic, utility. Prior to 1914, the rail system was quite weak. Russia's financial system vastly improved with the introduction of the **gold standard** in 1897 by Finance Minister **Sergei Witte.** The gold standard held down inflation and encouraged investment by stabilizing the currency. In short, the economy in the early twentieth century had problems but overall was experiencing modern economic growth and was not at all a failure that could by itself explain the eventual Bolshevik Revolution of 1917.

CULTURE AND SOCIETY

Imperial Russia had been for centuries divided into a system of **legal estates,** caste-like legal categories that included nobles, merchants, peasants, the clergy, and townspeople. These categories were usually inherited, but it was possible to change one's status and even become a noble through state service. The father of Vladimir Lenin, the founder of the Soviet state, became a nobleman by serving as a superintendent of a provincial school district.

Peasants were the largest such group or estate. Until the **Emancipation of 1861,** almost half of all peasants were *enserfed*, that is, tied to the land and treated little better than slaves: still considered to be moral human beings, serfs could nonetheless be punished at their master's discretion, sold, mortgaged, or even gambled away. After the Emancipation of 1861, almost all liberated serfs had to pay burdensome redemption payments to compensate their former owners for their loss. Noble landowners lost some of their land during the Emancipation but generally retained their wealth and their privileged access to education and state service. They also retained their power in the government in general, especially in the countryside among their former serfs. In addition, there was a growing middle class that included merchants, entrepreneurs, and various professionals.

Social Inequality

Many authors claim that the social gap between elites and common people in Russia was also a cultural one. Commoners were supposed to be truly Russian in their clothing, speech, and various social rituals, whereas the upper classes and the intellectuals—also known as the **intelligentsia**—supposedly had discarded their Russian heritage and embraced a common Western European culture. This picture is misleading, since even peasants actively participated in Russia's capitalist market economy, including its consumer culture, whereas nobles and rich merchants shared the Russian language and the Russian Orthodox faith and were also becoming more nationalistic on the eve of the First World War.

FOREIGN AFFAIRS

Russia was among the victors at the **Congress of Vienna** (1814–1815), which concluded the Napoleonic Wars, but in turn lost the **Crimean War** (1853–1856) against Great Britain, France, the Ottoman Empire, and Sardinia. Russia's defeat and subsequent military weakness facilitated the wars of German Unification. The rise of a powerful German state alarmed Russia and led to its unlikely alliance with republican France in 1893. Preparing to fight Germany in Europe, Russia was at the same time engaged in a competition with Great Britain in Central Asia known as the **Great Game,** with proxy wars and secret agents.

In the 1890s, Russia also intensified its efforts to develop and expand its Far Eastern possessions, coming into conflict with Japan in 1904–1905. It was a disaster for Russia, but it also enabled its army to learn from the defeat and to make a deal with Britain in 1908 that temporarily ended the Great Game. As a result, in 1914, Russia was a key member of the Triple Entente alongside Britain and France.

REVOLUTIONARY MOVEMENTS

Ironically—given that the Bolsheviks would make Russia the world's first communist state—radical socialist parties in late tsarist Russia tended to be small and without any broad external support. Russia avoided involvement in the European revolutions of 1848. More widespread was the populist movement of the 1860s and 1870s. Building on the ideas of Alexander Herzen and Mikhail Bakunin, **populists** sought to achieve social transformation by working through the common people, especially peasants, who resisted attempts at radicalization. In desperation, some populists turned to terror to force the government to make concessions. Tsar **Alexander II** was hunted down and assassinated in 1881. While small in numbers, Russian radicals created an image of a professional rebel who would give up all normal occupations and attachments to focus on revolutionary work.

Revolutionary Parties and Marxism in Russia in the Early Twentieth Century

In the late 1880s, another influential radical group appeared, basing its views on the teachings of **Karl Marx.** Political change, according to Marxists, would be enacted by rebelling industrial workers, who were better educated and organized than peasants and were deprived of all property. Yet Russian factory workers were relatively few in number, and this raised questions about how to adapt Marx's teachings. Around 1914, populists were still very influential in Russia, forming the **Socialist Revolutionary Party**, or the **SRs**.

The Origins of the Bolshevik Party

The leading Marxist party was the Russian **Social Democratic Workers' Party**, who split in 1903 into **Bolsheviks** and **Mensheviks**. The Bolsheviks, led by **Vladimir Lenin**, falsely claimed to be the majority wing. Lenin's followers believed in forming a small core of dedicated professional revolutionaries and that other less dedicated socialist groups could be more dangerous than bourgeois oppressors. The Mensheviks—the "minority"—were led by **Yulii Martov** and were more inclined to use legal channels and to cooperate with other radical groups. These parties were very active during Russia's first revolution in 1905–1907, but after the tsar granted a constitution and basic civil rights, revolutionaries lost almost all of their mass support and tacit backing of the liberal propertied classes. Socialist leaders, like Joseph Stalin, were arrested or went into exile (Lenin or **Leon Trotsky**). Surviving groups were heavily infiltrated by tsarist spies.

THE REVOLUTIONARY PERIOD: 1914–1921

The long history of tsarist Russia came to its end during the First World War, 1914–1918, during which Russia fought on the side of the **Triple Entente**, allied with Great Britain and France, against the **Central Powers** of Germany, Austria-Hungary, the Ottoman Empire, and Bulgaria. Russia left the war early in 1918 as the result of a separate peace treaty. The war led to the collapse of Russian, German, Austro-Hungarian, and Ottoman multiethnic empires, and it also enabled the Bolsheviks to seize power in 1917 during the October Revolution. The Bolsheviks were able to consolidate their power and defeat their opponents during the civil war that began in 1918 and ended in 1920 (1922 in the Russian Far East).

THE FIRST WORLD WAR

In 1914, Russia went to war with Germany and Austria-Hungary to protect Serbia, a small Orthodox Christian country in the Balkans, from an impending Austrian invasion. There were deeper reasons as well: an economic competition with Germany and geopolitical competition in the Balkans with Austria-Hungary. Russia's size made it very difficult to invade, while its huge population helped it to maintain the largest standing army in Europe. There are many myths about the imperial army's supposed inferiority and lack of weapons or training. In reality, it had many problems, but not more than every other European army.

The key weakness was the fact that the Russian economy as a whole, and especially its military industry, was too fragile to sustain a grueling war of attrition that tested industrial capacity and quickly devoured peacetime stocks of weapons and ammunitions.

Military Operations

During the opening battles, the Russian army had mixed success. One force attacked the German province of Eastern Prussia, while the Germans were busy invading France. However, the assault was hasty and poorly coordinated, and a smaller German force defeated General Samsonov's Second Army and captured about 50,000 prisoners. A clear and strategically important victory for Germany, the Battle of Tannenberg did not inflict any lasting damage on the Russian army.

At the same time, the Russians defeated Austro-Hungarian armies in Galicia, a borderland area in what is today Western Ukraine. But by the end of 1914, Russia's economy was barely coping with the war effort. Plans to increase production proved inadequate. Munition shortages became so acute in 1915 that the Russian artillery was unable to repel German offensives, which occupied Russian Poland and most of Lithuania. However, Germany failed in its objective to knock Russia out of the war or at least cripple it. In 1916, after the shortages were rectified, General **Aleksei Brusilov** inflicted a severe defeat on Austria-Hungary, and General Yudenich defeated the Ottoman Empire in Asia Minor. In sum, by the end of 1916, the military situation for Russia was stable despite severe losses. Some borderlands were lost to the Germans, but no major centers were captured or even threatened, as compared, for example, to France, which lost much of its industrial capacity to German attack.

Economy and Society During the War

Two other factors weakened Russia's war effort. First, its economic situation rapidly deteriorated. Tax revenues shrank, grain exports stopped due to enemy blockade, and inflation was rising, so that wages were losing their value. Conscription, refugee movements, and deportations of suspect groups (such as ethnic Germans) from areas close to the front created social dislocation. Second, politics and government were in a crisis. After the initial patriotic outburst, the losses of 1915 undermined the public's confidence in the tsar and his ministers. The Duma was convened only sporadically, and cabinet ministers were replaced every few months. There was no civilian leader on whom Nicholas II was willing to rely. In 1915, he even made himself a Commander-in-Chief—an unpopular move because it removed him from Petrograd (as St. Petersburg was renamed during the war).

Given the imperial family's withdrawn life and the absence of reliable information, rumors spread widely, blaming the Romanovs for military defeats and accusing the empress of being a German spy and a lover of the mystic **Grigorii Rasputin.** In short, Russia's elites no longer believed that the tsar could lead Russia to victory and avoid a serious crisis; they were willing to try something new.

FEBRUARY/MARCH REVOLUTION

The opportunity for change came in 1917. Economic problems and especially interruptions in food supplies in Petrograd led to strikes and then demonstrations and riots. The city garrison was ordered to fire on the protesters, but instead the soldiers started to join in. Nicholas II wanted to send loyal troops to regain control, but his top generals told him the revolution had gone too far and asked for his abdication. In March, Nicholas turned his throne over to his brother Michael who, in turn, immediately surrendered his power to a **Provisional Government** formed mostly by members of the liberal **Kadet (Constitutional Democratic) Party.** Nicholas and his wife and children were placed under house arrest and later transported to the interior of Russia to prevent them from fleeing the country. In 1918, they were executed by Bolshevik operatives in the city of Yekaterinburg.

INTERIM

The revolution in 1917 brought an end to centuries of tzarist autocracy. The sequence of events after Nicholas II's abdication served as milestones heading toward the communist revolution in Russia.

The Provisional Government's Policies and the Soviets

The Provisional Government's task was to govern until a **Constitutional Assembly** could be elected to determine Russia's new political structure. Meanwhile, it was to continue the war effort and make no major policy decisions. However, from the beginning this government had to operate in agreement with the **Petrograd Soviet**, a city council of deputies sent by factories and army units. Fearful that the Provisional Government would try to restore the "Old Regime," the Petrograd Soviet immediately issued its infamous **Order No. 1**, which created elected soldier committees in all military units (at first in Petrograd only but other garrisons soon followed their lead), whose authority superseded that of the officers. This decree crippled military discipline and thereby fatally undermined Russia's war effort. Soldiers started to surrender their trenches, refuse orders, murder their officers, or simply desert. Unlike the French Great Munity of 1917, Russian commanders were unable to restore order.

Lenin and the April Theses

The Soviet was dominated by socialists, mainly SRs and Mensheviks, as were the other Soviets that sprung up in most cities of the empire. The Bolsheviks initially played a minor role because most of their leaders were in exile abroad. Vladimir Lenin returned to Petrograd in April and issued his famous April Theses, in which he urged the Soviets to depose the Provisional Government; overturn the entire capitalist order, disband the army, the police, and the bureaucracy; nationalize all agricultural land; and refuse to support the war. This program met sharp criticism from the other parties and even from many Bolsheviks.

The July Days and the Kornilov Revolt

Many revolutionary leaders hoped that revolutionary ideas would improve morale and achieve a military breakthrough. However, the **June Offensive of 1917** was a great failure because, after initial successes, many units simply refused to advance. Only a few days later, this defeat led to another major uprising in Petrograd, known as the July Days. Started by conscripts trying to avoid being sent to the front, it was soon joined by the Bolsheviks. However, their first attempt to seize power through a mass popular uprising failed because their party lacked sufficient support and experience.

The result of the July Days was a rapid polarization of Russia's political life. The Bolsheviks were for a while viewed as traitors to the revolution. Liberal ministers were forced to resign and were replaced by moderate socialists led by former lawyer **Alexander Kerensky.** The military command was given to conservative General **Lavr Kornilov,** who was tasked with restoring military discipline. In late August, he sent some troops to Petrograd, apparently at Kerensky's request, to finish off the Bolsheviks and introduce direct military rule. However, Kerensky was reluctant to lose his power: he changed his mind and declared Kornilov a traitor. Kornilov's "rebellion" failed, but the Provisional Government lost most of its legitimacy, whereas the Soviets were becoming more influential and led by a resurgent Bolshevik party.

BOLSHEVIK REVOLUTION

Political crisis, lack of military success, and continuing economic decline all undermined the Provisional Government, and in October the Bolshevik Party organized a coup in the name of the Bolshevik-dominated Soviets. The Bolsheviks cooperated with the more radical members of the Social Revolutionary Party and enjoyed considerable support among the Petrograd garrison and among factory workers. Kerensky's government was unable to obtain emergency powers; most politicians also believed that the Bolsheviks' uprising would fail as it had in July.

Over the course of several days, Lenin's Bolsheviks seized control of the garrison, captured most militarily important points and finally, on November 7–8[1], arrested the Provisional Government itself without any significant bloodshed. This event became officially known as the Great October Socialist Revolution, or just the **October Revolution.** Two days later, Lenin formed a new government consisting only of Bolsheviks—the **Soviet of People's Commissars.** However, bloody street fighting continued in Moscow for another week and forces loyal to the Provisional Government continued to resist in many other cities. Elections to the Constitutional Assembly were held as planned. The result was that only about a quarter of all seats went to the Bolsheviks, and the Assembly was disbanded on its opening day, while a demonstration in its support was gunned down by Bolshevik troops. Meanwhile, the Soviets were purged of members who refused to support the Bolsheviks.

Bolshevik Policies and War Communism

Once they seized power, the Bolsheviks introduced a policy of "war communism" that was meant to jump-start Russia's crumbling government and the economy. Some measures were meant to win

---

1. The dates November 7–8 correspond to the New Style (Gregorian) calendar. Until 1918, Soviet Russia used the Old Style (Julian) calendar, on which the dates of the revolution were October 24–25.

popular support, such as the declaration of the 8-hour workday, the placing of all factories under workers' control, and granting all ethnic groups the right of self-determination.

Other measures were meant to secure Bolshevik power: political parties and newspapers opposing the Bolsheviks were prohibited, and the old-regime army, state service, courts, and the police were all disbanded and replaced with a new Bolshevik-controlled military force. A December 20, 1917, decree established the ChK (or **Cheka),** the Bolshevik secret police tasked with fighting counter-revolution, suppressing economic crime, and combating corruption within the Soviet government.

Nationalization of Private Property

Most important, the policy of war communism also included claiming complete control over the economy, seizing all banks and their deposits, nationalizing all large industry, prohibiting private entrepreneurship, and asserting complete monopoly over food supply and food trade, sending out food requisition squads into the countryside to ensure that the army and the most important factories would stay supplied. Not surprisingly, such policies led to mass uprisings and to runaway inflation and a flourishing black market. Eventually, in 1921–1922, Russia experienced one of the most terrible famines in its history, with approximately 5 million deaths from starvation.

Separate Peace with Germany

Finally, on March 3, 1918, Bolshevik Russia signed a separate peace treaty, the **Treaty of Brest-Litovsk**, with Germany, whereby it lost vast territories, including Poland, Ukraine, Belorussia, Finland, and the Baltic provinces, with almost a third of its population and a large share of its economic capacity. Lenin's government promised to make huge reparation payments and to demobilize Russia's military forces. Because of its separate peace with Germany, Soviet Russia was not included among the victorious powers during the Versailles negotiations in 1919. Taken together, Lenin's early policies were costly and arguably a failure overall, but they permitted the Bolsheviks to consolidate their power and defeat their armed opponents during the Civil War that began in early 1918.

CIVIL WAR

Anti-Bolshevik organizations and armed resistance began to appear everywhere soon after the October Revolution, but the Bolsheviks were able to maintain control in central Russia and especially in Moscow and Petrograd, arresting many conspirators and instituting a regime of **Red Terror**, which involved seizing and executing hostages. Anti-Bolshevik forces, known as the Whites, were made up of monarchists, liberals, and socialist revolutionaries, and they were more successful in the borderland territories.

Most White armies were led by former tsarist commanders with military experience, foreign assistance, and control over some important resources. Other White movements attempted to unite Russia against the Bolsheviks; in the process, they vowed to preserve private property and to leave the question of Russia's constitution to an elected assembly to be convened after their victory.

This project was not popular among non-Russian groups, among whom the Whites had to operate, or even among the mostly anti-Bolshevik **Cossacks.** Many regions were controlled by rebels hostile both to the Bolsheviks' **Red Army** and to the Whites. These were ironically known as the Greens. By late 1920, the Red Army had won the Civil War in European Russia because the Bolsheviks controlled Russia's central core, were more successful in economic and military mobilization, and were able to attract or conscript many military and other experts from the Old Regime.

NEW ECONOMIC POLICY (NEP)

Even after the Russian Civil War, "war communism" still dictated Soviet Russia's economic policy. As part of the policy, farmers and factory workers were ordered to produce food and goods, and these items were then taken and distributed at the discretion of the government. During the war, this distribution plan was in place to keep towns and troops stocked with food and weapons. The inefficient implementation of this policy was in part responsible for the devastating famine in 1921–1922. The resulting national discontent led to the development of a new economic policy for Russia.

Crisis of War Communism, 1920–1921

As the Civil War was nearing its end in 1920, other troubles plagued Soviet Russia. The newly independent Poland invaded Soviet Ukraine, Belorussia, and Lithuania, attempting to restore eighteenth-century borders. The Red Army counterattacked all the way to Warsaw, where it was, in turn, routed. The defeat in Poland cost Soviet Russia large swaths of territory and showed that Russia's army was exhausted after almost seven years of continuous warfare. Peasants were revolting throughout Russia, especially in the rich agricultural region around Tambov. Even revolutionary sailors in the Baltic fortress of Kronstadt revolted in early 1921, showing that the Bolsheviks were starting to lose support among their most faithful followers. Party members were beginning to quit, and many started to openly question Lenin's leadership.

Agriculture and Trade Under the New Economic Policy (NEP)

In March 1921, the Bolsheviks produced policies that reintroduced some aspects of capitalism in Russia that became known as the **New Economic Policy** (NEP). Most important, food requisitioning was replaced by a fixed food tax, and the amount of grain confiscated from the peasants went down from 70 to 30 percent of the harvest. Peasant farmers were allowed to sell their surplus, as markets and private trade were once more permitted. NEP became something of a golden age for Russian peasants, because they were now free from the most restrictive policies of the Old Regime and the Bolsheviks. Much of housing stock and small businesses were privatized, as well. Some foreign companies were allowed to do business in Soviet Russia. After years of privation, consumer goods and entertainment became more accessible, especially for the new entrepreneurial and property-owning class known as **NEPmen,** who were mostly not Old-Regime capitalists, but ordinary peasants and workers enriched by NEP policies. Some Bolsheviks became despondent at the apparent restoration of capitalism, but others viewed it as only a temporarily setback.

Limitations of NEP

At the same time, this restoration of capitalism was limited in scale. Most important, Lenin was adamant not to relinquish the Bolshevik's political monopoly. Non-Party periodicals or non-Bolshevik political groups were strictly prohibited. SR leaders and religious figures were put on massive show trials in the early 1920s (although the former were not executed because of protests by European socialists). The political structure was regularized by the formation of the **Union of Soviet Socialist Republics** in 1922. This was formally a union of independent republics that had the right to secede but were controlled by the Red Army and through the Communist Party.

Moreover, the government retained control over large-scale industry, especially heavy industry, and foreign trade. By reserving these powers, the Bolsheviks would be able to reverse NEP when and if they chose to do so.

PREWAR STALINISM

After Lenin died in 1924, Joseph Stalin emerged as his most powerful successor, sidelining other Old Bolsheviks and forcing Leon Trotsky to emigrate. Stalin had been one of the key Bolshevik leaders in 1917, although his military record during the Civil War was not spotless. Stalin came to power because of his control of the Bolshevik Party bureaucracy and because of his ability to forge temporary tactical alliances with other key Party members.

COLLECTIVIZATION

In 1926–1927, peasants could not or would not produce enough grain to afford to purchase manufactured goods from the state (which were often overpriced and of poor quality). The state needed food for export and to supply growing cities, so this created the so-called **"scissors crisis."** A "Right" opposition led by Nikolai Bukharin wanted to raise procurement prices to incentivize the peasants, purchase grain abroad, and stop persecuting better-off peasants (known as **Kulaks**). Stalin rejected this solution. Instead, his policy was to create large, more profitable grain farms using modern machinery that would be controlled by the state. However, he instituted this plan with no clear law or instructions. Starting in 1927, young party members were sent from cities to force peasants to surrender their land, livestock, and farming equipment to cooperatives (known as **collective farms, kolkhoz,** or **state-owned "Soviet" farms, sovkhoz).**

Ultimately the state's objective was not only to transform small-scale peasant farms into highly productive cooperatives but also to transfer resources from agriculture to industry.

The Great Break and Peasants' Resistance

In 1929, Stalin announced the **"Great Break,"** claiming that the Soviet Union now had sufficient resources for complete collectivization. This intensification resulted in increased peasant resistance, with violence in the countryside peaking from 1930–1933. Peasants killed their livestock rather than surrender it, refused to work, and even killed activists in open uprisings. The government responded with arrests, executions, and exile; approximately 2 million peasants were branded as **"kulaks"** and exiled to remote regions. In a 1930 speech using the phrase **"dizzy with success,"** Stalin falsely put the blame for these excesses on Trotsky's followers occupying local administrative posts. The state abandoned its demand for immediate collectivization and many nonviable collective farms were disbanded, but later the same year, the process was forcefully renewed.

The Great Famine in 1932–1933

Bad weather in 1931–1932 compounded the problems caused by badly organized collective farms, decimated livestock, and insufficient seed stocks and resulted in large losses at harvest. State procurements were reduced somewhat (by 22 percent for grain), and grain exports—necessary for the state to obtain hard currency—were also reduced, but neither measure was enough to prevent famine in the winter of 1932–1933. Estimates of the number of victims vary from 2 to 8 million deaths, and overall approximately 40 million people were starving.

Holodomor in the Ukraine

TIP

The literal translation of the Ukrainian word *Holodomor* is "death by forced starvation."

As the center of large-scale specialized farming, responsible for 25 percent of grain production, Ukraine's large peasant population resisted collectivization fiercely and consequently suffered greatly in the famine, called the *Holodomor* in Ukrainian. Some believe that Russian Bolsheviks committed an intentional genocide of Ukrainians. However, the famine was equally brutal in Kazakhstan and Russia (Siberia, the Volga region, the North Caucasus, and former Cossack areas). The famine was certainly largely man-made, not simply through the wasteful policies of collectivization but also through the seizures of grain used to punish peasants for resistance. In addition to the famine, peasants were arrested in large numbers for supposed sabotage of the harvest, and those remaining in the famine areas were not allowed to flee to the cities. The following year, peasants were allowed small garden plots for their own use, and centralized oversight improved the management of kolkhozes. Harvests improved, but isolated famines continued to recur throughout the 1930s.

INDUSTRIALIZATION

One of the goals of collectivization was to provide food for the industrial workers inhabiting Soviet cities. After the Civil War, Russian heavy industry was less competitive than ever compared to the leading capitalist states, and the Bolsheviks feared invasion from capitalist powers at any time. At the same time, industrial workers were assumed to be the base of Bolshevik support. Stalin introduced the **First Five-Year Plan** for 1928–1932, which was meant to guide a process of rapid modernization of industry at the expense of the peasants (a plan similar to Trotsky's). In its original form, the plan was well thought out and realistic. It involved 1,500 sites, of which fifty consumed half of all state investment. The major types of projects constructed included:

- **Infrastructure:** canals, railroads, the Moscow metro
- **Energy:** especially hydroelectric power plants
- **Processing raw materials:** especially iron and steel production
- **Machine-building plants:** tractors, automobiles

A further aspect of the Plan was to develop technical education, and universal elementary education was introduced in 1930. Foreign experts were widely used to guide the process, especially from Germany and the United States. **Albert Kahn** alone got contracts for $2 billion, while whole factories were assembled in the United States and then moved to Russia. Industrial production grew rapidly, at a rate of 10–16 percent per year. By 1937, the Soviet Union was able to boast the second-largest industrial capacity in the world, second only to the United States.

Limitations of Central Planning

Once the plan was in place, the leadership continually revised its goals upward until it became entirely unrealistic, which led to faked statistics. The state also encouraged a movement to exceed the plan, which defeated the purpose of thinking out the process in advance. The **Stakhanov movement** consisted of workers using organizational techniques borrowed from Taylorism and Fordism to exceed quotas at the expense of other workers. The plans were also executed in part by forced labor. The Second Five-Year Plan, covering 1933–37, was somewhat more modest and had better results. Yet many of its projects were badly built or simply unnecessary. Agriculture suffered from the process, but the failures were blamed on so-called "traitors" and "saboteurs." These accusations helped to encourage a culture of purges and denunciations.

Industrialization and Consumer Goods

Another criticism of the Five-Year Plans was that they slanted toward heavy industry at the expense of developing the domestic market. Consumer goods were insufficient in this period, even for those with enough money. Instead, the state organized a distribution system for consumer goods and food rationing. A system like this had already existed during the Civil War, in which party members and other privileged categories received better packages, and similar inequalities persisted in the 1930s. In the long term, Stalin's industrialization has been seen as the greatest achievement of the Soviet period, but its legacy should be weighed in terms both of its costs and relative efficiency.

REIGN OF TERROR

By the mid-1930s, many of the worst aspects of collectivization and industrialization were settling down, and life was becoming slightly better for many. Yet what followed, starting in 1933 and culminating in 1936–1938, were mass arrests, deportations, and executions of alleged domestic "enemies."

Origins of Terror

Mass state-organized terror as a political tool was not new: the Red Terror first appeared during the Civil War and targeted members of former elite groups, monarchists, clergy, capitalists, and members of rival parties, and during the Cultural Revolution certain "bourgeois specialists" were targeted (they were engineers and other professionals who joined the Bolsheviks but were suspect because their training had been under the tsars).

The Great Terror of 1936–1938 and the Moscow Show Trials

The Great Terror of 1936–38 was different because Bolsheviks themselves became victims, including prominent early members of the party. Much of the party's "Old Guard" had at some point in the 1920s been in opposition to Stalin and his policies and were targeted on these grounds. In 1937 especially, victims often included people completely loyal to Stalin and large numbers of the party apparatus.

Reasons for this purge no doubt included Stalin's personal paranoia, but it was also a means of consolidating control, especially over regions that in the early 1930s often resisted commands from Moscow.

Cases were crudely falsified, usually relying only on coerced testimony from the defendants themselves. Some trials were publicized "show trials," including three **Moscow Show Trials** that were widely watched abroad, resulting in the execution or imprisonment of a total of 54 defendants, ultimately including **Genrikh Yagoda,** the former head of the Soviet-Russian secret police, who had supervised the first of the show trials. Other trials took place in other cities, out of the spotlight. The majority of cases were secret extrajudicial prosecutions carried out by secret police tribunals without even perfunctory legal protections.

The Extent of the Great Terror

But these trials and prosecutions were only the tip of the iceberg. At the heart of the Great Terror were two massive operations. Their purpose seems to have been to liquidate potential "enemies within," who were seen as likely to turn against the Soviets in the event of a major war, and send millions to labor camps (collectively known as **GULAG**) to silence and punish the enemy while benefiting from their labor. In a departure from typical patterns, these purges were largely driven not by political rivalries or personal animosities but were planned from above and mostly carried out through lists approved by Stalin or regional authorities.

One action, **Order 00447,** created for each region minimum quotas of various undesirables, including former kulaks, White army personnel, former propertied classes, and even ordinary criminals, who were to be put into two categories: those who would be executed and those to be imprisoned. The other operation targeted numerous national minorities—including Germans, Poles, Finns, Serbs, Greeks, and Koreans—who were suspected of being capable of helping the enemy if the Soviet Union were attacked. In total, direct executions during the Great Terror probably numbered about 1 million. There were no legal protections and often no hearings or proceedings whatsoever, and bodies were buried in secret. Millions more were either sent to the aforementioned labor camps or simply lost their jobs or were forced to move to less prestigious and less prosperous regions. The secret police itself was heavily damaged by the purges, as was the Red Army, which lost virtually all of its top commanders and much of its mid-echelon, who were accused of being traitors and enemy spies.

Responsibility for the Great Terror

There is debate about the extent to which the Terror was initiated from the top. A key piece of evidence is that it was stopped immediately when Stalin gave the command. By 1939 many people who had helped to carry out Terror were themselves purged. Fabricated prosecutions and killings continued until after Stalin's death in 1953 but were much more limited for the rest of his rule. At the same time, denunciations from ordinary people played a role in how the secret police fulfilled (or exceeded) their quotas, and there was a large stratum of persons who benefited from the purges because they took the jobs of the victims. These younger people tended to be completely committed to the Soviet regime because they owed their education and rapid rise to it

STALINIST CULTURE

In addition to terror and the transformation of the economy and society, the Bolsheviks from the very beginning regarded culture and the arts as a key instrument of control and of socialist restructuring.

TIP

GULAG was the acronym for the Russian words that translate to "main camp administration." At the height of its use, the GULAG system consisted of a combination of nearly 500 camps and labor colonies.

The Cultural Revolution

The term "cultural revolution" was used from 1917 onward. Many intellectuals welcomed the Revolution as an act of creative liberation. The 1920s was a period of cultural experimentation and creativity building on the achievements of pre-1917 **Russian Silver Age** culture. In this period, cinema flourished creatively, as did art, literature, music, and theater. Mass celebrations were organized to honor the Revolution, with the intention of luring people away from religious observance. Mass campaigns were waged against religion, consisting mainly of propaganda (periodicals, posters, and lectures) but also open persecution of the clergy and practicing believers, directed against all confessions. The arts were also employed to construct a cult of the Revolution and its heroes and promote the "new" communist individual. Additionally, there was an attempt to purge the bourgeois academics, artists, and professionals. Until around 1935, there was little emphasis on Stalin himself, but by the mid-1930s, a cult of his supposed revolutionary achievements (many of them imaginary) began to dominate.

Education and Mass Culture Under Socialism

Another key component of the cultural revolution was a campaign against illiteracy and for mass elementary education. In 1917, literacy rates in Russia had been among the lowest in Europe, but the Soviets organized a massive literacy drive, promoted continuing education, and instituted a system of affirmative action in favor of students from the working classes. This effort did result in huge gains in literacy and was widely popular. The new generation of children who went to school in this system also became acculturated to the new regime and its values.

Cultural revolution also applied to daily life and affected housing, leisure, and food. Old "bourgeois" forms, with their emphasis on privacy, gave way to public forms, built on the models of pre-1917 industrial settlements that were already overcrowded and therefore boasted little privacy. The new ideal was that socialization, eating, and entertainment should take place in public spaces, and their content should be carefully chosen to reflect socialist values.

Part of this effort was intended to liberate women from domestic chores associated with the bourgeois family model. Soviet women enjoyed full political and civil rights and were encouraged to get an education and enter the workforce, while the state intended to provide childcare and collective food preparation. In reality, the state often had difficulty following through on these provisions, leaving women with a "double burden" of work and family responsibilities.

Socialist Realism Under Stalin

When the term "socialist realism" began to be used to describe an artistic style approved by the regime around 1932, it signaled an end to the Revolution in art. The new emphasis was on traditional models in literature, painting, and other art forms. **Maxim Gorky,** a prominent pre-1917 writer, came back from exile and headed the **Union of Writers,** which provided privileges in getting published, money, and housing, but also enforced norms in style and content. These norms endorsed traditional literary forms, but the subject matter had to reflect the goal of building socialism. In daily life, as well, the mid-1930s signaled the "Great Retreat," in which socialist ideology was preserved but was merged with "traditional" (and largely popular) values, such as prohibiting abortion; a renewed emphasis on family, including the subordinate position of women; and attention paid to consumer goods, simple entertainment, sports, and health.

NATIONALITIES

Imperial Russia had ruled over several hundred distinct ethnic groups, large and small. For the most part, its policies toward these groups were flexible and tended to involve limited recognition of local identity, including culture, language, religion, and accommodations with local elites. In the late nineteenth century, however, the government promoted a new policy of **"Russification,"** which meant extending the use of the Russian language and conversion to Russian Orthodoxy in several strategically important areas, especially among groups still developing their modern national consciousness. This policy created resentment in some areas like Finland and Poland, while in other areas, it was combined with Russian settlement, as in Central Asia and in the Caucasus. Jews were confined to living within the **"Pale of Settlement,"** an area in today's Poland, Ukraine, Lithuania, Belarus, and a few other areas. Jews converting to Christianity or falling under various exceptions were permitted to live outside the Pale but were generally discriminated against.

National Minorities Under Socialism

Most Marxists tended to neglect the importance of national and ethnic identity, but Stalin was exceptional in arguing that such identities were powerful and deeply rooted. In the 1920s, the Soviet government introduced many policies building on their early laws extending full tolerance and civil rights to all ethnic, national, and religious minorities. This was applied not only to large groups, such as Georgians, Ukrainians, or Volga Germans, but even to very small groups that then acquired semi-autonomous political units, including local government, schools, and other cultural institutions.

National literature, theater, and newspapers were promoted, sometimes causing tensions with the Russian majority. The one caveat was that national cultural leaders had to conform to socialist standards or risk being accused of "bourgeois nationalism" and on that basis possibly subjected to arrest or even execution. Prohibited activities included advocating for greater political autonomy or social arrangements different from those prescribed by the Soviet government. In the 1930s, after Stalin consolidated his power, the extent of national self-expression was circumscribed and the number of national units (autonomous regions and districts) was reduced, but the main principle of the Soviet Union being a multinational state was left untouched.

THE SECOND WORLD WAR

In 1917, many Bolsheviks, especially Leon Trotsky, believed that the Revolution in Russia would be followed by Communist revolutions elsewhere in Europe and eventually perhaps throughout the world. Groups and parties allied to the Bolsheviks were springing up everywhere, staging armed revolts in such places as Bavaria, Hungary, and Germany in the early 1920s. Their "internationalist" militancy made Bolsheviks feared by the property-owning classes throughout the world. Nonetheless, being a major military and economic power, the Soviet Union became intimately involved in international affairs in the 1920s and 1930s. In 1941, it was invaded by Nazi Germany and became one of the **Allied Powers** in the **Second World War.** Despite suffering heavy losses, the Red Army eventually defeated the German invasion and after 1945 was poised to become one of the world's two superpowers. The Soviet victory over Germany came to be viewed—in addition to the Revolution and the Civil War—as a key foundational event of Soviet history, and after the end of the Soviet Union, the **Victory Day,** celebrated in Russia on May 9, became its most important national holiday.

PREWAR FOREIGN RELATIONS

Soviet Russia emerged as an outcast in Europe's system of international relations, especially after it signed a separate peace treaty with Germany and refused to repay massive tsarist foreign loans. After the First World War, several independent nations emerged from the ruins of the Russian, German, Austro-Hungarian, and Ottoman empires, all of them hostile to the Bolsheviks. In Western Europe, they were viewed as a buffer against a Communist threat.

At the same time, Lenin's government successfully found a way out of this isolation: first, in 1921, Soviet Russia signed the **Moscow Treaty** with the emerging nationalist Turkish government of Mustafa Kemal, providing him with money and weapons. In that year, Soviet Russia also signed a trade treaty with Great Britain, which thereby recognized the new government in fact, though not officially. Finally, in April of 1922, Soviet Russia signed a key **Treaty of Rapallo** with the German Weimar Republic, Germany thus becoming the first major nation to formally recognize the Bolsheviks. Russia and Germany gave up all financial claims against each other and agreed to cooperate in several military projects. On December 30, 1922, Soviet Russia, the Transcaucasian Socialist Federative Soviet Republic (Armenia, Azerbaijan, and Georgia), the Soviet Socialist Republic of Ukraine, and the Soviet Socialist Republic of Byelorussia signed a treaty creating the **Union of Soviet Socialist Republics** (**USSR**), commonly known as the **Soviet Union**. During the 1920s, the Soviet Union was recognized by most major countries, although the United States did so only in 1933.

Foreign Relations in the 1930s

Soviet industrialization in the late 1920s and early 1930s largely relied on technical expertise and, indirectly (through grain exports), money from the West. Many Western European countries and the U.S. also had active socialist and communist movements that sought to turn their nations' public opinion in the Soviet Union's favor. After Hitler came to power in 1933, the Soviet Union began to participate in Europe's security arrangements, for example, through a loose mutual aid treaty with France in 1935. Nonetheless, Stalin and his government felt that Britain and France were unreliable as potential partners in a war against Hitler because of their pattern of failing to oppose Hitler's and Mussolini's advances in Ethiopia in 1935–36, in Spain during the Spanish Civil War in 1936–39, and during the Munich Crisis of 1938, when the USSR was excluded from the negotiations that handed Czechoslovakia over to Hitler.

The Molotov-Ribbentrop Pact

Although Stalin was wary of Hitler's avowed ambition to invade and colonize the Soviet Union, he ultimately chose to come to an agreement with him on August 23, 1939, signed as a **Soviet-German Nonaggression Treaty**, also known as the **Molotov-Ribbentrop Pact**, named for the two countries' respective foreign ministers. It contained a secret addition (or protocol) that divided much of Eastern Europe (Poland, Lithuania, Latvia, Estonia, Finland, and Romania) into Soviet and German spheres of influence. The Pact was not a formal alliance, and it did not require the USSR or Germany to invade any other country, even if the other side was attacked. It was, however, accompanied by economic treaties that supplied Germany with strategic raw materials in exchange for technological transfers. Britain and France began to regard Stalin as Hitler's ally and, after the beginning of the Second World War, started to make plans to attack objectives in the Soviet Union, such as the oil fields in Baku, to prevent them from benefiting Hitler.

The Pact in Action: Poland, the Baltic Republics, and the Winter War

After Hitler invaded Poland on September 1, 1939, Stalin waited until September 17, when Polish defeat was imminent, to order his troops to occupy Poland east of the so-called Curzon line, separating territories with primarily Ukrainian and Belorussian populations from the core Polish lands. While welcomed by some from the perspective of ethnic self-determination, the Soviet move resulted in rapid "sovietization" of these territories, with private property being nationalized and individuals suspected of anti-Soviet sentiments being arrested and deported or even executed.

Large numbers of Polish soldiers surrendered to the Red Army, and in 1940 over 20,000 Polish citizens, mostly captured military officers, were executed by the secret police without a trial in an action known as the **Katyn' Massacre.**

In the fall of 1939, Stalin coerced the authoritarian governments of the three Baltic republics (Estonia, Latvia, and Lithuania) to accept Soviet garrisons and, in 1940, forced them to appoint pro-Soviet cabinets and hold falsified elections, after which all three nations formally became constituent republics in the Soviet Union. Stalin's plans were less successful in Finland, another former part of the tsarist empire: After the USSR provoked a war in November of 1939, the small and poorly armed Finnish army effectively resisted the Red Army's attacks in the so-called **Winter War.** Although the Red Army defeated Finland in the spring of 1940, the war created the impression in the West that the Soviet Union was weak militarily as it did not gain the region of Karelia, and the successful, prolonged Finnish resistance provided a perception that ignored the Red Army's adaptability and high morale.

THE COURSE OF THE WAR

As World War II progressed, the USSR and Germany found occasions to modify the conditions of the pact, adjusting borders of occupied territories and addressing trade, shipping rights, and immigration issues. The union was often uneasy, and it began to deteriorate with the USSR's invasion of Bukovina, Romania, in 1940, which was located beyond the USSR's agreed-upon sphere of influence. But Nazi Germany's actions on June 22, 1941, would terminate the pact once and for all.

The Origins of Operation Barbarossa

Hitler began making plans to invade the USSR immediately after the fall of France in July 1940. He had never made a secret of his view of Russians as racially inferior beings destined to be colonized and exploited by Germans. Subsequently, he (as well as some Cold-War propagandists after the fact) claimed that the Nazi invasion, **Operation Barbarossa,** was preventive because of Stalin's own massive war preparations.

However, there is no evidence that Stalin actively planned such an attack. Hitler viewed the Red Army as weaker than the French one he had already beaten and intended to defeat it in a few weeks using rapid advances of his mechanized forces, supported by aircraft. German intelligence about Soviet military capabilities was poor and colored by ideological prejudice. At the same time, Stalin and his government knew that Hitler was about to attack but did not know the details and received reliable information only when it was too late to mobilize.

After the war, the Soviets created a myth that the Nazi attack was a complete surprise because Stalin trusted in his treaty with Hitler. Another myth is that the Red Army was poorly armed. In fact, in 1941, it had more armor and aircraft than the rest of the world combined. Though many of these were outdated, they were not obsolete, and up-to-date models were about as numerous as the German front-line strength. At the same time, though, the army's organization, doctrine, and training had suffered from the effect of the purges in the late 1930s and from rapid expansion and frequent reorganizations.

When Hitler's army began its attack on Sunday, June 22, 1941, the Soviet leadership expected that the Red Army would immediately counterattack and repel the invasion. Instead, German troops penetrated deeply behind Soviet lines and within a few days captured Belorussia and were beginning to threaten approaches to Leningrad. Hundreds of thousands of soldiers found themselves encircled and most became POWs. Despite its huge losses, the Red Army continued to fight and disrupted German plans.

The German assault against Moscow began on September 30, and it failed to capture the city. Soviet reserves began a counteroffensive in December and drove the Germans back in what was the first major Allied victory against Germany. Operation Barbarossa had failed.

From Moscow to Stalingrad, 1941–1942

In spite of its defeat of Operation Barbarossa, at the same time, the USSR failed to turn this victory into a rout, and, in the spring of 1942, Hitler was ready to attack once again, this time only in the southern portion of the front. His target was the city of Stalingrad (present-day Volgograd) on the Volga, important not only for its symbolic value but also because of its strategic location. Another army force turned south, trying to capture the oil fields in the Caucasus. Due to the strength of Soviet resistance, Germans were unable to reach either of these objectives, and in November, their Sixth Army was surrounded in Stalingrad and soon capitulated together with its commander.

The Soviet Victory

Stalingrad was a major victory for the Red Army, but elsewhere it was less successful: in the north, it failed to lift the German siege of Leningrad, a major war crime that caused over 600,000 civilian deaths from starvation. And northwest of Moscow, the Red Army failed to capture the Rzhev salient threatening the capital, despite repeated bloody assaults that resulted in over a million dead and wounded soldiers. In 1943, the German army once again regrouped and launched another assault near the South Russian town of Kursk in July. Known as one of the largest armored battles in history,

Kursk was a decisive loss for the Nazis. Between July 1943 and May 1945, the Red Army went on an offensive that the Germans were unable to repel—despite their desperate attempts to launch a "total war." In particular, the Soviet offensive in Belorussia, Operation Bagration, begun on June 22, 1944, rapidly overwhelmed the Germans and advanced into German-occupied Poland. In April 1945, the Red Army surrounded and stormed Berlin, whereas to the north and to the south of the city its soldiers met British and American troops on the river Elbe.

USSR's War Against Japan, 1945

Although the war in Europe was over in August 1945, the Soviet Union declared war on Japan to fulfill its pledge to its Western Allies. Within days, the Red Army destroyed Japan's powerful Kwantung Army and occupied Manchuria, North Korea, Sakhalin, and the Kuril Islands.

THE IMPACT OF THE WAR

During the war, the Soviet government continued to rely on existing mechanisms of coercion and ideological indoctrination, emphasizing the leading role of Stalin and the Communist Party and arguing that the war was started by German capitalists. However, these mechanisms were insufficient, and the state furthered the ideological and symbolic changes already begun in the 1930s. Stalin appealed to traditional Russian patriotism and used imperial-era heroes, such as Generals Suvorov and Kutuzov, as models.

Imperial-era military symbols were revived: uniforms were made according to pre-1917 patterns and officers' golden shoulder-badges were reintroduced in 1943. Religion, especially in the form of the Russian Orthodox Church, was rehabilitated, and surviving bishops met with Stalin and were allowed to elect a Patriarch. Although some military commanders blamed for the June 1941 defeat were executed, many purge victims from 1939–1940 were freed and allowed to join the army.

Industrial Mobilization; Women and Children

Even before the German invasion, large segments of the Soviet economy operated on a wartime footing, and the major impact of the attack was to continue the process of mobilization. This affected above all those civilian productive capacities that could be altered to produce military equipment and supplies. Immediately after the war began, Stalin ordered the evacuation of key military industries from the western regions of the USSR to the Urals and Siberia. But the German advance was so rapid that only around 10 percent of industry could be removed from affected areas. Evacuees often found themselves in open fields without any of their possessions. Those factories that remained operational had to rely on the labor of women and children. Most civilians, and especially those engaged in agriculture, were given low priority in receiving supplies and suffered extensive privations, even when they were not exposed to direct military action.

Soviet Losses

The USSR overall lost about 30 percent of its national wealth, and territories occupied by Germany lost about two-thirds. Approximately 4 million civilians died from hunger, disease, lack of medical care, and other privations. German soldiers were permitted to kill and molest Soviet civilians with impunity, and so losses were much greater for those directly affected by the invasion: almost 7.5 million civilians were murdered on occupied territory or died from enemy actions such as artillery strikes and bombing. Over 2 million more died performing slave labor in Germany, and more than 1.5 million Soviet POWs died.

In addition, a mass famine occurred in 1946, resulting in 1 to 1.5 million deaths. Two million people were war invalids who would not see much public assistance from their post-war government. In addition, the **Holocaust** was carried out partially on Soviet territory. Approximately 3 million Jews were in German-occupied parts of the USSR, and their mass murder began shortly after the invasion, with the assistance of local collaborators. There were several sites of mass execution, most notably **Babi Yar** in Kiev, where over 100,000 Jews were executed.

SETTLEMENTS OF WWII AND THE ORIGINS OF THE COLD WAR

The Soviet Union joined the **Atlantic Charter** in 1941. During the war, Stalin held three conferences with the leaders of Britain and the United States that decided on the post-war settlement (Tehran Conference in 1943; Yalta Conference and Potsdam Conference in 1945). The territorial rearrangement that emerged from these negotiations moved Poland's border westward, gave the USSR one-third of Eastern Prussia, demilitarized the German army, reduced German territory by 25 percent, and divided it into occupation zones. The USSR was also granted Japanese territories lost by Russia in 1905.

In addition, the Soviet Union joined in an agreement to create the United Nations, which gave the USSR the legitimacy of occupying a key position in the most important international organization throughout the Cold War.

The Origins of the Cold War

Post-war settlements also laid the foundation for the Cold War by creating a bipolar division of Europe and eventually the world into two spheres of interest, or blocs. The USSR was in effect allowed to control Eastern (and most of southeastern Europe,) but disagreements emerged quickly about Poland, the status of the Turkish Straits, Truman's nuclear threat, and more. The U.S. and Britain both desired influence in Eastern Europe but eventually settled for keeping the USSR out of having any say in Western Europe, such as West Germany, France, Italy, and Belgium.

POSTWAR STALINISM

While facing the task of rebuilding its war-shattered country after 1945, Stalin's regime partially returned to policies of repression, which continued until Stalin's death in 1953. The predominant post-war ideology of "Soviet patriotism" blended the existing Communist images and stories with the more traditional mythology of Russian nationalism.

TIP

Czechoslovakia, the
Soviet Union,
Bulgaria, Romania,
East Germany,
Poland, and Albania
comprised the
Communist Bloc
during the Cold War.

RECONSTRUCTION

Stalin rejected U.S. assistance from the **Marshall Plan**, believing its terms to be overly constraining economically and politically. Resources for rebuilding the Soviet economy included reparations from the Axis countries and forced labor (including that of POWs), but it was done primarily through continuing or even increasing the regime of total mobilization. The extensive black market that had been tolerated during the war was restricted again, but work continued to be carried out disproportionately by women and teenagers. In the post-war period, many families were headed by single mothers, since there were about 13 million fewer men than women in the age bracket between 20 and 44.

Less easy to measure is the psychological effect of years of extreme deprivation and trauma affecting the entire population. There were also long-term health effects: a contemporary study of working teenagers found that 35 percent were chronically ill. Much of Soviet housing stock was destroyed, and millions of people were dislocated through evacuation, forced displacement, or mobilization. The post-war period also saw a rise in violent and organized crime, especially in the larger cities.

NATIONALISM

Stalin's "Great Retreat" reached its high point after 1945, further developing the "Soviet patriotism" by mixing traditional Russo-centric civic nationalism and Communist ideology stripped of its internationalist aspects. Soviet patriotism used many traditional Russian symbols of power, historical figures, and monumental art, but was different in that writers and artists (such as Alexander Tvardovskii) who appeared too nationalist were chastised. Yet, intellectuals thought not to share these values—especially the poet Anna Akhmatova and satirist Mikhail Zoshchenko—faced brutal criticism by the Party and ostracism by their colleagues.

One particular element of this campaign was directed against Western (especially American) cultural and intellectual influences and targeted Jewish intellectuals, referring to them negatively as "Cosmopolitans." Almost all Jewish political and cultural organizations such as theaters were shut down. Shortly before Stalin's death, his secret police concocted the **Doctors' Plot of 1953** and arrested several physicians, most of them Jewish, for allegedly plotting to kill leading government figures. They were freed shortly after Stalin died.

THE ARMS RACE AND THE COLD WAR IN EUROPE AND ASIA

While British and American forces remained in Western Europe, the Red Army (partially demobilized but still large) occupied Eastern Europe. After the war, the Soviet Union committed to huge expenditures on new types of weapons: jet aircraft, missiles, radars, and especially nuclear weapons. The first Soviet nuclear weapon was successfully produced in 1949.

The Beginning of the Cold War in Europe

It was unclear in the first few years after the war what relations would be like between the USSR and the West. But President Truman was staunchly anti-Soviet, and Stalin took Churchill's 1946 "Iron Curtain" speech as a dangerous sign of the West's intentions. "Iron Curtain" referred to the fact that Stalin's government severely restricted travel from its sphere of influence and shut down almost all non-Communist political activities in the countries under its occupation. In a series of foreign policy crises, Stalin was careful not to overextend himself in the Greek Civil War, 1946–49, and the Iran crisis in 1946; however he did try to "Sovietize" both nations. On the other hand, he did stumble through some miscalculations: when Yugoslavia under Josip Tito broke from Soviet influence in 1948 and Stalin banished Yugoslavia from the Soviet bloc, and also the Berlin blockade (1948–49) that secured West Berlin for the Western powers and hastened the formation of NATO, an anti-Soviet military alliance. Stalin had ordered the blockade of Western-provided supplies to the people of West Berlin. Committed to reaching western Germans, the Americans and British circumvented the blockade and airlifted supplies, highlighting Stalin's miscalculation of the Western bloc's resolve. West Germany was then established in 1949, prompting the USSR to set up East Germany later the same year.

Soviet Rule in Eastern Europe

Stalin was more successful in Eastern Europe, where anti-Soviet guerillas were defeated all over, including in western parts of the Soviet Union itself. Pro-Soviet regimes were consolidated in Poland, Czechoslovakia, Hungary, Romania, and Bulgaria. Czechoslovakia was the most pro-Soviet of the satellite nations. These quickly became mini-Stalinist regimes with purges and secret police, where non-Communists, and then non-Stalinist communists, were often tried and executed.

Cold War in Asia, 1945–1953

Another key event was the victory of Chinese Communists in 1949. Mao Zedong was friendly to the USSR and dependent on its assistance. More questionable in its effects for the Soviet Union was the Korean War, 1950–53 (ending in July, a few months after Stalin's death). The USSR did not officially take part, but it did finance North Korea and supplied Chinese troops. Approximately 30,000 Soviet soldiers took some part, especially manning aircraft during a massive air war between U.S. and Soviet planes. For the USSR, the war was mostly a failure because it did not unite Korea. But it increased Soviet authority in third-world countries, where the USSR came to be seen as a potential source of real military and economic assistance.

THE KHRUSHCHEV YEARS

Nikita Khrushchev's rule (1953–1964) is usually interpreted as a period of relative liberalism, marked by the cultural "Thaw" and de-Stalinization. However, Khrushchev left intact, and indeed reaffirmed, the foundations of the Soviet regime, though he avoided the mass terror of Stalin's rule. In this style, he was able to gain and preserve his power by appealing to the Central Committee of the Party, as well as the army and the KGB. Khrushchev's unpredictability and mistakes in domestic and foreign policy eventually led to his removal by his close associates in the Communist Party.

SUCCESSION STRUGGLE AND DE-STALINIZATION

After Stalin's death on March 5, 1953, a struggle for leadership took place among **Lavrentiy Beria** (the head of the secret police), **Georgi Malenkov** (the head of the government), and **Nikita Khrushchev** (the Moscow party boss). Malenkov and Beria traditionally worked together, but Khrushchev managed to divide them and organize what was essentially a coup against Beria. Beria was arrested on June 26 and was most likely murdered on that same day. In September, Khrushchev was elected as the First Secretary of the Communist Party.

Stalin's Cult of Personality Dismantled

At the height of his rule, Joseph Stalin was portrayed by the Soviet press as the all-powerful and all-knowing Father of the Nations. He was revered by the people in communist countries. Expressions of devotion permeated all forms of media and his likeness was displayed everywhere. In Khrushchev's speech, "On the Cult of Personality and Its Consequences,"(commonly known as the **Secret Speech**), given at the 20th Party Congress on February 25, 1956, he condemned Stalin charging him with having encouraged a leadership personality cult despite his claims of maintaining support for the ideals of Marxist-Leninist communism. Khrushchev referred to this overwhelming cultural influence as Stalin's cult of the individual The "Secret Speech" initiated a political reform, known as De-Stalinization, that sought to eradicate Stalin's influence on the Soviet society.

In addition, Khrushchev criticized Stalin's reign of terror but mentioned only Stalin's persecution of Party personnel. Khrushchev said nothing about collectivization or the Soviet ex-POWs who had been put in filtration camps; former "opposition" members who had been purged, like Bukharin, were also not defended. Still, the overwhelming picture provided by the speech was of mass illegality, falsified evidence, torture, and extrajudicial killings, with an emphasis on Stalin's personal responsibility.

Khrushchev Criticized

Although officially secret, the speech was nonetheless widely circulated. Congress delegates were shocked, and many were dismayed. In June 1957, an **"Anti-Party group"** comprised of older, leading Stalin-era Communists (Molotov, Malenkov, Kaganovich, Voroshilov) attempted to remove Khrushchev from power. The KGB and the army, led by war hero **Marshal Zhukov**, helped Khrushchev to resist the coup attempt. But in the aftermath, the USSR started having more problems with its satellites. Stalinist Communists in Eastern Europe were also displeased with the new direction. In 1956 there were mass uprisings against Communist rule in Poland and an attempt to overthrow the Communist regime in Hungary, which was suppressed by the Soviet army after bloody street fighting.

Hungarian Uprising

In 1956, what began as a student-led protest against the Soviet-backed Hungarian People's Republic erupted into a nationwide revolt against the communist regime as Hungary vowed to disengage from the Warsaw Pact. Known as the **Hungarian Uprising**, the revolt took hold quickly and the government collapsed. After initially claiming their willingness to negotiate, the Soviets crushed the uprising, killing 2,500 Hungarians; 200,000 more fled as refugees.

The Cultural "Thaw"

Three waves of cultural "Thaw" continued the process of de-Stalinization in 1953, 1956, and 1962. A 1954 novel entitled *Thaw* by Ilya Ehrenburg signaled a liberalization in literature and film, which notably included the publication of Alexander Solzhenitsyn's novella *A Day in the Life of Ivan Denisovich* in 1962, the story of a prison camp inmate. With much stopping and starting, these waves would often be replaced by conservative attacks, as repressive measures were still common. For example, religion was prosecuted once again and thousands of churches shut down.

A campaign was waged against "idleness" that targeted individuals without official employment, including artists who were not members of the state-led unions, such as the poet Joseph Brodsky. In 1957, Boris Pasternak was persecuted because of the publication in the West of his novel *Doctor Zhivago*.

Society and Economy Under Khrushchev

During this time, ordinary people were not necessarily better off than they had been before the war. There was gradually increased attention paid to consumer goods, but the greatest push was made to provide desperately needed housing, in the form of cheap, mass-produced apartment buildings. Collective farmers were stripped of most of their private plots and food prices rose. Mass protests resulted, but were hushed up. In Novocherkassk in 1962, protestors were shot by the army.

In spite of the challenges people faced under the new regime, Khrushchev's de-Stalinization efforts were successful. Soon after Stalin died, his influence diminished; he was mentioned less often in newspapers, and his pictures, busts, and other images were removed. In 1961, Stalingrad, the city that had been renamed from Tsaritsyn in honor of Stalin in 1925, was renamed Volgograd.

SOVIET RELATIONS WITH THE U.S. UNDER KHRUSHCHEV

"Peaceful Coexistence" and the Space Race

Khrushchev pursued a policy of "peaceful coexistence" with the West after the end of the Korean War, based in part on the reality that nuclear arsenals on both sides meant "Mutually Assured Destruction" (MAD) would be the inevitable result of a direct military confrontation. The Cold War in this era was fought through the "space race," in which both sides sought to demonstrate their technical prowess and achieve parity in missiles and nuclear warheads. Until the 1960s, the Soviet Union had the capacity to destroy Europe but not really to reach the United States. But in 1957, when the Soviets launched the first satellite into space, **Sputnik**, they also demonstrated their ability to reach the U.S. with ICBMs (Inter-Continental Ballistic Missiles) and greatly reduced their conventional army. In 1961, Soviet cosmonaut **Yury Gagarin** became the first man in space, urging the U.S. to intensify its efforts in the same realm.

The Cold War in Europe Under Khrushchev

The **Warsaw Pact**, the Soviet counter to NATO (North Atlantic Treaty Organization), was created in 1955 to formalize Soviet dominance of the Eastern bloc. In 1959, Khrushchev visited the United States, putting on a show of one-upmanship but basically warming relations. However, in 1960, a United States U-2 spy plane was shot down over Russia, renewing tensions. In 1961, the German Democratic Republic began construction of the Berlin Wall, separating NATO-controlled West Berlin and Communist-controlled East Berlin and surrounding East Germany.

The Cuban Missile Crisis

Then, in 1962, Khrushchev secretly moved nuclear-tipped missiles to Cuba, ruled by Fidel Castro. His reasons are not entirely clear, but the move seems to have been intended to protect Castro's regime from an imminent U.S. invasion and to push the U.S. to remove its own nuclear missiles from Turkey. The U.S. detected the move late and declared a "quarantine," in effect a blockade that could be interpreted as an act of war. This stand-off was the closest the world has come to a massive nuclear war, but Khrushchev and President Kennedy never stopped talking to each other through the crisis, and it is clear that neither wanted to risk MAD. In the end, the USSR removed its missiles from Cuba and the U.S. agreed not to invade, as well as to remove its missiles from Turkey. However, this last provision was kept secret, making the outcome look like a Soviet defeat.

PROXY WARS

A proxy war is a conflict between major powers in which neither power fights the other directly. Rather, smaller countries fight on behalf of the major powers, who provide support through the supply of arms, equipment, military training, financial aid, and at times, military troops. During the Cold War, proxy wars served as a way for the United States and USSR to maintain their respective spheres of influence without getting into a direct conflict, which held the threat of nuclear war. Perhaps the most well-known proxy war during Khrushchev's leadership in the USSR is the **Second Indochina War**, also known as the **Vietnam War** (1955–1975).

The Suez Crisis

In July 1956, supported by Soviet funds, Egyptian President Gamal Abdel Nasser nationalized the Suez Canal, prohibiting its use by Israel. Israel, backed by the British and the French, launched an attack to retake the canal. Khrushchev, preoccupied with the Hungarian Uprising, threatened to launch a nuclear attack against the three nations if they did not withdraw and stop their offensive. President Eisenhower warned Khrushchev against such threatening rhetoric but also threatened the British, French, and Israelis with economic sanctions if they did not stop their offensive. Ultimately, the British and French withdrew in December and the Israelis, feeling pressure from the United States, withdrew the following March.

RIFT WITH CHINA

In 1960–1961, the USSR split with Communist China, a rift that persisted until 1989. **Mao Zedong** did not want to support or participate in Khrushchev's policy of "peaceful coexistence" with the West, nor did he approve of de-Stalinization. Chinese Communists viewed the USSR as revisionist traitors to the cause and unworthy of trust. The result was a kind of second Cold War between China and the Soviet Union, in which China built its own system of allies in Asia and Africa. The long-term effect of the rift was to alter the global power structure based in third-world allies and satellites in ways that did not favor Soviet interests.

THE BREZHNEV ERA

Khrushchev's successor, **Leonid Brezhnev**, ruled the Soviet Union from 1964–1982. This period came to be popularly known as "stagnation," referring to the sense of political and social stability, but also a slow-down in the growth of the Soviet economy.

GROWTH AND STAGNATION

In October 1964, Nikita Khrushchev was removed from power in a bloodless coup organized by the KGB. His position went to Leonid Brezhnev, who represented a younger generation untainted by direct participation in the Stalinist terror (though many had reached their positions by replacing purge victims).

Brezhnev's style of rule was very different from Khrushchev and Stalin: he reintroduced Lenin's earlier practice of "collective leadership," that is, of sharing power with a small group of senior Communists known as the **Politburo.**

Society and Economy During "Stagnation"

Although the Brezhnev period was marked by a slowdown in economic growth, at the same time, it was a period of social stability and a much higher standard of living for ordinary Soviet citizens. Successes in space exploration, aviation, nuclear energy, education, medical care and social services, arts and sciences, and sports created the impression of a stabilized regime after decades of upheaval. Under Brezhnev, Soviet citizens enjoyed free education, free basic healthcare, and very low housing costs.

In addition, the state invested in large-scale, long-term capital investment and infrastructure projects, such as housing, subways, and the complete electrification of rural villages.

In the 1970s, the Soviet Union finally acquired unified transportation and energy networks, and the government sponsored massive irrigation and reforestation programs.

Soviet Vulnerabilities

At the same time, the economy had become dependent on the export of raw materials, especially oil and gas after the 1973 oil crisis. Many high-tech industries such as electronics were not developing, and labor productivity was not high enough to compete with other major economies. Consumer goods were often of low quality and still insufficient to meet demand. Agriculture had been deprived of resources for so long that the USSR was forced to purchase grain abroad. People were eating better than in turbulent previous decades, but it was still not enough. Private garden plots were again allowed, and there were occasional attempts to introduce limited elements of the market, with the intention of making state-owned businesses accountable and profitable. Government effort was directed toward culture and leisure, but what developed instead was a working-class urban culture that led to frequent mass riots, usually aimed at police and the courts. These were not mentioned in the press, and rampant alcoholism and violent crime were similarly ignored. After 1969, modern terrorism began to affect the Soviet Union, with recurring plane hijackings and suicide bombings.

IDEOLOGICAL DISSENT

Soon after Brezhnev came to power, the policies of Thaw were abandoned, to be replaced with a cult of the "Great Patriotic War." Stalin was rehabilitated in a limited way, mentioned as part of the story of Soviet growth and victory in World War II, but not glorified. Ideological dissenters were persecuted, as in the 1965 trial of two writers, Siniavsky and Daniel, who had published abroad works that were censored in the Soviet Union. They were sentenced to prison amid public protests. Czech socialists rose up in the **Prague Spring of 1968** and were suppressed by tanks sent from Moscow to prop up the local regime. Human rights activists in the Soviet bloc were also harassed. But overall, the scale of dissent was small, involving relatively isolated intellectuals without broad social support.

Dissidents' Beliefs and Practices

The overwhelming majority of dissidents were actually pro-Soviet: they wanted to reform the Soviet system but leave its foundations untouched. Rather than another revolution, they hoped to hold the regime accountable to its official promises of justice and liberation. These protests were nonviolent and insisted on observing existing state law. They varied ideologically, with some emphasizing Communism, others western liberalism, and still others nationalist themes (Russian or other). Finally, there was religious dissent, including nonconforming Orthodox believers and other confessions or sects.

Official Persecution of Dissent

Dissidents were punished with imprisonment; forced commitment to psychiatric wards; and, for the most famous cultural figures, forced emigration from the USSR. Joseph Brodsky emigrated in 1972, and Alexander Solzhenitsyn published *The Gulag Archipelago* abroad in 1973 and emigrated in 1974. Andrei Sakharov (1921–1989), a nuclear physicist who became a human rights activist, was sentenced to internal exile from 1980 until 1986, when he was allowed to return to his home in Moscow.

DÉTENTE

Brezhnev created good working relationships with Western leaders, with the intention of preventing another Cuban Missile Crisis. The Soyuz-Apollo joint space mission beginning in 1967 reduced the antagonism of the space race, and a series of agreements in the 1970s reduced the risk of a major nuclear war. These included:

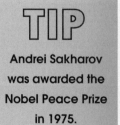

TIP

Andrei Sakharov was awarded the Nobel Peace Prize in 1975.

- The **Soviet-West German treaty**, 1970
- The **ABM and SALT-1 disarmament treaties**, 1972
- **Nixon's visit to Moscow**, 1972
- **Brezhnev's visit to the United States**, 1973
- The **Helsinki agreements** confirming European borders, economic cooperation, and human rights pledges
- The **SALT-2 disarmament treaty** signed in Vienna

Cultural and economic contacts also began to be encouraged within limits, as when Pepsi was brought to the USSR. At the same time, the Soviet Union continued to improve its armaments, reaching strategic nuclear parity with the U.S. and creating a powerful navy and air force. Détente ended in December 1979 with the Soviet invasion of Afghanistan.

PROXY WARS IN THE THIRD WORLD

Despite détente, the USSR had intensified its efforts in the Third World under Brezhnev. In early 1965, the Soviets provided massive aid to North Vietnam and actively cooperated with China. Few Soviet soldiers were directly involved in the fighting and generally worked only as military advisers and technical specialists. In addition, the USSR supported communist governments fighting civil wars against rebels supported by the U.S. or other western powers, as in Ethiopia after 1974, Angola after 1975, and Nicaragua beginning in 1981 (supporting the Sandinistas, who were militarily successful but agreed to a political compromise in 1988). In the Near East, the USSR provided massive aid to Egypt and Syria in the Arab-Israeli wars of 1967, 1973, and 1982, without success. In other areas, the Soviets supported Communist rebels or governments that were overthrown by pro-American forces, such as the Chilean socialist democratic government overthrown in 1973.

WAR IN AFGHANISTAN

The 1978 April Revolution in Afghanistan established a left-wing republic. The new government's social reforms were resisted by an Islamic opposition financed by the United States, resulting in a civil war. The Afghan government called for Soviet troops. The Kremlin at first declined, but changed its mind when Hafizullah Amin seized power in September 1979. Amin was seen as an unreliable and cruel dictator who launched mass executions, and the USSR feared that Amin would either defect to the U.S. or bring about the defeat of communism in Afghanistan. They therefore used Amin's own request for troops to overthrow him. Soviet troops seized key points in Afghanistan, killed Amin, and replaced him with the more moderate Babrak Karmal. However, the USSR had no plan for what to do next, including the potential for actual warfare, since it was assumed they would withdraw. But from the start, they engaged in open fighting with Islamists. The Soviets' heavily armed troops won the initial full-scale battles but after 1983 became beleaguered by ongoing guerilla warfare and terrorist attacks.

REFORM AND COLLAPSE

In the early 1980s, the Soviet Union was facing increased pressures abroad and a series of economic problems at home; however, none of these indicated its imminent fall. Mikhail Gorbachev was brought to power by his Politburo colleagues in 1985 with the expectation of a modest program of reforms, but within only a couple of years, Soviet ideology and the Communist Party's political control crumbled, and Gorbachev unexpectedly lost his predominance to Boris Yeltsin, who became the first president of the independent Russian Federation.

GLOBAL CHALLENGERS AND THE END OF DÉTENTE

With the election of Margaret Thatcher as Prime Minister of the UK in 1979 and of Ronald Reagan as U.S. President in 1980, détente was abandoned by the West, with Soviet actions in Afghanistan as the excuse. Both leaders were strongly ideological in their opposition to the Soviet Union, and they became swayed by intelligence reports that Soviet military capabilities were greater than they probably were, as well as by theories that increased military spending on their part could push the Soviet Union, in its efforts to respond, to collapse (this remains a popular theory to explain the eventual collapse, though there is little evidence to support it).

Pressure Against the USSR

Western pressure was applied in various ways. In 1980, most Western countries boycotted the Olympic Games in Moscow (in return, the USSR boycotted the 1984 Games in Los Angeles). In 1983, a Soviet airplane mistakenly shot down Korean Air Lines Flight 007 that had strayed over a restricted military area, thinking it to be a spy plane. President Reagan responded with a media campaign accusing the USSR of a "crime against humanity." Finally, the U.S. began to deploy intermediate-range Pershing II missiles to Europe, hoping to gain an advantage in nuclear arms. In a series of speeches, including one in 1983 that referred to the USSR as an "**evil empire**" living in "totalitarian darkness," Reagan called for an aggressive anti-Soviet strategy. Finally, the Soviet Union was sharply criticized for its poor human rights record.

Soviet Reaction

Soviet leaders in the early 1980s were of course aware of these challenges, but they thought Reagan to be a dangerous fanatic and were determined to invest in more advanced weapons to counter his threats (although this cannot be seen as an increase in Soviet spending on the military, since military spending was maximized almost throughout the Soviet period). The nonviolent "soft power" threat, however, could not be as easily addressed, and the exposure of Soviet human rights abuses did take a toll on the USSR's reputation and bargaining power.

EXTERNAL FACTORS (AFGHANISTAN, ISLAM)

Because their troops had been invited in, the Soviets considered Afghanistan to be an internal Communist matter, like Prague in 1968, but the West portrayed the Soviet entry into Afghanistan as

TIP

Pope John Paul II (elected 1978) was of Polish origin, and during his pastoral trips to Poland tacitly encouraged its anti-Communist Solidarity movement, although the latter's—and the Pope's—role in ending Communism is usually greatly exaggerated.

an unprovoked invasion and used it as an excuse to end détente. The West then imposed economic sanctions, although they were ineffective because Europeans did not fully participate. The U.S. had provided the Afghan mujahedeen with advanced weapons, only a few months before the Soviet invasion in 1979, including Stinger missiles.

Soviet Escalation and Withdrawal

The USSR in reply combined large-scale army operations with Special Forces raids to intercept weapon supplies smuggled from Pakistan. The Soviets were militarily successful, but, having from the start planned for a limited engagement, they were anxious to pull out. Large-scale fighting with significant casualties was deeply unpopular, but the Soviets could not find a political solution. Gorbachev's initial solution in 1985–1987 was not to pull out but actually to intensify warfare. Only in 1988, as part of the **Geneva Agreements**, did the USSR promise to pull out of Afghanistan while the U.S. and Pakistan promised to stop supporting the mujahedeen. The Soviet army pulled out by February 1989, but continued to support the regime, and the Americans and Pakistan continued to support the mujahedeen. The results of the conflict were inconclusive; instability in the region made Islamic terrorism a continuing problem as the population had been antagonized by external forces, but the effort was a military success as they were able to maintain the USSR's own safe borders while it lasted. Immediately after Soviet withdrawal, Islamist fighters started penetrating into Soviet Central Asia.

PERESTROIKA AND GLASNOST

In March 1985, Mikhail Gorbachev came to power, representing a younger generation educated in less chaotic and more idealistic circumstances than Brezhnev and his peers. However, for the first two years of his rule, no changes were made, although many Brezhnev-era bureaucrats were replaced with younger men during that period.

In January 1987, the Party announced a new policy of perestroika (restructuring) to be the official state doctrine. The policy dictated that the USSR would remain socialist, but the aim was to return to "Leninist norms," a rather idealized vision of the Party's first principles. Following a period of falling oil prices and the **Chernobyl nuclear disaster** in 1986, a limited economic liberalization was begun, allowing private business and trade (euphemistically called "cooperatives") to operate, especially after Gorbachev's Law on Cooperatives of 1988 that allowed the use of hired labor. Private trade and small-scale manufacture grew rapidly but did not produce the expected economic miracle. To the contrary, existing supply networks were disrupted and periodic shortages of staple consumer goods became common in 1987–1988. Additionally, Armenia suffered a devastating earthquake in Spitak in 1988, which exposed the inability of the Soviet government to financially support its satellite nations.

Another element of the new direction was glasnost (openness), which meant the relaxation of censorship on all levels. The government allowed previously prohibited works of literature to be published, including the incendiary works of Solzhenitsyn about the GULAG system. It also allowed public discussion of such problematic topics as the legacy of Stalinism, prostitution, drug problems, and more. Religious practice became completely unrestricted, and all dissidents were freed.

Aside from the economic and cultural liberalization, another key element of Gorbachev's reforms was to permit open political dialogue for the first time in Soviet history. The **19th Party Conference** in 1988 included delegates who were not appointed from above, and it decided that free elections to local councils (Soviets) would be held everywhere from then on. Finally, the first **Congress of People's Deputies** was convened in 1989, with many non-Communists elected as deputies. Sharp discussions at the Congress were televised, showing that the Party's monopoly on political life was coming to an end and exposing viewers to alternative points of view.

In foreign policy, Gorbachev at first sought to bargain with the West on equal terms and to recreate the détente of the 1970s, but he met resistance from Reagan and Thatcher, who rejected most of his arms control proposals. But after 1987, Gorbachev began to make significant and mostly one-sided concessions to the U.S., beginning with a treaty liquidating short- and intermediate-range missiles.

REEMERGENCE OF THE NATIONALITIES ISSUES

The power struggle in the Kremlin combined with, and in some cases rekindled, longstanding ethnic tensions and damaged the image of the USSR as a land where numerous national groups could live in peace and harmony. For instance, in 1986, there were anti-Russian riots in Kazakhstan. In 1987, the conflict between Armenians and the Azeri over the region of Nagorno-Karabakh (mostly populated by Armenians but administratively part of Azerbaijan) grew into open warfare using weapons stolen from Soviet police and the military. In 1988–1990, this conflict spilled into bloody pogroms against the large Armenian minority in Baku, Sumgait (Sumqayit), and other Azeri cities.

Time and again, Gorbachev sent additional troops to stop the fighting but was unable or unwilling to address the underlying causes. Mostly nonviolent nationalistic movements also developed in the Baltic republics, advocating for their autonomy and eventual independence. These were tolerated because they were officially formed to support Gorbachev and his reforms. By the time Gorbachev realized the danger and ordered his troops to suppress the separatists early in 1991, it was too late to have any effect.

Finally, Gorbachev's position was seriously undermined in 1990 by the election of **Boris Yeltsin** as the leader of the Russian Federation. The Russian Federation was the largest Union republic that had not had its own political identity throughout the Soviet period, even though it included most of Soviet population and economic resources. Yeltsin was determined to create his own power structure and to overcome Gorbachev by destroying the Soviet Union in the process, if necessary.

REVOLUTIONS IN EASTERN EUROPE

In 1989, Communist regimes fell throughout Soviet satellite states in Eastern Europe, including Poland, Hungary, East Germany, Czechoslovakia, Romania, and Bulgaria. This happened in part because Gorbachev's government felt that it did not have the moral and military-financial resources to maintain Soviet control (because it wanted to improve relations with the West) and also because Gorbachev felt that conservative Communist leaders in Eastern Europe were resisting introducing their own versions of perestroika, thinking that he and his policies would be short-lived. Gorbachev in effect ruled out the possibility that the USSR would support Communist regimes with military force if necessary.

The "Velvet" Revolution and the Fall of the Berlin Wall

As a result, on April 4, 1989, the Polish government legalized the anti-Communist Solidarity movement and permitted free elections. A similar process took place in Bulgaria and in Hungary, which permitted non-Communist parties and began to dismantle its fortified border with Austria. Czechoslovakia opened its borders and refused to forcefully quell protests, resulting in the "Velvet Revolution," ending Communist rule with the the installation of a new president, **Václav Havel**.

In the fall of 1989, East Germany's leader **Erich Honecker** faced mass protests from East Germans who wanted to leave the country. Honecker attempted to resist these pressures but eventually gave in to public protests and resigned on October 18, 1989. The nonviolent protests and growing numbers of East German refugees leaving the country continued until, at a press conference on November 9, the announcement was made that official border crossings through the Berlin Wall into West Berlin were open. People began tearing off pieces of the Wall to keep as souvenirs and creating unofficial border crossings. On June 13, 1990, the East German military began the official dismantling of the Berlin Wall. By August 1, 1990, most of the roads connecting East and West Berlin that had been severed by the Wall had been rebuilt and reopened.

Violence in Romania and the End of the Warsaw Pact

The only country in Eastern Europe where the fall of Communism involved considerable violence was Romania, whose dictator, Nicolae Ceauçescu, was determined to hold on to his power; he eventually faced the defection of his troops and was murdered with his wife Elena. Gorbachev refused to intervene in any of these events, and, on July 1, 1991, the Warsaw Pact was officially dissolved.

END OF THE UNION OF SOVIET SOCIALIST REPUBLICS

During 1989, as Gorbachev's regime gave up its control of Eastern Europe and was facing political dissent, separatist movements, and ethnic tensions on its own territory, the future fate of the Soviet Union came into question. Gorbachev's plan, shared by many in the leadership, was to revive the USSR by drafting a looser, more democratic Union treaty that would provide greater autonomy for the constituent republics.

A referendum on the future of the Soviet Union was held on March 17, 1991. Separatist authorities in Georgia, Moldavia (Moldova), and the Baltic republics refused to participate, although their citizens could still vote with the assistance of USSR officials. In the Baltic republics, especially, their large Russian minorities (up to 40 percent overwhelmingly voted against independence. Votes in favor of preserving the union were also very high in Azerbaijan and in Central Asian republics (over 90 percent), and even in Ukraine (over 80 percent). Overall, almost 78 percent of the vote was in favor of keeping a renewed version of the USSR. The new Union treaty was scheduled to be signed on August 20, 1991.

TIP

Although the fall of the Berlin Wall marked the beginning of the reunification of Germany, the official reunification happened on October 3, 1990, with the dissolution of East Germany.

The Coup Attempt in August 1991

A number of key Soviet officials believed that the new treaty would amount to a breakup of the USSR and would violate the popular will expressed in the March referendum. They formed a conspiracy to introduce a state of emergency and remove from power secession-minded figures, especially Boris Yeltsin. It is unclear how much Gorbachev knew about the proposed coup or whether he approved.

The coup began on August 18 when Gorbachev was vacationing in Crimea and the public was told that he was sick. Gorbachev claimed that he was put under house arrest. Coup leaders brought large numbers of loyal troops into Moscow, but they quickly lost their nerve and refused to take more decisive and violent measures, especially against Boris Yeltsin, who was barricaded in his headquarters, known as the White House. By August 21, the troops were ordered out and the coup leaders surrendered (but were eventually pardoned).

Dissolution of the Soviet Union

The failed coup made it politically impossible to revive the Soviet Union under its own name and Gorbachev quickly lost whatever remained of his power. On December 8, 1991, Boris Yeltsin met with leaders of Ukraine and Belorussia, known as the **Belavezha Accords**, without Gorbachev's knowledge, and agreed to formally dissolve the Soviet Union and to replace it with a loose alliance known as the Commonwealth of Independent States.

Causes of the Soviet Collapse

The collapse of the Soviet Union, though it came suddenly and surprised many observers, can now be seen to have had deep roots in a wide variety of irresolvable conflicts and challenges, in which foreign policy disasters and competition with the West played a relatively minor role.

Recognized factors destabilizing the Soviet regime include the following:

- The centralized economy was overextended and inflexible after over-investment in heavy industry in the early Brezhnev years.

- Soviet science education was compartmentalized and overly technical, impeding the development of technological innovation and problem-solving and contributing to disasters such as the Chernobyl nuclear meltdown.

- The maintenance of the Soviet bloc had become an economic and political liability.

- Increased reliance on oil and gas exports made the Soviet Union economically dependent on complicated conflicts in the Middle East.

- The Brezhnev-era leadership was riven with corruption and embedded in organized crime rings.

- Marxist ideology had lost its grip on ordinary people, who had sacrificed a great deal for the promise of socialist equality and liberation only to see corrupt officials continue to ignore or suppress the demands of ordinary workers, while the publications released under glasnost made people mistrustful of anything coming from the government.

- The development of nationalist movements in several parts of the Soviet Union challenged the center's overall ideological and political control and led to violence and separatist pressures.

- Increased access to information through the spread of television and eventually the lessening of censorship highlighted unflattering comparisons with the West, which made people dissatisfied with the state's weak attempts to meet demand in consumer goods and standards of living.

- Increased media attention on Brezhnev and his leadership in their later years made them appear out of touch, weak, and ridiculous.

- Reagan's decision to use the arms reduction talks of the 1980s to publicly hold the USSR accountable for human rights abuses according to the terms of the 1975 Helsinki Accords created international pressure, at a time of military and diplomatic embarrassments.

On the whole, while the USSR's inability to compete with the West on a wide range of fronts was a major factor in its collapse, this inability was due to problems long pre-dating Reagan's election and may not have been decisive in itself. It was the combination of these factors with serious internal instabilities and the disaffection of the Soviet population with its own regime that resulted in the total lack of support for either the coup leaders or for Gorbachev in August 1991, and the relative openness on the part of sufficient numbers of people (though not a majority) for the nation-based breakup of republics represented by Yeltsin and fulfilled by the formation of the Commonwealth of Independent States.

GORBACHEV'S LEGACY

Mikhail Gorbachev has been much lauded in the West since the collapse of the Soviet Union. He is credited with eliminating the most oppressive aspects of Soviet rule and helping to bring about a relatively bloodless end to the Cold War and the Soviet Communist experiment, in the process opening the Russian Federation and other newly independent states to the global marketplace (which was expected to bring prosperity to the region, though that has not been the case).

Within Russia, Gorbachev's leadership is viewed as a failure that lost Russia its position as a great power, as the second largest economy in the world, and as a stable social system with a functioning safety net for its most vulnerable citizens. Meanwhile, some foreign policy observers have noted that the Cold War was also a long period of relative peace, when major warfare was avoided.

Gorbachev's legacy is mixed: the roots of collapse were deep, pre-dating his rise and thus making it doubtful that he could have done anything to prevent it. Several former Soviet satellite states in Eastern Europe, such as Poland and the Czech Republic, have developed into peaceful and relatively prosperous democracies. Yet the consequences of Communist collapse have been costly for many people of the former Soviet Union and some of its satellites. Regional conflicts there and in the Middle East have emerged or intensified since the Soviet collapse, often fueled by competing nationalist movements, resurgent right-wing politics, and/or competition over oil and gas resources. Authoritarian successor regimes have replaced Soviet power in many places, displaying many of the worst aspects of the Communist Party. Post-Soviet leaders in Russia and other successor states have also presided over economic systems as deeply corrupt as ever but lacking the relative stability and safety net provided under late Communism; enormous wealth has been amassed by a few, while the economic circumstances of most people remain shaky and rocked by frequent crises.

SUMMING IT UP

- Today's **Russia rose to power in the late fifteenth century**, when Muscovy grew to become the largest state in Europe and eventually in the world. Tsar Peter the Great changed Russia's politics and culture and adopted the title of "emperor" to assert his dominance.

- In the early twentieth century Russia was the only major European state ruled by an **autocracy** (under Nicholas II). During the Revolution of 1905–1907, Nicholas II was persuaded to establish the **State Duma**, which could control the budget and grant basic civil rights. The **Russian Orthodox Church** remained Russia's state religion.

- **Russia's economy in the early twentieth century was one of the largest in the world** due to agriculture. Still, per capita incomes remained among the lowest in Europe.

- **Industrial enterprises** appeared in Russia in the seventeenth century, and Peter the Great made an effort to establish a metalworking industry in the Ural Mountains. Russia's rail network was the largest in Europe in 1914—the Trans-Siberian Railroad connected European Russia to the Pacific Ocean. Russia's financial system improved with the introduction of the gold standard in 1897.

- Until the **Emancipation of 1861**, almost half of all peasants were enserfed. After, noble landowners lost some of their land but generally retained their wealth, access to education and state service, and power in the government. At this time, there was a growing middle class that included merchants, entrepreneurs, and various professionals.

- **Russia was among the victors at the Congress of Vienna** but lost the Crimean War, which facilitated the wars of German Unification. The rise of a powerful Germany led to an alliance with France in 1893. At this time, Russia was also engaged in the Great Game with Great Britain and came into conflict with Japan in 1904–1905.

- The **populist movement** was widespread in the 1860s and 1870s. Populists sought to achieve social transformation by working through the common people; some turned to terror to force the government to make concessions. Tsar Alexander II was hunted down and assassinated in 1881. Populists were still very influential in Russia, forming the Socialist Revolutionary Party in 1914.

- In 1903, the leading Marxist party, the **Social Democrats**, split into two parties: the **Bolsheviks** (led by Vladimir Lenin) and the **Mensheviks** (led by Yulii Martov. By 1914, Marxist leaders like Lenin and Leon Trotsky had fallen out of favor and gone into hiding, and others, including Joseph Stalin, had been arrested.

- **Russia entered the First World War on the side of Great Britain and France to protect Serbia**, but by 1918 Russia's empire had collapsed as a result of not being able to withstand the costs of the war. Following the collapse, the Bolsheviks reemerged to seize power and overthrow the tsarist government during the 1917 revolutions. The February/March Revolution of 1917 forced Nicholas II to step down. The October Revolution that year brought the Bolsheviks to power. The Romanov family was later executed by Bolshevik operatives.

- Under the Bolsheviks and Lenin, Russia adopted a policy of **war communism**, which included complete control over the economy (seizing all banks and deposits, nationalizing all large industries, banning private entrepreneurship, and assuming total control over food supplies and trade). The fallout from these policies led to out-of-control inflation, a massive black market, and eventually a famine that claimed 5 million lives. Despite this, the Bolsheviks maintained control after a civil war with the Cossacks.

- Russia formally became the **Union of Soviet Socialist Republics** (USSR, Soviet Union) in 1922, with power over the republics held by the Red Army and the Communist Party.

- After Lenin's death, **Joseph Stalin** emerged as the new leader of the USSR. He began to implement state-controlled collective farms to replace private farms that were unable (or unwilling) to keep up with the state's food and export needs. The poor organization of these farms, coupled with environmental factors, led to the Great Famine in 1931–1932, during which 2–8 million people died and more than 40 million people suffered.

- Stalin's **First Five-Year Plan (1928–1932)** was intended to modernize the USSR's infrastructure, energy plants, raw materials processing, and machine-building plants. Industrial production grew rapidly (leaving the USSR second only to the U.S.), but unrealistic goals and faked statistics undermined the program's success.

- The **cultural revolution** established state-sponsorship of art, film, literature and music and theater and encouraged literacy. It created a boom in the arts, but was also used to circulate anti-religion/pro-Stalinist-government propaganda.

- **In the Second World War, the Soviet Union eventually joined the Allied Powers** against Germany, breaking the Soviet-German Nonaggression Treaty and ending a long period of diplomatic isolation. After the war, Russia received Eastern and Southeastern European territories that were formerly under German control.

- After the war, Stalin's regime instituted a strict program **of Russian and Communist nationalism**, backed by force and propaganda. Conflicts over USSR territory formed the basis of the Cold War with the U.S. and western European nations.

- Stalin's successor, **Nikita Khrushchev**, reinforced the Soviet regime and introduced a cultural "Thaw," though repressive force was still common. Khrushchev sought diplomacy with the West in the 1950s, while introducing the concept of "Mutually Assured Destruction" (MAD) as a consequence for military confrontation with Western nations.

- The USSR also invested heavily in the "**space race,**" with cosmonaut **Yuri Gagarin** becoming the first man in space.

- The **Cuban Missile Crisis of 1962** was caused by Khrushchev sending nuclear missiles to Cuba. The threat of MAD led to an agreement between Khrushchev and U.S. President John F. Kennedy, though the Cold War would continue until 1989.

- Khrushchev's successor, **Leonid Brezhnev**, presided over "stagnation" as the Soviet Union's economic growth slowed. He also presided over "détente," or improved diplomatic relations with Western nations.

- **Détente ended under Mikhail Gorbachev's regime** when UK prime minister Margaret Thatcher and U.S. president Ronald Reagan came to power, as they were ideologically opposed to the USSR.

- **After a failed coup in 1989** that was supposed to maintain central USSR control over its republics, **Boris Yeltsin**, Gorbachev's successor, **agreed to formally dissolve the USSR into independent states**. Among the primary factors for this were the Soviet Union's collapsing nationalized industries and the USSR's inability to compete with the United States.

HISTORY OF THE SOVIET UNION POST-TEST

Directions: Carefully read each of the following 60 questions. Choose the best answer to each question and fill in the corresponding circle on the answer sheet. The Answer Key and Explanations can be found following this post-test.

1. What happened to Soviet territory in Europe as a result of the Second World War?
   A. The USSR received part of Eastern Prussia and kept the lands it annexed in 1939–1940.
   B. The USSR annexed Finland and Denmark as the Scandinavian Soviet Socialist Republic.
   C. The USSR took parts of German territory but restored independence to the Baltic states.
   D. The USSR directly incorporated East Berlin as an exclave of the Russian Federation.

2. Which of the following was NOT one of the Great Reforms of the 1860s?
   A. Serf emancipation
   B. Judicial reform
   C. Freedom of speech
   D. Local self-government

3. What happened to Leningrad in 1941–1944?
   A. It was besieged and much of its population starved to death, but it was never captured.
   B. It was captured by the German Army and its large Jewish population murdered.
   C. It served as a temporary capital of the USSR despite the danger of being captured.
   D. It became known as Tankograd because Soviet tank factories were evacuated there.

4. What happened to Russia's industrial production in the 1890s?
   A. Growth was limited to textiles and food processing.
   B. Growth was most notable in heavy industry and railroad construction.
   C. Industry stagnated because it could not face competition from Germany.
   D. Industry declined because Old Believer merchants opposed capitalism.

5. Russia's performance during the First World War suffered because of a lack of
   A. industrial capacity leading to munitions shortages.
   B. sufficient manpower to make up for battle casualties.
   C. naval power, such as submarines and battleships.
   D. powerful fortresses to protect western borders.

6. The February Revolution of 1917 started when
   A. the German threat to Petrograd induced the Duma to call for emergency laws.
   B. the assassination of Rasputin started anti-clerical demonstrations in Petrograd.
   C. interruptions of the food supply in Petrograd led to strikes and riots by workers.
   D. the Socialist-led Petrograd garrison demanded that Alexei replace Nicholas as the tsar.

7. Soviet economic planning in the 1930s
   A. was overly rigid but overall set realistic production goals and growth rates.
   B. used the earliest analog computers to balance economic inputs and outputs.
   C. set unrealistically large production goals and often treated failure as treason.
   D. set intentionally modest production targets that could be easily exceeded.

8. All of the following contributed to the beginning of the Cold War EXCEPT:
   A. Longstanding mistrust between Soviet Communists and Western leaders
   B. The Soviet Union's determination to continue its occupation of Eastern Europe
   C. Stalin's refusal to de-Nazify its occupation zone in Germany and to try war criminals
   D. Stalin's attempt to Sovietize Greece in 1946-1949 and annex parts of Iran in 1946

9. What happened during the "July Days" of 1917?
   A. Monarchists temporarily arrested Lenin and Trotsky.
   B. Anarchists tried to assassinate the leading Bolsheviks.
   C. The Bolsheviks unsuccessfully attempted to seize power.
   D. The Kadets purged the Petrograd Soviet of pro-Bolshevik deputies.

10. What was the effect of the New Economic Policy on Russia's peasant farmers?
    A. They were not affected because NEP applied only to large-scale urban industry.
    B. They were impoverished by Stalin's policy of excessive taxation of grain surplus.
    C. They prospered because of lower grain taxes and the resumption of private trade.
    D. They prospered culturally but were impoverished by NEP's collectivization drive.

11. The key objective of Stalin's GULAG camps was to
    A. neutralize and punish political enemies while the state benefited from their labor.
    B. make a profit from the prisoners' labor, while treating them relatively humanely.
    C. house inmates temporarily until they could be murdered and buried in secret.
    D. force prisoners to learn Marxism and be reintegrated into the socialist system.

12. The Bolshevik Party evolved from the
    A. Russian Social Democratic Workers' Party.
    B. Socialist Revolutionary Party.
    C. Union of the Russian People.
    D. Constitutional Democratic Party.

13. What happened to Russia's heavy industry during NEP?
    A. It was temporarily returned to its pre-1917 owners.
    B. It was retained under state ownership and control.
    C. It was leased out to investors from Germany and the U.S.
    D. It was confiscated from owners who were disloyal.

14. Which of the following was NOT an important motivation for the Soviet collectivization drive in the late 1920s?

  A. Building socialism while at the same time destroying private property entrenched in villages

  B. Forcing peasant farmers to sell grain at low prices so that the Soviet government could feed urban workers

  C. Creating a stable food supply to maintain and expand a large army necessary to deter enemy invasions

  D. Reducing the number of Russian peasant villages because of the peasants' strongly nationalist sentiments

15. A Soviet nuclear weapon was first created in

  A. 1945.

  B. 1953.

  C. 1960.

  D. 1949.

16. Which of the following best describes late imperial Russia's religious policies?

  A. They supported Russian Orthodoxy as the official state religion.

  B. They extended full tolerance to Judaism and other non-Christian faiths.

  C. They secularized public schools and universities but not private ones.

  D. They mended the ancient schism with the Roman Catholic Church.

17. What was the result of Stalin's industrialization drive?

  A. It jump-started Soviet heavy industry but involved high costs and sacrifices.

  B. Russian nationalist reaction caused Stalin to abandon the worst excesses.

  C. It was originally a failure but improved once free labor was introduced.

  D. It was a complete failure and the Soviet economy largely deindustrialized by 1941.

18. Russia's peasant agriculture under the Old Regime was

  A. growing rapidly and known as the "Peasant Miracle."

  B. growing modestly and providing grain surplus for export.

  C. stagnant aside from the fertile lands in northeast Russia.

  D. depressed and requiring food imports from the United States.

19. The term "Cosmopolitans" in post-war Soviet propaganda referred to

  A. intellectuals, many of them Jewish, deemed to be too friendly toward the West.

  B. communists who thought that the Soviet victory would bring a worldwide revolution.

  C. communist intellectuals who were displaced or lost their homes during the war.

  D. anti-communist activists who wanted to bring the USSR into the United Nations.

20. The Belavezha Accords of 1991 declared that

  A. Russia would be permitted to station troops in Poland.

  B. Russia would pursue an affiliated status within NATO.

  C. the Commonwealth of Independent States (CIS) would replace the USSR.

  D. Russia, Belarus, and Ukraine would form the National Slavic Union.

21. Targets of Stalin's Terror in the 1930s included all of these groups EXCEPT:

  A. Individuals trained or educated in their professions before 1917

  B. Communists who at one point opposed Stalin's policies or power

  C. Individuals previously arrested as kulaks or who had served the Whites

  D. Jewish intellectuals and doctors regarded as potential enemy spies

22. Khrushchev gained and preserved his power by appealing primarily to
    A. the Central Committee of the Party, as well as the army and the KGB.
    B. technical experts who ran the Soviet Union's vast military-industrial complex.
    C. communists from Ukraine, Georgia, and the Baltic republics.
    D. grass-roots local Communist organizations who wanted reform.

23. All of the following contributed to the fall of the Soviet Union EXCEPT:
    A. Terrorist attacks
    B. Low oil prices
    C. Chernobyl accident
    D. The Spitak earthquake in 1988

24. As a result of the Winter War of 1939–1940, Finland was
    A. defeated and incorporated into the Soviet Union together with the Baltic states.
    B. victorious, inducing Stalin to accept pre-war borders and economic concessions.
    C. defeated after prolonged and brave resistance and deprived of the region of Karelia.
    D. victorious after the British and French armies landed in Narvik and rescued the Finns.

25. The 1975 Helsinki agreements required the Soviet government to
    A. release all remaining POWs.
    B. stop supporting terrorism.
    C. observe human rights.
    D. allow private small businesses.

26. Khrushchev's attitude toward the United States is best described as believing
    A. that the USSR had to use its tactical nukes to demonstrate resolve.
    B. in "peaceful coexistence" while pursuing a nuclear and space program.
    C. in "rollback", i.e., forcefully expanding the Soviet sphere of influence.
    D. that the USSR had to adopt some elements of American democracy.

27. In contemporary Russia, Gorbachev is regarded mostly as a
    A. mad fanatic because he stuck to his Communist beliefs to the end.
    B. great success because he ended the Cold War without violence.
    C. Russia's greatest ruler because he overthrew the Communist Party.
    D. failure because perestroika failed to preserve the Soviet Union.

28. Brezhnev-era investments in infrastructure
    A. included nationwide transportation and energy networks and industrial modernization.
    B. were limited to high-tech industries, especially electronics.
    C. focused on consumer goods, to the detriment of military industry.
    D. focused on oil and gas extraction, to the detriment of all other areas.

29. The main strategy of the Provisional Government was to
    A. postpone major reforms until the Constitutional Assembly was elected and the war won.
    B. call for British, French, and American military help to suppress Bolshevik uprisings.
    C. improve land and labor laws so as to win the majority in the Constitutional Assembly
    D. conclude a separate peace treaty with Germany and then carry out land reforms.

30. The "Velvet Revolution" of 1989 took place in

A. Czechoslovakia

B. East Germany

C. Hungary

D. Bulgaria

31. What was the condition of the Red Army on the eve of the German invasion in 1941?

A. It lacked enough soldiers because the invasion was so sudden.

B. It was completely demoralized after the defeat at Nomonhan against Japan.

C. It was well-motivated but armed entirely with obsolete armor and aircraft.

D. It was well-armed but weakened by purges and organizational problems.

32. Gorbachev's perestroika in 1987–1990 meant

A. retaining the planned economy but radically reducing military expenses.

B. easing censorship, ending the planned economy, and improving relations with the West.

C. disbanding the Communist Party and dismantling the Warsaw Pact.

D. permitting non-Communist parties but tougher policies toward the U.S.

33. The Soviet breakup with China happened because Mao Zedong thought

A. the Soviet Union was irresponsible in almost starting a world war over Cuba.

B. de-Stalinization was wrong and Khrushchev had failed to stand up to the U.S.

C. Khrushchev was too aggressive in attempting to restart the Korean War.

D. Khrushchev's Secret Speech failed to apologize for Stalin's purges of ethnic Chinese.

34. Reagan's reaction to the Soviet shoot-down of Korean Air Lines Flight 007 in 1983 was to

A. admit that the flight was intended to probe Soviet air defenses.

B. recognize that the shoot-down was negligent but not intentional.

C. sharply criticize it as an intentional "crime against humanity."

D. threaten the USSR with military action if it did not offer compensation.

35. Soviet policies in the 1920s with respect to national minorities

A. continued tsarist policies of oppression and ignored minorities' needs.

B. made an exception for national minorities when introducing socialist policies.

C. assumed that non-Russian identities would naturally die out under socialism.

D. promoted minority cultures and identities as long as they adhered to socialism.

36. The USSR participated in the Arab-Israeli Wars of 1967 and 1973 by

A. providing financial and diplomatic assistance to Israel.

B. providing massive military and other aid to the Arabs.

C. officially refusing to be involved but secretly helping both sides.

D. sending large numbers of ground troops disguised as Cubans.

post-test

37. Which of the following was NOT a site of a major ethnic or national conflict in the early 1990s?

    A. Nagorno-Karabakh

    B. Transnistria

    C. South Ossetia

    D. The Don Cossack District

38. What was the extent of "proxy wars" under Khrushchev?

    A. The USSR and the U.S. fought proxy wars in Namibia, Iran, and Guatemala.

    B. The Soviet Union trained and armed the Democratic Army of Greece in 1946.

    C. Conflict in the Suez Canal prompted Khrushchev to threaten to launch nuclear missiles against the British and French.

    D. USSR-trained forces in Eastern Europe fought against pro-U.S. guerillas.

39. After promising to invade Japan in August 1945, Stalin

    A. broke his promise because the USSR had a nonaggression pact with Japan.

    B. declared war on Japan but never commenced active operations.

    C. kept his promise and defeated Japan's powerful Kwantung army.

    D. attacked Japan as promised but also fought against Nationalist China.

40. All of the following are true of the Hungarian Uprising EXCEPT:

    A. It began as a student-lead revolt

    B. It ended in a violent Soviet silencing of opposition

    C. It left 200,000 Hungarians as refugees

    D. It dismantled the Warsaw Pact

41. What changed in the status of the Russian Orthodox Church in 1941–1945?

    A. It was blamed for the German invasion and almost all churches were closed.

    B. It was allowed to function as long as it promoted prayers for Communism and Stalin.

    C. It was greatly expanded and revived to provide support for the war effort.

    D. It was reestablished as the Soviet Union's official religion under Stalin's tutelage.

42. Which Eastern European nation was most pro-Soviet after 1945?

    A. Hungary

    B. Czechoslovakia

    C. Poland

    D. Romania

43. What caused the famine of 1932–1933 in the Soviet Union?

    A. A bad harvest in 1932 that could not be helped by any amount of state aid

    B. Stalin's desire to break the peasants' resistance to collectivization

    C. Stalin's desire to ethnically cleanse the Soviet Union of Ukrainians and Kazakhs

    D. Stalin's paranoia that peasants were sheltering anarchist leaders

44. When the U.S. invited Stalin to participate in the Marshall Plan, he

    A. accepted the offer unconditionally because the USSR needed all the aid it could get.

    B. refused the offer except for the U.S. program of food assistance in Ukraine.

    C. accepted the offer, as long as the USSR's planned economy would not be threatened.

    D. refused the offer when he learned about the Plan's terms.

45. The White Movement during the Russian Civil War was a

    A. mass movement of peasants who resented both the Bolsheviks and their former noble masters.

    B. coalition of regional governments who wanted to divide Russia into separate republics.

    C. small, disciplined group of monarchist conspirators who supported Grand Duke Michael.

    D. coalition of anti-Bolshevik forces that included monarchists, liberals, and the socialist revolutionists.

46. The large-scale Soviet military presence in Afghanistan ended in

    A. 1988, after the Geneva Agreements with the U.S.

    B. 1985, as soon as Gorbachev came to power.

    C. 1991, as soon as the Soviet Union fell.

    D. 1984, after U.S. Stinger missiles grounded Soviet aircraft.

47. The Treaty of Rapallo of 1922 involved mutual diplomatic recognition between the USSR and

    A. Fascist Italy.

    B. Weimar Germany.

    C. Kemalist Turkey.

    D. Republican Spain.

48. The Berlin Blockade of 1948–1949 was

    A. a miscalculation by Stalin because the Western bloc did not back down.

    B. inconclusive because the Soviet Army continued to control West Berlin.

    C. a victory for Stalin because his authority in East Germany was strengthened.

    D. a major defeat for Stalin because he had to allow U.S. observers into East Berlin.

49. Mikhail Gorbachev came to power because he

    A. was viewed by the aging Politburo as a younger, more energetic type of leader.

    B. promised to do everything in his power to overthrow Communism in Russia.

    C. promised to do everything in his power to preserve Communism in Russia.

    D. was viewed by the Politburo as an ignorant upstart who could be easily dominated.

50. How extensive was the Holocaust in the Soviet Union?

    A. The Germans were more lenient towards Soviet Jews, as opposed to Polish Jews.

    B. Most Soviet Jews were forewarned and managed to escape to the East.

    C. Most of the Jews in German-occupied territory were killed, totaling between 2 and 3 million.

    D. The Germans spared those Jews who openly condemned Stalin and Communism.

51. The extent of Soviet participation in the Korean War was that it

    A. sent over 250,000 Soviet Army "volunteers" masquerading as Chinese troops.

    B. refused to support North Korea and antagonized Mao Zedong's China.

    C. financed and armed North Korea, sent military advisers, and provided air cover.

    D. supported North Korea only diplomatically and by promising economic aid.

52. Who was the most likely successor to Stalin in 1953?

    A. Marshal Zhukov

    B. Leonid Brezhnev

    C. Lavrentiy Beria

    D. Vyacheslav Molotov

53. Socialist Realist art under Stalin meant
    A. returning to traditional realist forms while glorifying new communist values.
    B. discarding communist ideology and relying on traditional pre-1917 artistic forms.
    C. avoiding any realistic subjects and developing unique, ideology-driven artistic forms.
    D. continuing the Avant-Garde art of the 1920s but depicting working-class subjects.

54. Which of the following most accurately describes the cultural "Thaw" under Khrushchev?
    A. It was a propagandistic fiction, because Thaw leaders were coached to appear independent.
    B. It proceeded in fits and starts, with liberal waves replaced by conservative attacks.
    C. Political topics could be discussed but only in Aesopian language.
    D. The topic of Stalin's terror was freely discussed in print under Khrushchev.

55. Gorbachev's 1988 Law on Cooperatives
    A. for the first time permitted private businesses to use hired labor.
    B. prohibited most forms of private business as contrary to glasnost.
    C. allowed private business under oversight from state-owned organizations.
    D. allowed private business as long as hired labor was not "exploited."

56. Most of the intellectuals known as "dissidents"
    A. emphasized right-wing versions of ethnic Russian nationalism.
    B. wanted the Soviet government to accurately observe its own laws.
    C. used terror to overthrow the government for their personal gain.
    D. thought that socialism as an ideology was completely wrong-headed.

57. The only anti-Communist revolution in Eastern Europe in 1989 that involved large-scale violence took place in
    A. Poland.
    B. Hungary.
    C. Bulgaria.
    D. Romania.

58. U.S. support of Islamist fighters in Afghanistan began
    A. never, because the U.S. only supported the secular opposition.
    B. a few months before the Soviet invasion in 1979.
    C. a few months after the Soviet invasion in 1979.
    D. only in 1982 after the Soviets appeared to be winning.

59. The Soviet war in Afghanistan can be best described as a
    A. clear win because Islamic militancy was contained.
    B. clear loss because it led directly to the Soviet collapse.
    C. military success but political failure because the Afghan population was antagonized.
    D. military failure but political success because the Afghan population was won over.

60. Brezhnev-era "stagnation" refers to the fact that
    A. the Soviet middle class became increasingly impoverished.
    B. Soviet military equipment was inferior to that of the U.S.
    C. Soviet culture and the arts lacked vitality and originality.
    D. the rate of Soviet economic growth was slowing down.

ANSWER KEY AND EXPLANATIONS

1. A	13. B	25. C	37. D	49. A
2. C	14. D	26. B	38. C	50. C
3. A	15. D	27. D	39. C	51. C
4. B	16. A	28. A	40. D	52. C
5. A	17. A	29. A	41. C	53. A
6. C	18. B	30. A	42. B	54. B
7. C	19. A	31. D	43. B	55. A
8. C	20. C	32. B	44. D	56. B
9. C	21. D	33. B	45. D	57. D
10. C	22. A	34. C	46. A	58. B
11. A	23. A	35. D	47. B	59. C
12. A	24. C	36. B	48. A	60. D

1. **The correct answer is A.** The USSR was given about one-third of Eastern Prussia as part of its share of war reparations from Germany. While Western Allies were uneasy about the USSR's continued occupation of some of its gains from 1939–1940 (such as the Baltic Republics), these gains were de facto recognized by the Yalta Agreement.

2. **The correct answer is C.** Freedom of speech was not introduced during the Great Reforms. Choices A, B, and D are incorrect because all of these items were part of the Great Reforms.

3. **The correct answer is A.** The Germans failed to capture Leningrad but cut it off from most supplies, so that over 600,000 of its citizens died of starvation. Choice B is incorrect because Leningrad was never captured. Choice C is incorrect because Leningrad was not a temporary capital during that period. Choice D is incorrect because Tankograd was located in Chelyabinsk in the Urals, and not in Leningrad.

4. **The correct answer is B.** Russia's heavy industry and railroad network grew particularly rapidly in the 1890s. For this reason, choice A is incorrect. Choice C is incorrect because industry did not stagnate. Choice D is incorrect because industry did not decline and Old Believer merchants supported capitalism rather than opposed it.

5. **The correct answer is A.** The Russian army suffered its most serious defeats during the munitions shortages in 1915. Choice B is incorrect because Russia did not suffer manpower shortages during the First World War. Choice C is incorrect because lack of naval power did not seriously hinder Russia's war effort. Choice D is incorrect because fortresses did not play a significant role in Russia's war effort.

6. **The correct answer is C.** The tsar's government lost control of Petrograd after food shortages led to strikes and violent riots and the city's garrison had rebelled as well. Choice A is incorrect because Germans were not threatening Petrograd in February 1917. Choice B is incorrect because Rasputin's assassination occurred months before the revolution and did not lead to anti-clerical riots. Choice D is incorrect because the Petrograd garrison did not want Nicholas' son, Alexei, to be the next tsar.

7. **The correct answer is C.** Soviet five-year plans were impossible to meet because of their unrealistic goals. Choice A is incorrect because production goals were not realistic. Choice B is incorrect because computer-assisted calculations were not used. Choice D is incorrect because production targets were excessively high rather than modest.

8. **The correct answer is C.** Stalin did not refuse to de-Nazify its occupation zone or to try war criminals. Choices A, B, and D were all factors in worsening relations between the USSR and the Western Allies.

9. **The correct answer is C.** In July 1917, the Bolsheviks tried to seize power in the wake of popular uprisings, but failed. Choice A is incorrect because monarchists were not a major political force in Petrograd. Choice B is incorrect because no one tried to assassinate Bolshevik leaders. Choice D is incorrect because it was the Kadets who were purged after the July days.

10. **The correct answer is C.** NEP involved a much better treatment of peasants by the Bolshevik government. Choice A is incorrect because NEP policies did not apply to large-scale industry. Choice B is incorrect because peasants were not impoverished under NEP and excessive taxation was not one of NEP's features. Choice D is incorrect because NEP did not involve a collectivization drive.

11. **The correct answer is A.** Stalin's GULAG camps were punitive in nature, but at the same time were intended to contribute economically by providing labor for those sectors to which free labor could not be easily attracted. Choice B is incorrect because GULAG prisoners were not treated humanely. Choice C is incorrect because GULAG camps were not set up to intentionally murder large numbers of inmates. Choice D is incorrect because reeducation was occasionally an element of GULAG camps but a very minor one.

12. **The correct answer is A.** The Russian Social Democratic Workers' Party split off into Bolshevik and Menshevik branches. Choices B, C, and D are incorrect because these were different political parties not related to the Bolsheviks.

13. **The correct answer is B.** NEP's policy of economic liberalization did not apply to heavy industry. Choice A is incorrect because heavy industry was not privatized. Choice C is incorrect because heavy industry was not leased out to foreign firms. Choice D is

incorrect because all heavy industry in Russia had been nationalized in 1918–1919.

14. **The correct answer is D.** Peasants' nationalism was not a major concern during collectivization. Choices A, B, and C are incorrect because these items were all among the reasons for undertaking the collectivization of Soviet agriculture.

15. **The correct answer is D.** The Soviet nuclear bomb was tested in 1949. For this reason, choices A, B, and C are incorrect.

16. **The correct answer is A.** Russian Orthodoxy was the official state-supported religion in the Russian Empire. Other religions were tolerated to a limited extent. Choice B is incorrect because non-Christian faiths and Judaism in particular did not enjoy full tolerance. Choice C is incorrect because public schools required mandatory catechism lessons. Choice D is incorrect because the official policy was not striving to mend the schism between the Orthodox and Catholic churches.

17. **The correct answer is A.** Stalin's industrialization made Soviet industry the second-largest after that of the U.S. but at a high cost in human lives and suffering. Choice B is incorrect because there was no Russian nationalist reaction. Choice C is incorrect because, while free labor was used alongside GULAG inmates on most major sites, it did not ensure that industrialization was a success. Choice D is not correct because only a few of the Soviet industrial projects of the 1930s can be described as clear failures.

18. **The correct answer is B.** While per capita incomes in late imperial Russia were low, its vast agricultural sector was growing modestly, and Russia was the world's leading wheat exporter. Choice A is incorrect because Russian agriculture did not grow rapidly. Choice C is incorrect because agriculture was not stagnant and northeast Russia was not fertile. Choice D is incorrect because domestic food supplies were sufficient under the Old Regime.

19. **The correct answer is A.** The campaign against "rootless cosmopolitanism" was intended to root out any support or sympathy

for the West among Soviet elites. Choices B, C, and D are incorrect because these groups were not specified as targets of the campaign against cosmopolitans.

20. **The correct answer is C.** The 1991 agreement among the leaders of the Russian Federation, Ukraine, and Belarus in effect disbanded the Soviet Union and replaced it with the CIS. Choices A, B, and D were not issues addressed by the Belavezha Accords.

21. **The correct answer is D.** Jewish intellectuals and doctors were targeted in the late 1940s and early 1950s but not during the pre-war terror. Choices A, B, and C are incorrect because all of these groups were targeted in the 1930s.

22. **The correct answer is A.** Khrushchev maintained his power by reaffirming the privileged position of the Communist Party and its Central Committee. In addition, he was supported by important military and KGB figures who did not want a return of Stalinist politics. Choice B is incorrect because technical experts were sidelined under Khrushchev. Choice C is incorrect because non-Russian leaders were not regarded as a significant source of support in their own right. Choice D is incorrect because there were no independent grass-roots Communist organizations under Khrushchev.

23. **The correct answer is A.** Terrorist attacks did occur in the Soviet Union in the 1970s and 1980s but they were not frequent enough or violent enough to undermine the Soviet regime. Choice B is incorrect because low oil prices deprived the USSR of its source of hard currency. Choice C is incorrect because the Chernobyl nuclear accident was expensive and undermined public confidence in the Communist Party. Choice D is incorrect because the Spitak earthquake in Armenia was hugely expensive to repair and thus damaged the Soviet economy.

24. **The correct answer is C.** Although Finland put up a good fight, it was defeated and lost some of its territory in Karelia. Choice A is incorrect because the USSR failed to annex Finland. Choice B is incorrect because

Finland did not win the war. Choice D is incorrect because the British and the French did not join the war on the Finns' side, although they did send some weapons and supplies.

25. **The correct answer is C.** The Soviet Union agreed to observe human rights. Choice A is incorrect because POWs were not an issue in 1975. Choice B is incorrect because in Helsinki, the USSR was not accused of supporting terrorism. Choice D is incorrect because private business was not a topic discussed at Helsinki.

26. **The correct answer is B.** Khrushchev believed that nuclear war was not inevitable, but he was determined to build up Soviet nuclear and missile strength. Choice A is incorrect because Khrushchev did not want to use nuclear weapons. Choice C is incorrect because he did not believe in a forceful "rollback" of the Western bloc, although he did suppress attempts to reduce Soviet influence in Eastern Europe. Choice D is incorrect because there was no question of adopting American democracy even in part.

27. **The correct answer is D.** In today's Russia, Gorbachev is widely criticized for failing to preserve the Soviet Union. Choice A is incorrect because it is not commonly believed that Gorbachev did stick to his Communist beliefs. Choice B is incorrect because Gorbachev's role in ending the Cold War is not widely viewed as an accomplishment in Russia, because he failed to secure terms advantageous to the Soviet Union. Choice C is incorrect because Gorbachev is not viewed as a great (or the greatest) ruler or as having intentionally overthrown the Communist Party.

28. **The correct answer is A.** Brezhnev-era investments emphasized long-term capital projects. Choice B is incorrect because investments went to all areas, and electronics were not privileged. Choice C is incorrect because military industry still had priority. Choice D is incorrect because oil and gas were important, but other areas of the economy were being developed as well.

29. **The correct answer is A.** The Provisional Government was formed to run the country until nationwide elections could be held and to make sure that the war effort was maintained. Choice B is incorrect because Bolshevik uprisings were not originally seen as a major threat and foreign assistance was not requested. Choice C is incorrect because the Provisional Government refused to introduce major social reforms. Choice D is incorrect because the Provisional Government ruled out both a separate peace and land reform.

30. **The correct answer is A.** The term "Velvet Revolution" is applied to Czechoslovakia's overthrow of Communism in 1989. Choices B, C, and D are incorrect.

31. **The correct answer is D.** The Red Army had sufficient numbers of modern weapons, but its morale and organization were weakened by the purges and rapid expansion in the late 1930s. Choice A is incorrect because the Red Army was not smaller than the German Army. Choice B is incorrect because the Red Army won the battle of Nomonhan. Choice C is incorrect because the Red Army had large numbers of modern weapons in addition to even larger numbers of out-of-date ones.

32. **The correct answer is B.** Important aspects of Gorbachev's policies were glasnost (the relaxation of censorship), permitting private business, and easing the USSR's confrontation with the West. Choice A is incorrect because the planned economy was widely seen as untenable. Choice C is incorrect because perestroika was meant to preserve the Communist system. Choice D is incorrect because perestroika involved a more conciliatory policy toward the U.S.

33. **The correct answer is B.** Mao broke with Khrushchev over his de-Stalinization and because he failed to respond more forcefully to the crisis with the U-2 spy plane in 1960. Choice A is incorrect because the Cuban crisis happened after the break with China. Choice C is incorrect because Khrushchev did not attempt to restart the Korean War. Choice D is incorrect because purges of ethnic Chinese people or a failure to apologize for them were not a factor in the Sino-Soviet rift.

34. **The correct answer is C.** Reagan criticized the incident as if it were an intentional murder of civilians by the Soviets. Choice A is incorrect because Reagan never admitted that the CIA may have been involved in the incident. Choice B is incorrect because Reagan claimed that the Soviets knew that the plane was full of civilians. Choice D is incorrect because Reagan did not threaten to go to war with the USSR over this incident.

35. **The correct answer is D.** Bolshevik nationalities policy in the 1920s reversed the tsars' policy of Russification and promoted national and ethnic minority cultures. Choice A is incorrect because tsarist nationalist policies did not always involve oppression and in any case were not imitated in the 1920s. Choice B is incorrect because no significant exceptions were made for national minorities. Choice C is incorrect because Stalin believed that national identities would survive even after the USSR became fully socialist.

36. **The correct answer is B.** The Soviet Union provided massive military aid to Egypt, Syria, and other Arab countries. Choice A is incorrect because the USSR only supported Israel briefly and indirectly in the late 1940s. Choice C is incorrect because the Soviet Union openly supported the Arabs. Choice D is incorrect because the Soviet Union sent pilots, sailors, and surface-to-air missiles to assist the Arabs but no ground troops, disguised or otherwise.

37. **The correct answer is D.** Don Cossacks are not usually regarded to be an ethnic or a national group, and they were not directly involved in any conflicts. Choices A, B, and C are incorrect because all of these areas involved inter-ethnic conflicts in the early 1990s.

38. **The correct answer is C.** The Cold War under Khrushchev focused on the space and nuclear race and on maintaining Soviet control in Eastern Europe; however, he did back the Egyptian leader when he nationalized the Suez Canal. After the British

and French supported Israel in its attack on Egypt, Khrushchev threatened to launch a nuclear attack on all three nations. Choices A, B, and D are incorrect because these conflicts did not take place under Khrushchev's regime.

39. **The correct answer is C.** The USSR invaded Japan and defeated its forces in Manchuria and North China. Choice A is incorrect because the USSR abrogated its nonaggression pact with Japan when it attacked in August 1945. Choice B is incorrect because the Red Army did actively attack the Japanese forces. Choice D is incorrect because the Red Army did not fight against Nationalist Chinese forces in 1945.

40. **The correct answer is D.** The uprising was unsuccessful and the Warsaw Pact remained intact. Choice A is incorrect because the Hungarian Uprising began as a student revolt as an attempt to deflect from the Warsaw Pact. Choice B is incorrect as it ended in Soviet troops crushing the opposition. Choice C is incorrect because the uprising did indeed result in 200,000 Hungarian refugees.

41. **The correct answer is C.** Stalin's policy was to expand and support the Church during the war. Choice A is incorrect because the Church was not blamed for the German invasion. Choice B is incorrect because praying for Stalin and Communism were not conditions for allowing the Church to revive its organization. Choice D is incorrect because the Russian Orthodox Church was greatly strengthened during the war, but it was not made an official church.

42. **The correct answer is B.** Czechoslovakia's leaders and ruling elites were relatively well disposed toward the USSR after 1945. Other Eastern European countries were much less friendly, so choices A, C, and D are incorrect.

43. **The correct answer is B.** The key cause of the famine was the government's policy of forced collectivization and its determination to overcome the peasants' resistance by confiscating a large proportion (up to 40 percent) of their 1932 harvest. Choice A is incorrect because the harvest in 1932 was bad but not catastrophically so. Choice C is incorrect because Stalin's hostility was toward peasants as socially alien elements and not toward any particular ethnic groups. Choice D is incorrect because anarchist leaders were not a major concern at that time.

44. **The correct answer is D.** Stalin considered accepting the Marshall Plan in the form of a money loan from the U.S. but declined when he found out the details of its terms. Choices A and C are incorrect because Stalin did not accept the Plan. Choice B is incorrect because there was no U.S. program to assist Ukraine.

45. **The correct answer is D.** The White Movement consisted of numerous organizations and armies of different political persuasions. Choice A is incorrect because the Whites failed to secure the loyalty of large numbers of peasants. Choice B is incorrect because major White leaders wanted to preserve a single and indivisible Russia. Choice C is incorrect because monarchists were not the only members of the White Movement. Grand Duke Michael had been killed in 1918 and so could not take part in it.

46. **The correct answer is A.** The U.S. and the USSR agreed to end their respective involvement in Afghanistan in 1988. Choice B is incorrect because Gorbachev initially wanted to escalate the war, not end it. Choice C is incorrect because Soviet involvement ended long before the fall of the Soviet Union. Choice D is incorrect because the Soviets suffered from the Stinger missiles supplied to the mujahedeen but quickly captured a sample missile and developed countermeasures.

47. **The correct answer is B.** The Treaty of Rapallo was a landmark agreement between Soviet Russia and Weimar Germany. Choices A, C, and D are incorrect because these countries were not parties to the Treaty of Rapallo.

48. **The correct answer is A.** Stalin expected that the U.S. and its allies would meet his

demand and did not anticipate that they would instead run an airlift. Choice B is incorrect because the Soviet Army did not control West Berlin. Choice C is incorrect because his authority in East Germany was weakened, rather than strengthened, as a result of the blockade. Choice D is incorrect because Stalin neither suffered a major defeat nor had to allow U.S. observers into East Berlin.

49. **The correct answer is A.** Gorbachev was promoted because he was seen as younger and more energetic but holding the same beliefs and values as his older comrades. Choices B and C are incorrect because overthrowing or maintaining Communism was not an issue in deciding whether Gorbachev would become the next leader. Choice D is incorrect because Gorbachev was recognized as intelligent and well-connected to influential older Communists.

50. **The correct answer is C.** While many Jews did escape the German onslaught, most of those who stayed behind were killed. Choice A is incorrect because the Germans were equally brutal toward Soviet and Polish Jews. Choice B is incorrect because most Soviet Jews were unable to escape the Germans in time to save themselves. Choice D is incorrect because the Germans were not interested in recruiting collaborators from among Soviet Jews.

51. **The correct answer is C.** The USSR sponsored North Korea and provided fighter aircraft and pilots. Choice A is incorrect because Soviet troops did not intervene in large numbers. Choice B is incorrect because Stalin actually did support North Korea. Choice D is incorrect because Stalin also provided considerable military aid.

52. **The correct answer is C.** Until his arrest and likely murder on June 26, 1953, Lavrentiy Beria was the most powerful figure in the Soviet Union. Choice A is incorrect because Zhukov was removed from active political life during Stalin's last years. Choice B is incorrect because Brezhnev was too junior to succeed Stalin. Choice D is incorrect because Molotov had been disgraced by Stalin and removed as a likely successor.

53. **The correct answer is A.** Writers and other cultural figures were expected to glorify communism while using traditional forms that would be easily appreciated by workers and peasants. Choice B is incorrect because communist ideology was not to be discarded. Choice C is incorrect because realistic forms and subjects were required. Choice D is incorrect because the Avant-Garde art of the 1920s was viewed with suspicion in the 1930s and largely avoided.

54. **The correct answer is B.** There were several periods of cultural liberalization, known as the Thaw, always followed by periods of tighter censorship and attacks in the press by conservative intellectuals. Choice A is incorrect because the Thaw was a real event. Choice C is incorrect because many important political problems were discussed directly (if only intermittently). Choice D is incorrect because Stalin's terror was discussed in print but in carefully measured ways.

55. **The correct answer is A.** Private businesses, labeled as cooperatives, were allowed to function virtually without restrictions. Choices B, C, and D are incorrect because none of these restrictions applied under the terms of the 1988 law.

56. **The correct answer is B.** Dissidents demanded above all that the Soviet government at least observe the laws that it itself issued. Choice A is incorrect because right-wing Russian nationalist dissidents were few in number. Choice C is incorrect because dissidents did not use terror. Choice D is incorrect because dissidents did not oppose socialism.

57. **The correct answer is D.** Mass violence took place in Romania only. For this reason, choices A, B, and C are incorrect.

58. **The correct answer is B.** The U.S. began to support Islamist forces in Afghanistan approximately six months before the Soviet invasion. Choice A is incorrect because there was no significant secular opposition in Afghanistan during the period in question, and the U.S. supported the Islamic opposition (mujahedeen). Choice C is incorrect

because the U.S. started to support the mujahedeen hoping to undermine Soviet influence before the actual invasion. Choice D is incorrect because the U.S. started to support the mujahedeen long before 1982.

59. **The correct answer is C.** The Soviet Army won all major battles and operations but was unable to secure Afghanistan's pro-Soviet regime politically. Choice A is incorrect because Islamic militancy continued to grow in the 1980s. Choice B is incorrect because the war was only a minor factor in undermining Gorbachev's power. Choice D is incorrect because the Soviets failed to win over Afghanistan's population.

60. **The correct answer is D.** The Soviet economy was growing under Brezhnev but not fast enough to ensure parity with the West. Choice A is incorrect because the Soviet middle class was much better off under Brezhnev than ever before. Choice B is incorrect because Soviet weapons were often equal or superior to American ones. Choice C is incorrect because the Soviet Union developed brilliant artistic and cultural productions under Brezhnev.

answers post-test

Substance Abuse

OVERVIEW

- Test Answer Sheets
- Substance Abuse Diagnostic Test
- Answer Key and Explanations
- Diagnostic Test Assessment Grid
- Overview of Substance Abuse and Dependence
- Classification of Drugs
- Pharmacological and Neuropsychological Principles
- Alcohol
- Antianxiety and Sedative-Hypnotics
- Inhalants
- Tobacco and Nicotine
- Psychomotor Stimulants
- Opioids
- Cannabinoids
- Hallucinogens
- Other Drugs of Abuse
- Antipsychotic Drugs
- Antidepressants and Mood Stabilizers
- Summing It Up
- Substance Abuse Post-test
- Answer Key and Explanations

Chapter 12

The DSST® Substance Abuse exam consists of 100 multiple-choice questions that cover the history, effects, uses, administration, tolerance, withdrawal, overdose, prevention, and treatment of such substances as alcohol, antianxiety and sedative-hypnotic drugs, inhalants, tobacco and nicotine, psychomotor drugs, opioids, cannabinoids, hallucinogens, antipsychotics, antidepressants, and mood stabilizers. Careful reading, critical thinking, and logical analysis will be as important as your knowledge of substance abuse and treatment.

DIAGNOSTIC TEST ANSWER SHEET

1. Ⓐ Ⓑ Ⓒ Ⓓ 5. Ⓐ Ⓑ Ⓒ Ⓓ 9. Ⓐ Ⓑ Ⓒ Ⓓ 13. Ⓐ Ⓑ Ⓒ Ⓓ 17. Ⓐ Ⓑ Ⓒ Ⓓ
2. Ⓐ Ⓑ Ⓒ Ⓓ 6. Ⓐ Ⓑ Ⓒ Ⓓ 10. Ⓐ Ⓑ Ⓒ Ⓓ 14. Ⓐ Ⓑ Ⓒ Ⓓ 18. Ⓐ Ⓑ Ⓒ Ⓓ
3. Ⓐ Ⓑ Ⓒ Ⓓ 7. Ⓐ Ⓑ Ⓒ Ⓓ 11. Ⓐ Ⓑ Ⓒ Ⓓ 15. Ⓐ Ⓑ Ⓒ Ⓓ 19. Ⓐ Ⓑ Ⓒ Ⓓ
4. Ⓐ Ⓑ Ⓒ Ⓓ 8. Ⓐ Ⓑ Ⓒ Ⓓ 12. Ⓐ Ⓑ Ⓒ Ⓓ 16. Ⓐ Ⓑ Ⓒ Ⓓ 20. Ⓐ Ⓑ Ⓒ Ⓓ

POST-TEST ANSWER SHEET

1. Ⓐ Ⓑ Ⓒ Ⓓ   13. Ⓐ Ⓑ Ⓒ Ⓓ   25. Ⓐ Ⓑ Ⓒ Ⓓ   37. Ⓐ Ⓑ Ⓒ Ⓓ   49. Ⓐ Ⓑ Ⓒ Ⓓ
2. Ⓐ Ⓑ Ⓒ Ⓓ   14. Ⓐ Ⓑ Ⓒ Ⓓ   26. Ⓐ Ⓑ Ⓒ Ⓓ   38. Ⓐ Ⓑ Ⓒ Ⓓ   50. Ⓐ Ⓑ Ⓒ Ⓓ
3. Ⓐ Ⓑ Ⓒ Ⓓ   15. Ⓐ Ⓑ Ⓒ Ⓓ   27. Ⓐ Ⓑ Ⓒ Ⓓ   39. Ⓐ Ⓑ Ⓒ Ⓓ   51. Ⓐ Ⓑ Ⓒ Ⓓ
4. Ⓐ Ⓑ Ⓒ Ⓓ   16. Ⓐ Ⓑ Ⓒ Ⓓ   28. Ⓐ Ⓑ Ⓒ Ⓓ   40. Ⓐ Ⓑ Ⓒ Ⓓ   52. Ⓐ Ⓑ Ⓒ Ⓓ
5. Ⓐ Ⓑ Ⓒ Ⓓ   17. Ⓐ Ⓑ Ⓒ Ⓓ   29. Ⓐ Ⓑ Ⓒ Ⓓ   41. Ⓐ Ⓑ Ⓒ Ⓓ   53. Ⓐ Ⓑ Ⓒ Ⓓ
6. Ⓐ Ⓑ Ⓒ Ⓓ   18. Ⓐ Ⓑ Ⓒ Ⓓ   30. Ⓐ Ⓑ Ⓒ Ⓓ   42. Ⓐ Ⓑ Ⓒ Ⓓ   54. Ⓐ Ⓑ Ⓒ Ⓓ
7. Ⓐ Ⓑ Ⓒ Ⓓ   19. Ⓐ Ⓑ Ⓒ Ⓓ   31. Ⓐ Ⓑ Ⓒ Ⓓ   43. Ⓐ Ⓑ Ⓒ Ⓓ   55. Ⓐ Ⓑ Ⓒ Ⓓ
8. Ⓐ Ⓑ Ⓒ Ⓓ   20. Ⓐ Ⓑ Ⓒ Ⓓ   32. Ⓐ Ⓑ Ⓒ Ⓓ   44. Ⓐ Ⓑ Ⓒ Ⓓ   56. Ⓐ Ⓑ Ⓒ Ⓓ
9. Ⓐ Ⓑ Ⓒ Ⓓ   21. Ⓐ Ⓑ Ⓒ Ⓓ   33. Ⓐ Ⓑ Ⓒ Ⓓ   45. Ⓐ Ⓑ Ⓒ Ⓓ   57. Ⓐ Ⓑ Ⓒ Ⓓ
10. Ⓐ Ⓑ Ⓒ Ⓓ   22. Ⓐ Ⓑ Ⓒ Ⓓ   34. Ⓐ Ⓑ Ⓒ Ⓓ   46. Ⓐ Ⓑ Ⓒ Ⓓ   58. Ⓐ Ⓑ Ⓒ Ⓓ
11. Ⓐ Ⓑ Ⓒ Ⓓ   23. Ⓐ Ⓑ Ⓒ Ⓓ   35. Ⓐ Ⓑ Ⓒ Ⓓ   47. Ⓐ Ⓑ Ⓒ Ⓓ   59. Ⓐ Ⓑ Ⓒ Ⓓ
12. Ⓐ Ⓑ Ⓒ Ⓓ   24. Ⓐ Ⓑ Ⓒ Ⓓ   36. Ⓐ Ⓑ Ⓒ Ⓓ   48. Ⓐ Ⓑ Ⓒ Ⓓ   60. Ⓐ Ⓑ Ⓒ Ⓓ

answer sheets

SUBSTANCE ABUSE DIAGNOSTIC TEST

Directions: Carefully read each of the following 20 questions. Choose the best answer to each question and fill in the corresponding circle on the answer sheet. The Answer Key and Explanations can be found following this Diagnostic Test.

1. Smoke released into the air from a lighted cigarette is known as
   A. mainstream smoke.
   B. nicotine smoke.
   C. sidestream smoke.
   D. active smoke.

2. Alcohol and tobacco are considered
   A. opioids.
   B. OTC drugs.
   C. illicit drugs.
   D. gateway drugs.

3. In general, how would you calculate the length of time it will take an individual to metabolize the alcohol he or she drinks?
   A. Multiply the number of drinks by 2 hours each.
   B. Each drink takes about 30 minutes to metabolize.
   C. Beer and wine take about 30 minutes to metabolize, and hard alcohol takes about 2 hours to metabolize.
   D. Each drink takes about 1 hour to metabolize.

4. When an individual is in withdrawal from alcohol abuse, which of the following could occur in Stage 3?
   A. Insomnia
   B. Delusions
   C. Tremors
   D. Seizures

5. Dr. Sigmund Freud advocated cocaine usage to treat
   A. schizophrenia.
   B. hallucinations.
   C. depression.
   D. anxiety.

6. Which region of a neuron stores neurotransmitters?
   A. Presynaptic terminals
   B. Cell body
   C. Dendrites
   D. Axon

7. One of the most common side effects of low doses of opioids is
   A. diarrhea.
   B. headaches.
   C. alertness.
   D. constipation.

8. Sedative-hypnotics often come in the form of
   A. leaves.
   B. pills.
   C. liquid.
   D. nasal spray.

9. An individual takes substances that create an antagonistic interaction. What does this mean?
   A. The individual takes more than one substance in which one enhances the effects of another.
   B. The individual ingests a combination of drugs in which one activates the dormant properties of another.
   C. The individual ingests a combination of drugs in which one drug blocks the effects of another drug.
   D. The individual takes a combination of more than one substance in which one causes no effect based on the properties of the other.

10. Which of the following is the most common physiological effect of using marijuana?
    A. Decreased blood pressure
    B. Increased aggression
    C. Decreased appetite
    D. Increased heart rate

11. What of the following is a characteristic of antipsychotic drugs?
    A. They are highly addictive.
    B. They block the effects of other substances.
    C. They are most often obtained by prescription.
    D. Discontinued use will lead to severe withdrawal.

12. Cocaine is categorized as a
    A. stimulant.
    B. depressant.
    C. hallucinogen.
    D. psychotherapeutic.

13. A long-term effect known to be associated with extensive marijuana smoking is
    A. seizures.
    B. lung damage.
    C. mouth cancer.
    D. brain damage.

14. What is the alcohol content of an 80-proof bottle of whiskey?
    A. 20 percent
    B. 40 percent
    C. 80 percent
    D. 100 percent

15. Which of the following asserts that drug abuse is the result of a biological condition?
    A. Personality predisposition model
    B. Characterological model
    C. Disease model
    D. Moral model

16. Which of the following is another name for hallucinogens?
    A. Analgesics
    B. Cannabis
    C. Depressants
    D. Psychedelics

17. Which type of drug is abused by placing a bag over the head?
    A. Opioids
    B. Inhalants
    C. Nicotine
    D. Antipsychotics

18. MDMA, GHB, and Rohypnol are examples of
    A. club drugs.
    B. herbal drugs.
    C. antidepressants.
    D. anabolic steroids.

19. A drug that requires a written prescription and cannot be refilled by phone-in requests is classified under which DEA schedule?
    A. Schedule I
    B. Schedule II
    C. Schedule IV
    D. Schedule V

20. Prozac is the most popular
    A. anabolic steroid.
    B. antidepressant.
    C. antipsychotic.
    D. mood stabilizer.

ANSWER KEY AND EXPLANATIONS

1. C	5. C	9. C	13. B	17. B
2. D	6. A	10. D	14. B	18. A
3. D	7. D	11. C	15. C	19. B
4. B	8. B	12. A	16. D	20. B

1. **The correct answer is C.** Sidestream smoke refers to the smoke that is released into the air from the end of a lighted cigarette. Mainstream smoke (choice A) is the smoke that a smoker inhales directly from the mouthpiece of a cigarette. Sidestream smoke does contain high levels of nicotine, but nicotine smoke (choice B) is not the correct terminology. Active smoke (choice D) is the smoke intentionally inhaled.

2. **The correct answer is D.** Alcohol and tobacco are considered gateway drugs. Gateway drugs are typically used first by individuals who later move on to illicit drugs, such as heroin and cocaine. Choice A is incorrect because alcohol and tobacco are not derived from opium. Alcohol and tobacco are licit drugs, so choice C is incorrect. Over-the-counter (OTC) drugs (choice B) are medicines purchased without prescriptions, such as antihistamines and aspirin.

3. **The correct answer is D.** Each drink takes about 1 hour to metabolize, regardless of the type of alcohol. The drink would need to be the standard size used for calculation. If an individual has three drinks, it will take about 3 hours to metabolize. Choices A, B, and C are incorrect.

4. **The correct answer is B.** Delusions are a symptom of withdrawal associated with Stage 3. Insomnia and tremors are associated with Stage 1, so choices A and C are incorrect. Seizures are associated with Stage 4, so choice D is incorrect.

5. **The correct answer is C.** Freud recommended the use of cocaine in the treatment of depression. Physicians prescribed cocaine for a number of medical purposes until the Harrison Act of 1914 made it illegal to use or distribute cocaine. Choices A, B, and D are incorrect.

6. **The correct answer is A.** The presynaptic terminals store neurotransmitters, which act as chemical messengers. The cell body (choice B) contains the nucleus, and the dendrites (choice C) are treelike branches that receive transmitter signals. The axon conducts electrical signals, so choice D is incorrect.

7. **The correct answer is D.** Constipation is one of the most common side effects of opioids. Because of this side effect, opioids are used to treat severe diarrhea, so choice A is incorrect. Opioids relieve pain rather than cause pain, so choice B is incorrect. Opioids are not stimulants, so alertness (choice C) is not a side effect.

8. **The correct answer is B.** Sedative-hypnotics often come in the form of pills and are most widely dispensed as prescription drugs. Choices A, C, and D are incorrect.

9. **The correct answer is C.** An antagonistic interaction occurs when one drug blocks the effect of another drug. A reaction does occur, which eliminates choices B and D. Choice A is indicative of a potentiating effect.

10. **The correct answer is D.** Marijuana increases the heart rate among almost all users. Choice A is incorrect because marijuana's effect on blood pressure varies from slight increases to no change among users. Aggression (choice B) is not a typical effect of marijuana because most people feel relaxed. Appetite increases with marijuana, so choice C is incorrect.

11. **The correct answer is C.** Antipsychotics are most often obtained by prescription. Antipsychotics are not addictive, so choice

answers diagnostic test

A is incorrect. They enhance the effects of other drugs, so choice B is incorrect. Because they are not addictive, withdrawal symptoms would not be severe, so choice D is incorrect.

12. **The correct answer is A.** Cocaine is a stimulant that triggers excitement and paranoia among frequent users. Alcohol and sleeping pills are categorized as depressants, so choice B is incorrect. Hallucinogens (choice C) alter the perceptions of users, which is not an effect of cocaine usage. Psychotherapeutic drugs, such as Prozac, are used to treat patients with extensive mental problems, so choice D is incorrect.

13. **The correct answer is B.** Experts agree that long-term smoking of marijuana decreases pulmonary capabilities, causes chronic lung diseases, and raises the risk of lung cancer. Seizures and mouth cancer are not linked with smoking marijuana. Some people believe that marijuana causes brain damage, but there is no evidence to support this suspicion.

14. **The correct answer is B.** The alcohol content of an 80-proof bottle of whiskey is 40 percent. Proof is double the alcohol percentage. The proof of a bottle of alcohol is printed on its label.

15. **The correct answer is C.** According to the disease model of dependency, people abuse drugs and alcohol because of biological conditions. The moral model asserts that people make the choice to abuse drugs and alcohol. Choices A and B suggest that people develop chemical dependencies because their personality traits are predisposed to doing so.

16. **The correct answer is D.** Psychedelics are hallucinogens. Choice A refers to an opioid, choice B refers to a cannabinoid, and choice C is is a separate category of drugs called depressants.

17. **The correct answer is B.** Inhalants can be ingested by placing a bag over the head with the substance released in the bag so the individual can breathe it in. Choices A, C, and D are incorrect.

18. **The correct answer is A.** MDMA, GHB, and Rohypnol are all examples of club drugs. Both GHB and Rohypnol have been used as date-rape drugs to incapacitate victims of sexual assaults. MDMA, which is known as Ecstasy, is used at raves and nightclubs to increase sensory experiences. Choices B, C, and D are incorrect.

19. **The correct answer is B.** Schedule II drugs (such as hydrocodone) have a high risk for abuse and dependence and require a written prescription in order to be filled at a pharmacy. Schedule I drugs (choice A) are illicit drugs (such as heroin) and are not prescribed. Schedule IV drugs (choice C) have a low risk of dependence and can be refilled by a phone request. Schedule V drugs (choice D) are over-the-counter medications and do not require a prescription.

20. **The correct answer is B.** Prozac is the most commonly prescribed antidepressant. Prozac, Paxil, and Zoloft are selective reuptake inhibitors. SSRIs are antidepressants considered safer than MAOIs and tricyclics because they have fewer adverse side effects. Choices A, C, and D are incorrect.

DIAGNOSTIC TEST ASSESSMENT GRID

Now that you've completed the diagnostic test and read through the answer explanations, you can use your results to target your studying. Find the question numbers from the diagnostic test that you answered incorrectly and highlight or circle them below. Then focus extra attention on the sections within the chapter dealing with those topics.

Substance Abuse		
Content Area	**Topic**	**Question #**
Overview of Substance Abuse and Dependence Abuse	• Terminology • Theories and models of abuse and dependence • Demographics • Costs to society and associations with social problems • Screening and diagnosis	2, 15
Classification of Drugs	• DEA schedule • Pharmacologic effect • Regulations	19
Pharmacological and Neuropsychological Principles	• Nervous system • Actions of drugs • Drug interactions	6, 9
Alcohol	• History and types • Determinants of blood alcohol level • Effects • Uses and administration • Tolerance, withdrawal, and overdose • Dependency issues • Prevention and treatment	3, 4, 14
Antianxiety and Sedative-Hypnotics	• History and types • Effects • Uses and administration • Tolerance, withdrawal, and overdose • Dependency issues • Prevention and treatment	8

Substance Abuse		
Content Area	**Topic**	**Question #**
Inhalants	• History and types • Effects • Tolerance, withdrawal, and overdose • Dependency issues • Prevention and treatment	17
Tobacco and Nicotine	• History and types • Effects • Uses and administration • Tolerance, withdrawal, and overdose • Dependency issues • Prevention and treatment	1
Psychomotor	• History and types • Effects • Uses and administration • Tolerance, withdrawal, and overdose • Dependency issues • Prevention and treatment	12
Opioids	• History and types • Effects • Uses and administration • Tolerance, withdrawal, and overdose • Dependency issues • Prevention and treatment	7
Cannabinoids	• History and types • Effects • Uses and administration • Tolerance, withdrawal, and overdose • Dependency issues • Prevention and treatment	10, 13

Substance Abuse		
Content Area	**Topic**	**Question #**
Hallucinogens	• History and types • Effects • Uses and administration • Tolerance, withdrawal, and overdose	16
Other Drugs of Abuse	• Anabolic steroids • Over-the-counter (OTC) substances • Synthetic substances • Club drugs	2, 18
Antipsychotic Drugs	• History and types • Effects • Uses and administration	11
Antidepressants and Mood Stabilizers	• History and types • Effects • Uses and administration • Tolerance, withdrawal, and suicidal behaviors	20

GET THE FACTS

To see the DSST® Substance Abuse Fact Sheet, go to **http://getcollegecredit.com/exam_fact_sheets** and click on the **Social Sciences** tab. Scroll down and click the **Substance Abuse** link. Here you will find suggestions for further study material and the ACE college credit recommendations for passing the test.

OVERVIEW OF SUBSTANCE ABUSE AND DEPENDENCE

For thousands of years, alcohol and drugs have been used in society for medicinal and recreational purposes. Evidence suggests that substance abuse plagued societies of the past just as it does modern societies. Before addressing the different types of drugs and their unique effects, it is important to understand the terms and theories associated with substance abuse.

TERMINOLOGY

Drugs are natural or artificial substances that improve, obstruct, or alter mind and body functions. The term **illicit drug** refers to substances that are illegal to possess, such as heroin and cocaine. In contrast, **licit drugs** are legal and include caffeine, alcohol, and nicotine. Licit drugs also include over-the-counter (OTC) drugs, which are available for purchase without a prescription, such as aspirin, cold remedies, and antihistamines. Alcohol and nicotine are considered **gateway drugs** because most people who abuse illicit drugs first try liquor and/or cigarettes.

Illicit substance use often begins with experimental or recreational use that becomes routine and expected in some way. While the user might not yet feel physical and psychological pulls, there is a strong desire for continual use. This use does not yet cause problems, but it signals the start of a problem as the user begins a regular habit of use, or **habituation**.

Psychoactive drugs mainly affect the central nervous system, and they result in changes to consciousness, thought processes, and mood. Many psychoactive drugs are prescribed for physical and mental problems, but it is when such drugs are misused or abused that problems can occur. **Drug misuse** refers to using prescribed drugs in ways other than recommended by a physician, such as taking too many pills at one time. **Drug abuse** occurs when a substance, either prescribed or illicit, is used in a manner that causes social, occupational, psychological, or physical problems.

Although the terms **dependence** and **addiction** often describe the same condition, medical professionals typically prefer the term **dependency**. The common use of **addiction** to describe people's overindulgence in everything from gambling to chocolate makes *dependence* a better and more specific term in discussing drug use. **Drug dependency** occurs when an individual uses a drug so regularly that going without it is physically and psychologically difficult and results in withdrawal symptoms. Withdrawal symptoms frequently include nausea, anxiety, muscle spasms, and sweating, but they vary with different substances.

The criteria used to determine levels of abuse and dependency include frequency of use—how often does the individual use the substance? As use becomes more frequent, criteria move from habituation to abuse to dependence. Is the drug obtained through illegal means? Alcohol is legal for individuals who are 21 and over, but cocaine is illegal. Reasons for use also factor in, as some individuals might use alcohol to relax after a long day, while others need it to stop tremors in their hands. Finally, the effects of the use are a factor. Some people exhibit symptoms of tolerance and withdrawal, which indicate a higher level of abuse and dependence.

THEORIES AND MODELS OF ABUSE AND DEPENDENCE

Experts have analyzed and described drug addiction over the years and have developed three theories of dependency: **biological**, **psychological**, and **sociological**. The **biological theory** proposes that substance abuse stems from physical characteristics related to genetics, brain dysfunction, and biomedical patterns. People with such traits experiment with drugs and then crave them. The **psychological theory** proposes that the mental and emotional status of an individual leads to substance abuse. The **sociological theory** proposes that social and environmental factors influence substance abuse. Several additional theories stem from the sociological theory:

- **Social learning theory** emphasizes that individuals learn drug use behaviors from society, family, and peers.
- **Social influence theories** claim that a person's daily social relationships are the cause of substance abuse.
- **Structural influence theories** assert that substance abuse occurs because of the organization of an individual's society, peer groups, and subculture.

Models of abuse and dependence include the **moral model**, which states that a person chooses to abuse drugs and alcohol. The **disease model** indicates that a person abuses drugs and alcohol because of a biological condition. The **characterological or personality predisposition model** proposes that a person is inclined to develop a chemical dependency because of certain personality traits. Although the moral model is generally considered outdated by the scientific community, many people maintain that lifestyle choices and immorality lead to drug dependency. Supporters of the disease model assert that dependency is a chronic disease that progresses with time and requires treatment and therapy. Recovery groups like Alcoholics Anonymous and Narcotics Anonymous adhere to the disease model. The fact that a number of people with chemical dependencies are also diagnosed with personality disorders supports the personality predisposition model. Consensus does not exist with regard to any of the dependency models or to the three theoretical explanations of drug dependency.

DEMOGRAPHICS

Although drug abuse occurs in all areas of society, researchers have detected certain trends. Among American college students, approximately 70 percent drink alcohol and about 25 percent smoke cigarettes. A smaller number uses illicit drugs: 20 percent admit to smoking marijuana and 2 percent use cocaine. Based on race and ethnicity, Asians have the lowest percentage of illicit drug use, while Native Americans have the highest percentage. Substance abuse is also more common among men.

Researchers have also discovered that teens who use illicit drugs are more likely to know drug-abusing adults. The same adolescents typically associate with peers who use drugs, have academic difficulties, and believe their parents are not sources of support or encouragement. In general, experts believe that society, community, and family influence an individual's first use of drugs or alcohol. However, long-term usage is determined by an individual's experience with the drug. Once a person becomes truly dependent, social factors like laws, costs, and availability have very little bearing.

COSTS TO SOCIETY AND ASSOCIATIONS WITH SOCIAL PROBLEMS

Substance abuse is a costly habit to maintain. According to the National Institute on Drug Abuse, a drug abuser needs $100 every day to support a narcotics habit. Unfortunately, criminal activity is the primary source of funds for many drug abusers. Burglary and shoplifting are the crimes primarily associated with drug abusers in need of money, and many heroin abusers become involved in prostitution. Researchers have identified at least three correlations between drugs and crime:

- Drug users commit more crimes than individuals who don't use drugs.
- Violence is frequently associated with the use of narcotics, such as cocaine.
- Crimes are often committed while under the influence of drugs.

In addition to criminal activity, substance abuse affects the healthcare system. Diseases associated with intravenous drug use, such as hepatitis B and HIV, require expensive treatment. Automobile accidents, drug overdoses, and babies born with fetal alcohol syndrome require costly medical intervention as well. Substance abuse also affects productivity in the work place. Unlike people who abuse drugs such as heroin and LSD, most alcoholics are able to hold jobs. However, alcoholics have a tendency to be late for work, have on-the-job accidents, and miss work. Many employers require employees to take drug screening tests and are making drug and alcohol assistance programs more available to employees with dependency issues.

SCREENING AND DIAGNOSIS

Substance abuse problems are often identified when an individual begins to get into trouble with family, at work, with the law, or with their finances. As trouble develops and use continues, it is often a sign that an individual has developed a diagnosable **substance abuse disorder**. Diagnosis and screening for this type of disorder is normally conducted in a clinical setting by someone who has formal training in substance abuse evaluation and treatment, often a substance abuse counselor. The evaluation itself often takes two to three hours as the counselor asks many questions designed to gain a complete picture of an individual's life. The **biopsychosocial approach** looks at biological factors, such as medical conditions; psychological factors, such as the presence of other mental health issues; and social factors, such as the environment and support system the individual has.

CLASSIFICATION OF DRUGS

Drug classification varies by the purpose of the drug. For example, a physician may categorize an amphetamine as a weight-control tool because of the drug's ability to suppress food consumption. However, law enforcement may refer to that same drug as a Schedule II controlled substance. The following table shows the major drug categories and provides examples of the types of drugs in each category.

Category	Examples
Stimulants	Cocaine, Amphetamines, Ritalin, Caffeine
Depressants	Alcohol, Barbiturates, Sleeping Pills, Inhalants
Hallucinogens	LSD, Mescaline, Ecstasy, PCP
Opioids	Opium, Morphine, Codeine, Heroin, Methadone
Cannabis	Marijuana, THC, Hashish
Nicotine	Cigarettes, chewing tobacco, cigars
Psychotherapeutics	Prozac, Haldol

DEA SCHEDULE

The U.S. Drug Enforcement Administration (DEA) has created a classification system placing drugs, substances, and the chemicals used to make drugs into five categories. Drugs are placed into these different categories based on the chemicals used to make the drugs, the drugs' acceptable medical use, and the drugs' potential for abuse and dependency. The drugs are divided into schedules based on the abuse and danger risks ranging from the most serious in Schedule I to drugs with lower potential for abuse in Schedule V.

Schedule	Characteristics	Risk	Examples
Schedule I	Drugs with no currently accepted medical use with a very high potential for severe psychological and physical dependence	Severe risk of abuse and dependence	Heroin, lysergic acid dithylamide (LSD), marijuana, 3,4-methyleneioxymethamphetamine (ecstasy), methaqualone, peyote
Schedule II	Dangerous drugs with high potential for severe psychological and physical dependence	High risk of abuse and dependence	Hydrocodone, cocaine, methamphetamine, methadone, oxycodone, fentanyl, Adderall, and Ritalin

Schedule	Characteristics	Risk	Examples
Schedule III	Drugs with moderate-to-low potential for psychological and physical dependence	Moderate-to-low risk of abuse and dependence, but less than Schedule I and II drugs	Ketamine, anabolic steroids, testosterone, Tylenol with codeine
Schedule IV	Drugs with low potential for psychological and physical abuse and dependence	Low risk of dependence	Xanax, Soma, Darvon, Darvocet, Valium, Ambien, Tramadol
Schedule V	Drugs with the lowest potential for psychological and physical abuse and dependence	Lowest risk of dependence of the Schedule drugs	Robitussin AC, Lomotil, Motofen, Lyrica, Parepectolin

PHARMACOLOGIC EFFECT

When drugs are ingested, they act to create a change in the function of certain cells within the body which, in turn, leads to changes in body function and behavior. This occurs as the drug interacts with the parts of the cell receptor. Some drugs exert stronger influences on the receptors than others, and more than one drug could affect the same receptor. For example, amphetamine and methamphetamine are both stimulants that would affect the same receptors, but methamphetamine would have a stronger effect on these receptors.

The concentration of the drug at the site of the action also plays a part in the effects of the drug on the central nervous system: the greater the concentration, the stronger the reaction. This is often described with a **dose-response curve**. The dose-response curve indicates the quantity, or dosage, of a drug that will cause a given response. The response could be all-or-none, such as death, or continuous, such as changes in blood pressure, respiration rate, etc., that increase with increases in the drug.

Some target cells are more sensitive to the effects of the drugs based on genetic factors and changes made to the cells by previous use of the drug. Continued use of the drug on the target cells often results in a loss of sensitivity, called **tolerance**. Tolerance occurs as an individual's body adapts to the presence of a given drug. As the body adapts, an individual must take more of the drug to create the same desired effects.

The adjustment to the presence of the drugs over time can also lead to dependence. **Physical dependence** occurs as the body adapts so completely to the presence of the drug that removal of the drug from the system causes physical symptoms ranging from headache and nausea to insomnia and even heart failure. The body creates a new "normal" that includes the drug. When the drug is removed, the body physically tries to compensate. Often the drug user will take the drug again in order to alleviate the painful symptoms, thus reinforcing the abuse of the drug.

Adjustment to the presence of the drug also leads to **psychological dependence** on the drug. Individuals who become dependent on the drug spend a lot of time fixating on the drug's effects and feel continuous cravings for the drug. This leads to impulsivity and compulsive use of the drug based on a perceived emotional and psychological need for it.

When taken in moderate doses, **stimulants**, such as caffeine, provide energy to users. However, powerful stimulants, such as cocaine, often trigger manic excitement and paranoia, which is why stimulants are referred to as "uppers." **Depressants**, known as "downers," have the opposite effect of stimulants on the body. Low to medium doses lead to relaxation, a loss of inhibition, slow reaction times, and uncoordinated movements. The regular use of depressants may cause hallucinations and restlessness.

As implied by the name, **hallucinogens** cause users to have hallucinations and experience a distorted reality. Often referred to as psychedelics, hallucinogens alter a user's perceptions, such as taste, smell, hearing, and vision. Higher amounts of hallucinogens are needed to achieve the same effects because tolerance for such drugs builds up quickly. **Opioids** are categorized as analgesics, painkillers, or narcotics. Low doses lead to a relaxed state, while higher doses may induce sleep. Unlike depressants that cause reckless behavior and slurred speech, opioids lead to users being in a stupor. Individuals who regularly take heroin, codeine, or morphine may become withdrawn. The most commonly used illegal drug in the United States is marijuana, which is also known as **cannabis**, as it is made from the crushed parts of the *Cannabis sativa* plant. The main psychoactive ingredient in marijuana is delta 9-tetrahydrocannabinol (THC), which generates the "high" experienced by users. **Nicotine**, which is considered a gateway drug, is extremely addictive and found in cigarettes, chewing tobacco, and cigars. Although nicotine is legal, it causes respiratory problems and cancer among some long-term users. Medical conditions associated with secondhand smoke have inspired the creation of "smoke-free" policies for buildings, businesses, and restaurants.

Psychiatrists and physicians often prescribe **psychotherapeutic drugs** to control mental problems in patients. Antipsychotics, such as haloperidol, are a type of psychotherapeutic drug that have a calming effect on patients and help control hallucinations. Antipsychotics are often prescribed to patients diagnosed with schizophrenia, mania, and delusional disorder. Antidepressants, such as Prozac, are psychotherapeutic drugs prescribed to patients with severe depression.

REGULATIONS

Laws and regulations differ based on the pharmacological effects of the different drugs based on their status in the DEA schedule:

DEA Schedule	Regulation of Availability
Schedule I	Illegal for consumer distribution; for research use only in a controlled setting
Schedule II	Requires written prescription—no refills and no phone-in prescription; often requires drug testing in physician's office before a new prescription can be written
Schedule III	Requires prescription—written or oral; refills are legal without drug testing
Schedule IV	Requires prescription—written or oral; refills are legal without drug testing
Schedule V	Over the counter availability with proof of age

PHARMACOLOGICAL AND NEUROPHYSIOLOGICAL PRINCIPLES

NERVOUS SYSTEM

The human body is constantly attempting to maintain internal stability, or **homeostasis.** Homeostatic mechanisms regulate body temperature, blood pressure, and glucose concentrations, as well as many other physiological functions. The human body works to maintain its internal stability to keep its organs and systems functioning properly, which is key to its survival. For example, a consistent body temperature of 98.6°F is optimal because a temperature that is too high or too low causes problems in certain parts of the body.

One area where body regulation is influenced is in the nervous system. The nervous system sends messages to and from the brain, and these messages are influenced by outside agents that act on the components of the nervous system. The nervous system is composed of **neurons**, which are specialized nerve cells that transfer messages throughout the body. The human brain contains billions of neurons, which are all close to each other but never touch. All neurons consist of four regions:

1. *Cell body*: contains the nucleus
2. *Dendrites*: treelike branches that receive transmitter signals

3. *Axon*: long extension of the cell body that conducts electrical signal

4. *Presynaptic terminals*: store chemical messengers, which are known as **neurotransmitters**

Neurons communicate with each other by releasing neurotransmitters. A **synapse** is the point of communication between a neuron sending a message and a neuron receiving a message. The small gap between one neuron and another is known as the **synaptic cleft.** Neurotransmitters travel across the synaptic cleft and bind to special proteins known as **receptors** on the outer membranes of target cells. The activation of receptors leads to a change in cell activity and is accomplished by both natural substances and drugs.

The nervous system is divided into the **somatic nervous system**, the **autonomic nervous system**, and the **central nervous system.** Neurons in the somatic nervous system are associated with voluntary actions, such as seeing, hearing, smelling, chewing, and moving one's arms and legs. The autonomic nervous system monitors involuntary actions, such as heart rate and blood pressure. The central nervous system consists of the brain and spinal cord and is responsible for learning, memory, and activity coordination.

The drugs in the major drug categories are designed to affect the central nervous system in order to produce a response that could ease negative physical effects of a health issue or treat a specific medical condition. As these drugs act to alleviate the pain or discomfort, they might also produce calming or euphoric effects that an individual may seek to continue to experience. In addition, some drugs are created to mimic or influence how the central nervous system responds, again creating euphoria and freedom from pain.

ACTIONS OF DRUGS

Drugs have varying effects on the human body, including excitement, relaxation, and addiction. Analyzing how the nervous system works will lead to a better understanding of the variation in drug effects. As mentioned previously, neurotransmitters are chemical messengers released by neurons that have brief effects. Some drugs alter how neurotransmitters function. Certain neurotransmitters are associated with the introduction of psychoactive drugs into the nervous system, especially dopamine, acetylcholine, norepinephrine, serotonin, GABA, glutamate, and the endorphins. Many drugs that are abused, such as amphetamines and cocaine, alter dopamine neurons and cause paranoia, agitation, and euphoria. Serotonin is responsible for controlling mood, appetite, and aggressiveness, and substances such as LSD have been found to affect serotonin levels.

Different routes of administration have different effects. Drugs applied topically, such as ointment on the skin, tend to remain in the applied area. Transdermal application can be achieved by placing a patch on the skin with drugs that will release slowly from the patch over a period of time. Oral administration involves placing the drug in the mouth and swallowing, which allows the stomach or small intestine to absorb it into the bloodstream. Drugs can also be administered sublingually by placing them under the tongue and allowing them to disintegrate in the mouth. Nasal administration involves spraying the drug in the nasal cavities. Inhalation involves inhaling drugs that are in gas, liquid, or powder form. Drugs can also be injected with a needle and syringe. The injection can be subcutaneous, which injects the drug in liquid form into the subcutaneous tissue that lies just beneath

TIP

Light drinking may reduce the likelihood of heart disease, perhaps because it reduces stress and increases high-density lipoproteins that carry fat through the bloodstream.

the dermis of the skin. Intramuscular injection occurs in the muscular areas of the body. Intravenous injection administers the drug directly into a vein.

Drugs are metabolized, or processed, from an active form to a less active, potentially inactive form. The principle organ of metabolism is the liver. Drugs administered orally are absorbed into the bloodstream via the stomach or intestines where they are immediately available for metabolizing by the liver before they create an effect on the target cells. Intravenous administration is often one of the most dangerous forms of administration because the drug avoids the absorption phase and potential partial inactivation by the liver.

DRUG INTERACTIONS

Physicians prescribe medication to patients in order to treat an illness or relieve pain associated with a condition. In some cases, medication causes side effects, which are the unintended effects of a drug. Common side effects, such as nausea, vomiting, nervousness, breathing difficulties, dependence, and changes in cardiovascular activity, illustrate the fact that risks are associated with the consumption of any drug—over-the-counter, prescribed, and illicit. For example, morphine relieves pain, but it depresses breathing and causes constipation. Cocaine works well as a local anesthetic, but the drug's addictiveness outweighs its value in that capacity.

Both intended and unintended effects of a substance correspond to the amount consumed. **Potency** refers to the quantity of a drug that is required to produce an effect. In other words, a highly potent drug, such as LSD, requires a small dose to achieve a specific effect. **Toxicity** is a drug's capacity to harm the body, which may occur when any substance is taken in high doses. The consumption of extremely potent drugs, such as heroin, can cause serious damage to the body and possibly death. The presence of one drug can affect how another drug works in the body, a process known as drug interaction. Drug interactions are categorized into three types.

1. *Additive interaction*: Two drugs taken together equal the sum of the effects of each drug taken separately; occurs when both drugs are similar in structure (e.g., aspirin and acetaminophen).

2. *Antagonistic interaction*: One drug blocks the effect of another drug—also known as **inhibitory interaction**; this type of interaction is the basis for poison antidotes.

3. *Synergistic interaction*: The sum of the effects of two drugs taken together is greater than the effects of each drug taken separately (e.g., alcohol and acetaminophen).

Related to synergistic interactions are **potentiating effects**, in which one drug enhances the effect of another drug so that the combined effect is greater than the sum of the effects of each drug taken separately.

One of the most dangerous drug interactions involves any combination of depressants, alcohol, or narcotics. Since all three substances act in slowing down the breathing rate, a combination of any of them may result in one of the most common types of drug overdoses: respiratory depression. People who experience respiratory depression stop breathing and usually die without intervention. An example of an antagonistic interaction often initiated by drug abusers is the combination of alcohol and cocaine. The cocaine chemically combines with the ethyl alcohol in the body to create an extremely potent and toxic stimulant known as **cocaethylene**. Cocaethylene is suspected of causing a greater sense of euphoria than cocaine alone because it increases dopamine transmission.

ALCOHOL

As illustrated in the previous section, alcohol is dangerous when combined with other substances. However, consuming alcohol by itself also leads to problematic behavior, such as drunk driving, risky sexual behavior, and blackouts.

HISTORY AND TYPES

Alcoholic beverages have been an aspect of society since ancient civilizations discovered fermentation, the chemical reaction that occurs when yeast converts sugar into alcohol. Mead, an alcoholic drink made from honey, was invented around 7000 BCE. Beer and berry wine were developed around 6400 BCE and grape wine in 300 BCE.

Distilled alcoholic beverages, such as brandy and whiskey, have alcohol concentrations greater than 15 percent. Distillation involves heating the mixture containing alcohol, collecting the vapors, and condensing the solution into a liquid once again. The process most likely originated in Asia around 800 CE. Today, proof indicates the alcohol content of a distilled beverage. Proof is twice the alcohol percentage, which means that a bottle of 100-proof vodka is 50 percent alcohol.

During the late eighteenth century, American citizens preferred alcoholic beverages to water partially because of water contamination issues. Much of society did not view alcohol negatively until after the Revolutionary War, when distilled spirits were associated with immoral and criminal activities. The heaviest period of alcohol consumption in the United States occurred between 1800 and 1808. The idea that people should avoid hard liquor, such as whiskey and vodka, and should only drink beer or wine in moderation was the basis of the **temperance movement** of the 1800s. The temperance movement eventually advocated complete abstinence from all alcoholic beverages. The Eighteenth Amendment to the U.S. Constitution, enacted in 1920, prohibited the production, sale, and transportation of alcohol. However, Prohibition only pushed alcohol consumption underground. People could purchase alcoholic drinks at illegal bars known as speakeasies, and bootleggers made and sold moonshine throughout the country. Prohibition was repealed in 1933 for a number of reasons: lost tax revenue, enforcement difficulties, black market liquor sales, police corruption, and political pressure.

DETERMINANTS OF BLOOD ALCOHOL LEVEL

The rate of alcohol absorption plays a significant role in **blood alcohol content** (**BAC**) level. Alcohol consumed on a full stomach is absorbed into the bloodstream slower than alcohol consumed on an empty stomach. Drinking water also slows the rate of alcohol absorption, while carbonated beverages increase it. Estimates of BAC levels are based on an individual's gender, weight, and alcohol consumption. Since alcohol does not dissolve into fatty tissues, a lean 200-pound man will have a lower BAC than a fat 200-pound man, all other variables being equal. Body weight is a significant factor as well. A 200-pound woman who drinks one beer will have a BAC of 0.022 percent, while a 100-pound woman who drinks the same amount will have a BAC of 0.045 percent. Blood alcohol content level is used as a measurement of intoxication and impairment for the legal and medical systems. A BAC level greater than 0.08 percent is illegal in every state in the United States. A BAC level of 0.4 percent to 0.6 percent is lethal because respiration is severely depressed. The following table shows the correlation between BAC and behavior.

BAC	Common Behavior
0.05%	Reduced inhibition, decreased alertness, impaired judgment, relaxed mood
0.10%	Decreased reaction time, impaired motor skills
0.20%	Significant reduction in sensory and motor skills
0.25%	Staggering, severe motor skill disturbance
0.30%	Conscious but in a stupor
0.40%	Unconsciousness

Alcohol stays in the bloodstream until it has metabolized, or been broken down by enzymes. More than 90 percent of alcohol metabolism takes place in the liver, which is why chronic drinkers often experience liver disorders, such as alcoholic hepatitis and cirrhosis. The liver metabolizes alcohol at a constant rate, no matter how much alcohol is consumed or the size of the person drinking. In general, the number of drinks consumed is the number of hours it takes a person to metabolize the alcohol.

EFFECTS

Previous drinking experiences, mood, attitude, expectations, and circumstances are factors in an individual's behavior while drinking. However, when a person consumes alcohol, the effect of the alcohol depends mainly upon the amount of alcohol that is concentrated in the blood system. A person's blood alcohol content level determines how he or she behaves in response to alcohol consumption.

In addition to liver diseases, heavy alcohol use is linked to the damage of almost every organ and bodily function. Alcohol affects the digestive system by irritating tissue and damaging the stomach lining. Neurological damage is apparent because many heavy drinkers suffer from irreversible impairment to memory and judgment.

USES AND ADMINISTRATION

Alcohol is a chemical group of compounds that includes ethanol, methanol, propanol, and pentanol. While ethanol is used to create alcoholic drinks used for recreation and relaxation, ethanol is also used as a form of fossil fuel and can be diluted and distilled into perfumes. It is also used as a cleaning agent for general household cleaning and is also used topically in first aid as a wound cleaner. Alcohol is ingested orally in liquid form for recreational purposes. It is absorbed into the bloodstream quickly, based on the amount of food present in the stomach and the strength of the alcoholic drink.

TOLERANCE, WITHDRAWAL, AND OVERDOSE

The socially acceptable nature of drinking lends itself to both psychological and physical dependency. The relaxation and positive feelings that occur with drinking make it routine for many people. The regular use of alcohol often leads to increased tolerance levels and decreased pharmacological effects, which may increase consumption and cause physical dependence. Alcoholics are individuals who are unable to function normally without consuming alcohol. Physical dependence becomes evident when alcohol consumption stops and withdrawal symptoms occur. Withdrawal effects from alcohol and barbiturates are more severe than effects associated with other substances. Withdrawal occurs in a progression of four stages.

> **Stage 1:** tremors, restlessness, insomnia, rapid heartbeat, and heavy sweating
>
> **Stage 2:** stage 1 symptoms plus hallucinations and vomiting
>
> **Stage 3:** delusions, disorientation, and fever
>
> **Stage 4:** seizures that are life-threatening in some cases

DEPENDENCY ISSUES

Dependency becomes a factor when an individual shows issues with use, continues to use, and becomes physically dependent on alcohol. If an individual ingests consistently larger quantities of alcohol for a period of time, the body will likely become dependent upon the substance. In the case of alcohol, body chemistry changes and withdrawal from a dependent state can become a serious medical concern. Individuals who decide to stop drinking after they have become dependent on alcohol are often weaned off of the substance under medical supervision.

PREVENTION AND TREATMENT

Once an individual has been diagnosed with an alcohol issue, the treatment process begins. First, there is an initial evaluation interview, after which a diagnosis is determined. Once the counselor has a diagnosis, the client and the counselor develop a treatment plan, which outlines the issues they will work on for a treatment period, usually 90 days. For chronic users who cannot stop without medical intervention, there are medications that, when taken, can create a very negative reaction when alcohol is ingested. These medications create a negative physical and psychological association with alcohol. In general, treatment seeks to establish the reasons for the use, help the client stop using, and set up methods to maintain sobriety. These methods include attending twelve-step programs that provide peer support and attending individual and group counseling sessions.

Recovering alcoholics often face a more difficult journey than those who are dependent on other drugs, such as cocaine or heroin, because society generally finds drinking acceptable. Alcoholics Anonymous encourages addicts to stay connected with other alcoholics by attending chapter meetings and avoiding the social isolation that can trigger a relapse. Some alcoholics seek help from residential treatment centers for one or two months in order to avoid relapses.

ANTIANXIETY AND SEDATIVE-HYPNOTICS

Sedative-hypnotics, also known as **central nervous system** (**CNS**) depressants, are frequently abused substances because of their ability to reduce CNS activity, decrease the brain's level of awareness, and relieve anxiety. Within the category of CNS depressants, sedatives relieve anxiety and fear, while hypnotics induce drowsiness and sleep.

HISTORY AND TYPES

Prior to the development of CNS depressants, alcohol was commonly used to treat anxiety and nervousness. In the 1800s, bromides were introduced as a way to induce sleep, but they were later found to be highly toxic. In the early part of the twentieth century, barbiturates such as phenobarbital replaced bromides as an antianxiety medication. However, scientists and physicians noticed a number of problems associated with barbiturates—tolerance, dependence, and respiratory depression. While many people safely took barbiturate sleeping pills, the medical community sought a better drug for the treatment of anxiety and sleep disorders.

During the 1950s, benzodiazepines were marketed as CNS depressants that offered a safe alternative to barbiturates. Benzodiazepines remain the most popular and safest CNS depressants prescribed by doctors today and include brand-name pharmaceuticals such as Valium, Ambien, and Xanax. Benzodiazepines are prescribed for the treatment of anxiety, neurosis, muscle tension, lower back pain, and insomnia. Like barbiturates, benzodiazepines increase the actions of the neurotransmitter GABA. GABA is the primary inhibitory neurotransmitter in the central nervous system and acts as the body's tranquilizer by inducing sleep and promoting calmness.

EFFECTS

Small amounts of these drugs can relax muscles and calm the nervous system, easing symptoms of chronic anxiety or insomnia. Larger doses can reduce alertness, impair reflexes, cause irritability, and slur speech. Problems associated with barbiturates and benzodiazepines occur when they interact with other depressants, such as alcohol. Combining benzodiazepines with illicit drugs, such as heroin and cocaine, is common among substance abusers. Both barbiturates and benzodiazepines can cause physical and psychological dependence. Mothers who take these drugs during pregnancy can create dependency in their unborn children. Barbiturate overdoses can lead to suicide and accidental drug poisoning. Reduction of benzodiazepine use should occur over a period of time in order to minimize withdrawal symptoms and avoid complications.

USES AND ADMINISTRATION

Antianxiety drugs and sedative-hypnotics are most often abused as prescription drugs. An individual either convinces the doctor of a need for the drugs and sells them to others or uses and abuses their own prescription. In most cases, these drugs are in pill form and are available as prescription phar-maceuticals, which means there is a higher level of regulation related to their distribution. Many of the drugs in this category are distributed legally as prescription drugs. Unfortunately, there is a common, and erroneous, belief that prescription drugs are safer than illicit drugs. Antianxiety drugs operate on the neurotransmitter GABA, which regulates a sedative effect.

TOLERANCE, WITHDRAWAL, AND OVERDOSE

Use of barbiturates and benzodiazepines over an extended period of time can result in tolerance, which means that individuals who take them need to take increasingly more of the substance in order to experience the same effects. When the individual attempts to stop the use after a period of time, he or she would likely experience physical symptoms of withdrawal, including restlessness, insomnia, and potentially convulsions and death. Some individuals experience hallucinations, seizures, disturbed heart rhythm, and vomiting. Behaviorally, individuals might take less time with personal hygiene, experience psychomotor agitation and exhibit irritability and inability to focus. Individuals are often disoriented and have trouble determining person, place, and time when asked. There is reduced memory function and disorganization. Withdrawal effects can last as long as three weeks after the drug is no longer ingested. Individuals might experience increased sleeplessness and anxiety. Overdoses of these substances are often lethal, as nearly one-third of all reported drug-related deaths involve barbiturates and benzodiazepines.

DEPENDENCY ISSUES

Drugs in this class can create a pattern of behaviors that result in psychological and physical dependence. In the case of benzodiazepines, individuals find it hard to sleep without the drugs, and they become dependent upon them. Since quick cessation of benzodiazepine use can result in severe physical withdrawal symptoms, it is important to wean from them under the supervision of a physician, while also attending mental-health counseling.

PREVENTION AND TREATMENT

In many cases, use of this category of drugs is related to stress and/or anxiety management. Many individuals start use as a prescription treatment for symptoms of anxiety and develop a psychological and physical dependence on the drugs. Treatment must address all aspects of the drug use and will include counseling and other behavior therapies. In this case, it is important to treat the issues that brought about the need to use and abuse antianxiety medications in the first place.

INHALANTS

Many everyday products normally found in a home have volatile ingredients that can cause psychoactive reactions when inhaled. While they are abused mainly by younger populations of children and adolescents, they are also abused by adults.

HISTORY AND TYPES

Gasoline, paint, glue, air freshener, and nail polish are volatile substances that elicit euphoric feelings when inhaled. Although inhalant abuse may seem to be a modern trend, it actually dates back to the eighteenth century, when people inhaled nitrous oxide to attain a state of drunkenness. Inhaling nitrous oxide, or laughing gas, for recreational purposes continued for many years, and the inhalant is still used for some medical procedures such as dental work. During the 1950s, the public was made aware of teenagers becoming "high" by sniffing glue. Currently, teenagers and adolescents misuse over a thousand different products as inhalants.

There are three categories of inhalants: **gaseous anesthetics**, **nitrites**, and **volatile solvents**.

Inhalants	
Category	**Examples**
Gaseous anesthetics	Nitrous oxide ("laughing gas"), ether, chloroform
Nitrites	Amyl nitrite ("poppers")
Volatile substances	Aerosols, toluene, butane, propane, gasoline, Freon

As previously mentioned, nitrous oxide is safe to use as a light anesthetic for outpatient procedures performed by dentists and physicians. Its availability in the medical community has led to its abuse by medical professionals who have access to it. The colorless gas is found in large balloons and in cartridges called whippets that are included in containers of whipping cream. Both are sources for inhalant abusers.

Nitrites are chemicals that cause a rapid dilation of the arteries combined with a reduction in blood pressure to the brain. The result of this vasodilation is a short feeling of faintness and sometimes unconsciousness. Nitrites were sold in small vials over the counter in the 1960s and were "popped" between the fingers and held under the nose for inhalation. Nitrites have not been available to consumers since the early 1990s.

The most prevalent category of inhalants is volatile substances. The easy availability and low cost associated with volatile substances makes them especially appealing to children and teenagers. Some states have passed laws to limit the sale of volatile solvents to young people, but, with so many kinds on the market, the effect has been minimal.

Types of Volatile Substances	
Substance Type	**Sources and Hazards**
Aerosols	High concentration of chemicals from spray paint and other spray cans
Toluene	Chemical found in glues, paints, and nail polish; quickly absorbed by the lungs, brain, heart, and liver
Butane and propane	Highly flammable, especially when combined with smoking; found in lighter fluid
Gasoline	Widely available and highly flammable
Freon	Found in refrigerators, airbrushes, and air conditioners; danger of freeze injuries

Methods of inhalation vary. *Sniffing* or *snorting* refers to inhaling vapors straight from the product's original container. *Huffing* refers to soaking rags in a solvent and holding the rag over one's mouth. If highly concentrated substances are inhaled directly, it can lead to heart failure and death. *Bagging* is the term used to describe inhaling solvents that have been placed in paper or plastic bags. The high from inhaling lasts only a few minutes, which often means the individual inhales repeatedly over the course of a short period of time.

EFFECTS

The initial effects of inhaling volatile chemicals are nausea, coughing, and sneezing. Low doses generate feelings of lightheadedness, disorientation, mild stimulation, and dizziness. High doses act like CNS depressants by producing relaxation, sleep, slurred speech, and possibly coma. Hypoxia (oxygen deficiency), brain damage, suffocation, and death may occur in some cases. In addition to the short-term health effects of inhalant abuse, users may experience permanent damage. Although teenagers who abuse inhalants typically move on to other drugs or alcohol, the damage of inhalant abuse is permanent. The inhalation of high concentrations of household products that contain multiple chemicals damages vital organs that absorb the inhaled substances. In addition, young abusers of inhalants are still growing and developing, and the toxic nature of inhalants may interfere with their mental development.

TOLERANCE, WITHDRAWAL, AND OVERDOSE

Addiction to inhalants is not common but can arise with repeated use. Since the high is of such short duration, individuals often inhale numerous times over a short period. This can lead to overdose. Repeated use over longer periods of time can lead to symptoms of tolerance. Mild withdrawal can occur with long-term inhalant use over periods of many days.

DEPENDENCY ISSUES

Prolonged heavy use of inhalants could lead to dependency issues, although it is not common. More common is graduation to stronger substances that do have a higher addiction and dependence risk. The aftereffects are not long lasting but can be quickly lethal without warning.

PREVENTION AND TREATMENT

Since the population associated with inhalant use is younger, efforts to prevent this behavior often begin in school with information sessions. Students identified as at-risk will be given additional counseling and information. Parents can be included in the process so they know what to look for at home. Since most products used for inhalation are found in the home, it is important for adults to understand the signs and consequences of even a single huff.

TOBACCO AND NICOTINE

Despite the fact that tobacco contributes to deaths related to cardiovascular disease and cancer, smoking remains a habit for nearly 17 percent of the U.S. population aged 18 years or older (approximately 40 million adults). The deadly addiction is unlikely to cease anytime soon because each day in America almost 4,000 teenagers and young adults try smoking for the first time. Tobacco will likely remain part of America's future just as it has been part of America's past.

HISTORY AND TYPES

The indigenous people of the New World introduced Christopher Columbus to tobacco in 1492, but native populations in North and South America had likely been smoking tobacco leaves for centuries. Explorers brought tobacco back to Europe, where it was initially viewed as an oddity. However, its use soon became popular. Europeans used tobacco leaves to treat over thirty different medical conditions, including headaches and abscesses. Some Europeans, such as King James I, believed that tobacco was evil because of its association with Native American religion and magic. He attempted to curb the use of tobacco by raising the import tax on it, but tobacco continued to be popular. Across the Atlantic, the tobacco industry flourished in Virginia and became a significant export of the American colonies.

Until the late nineteenth century, pipes, chewing, and snuff were the most popular methods of using tobacco, although some people enjoyed smoking cigars. The invention of a cigarette-rolling machine in the 1880s gave rise to the cigarette industry and forever changed the way people used tobacco. In 1885, American tobacco companies sold 1 billion cigarettes. Sales continued to rise over the years, reaching 702 billion cigarettes in 1992. Although American demand for cigarettes has dropped, more than 64 billion cigarettes were sold in the United States in 2015.

EFFECTS

Nicotine entering the central nervous system triggers the release of the neurotransmitter dopamine, which causes feelings of pleasure. Within ten seconds of smoking a cigarette, nicotine reaches the brain, which may partially explain the abuse potential. Nicotine affects the body in a number of other ways as well:

- Decreases ability of blood to carry oxygen
- Increases blood pressure, heart rate, and blood flow
- Diminishes desire to eat for a short time

Although cigarette smoking has declined over the last twenty years, over 40 million adults smoke cigarettes on a regular basis. One out of every five deaths that occurs in the United States can be traced to smoking—a preventable cause of death. Lung cancer, heart disease, stroke, and chronic lung disease are some of the specific causes of death for smokers.

The leading cause of death in the United States is cardiovascular disease, and research suggests that smoking increases a person's risk of having a heart attack. Fat deposits block the arteries of smokers and prevent blood from reaching the heart. However, the damage is not necessarily permanent. Studies have shown that people who stop smoking are able to lower their risk of heart disease over time.

Cancer is the second leading cause of death in the United States, and the risk of cancer increases with three factors:

1. Number of cigarettes smoked daily
2. Number of years spent smoking
3. Age at which smoking began

Although lung cancer is not highly common, it can be directly linked to smoking in approximately 85 percent of all cases. Cancers of the mouth, larynx, and esophagus are associated with smoking cigars and pipes. Like heart disease, cancer risks drop when smoking ceases, although it may take many years to reach the same risk level as nonsmokers. Lung ailments such as pulmonary emphysema, chronic bronchitis, and respiratory infections are more common among smokers than among nonsmokers.

The adverse health effects of tobacco are not limited to smokers. Passive smoking refers to the inhalation of cigarette smoke in the environment by nonsmokers. The smoker draws mainstream smoke directly from the mouthpiece of a cigarette. In contrast, sidestream smoke, which is also known as secondhand smoke, is the smoke that comes from the lighted end of a cigarette. Sidestream smoke pollutes the air breathed by both smokers and nonsmokers, and it contains high concentrations of carbon monoxide, nicotine, and ammonia. In conditions of limited ventilation and heavy smoking, sidestream smoke is responsible for numerous respiratory tract infections among children each year.

Most people are aware that cigarette smoking during pregnancy can be detrimental to a developing fetus. Women who smoke during pregnancy have a higher risk of a stillbirth and premature delivery. Babies of smokers usually have below-average weight and length because nicotine and carbon monoxide reduce the amount of oxygen and nutrients that flow to the placenta.

USES AND ADMINISTRATION

Tobacco is often ingested through cigarette smoking. Individuals inhale the substance through the cigarette, either filtered or unfiltered. Other individuals use smokeless tobacco that comes in the forms of chewing tobacco and snuff. Chewing tobacco is placed between the gum and teeth and absorbed through the saliva and bloodstream. Snuff can be used by sniffing or inhaling the tobacco into the nose. Individuals can also use pipes to smoke the tobacco. Pipes are reusable and the tobacco is placed in a bowl at the end of a stem. The other end of the stem contains the mouthpiece through which the smoke is drawn. E-cigarettes are battery operated electronic devices that are designed to produce a flavored nicotine vapor similar to tobacco smoke. The user puffs on it like they would a cigarette, which releases a vaporized solution of chemicals. Although they have been marketed as safe, they contain many known carcinogens and toxic chemicals. A hookah is a pipe used to smoke a combination of produce and tobacco called a Shisha that is heated. The smoke created by the heating is filtered through water. The filtration with water does not reduce the ingestion of toxic chemicals, and hookah smoking has been associated with many negative health risks. A new form of administration is dissolvable tobacco, which comes in the form of strips, sticks, or lozenges. They are smoke and snuff free and are dissolved on the tongue or in the mouth like a breath mint or hard candy.

TOLERANCE, WITHDRAWAL, AND OVERDOSE

As the nicotine is absorbed into the bloodstream, it immediately stimulates the adrenal glands to produce epinephrine, which stimulates the central nervous system. It also increases the activation of the neurotransmitter dopamine, which influences brain pathways that elicit reward and pleasure. After a period of time, these effects alter brain chemistry, causing the brain to need ever-increasing doses to produce the same effect. This causes tolerance. When an individual ceases tobacco use after a period of time, they often experience withdrawal symptoms, including irritability, sleep disturbances, and strong tobacco cravings. While there is no direct overdose potential, the more individuals smoke, the more they increase their risk of heart disease, stroke, cancer, and many other terminal health issues.

DEPENDENCY ISSUES

The nicotine in cigarettes is highly addictive, which makes stopping the habit extremely difficult. Nicotine gum, nicotine skin patches, self-help classes, and counseling are all methods commonly employed to help smokers stop lighting up. Regular smokers who stop smoking without the use of cessation aids, such as nicotine gum, typically experience withdrawal symptoms, including irritability, insomnia, anxiety, poor judgment, and tobacco cravings. In some cases, signs of withdrawal may appear only a few hours after quitting and may last for months. Studies indicate that smoking cessation should be gradual rather than sudden, in order to avoid a relapse. Many smokers admit to a desire to quit, but most of those who try to quit on their own relapse within one week.

PREVENTION AND TREATMENT

Nicotine is only one of over 4,000 chemicals in tobacco smoke, but it is the key to dependency. Nicotine is a colorless, volatile liquid alkaloid that is highly addictive. When a person smokes a cigarette, the nicotine is absorbed into the bloodstream. Nicotine activates the reward pathways through the increased release of dopamine. The effects peak within 10 seconds of inhalation and dissipate quickly, which encourages the need to continue smoking in order to maintain the pleasant feelings. A smoker experiences long-term brain changes with continued use of nicotine, which results in the addiction and dependency issues.

PSYCHOMOTOR STIMULANTS

Stimulants are substances that increase energy levels and generate a euphoric state for users. Cocaine and amphetamines are stimulants. Xanthine and caffeine, a type of xanthine, are stimulants often contained in foods and beverages such as chocolate, coffee, tea, and soft drinks. We will discuss each of these stimulants separately in the next few sections.[1]

HISTORY AND TYPES

Cocaine

Cocaine comes from the coca plant that grows in the Andes Mountains in South America. Citizens of the Inca Empire in Peru chewed coca leaves to provide relief from fatigue and to boost endurance for carrying loads over mountains. Coca leaves were used as currency at the time of the Spanish invasion in the sixteenth century. During the nineteenth century, French chemist Angelo Mariani used extractions from the coca leaf in a number of products, such as cough drops, tea, and wine. Mariani's cocaine extract was advertised as a magical drug that would lift the spirits and end fatigue. The chemist even received a medal of appreciation from the Pope for Vin Mariani, a red wine created with cocaine extract. In the 1880s, Dr. W. S. Halsted, an American physician, experimented with cocaine as a local anesthetic. Dr. Sigmund Freud also advocated the use of cocaine to treat depression and morphine dependence. Most physicians, however, realized that frequent recreational use of cocaine was dangerous, and the Harrison Act was enacted in 1914 to regulate use and distribution of the substance.[2]

Amphetamines

Patented in 1932, amphetamines were initially used for the treatment of asthma because of their ability to dilate bronchial passages. People soon realized that the over-the-counter amphetamine inhaler allowed users to stay awake for extended periods. During World War II, German, British, and Japanese soldiers used amphetamines to counteract fatigue, and U.S. soldiers used it for the same reason during the Korean War.

In the 1960s, intravenous abuse of amphetamines began because the drug offered effects similar to cocaine when injected with heroin. At the time, doctors prescribed amphetamines for depression

---

1. Carteret Community College (n.d.). Xanthines. Retrieved from: http://web.carteret.edu/keoughp/LFreshwater/PHARM/NOTES/Xanthines.htm

2. National Institute on Drug Abuse (n.d.) Drugfacts: Cocaine. Retrieved from: https://www.drugabuse.gov/publications/drugfacts/cocaine

and obesity, so legal acquisition of the drugs was not an issue. Currently, methamphetamines, which are similar in structure to amphetamines and highly addictive, are rising in popularity among drug users. Methamphetamines offer longer-lasting effects than cocaine, and they can be made very easily and inexpensively in home laboratories.

Xanthines

Xanthine is a type of purine that is produced by all human cells and by some plants and animals. Caffeine is one of the main types of xanthines and can be found in many food and drink products. Any food, drink, or medication containing caffeine contains xanthines.

The various types of xanthines include caffeine, theobromine, theophylline, and paraxanthine. Caffeine and theophylline can be found in tea, yerba mate, and kola, while theobromine can be found in cacao, yerba mate, and kola. Paraxanthine is found in animals that have consumed caffeine. Xanthines are a group of alkaloids that are used as mild stimulants in treatment of certain respiratory issues.[3]

Caffeine is a chemical believed to be in use as a stimulant in one form or another since the year 850. In the time of explorations by Columbus, cocoa beans were used as money in Central America, or New Spain as it was termed at the time. In the early 1600s coffee was introduced to Europe and its introduction as a mainstay in society was cemented. Since that time caffeinated drinks in various forms have become a regular item on the daily menus of many families. Although caffeine poses less of a danger risk than cocaine and amphetamines, heavy use can cause health problems. It is considered the world's most widely used psychoactive drug, and it is legal.

EFFECTS

Cocaine

Cocaine is a highly addictive substance that produces short-term euphoria, energy, talkativeness, and dangerous increases in heart rate and blood pressure. It stimulates the central nervous system and increases the levels of dopamine, which regulate reward and pleasure. Cocaine can decrease appetite while increasing body temperature. Blood vessels constrict and pupils dilate as a result of use. Additionally, judgment is often impaired, leading to adverse behaviors.

Amphetamines

In addition to alertness, amphetamines cause arousal and activate the fight-or-flight response in users. Effects associated with low doses of amphetamines include increased heart rate, blood pressure, and breathing, as well as decreased appetite. High doses may lead to convulsions, fever, and chest pain. Heavy amphetamine usage has also been associated with behavioral stereotypy, which is the meaningless repetition of a simple activity, such as repeating a word or cleaning an object. Chronic amphetamine usage damages brain cells and reduces the number of dopamine and serotonin neurotransmitters and can result in cardiovascular issues.

---

3. Carteret Community College (n.d.). Xanthines. Retrieved from: http://web.carteret.edu/keoughp/LFreshwater/PHARM/NOTES/Xanthines.htm

Xanthines

Caffeine increases energy utilization and efficiency in neurotransmissions involved in the cerebral cortex, which provides heightened alertness, concentration, and neuromuscular coordination. Caffeine can also be used to increase mood. Caffeine can produce negative side effects. Larger doses of caffeine can produce moodiness, anxiety, jitters, headaches, and fatigue. It has also been thought by some to be a gateway drug to other, stronger substances.

USES AND ADMINISTRATION

Cocaine

In the early 1980s, cocaine was perceived as a safe and glamorous drug used by the wealthy and the famous. Its cost was too high for most people, until drug dealers in 1985 began selling crack, an inexpensive variety of freebase cocaine smoked in a glass water pipe. **Freebasing** is a method of reducing the impurities in cocaine to prepare the drug for smoking. The method by which cocaine is administered affects the drug's intensity, abuse potential, and toxicity level.

Methods of Using Cocaine	
Method	**Effects/Abuse Potential**
Chewing coca leaves	Least potent method; not likely to cause dependence or health issues; uncommon in United States
Intranasal (snorting cocaine powder)	Quick stimulation of CNS that lasts up to 40 minutes and is followed by "crashing"; most common administration method for recreational users
Intravenous	Delivers high amount of cocaine quickly to the brain; intense "high" that lasts up to 20 minutes followed by "crashing"; dependency likely
Smoking crack cocaine (freebasing)	Similar effects to intravenous usage but more intense; preferred by some users over intravenous because no needles required; most addictive method

Amphetamines

Amphetamines were once prescribed for depression, fatigue, and long-term weight loss, but the Food and Drug Administration restricted amphetamine usage in 1970. Physicians may now only prescribe amphetamines for three medical conditions.

1. *Narcolepsy*: A condition that causes sudden sleeping; low doses of amphetamines enable narcoleptics to remain alert.

2. *Attention Deficit Hyperactivity Disorder* (*ADHD*): Behavioral problem in children and adolescents involving high activity levels; Ritalin is a stimulant used for treatment.

3. *Obesity*: Short-term use of amphetamines in weight reduction programs; helps control appetite.

Medical use of amphetamines runs the risk of abuse potential and cardiovascular toxicities. Amphetamines increase heart rate, increase blood pressure, and damage veins and arteries, which may be especially fatal for patients with hypertension or heart arrhythmia.

Xanthines

Xanthines are alkaloids that can act to help open air passages in the lungs. As such they have been used in the treatment of asthma, bronchitis, emphysema, and other respiratory issues. They have also been used in treatment of apnea and chronic obstructive pulmonary disease. Some forms of xanthine, such as theophylline, can have toxic effects with use, and often have drug-drug and drug-condition interactions. There is a very fine line between beneficial doses and doses that can produce toxic side effects.

TOLERANCE, WITHDRAWAL, AND OVERDOSE

Withdrawal effects from cocaine depend on the amount of time a person has been a user and the intensity level of the abuse. Short-term withdrawal effects may include depression, insomnia, agitation, and drug cravings. Anhedonia, which is the inability to feel pleasure, is also a short-term effect of cocaine withdrawal. Long-term effects include mood swings and occasional cravings.

Overdose of amphetamines can cause restlessness, tremors, rapid breathing, panic, and aggression. It can promote nausea, vomiting, diarrhea, and fainting. Harmful side effects are most likely to occur when amphetamines are paired with alcohol. After continued use for a long period of time, coming down from amphetamines can be challenging. The body builds up a tolerance to the drug, and withdrawal symptoms will likely occur. Withdrawal can include aches and pains, confusion, irritability, restlessness, anxiety, depression, and paranoia.

Caffeine can produce tolerance and withdrawal symptoms as an individual could need increasing levels of a substance to produce the same effects of alertness. Continued use and subsequent cessation of use could result in symptoms of withdrawal. Caffeine withdrawal symptoms tend to be the opposite of the benefits of caffeine use—headaches, difficulty concentrating, irritability, and fatigue. Overdoses can occur in extremely high doses, such as 80 cups of coffee in one day; ingesting levels of caffeine this high could result in overdose and death.

DEPENDENCY ISSUES

Cocaine is a highly addictive drug that acts directly on the brain. Long-term use makes an individual more sensitive to the drug and its anxiety-producing effects. Users often go on binges, during which they use increasingly higher doses. Cocaine alters reactions in chronic users' brains so that even after a period of disuse, triggers can lead to relapse and overdose. Amphetamine use long-term can also cause dependency issues. Dependence can occur even if the prescription is taken according to doctor direction. Risk of amphetamine dependence increases if mental health issues exist, if there is a great deal of stress, if emotional problems are present, and if the individual has low self-esteem.

PREVENTION AND TREATMENT

Acute toxicity treatment to prevent or treat overdose occurs in a medical setting. No clear-cut treatment program exists for cocaine or amphetamine addiction, but many people seek help from inpatient and outpatient facilities. Most treatments attempt to curb a person's craving for cocaine and to relieve mood swings. Counseling and support groups are typical elements of treating cocaine addiction. At this time there are no FDA-approved medications available to treat cocaine addiction, but recent brain imaging studies have shown which areas of the brain could be targeted in the development of treatment drugs. Individuals must distance themselves completely from others who use or supply any illicit drugs. Proximity to people who use can create triggers that cause instant strong cravings for the substance. It is also important to address issues with impulsivity, risk-taking, and rule-breaking, as these behaviors often lead to a return to use. Individuals must build a strong non-using support base of friends and family and occupy time with positive activities that do not involve drug use.

OPIOIDS

An opioid, also known as a narcotic, is any drug derived from opium, such as morphine and codeine, or any synthetic drug that has opium-like effects, such as oxycodone. Opioids act like two kinds of pain-suppressing neurotransmitters found naturally in the brain—encephalins and endorphins. Although opioids are associated with drug abuse, they remain useful for therapeutic purposes because of their analgesic properties.

HISTORY AND TYPES

Opium is a raw plant substance that contains both morphine and codeine, and its medical and recreational use dates back thousands of years to the Middle East. The introduction of opium poppies to China and India led to significant addiction problems. In 1729, China banned the sale of opium, but opium continued to be smuggled from India where it was primarily grown; the British government in India encouraged the profitable cultivation and smuggling of opium to China. Trade disputes and conflicts between the Chinese and British governments triggered the Opium War, which lasted from 1839 until 1842. In 1803, Frederick Serturner extracted and isolated the main active ingredient in opium, which was ten times more potent than the opium itself. Serturner named his extraction morphine. Thirty years later, codeine was extracted from the poppy plant. In 1874, Bayer Laboratories made changes to the morphine molecule to create heroin, which has three times the potency of morphine. Initially, the medical community was unaware of dependency issues associated with heroin, but federal laws were enacted in the early 1900s to regulate heroin.

Medical Uses of Opioids	
Opioid	**Medical Use**
Morphine	Used to relieve moderate to severe pain without inducing sleep
Codeine	Used for treating mild to moderate pain and as a cough suppressant
Fentanyls	Synthetic opioids that are highly potent; used for general anesthesia and chronic pain
Oxycodone	Analgesic used for severe pain related to cancer or other lingering diseases
Dextromethorphan	Synthetic used in OTC cough medicines; high doses may cause hallucinations
Buprenorphine	Analgesic used to treat narcotic abuse and dependence; low potential for dependence
Meperidine	Synthetic drug used to treat moderate pain; associated with dependence

Constipation is one of the most common side effects of opioids, but other side effects include drowsiness, respiratory depression, nausea, and itching. Opioids have been used to treat severe diarrhea, especially in patients with dysentery.

EFFECTS

Opioids provide relief from pain and provide a sense of euphoria that make them highly addictive. Opioids affect the brain regions involved in reward and act on cell receptors to reduce the perception of pain. Many opioids are prescribed as a pain medication after a medical procedure or for injury. Unfortunately, the highly addictive nature of the opioids makes even legal use monitored by a doctor very risky, as individuals seek to extend or intensify the feelings of euphoria. For individuals with chronic pain, this can become even more tempting.

USES AND ADMINISTRATION

Opioids have historically been used as painkillers, dispensed legally through prescription. Many opioids, however, come with a heavy price. Drug enforcement agents report that many who turn to heroin begin with hydrocodone. Hydrocodone is often prescribed by a doctor in pill form, yet these pills have a high street value and often end up for sale. Unfortunately, hydrocodone, oxycodone, morphine, and codeine are expensive on the street, leading the way to heroin. Heroin comes in powder form and is crushed and mixed with other substances. It is diluted with water, heated to liquid form, and injected intravenously. Fentanyl, which has recently been mixed with heroin with fatal results, is another form of opioid. Fentanyl is often prescribed as a transdermal method of pain relief. In its intended form it provides a slow release of medication, but delayed onset of action and side effects can lead to problems that are not quickly reversed. Opioids can also be administered sublingually or subcutaneously for slow and controlled relief.

TOLERANCE, WITHDRAWAL, AND OVERDOSE

Unlike morphine and codeine, which may be used for medical purposes, heroin cannot be prescribed or used in any U.S. clinics. Heroin is deadly and the most likely opioid to be abused. All opioids have the potential for abuse because they cause tolerance, dependence, and withdrawal effects. Opioids prescribed for pain relief will require increased doses to maintain the needed effect, and recreational users will need additional amounts to achieve the desired euphoria. Physical dependence on opioids is likely for people who use high doses on a regular basis.

The initial stage of heroin usage brings euphoria and positive effects that encourage further abuse. Later stages require users to continue taking the drug to avoid withdrawal symptoms. Most heroin users inject themselves three or four times each day because withdrawal signs usually begin 6 hours after each dose.

The following is a list of withdrawal symptoms associated with opioid abuse:

- **6 hours after last dose:** anxiety and drug cravings
- **14 hours after last dose:** runny nose, perspiration, and yawning
- **16 hours after last dose:** pupil dilation, tremors, hot and cold flashes, and achiness
- **24–36 hours after last dose:** insomnia, nausea, and increased blood pressure, temperature, and pulse
- **36–48 hours after last dose:** vomiting, diarrhea, and increased blood sugar

Each withdrawal symptom builds on the previous one, so, by the final stage, a person may experience all of the effects at once. Opioid withdrawal is not typically life-threatening, but it is extremely painful. Withdrawal from methadone, which is a long-lasting synthetic opioid, is associated with the first three symptoms but with less severity. Craving for methadone does not begin until 24 hours after the last dose, which is why oral methadone is often employed in the treatment of heroin dependency. Although methadone causes dependence as well, it is less addictive than heroin and easier to manage. However, buprenorphine has a lower risk of dependence than methadone and provides an alternative form of treatment for heroin addicts.

DEPENDENCY ISSUES

The presence of severe withdrawal symptoms often reduces an individual's willingness to stop use. The individual will also experience severe cravings for the substance. These factors make it very hard for an individual to psychologically separate from the substance, and physical issues such as diarrhea and vomiting, cold flashes, and muscle pain decrease motivation to quit. Individuals addicted to opioids are often willing to lie, cheat, and steal in order to maintain the physical and psychological dependence on the substance. They are willing to lose family and home in order to continue use. This makes treatment very challenging.

PREVENTION AND TREATMENT

Some studies indicate the use of the prescription opioids Vicodin and OxyContin could be the gateway to heroin use. Prevention programs target younger populations in an effort to stop the use before it starts. Since opioid addiction can be so pervasive, it is often treated with the use of other drugs designed to mimic the effects and reduce the lethality while incorporating mental health treatment options. Inpatient treatment is often recommended in order to monitor health with medications and surround the individual with supportive, knowledgeable help and therapy. Individuals often explore attitudes and behaviors related to drug use and learn new and healthier means of living and problem solving.

CANNABINOIDS

Marijuana has properties similar to a variety of substances, so it is typically given its own classification. Marijuana has been described as a depressant, hallucinogenic, and an analgesic, which makes it a unique substance. The chief psychoactive ingredient of marijuana, delta-9-tetrahydrocannabinol (THC), is found in the resin of the cannabis sativa plant, especially in the flowering tops of female plants. The woody fibers of the cannabis stem are used to make hemp cloth and rope.

HISTORY AND TYPES

Cannabis plants have been cultivated for thousands of years, since the discovery that smoking the dried and crushed leaves produced intoxicating effects. Marijuana has a history of usage in India as part of religious ceremonies. The use of marijuana spread from India to the rest of the world: Asia, Africa, Europe, and the Americas. In the United States during the 1930s, public concerns were raised about marijuana as a cause of violent crimes. Although little evidence supported a link between marijuana and violence, the substance was outlawed in 1937. During the 1960s and 1970s, marijuana served as a symbol for rejecting authority, and its usage peaked in 1980.

EFFECTS

Marijuana contains over 400 chemicals, but THC is the most active one. When marijuana is smoked, THC absorbs rapidly into the blood, distributes into the brain, and then redistributes to the rest of the body. Within 5 to 10 minutes, a user experiences the peak psychological and cardiovascular effects of the drug, and within 30 minutes most of the THC is out of the brain. However, reduced percentages of THC linger in a user's body for days, and large doses may take weeks to eliminate from the body. THC taken orally absorbs slowly and incompletely, so it takes longer for a user to experience its effects. The THC level in marijuana varies, but most marijuana sold by dealers in the United States has a THC content of 0.5–11 percent. Such levels are believed to be 20 percent greater than marijuana that was smoked in the 1960s and 1970s because of more efficient cultivation methods. Hashish, which is another derivative of cannabis, contains the purest version of the plant's resin. Hashish has THC levels anywhere from 3.6–25 percent, so it is a more potent version of marijuana that may generate hallucinogenic effects.

Marijuana affects both the body and the mind in a variety of ways. The primary and most consistent physiological effect of marijuana usage is an increased heart rate. Other bodily effects include reddening of the eyes and drying of the mouth and throat. Low doses of marijuana typically produce feelings of euphoria, tranquility, and relaxation. Loss of coordination and balance and slowed reaction times often accompany marijuana usage as well, which is why driving or operating heavy machinery is extremely dangerous after using marijuana. Marijuana users also experience an increased appetite.

The "high" experienced from smoking one marijuana cigarette usually lasts 2 or 3 hours and may be accompanied by impaired memory and an altered perception of time and events. In contrast, smoking a larger dose of marijuana may result in anxiety, panic, hallucinations, delusions, and paranoia, especially with people who are already feeling anxious or depressed.

Long-term effects of heavy marijuana usage are inconclusive. However, experts agree that long-term smoking of marijuana decreases pulmonary capabilities, causes chronic lung diseases, and raises the risk of lung cancer. Whether or not there are long-term cognitive effects of marijuana usage is a controversial subject. Some studies have shown that heavy marijuana usage causes amotivational syndrome, a psychological condition marked by decreased motivation and productivity, problems with concentration and memory, and disinterest in normal social activities. Critics of these studies, however, argue that there is no direct correlation between marijuana usage and amotivational syndrome, and some even argue that the syndrome is nonexistent. Frequent high doses of marijuana produce tolerance, so higher doses are needed to achieve effects of similar intensity. In addition, mild physical dependence can develop in people who often use high doses of marijuana, but physical dependence is typically very low. Mild withdrawal symptoms may include irritability, insomnia, and loss of appetite.

USES AND ADMINISTRATION

Over the last decade, questions have arisen regarding the medical use of marijuana. Advocates of using marijuana for medical purposes assert that the substance has many possible applications. The Food and Drug Administration (FDA) approved Marinol, a legal form of synthetic THC that is available in a capsule by prescription, to treat nausea associated with cancer chemotherapy and to stimulate the appetite of HIV/AIDS patients. However, marijuana legalization supporters claim that THC is more effective when it is smoked and that medical conditions like migraines, depression, and seizures could be relieved by smoking marijuana. However, critics point out that smoking is a poor delivery system for medication because of questionable dosage regulation and possible pulmonary damage. Limited studies are available regarding the actual medical benefits or potential dangers of marijuana, so the controversy is likely to continue. Some states have legalized marijuana for medical purposes. These states include Colorado, Alaska, Delaware, California, New York, and Maryland. To date, twenty-five states have legalized marijuana use in some form, with many others exploring legislation now.

TOLERANCE, WITHDRAWAL, AND OVERDOSE

Marijuana is rarely addictive, and while instances of withdrawal have been reported, many health officials do not acknowledge this. Synthetic cannabinoids, on the other hand, are addictive and can cause withdrawal symptoms of headaches, anxiety, depression, and irritability. They can raise blood pressure and affect the blood supply to the heart, in some cases resulting in death.

DEPENDENCY ISSUES

At this time, cannabis is not recognized as a drug that produces life-threatening risks and does not meet the criteria for dependency. While it can have a negative impact on an individual's physiological and psychological health when it is taken regularly in larger quantities, many of the more lethal risks are secondary, such as driving under the influence and getting into an accident.

PREVENTION AND TREATMENT

Treatment of cannabinoid abuse tends to follow the same path as treatment of other drugs, including counseling. Medications have not been tested for treatment of cannabinoid abuse to a great extent and, as such, are not approved for treatment.

HALLUCINOGENS

HISTORY AND TYPES

For many centuries, medicine men, shamans, and mystics have used hallucinogenic plants and herbs as part of spiritual events in different cultures around the world. Hallucinogens, such as LSD, are substances that generate perceptual disturbances and produce visions for those who use them. Since many substances generate hallucinogenic effects at certain doses, the determination of whether a drug is classified as a hallucinogen has been debated for many years. In general, a drug's tendency to produce hallucinations places it in the hallucinogen category.

EFFECTS

Within the hallucinogen classification, there are variations. **Phantastica hallucinogens** are those that create a fantasy world for the user, and they are divided into two categories: **indole** and **catechol**. Phantastica hallucinogens are also known as **psychedelic** and **psychotomimetic drugs**.

Phantastica Hallucinogens	
Indole hallucinogens	Indole is a chemical structure found in the neurotransmitter serotonin and also in LSD and psilocybin, which is derived from the Mexican mushroom.
Catechol hallucinogens	Catecholamines include the neurotransmitters norepinephrine, epinephrine, and dopamine, and they are found in the peyote cactus, which contains mescaline.

In 1938, Dr. Albert Hofmann, a Swiss scientist, discovered lysergic acid diethylamide (LSD) while searching for active chemicals in ergot compounds. Ergot is a type of fungus that grows in rye and other plants. Hofmann's synthetic drug became one of the most widely known hallucinogenic drugs.

The effects associated with using LSD are typical of many other hallucinogenic substances, including peyote, but effects vary, depending upon the individual and the environment. The following is a list of possible effects related to LSD usage:

- Hallucinations
- Heightened sensory awareness
- Enhanced emotions
- Exaggeration of perceptions
- Awareness of both fantasy world and real world
- Time distortion
- Awareness of inner thought

Hallucinogens such as LSD and peyote have similar effects and do not cause psychological or physical dependence. Phencyclidine (PCP), also known as angel dust, is a different kind of hallucinogen that does cause psychological dependence. Originally developed in the 1950s as an anesthetic, PCP generates a number of unique effects:

- Numbness in low doses and unconsciousness in higher doses
- Coma, fever, seizures, and death linked to high doses
- Altered body perception and feelings of strength, power, and invincibility
- Schizophrenic-type episodes that may include violent behavior

USES AND ADMINISTRATION

Hallucinogens are ingested in a variety of forms, including tablets or pills, liquid, raw or dried plant, tea, snorting, injecting, inhaling, and absorption in the mouth. In some cases, the plant is ground into a powder, and in others it is soaked into a piece of paper that is then placed in the mouth. The rate of absorption depends on the method of ingestion and often begins between 20 and 90 minutes after administration. The effects can last up to 12 hours.

OTHER DRUGS OF ABUSE

ANABOLIC STEROIDS

Androgens are a group of hormones frequently abused by athletes. **Testosterone** is the primary natural androgen responsible for growth spurts during adolescence, as well as the growth of the male sex organs, body hair, muscles, and vocal cords. **Anabolic steroids** are a type of steroid hormone related to the male hormone testosterone. Male and female athletes have abused anabolic steroids in the attempt to build muscle mass and improve physical performance. The negative side effects of taking high doses of anabolic steroids include muscle tears, increased aggression, uncontrolled rage, headaches, insomnia, and anxiety. The use of anabolic steroids is banned by nearly all major sporting organizations.

OVER-THE-COUNTER (OTC) SUBSTANCES

Over-the-counter substances can be addictive and dangerous when used improperly. Cold and cough medicines taken in large doses can create a high and cause hallucinations. This can also cause vomiting, rapid heart rate, and sometimes brain damage in extreme cases. Decongestants are also abused; pseudoephedrine, for example, contains the active ingredient used to make methamphetamine.

SYNTHETIC SUBSTANCES

Synthetic drugs are substances that are constructed of man-made chemicals that are added to plant material in some way, often through spray. They are then marketed as legal highs that mimic marijuana. Synthetic drugs can be called "synthetic marijuana," "K2," or "Spice." They are often marketed legally as herbal incense, potpourri, bath salts, or jewelry cleaner. Synthetic cannabinoids are the second most frequently used illegal drug reported by high school students; they are second to marijuana.

Synthetic cathinones are man-made chemicals that mimic amphetamines. The contents of both synthetic cannabinoids and cathinones are constantly changing as the manufacturing process has no restrictions or regulations. This leads to risk of accidental poisoning, severe anxiety, nausea, vomiting, racing heart, hallucinations, and increased suicide risk. Synthetic cathinone causes adverse side effects similar to the amphetamines it mimics, and it can cause the same paranoia, delusions, and violent behavior.

Synthetic substances are labeled "not for human consumption" in an effort to avoid regulation by the Food and Drug Administration. The synthetic substances are available in retail stores and online, and federal agencies are working to ban many of them. The Synthetic Drug Abuse Prevention Act of 2012 placed twenty-six types of synthetic mixtures into the Schedule I tier of controlled substances, which allows drug enforcement agents to take harsh action to remove supply.

CLUB DRUGS

Club drugs are those associated with all-night raves, parties, bars, and nightclubs. The club drug group includes MDMA (Ecstasy), GHB, and Rohypnol. MDMA is a synthetic amphetamine that gained popularity among young adults at raves and nightclubs in England and the United States. The effects of MDMA include increased empathy, distortions of time, increased energy, and euphoria. A number of psychiatrists advocate the use of MDMA for the treatment of mental disorders such as fear and anxiety. Inconclusive laboratory studies of MDMA have shown that the drug may cause brain damage.

Gamma hydroxybutyrate (GHB) is found naturally in the body and has a structure similar to the inhibitory neurotransmitter GABA. GHB is a depressant that has been used as an anesthetic and a dietary supplement. Athletes have used GHB as a way to stimulate muscle growth. GHB is considered a club drug because it has been linked to date rape. Clear and odorless, GHB can be easily mixed with the beverage of an unsuspecting victim. The substance has amnesiac and sedative characteristics that make victims vulnerable to sexual predators. Legal prosecution is often hindered because victims cannot recall details of the crime and the substance leaves the bloodstream quickly.

Rohypnol, which is illegal in the United States, is a benzodiazepine. Benzodiazepines are depressants taken for anxiety and sleep. Rohypnol is linked to date rapes. Sexual predators dissolve the drug in a victim's drink, and sexual assault victims are unable to recall any specific details because Rohypnol blocks short-term memory.

ANTIPSYCHOTIC DRUGS

HISTORY AND TYPES

A group of drugs called **phenothiazines** was introduced in the 1950s as a way to treat psychosis. These **antipsychotics**, or **neuroleptics**, revolutionized the mental health-care system by reducing the need for physical restraints and electroshock treatment of unmanageable patients. Antipsychotics decrease psychotic symptoms without sedation and enable patients to remain subdued enough to take care of their physical needs and to participate in social activities. Phenothiazines have been shown to help most schizophrenics, although the drugs are not a cure. Discontinuing the medication leads to a relapse of most symptoms, but the situation can be reversed by resuming treatment. **Typical (first-generation) antipsychotic drugs** include haloperidol and chlorpromazine. Some types of **atypical (second-generation) antipsychotic drugs** include risperidone, quetiapine, olanzapine, clozapine, and aripiprazole.

EFFECTS

Antipsychotic drugs act to take away many of the symptoms of such psychotic illnesses as schizophrenia. They do not cure psychotic illnesses, but they do make the symptoms milder, and sometimes they can shorten the course of a current psychotic episode. Newer atypical antipsychotics have fewer side effects than the older antipsychotics and are often used first. Some of these drugs take effect quickly, easing symptoms within the first day. Antipsychotics are not addictive, but they have some side effects. Movement disorders similar to Parkinson's disease, such as hand tremors, muscular rigidity, and a shuffling stride, may occur with patients taking antipsychotics. Most side effects of antipsychotics are mild, but there are some risks. One atypical antipsychotic, clozapine, can cause a serious blood disorder, which means patients on this drug must have their blood tested every week or so. Weight gain is also a side effect of the medications, which could require adjustments to diet and exercise. One significant risk is that when patients begin to feel better, some decide to stop taking the medication. This signals a return of the symptoms that were controlled by the medication. Maintenance treatment is often required, although it is important to determine what other medications an individual might be on. Some drug interactions can occur, leading to increased depression or interference with the medicinal value of the other medications. Long-term use can result in tardive dyskinesia, a condition characterized by tics or involuntary motions.

USES AND ADMINISTRATION

Antipsychotics are obtained with a prescription for certain mental health issues. Unfortunately, some individuals have discovered that they can be used to enhance the effects of illicit substances. For this purpose, individuals might obtain the drugs through improper prescription practices or through someone who sells them illegally.

ANTIDEPRESSANTS AND MOOD STABILIZERS

Depression is one of the most common psychiatric disorders and is characterized by sleep disturbances, diminished pleasure in normal activities, feelings of guilt and pessimism, and, in severe cases, suicidal thoughts. **Antidepressant medication** is typically prescribed to patients who have endogenous major depression, which is caused by either a genetic disorder or imbalanced brain chemistry.

HISTORY AND TYPES

Antidepressant drugs were discovered in the 1950s as researchers sought a treatment for schizophrenia. They created a drug that was able to control mood, pain, and other sensations. This did not help patients with schizophrenia, but it did help patients with depression. This first form of antidepressant was categorized as **tricyclics**. Tricyclics helped many who experienced symptoms of depression, but side effects prompted exploration for a different form. The second type of antidepressants were **monoamine oxidase inhibitors** (**MAOIs**), which were effective but again carried some serious side effects. In the late 1980s drug research was able to produce a new form of antidepressants termed **selective reuptake inhibitors** (**SSRIs**). The SSRIs did not produce the serious side effects of the first two forms. The SSRIs more specifically targeted the neurotransmitter serotonin and proved to be just as effective as tricyclics and monoamine oxidase inhibitors.[4]

---

4. Fitzpatrick, L. (2010). A brief history of antidepressants. Retrieved from: http://content.time.com/time/health/article/0,8599,1952143,00.html

Types of Antidepressants	
Tricyclics	Side effects include drowsiness, dry mouth, and blurred vision; patients develop tolerance. Drugs in this group include Elavil, Tofranil, Sinequan, and Pamelor.
Monoamine oxidase inhibitors (MAOIs)	Limited use because of significant side effects when combined with food, wine, and other medications. Side effects include dizziness, headaches, and trembling. Drugs in this group include Nardil and Parnate.
Selective reuptake inhibitors (SSRIs)	Considered safer than other types; fewest side effects. Prozac is the most prescribed; others brands include Paxil, Zoloft, and Celexa.

EFFECTS

Antidepressants work by making either norepinephrine or serotonin more readily available to the brain. Despite the differences between the three types of antidepressants, patients who take any of them typically do not see improvements in mood for approximately two weeks. The medication reaches a patient's brain quickly, but experts believe that repeated exposure to antidepressant medication is necessary before symptoms of depression diminish. Antidepressants can cause some unpleasant side effects, including nervousness, headache, and upset stomach. These side effects often fade over the course of time as the individual's body system gets used to the drug. There have also been links between antidepressants and suicide and violent behaviors.

USES AND ADMINISTRATION

Antidepressants normally come in pill form and are prescribed by a physician. SSRIs are considered nonaddictive, but they can create a dependency with continual overuse, especially when the user crushes and inhales the drug. Antidepressants act to restore balance in neurotransmitters involved in regulating mood, including serotonin, norepinephrine, and dopamine. Choice of antidepressant often relies on potential side effects based on an individual's physical status. Antidepressants are used with a wide range of ages, including children as young as 12 years old. Some believe that antidepressants are overprescribed and mental health therapy is underused. There is a need to approach treatment of depression from both physical and psychological forms in order to minimize risk of suicide and increase efficacy of treatment.

TOLERANCE, WITHDRAWAL, AND SUICIDAL BEHAVIORS

Dependency can arise with consistent abuse of antidepressants, and an individual will likely experience side effects if he or she ends use quickly. Side effects can include tremors, insomnia, nausea, fatigue, drowsiness, and dizziness. Some studies have indicated symptoms of tolerance and withdrawal with discontinued use of antidepressants after long-term use. Recurrent bouts of depression have been indicated as a long-term situation that increases risk of relapse, reduces antidepressant efficacy, and increases tolerance and withdrawal risk. Addiction to antidepressants can also have psychological side effects, including suicidal thoughts, increased depression, psychosis, and confusion. Some evidence suggests that SSRIs can, in some cases, increase suicidality, with a higher risk in children and adolescents who use them. The cause of this increased risk is still under investigation, although theories propose that it might be the result of the increased energy to act that occurs with SSRI use occurring before individuals are psychologically stable. Thus, they feel physically able to perform activities, but psychologically they are still in a great deal of pain they want to end.

SUMMING IT UP

- **Drugs** are natural or artificial substances that improve, obstruct, or alter mind and body functions. **Illicit drugs**, such as marijuana and cocaine, are illegal to possess. **Licit (legal) drugs** include caffeine, alcohol, nicotine, and over-the-counter (OTC) drugs like cold remedies. Alcohol and nicotine are considered **gateway drugs** because most illicit drug abusers first try liquor and/or cigarettes.

- **Psychoactive drugs** mainly affect the central nervous system, and they result in changes to consciousness, thought processes, and mood.

- **Drug dependency** occurs when one uses a drug so often that going without it is physically and psychologically difficult and results in such withdrawal symptoms as nausea, anxiety, muscle spasms, and sweating.
  - o The three models of dependency are **moral**, **disease**, and **characterologica**l or **personality predisposition**.
  - o Theories of dependency are **biological**, **psychological**, and **sociological**.

- Drug classifications are **stimulants** (cocaine, amphetamines, Ritalin, caffeine), **depressants** (alcohol, barbiturates, sleeping pills, inhalants), **hallucinogens** (LSD, Mescaline, Ecstasy, PCP), **opioids** (opium, morphine, codeine, heroin, methadone), **cannabis** (marijuana, THC, hashish), **nicotine** (cigarettes, chewing tobacco, cigars), and **psychotherapeutics** (Prozac, Haldol).

- When drugs are ingested in the body, they interact with the **cell receptors** of certain cells and change the function of those cells. This interaction results in changes in body function and behavior.

- The human body constantly attempts to maintain internal stability, a process known as **homeostasis**. Homeostatic mechanisms regulate body temperature, blood pressure, and glucose concentrations, as well as many other physiological functions.

- The **nervous system** is composed of neurons, which are specialized nerve cells that transfer messages throughout the body.
  - o The brain's billions of neurons communicate with each other by releasing chemical messengers known as **neurotransmitters**.

- o The nervous system is divided into the **somatic**, **autonomic**, and **central nervous systems**.

- The three main types of **drug interactions** are **additive**, **antagonistic**, and **synergistic**.
  - o A **potentiating effect** is a type of synergistic interaction.
  - o Any combination of depressants, alcohol, or narcotics can lead to respiratory failure and death.

- **Blood alcohol content (BAC)** estimates are based on a person's gender, weight, and alcohol consumption. A BAC level greater than 0.08 percent is illegal in every U.S. state. A BAC level of 0.4–0.6 percent is often lethal, as breathing can stop.

- Withdrawal effects from alcohol and barbiturates are more severe than withdrawal from other substances. The **four states of withdrawal** start with **tremors, insomnia**, and **rapid heartbeat** and end with life-threatening **seizures**.

- **Sedative-hypnotics**, also known as **central nervous system (CNS) depressants**, reduce CNS activity, decrease the brain's level of awareness, and relieve anxiety.

- The **three categories of inhalants** are **gaseous anesthetics, nitrites**, and **volatile solvents**.
  - o Inhaling methods include sniffing or snorting, bagging, and huffing.

- **Nicotine** is a colorless, volatile liquid alkaloid that is highly addictive. Nicotine decreases ability of blood to carry oxygen; increases blood pressure, heart rate, and blood flow; and diminishes one's desire to eat for a short time.
  - o **Passive smoke** is the cigarette smoke in the environment inhaled by nonsmokers.
  - o **Mainstream smoke** is drawn in directly from the mouthpiece of a cigarette.
  - o **Sidestream** or **secondhand smoke** comes from the lighted end of a cigarette.

- **Stimulants** (uppers) increase energy levels and generate a euphoric state for users. Cocaine and amphetamines are stimulants. Cocaine use includes chewing coca leaves, snorting, intravenous, and smoking crack cocaine. Amphetamines can increase heart rate and blood pressure and damage veins and arteries.

- **Opioids** or **narcotics** are drugs derived from opium that suppress pain and include morphine, codeine, Fentanyl, oxycodone, Dextromethorphan, Buprenorphine, and Meperidine. Heroin is the most likely opioid to be abused and can be deadly.

- **Marijuana**, a depressant, hallucinogenic, and analgesic, is a unique substance. Its chief psychoactive ingredient, delta-9-tetrahydrocannabinol (THC), is found in the resin of the cannabis sativa plant.
  - o **Hashish**, another derivative of cannabis, has THC levels of 3.6–25 percent, making it a more potent version of marijuana that may generate hallucinogenic effects.

- **Hallucinogens**, such as LSD, are substances that generate perceptual disturbances and produce visions for those who use them.

- **Phantastica hallucinogens** create a fantasy world for the user and are divided into two categories: **indole** and **catechol**.

- **Synthetic drugs** are substances that are constructed of man-made chemicals that are added to plant material in some way, often through a spray.

- **Club drugs** are those associated with all-night raves, parties, bars, and nightclubs. The club drug group includes MDMA (Ecstasy), GHB, and Rohypnol.

- **Anabolic steroids** are related to the male hormone testosterone and have been abused by athletes wanting to build muscle mass and improve physical performance. Negative side effects include muscle tears, uncontrolled rage, insomnia, and anxiety.

- **Phenothiazines**, or **antipsychotic drugs**, decrease psychotic symptoms without sedation, allowing patients to participate in social activities. Phenothiazines help most schizophrenics but are not a cure.

- **Antidepressants** can be divided into three main categories: **tricyclics**, **monoamine oxidase inhibitors** (**MAOIs**), and **selective reuptake inhibitors** (**SSRIs**).

SUBSTANCE ABUSE POST-TEST

Directions: Carefully read each of the following 60 questions. Choose the best answer to each question and fill in the corresponding circle on the answer sheet. The Answer Key and Explanations can be found following this post-test.

1. Amphetamines may be prescribed for which of the following medical conditions?
   A. Depression
   B. Asthma
   C. Epilepsy
   D. ADHD

2. The process used to make whiskey that involves heating an alcoholic mixture and collecting the vapors is known as
   A. fermentation.
   B. inhalation.
   C. distillation.
   D. prohibition.

3. How long do the effects of hallucinogens tend to last?
   A. Up to 12 hours
   B. Up to 16 hours
   C. Up to 20 hours
   D. Up to 24 hours

4. How long does a treatment plan normally last?
   A. 30 days
   B. 45 days
   C. 60 days
   D. 90 days

5. A side effect of antipsychotic drugs is
   A. short-term memory loss.
   B. suicidal thoughts.
   C. hand tremors.
   D. depression.

6. Of the following, the substance with the lowest possibility of physical dependency is
   A. methadone.
   B. marijuana.
   C. alcohol.
   D. codeine.

7. The most commonly used illicit drug in the United States is
   A. barbiturates.
   B. marijuana.
   C. cocaine.
   D. alcohol.

8. Which of the following statements is accurate?
   A. Bromides replaced barbiturates as a safer antianxiety alternative.
   B. Benzodiazepines are safe and do not produce any withdrawal or dependency effects.
   C. Most illicit use of antianxiety drugs is the result of private manufacture and sale.
   D. Prescriptions drugs can be just as dangerous as illicit drugs.

9. According to the moral model of drug dependency, people are dependent on drugs because of
   A. peer pressure.
   B. personal choices.
   C. personality traits.
   D. biological conditions.

10. The original concept behind the temperance movement was
    A. alcohol abstinence.
    B. marijuana legalization.
    C. drinking in moderation.
    D. prohibition of smoking.

11. Which part of the neuron is responsible for carrying a message across the synapse from one neuron to the next?
    A. Cell body
    B. Neurotransmitter
    C. Dendrite
    D. Axon

12. Which schedule of drugs can be dispensed without a prescription?
    A. Schedule II
    B. Schedule III
    C. Schedule IV
    D. Schedule V

13. Which of the following neurotransmitters would include an indole chemical structure?
    A. Norepinephrine
    B. Dopamine
    C. Epinephrine
    D. Serotonin

14. Which of the following was the first known abused inhalant?
    A. Amyl nitrite
    B. Ether
    C. Nitrous oxide
    D. Chloroform

15. Withdrawal symptoms are most associated with
    A. drug misuse.
    B. substance abuse.
    C. psychoactive drugs.
    D. drug dependency.

16. The primary active ingredient in marijuana is
    A. THC.
    B. MDMA.
    C. cannabis.
    D. Marinol.

17. All of the following factors increase a smoker's risk of having cancer EXCEPT:
    A. Daily number of cigarettes smoked
    B. Number of years spent smoking
    C. Gender and body weight
    D. Age when smoking began

18. Prohibition laws led to
    A. decreased criminal activity.
    B. dependence upon narcotics.
    C. reduction in alcohol usage.
    D. black market alcohol sales.

19. Which of the following is an effect associated with cocaine withdrawal?
    A. Heavy sweating
    B. Deadening of taste buds
    C. Life-threatening seizures
    D. Inability to feel pleasure

20. Which of the following is true of cannabinoids?
    A. The high from smoking a marijuana cigarette lasts about 6 to 7 hours.
    B. Marijuana users tend to exhibit problems with concentration and memory.
    C. Synthetic cannabinoids are rarely addictive and do not produce withdrawal effects.
    D. One of the primary consequences of smoking marijuana is a stimulant high that keeps individuals awake all night.

21. Which of the following are used to relieve anxiety and fear?
    A. Steroids
    B. Hypnotics
    C. Opiates
    D. Sedatives

22. Which of the following is most likely supported by Alcoholics Anonymous?
    A. Moral model
    B. Disease model
    C. Sociological model
    D. Predisposition model

23. Smoking cigars and pipes is closely correlated with a higher risk of
    A. esophageal cancer.
    B. bladder cancer.
    C. pancreatic cancer.
    D. lung cancer.

24. A protein to which neurotransmitters or drugs bind is a(n)
    A. axon.
    B. hormone.
    C. synapse.
    D. receptor.

25. Which of the following is an effect of inhalant usage?
    A. Paranoia
    B. Hallucinations
    C. Manic excitement
    D. Uncoordinated movements

26. A highly potent form of marijuana is
    A. hashish.
    B. opium.
    C. cannabis.
    D. hemp.

27. How soon after a dosage does a heroin addict usually experience the onset of withdrawal symptoms?
    A. 3 hours
    B. 6 hours
    C. 12 hours
    D. 24 hours

28. All of the following factors are used to estimate a person's blood alcohol level EXCEPT:
    A. Alcohol consumption
    B. Gender
    C. Alcohol metabolism
    D. Weight

29. Which of the following is a group of hormones abused by athletes to increase muscle mass?
    A. Amphetamines
    B. Androgens
    C. Creatines
    D. Opiates

30. Which of the following is a stimulant most likely to produce paranoia during use?
    A. Cocaine
    B. Alcohol
    C. Hashish
    D. Ecstasy

31. Which of the following consists of the brain and the spinal cord?
    A. Peripheral nervous system
    B. Central nervous system
    C. Autonomic nervous system
    D. Somatic nervous system

32. Low doses of inhaled aerosols most often cause
    A. dizziness.
    B. suffocation.
    C. sleep.
    D. hypoxia.

33. Where does the majority of alcohol metabolism take place?
    A. Kidneys
    B. Pancreas
    C. Liver
    D. Stomach

34. The idea that drug use behaviors are established by observing family and friends is the
    A. structural influence theory.
    B. cultural trend theory.
    C. social learning theory.
    D. biological theory.

35. All of the following are effects of nicotine EXCEPT:
    A. Increased desire to drink
    B. Decreased oxygen in blood
    C. Increased blood pressure
    D. Decreased desire to eat

36. The inhalation of cigarette smoke in the environment by nonsmokers is referred to as
    A. mainstream smoke.
    B. secondhand smoke.
    C. sidestream smoke.
    D. passive smoke.

37. Which of the following is used as a cough suppressant?
    A. Amphetamines
    B. Codeine
    C. Barbiturates
    D. Morphine

38. The loss of sensitivity to the use of a given drug by target cells results in which of the following?
    A. Dependence
    B. Habituation
    C. Reinforcement
    D. Tolerance

39. Which of the following would be considered a gateway drug?
    A. Heroin
    B. Cocaine
    C. LSD
    D. Nicotine

40. The neurotransmitter that is associated with intense euphoria is
    A. norepinephrine.
    B. acetylcholine.
    C. dopamine.
    D. GABA.

41. During which stage of alcohol withdrawal do hallucinations typically first occur?
    A. Stage 1
    B. Stage 2
    C. Stage 3
    D. Stage 4

42. Until the 1800s, the most popular way to use tobacco was by
    A. rubbing it on the gums.
    B. smoking cigarettes.
    C. smoking cigars.
    D. dipping snuff.

43. Which of the following ethnic groups accounts for the lowest percentage of illicit drug use in America?
    A. Asians
    B. Latinos
    C. African Americans
    D. Native Americans

44. Marijuana has been approved for the medical treatment of
    A. glaucoma.
    B. depression.
    C. appetite stimulation in anorexics.
    D. nausea caused by chemotherapy.

45. What of these statements best describes amotivational syndrome?
    A. Smoking marijuana produces motivation in smaller doses.
    B. Smoking marijuana creates a lack of motivation in the user.
    C. Smoking marijuana leads to brain damage.
    D. Smoking marijuana creates physical dependence that affects motivation.

46. Which of the following is true of antipsychotic drugs and their effects on schizophrenia?
    A. Antipsychotics cure symptoms of schizophrenia.
    B. Antipsychotics can often shorten the course of a schizophrenic episode.
    C. Atypical antipsychotics have more side effects than other antipsychotics.
    D. Atypical antipsychotics take at least one to two weeks to begin to take effect.

47. Which nervous system would be responsible for smelling a flower?
    A. Autonomic
    B. Central
    C. Somatic
    D. Involuntary

48. One of the potential side effects related to the medical use of amphetamines is
    A. Alzheimer's disease.
    B. neuromuscular damage.
    C. Parkinson's disease.
    D. cardiovascular damage.

49. Which of the following is a colorless, volatile liquid alkaloid that is highly addictive?
    A. Nicotine
    B. Heroin
    C. Alcohol
    D. Toluene

50. Which of the following would relieve pain?
    A. Amphetamines
    B. Cocaine
    C. Prozac
    D. Opium

51. Which of the following drugs would have the highest potential risk for abuse?
    A. Ketamine
    B. Ritalin
    C. Heroin
    D. Ambien

52. Which of the following has the fewest side effects in the treatment of moderate to severe depression?
    A. MAOIs
    B. Lithium
    C. SSRIs
    D. Tricyclics

53. Which drug is a member of the barbiturate category and would help an individual sleep?
    A. Ambien
    B. Phenobarbital
    C. Valium
    D. Xanax.

54. Which of the following increases the rate at which alcohol is absorbed in the body?
    A. Soda
    B. Food
    C. Water
    D. Coffee

55. Side effects of high doses of anabolic steroids may include all of the following EXCEPT:
    A. Uncontrolled rage
    B. Frequent headaches
    C. Visual hallucinations
    D. Increased aggression

post-test

56. All of the following are associated with employees who abuse alcohol EXCEPT:
    A. Criminal activity
    B. Absenteeism
    C. Accidents
    D. Tardiness

57. Which neurotransmitters are made more available to the brain with antidepressant medication?
    A. Serotonin and dopamine
    B. Acetylcholine and dopamine
    C. Norepinephrine and serotonin
    D. Glutamate and norepinephrine

58. Which of the following is an opioid?
    A. Ritalin
    B. Codeine
    C. Prozac
    D. Ecstasy

59. Which of the following neurotransmitters would provide a sedative effect?
    A. GABA
    B. Acetylcholine
    C. Epinephrine
    D. Norepinephrine

60. Which of the following drugs would be a low risk for potential abuse?
    A. Adderall
    B. Peyote
    C. Fentanyl
    D. Motofen

ANSWER KEY AND EXPLANATIONS

1. D	13. D	25. D	37. B	49. A
2. C	14. C	26. A	38. D	50. D
3. A	15. D	27. B	39. D	51. C
4. D	16. A	28. C	40. C	52. C
5. C	17. C	29. B	41. B	53. B
6. B	18. D	30. A	42. D	54. A
7. B	19. D	31. B	43. A	55. C
8. D	20. B	32. A	44. D	56. A
9. B	21. D	33. C	45. B	57. C
10. C	22. B	34. C	46. B	58. B
11. B	23. A	35. A	47. C	59. A
12. D	24. D	36. D	48. D	60. D

1. **The correct answer is D.** Amphetamines may be prescribed for attention deficit hyperactivity disorder (ADHD), narcolepsy, and obesity. In the past, amphetamines were prescribed for depression (choice A) and asthma, (choice B) but the FDA ended that practice in 1970. Amphetamines were never used in the treatment of epilepsy, so choice C is incorrect.

2. **The correct answer is C.** Distillation is the process of making a concentrated spirit, such as brandy or whiskey, by heating the mixture, collecting the vapors, and condensing the vapors back to a liquid form. Fermentation, (choice A) is used to make beer and wine and involves a combination of yeast, sugar, and water but no heat. Prohibition (choice D) was the period from 1920–1933 when the manufacture and sale of alcohol was illegal in the United States. Inhalation (choice B) is unrelated to the whiskey-making process.

3. **The correct answer is A.** The effects of hallucinogens can last up to 12 hours, but rarely beyond that point. Choices B, C and D are incorrect.

4. **The correct answer is D.** A treatment plan normally lasts 90 days, after which the client and counselor must construct a new plan with new objectives and review what has and has not been accomplished. Choices A, B, and C are incorrect.

5. **The correct answer is C.** One of the side effects of antipsychotic drugs is movement disorders similar to Parkinson's disease. Hand tremors, muscular rigidity, and a shuffling walk occur in about 20 percent of patients taking phenothiazines. Choices A, B, and D are not common side effects of antipsychotic drugs.

6. **The correct answer is B.** Marijuana has a very low physical dependency level. Methadone has a high physical dependency level, so choice A is incorrect. Both alcohol (choice C) and codeine (choice D) have moderate dependency levels.

7. **The correct answer is B.** Marijuana is the most commonly used illicit drug in the United States. Alcohol is a legal substance abused by many people, so choice D is incorrect. Barbiturates (choice A) and cocaine (choice C) are illicit drugs, but they are not used as commonly as marijuana.

8. **The correct answer is D.** Prescription drugs can be just as dangerous as illicit drugs. Barbiturates replaced bromides due to the toxic nature of bromides. Benzodiazepines do produce withdrawal and dependency effects. Most illicit use of antianxiety drugs is due to prescription misuse.

9. **The correct answer is B.** According to the moral model, lifestyle choices and immorality are the reason people become drug

dependent. Peer pressure is a sociological reason for drug dependency, so choice A is incorrect. Choice C refers to the personality predisposition model, and choice D refers to the disease model of dependency.

10. **The correct answer is C.** The temperance movement of the 1800s began as an attempt to encourage moderate drinking of beer and wine when the consumption of hard liquor was associated with criminal activity. The movement later advocated abstinence from all alcohol, so choice A is close but incorrect. Marijuana legalization (choice B) is not related to the temperance movement. Prohibition laws of 1920 outlawed alcohol in the United States and developed out of the temperance movement, so choice D is incorrect.

11. **The correct answer is B.** The neurotransmitter is responsible for carrying messages across the synapse from one neuron to the next. The cell body (choice A) contains the nucleus and resides within the neuron. The dendrites (choice C) receive the transmitted signals. The axon (choice D) is the long part of the cell body.

12. **The correct answer is D.** The only schedule of drugs that can be dispensed without a prescription is Schedule V. Answers A, B, and C represent schedules with stronger restrictions for prescribing medication, and all require a prescription of some sort.

13. **The correct answer is D.** Norepinephrine (choice A), dopamine (choice B), and epinephrine (choice C) are neurotransmitters that are considered catecholamines. Serotonin (choice D) includes indole.

14. **The correct answer is C.** Nitrous oxide, known as "laughing gas," was first abused in the eighteenth century. People inhaled the substance to achieve a quick state of drunkenness. Ether (choice B) and chloroform (choice D) are two other types of gaseous anesthetics, but they were not used first. Amyl nitrite (choice A) became popular in the 1960s.

15. **The correct answer is D.** Withdrawal symptoms are most associated with drug dependency, which means that a person uses a drug so frequently that going without it causes physical and psychological problems. Drug misuse (choice A) refers to using a prescription drug incorrectly, which is not likely to lead to withdrawal symptoms. Substance abuse (choice B) may lead to dependency, but the abuse of alcohol or drugs does not necessarily cause withdrawal symptoms. Psychoactive drugs (choice C) lead to withdrawal symptoms only if a person becomes dependent on them.

16. **The correct answer is A.** THC, which is delta-9-tetrahydrocannabinol, is the main active ingredient in marijuana. MDMA is an amphetamine derivative, so choice B is incorrect. Cannabis is the plant from which marijuana is derived, so choice C is incorrect. Marinol (choice D) is a synthetic THC prescribed for the treatment of nausea in cancer patients.

17. **The correct answer is C.** Gender and body weight are less likely to affect a smoker's risk of cancer. A smoker's risk of cancer increases with the number of cigarettes smoked on a daily basis, the number of years spent smoking, and the age when smoking began.

18. **The correct answer is D.** Bootlegging and black market liquor sales increased during Prohibition because these were the only ways to acquire alcohol between 1920 and 1933. Criminal activity and corruption increased during Prohibition, so choice A is incorrect. Alcohol consumption did not decrease during Prohibition because people who wanted to drink went to speakeasies or bootleggers, so choice C is incorrect. Narcotics usage did not change because of Prohibition, so choice B is incorrect.

19. **The correct answer is D.** Anhedonia, which is the loss of pleasure, is a short-term effect of cocaine withdrawal. Heavy sweating (choice A) and seizures (choice C) are associated with alcohol withdrawal. Heavy smokers lose some sensitivity in their taste buds, so choice B is incorrect.

20. **The correct answer is B.** Marijuana users tend to exhibit problems with concentration and memory. The high from smoking a marijuana cigarette lasts about 2 to 3 hours, so

choice A is incorrect. Synthetic cannabinoids are addictive and produce withdrawal effects, so choice C is incorrect. One of the primary consequences of smoking marijuana is the lack of focus and motivation, so choice D is incorrect.

21. **The correct answer is D.** Sedatives are CNS depressants used to relieve anxiety and fear. Hypnotics (choice B) are also CNS depressants, but they are intended to help people sleep. Steroids and opiates (choices A and C) are not drugs used for the relief of nervousness or anxiety.

22. **The correct answer is B.** Alcoholics Anonymous (AA) and Narcotics Anonymous advocate the disease model, which asserts that people abuse drugs and alcohol because of biological conditions. Choices A and D are two other dependency models that are less likely to be supported by AA. Sociological theories of drug dependency (choice C) suggest that social relationships lead to substance abuse.

23. **The correct answer is A.** Cancers of the esophagus, mouth, and larynx are more common among pipe and cigar smokers. Cigarette smoking increases the risk of lung, bladder, pancreas, and kidney cancer.

24. **The correct answer is D.** Receptors are special proteins to which neurotransmitters and drugs bind, which causes the cell function to change. The axon is part of the neuron, so choice A is incorrect. Hormones are chemical messengers released by glands, so choice B is incorrect. The synapse is the location at which two neurons communicate, so choice C is incorrect.

25. **The correct answer is D.** Uncoordinated movements and slurred speech are the typical effects associated with inhalant usage. Inhalants are categorized as depressants because they have similar effects to the use of alcohol and barbiturates. Paranoia and manic excitement (choices A and C) are effects of stimulants, such as cocaine and amphetamines. Hallucinations (choice B) are linked to using hallucinogens, such as Ecstasy and LSD.

26. **The correct answer is A.** Hashish is a potent form of marijuana that contains high levels of THC and may cause hallucinations. Opium is not a form of marijuana, so choice B is incorrect. The wood stem of the cannabis plant is used to make hemp cloth and rope, so choices C and D are incorrect.

27. **The correct answer is B.** Six hours after a dose, a heroin addict is likely to experience anxiety and cravings, which are the first signs of withdrawal. Most heavy users inject themselves every 4 to 6 hours to avoid the unpleasant effects of withdrawal, which can last for two days.

28. **The correct answer is C.** The amount of alcohol consumed and the gender and weight of an individual are factors used to estimate a person's blood alcohol level, so choices A, B, and D are incorrect. Alcohol metabolism refers to the way alcohol is broken down by enzymes in the body. Alcohol metabolism occurs at a constant rate no matter a person's weight or gender

29. **The correct answer is B.** Androgens are hormones abused by athletes that are found in anabolic steroids. Athletes have used both amphetamines (choice A) and creatine (choice C), but neither one is a hormone. Opiates are not hormones, so choice D is incorrect.

30. **The correct answer is A.** Cocaine is a stimulant that can cause feelings of paranoia during use. Alcohol (choice B) is a depressant. Hashish (choice C) is a cannabinoid. Ecstasy (choice D) is a hallucinogen.

31. **The correct answer is B.** The central nervous system consists of the brain and spinal cord and is responsible for learning and memory. The autonomic nervous system controls involuntary actions of the body like blood pressure. The somatic nervous system controls voluntary actions like chewing. The autonomic and somatic nervous systems comprise the peripheral nervous system, so choices A, C, and D are incorrect.

32. **The correct answer is A.** Dizziness and lightheadedness usually occur with low doses of aerosols such as spray paint. Sleep occurs with high doses, so choice C is incorrect.

Suffocation (choice B) and hypoxia (choice D) can occur in some cases, especially when extremely large doses are inhaled.

33. **The correct answer is C.** The liver metabolizes over 90 percent of all alcohol that a person consumes, which is why liver problems occur among heavy drinkers. Alcohol damages all organs of the body when consumed in large amounts over many years, but choices A, B, and D are incorrect.

34. **The correct answer is C.** According to the social learning theory, individuals learn drug use behaviors from family and friends., Structural influence theory (choice A) points to the organization of a society or subculture as the greatest influence on an individual's drug use. Biological theories (choice D) suggest that substance abuse derives from genetics and biological conditions. Choice B is not a drug use behavior theory.

35. **The correct answer is A.** Nicotine increases blood pressure (choice C), heart rate, and blood flow. The desire to eat decreases with smoking (choice D), at least for a short time. The ability of blood to carry oxygen is decreased by nicotine, so choice B is incorrect. Although smokers may drink alcohol while smoking, there is no indication that nicotine increases the desire to drink.

36. **The correct answer is D.** Passive smoke is the smoke inhaled from the environment by a nonsmoker. Mainstream smoke is the smoke a smoker directly takes in when they inhale. Secondhand and sidestream smoke are the same and refer to the smoke that comes off of the lit end of the cigarette.

37. **The correct answer is B.** Codeine is used for treating moderate pain and as a cough suppressant. Morphine (choice D) is another opioid used to relieve pain without inducing sleep. Amphetamines and barbiturates are not used for cough suppression, so choices A and C are incorrect.

38. **The correct answer is D.** When target cells lose their sensitivity to a substance, more of the substance is needed to create the same feeling because the body has developed a tolerance for the substance. Habituation (choice B) describes a process in which an individual fails to react to a given external stimulus as forcefully as the stimulus is continuously presented. Reinforcement (choice C) refers to a method of strengthening a given response to a behavior. Dependence (choice A) is the physiological consequences exhibited when an individual stops using a substance they have become tolerant to.

39. **The correct answer is D.** Nicotine is considered a gateway drug. Gateway drugs are defined as drugs that have relatively low psychotic effects, such as nicotine or marijuana. Gateway drugs lead to more serious drugs such as heroin (choice A), cocaine (choice B), and LSD (choice C).

40. **The correct answer is C.** Dopamine is associated with mood elevation, and many abused drugs alter the dopamine neurons of the body. Norepinephrine (choice A) is associated with arousal and attentiveness. Acetylcholine (choice B) is linked to mild euphoria, excitability, and insomnia. GABA (choice D), which is linked to alcohol and barbiturates, causes depression and drowsiness.

41. **The correct answer is B.** Hallucinations usually first appear in the second stage of alcohol withdrawal. Stage 1 involves tremors and restlessness, while Stage 3 involves disorientation. Seizures are symptomatic of the fourth stage of alcohol withdrawal.

42. **The correct answer is D.** Dipping snuff, chewing tobacco, and smoking pipes were the most popular methods of using tobacco. Native Americans often made syrup out of tobacco and rubbed it on their gums. Some people enjoyed cigars, but snuff was considered fashionable. Cigarettes did not become popular until the late 1800s, when a cigarette-rolling machine was invented.

43. **The correct answer is A.** Asians have the lowest percentage of illicit drug use, while Native Americans have the highest. Latinos and African Americans are both more frequent users than Asians but less frequent users than Native Americans.

44. **The correct answer is D.** Nausea caused by chemotherapy may be treated with Marinol, a synthetic THC. Marinol may also be given

to AIDS patients to help with appetite stimulation, but not to anorexics (choice C). Marijuana may be beneficial to the treatment of patients with glaucoma (choice A), and depression (choice B), but the FDA has not given approval for such use.

45. **The correct answer is B.** The theory behind amotivational syndrome is that smoking marijuana leads to a decrease in motivation. Choices A, C, and D are incorrect.

46. **The correct answer is B.** Antipsychotics do not cure symptoms of schizophrenia, choice A. Atypical antipsychotics have fewer side effects than other antipsychotics (choice C) and can begin easing symptoms as quickly as the first day (choice D).

47. **The correct answer is C.** The somatic nervous system is responsible for voluntary actions, such as smelling a flower. The autonomic nervous system (choice A) is responsible for involuntary actions such as heart rate. The central nervous system (choice B) is responsible for learning and memory. Choice D is not the name of one of the nervous systems.

48. **The correct answer is D.** Cardiovascular damage is a potential side effect of therapeutic amphetamine usage. Amphetamines increase heart rate and blood pressure and may damage veins and arteries. Patients with a history of heart attacks, hypertension, or heart arrhythmia are at an even higher risk of cardiovascular damage. Choices A, B, and C are not side effects known to be associated with amphetamine usage.

49. **The correct answer is A.** Nicotine is a colorless, volatile liquid alkaloid that is highly addictive and found in tobacco. Heroin (choice B) is addictive, but it is not a liquid alkaloid. Alcohol (choice C) is addictive for some people, but not everyone. Toluene (choice D) is a chemical found in glues and paints.

50. **The correct answer is D.** Opium is an opioid. Opioids are used to help manage pain symptoms. Amphetamines (choice A) are stimulants, as is cocaine (choice B). Choice C (Prozac) is a psychotherapeutic drug.

51. **The correct answer is C.** According to the DEA schedule, heroin is classified as a Schedule I drug, which presents the highest risk for substance abuse. Choice B is a Schedule II drug, which carries a lower risk than a Schedule I drug. Choice A is a Schedule III drug, and choice D is a Schedule IV drug.

52. **The correct answer is C.** Selective reuptake inhibitors (SSRIs) are considered the safest antidepressant medication with the fewest side effects. Both tricyclics and MAOIs are antidepressant medications, but they both have significant side effects. Lithium is a mood stabilizer used for the treatment of bipolar patients.

53. **The correct answer is B.** Phenobarbital is a barbiturate that acts to help an individual sleep. Barbiturates have been widely replaced with benzodiazepines, including Ambien, Valium, and Xanax. Choices A, C, and D are incorrect.

54. **The correct answer is A.** Carbonated beverages increase the rate that alcohol is absorbed in the body. Food and water decrease the rate of absorption, so choices B and C are incorrect. Coffee is falsely linked to the metabolism of alcohol, and it does not affect alcohol absorption.

55. **The correct answer is C.** Negative side effects of taking high doses of anabolic steroids include uncontrolled rage, headaches, aggression, anxiety, and insomnia. Visual hallucinations are not known side effects associated with anabolic steroid usage.

56. **The correct answer is A.** Being absent from work or frequently late are typical characteristics of alcoholic employees. Employees who have alcohol or drug abuse issues are also involved in more accidents than employees who do not abuse drugs or alcohol. Therefore, the correct answer is choice A. Unlike individuals who abuse narcotics, most alcoholics are able to support themselves with employment instead of criminal acts.

57. **The correct answer is C.** Antidepressants trigger either norepinephrine or serotonin in the brain to help relieve depression

symptoms. Dopamine is made more available to the brain by cocaine and causes euphoria and agitation, so choices A and B are incorrect. Glutamate is found throughout the body and is not specifically triggered by antidepressants.

58. **The correct answer is B.** Codeine is an opioid, which is a category of drugs that relieves pain. Ritalin is a stimulant, so choice A is incorrect. Prozac is a psychotherapeutic, so choice C is incorrect. Ecstasy is a hallucinogen, so choice D is incorrect.

59. **The correct answer is A.** GABA is the neurotransmitter that would have a sedative effect in the brain. Choices B, C, and D are incorrect.

60. **The correct answer is D.** Motofen is a Schedule V drug, which is the lowest risk category in the DEA schedule. Choice B is a Schedule I drug, with the highest risk, and choices A and C are Schedule II drugs, with higher risks than a Schedule V drug.

NOTES

NOTES

NOTES

NOTES

NOTES

NOTES

NOTES

NOTES

NOTES

NOTES